STRANGE STORIES OF SPORT

From The Badminton Magazine of Sports and Pastimes

Chris Harte

This Book has been Published in a Limited Edition
of One Hundred copies of which this is Number 39

Sports History Publishing

Alfred Watson

Daniele Vare

Herbert Knight-Horsfield

Geoffrey Williams

Sports History Publishing

First published in 2021

ISBN : 978-1-898010-15-9

Editor : Susan Lewis

Consultant Editor : Nicholas Harcourt-Hinds

Series Editor : Rupert Cavendish

Layout : Nick Beck

Contact : chrismedia47@yahoo.co.uk

Printed and bound in Wales

Recent Books by the Author include

The Badminton Magazine: A History, Index and Bibliography (2021)
The Captain Magazine: A History, Index and Bibliography (2021)
The Sporting Mirror: A History, Index and Bibliography (2020)
Hunting in Carmarthenshire 1741-1975 (2019)
A History, Index and Bibliography of Baily's Magazine (2017)
A Season With the Carmarthenshire Hunt (2016)
Old Gold: Carmarthen Town Football Club (2013)
Watching Brief (2010)
Recollections of a Sportswriter (2009)
The History of Australian Cricket (2008)
Rugby Clubs and Grounds (2005)
English Rugby Clubs (2004)
Britain's Rugby Grounds (2003)
Australian Cricket History (2003)
Reminiscences of a Sportswriter (2002)
Menston Actually (2001)
Sports Books in Britain (2000)
Ramblings of a Sportswriter (1999)
A Year in the Sporting Pressbox (1998)
The Twickenham Papers (1997)
A Sportswriter's Year (1997)
Sporting Heritage (1996)
One Day in Leicester (1995)
A History of Australian Cricket (1993)
Cricket Indulgence (1991)
History of South Australian Cricket (1990)
South African International Cricket (1989)
Two Tours and Pollock (1988)
Seven Tests (1987)
Australians in South Africa (1987)
Cricket Safari (1986)
Australian Cricket Journal (1985)
Cricket Rebels (1985)
The History of the Sheffield Shield (1984)
The Fight for the Ashes (1983)
Cathedral End (1979)

In Preparation

A History, Index and Bibliography of Fores's
Sporting Notes & Sketches Magazine
(to be published in 2022)

STORY INDEX

Charles Edwardes

George Charlton-Anne

John Nugent

Elizabeth Savile
(co-writer)

Alfred Watson   Alfred Watson   Alfred Watson

Alfred Watson   Charles Edwardes   Charles Edwardes

Charles Edwardes   Charles Edwardes   Henry Bryden

STRANGE STORIES OF SPORT

The series of forty-six stories ran in the *Badminton Magazine of Sports and Pastimes* from March 1905, Issue 116, until March 1909, Issue 164. Twenty-one writers contributed tales with the most, eleven, coming from the pen of Frank Savile.

The magazine's editor from 1895 until 1922 was Alfred Edward Thomas Watson. He had previously been the editor of *The Illustrated Sporting and Dramatic News* and had been both a leader writer and dramatic critic on London's *Evening Standard*. Watson had also written for the *London Figaro, London Society, Punch, Saturday Review, English Illustrated, Fores's, Lloyd's, Longman's, Grand, Idler, Belgravia* and *The Referee*. He produced a number of books and owned part of the publishing house of *Lawrence & Bullen*. For many years he was the Turf Correspondent of *The Times*.

The idea for the series came from a lunch Watson had at the Beefsteak Club in the autumn of 1904 with the Northamptonshire based novelist Frank Savile. They had just finished writing jointly a book which would be titled *Fate's Intruder* and published by William Heinemann. It was a thriller set partly around horse racing and partly in Algeria.

Frank Hope Mackenzie Savile (1865-1950) was born in Matlock, Derbyshire and started writing short stories at an early age. Numerous magazines of the time accepted his work including *Pall Mall, Strand, Argosy, Red, Novel, Munsey's, Ainslee's, Pearson's, Grand, Lippincott's, Cornhill, Harper's* and *English Illustrated*.

He was trained as an Estate Agent and was fortunate to obtain the post of Estate Manager to the Compton Estates. This position gave him plenty of free time in his office which he put to full use. His first book, *John Ship, Mariner* was published in 1898 by Sampson Low followed by *The Blessing of Esau* and other historical adventures. Then came *Fate's Intruder* after which the Edward Arnold and Thomas Nelson companies published his work. Following retirement he became an explorer and big-game hunter in Africa.

Watson took up the idea and went around commissioning authors for the magazine. He and Savile shared the first four stories out of the forty-six which eventually saw the light of day. The writers were:

Frank Savile: 2, 4, 6, 8, 10, 11, 15, 18, 22, 25, 36
Alfred Watson: 1, 3, 27, 32, 33, 35
Herbert Knight-Horsfield: 5, 9, 12, 19
Geoffrey Williams: 26, 30, 39, 45
John Sanderson: 37, 40, 43
Miriam Alexander: 20, 44
Charles Edwardes: 21, 31
George Charlton-Anne: 7
Alma Scriven: 13

Charles Mott / Edith Mott: 14
Charles de Courcy-Parry: 16
Daniele Vare: 17
Ralph Richardson: 23
John Nugent: 24
William Austin: 28
Laurence Hornibrook: 29
Henry Bryden: 34
Lewis Shaw: 38
Norman Phillips: 41
John Dodington: 42
Edward Morphy: 46

Henry Bryden

Daniele Vare

Daniele Vare

Daniele Vare

Daniele Vare

Daniele Vare

Daniele Vare

Daniele Vare

Amy
Charlton- Anne

Herbert Knight-Horsfield (1856-1932) was born in Hunslet and became a naturalist, particularly in ornithology. He was a regular contributor to *Badminton* and *Royal* magazines. His main publications were *English Bird Life* (1908) and *Side Lights on British Birds* (1923).

Geoffrey Williams (b.1871) was both a journalist and publisher who took over the editorship of *The Publisher & Bookseller* in 1928. Little is known of John Sanderson who wrote a few articles for both the *Badminton* and *Pall Mall* magazines.

It was Alfred Watson's proud boast that he was the first editor to accept a story from Miriam Alexander. She was born in Birkenhead in 1879 and educated at home before going to Alexandra College in Dublin. She made her literary debut with her novel *The House of Lisronan*, a story of the Williamite wars, which sold six editions in less than two months. For this she was awarded the Melrose Prize for 1911. Her historical novels all had Irish settings and included *The Port of Dreams* (1912), *The Ripple* (1913), *Miss Noreen O'Corra, MFH* (1915) and *The Green Altar* (1924). She also contributed stories to *Fry's, Pall Mall* and *The Grand* magazines.

Charles Edwardes was a prolific writer for magazines. His contributions appeared in *Bystander, Black and White, Boy's Own Paper, Chambers, Cornhill, Chapman's, Cassell's, Chums, Nation, Punch, English Illustrated, Sketch, Outlook, Pearson's, London, Harmworth's, Temple Bar* and *Red* along with *The Daily News, Pall Mall Gazette* and *The Manchester Guardian*. He wrote several books for boys but is probably best known for his travel books, the most popular being *Rides and Studies in the Canary Islands; Letters From Crete* and *Sardinia and the Sardes*.

George Charlton-Anne (1886-1960) was an occasional writer whose work also appeared in *The Captain* and *Cornhill*. Alma Scriven (b.1855) was also in the *London* while the senior Charles de Courcy-Parry (1869-1948) only had one other article published in *Badminton*. Charles Frederick Mott had stories in the *Boy's Own Paper* while his wife, Edith (1875-1920) is only noted as having this one Strange Story. After his wife's early death, Charles became known as a 'Ladies Man' around the East End of London and his writing appeared to cease. Daniele Vare (1880-1956) appeared in *Temple Bar* and *Cornhill*.

Ralph Richardson (1845-1933) was born in Edinburgh and became a solicitor, rising through the judicial system to eventually hold one of Scotland's highest legal ranks. He wrote law books but did not seem to appear in any of the popular journals. John Nugent (1837-1915) was a journalist who had stories published in *Pall Mall*. Likewise William Austin worked in newspapers.

John Laurence Hornibrook (1862-1934) was a popular writer appearing in *Argosy, Captain, English Illustrated, Harmworth's, Novel, Royal* and *Strand*. His fiction books included *The Shadow of a Life* (1888) and *Queen of the Ranche* (1890). He produced many children's titles.

Henry Anderson Bryden (1854-1937) was a very talented sportsman who played rugby for England and also for a number of London clubs. He trained as a solicitor but writing took much of his time. He became an authority on wildlife with a number of books to his name. Bryden contributed to various magazines including *Cornhill, English Illustrated, Chambers, Lippincott's,*

Temple Bar, Novel, Longman's, Pall Mall and *Windsor*.

Lewis Hugh de Visme Shaw (1865-1931) was born in rural Sussex and gained his love of wild birds at an early age. His most popular book was *Snipe and Woodcock*. His contributions to magazines was limited to *The Grand* and one of *Phil May's Annuals*.

Little is known of Norman Phillips or John Dodington although the latter supplied a number of stories for Watson to use. He was also in *Fry's, Blue* and *Pearson's*. Edward Morphy (b.1867) was a journalist who contributed short stories to a number of magazines which included *Argosy, Cavalier, Grand, Nash's, Novel, Pearson's, Red, Royal* and *Strand*.

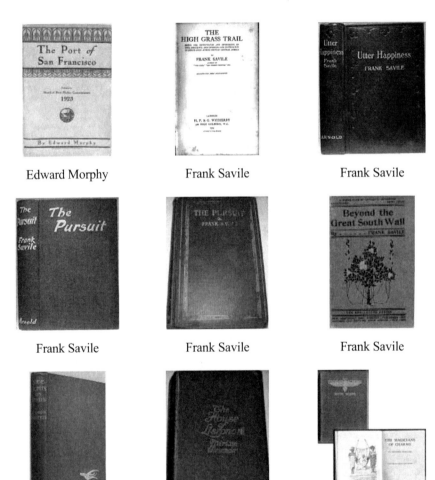

Edward Morphy	Frank Savile	Frank Savile
Frank Savile	Frank Savile	Frank Savile
Herbert Knight-Horsfield	Miriam Alexander	Geoffrey Williams

STRANGE STORIES OF SPORT

I.—THE MYSTERIOUS TELEGRAMS

BY ALFRED E. T. WATSON

CHAPTER I.

"WELL!" Davern said, sitting in thoughtful perplexity with his extinguished cigar in his hand, "it's the strangest thing I have ever known in all my life!"

The other occupant of the smoking-room of Davern's flat was his close friend Dick Aldwyn, who nodded entire acquiescence.

"Let's have another look at Jacobson's letter," he said.

Davern took the envelope from the table by his side and handed it to Aldwyn, who again read:

> "013, Cork Street, S.W.
> "October 9.

"DEAR SIR,

"I can only state the plain facts of the case once more. A wire came from you—that is to say, in the cipher which we have both always understood is known to nobody except us two—saying that you wanted to have £1,200 on your horse Seagull if I could lay you 10 to 1. You instructed me to reply to Kempton Park Racecourse, where you would be in the afternoon. I did so, saying that you were on.

"That is all; but I want to make one remark and to ask one question. Seagull went to fours, and, as you may imagine, the big bet I had laid you upset my book considerably. That is the remark. As to the question, I should like to ask if you think it is quite right that I should suffer because you have been careless in letting somebody get hold of your cipher code? I only just want to put that to you.

"Yours faithfully,

"HARRY JACOBSON.

"Sir James Davern, Bart., etc."

"It *is* odd!" Aldwyn agreed, as he replaced the letter in the envelope and passed it to Davern. "You say you never spoke to Jacobson about the horse?"

"Never a word. I seldom bet with anyone else, as you know, but quite by accident I chanced to run up against Cooper in the street just after meeting Laverton, and hearing from him that he had tried to get tens in vain, I asked Cooper how they were betting on the race. He said 10 to 1 Seagull amongst others, and I took the odds to a monkey—quite as much as I wanted on; indeed, I should not have had so much except that I thought that some fellows I knew would like to stand in."

"And you weren't at Kempton at all?" Aldwyn rejoined.

"No, and never had any intention of going. I was shooting all that week," Davern answered. "Of course the thing is simple. Somebody sent this wire to Jacobson—it went, that is beyond doubt, from the Bury Street office. The idea was, if the horse won, to tell Jacobson to forward the cheque to some place where the sender of the message would be able to get hold of it; if the horse lost, naturally Jacobson would come down on me. 'Heads I win, tails you lose'—that was about the notion. But who sent the wire?"

"How could anyone get hold of your cipher? That is the point. You have not had Perkins with you very long—are you quite sure of him?"

"Yes, I have every confidence in his honesty," Davern replied. "He's a thoroughly steady, straight-going servant—and not nearly sharp enough to have thought of such a thing, besides."

"Good stock-in-trade for a rogue," the other suggested, "a reputation for honesty and for being a bit of an ass!"

But Davern shook his head and declined to consider the possibility of his man's guilt.

"I suppose Jacobson cannot be playing a little game of his own?" Aldwyn suggested.

Davern shook his head again still more emphatically.

"Oh, that idea would be absolutely mad," he said; "there is not a more straightforward old boy in the world. He's full of money, too, for the matter of that, and £1,200 more or less is of no importance to him. No; the telegram went all right, I have not the shadow of a doubt."

"That precious cousin of yours, if you won't mind my abusing your family—though, by the way, I suppose he is a cousin of mine too? You lent him these rooms for two or three weeks, I remember, and I've heard you say he would do anything for a tenner?"

"Yes, but he wouldn't do that sort of thing—he's not as bad as that," Davern replied.

"There are many tenners in £12,000, you know?" Aldwyn continued.

But Davern would not for a moment accept the idea as possible.

"Well, the telegram was sent, and therefore I suppose we are justified in concluding that someone sent it. It must have been someone, too, who has the run of the place, though I can't quite see why you want a cipher—why ordinary English isn't good enough?"

"There are reasons, my dear fellow, why a code is better, and the likelihood of mistake is—well, we have never had a figure wrong before. Jacobson sits in his office all the flat-racing season every day from eleven till five and looks after everything himself."

"I suppose there is a key to the cipher. Where do you keep it? I wonder, by the way, if anybody, knowing that we see so much of each other, will believe that I am the culprit? Oh! you don't know," he continued, noting Davern's smile. "It was sent, as you say, and therefore someone must have sent it. Where *do* you keep the code?"

"It's in that drawer," Davern said, pointing to his writing-table, "and I confess that I am beastly careless. I often forget to lock the drawers up, or rather have a habit of leaving the key in the lock of any drawer I may have opened. To be quite frank I'm almost sure I had left it when Heatherley was here; but he'd never do *that!*"

"Who is there who could have done it?" Aldwyn continued. "That girl—don't be angry—Miss Bessie Richardson, makes herself very much at home here. She was turning over the papers on the table when we came in the other day in a very unconventional manner."

"Looking for something to read while she waited," Davern said.

"Perhaps, but she was rummaging about, and that pasty-faced fellow who hangs about after her and looks so sanctimonious strikes me as capable of anything."

"There's not an ounce of harm in Bessie," Davern rejoined. "I have encouraged her perhaps a bit too much; but, as I think I've told you, she is the daughter of the old head-keeper at my uncle's who taught me to hold a gun. I've known her from a child—I am

15

glad you have given up your old idea that I was ever in the least fond of her—and when she turned from a nursery governess to a music-hall singer I felt bound to look after her a little. No; Bessie is, as you say, unconventional, but——"

At this moment Perkins opened the door to announce that Mr. Jacobson had called, and was told to admit him; the visitor, however, was not the old man of whom Davern had spoken so highly, but his son, a youth with prominent eyes, rather purple as to what should have been the white, and a somewhat aggressive manner.

"I called, Sir James," he began, "because my father thought that perhaps you would like to see this certified copy of the telegram that reached his office in your name."

"Thank you," Davern answered. "I was not in the least anxious to do so, for I have had no doubt that the message arrived."

"Of course it did!" Jacobson junior answered. "Haven't you any idea yet who sent it—as you didn't?" and the last three words brought an angry flush to Aldwyn's face, seeming as they did to throw something of doubt on Davern's denial.

"I much regret to say that I cannot form the slightest conjecture," Davern, with something of a frown on his forehead, replied.

"Rum thing, isn't it, sir?" the youth went on; "about the rummest I've ever heard of! It isn't as if——"

"Had you any further message to deliver?" Davern rather impatiently broke in.

"No, Sir James. I was only asked to bring you that copy of the telegram; but father is anxious to know what you are going to do about it—at least, not what you'd call anxious, but he'd like to know. He says he's not sure he shouldn't be wise to let it drop, so far as that goes, for he heard from a very good man that there's something wrong about the winner, and he might have to pay you after all, as you may get the race. I thought you were going to win at the distance, but the other stayed on better. But you see father likes to go straight, and—well, you know, the message came in your cipher, Sir James, and of course there's not much doubt that the Committee of the Newmarket Rooms would soon say——"

"Your father did not ask you to express these opinions, I presume?" Davern interrupted. "I will write to him on the subject: I scarcely think you and I need discuss it."

"I dare say you are right, only—— Well, good afternoon, Sir James. Of course, we know that you'll do the right thing——"

"Yes; very kind of you to say so. Good day, Mr. Jacobson," Davern cut in impatiently, and the cub retired.

" Insolent little beast ! " Aldwyn ejaculated as the door closed. " ' Knows you'll do the right thing ! ' Confound his impudence ! And the stupid little bit of temptation that the winner may be disqualified ! I expect that's what the creature regards as a brilliant idea of his own. ' The right thing ! ' Why should you pay a debt you never incurred ? That seems to be infernally hard, not to say ridiculous."

" I regard it as a fine on my carelessness. The cipher has been in an unlocked drawer, and though I can't imagine who ferreted it out, someone must have done so, I suppose."

" Well, I call it Quixotic," Aldwyn rejoined; "and as for the Newmarket Committee, you can't suppose that they would refuse to take your word that you never sent the message—had no notion of the bet till you received Jacobson's request for payment ? "

" There's another side of the question, you know," Davern answered. " The old man had to square his book, and I can't blame him for supposing that a telegram which came in my cipher was from me ? It's hard that I should have to pay, I fully agree with you; but it would be harder, I think, that Jacobson shouldn't be paid."

" I don't know—it's hard either way. That little beast who was here just now believes in his heart that you did send it, I'm convinced—that's what made me so angry. He spoke as if he thought that you wanted to compromise, to come to an understanding, to delay payment at any rate—I don't know what. Confound him ! He's made me lose my temper. I *can't* see why you should pay, though all the same I admit that it is rough on Jacobson. The only thing certain seems to be that it is a most amazing business altogether ! "

CHAPTER II.

ABOUT a week later Davern and Aldwyn were shooting with a friend in a rather remote part of Wiltshire. A familiar group was assembled at the end of a muddy lane, by a gate through which the company of beaters had just passed on their way to the wood at which operations were to begin. Keepers and loaders were taking the gun-cases from the host's brake, and from a motor that had brought a couple of friends who lived some twenty miles away— neighbours now, though they had been practically out of reach in pre-motor days. The dogs, excited by the prospect of sport, wagged their tails and occasionally vented an uncontrollable yelp of satisfaction. Only one guest had not arrived, and his cart was soon descried rapidly approaching.

"Congratulate you, my dear fellow," he said, when after alighting from his trap and shaking hands with his host he came to greet Davern.

"Thank you. Very kind of you, I'm sure—but I don't know what it's about?" Davern replied.

"Why, haven't you heard, really?" the other rejoined. "You've got that race. The winner's disqualified—in the Irish Forfeit list. Do you mean to say you know nothing about it?"

"No idea of it, not even that there was an objection. We've none of us really read a paper for a couple of days; though, by the way," he added, turning to Aldwyn, "young Jacobson said something about it, I remember, which I thought was rubbish at the time."

"Well, I hope you backed yours, at any rate," the friend went on.

"He did, and so did I—nine ponies, me. Good business! It's a most wonderful story about this bet of his," Aldwyn broke in.

"Yes, too long to tell you now," Davern said. "You shall have it at lunch, if you like," and after having drawn for places and been instructed to move up two each time, the party marched off across the field to take their stands and wait developments.

"Strange, isn't it?" Davern observed to Aldwyn as they walked together. "I don't know what to do, for I shouldn't feel quite comfortable in taking a large sum from Jacobson when I never really backed the horse with him."

"I don't see that," Aldwyn answered. "You sent him the money he claimed—for he did claim it, though he did it in the 'leave it to you' style; and if that doesn't constitute a bet I don't know what does! You paid him thinking you were beaten: why shouldn't he pay you now you've won? Quixotic, old boy, as I told you before! Bets follow stakes, and you won the race."

But Davern shook his head as he looked at the number on the bit of paper in the cleft of the stick that marked the position of one of the guns, and found that it was his place.

At lunch-time the story was told, but naturally the hearers were as much puzzled as the two friends had been, and could not suggest a reasonable or even unreasonable explanation, especially as only Aldwyn, who had given up all efforts to solve the problem, knew the frequenters of Davern's flat. Jacobson's character for straightforwardness was, however, well recognised; most of the party had betted with him, and that he could possibly be in any way an accomplice to the fraud no one would for a moment believe. The certified copy of the telegram proved nothing, one of the men pointed out, as—without a suggestion that such a thing had been done—he or some agent of his might have sent the message; but the man who remarked this was careful to add that he knew the old boy was as straight as a die.

A couple of evenings afterwards Aldwyn was sitting in the Mutton Chop Club waiting for Davern to come and dine, the pair having reached town just in time to dress, when the latter entered, and without a word put a letter into his friend's hand. Aldwyn read—

013, Cork Street, S.W.

" Dear Sir James,

"I am a little upset at not receiving a written acknowledgment of the cheque for £13,200 which I sent you last Monday. I got your wire asking me to forward it to the Empire Hotel, Seaford, and duly received another message saying that you had it; but as it is a large sum I thought you would have been sure to send an acknowledgment in your own hand. I hope it is all right, but shall be pleased to hear from you.

" Yours faithfully,

" Harry Jacobson.

" Sir James Davern, Bart., etc."

" I found that on my return," Davern said, as his friend, with a blank look on his face, gave him back the epistle. "Of course, as you know, I've not been near Seaford, and had no intention of going," he continued.

" He has sent you cheques to the hotel there, I suppose? " Aldwyn inquired.

" Oh, yes, several times. This rogue is someone who knows my habits and movements thoroughly. It's getting on my nerves! "

Davern had a large property near that popular watering place, but the Manor House was let to a Lord Hubert Merrow, and when he visited the estate he had been in the habit of staying at the hotel.

" What have you done? " Aldwyn asked.

" He'd left his office, of course, when I got the letter about half-past six, so I sent Perkins to his private house—he lives at Beckenham. I wrote that I had not asked him to forward the money, and knew nothing of any telegram—that the sender of the first message must have sent the second and got hold of the cheque. It's too late to stop it, of course! "

" Yes, but it must have been crossed. It will have to be passed through a bank, and the man who has presented it can be traced, can't he? " Aldwyn replied.

" I'm not so sure of that," Davern rejoined. " A clever rogue like this fellow would find some way of getting the money, I expect.

However, we must dine, and then, perhaps, you can come back with me and see what news Perkins brings. He should be home before ten."

Perkins's quest, however, proved vain. He had been to Beckenham, he reported, but Mr. Jacobson was not there, and furthermore not expected home that night; had gone to Brighton, where he had a daughter at school, and his servant did not know at what hotel he stayed nor the name of the school, so that it was impossible to communicate with him. There was nothing for it but to wait till morning, which Davern did impatiently enough. At least Jacobson was certain to be at his office by eleven or there-abouts, and at that hour Davern, who was going to motor into the country, stopped his car at the bookmaker's door, his friend accompanying him as usual.

Jacobson was at home, a clean-shaven, benevolent-looking old gentleman, who might, from his appearance, have been a member of any learned profession, and whom no one would ever have taken for a layer of odds. The office, too, suggested the parlour of a prosperous banker, with its old-fashioned solid mahogany furniture. The bookmaker rose from his chair and greeted his visitors warmly.

"I'm very glad indeed you've come, Sir James," he said, "for I really was growing anxious. I begged you to let me see you personally, indeed, in answering your wire."

"My wire! What wire *now*? I've sent you no wire at all. What do you mean?" Davern broke in.

Jacobson gazed with an expression of amazement and perplexity.

"Why," he rejoined, "I found a message here this morning from you—here it is, sent from Bury Street 9.27—saying you wanted a monkey each way on The Corner for the Cesarewitch. Is this one wrong, too?"

"I sent no message at all; is it in code?" Davern asked.

"No, plain wording; and I wasn't surprised that you had given up the cipher—indeed that, I rather believe now I think of it, prevented me from having any doubt about its being genuine," and Jacobson handed the other the telegram which ran: "Want monkey each way The Corner Cesarewitch. Please reply to Sandown. Am writing."

"'Am writing.' That's rather a cunning stroke, isn't it?" Aldwyn observed. "He's certainly a clever devil. I needn't ask if you ever got the letter," he added to the bookmaker.

"We're being robbed, Jacobson, by some shrewd rascal—who, I can't for the life of me guess. About that cheque. I never wrote a word to you. I've not been near Seaford, and had no intention of going there. Has it been presented?" Davern asked.

"It has indeed," the bookmaker answered. "I had inquiries about it made. A groom—very smart groom, the hall-porter said—rode up to the hotel and asked for your letters and telegrams. He had your card with him, and said you were staying with Lord Hubert Merrow at the Manor House. Of course, the hall-porter had no suspicion that there was anything wrong, and brought out a bundle of letters."

"A bundle?" Davern interrupted. "I should not have supposed there could have been one. My visits to the hotel are quite casual, and nobody I can think of would write to me there. How came there to be a bundle?"

"Part of the plant, my dear fellow," Aldwyn put in. "If there had been a single letter special notice would have been taken of it, but when there were a lot of them it would seem as if you had intended to come or were likely to send. Our rogue wrote the lot, I have no doubt. He's clever, that's very certain, and seems to think of everything. He'll want catching!"

"But what of the cheque?" Davern continued. "Where did it come from? Who paid it into your bank?"

"I thought we might get a clue there, but it's no good," Jacobson answered, with a despairing shrug of the shoulders. "My cheque was paid into the Crédit Lyonnais in Paris by someone who signed your name and asked that the Monte Carlo branch might be requested to honour cheques. Of course they were instructed to do so. My cheque was negotiated on the 7th, and on the 10th the money was drawn out of the Crédit Lyonnais at Monte Carlo in two sums, £11,000 in the morning and the balance just before the place closed. It had been ascertained, you see, that the cheque was good, and then very little time was lost."

"He gets the best of us at every turn, our robber!" Davern ejaculated. "Far from asking you for the money, I had not made up my mind to accept it, for—— "

"Oh, Sir James, there can't be a question about that! I asked you for what seemed to me—— "

Aldwyn suddenly clutched Davern by the arm.

"My dear fellow!" he said hastily, "we are wasting most precious time! Jacobson has sent a reply to what he supposes to be your message to Sandown. The telegram will be in the rack there, either in Tattersall's Ring or the Club Stand."

"The Club Stand," Jacobson interjected.

"Very well," Aldwyn went on. "We shall reach the course, if we're lucky, as soon as the first train from town gets there. Let us start off at once, see if the telegram is in the rack, and watch who comes for it! We ought to have him that way! He had some reason to imagine you wouldn't be at Sandown, no doubt."

"What a fool I was not to think of it! Excellent idea, of course! Come on; we'll go this moment!" Davern said, delighted at the scheme.

"And good luck, gentlemen," Jacobson said, as they hurried out. "I've seen some funny things in my time, but never anything quite so odd as this!"

Davern was a skilful driver. Along Piccadilly he manœuvred skilfully in and out of the traffic, made spurts through Putney, dashed along by Wimbledon Common, and tore, reckless for once of legal enactments, through Richmond Park. Kingston was soon reached, not long afterwards the gates of Sandown; over the grass to the place reserved for automobiles, and then he and Aldwyn ran like hares to see if the message was waiting, and to leave it carefully as bait if it were. The one fear was that the artful enemy might have driven down from London, or come to some convenient station and walked or hired a fly, so that the all-important missive would be gone. A number of telegrams were exposed. "Dalrymple," "Davies"—yes! "Sir James Davern." There it was, and now who would come and take it, and what explanation could he give? If no one came! That would be most exasperating of all, for here the solution of the mystery did really seem to be impending. And who *could* it be! The friends entered the refreshment-room, which gave them a view of the board through the windows, and a few moments after their arrival, from right and from left began to stream up those who had arrived by the first train, a large proportion of the increasing throng going to look at the board; for devotees of the sport are much given to the receipt and despatch of telegrams. A man in a long covert-coat came up quickly, but it was the line headed by "W" that he began to investigate. A foreign-looking personage with upturned moustache—who could he be? It was, at any rate, down the "S's" that he searched hesitatingly, as if not sure that the envelope which arrested his attention was addressed to him; but he presently took it, and from his face it was evident that it was something he expected. A youth comes up, glances vaguely from the "A's" to the "Z's," and turns away with an exclamation of annoyance.

"There's Etheridge!" Aldwyn said quickly, as someone investigated the earlier letters of the alphabet.

The friends chafed. This waiting, anxiety, and excitement tried them. Ah! here is someone, a stout, coarse-featured, fur-coated man of middle age, who is occupied with the "D's." He stretches out his hand, and actually touches the envelope addressed to Davern; its legitimate owner is about to rush forward when the man glances at the board again and takes the message below—he is apparently a Davis.

The members now begin to arrive in streams, and some passing to the right, others to the left, occasionally obscure the board and confuse the watchers; but through the crowd—for their eyes are glued on to the message—they suddenly observe someone stop, look at the " D's," and—yes! no doubt about it this time!—take the telegram from the rack. At last! Rushing to the place Davern seizes the long-sought rascal's arm before he has time to open the envelope.

" So it's *you*, is it ? " he exclaimed, as the man turned round in amazement and fright, and disclosed the features of Jacobson, junior.

The detected rogue gasped, stared, and went deadly pale as he gazed on the face of his captor. He could say nothing; there was, indeed, nothing to be said. Denials would have been worse than useless now that he was caught in the act.

" You precious villain ! " Davern murmured, as the three walked on together, Aldwyn on the other side; for it was desirable not to make a scene. " You precious villain ! Not only to rob me, but to rob your own father—for you had the cheque, of course; I needn't ask ! "

The wretch could hardly articulate.

" Oh, Sir James," he whispered, hoarsely, "if you could only forgive me and say nothing ! I won't deny it, but my father is so strict—and so rich. If he knew, I should be done for for ever ! "

" I have nothing to say to you," Davern replied, turning scornfully aside. It was a grief to him to distress the father by a revelation of the son's iniquities, but of course the thing had to be done. Jacobson was indeed heart-broken; he had trusted the youth implicitly, and access to the key to the cipher was easy for him. The rogue disappeared without seeing the old man, and is understood to have taken his talents to the Colonies.

STRANGE STORIES OF SPORT

II.—A TRAINING TREACHERY: A TALE OF THE BOAT RACE

BY FRANK SAVILE

"I'M quite ready to back my opinion," said Stanger. "I'll lay you 3 to 1—in tenners, shall we say?—on Cambridge."

The club smoking-room contained three young men, and one considerably older. The youths, all intimates, were discussing the chances of the 'Varsity Boat Race with the enthusiasm and with the self-satisfied confidence which is in its manifest prime when its owner counts little more than twenty as the number of his years. Each individual member of the crews had been the subject of argument. From bow to stroke the most recondite faults had been demonstrated in each and every oar, while minute excellences which had escaped the less intelligent criticism of the man in the street were widely canvassed from the point of view of experts. Stanger had crystallised the prevalent opinion in the speech with which this story opens. Hussey, to whom it had been addressed, shook his head.

"I never bet against my own side," he answered shortly.

"Very good principle," said Latham, the Oxford man. "From what I've seen of the practice, I'm sorry to say I have to agree with your conclusions, Stanger ; but I'll take you—merely in sovereigns— 'just for a bit o' sport, like,' as Jerry Bindloss, our local bookie, calls it."

"Right," said Stanger, nodding and booking the bet. "There's one thing about it, you're sure of a run for your money. Your choice in this event will always win—if there's a chance of winning."

"And can't be got at," added Hussey.

The man in the corner suddenly looked up over the edge of his newspaper. He was a burly, clean-shaved elder of a legal caste of countenance. The slight grizzling of the hair beside his temples proclaimed his age a full generation ahead of the boys by whose conversation he had been both amused and interested. He seemed to hesitate momentarily. Then he made rejoinder to the last speaker's remark.

"Are you quite sure?" he asked, gently.

The three swerved round, and stared at him as three well-bred fox-terriers might eye an intrusive mastiff.

"I beg your pardon?" answered Hussey, with ceremonious politeness.

The man smiled.

"I was merely asking, in reply to your confident statement that a crew could not be got at, if you were sure of that fact."

The youth looked at his companions for support. They encouraged him with appreciative nods.

"It has never, to my knowledge, been heard of," he submitted.

The questioner gave a short shrug of his shoulders.

"Ah," he answered, meditatively. He encompassed the youths with a gaze of stolid benignance, while he played abstractedly with his pince-nez. He seemed like one forming a decision. Finally, as if he rent some tension of the mind, he spoke with sudden abruptness. "It was done—once," he said, "something like thirty years ago."

Hussey's eyebrows were lifted.

"Indeed," he responded, politely, but with a distinct want of conviction in his tone. The other two echoed the dissyllable with the same lack of enthusiasm.

The intruder laughed.

"You don't believe my unsupported word?" he said. "Indeed, why should you? Let me introduce myself. My name is Seton-Leathes. Many members of the club will vouch for that if you ask them, and if you consult authorities you will see that I stroked Cambridge three years in succession."

An instant change suffused the ingenuous countenances of the young men. Genuinely, if a little incoherently, they murmured the pleasure which this introduction gave them.

"Of course your name is very familiar to us," said Stanger. "You won twice, and lost by a yard the third time."

"Yes—after leading by eight lengths," said Seton-Leathes, with a very wry face.

"Eight lengths!" They echoed the words incredulously. "I couldn't have believed *that* was possible," said Latham. "It—it wasn't the year you *sank*?"

The older man laughed again.

"By no means," he returned; "we finished. About the best Cambridge crew which ever sat in a boat were vanquished by about the worst Oxford eight which was ever scratched together. Time something like five and twenty minutes; Cambridge, going easy, passed under Hammersmith Bridge at least six lengths ahead."

"Surely there was some explanation," said Stanger. "Were you overtrained?"

Seton-Leathes rubbed his nose reflectively.

"That was the explanation furnished by the comments of every newspaper," he answered. "I wonder if I ought to tell you the real one?"

The three grinned.

"If you can't," began Hussey, "I think it was hardly fair ——"

"To raise your curiosity up to fever point," interrupted the other. "Well, I dare say you're right. And as a matter of fact the villain of the piece has been dead this twenty years, and I don't propose to tell you his real name. You won't go leaking the yarn to any of these dashed magazines or papers, will you?"

They promised unanimously. Three cigarette-cases were produced. Three voices suggested a refilling of this notable veteran's glass. Accepting tobacco but declining drink, he plunged into his story forthwith.

"When we went up to tidal waters the third year that I stroked our boat," he began, "I think I may say that the odds on us were anything you liked to mention. Not only were we an intrinsically strong crew, but seven, five, and bow had rowed behind me in the two previous years, while of the remaining four only one was new to the race. And as he was Lloyd, the Australian, who won both the Wingfields and the Goblets afterwards—though I don't say that is proof that a man is fit to sit in an eight-oar—you can see that we didn't want for material. The only possible defect about so much excellence was the chance of going stale. And that our trainers scoffed at. They worked us lightly but steadily, and the first trial they sent us on the flood surprised the critics, expectant of great things though they were. Against a head wind we did 18.30. It was reckoned that under good conditions we should have lowered the record to somewhere about seventeen!

"Now Oxford, on the other hand, had had just about the hardest of hard luck. It was before the days when influenza was fashionable, but that was probably the foundation of their misfortunes. No fewer than three of their men were crocked up within a fortnight of the race, and their reserves were of the very weakest. It really went to our hearts, watching them practise, to think how we were being wasted on such opponents! Certainly pride had the very heaviest of falls.

"The trainers we had were of the very best. Arthurs, a former President, and Barrington—suppose we call him. For good, solid, ding-dong hammering a crew into shape I don't suppose Arthurs has ever been excelled. Not a nagger, souring his men, you'll understand; but one who would have *what* he meant *as* he meant, and would take no denial. He laid the foundations of five as good crews as ever practised on the Cam, and took his own college to the head of the river and kept it there all the time he was in residence. He was our first slogger. But when it came to finish—well, Barrington made rings round him.

" Barrington showed signs of being what I sometimes think is a most unfortunate thing to be—a genius. Whatever he touched, from a social, intellectual, or athletic point of view, he made a success of. And the last of these three, at that time, had much more attraction for him than the other two. He was mad on what he called the ' poetry ' of rowing. For subtle insight into an oar's tricks and failings, for perception of what was lacking to a finish, what was exaggerated in a beginning, he had no equal. And he could make the pupil see with his own master eye. Whatever I learned of oarsmanship I learned from him and Arthurs, and there was no question which of the two left the deeper impression. They say Barrington went down to the medical school and got a friend to dissect a couple of forearms for him when the wrist work of a crew he was coaching went more than ordinarily wrong. He came back and explained intricate muscular matters to those louts with an intuition and enthusiasm which gained them four bumps in three evenings !

" It had been quite by chance that we had had the luck of getting him as trainer. Since he had left the 'Varsity two years before he had disappeared—to America, it was reported. Arthurs, stumbling up against him in town at Christmas time, and finding that he was on the beach as far as employment went, had been quick to seize on the opportunity. Barrington had accepted the Boat Club's invitation to train with an eagerness which led one to suspect that his mere board and lodging had become questions of difficulty with him. I heard him bemoaning to Arthurs one day that the overpowering excellence of our crew made it impossible for a man to make anything on our efforts.

" ' I have tried a score of bookies if I have tried one,' he said, ' but not a fielder of the lot but asked 8 to 1 or worse. It is most discouraging to a man.'

" ' You shouldn't have put such an extra superfine polish on them,' laughed Arthurs. ' I'd give anybody 10 to 1 with a light heart myself.'

" ' We couldn't get them to look stale and affect the odds that way ? ' suggested Barrington; and Arthurs said it was quite possible that we should stale ourselves without any help. 'But not to the extent of getting laid out by that little lot,' he added as Oxford went by, feathering under water in a cloud of spray.

"Within ten days of the race we were going with such clock-work precision that both trainers began to look dissatisfied. There was very little to comment on in our work, and the shadow of overtrain began to loom in their minds. To bring a crew up to concert pitch ten days too soon is, as you well know, a trifle worse than doing so ten days too late. Now and again I caught a look in Arthurs's face when we came in from a spin as if he *wished* to see us ragged. Then, from self-interested motives, I made a suggestion to him myself.

"'My old dad is running a likely three-year-old at Leicester, Arthurs,' said I. 'What is the objection to having an early spin on Wednesday and letting us have the afternoon off? You can tub what men you like afterwards, if you see the necessity.'

"'What!' he shouted. 'Let you go risking chills on a nasty draughty racecourse! As likely as not, too, you'd do something ridiculous and throw the whole crew out for a week!'

"'And jolly glad you'd be if I did, and you know it,' said I, bluntly. 'What do you want to *massacre* the poor Oxford devils for? We could lick them as it is with our left hands and our eyes shut.'

"Well, we argued it up and down for some time, but in the end he gave in, with the consequence that the following Wednesday afternoon I found myself with Barrington at Euston, taking the mid-day train to Leicester with about a couple of hundred other racegoers. Arthurs had quieted down when his colleague agreed to accompany me. He had every confidence that Barrington would see that I did nothing foolish.

"Just before the train started I was at the bookstall. Two men, bookies in every outline, passed me, going down the platform. I saw one of them come to a stop opposite Barrington, who was standing at the carriage door. The man smiled broadly and nodded.

"Barrington was staring at him in a hesitating sort of way. The man spoke. Then I saw every shred of colour vanish out of Barrington's face. With what was evidently an unconscious gesture his hand went up towards his throat, as if something choked him.

"The man went a step nearer and spoke again. Barrington replied. At which the other smiled again, shrugged his shoulders, and passed on. The whole incident was over in a few seconds.

"There is no doubt that my curiosity was aroused, but it remained unslaked. Barrington was remarkably silent during the journey down, and when we arrived on the course looked about him furtively several times. I, who was concerned to find my old dad, soon lost sight of him. In fact it was a couple of hours later when I saw him again. He was in the ring, talking to the same man who had addressed him at Euston, and this time they seemed to have a certain amount to say to each other. The bookie, leaving business for the moment to his partner and clerk, was talking in an impressive undertone. Barrington was listening, merely shaking his head at intervals with a sort of hopeless gesture. The other grew more and more vehement. Barrington shrugged his shoulders. The bookie at last, and I was close to them by this time, pointed angrily in the direction of the town.

"'Now and here!' I heard him say. Barrington was looking at him out of a white, set face. Then some sort of tension seemed to break in his attitude.

"'Very well,' he said, grimly.

"A gratified smile suffused the bookie's face.

"'Thank you, Mr. Barrington,' he answered. 'I'll take it for you in thousands? Eh?'

"Barrington nodded and turned away.

"I must say that the idea of Barrington, who was supposed to be permanently located in Short's Gardens, with Queer Street as a prospect, betting a thousand pounds, came to me as a shock. But I reflected that his impecuniosity was only a matter of report, and for the time being the matter passed from my mind. I failed to meet Barrington at the station, but was not a little interested to note that among my fellow passengers were the bookie of his acquaintance and his partner. In fact the whole compartment seemed to be filled by members of the ring, judging by their talk. Barrington's friend came in for a little professional chaff.

"'You were seen at Altcar, Billy,' cried one of his fellow passengers. 'What in the name of wonder do you think you know about dogs?'

"'I knows about dogs just what you think you know about 'osses,' replied Billy, in nowise abashed; 'what I reads in the *Sportsman*. Candid now, is there a much better way of goin' racin' than by takin' the market odds, givin' yourself a trifle the best of it when you gets the chance, and leavin' private gas alone. Give me the *Sportsman*, ten minutes to read it, and a pencil, and I'll be pleased to drop myself on any racecourse in England. I've made a book on rabbit coursin' before now.'

"There was no doubt from Billy's self-satisfied aspect that he had been imbibing pretty freely without being exactly intoxicated. His friends were quite aware of the fact.

" 'Don't you talk back at Billy' said one. ' He's been keepin'
company with the highest in the land to-day.'

" There was a general laugh at this—one which I did not understand at first. The next remark enlightened me.

" ' 'E *is* a grenadier, ain't he ? ' said Billy. ' Six foot five if he's
an inch, and quite the gentleman.'

" My heart gave something of a jump. I don't know if I mentioned it, but Barrington was the tallest man of his year at the
'Varsity—a long six foot four which might easily be described as five.

" ' Quite the gentleman, is he ? ' said a man in the corner who
had not yet spoken. ' I wasn't sure enough to interrupt you on the
course, but he's the image of a cove named Barrington who passed
a Monday with me two years back to the tune of eighty pounds.'

" Billy looked at him with his little pig's eyes.

" ' Eighty pounds—did he ? ' he said. ' Well, he'll pay you.
I'll draw his attention to it. He's come—or he's coming—into
money, and you'll be paid.'

" ' Glad to hear it,' said the other, incredulously. ' Did you do
any business with 'im yourself ? '

" ' No,' said Billy, tersely enough, and swerved the conversation
into other channels. My pulse gave another little throb. Had I
not myself heard of business being done—and in thousands too.
What was the bookie lying for ? It seemed unnecessary.

" Arthurs was pleased to say the next day that my expedition had
upset me and that I had upset the whole crew. With joy he found
quite half-a-dozen things to anathematise in our rowing, and there
is no doubt that we were not on the top of our form. We had gone
back a little suddenly, and Arthurs recognised the fact gladly.
Now he could hammer us back to full pitch without the danger of
overtraining.

" Barrington, on the other hand, worried himself about us little
enough. He seemed a different man since that journey to Leicester.
He took things in a perfunctory, uninterested way which would have
made a vast difference to our polish if he had used it two months
before. The quaint, intuitive, biting sentences with which he would
show a man his defects were gone, and the coaching he left almost
entirely to Arthurs. He had developed a sudden fussiness about our
boat.

" It will show you how long ago it was when I say that it was
in quite the first days of sliding seats. Both Arthurs and Barrington
had rowed on solids themselves, and had their own opinions about
the new arrangement. Barrington several times got nervous about
the sit of the shell. He had the slides shifted more than once in
spite of our protests, though as a matter of fact it ended in there

being no rearrangement. But on the morning of the race he fussed about with an oil-can nervous as ever. Arthurs made a mock of him.

"'My good chap,' he said, 'two penn'orth of oil isn't going to make the difference between victory and defeat to-day. Don't be such an old hen.'

"Barrington gave a queer shake of the head, but said nothing. He was making off for the umpire's launch and didn't even see us into the water. Arthurs spared us many injunctions.

"'I don't say make a procession of it from the start,' he advised me, 'but, on the other hand, don't *ever* let them wash you. They mean to start at forty on the bare chance of flustering you. You know what to do quite as well as I can tell you.'

"I will own that of the many races I've rowed in I don't think I ever started one with less anxiety. I had the measure of our opponents, and I knew the men behind me. Bar miracles, there did not seem one single ghostly chance of being beaten. Tow-path bookies were offering to take 6 to 1 here and there in a desultory sort of way we were told, but at these prices business was pretty much at a standstill.

"They say that for a matter of half a minute Oxford, pulling forty-two, kept us overlapped. It was very likely so. All I know is that I had not pulled half a hundred strokes before I keeked my eye out of the boat to get a clear view of their number five without turning my head a hair's breadth. The next time I stared I saw their bow, and a few seconds later the end of their prow. Mainwaring, our cox, allowed himself to smile. It was a breezy day, and the dark blue oars were sending up a smother of spray that was actually blown upon our backs, while our own eight blades slipped over the tips of the ripples like clockwork. Our starting pace of thirty-six we kept up till we were a fair two lengths clear. Then I slipped gradually down through thirty-four to thirty-two, pulling it long and clean, and getting every ounce out of it. I'm bound to say we travelled a good deal faster than many boats I have seen going ten more to the minute.

"For two miles we kept the pace faultlessly, Oxford slipping further and yet further back into the distance till at Hammersmith Bridge I wouldn't be surprised to hear that there was a furlong between us. It was just there that I began to feel a queer sensation in my nostrils. There was a suspicion of an ache in my eyes, too.

"I went on swinging backwards and forwards with mechanical regularity, but the queer sensation seemed to crawl into my throat. There was a stuffy feeling about my chest. And it struck me with sudden force that my seat ran very hard upon the slides.

"The boat gave something of a roll. I frowned. 'Steady, behind there!' I cried, and looked at Mainwaring. 'Who is it?' I said, rather testily.

"Then I noticed that his face had got a bloated, flushed appearance as if he had been drinking. His voice as he answered me was noticeably thick.

"'If it is anybody it is *you!*' he said, unsteadily. 'You're going back right aslant the trim!'

"At his words I straightened my shoulders instinctively, and of course the boat rolled again. I swore under my breath and set my teeth. The queer ache in my throat was more acute by now, and it was accompanied by a sense of impotence. Suddenly I became aware of the fact—and any of you who have tried to row when you are seedy will realise what I felt—that I was a *passenger*. I was still swinging—irregularly. I could feel that I was ragged and completely out of touch with my crew. No doubt it was impossible for them to keep the jerky time I was setting.

"Mainwaring's voice was in my ears. As he leaned forward with the swing his face seemed to peer within touching distance of mine, but I heard his words as if they were a whisper, and miles away. All sense of dimension seemed leaving me.

"'Are you ill, old man?' he asked. I looked at him with a sort of detachment. It is quite impossible for me to describe my sensations. It seemed as if a stifling gas was rising between my feet to transform my surroundings. I thought of myself as watching myself. I seemed to float above an eight which my body was stroking, but with which my soul had no concern. Yet I saw with my bodily eyes that Oxford had decreased our lead and were appreciably nearer, and my ears informed me that the crowd upon the banks was perfectly cognisant of the fact. Mechanically I went on dropping my hands and passing my blade through the water, but there was no *bite* about my stroke. I felt that I did no work; and yet I remember wondering, in my dazed way, *why*—not that I cared, do you understand. My feelings were too utterly inconsequent for any sense of duty or enthusiasm. The only thing that was definite to my sensation was the fact that my slides, which had worked harder and harder, had now absolutely stuck. I pulled a couple of strokes with one hand as I put my left down to feel if there was any obstacle jammed in them. I nearly shrieked as I did so. There was not a trace of oil left upon them, and the friction had made them nearly red-hot!

"From that moment onwards everything was a blur. I heard the din from the banks as if it was so much thunder. I rowed in a thick mist myself, which seemed to open momentarily now and

32

then to disclose the Oxford boat first within a length, then over-lapping, finally alongside. Mainwaring's voice, hoarse and muffled, was yelling encouragements at first, but this soon ceased. Finally a bump upon my knees roused me to the fact that his head, bowing forward, had not gone back. He was lying upon his face between my legs! And at the same moment a hand reached over my shoulder and gripped my arm. Argles, my number seven, was roaring at me to stop—to stop! Another bump showed me that somehow we were alongside the raft, while staring at me with great amazement I recognised old Doctor Beck, who had medical charge of us during training. Everything else was a misty twilight, peopled by chattering shadows.

"I have a hazy remembrance of being half lifted from the boat and supported on two men's shoulders as they hurried me up to a dressing-room. And I realised after a bit that the extraordinary depression which was over all my senses was lifting since old Beck had given me a draught which had made me horribly and outrage-ously sick. He had allowed no one to be present, and he divided his attendance between Mainwaring and myself. We had been stretched upon heaps of coats and sweaters upon the floor.

"Only twice did he leave us—the first time to hold a short conversation with somebody at the door whose voice I recognised as that of Tom Barrett, our waterman; the second time to call a messenger to take a telegram which he wrote hastily.

"When at last I found myself strong enough to sit up I dis-covered that Mainwaring was doing the same. We raised ourselves upon our elbows and stared at each other ruefully.

"'Were we licked?' I asked him. It was the thought that was naturally most dominant in my mind. Before he had time to reply old Beck interrupted.

"'Licked? Of course you were licked,' he said, sharply. 'When the skipper sways about so that the boat rolls gunwale under at every stroke, when he feathers under water, and when cox and he finally take it into their heads to collapse in a heap, a Noah's Ark under sail will lick them. What have you chaps been doing to yourselves? Why did you start at all if you were feeling as you must have felt?'

"I never felt better in my life!' protested Mainwaring, and I echoed the sentiment with vehemence.

"'Till we were past Hammersmith Bridge and my slide began to work stiff I never noticed a thing wrong,' I went on. 'I was fit to row twice the race when I started.'

"He looked at me sharply.

"'Your slides worked stiff?' he said, interrogatively.

" I nodded. ' They were hot enough to burn me from friction,'
I declared.

" For a moment he was silent, biting at his stubbly moustache.
Then he strode to the door, went out, and locked it after him.
Mainwairing and I looked at each other, still bewildered. We begin
to exchange experiences.

" ' You were rolling very jerkily before I noticed anything wrong
with myself,' he told me. ' Then it seemed to me as if the air had
gone suddenly stuffy. Then my mouth parched and things began
to blur. Finally, my throat seemed filled with murk; I could hardly
feel the lines between my fingers; I leaned forward, tried to tell you
about it, and remember no more.'

" ' My symptoms exactly,' said I, ' except that I never went
right off as you did. There is only one sensation I can compare it to, and that is a very long drawn out administration of
laughing gas to have a tooth out.'

" A knock came at the door. We heard Barrington's voice, and
then Arthurs clamouring for admission. We explained that we
were prisoners till old Beck returned, but at almost the same moment
we heard his voice. He came in, bringing the two trainers with
him. A reporter tried to bully an entrance, but the doctor made
short work of him. By this time Mainwaring and I were feeling
moderately convalescent and fit for conversation. Beck planted a
chair in front of us and began an interrogation.

" ' Did you eat anything before starting?' he demanded, and
we shook our heads. ' Nor drink?' he continued, and we laughed
him to scorn. ' And yet,' he went on, turning to the other two,
' within twelve minutes of the start they are both found suffering
from incipient narcosis! I don't think much of the way you look
after your men!'

" I looked at the two of them. Arthurs flushed a royal red with
rage, but Barrington was white as a sheet. And it was at him, too,
that Beck was staring with his little gimlet eyes.

" ' Narcosis?' Barrington repeated the word inquiringly.
' Narcosis?'

" ' Insensibility from anæsthesia, if you want it in plain English,'
said Beck, and went to the door again in answer to an imperious
knock. He came back reading a telegram. He crammed it in his
pocket, and when he spoke again his voice cut like the lash of a
whip.

" ' And now I want to know, Mr. Barrington,' he added, suddenly,
' what you have gained by administering that same anæsthetic?'

" A bombshell couldn't have made the four of us jump quicker.
Mainwairing and I yelled indignant denials. ' Nothing was ad-

ministered to us—nothing!' we protested. Barrington stuttered almost incoherent curses. Old Beck swung himself up to his full height. He is a little man, but from the summit of his passion he dominated us.

" 'Silence, all of you!' he cried. 'I'm going to give you a few facts, and then you can call on me for an apology if you like.'

" Barrington strode towards the door.

" 'I'm not staying here to be insulted!' he cried. 'The apology must come before I listen to anything else.'

" Beck was too quick for him. He darted across the floor, turned the key in the lock, and shoved it in his pocket.

" 'You, Barrington!' he cried, imperiously, 'sit down! For the credit of the 'Varsity I meant to cover this up. I'm not going to stand any nonsense. I'll give you away to every reporter in the place!'

" Barrington stood still, seemed to sway a little, and then fell rather than sat upon a chair. You could have heard a pin drop as we three looked at each other. The very foundations of sporting honour seemed uprooted.

" 'This—fellow,' said Beck, pointing at him, 'oiled your slides —did he not, Seton-Leathes?'

" I nodded, silently.

" 'So you think,' went on Beck; 'as a matter of fact he really covered them with turpentine and blacklead. That is evident by the state they are now in—not a vestige of oil on them, and jammed. But a jammed slide would not have been enough to stop you—not enough to stop a crew that everybody was laying any odds on. You would have swung on, and let the men behind you get you home. The sticking of the slides was only a part of the most ingenious knavery it has ever been my lot to investigate. He nobbled you and Mainwaring as well.'

" 'He didn't, I tell you!' I denied, hotly. 'He never touched me! I took nothing from him!'

" 'Shut up!' said Beck, curtly. 'The facts are these: Barrington busied himself with oiling the boat, which is Barrett's job. Barrett happened to notice that Barrington used his own oil, and flung away the bottle. He flung it into the river, as he thought, but it didn't happen to sink, and when it washed up on the gravel, Barrett, with natural curiosity to see what this new-fangled oil was, picked it up and looked at it. The bottle bore the label of a chemist in the Strand.'

" For the first time Barrington made a movement—one of irritation, it seemed. He kicked his foot restlessly against the chair leg.

"'My nose told me as soon as I helped to lift Mainwaring out of the boat what was the matter with him,' Beck went on. 'When ten minutes later Barrett brought me that bottle there was only one person left to suspect, though I'll own it came as a shock to me.'

"'So you take Barrett's bare word to father this thing on me!' cried Barrington. 'I deny his story absolutely.'

"'You do, do you?' answered Beck, calmly. 'Then let me tell you that it is a deuced funny thing that a gentleman six feet four in height should have had that bottle filled at that chemist's shop only yesterday. Will you come down with me and interview him? There aren't too many men of your stature in London to make it hard to find the right man if you're the wrong one. And the answer I have just received to the telegram I sent him is quite explicit.'

"Barrington collapsed. Beck eyed him for a moment, and then resumed, dispassionately:

"'I went out and examined Seton-Leathes's seat and slides just now,' he said. 'They reeked of what this bottle reeks of—bichloride of methylene, as I expected they would. On the woodwork of the shell below the seat I found some drippings of green wax. That made me think, for both Mainwaring and Seton-Leathes assured me that they noticed no smell and no oppression when they started. Very little further investigation showed me that the slides, which as you know are hollow tubes, exhibited traces of green wax on each end. That completed the evidence.'

"Arthurs and I looked at him uncomprehendingly. 'How?' we stammered, and the old chap gave us a pitying look.

"'You have little enough imagination, you two,' he answered. 'He had *filled the slides with the stuff and then waxed up the ends.* Now do you understand why he wanted your slides to run hot? The friction melted the wax just soon enough to let the stuff out, evaporate under your noses, and bowl you both over. And now I want to know,' he went on, turning to Barrington, 'just exactly what you stand to win over this villany, and who put you up to it?'

"For ten seconds there was complete silence in the room. Barrington did not raise his eyes. Only the working of his face betrayed his emotion. Suddenly he threw out his hands with a gesture of despair, and dropped his head upon the table. His great shoulders shook convulsively.

"Through a long tense minute he lay there motionless. When he raised his face at last the shock of his appearance drew a gasp from all three of us. Twenty years seemed to have been added to his age—he looked haggard—wan—hopeless. His voice was hardly recognisable.

" 'The beginning of it all was two years ago,' he said, wearily. 'I came up to town, went the pace, plunged, and found myself at last on a certain Monday with nothing in the world but a cheque for fifteen pounds which I had received at a bookmaker's settling. The man was one with whom I had betted frequently. The same evening, when I was playing billiards at the club, in came a friend reporting that the fellow—Gates by name, commonly known as Billy—had been run over in the Strand, taken to a hospital, and had been pronounced fatally injured. He was expected to die before morning.

" 'How exactly the temptation first came to me I don't know, but I was desperate. I made the cheque for fifteen hundred, took a ticket for America, and disappeared. A bookmaker's accounts are not often so exact that his executors can fix his debts to a penny. The bank cashed the cheque with no demur, and no inquiry, as far as I knew, was made. I went to Leicester ten days ago, and the man Gates then and there confronted me. The report of his injuries had been a mere rumour—he had never been in danger of death at all.

" 'How he knew my position with the crew I can't tell. I needn't worry you with the threats and arguments he used. But the alternative was instant disgrace '—(how well I remembered that vehement 'Here and now' which I had overheard)—'if I did not lend myself to this plot. He engineered it. He was a chemist's assistant once, and he told me that the notion of the thing had been in his head for years, only he had never seen an opportunity of working it. As to what I was to get? The results of a thousand laid out at current odds, out of which I was to refund him the £1,500. Now you know all there is to know.'

" And that, when all is said and done, is all that I have to tell. Of the hushing up of the matter for the good name of 'Varsity sport; of the penalty exacted from Gates; of the second and final disappearance of Barrington into an American limbo, I needn't tell. I am not sure that I ought to have told you what I have done. But the matter is a quarter of a century old and Barrington is dead. And after all "—he looked smilingly at Latham—"it can do you Oxford men no harm when you talk patronisingly of being six wins ahead to know that you have a right to only five of them."

STRANGE STORIES OF SPORT

III.—A DECEPTIVE MESSAGE

BY "RAPIER"

"THERE never was an easier race to sum up than the Loamshire
Handicap—that is to say, assuming that the horses are fit and well.
One stands out by himself, The Viking. As a two-year-old he was
among the best of a more than average lot, and had he been entered
for the Derby his chance would have had to be seriously considered.
He won, however, at Ascot, and again at Goodwood; but there are
of course two unaccountable defeats in the autumn to be explained
away. This is a task we do not for a moment propose to undertake. It is obvious that The Viking did not run up to within a
good 21 lb. of his form; it would be useless to speculate why. It
is said, however, that he is now himself again, and if so, this handicap is a mere exercise canter for him. In his absence, or if he has
really deteriorated, Centrebit stands out almost equally in front of
the unusually ragged lot engaged. Though he has never won a race
he has been close up in good company; he is a very useful colt,
perhaps more than useful, though we think not in the same class
as The Viking. Nothing else need be seriously considered, though
Rosamund is reported to have come on. It will be necessary for
her to have come on a very long way in order to have the remotest
chance against the two mentioned."

It was after dinner at the Carlton Hotel that Winthorpe read
this in an evening paper, seated, smoking, at a table with Reade,
the owner of The Viking, and his friend, Hazel.

"A very sensible little article, I call it," Winthorpe remarked;
"at least I suppose it is. You think so, don't you?"

"Yes, it's right enough," Reade answered, "but I don't know what the fellow means by his references to loss of form—whether he's insinuating anything or not, confound him!" and he endeavoured to soothe his indignation with a second liqueur.

"I forget what time your train goes?" Winthorpe observed.

"It's 8.5," the other returned. "We drive straight to the Downs, and the gallop is to come off at half-past ten. We shall be back at the hotel by eleven; so between eleven and a quarter past I'll telephone the result to you."

"All right, I understand," Winthorpe said. "But if The Viking wins, are you sure you would not like me to do anything for you?"

"No, my dear fellow, thanks; I've arranged all that, but I've left the three bookies you generally deal with untouched, so that you can go and do what you like with them as soon as you get my message. And if I tell you to back it, you may be pretty sure it's good enough. But you need not be surprised if you hear that the three-year-old is very close up, and if he is he will be well worth the four thousand I want for him."

None of the three observed how a black-visaged, hook-nosed man, seated with his back to them at another table, was eagerly straining his ears to catch the conversation. He, Myers, was an owner of horses, Centrebit, amongst others, being his property, and he had carefully manœuvred to get a seat near enough to the little party to hear what was said in the not improbable event of its turning on the next week's meeting. Myers raced in an entirely commercial spirit, caring nothing whatever for the sport except as an investment. So little interest did he take in it that he seldom went to a meeting, though now and then he turned up at Sandown or Kempton, with a carriage full of lunch, which he spent the afternoon in devouring and distributing, seldom crossing the course to the enclosures, so that few men who went racing even knew him by sight.

"Well," Winthorpe presently said, "you will want to go home as you have to be away so early. I'll be waiting at my telephone at eleven o'clock, and I need not tell you how grateful I am for what you are going to do, for, as you know, I have been having a desperately bad time of late. I should like the three-year-old, but if things don't get better I shall have to sell instead of buying—in fact I'm rather in a hole."

And so they went to get their coats, Winthorpe took a hansom, leaving the other two to stroll off down Pall Mall.

"He's a good little fellow," Hazel said. "I'm sorry he's got to lose his money."

" So am I," Reade rejoined, without, however, any very poignant suggestion of sympathy in his voice or expression of face. " But *someone's* got to back The Viking. We can't afford to do it ourselves, and he's the only fellow I can think of. If there's no money for him next week, these infernal newspaper fellows will begin to write about his being beaten; and when he wins, as likely as not there'd be a fuss. If we can get him to a nice short price and he is beaten, as of course he will be, no one can very well say anything. It's the market that gives these things away."

" Well, I can only say I'm sorry," Hazel went on, " but I suppose it's got to be done. You're going to let The Rover win the gallop to-morrow, I suppose? But, if Winthorpe's hard up, he can't give you four thousand for it ? "

" No, he can't, but one of his pals very likely will. That little ass Parkinson he's been about with lately is full of money, I'm told. It all fits in so nicely! Perkins will ride, he knows just what he's got to do, and he is sure to do it cleverly. The Rover will beat him a length or so, and then the idea will be that he's a smasher, and that in spite of being just beaten The Viking is sure to win on Wednesday. Then we shall get The Viking well backed, and, with luck, find someone to pay the price for the three-year-old. Of course The Viking not winning his race will discount The Rover a bit, but we can explain that away and he won't be beaten far. After being beaten three times, they can't give the horse much to carry in the Hunt Cup, and you know as well as I do what he can do when he's wanted. So we'll go down and have our gallop and send him the news."

Hazel was not quite without conscience.

" Well, we might perhaps tell Winthorpe to save on Centrebit ? I don't want him to go broke," he said.

" Perhaps we will, later on. We'll see how they bet. There's plenty of time to think about that. Good-night. Waterloo, ten minutes to eight sharp in the morning ! "

And the two parted.

Meantime, Myers still sat at the Carlton, trying to solve an exceedingly difficult problem, the solution of which he had not reached when he, too, left the restaurant, put his companion in a cab—a good-looking woman who was not too well pleased at the small effort her silent thoughtful host had made to entertain her—and walked off down the street still wrapped in thought. How to tempt a man out of his own room at a time when he had urgently pressing reasons to be in it, and how to get the free run of the place himself—that was the puzzle which perplexed Myers.

" Yes, by Jove! that's it ! " he suddenly exclaimed; " that 'll do! I'll telephone to him in the morning to tell him the gallop's put off for an hour, send him an urgent wire begging him to go down to his club, where someone is particularly anxious to see him—there's no reason why he shouldn't go if he thinks he's not wanted till twelve—then I can call at his flat, tell his man I have urgent business with him, and must wait till he comes in, and then with luck I shall get the message!"

Two years before, when Winthorpe came of age, he had found himself master of a handsome fortune, a sheep with golden fleece ready to be shorn by any particularly ingenious shearer who might devote himself to the task. He had met Reade, and though Winthorpe was not exactly a fool, the ingenuity of the other had been too much for him. His racing, under Reade's guidance, had made a serious hole in his finances, and thus had incidentally caused him to lose a good deal of his keenness for the sport, the more so as he was engaged to marry an exceptionally charming girl who had no sympathy for his chosen companions; entertained, indeed, much distrust and dislike of them. His anxiety was to get back at any rate a few of the thousands he had lost; and as, so far, no suspicion of Reade had entered his mind, he still believed that he might benefit by his false friend's assistance.

He was engaged next morning in figuring out a rather melancholy statement of his affairs on a sheet of paper, when a ring at his telephone drew him to the instrument. Reade, it appeared, was speaking to him from the hotel at Chesterton, the town near to which his horses were kept.

"That careless little devil Perkins has missed his train," the voice said, "can't get here for nearly an hour; so I shan't be able to ring you up and tell you what's happened till about a quarter past twelve. I hope it isn't putting you out?"

Winthorpe replied that it was all right, he would be waiting for the message at the time, and just then his servant entered with a telegram: "Want to see you most particularly, shall be at club from eleven to half-past. Do come if you possibly can." So the message ran, and it was unsigned, which Myers, from whom of course it came—that he likewise had spoken on the telephone will be understood—regarded as rather a clever stroke. He had not known whose summons Winthorpe was most likely to obey, and had shrewdly imagined that the recipient would think of a presumptive sender whom he would not like to disappoint. As for Winthorpe, if he was not to hear anything from Chesterton till a quarter past twelve, there was no use his hanging about his flat; so after another investigation of the ugly array of figures, he strolled off to St. James's Street, wondering which of two or three friends had telegraphed to him and carelessly omitted the signature; and he had not been gone many minutes when a ring came at his door.

"Is Mr. Winthorpe in?" the caller inquired.

His master was not at home, the servant replied.

Myers pulled out his pocket-book, looked into it, and presently said, "I find I haven't a card—I am Mr. Somerton"—it was a name under which he did business as a money-lender, and would serve as well as another—"and I must see Mr. Winthorpe without delay. I understood that he would be at home this morning, and I think I'd better wait."

"Certainly, sir; will you step in?" the man politely replied; and Myers entered, was begged to take a chair, and provided with a pile of papers which he apparently settled down to read as the servant left the room.

"His anxiety was as to what would happen. Would the servant hear the bell of the telephone and come in to receive the message? Was there any means of mitigating the sound? He sat for some time looking at the paper without reading it, when the tinkle came, and dashing to the instrument he waited for the information he was so eager to gain.

"Is that you, Winthorpe?" came the question.

"Yes. How have things gone?" Myers replied.

"Well, The Viking didn't win, but he was close up. I'm not in the least disappointed, for Rover has come on wonderfully the last two or three weeks. He's been doing so well that I expected he'd win almost comfortably, but The Viking stuck to him and was only just beaten at the finish. It's quite good enough, and I'm convinced that the other's worth a lot more than what I want for him. They came clean away from the other two, Snowflake and Fox, beat them thirty or forty lengths, though they were carrying nothing."

"And you think I ought to back The Viking?"

"I do, indeed. Hawkins has got a line too, says he's better than Chain Mail that won last week. The old man's wonderfully shrewd, though he's as blind as a bat, and he gets to hear all that's going on."

"All right; many thanks, old fellow. I'll go and do it at once. Good-bye," Myers said aloud; and then to himself, "That's exactly what I wanted to know! If this Viking of theirs isn't a good lot better than Chain Mail, he won't beat me, for mine hasn't been particularly busy just of late."

Meantime, Winthorpe had been waiting at his club, patiently until the half-hour nearly struck, impatiently afterwards. He gave his unknown correspondent ten minutes' grace and then left a message with the hall porter saying that he had waited as long as he could,

42

but had an important engagement to keep. Reaching his rooms a little before twelve, another tedious period of suspense was before him—nothing occurred. He watched the instrument so pregnant at times with good news, bad news, and all sorts of surprises, but it remained exasperatingly placid. The half-hour struck—what could have happened? Reade had said from 12 to 12.15. He waited till half past, till a quarter to one, and then rang up the hotel at Chesterton. " Is Mr. Reade there? " he asked. Burley the landlord replied that he and his friend had been there, but had left about an hour before.

He had been expecting a message from Mr. Reade, Winthorpe said, explaining who he was and where he lived.

" Why, that was the number Mr. Reade had looked up in the book, not being quite sure of it, and so he must have telephoned," Burley said.

" What time was he back at the hotel? " Winthorpe asked.

" It must have been a little before eleven. He went to the telephone at once, then he had a sandwich, and drove off to see some horses at a farm in the neighbourhood. He was going down to Brighton by the 4.30."

Winthorpe was puzzled. He had been distinctly warned that the message could not reach him before twelve. He had, however, been called up at eleven, according to the first arrangement, when most unfortunately he was away. How could he ascertain what had taken place? Reade was not very likely to have told the landlord much, but he might possibly have said something.

" Did Mr. Reade tell you anything about what he had been doing? " Winthorpe asked on the telephone.

" No, sir," came the reply. " I made out that he had been to see the horses at their work, but he said nothing in particular."

" He didn't say anything about a trial, I suppose? Did he look pleased? " This, Winthorpe thought, might afford some sort of clue to what had been going on—if the horse had been beaten, Reade's manner would perhaps have shown disappointment or annoyance.

" Yes, sir, he seemed particular light-hearted, and so did his friend ; they were laughing and joking all the time they were here. I am sure they were satisfied with what had been going on."

This was, at any rate, something to know ; but what should he do? There was no means of communicating with Reade, who had, as well as he could understand, been ringing up an unresponsive telephone, and it behoved him to do something ; for Reade's other commissioners, he imagined, were already at work ; and as he supposed that they had a great deal of money to put on, the price would naturally soon shorten. He had not, of course, the least idea that he was to have the market all to himself and to put his money on a horse who was not intended to win, who was to be stopped in the race, as he had been stopped in the trial. The thing to do, in his futile opinion, was to go and back it at once, and off he went accordingly. The price was short, for the class of the horse was fully recognised. Nothing else but Centrebit was really mentioned with the exception of an outside shot now and then at Rosamund, both ways, and he was obliged to venture £4,000 to win something under rather than over £11,000.

Reade was accustomed to pass his week-ends out of town; it was not until Monday morning that Winthorpe could get speech with him, but on that day The Viking's owner paid him an early visit.

" Well, are you having a dash ? " he asked, cheerily.

" Yes, I am indeed," Winthorpe replied, "and I hope I am doing right, but not hearing from you as arranged I was only guessing. Indeed, I only betted because Burley said you seemed to have been satisfied with what had been done. There must have been some mistake about your telephoning."

" I don't understand you," Reade rejoined. " What do you mean by ' not hearing from me as arranged ' ? "

There was no doubt about it, Reade was honestly puzzled.

" Why, I mean, my dear fellow, that you didn't telephone when you said you would. I waited from twelve to a quarter to one, then rang up Burley and tried to find out something about you, and he thought you had talked to me before. I can't understand it ! "

" Twelve to a quarter to one ? " Reade said with surprise. " I told you from eleven to a quarter past, and it was striking eleven when I rang you up. Good heavens, man ! you talked to me— either I must be mad or you must ! I told you what had happened, and that you had better go and back the horse, and I gathered from you that you were going to."

" ' Gathered from me ' ? Why, I wasn't here at eleven o'clock. Nearly an hour before that a telegram came asking me to go down to the club to meet somebody, and as you had rung me up to say that you wouldn't have finished before twelve, I went off to see who wanted me."

Reade shook his head slowly.

" You are talking riddles," he said; " I never rang you up and told you anything about twelve. The last communication I had with you was when we parted at the Carlton. I told you I would let you know between 11 and 11.15 next day what had happened, and I did so."

44

" Well, I didn't get your message, simply because I wasn't here; and if anyone replied it was not I ! "

Winthorpe rang for his servant, and asked him if he could recall the morning in question. He did so readily. A gentleman had come very anxious to see his master, had waited some twenty minutes or so and then gone away, saying that he would write. He gave the name of Somerton. " Yes, he looked like a gentleman," the man said after some hesitation ; but all this really threw no light on the subject. Who could have known that a telephone message was coming at a certain time ? And yet this previous message, which was supposed to have come from Reade, saying that the trial was postponed for an hour, wanted a vast deal of explanation. There was an insoluble mystery, in fact, which grew more complicated the more it was examined. However, the important thing was that the horse had been backed ; and great was the satisfaction of Reade on the morning of the race to find that 2 to 1 was not obtainable. Winthorpe's £4,000 had been followed by some big bets from his friends, Reade having served his own ends by telling Winthorpe that, the stable commission being executed, he didn't care who participated in the good thing. The public followed suit, 7 to 4, then 6 to 4 was taken. Centrebit stood at 6 to 1, 13 to 2 in places, which well suited Reade and Hazel, who perceived that, Perkins having his instructions and being sure to carry them out, Centrebit could not be beaten.

The race need not be described at length. The Viking, it was generally agreed, had cruelly bad luck, Perkins not riding with anything like his accustomed discretion. At the turn into the straight he was badly hampered, his jockey pulled out as if intending to come on the outside, but—and here it was generally agreed he made his mistake—he changed his mind, pulled in again, and waited for an opening on the rails until the race was practically over. It was too late when he set off in pursuit of the leader, to be beaten two lengths. The truth was that Perkins had been hard put to it to prevent The Viking from winning easily. He might conceivably, by very bad judgment, have made the mess of it at the bend, but his attempt to get through on the rails was perceived by experts to be so clumsy that some good judges of riding shrewdly suspected what was being done, and one of the stewards was more than half inclined to send for the jockey and ask him to explain his riding. The horse had, however, unquestionably been backed, Winthorpe and some of his friends were known to have betted heavily, they were supposed to be in the confidence of Reade, who, it was assumed, had betted also, and so nothing came of the business, except that the handicappers made a mental note that The Viking was not to be dropped.

Reade had had a very good race, as had Myers. Hazel had won more money than he had ever been possessed of before; but poor Winthorpe, disdaining a furtive hint from Hazel that it might be judicious to save on Centrebit, stuck to his colours, and went down heavily. He dined with Reade at the hotel where he and Hazel were staying, and was distinctly glum. The result, The Viking being second instead of first, made a difference of £15,000 to him.

It was with quite another sort of face that Winthorpe entered Reade's sitting-room next morning. Evidently he had something important to say—something which he thought would afford a great deal of gratification.

"I hope to have to congratulate you in the course of the day, old fellow," he burst out.

"It is very kind of you; but what about?" Reade answered, looking up in surprise.

"Why, I believe you have a great chance of getting the race."

"Why, what on earth do you mean?" Reade exclaimed, momentarily losing his self-possession, and speaking with anxiety rather than satisfaction at the prospect.

"Parkinson is going to object to the winner; he was fourth, you know. He had backed his horse for a lot of money for a place, and says he is quite certain to get it."

"But what the devil is he objecting about? Surely everybody knows everything that is to be known about Centrebit? I am afraid your friend has found an exceptionally capacious mare's nest!"

"I don't know what it is," Winthorpe rejoined. "He said he wouldn't tell me till he had made sure; but he was as certain as he could be, all the same, and said he'd lay me 6 to 4 he got his place money. I'm in a hurry, but I thought I would just run in and tell you, because I knew how glad you'd be. I'll let you know as soon as I hear anything for certain," and, with a nod to the pair of them, he left the room.

"Glad?" Reade said. "Oh, yes, delighted, of course, after taking 6,000 to 1,000 about the winner, and laying just a little against my own. A few years ago, if what one hears is true, I might have made a little fortune that way; but it is almost impossible to manage now, though I did get a bit. I wonder what Parkinson thinks he knows?"

"But there can't be anything in it, can there?" Hazel asked.

"The most preposterous idea! If there's a horse everyone knows all about, surely it is Centrebit, bred at what you may call an historical stud, his dam the dam also of a Derby winner, sold at the Duke's death to the man who has had him ever since. You don't suppose I'd have a lot of money on a horse unless I was sure that it was right, do you?"

"Who is Myers? I know most people, but I don't even know him by sight."

"He's what they call a 'financier,' which may mean anything; and he 'finances' under all sorts of names; but his real name is Myers, I chance to know—I've had dealings with him. He doesn't understand much about racing—practically nothing, I expect—but he's a long-headed fellow himself, and his horses are managed by Lindsay; and I needn't tell you how little likely *he* is to go wrong. I must confess I'm curious to know what Mr. Parkinson has blundered into, all the same. But it's mere curiosity; I'm not anxious."

"I can't imagine," Hazel remarked. "Centrebit is certainly a four-year-old, and he is certainly a chestnut. Do you remember the objection to Rusticus because he was entered as a chestnut and the owner of the second declared that he was a black? As you say, with Lindsay looking after the horses there simply couldn't be a mistake about the entry, and we know there couldn't either about the weight. He can't be in the forfeit list, English or Irish—that Irish forfeit list has tripped up more than one man who thought he was safe."

"Yes, I've paid for carelessness about that, but Centrebit has never had anything to do with Ireland. I wish Parkinson would lay me 6 to 4 about getting his place money, I'd go on taking it till the cows came home. I never regarded Parkinson as a genius; to be frank, I always thought he was a silly little ass, but I didn't think he was such a silly little ass as that!"

When they arrived at the course, bookmakers were busy offering to bet on the objection, and Reade's views were confirmed by the market, for the ring were offering to lay 4 to 1 that the winner got it.

Laying the odds struck Reade as coining money. It occurred to him that he might just as well get another monkey out of the race if he could find anyone sufficiently infatuated to bet, and he looked about for Parkinson or any of his friends accordingly, in the hope that they might be inclined to support their eccentric opinion. At last he found the object of his quest.

"I'm making your fortune, you see," Parkinson said as he greeted Reade.

"I hope you are, indeed," the other replied untruthfully, "though I'm bound to say I don't understand how you are doing it, and I am curious to know."

"Well, my dear fellow, I think you are certain to get the race at any rate," Parkinson answered; "and I should strongly advise you to take these very liberal odds. They will lay you 4 to 1 against yours."

" I needn't tell you how much I hope you are right," Reade rejoined, " but I confess I am far more inclined to lay odds on the winner. What is it ? "

" I don't like to say until I am quite certain. I've wired up to town for confirmation, though all the same I *am* as certain as I can be. But take my advice and see if Cooper will lay you four monkeys."

" You wouldn't like to do it yourself, I suppose ? I confess it seems to me a good hedge," Reade asked.

" I would, gladly, only I don't like betting with a pal; but if you really want to hedge I don't mind, though I feel sure you will lose your money. I persuaded Winthorpe to back yours again."

" Well, put it down," Reade said, " 4,000 to 1,000 if you like. I'll lay you 4,000 to 1,000 on Centrebit." And the bet was booked.

The numbers for the first race were by this time hoisted. Betting on it had begun. Reade and Hazel strolled off to the paddock to see what was going on ; but there was a big field, several with evenly-balanced chances. Reade saw nothing to bet on, and thought it, on the other hand, a pity not to get a bit more out of his certainty ; so returning to the ring he quietly asked the first big man he came to on the rails what he was doing about the objection. The answer astonished him :

" Why, they are laying 7 to 4 on you, sir; but I'm not betting. I think you are sure to get it."

Reade was simply thunderstruck. Never had he known such a reversal of the odds, and now, too, he began to feel that something must indeed be wrong. But he must not show it.

" I wish you were right," he replied, for of course it had to be assumed that he was anxious for the victory of his own horse; "but I don't see that I have a chance. Have you any idea what's supposed to be wrong ? "

" Well, sir, they say something about the horse having been foaled abroad. The mare was sent to France, I'm told. I don't know the rule, but a very clever man told me you were sure to get the race."

Reade did know the rule to which the man referred. There it was in black and white.

" Foreign Horses.

" A horse foaled out of the United Kingdom shall not be qualified to start for any race until there have been deposited at the Registry Office and a fee of 5s. paid on each certificate : (1) Such a foreign certificate, and (2) such a certificate of age as are next mentioned. The foreign certificate must state the age, sex, pedigree, and colour of the horse, and any mark by which it may be distinguished, and must be signed by the secretary or other officer of some approved racing club of the country in which the horse was foaled, or by some magistrate, mayor, or public officer of that country."

If this had been omitted the objection was necessarily fatal; and, silly little ass as Parkinson might be, for once it presently appeared that he had stumbled upon a hard fact. There was no mistake about it; Centrebit's dam, The Safe, had been sent across the Channel to visit a sire for whom her owner had especial admiration. Her foal, Centrebit, had been born in France, and was consequently a foreign horse, according to the Rules of Racing. Every possible ground of objection except this one had been thought of by Reade—the fatal flaw had never occurred to him. It was cruel luck, he felt—people have such extraordinary views about that sort of thing—to lose his money over The Viking; harder still to part with what he had lost by laying against his own horse; and perhaps hardest of all to have to assume a smile and try to look gratified at the congratulations of the jubilant Winthorpe.

It was the beginning of Reade's downhill career, and when he started he travelled quickly. Winthorpe goes racing with his wife, but only bets ponies, and so avoids anxiety. The Rover was disposed of at the sale of Reade's horses for 480 guineas, and wins selling plates.

STRANGE STORIES OF SPORT

IV.—FIRST SPEAR: A PIG-STICKING TALE

BY FRANK SAVILE

CARWARDINE'S horse stumbled wearily as it thrust through the thicket of Spanish broom, and Carwardine swore with the exasperation of fatigue. He looked round at his companion. Hassan, his Moorish guide, stared back at him stolidly. The mule he rode was lathered and drooping, its ears drawn back along its sweating neck. Men and beasts were in the same evil case—reaching the last limits of exhaustion.

"How far?" asked the Englishman. "How far *now*?"

Hassan made an expressive gesture.

"Ten miles—or twelve, as the sand has shifted or the broom thickened," he answered briefly, and Carwardine swore again.

"I must be in Ceuta in three hours—I must—I must!" he insisted.

Hassan shook his head.

"*Mektub!*" he said, fatalistically. "It has been written by the All Merciful that we shall not do it. The beasts are beyond it."

Carwardine concentrated into a torrent of abuse every evil word of Arabic he knew. He cursed Hassan, the horse, the mule, the Moroquin Empire from Tangier to the Sus, but left his companion still indifferent. "Fool that I was to come this infernal expedition," he concluded to himself, in English. "I'd give a thousand for a sound horse this minute!"

Hassan's lack-lustre eyes suddenly brightened. His knowledge of his employer's tongue was limited, but in questions of finance his intelligence matched his self-interest.

"The English lord said——?" he suggested, interrogatively, and Carwardine recognised, with a sudden spasm of hope, a new tone in his henchman's voice.

"I said I would give a thousand dollars for a horse!" he replied. "Is there a village anywhere handy—a rest house—a Berber camp—where we could get one?"

"No," said the Moor, curtly; "but if you will I can arrange that these beasts get us to Ceuta in time—on conditions. You must buy them of me at my own price."

Carwardine's need was too pressing to desire explanations. "How much?" he asked, with a curtness that matched his companion's.

"Five hundred dollars each," said the other.

For a moment the Englishman hesitated. The terms were extortionate, but needs must when a certain Personage drives. And Carwardine was a wealthy man. He nodded.

The Moor nodded back. "And you must go waterless yourself till we reach Ceuta," he added.

Carwardine shrugged his shoulders in assent.

Hassan showed a sudden liveliness. With a quick direction to the Englishman to follow, he turned aside, forced a passage through the centre of a patch of alfa, and looked keenly on the earth. Five minutes later he gave a grunt of satisfaction and leaped to the ground.

Carwardine dismounted in his turn and took the mule by the bridle, for Hassan was digging furiously. It was not long before his search was rewarded. He had cut directly into the centre of an anthill, and the busy inhabitants swarmed out in indignation to resent this wanton attack upon their stronghold. The Moor brushed them aside till the rows of white eggs began to show amid the brown of the earth.

He swept them up in handfuls till they lay in a heap upon a corner of his *djelab* which he had taken off. Then he sprang to his feet, and took from the mule's pannier a cooking-pot and the water-skin—that water-skin which the day's thirst had already made all too light.

He filled the cooking-pot with his spoil, kneading it down with his knuckles till it made a paste of the consistency of honey. Even then he hardly appeared satisfied. He began to gather up the ants themselves and add them to the eggs, still pressing them down till the pot overflowed with their life juice. Then he took from Carwardine's saddle the other water-skin which hung there empty. He slashed it open, emptied the paste upon it, squirted the few pints of water left over the mass, and stirred it furiously for nearly a quarter of an hour. Finally he spread another corner of his *djelab* over the mouth of the cooking-pot, and through this improvised filter dripped all the liquid which he could press from his decoction.

He thrust it to the horse's lips. The poor brute drank greedily, but not his fill, for the pot was snatched from him half-emptied and transferred to the mule, who sucked up the remainder to the last drop.

Hassan gathered up his belongings swiftly.

" Mount !" he cried. " Mount while you can !"

Wondering, but silent, Carwardine did as he was told. A sudden animation seemed growing in his horse's action. His ears were aprick—he pawed the sand. The next instant the animal, which half an hour before had seemed within measurable distance of its last breath, gave a mighty buck, and set off across the sandhills at a gallop. The mule followed emulously.

" Ride hard !" shouted Hassan, as he thundered behind. " At most the effect will last but a hundred minutes, and we have three leagues to go !"

Carwardine heard as in a dream. A patent miracle had been done before his eyes, and he found no words as yet to cope with the situation. But he obeyed dumbly and sent his spurs into the sweat-smothered flanks. The horse responded like a four-year-old fresh from its stall.

Three hours later Hassan sat beside the dead bodies of both horse and mule within a mile of Ceuta. He was fingering with reverent hands a cheque on the well-known firm of Guzman and Co. for two hundred English pounds. The smoke of the Gibraltar steamer floated on the western breeze as it left the harbour, and Carwardine was exultantly pacing its decks.

*   *   *   *   *

The strains of the third waltz were dying away as Carwardine came into the ballroom and looked eagerly around. The dancers were crowding in pairs to sitting-out places in the verandah or to tiny tents and canopies among the cactus and in the aloe-hedged garden. His eyes brightened as they fell upon a girl coming towards him—a girl whose hand lay upon the arm of a tall Hussar-uniformed man. She was looking up at him with an intentness which made her oblivious of her surroundings. She gave a little start as Carwardine's voice greeted her as she passed.

"*You!*" she cried, in genuine surprise. "We heard you were up among the Atlas. I didn't expect to see you again till—till we should happen to meet in England," she concluded, a little incoherently.

Carwardine looked at her steadily.

" I met Morrison going up to Fez," he said, quietly. " He told me that you left for England to-morrow."

The colour rose suddenly to her face. She looked hurriedly at her companion. The Hussar was staring at Carwardine with half-curious, half-pitying eyes.

"As I *am* here," went on the other, in his even, unemotional tones, " I hope you have a dance for me ? "

She gave a tiny little shrug of her shoulders.

" They were all gone a week ago," she answered, "unless you can get Captain Beresford to forego you one ; " and she looked up again at her companion with a whimsical smile of inquiry.

For a moment the Hussar hesitated. Then the pity in his eyes extinguished mere curiosity.

" I think perhaps he deserves it," he said, gently. " The next, Carwardine, if Miss Fellowes will transfer it to you ; " and as he spoke he relinquished his partner's arm.

For a moment she showed surprise—almost annoyance. Her eyes sought Beresford's, seemed to read a message, and fell again. She laughed pleasantly, took Carwardine's proffered arm, and led him back towards the ballroom, where the band was playing the preliminary flourish of a set of Lancers.

Ten minutes later Miss Fellowes sat in the shadow of a flowering aloe, listening to the second proposal of marriage which she had received that evening. Her eyes were dim, and her voice extremely gentle.

" I am so grieved—so very, very grieved," she was saying, in answer to Carwardine's vehement words. " And after all your suffering and fatigue, too, in getting here to-night it sounds so dreadfully hard-hearted ; but I accepted Arthur Beresford half an hour ago, and—and I *love* him."

For ten seconds Carwardine's only answer was silence—a silence which could be felt. Then he rose.

" Shall we go back to the ballroom ? " he said, quietly, offering his arm. She rose in her turn and took it, but she hesitated.

" Captain Beresford is—is your friend," she said. " You—you won't—— "

" Forget it ? " he interrupted, slowly. " No, Miss Fellowes, I shan't forget it, on my honour." And so led on out of the shadows of the garden into the brilliance of the hall.

* * * * *

Hassan lay back on the pile of cut alfa grass in the thicket clearing and looked at his companion, who for the second time that month was Major Carwardine. The Moor's brown eyes shone dully over the bowl of kif which he had set alight in his pipe. His face wore a great impassivity.

" So," he said, " if I have understood you aright, the meeting next week is of a new arrangement ? You do not all of you ride the boar ? It is left to each pair to deal with him separately, man to man ? "

Carwardine nodded.

" We call it a tournament. As each boar is found, two men as arranged ride forth upon it and count merit for the planting of the first spear in his body or for his death, as you have seen aforetime. Winner continues to compete with winner till the ultimate victor be found."

" It agrees well with other madnesses of your nation which I have witnessed," said Hassan, reflectively. " You wish, then, that I get news of pig within a score of miles ? "

Carwardine nodded.

" Yes," he said, " I require that of you, and more. I require that you take me one boar, of full age and fierce, alive."

Hassan's face lost a shade of its wonted immobility.

" Alive ! " He pondered. " That would have need of men— six men—eight men, possibly ten men ; and ropes, and nets. Wounds might be received—even death. Nets will be broken—nets expensive to replace. Even my respect for your excellency will not permit me to say that it would cost any sum less than five hundred dollars."

Carwardine laughed harshly.

" You have monotonous notions in finance," he said. " A boar costs the life of a horse. So be it ; the more especially as I would have you treat this boar as you, within the last fortnight, treated my horse. The *ant drink* has to be administered to him as I will show you."

Hassan's eyes were bright by now.

" Name of Allah ! " he swore, softly. " What is your excellency's purpose ? "

" When I and he whom I shall emulate ride forth, I would have you and your underlings prepared within a thicket," said Carwardine, distinctly. " Thence, at a signal arranged, you will let loose your captive. You will have your price if he be of such fierceness as I approve ; you will have your price doubled if——"

The Moor interrupted with an expressive wave of the hand.

" Your excellency need have little fear of his fierceness if *I* have dealings with him such as you saw me work upon your horse. But think first, excellency. A boar is already a fighter among fighters. If such as *he* become intoxicated with the blood of ants he becomes an Afreet, a devil of the pit, a seeker of blood, terrible, careless of his life, ready to risk all that he may kill, kill, kill ! "

Carwardine nodded again.

" Yes," he answered, " so would I have him. Since I saw you work upon my horse I have made inquiries, and it is as you say. See to it, my friend, and you will find me generous as before."

He rose and faced towards the town. Hassan rose in his turn.

"And the meeting of the Tent Club is ——?" he asked.

"Eight days from now," said Carwardine, curtly. "Remember, a boar of full age, and fierce—*fierce!*"

*   *   *   *   *

The winter sunshine lit up the camp at Awara as the members of the Tent Club foregathered after their early breakfast. Away to the north the ocean gleamed dazzlingly in front of Spartel; inland the marshes were silver ribands across the mimosa-covered plain, while the mists hung in soft grey canopy over the Red Mountain.

It was a cosmopolitan assembly, Britons being in the majority, though each of the Tangier Legations supplied one or more members to this sporting contingent. The beaters were a motley crew, clad in every fabric from tattered lawn to sackcloth; Moors for the most part, they included one or two human derelicts whose European garb revealed the fact that they were *Kaffir-billahs*—dogs of unbelievers who would not refuse to act the butcher's part upon the slain pigs, a duty which a son of Islam would not undertake for any bribe. A pack of mongrel hounds bayed and quarrelled around their masters' feet.

Hassan, the head man, drew out from among his underlings. Carwardine joined him, and drew him aside.

"We have *him*, even as you desired, tethered among the cork trees below Hafa," said the Moor.

Carwardine nodded gravely.

"A full-grown boar?" he questioned.

Hassan held up his open palm suggestively the height of his own hip. "A forty-inch tusker!" he averred. "Name of Allah! A monster—the father of all pigs!"

There was a gleam of doubt in Carwardine's smile.

"I hope he may reach within four inches of your description," he answered." "Have you prepared the draught?"

Hassan nodded energetically.

"It lies beside him in an earthen-stoppered vessel," he replied. "Scarcely does he need it. His eyes are already of the colour of blood—his desires run to killing—he voices his anger."

"Good," interrupted Carwardine. "How will you administer it?"

The Moor touched the bosom of his *djelab*.

"I have here a ram's horn," he explained. "With this aid Manuel will sluice what I have prepared down the beast's evil throat till his rage grows upon him into madness. He will be a devil of devils—*ghazi*—careless of life."

"Allah send it!" said Carwardine, piously. "Why must Manuel deal with him and not yourself?"

The other flushed angrily.

"Would a son of the true faith defile himself with swine carrion?" he answered. "Nay; I have Manuel, Pedro, and the renegade Frenchman from Oran. They have their orders, and claim twenty dollars apiece," he added, with an avaricious gleam in his eyes.

"See that they earn it!" said Carwardine, coldly. "For the present beat as usual. But when you see me ride forth for my course, and I raise my arm to my helmet—so, then follow your instructions."

"On my head be it," said Hassan. "May my bones lie eternally within the jaws of jackals if it be not so!"

Nodding again solemnly the Moor drew his garments about him and roared his hoarse commands. Chattering, yelling to their dogs, and shouting farewell ribaldries to the servants left in camp, the crowd of beaters moved off in a ragged procession, while Carwardine rode back to the tents. A few minutes later the horses were brought up, and about a score of men, with two or three ladies, mounted and ambled gently after the beaters.

Before they reached the cover the horsemen divided, the majority of them riding towards the crest of the low hill which commanded an extensive view; but two, who carried spears, cantered towards the banks of a mud lake where the scrub ended. A couple of mounted natives with spare spears followed them.

As soon as these latter reached the edge of the marsh pandemonium broke out among the beaters on the hill. Men began yelling vociferously, beat their staves together, and urged their dogs to stupendous exertions in the way of barking and rushing from tussock to tussock. Birds whirred up here and there. A jackal slunk furtively from a patch of Spanish broom, rabbits were afoot, pattering over the sun-dried alfa. But so far no heavier game gave sign of its presence.

Suddenly a dog bayed loudly. A score took up the chorus. A Moor howled some excited words, and Hassan came pounding through the scrub to his side. He put his hands to his mouth and sent a warning halloa to the two upon the marsh edge. With a crash of dry cork branches a tawny grey shadow seemed to swing out across the yellow glare of the plain.

The boar had struck the open mid-way between the spectators on the hill and the two competitors at its foot. The latter came at a stretching gallop towards him, reckless of rabbit-holes and boulders. Their quarry had set his snout for the cover on the western side of the plain a full mile away.

Robertson, of the Fusiliers, was the better mounted of the two riders; but Arthurs, the gunner, was the more experienced spearsman. He dropped away behind his companion to the right, taking the upper ground of the slope. Robertson, believing that he gained an advantage, spurred on his horse eagerly, and drew ahead yard by yard.

The pig's short legs moved incredibly fast. For a full minute he held his distance, but then pace and gradient both began to tell. Robertson neared him, overhauled him, poised his spear for the underhand stab, seemed to hover over the dun hide for a single waiting instant, and delivered his stroke—into the empty air!

With astounding quickness and at full pace the boar had jinked! The fusilier went thundering on half a furlong before he could rein in his excited charger, while the boar, swerving uphill, found himself bearing full-tilt towards the imperturbable Arthurs.

The latter steadied his horse to a canter and looked keenly at the boar, recognising in an instant that the latter meant a charge. The little deep-set eyes were twinkling fiercely: the snout was sunk: the neck ridged up in wrath. The gunner, with pressure of bridle and knee, swung round his horse to meet the crucial moment.

It came. With a sound half grunt, half snarl, the brute dashed towards the horse's knees.

No stroke seemed to be delivered. The beast appeared to bring about its own destruction. Full into its chest the point went home, buried up to the wood. As the shaft broke the boar ploughed a groove through the sand almost between the horse's fetlocks, while the latter bucked aside from its sprawling body. A spasmodic spurning of the dust, a coughing grunt or two, and the beast was dead. A smashing victory for Arthurs, as his opponent, Robertson, was the first cheerily to acknowledge.

So with varying success the sport went on till three more courses had been run. Pig were numerous and the next beat produced a whole sounder, which was the cause of an amusing incident. Bingham, a young subaltern and a green hand, selected with enthusiasm the largest animal in view, raced upon it, broke his spear with an ineffectual stroke, and letting his horse get out of hand, was chased half a mile by the infuriated porker before an orderly could give his master a new spear and the information that he had been wasting his energies upon a sow. The second course ended in a draw, each competitor getting in first spear upon his selection at identically the same moment, while each also permitted his quarry to escape unslain to cover. In the third course, Montesquieu, the French attaché, won a handsome victory from Saunders, a naval lieutenant, a win provoking great enthusiasm among promoters of the *entente cordiale.*

There was an obvious hush in the chattering crowd of onlookers as spears were produced for the fourth round. Gibraltar is a place distinctly parochial in its interests, and individuals are apt to claim more attention than public affairs. If it had not been expressed in so many words it was certainly understood that Carwardine and Beresford were rivals. That both had aspired to the hand of General Fellowes's daughter was common knowledge. That Carwardine had taken his defeat in this quarter like a gentleman was the general opinion, but the fact that the two competitors in the coming course had met in other lists added piquancy to the situation. It had been much discussed since the draw took place a month before.

Each had a reputation for horsemanship; each had ridden and killed his boar over a score of times; each was well mounted and knew his country as the palm of his own hand. Onlookers hastened to take up positions which would command a wide view as the beaters slouched with shouting into the first cork patch of the Hafa woods. It was a famous beat, not drawn blank twice in a season.

The two riders cantered up towards the apex of the cover, chatting amicably. Carwardine's horse seemed strangely excited. Beresford looked at the lathering animal.

" You're handicapping yourself with that brute, my boy," he said, earnestly. " Go back and change. One of Hassan's would do you better."

Carwardine's lip curled.

" Many thanks, old chap," he answered, drily. " I've sat a horse before."

Beresford shrugged his shoulders.

" Sorry," he said, briefly. " Will you take right or left ? "

" Left," said Carwardine, laconically, and plunged on to take up a position about a hundred yards from his opponent. As he did so he raised his hand with what seemed an elaborated gesture towards his helmet, and lifted it from his brow.

A moment or two later a yell chorused up from the beaters, echoed by the barkings of a score of dogs. A cork bush crashed in the heart of the cover and the swish of the alfa grass announced that a more than usually bulky carcase was grooving a way through it. The two riders scanned the bush keenly.

The next instant a long, lean, deep-flanked boar burst into the open, the great bristles ridged up like quills between his shoulders. His eyes flamed; he bounded forward with a furious motion utterly unlike the business-like scuttle of pig when ordinarily disturbed; his grunts shrilled up into a sort of hissing snarl. He flung his glance from right to left, half halted for a moment indeterminate, and then saw the horsemen who were just spurring their nags towards him. Like a bolt from a catapult he rushed—not away from, but directly towards them.

Beresford, who was nearest, steadied his horse, lowered his hand, and prepared to receive the charge. Beneath his breath he was softly congratulating himself upon the luck which had given him the right-hand position. Bar accidents, he felt confident of accounting for this brute before Carwardine had done much more than see him. A direct charge? Nothing was easier for a cool hand to compete with.

He had reckoned without his host. This was no ordinary brute that was racing upon him, blind with mere terror or animal rage. It was, as Hassan had predicted, a devil of devils—killing mad—endowed with all the maniac agility which the drug had set running in its fevered veins. Within a fathom of the waiting spear-head it swerved, plunged aside, whisked round furiously below Beresford's stirrup, and cut savagely with its tusks at his horse's flanks. The poor brute leaped in its sudden agony and staggered, while the boar, catching sight of Carwardine, continued its charge. Before the beast was within twenty yards of it Carwardine's horse was frankly running away. Pig it knew—boar, sow or sounder—but this was something beyond its experience. Never had snarls like those issued before from porcine lips—never had one of the accursed race of swine shown such swiftness of attack and such fury. Tugging madly at the reins Carwardine flew past Beresford as the latter became aware that in his horse's leg an artery was severed.

The boar's nostrils quivered as they scented the crimson puddle. Its little eyes shifted from Carwardine's flying steed to Beresford's, which blundered and rocked as it cantered heavily up the slope. With a whisk and a wriggle of its curly tail the dun snout swerved and steered its owner towards this easier prey.

There was a shock as the cruel tusks came home again into the sweating flanks. The horse screamed, staggered, and fell, and Beresford's leg was between the saddle and the sand. The spear dropped from his hand. With a desperate effort he rolled clear, only to know that his leg was broken. Twice the maddened pig dashed its tusks into the struggling horse's belly, and twice its victim responded with a scream—the shriek of agony which from a horse's throat is pitiful beyond all hearing. It roused in Beresford the sensibility which the shock of his fall had numbed. Despite his pain he crawled to and reached the spear. A shout made him look up. Carwardine was riding towards him, but the terror and unwillingness of his horse seemed to make his progress appallingly slow. He was a couple of hundred yards away, seeming to be thrusting his charger along by mere force of spur and blows. The onlookers were half a mile up the slope. For the next minute Beresford had only himself to look to in his moment of peril.

The flaming eyes glanced upon him over his struggling horse's flank: he realised that within a second the long white fangs would be stabbing at his body. And then, as he grasped his spear, and tensed his muscles for the encounter, the boar's gaze swerved. The sound of Carwardine's horse pawing the sand, the cloud of dust that rose from its uneasy feet, attracted his attention and his rage. With a grunt he whirled away to find other victims--ones worthier the strength of his fierce anger still unslaked.

Carwardine lowered his spear unsteadily. Beresford, as he lay helpless, could but notice how unlike his imperturbable self the other sat his plunging horse. A sudden pang pulsed into the Hussar's heart. Was Carwardine's nerve giving--was he, too, going to miss and thus share, not shorten, his comrade's danger?

The boar charged on. As he approached he squealed—fiercely, shrilly. The sound was too much for Carwardine's horse. He bucked, reared, made as if he would swerve upon two legs, crossed them, and with a thud came down. Carwardine was underneath—received the full weight of his body, and so lay not twenty yards from his companion, but helpless as Beresford's self!

The next few minutes for the Hussar were a sort of nightmare, in which impossibilities became accepted facts. How else can it be explained that a man with a broken leg dragged himself, spear in hand, a distance of over sixty feet, to stab and stab again into a bristling hide which seemed to have all the impenetrability of armour plate. The glare of the desert danced about him like the glare of red-hot steel; the dust ringed him in—covered him—suffocated him. And through the veil of it the boar's mask swerved back and forth, its jaws a-champ with rage, its eyes red and flaming, its limbs trampling Beresford's shattered bone and quivering flesh as it fought across his body to reach his face. And still as in a dream, with all the obstinacy of growing unconsciousness, he held the point of the spear buried in that advancing chest, and thrust the point deeper and deeper towards that fiery heart!

*   *   *   *   *

A minute later the crowd of onlookers swarmed down to find a dead horse, a dead boar, and two men living, but senseless as the carcases beside them. Under the direction of Gilliatt, the surgeon of the gunners, litters were improvised, and half an hour later the

60

dining marquee had become a hospital. There through the night Carwardine threshed out the hours of delirium, and Gilliatt, listening, grew wide-eyed with wonder as the self-revealing words were poured out in a ceaseless stream. Before the dawn the doctor had learned enough to make strenuous inquiries for Hassan, and to be told that that most versatile of headmen had not been seen since the previous afternoon. His next inquiry was for Carwardine's Colonel, Halkett, to whom he made a communication which made that worthy soldier stare incredulously.

"If Carwardine likes to send in his papers after I have interviewed him, well and good," said Halkett at last; "but if he does not, how am I to act? No Court of Inquiry would receive such evidence—the whole thing is a nightmare—and outside the plane of practicalities. How can a man endow a pig with the strength and fury of a tiger simply by dosing him with a decoction of ant eggs? It's absurd!"

Gilliatt shrugged his shoulders and smiled.

"The funny thing is that I got corroborative evidence by last mail!" he answered.

Halkett looked at him as if he thought that the mantle of the boar's madness had descended upon the doctor.

"What d'you mean?" he rapped out.

"Simply this," said Gilliatt, quietly. "In the last quarterly number of my medical journal is an account of the properties discovered lurking in formic acid, so that dilute doses administered to a patient induce in him five-fold muscular powers. Perhaps I need hardly remind you that formic acid—as its name implies—is the product of ants!"

Halkett gasped.

"Good Lord!" he cried.

Gilliatt nodded.

"It's the old story," he said, simply. "The Discoveries of the West are the Traditions of the East. We think they are behind us all the time, these Moors and Arabs. They alone know how far they are in front, my friend—how very far in front!"

61

STRANGE STORIES OF SPORT
V.—THE GHOSTLY POACHER.

BY H. KNIGHT HORSFIELD

EARLY in January I found a letter upon my breakfast table. I read it casually and threw it amidst the *débris* of my other correspondence. It was the kind of letter one often receives, and comes to regard rather as a nuisance, involving as it does an immediate reply and the need of inventing more or less plausible excuses; in brief, an invitation to be declined. It was an invitation from a man whom I had known and shot with abroad, a certain Colonel Gilroy, and he asked me to stay with him, for a week's shooting, at the great red-brick Georgian monstrosity which formed the residence on his family estate, in the East Riding of York. I had seen the hard, forbidding face of the house, set in low-lying and uninteresting surroundings, many times from the railway-carriage window, and I had never felt in the least tempted to take up even a temporary abode there. In addition, I had never quite liked the man. He was subject to moods, to long fits of what seemed to be a morose silence; moreover, he was a bachelor living practically alone. So that, on the whole, with other and more entertaining engagements on hand, I had no leaning to a six days' *tête-à-tête* with a host so little congenial.

Still, as I reflected upon the form of my reply, I found that something in the wording of his letter stuck in my mind. It worried me. The opening sentences were cold and formal enough: a brief reminder that we had shot together before, an equally brief hope that the acquaintanceship might be renewed; then the stiff handwriting had changed. In hurried, sprawling characters he had written the word, "Come." Below the signature, isolated from the text, he had written it, doubly underlined.

My mind went back to a sandy nullah in Somaliland. Around, the great prairie rolled in endless undulation. A few trees fringed the nullah, their great leaves drooping motionless in the heat. Gilroy was stretched lazily on the sand, availing himself of the bare shelter. At his feet a blesbok was lying, the white blaze on its forehead snowily pure against the darker ground. There was no need for the *coup de grâce*; it had clearly been *in extremis* when we came up. Gilroy was watching it intently. A shudder like a gentle wind flowed through its slender limbs, stirred in its breast, and passed from its mouth in a sigh. Gilroy leapt up. "Man," he exclaimed, "I—I saw something go!" I was lighting my pipe at the time. I thought he had a touch of the sun, and did not reply. He made no reference to the matter again, in fact for two days he barely opened his lips. Now this incident came back to me. I saw him again in the desert, a sudden wave of emotion breaking down for a moment the wall of icy taciturnity which usually hemmed him in. And it seemed to me that such a wave had swept across his soul when he had written that one word "Come." As I looked at it, it became more than a mere word; it became a cry—almost a command.

So I decided to set aside the chance of some 400-head days, with Bridge and bright eyes and laughter to follow, and to immure myself for a week in the red-brick monstrosity, with its grim array of flat windows, and with a hard-faced, silent man for a gaoler, in the hope that it might be counted to me for righteousness. After all, I reflected, we spent months together in the waste places of the earth without any serious difference—there must have been some bond of sympathy between us. Perhaps we were both a little superstitious; some common taint in our blood, it might be, derived from a savage, fetish-loving ancestry, which had survived even to these radiant days of School Boards and County Councils. In any case, I decided to go, and I wrote my acceptance in the properly accredited formula; yet all the while I felt deep down in my heart that I was being called to a man in need.

*   *   *   *   *

It was a cold, black night when I drove up the long carriage sweep. The blank face of the house, unrelieved by creeper or any growing thing, looked strangely inhospitable. Gilroy received me as genially as his nature would permit, but a sense of gloom still pervaded the place. Certainly the personality of my host did little to dispel it. Always thin and hard-featured, he appeared to have grown more cadaverous; yet when I made some reference to his health he waved the matter aside with almost petulant impatience. On my arrival Gilroy had been engaged with a florid, clean-shaven man, to whom he introduced me, if the bare indication of his companion's existence could be called an introduction, but I had failed to catch the name. The man was plainly not a retainer, but it was equally clear that he was not a guest in any ordinary sense. His manner was deferential, yet he moved about the room, examined the papers and so on, with the air of one whose position was assured. Soon after my coming he quietly withdrew, leaving me with my host.

The thought occurred to me here that the man was present in the capacity of a medical attendant, but in this I was wrong. Gilroy and I dined together alone, and I tried to the best of a somewhat poor ability, for I felt flat and depressed, to enliven the proceedings with reminiscences of the olden days. Still the evening dragged its slow length wearily along. As soon as I decently could, I called attention to the hour, and suggested that I should turn in. Then it was that Gilroy spoke. He had been silent for quite a long time, but now I noticed a curious flickering of his eyelids, and he waved me back to my seat.

" You were surprised to hear from me ? " he said, abruptly.

I admitted it, throwing in a few civil commonplaces.

" The fact is," he went on, " I wanted you—wanted you badly. You are the one person I know whose assistance may be of great use to me."

I bowed in acknowledgment of the compliment, feeling at the same time not altogether comfortable in regard to the honour about to be thrust upon me.

" You saw that man," Gilroy proceeded. " He is a detective—a clever one, I am told. I asked for the best procurable. But he will approach my problem from one direction only—the material. He will probably find the solution there; I hope he may. But if he fails there is another point of view—the immaterial, psychical, supernatural, what you will. And you are the man to deal with that." He passed his hand with a distressed movement across his brow. " I will spare no trouble, no thought, no money, to sift this matter to the very bottom," he added, almost fiercely.

It did not seem to occur to him that he was also likely to be lavish of the trouble of his friends, but I did not refer to this.

" But you have not told me yet what the question is," I said ;
" I am quite in the dark."

I again noticed the curious flickering movement of the eyelids.
He seemed to have difficulty in speaking.

" There is something going on here," he said at last, " something which evades every solution I can suggest. I admit that the
thing is getting on my nerves. Night by night we have a poacher
in the woods. No common poacher."

" What have your keepers to say ? " I asked.

He made a quick, angry gesture. " This is no common poacher,
I tell you. In the dead of night a figure appears, armed, clad in
white. It has been seen, time after time, by a number of men, upon
all of whom I can rely. They say it moves down the rides in the
covert, slowly and deliberately. It makes no attempt at concealment
or escape ; then it abruptly disappears. Whatever it may be, it has
some quality which demoralises the watchers. They refuse to enter
the woods."

" You have not chanced to encounter it yourself? "

" No ; I have been out several times, but I have had no luck.
I should like to meet it. The 'material' question should be settled
finally. I should shoot at sight."

I remembered that the Colonel had a reputation for drastic
methods where poachers were concerned. Ignoring the law, his
keepers had strict injunctions to carry their guns when engaged in
night watching. " I decline to submit for one moment to the
absurd sentimentalism of our law-givers," he had once said to me.
" An armed man, or, it may be, a gang of armed men, enter upon
my property. There are three courses open to me : I may permit
them to rob my coverts unmolested ; I may send out my men
unarmed to cope with murderous ruffians, able, and in most cases
ready, to drop them at twenty paces ; or I may instruct my servants
always to carry firearms, and to use them freely if there is reason to
fear that their life or limb is in danger. I choose the last course,
notwithstanding the law. My keepers are engaged in a lawful duty.
They have wives and families to consider as well as their own safety.
In the event of a fatality on his side, the poacher has no cause for
complaint ; the risk is incident to his calling. For us it is a mere
choice of evils. I prefer to risk the puny terrors of the law. The
punishment, if any, which an English judge would dare to mete out
to an honest man defending, to the best of his ability, his own life
and his employer's property, is scarcely likely to equal the loss of an
eye or a limb."

I remembered this ethical code of the Colonel's as he spoke.
His opinions were well known in the district, and it occurred to me

that if any local humourist was playing the ghostly part for his amusement, he was indeed a bold man.

" Have you no solution which will at all meet the case ? " I asked at length.

I noticed that Gilroy's flickering eyelids drooped. He looked tired and ill, and his head was bent.

" No," he said, wearily. " The detective suggests that it is the prank of some village idiot. He even hints at the servants here, but I will answer personally for every man on the place. No ; the thing goes deeper than that. You know how the world is mainly divided : into fools who believe everything, and fools who believe nothing. There is another class to which you and I may fairly claim to belong. There are facts in this strange world of ours which only the man with the brain of the scientist and the heart of the poet can hope to grasp truly. You—oh, I am not going to flatter you—are an indifferent enough example of this latter class; but you may serve. This visitant in the woods has some reference to me. I feel it. I can't tell you how, any more than Huxley or Tennyson could have told you how the music of the moon comes to be hidden in the plain eggs of the nightingale. Anyhow, the feeling is there. What do you make of it ? "

I remained silent, trying to think.

" You know the legend of the place, that when the ghost comes three times the owner or one of his kin—some known person, any-how—goes mad or dies. Rot, of course, but with some residue of truth in it. What is that residue ? Put your brain to work on it. All hope for me, all real discovery in the mystery of life, lies that way."

I looked at him attentively. His pale face was strained. Some faint theories were moving, trying to uplift their heads in the slug-gish waters of my mind.

" I want to go to bed," I said. " When your keepers go into the coverts again, forbid them to take their guns."

*   *   *   *   *

On the morrow I interviewed the detective. He was a cheery, companionable man. We talked, of course, about the ghost.

" You're a bit of a spiritualist yourself, sir, like the gov'nor," indi-cating the Colonel, who was standing apart. " Well, I think we shall get at the truth of this without the help of either Mrs. Piper or Mas-kelyne and Cooke. You see," he went on, confidentially, seeing that he had no rival to fear in me, " it is as well to begin at the beginning. The head-keeper now is a decent man, so is the under-keeper; we needn't count the boy who looks after the dogs, he's too little. Then we come to the butler, to the coachman, and to the stable helper. The stable helper is a nice lad, not very keen-witted, but no fool."

"No," I said, not seeing very clearly where these remarks tended.

"No. Now, what I'm looking for just now is a fool."

"Really," I said; "that seems rather a strange lack."

"Well, who but a fool would risk his place, and his life even—for that old fire-eater would shoot him as soon as he would a rabbit—to go poaching, and then leave the dead pheasants where they fall in the woods?"

"Does our ghost do this?" I asked.

"Of course it does. Shots are heard in the woods, the ghost is seen walking calmly down the rides like a duke, and the dead pheasants are found where they fall. No man other than a fool or a lunatic would act in such a way."

"You appear to believe that the culprit is a member of the household. How is that?"

He winked impressively. "I'll tell you later," he said.

*　　*　　*　　*　　*

I spent the morning trying for rabbits in a long bank near the house, but the ferrets were lazy, and the short January day soon closed in. In a little while I found myself again with Gilroy, alone in the dim lamp-lighted room. He did not refer to the ghost. He looked tired and ill. Soon after dinner he asked to be excused, took his candle, and went to bed, and I am bound to admit that I found his absence a relief. Then I lighted a pipe and sat by the fire to think. When it had grown quite late the detective came in.

"I think something may happen to-night," he said. "May I sit down?"

I indicated the opposite chair, which he took, and I handed my pouch, from which he filled his pipe.

"Have you noticed anything to-day, sir?" he asked.

I reflected. I had seen the stableman cleaning some harness. I had seen the spectacled housekeeper on the stairway, and the maid, a girl with rather prominent blue eyes, dusting the large glazed gun-case in the hall, in which were many fowling-pieces of present and bygone dates. These observations did not appear to amount to much; still, I named them, not knowing what chance material might prove meat for my friend's professional acumen to feed upon.

"I looked through the guns this morning, sir. One of them had been recently used. It had been replaced uncleaned."

"Indeed!" I said, in some surprise, knowing that Gilroy was most particular about his guns.

" Yes—a 20-bore. A nice, handy little weapon, sir. Who is likely to have access to the hall, and to use a 20-bore ? "

I had no means of knowing. I paused. My meditations were cut short by two shots, fired in quick succession, in the covert close to the house.

The detective rose quietly. " The ghost walks," he said. " Come with me. We'll settle this matter to-night."

So together, armed only with sticks, we passed out into the night. As we went through the hall the detective glanced at the gun-case in the dim lamp-light.

" The 20-bore has gone," he whispered ; " as I thought."

The night was perfectly still, and the stars were shining brightly. A slight snowfall had touched the leafless trees with a film of white. Without speaking, we traversed the long rides within the covert, stopping at intervals to listen. The shots were not repeated. No sound or sight unusual greeted us, and the hour of midnight went by. Thinking that our ghostly visitant had got wind of us, and had sought safety in flight, we were about to return. A cluster of fir trees edged the ride for a little way, and their plumed branches cast a heavy gloom below. Beyond, the trees were thinner, and the path, whitened by the driven snow, became clearly visible. In the shadow of the firs I paused, and feeling that the time for circumspection had gone by, I struck a match, and proceeded to ignite a pipe. Suddenly the light was dashed from my shading hands, and the strong grip of my companion forced me into the brushwood.

" It is coming," he whispered, almost inaudibly. " Look ! "

Peering through the dim vista I saw a figure moving. It was clad in white, or what seemed to be white, for, chameleon-like, it appeared to take its hue from its surroundings, and save for the faint moving outline it might have been part of the wintry scene. It showed no haste, and gave no furtive sign, as a man might who walks by night upon forbidden ground. On the contrary, it advanced in the leisurely fashion of one without a fear or a care, and as it bore down straight upon us I saw a stray star-beam glint on the barrel of its gun.

I admit that my heart quickened and my breathing stopped. In a moment more it would be upon us, and the time for action would have come. Then, when barely two yards away, the hand which had tightened on my club fell to my side. For the first time I saw the face clearly, strangely transfigured, wide-eyed, open-lipped, yet still the face of my friend and host—the face of Gilroy.

*   *   *   *   *

In a little over twelve hours I was in Harley Street, and the great specialist in mental complications—the small gentleman with the spectacles and the manners of a dancing master—had listened to my tale. If I had any thought to surprise him I had reckoned without my specialist.

"Duplex personality," he said. "Interesting, of course, but by no means uncommon. Let me see. A case on all fours. Ah!" turning to a well-filled bookcase, "'Journal of Medical Association— Dr. Mason.' We will see what Mason has to say: 'In another patient of my own a second personality assumed absolute control of the physical organisation. During the stay of the second personality the primary or original self was entirely blotted out, and the time so occupied was a blank. Primary self no knowledge of second personality except from report of others.' Ah! yes. I had better see Colonel Gilroy. No cause for anxiety; treatment—care. Of course we all pass normally into a second phase of personality, alternating with the first, when we go to bed and sleep. Yes. I had better see your friend Colonel Gilbert—I beg your pardon, Gilroy. Good day to you. Wretched weather, isn't it?"

      *   *   *   *   *

So I passed out into the bitter street. Why, I wondered, did this strange, wandering other self of poor Gilroy select the old greyish-white khaki and sun helmet—the garb we had worn in Somaliland—for his mid-winterly wanderings? Why? But there are so many whys in this strange world. And the specialists are not so explicit as they might be.

STRANGE STORIES OF SPORT

VI.—BROTHERTAP MOOR

BY FRANK SAVILE

SIR WILLIAM CRUNDAL was a scientist first and a sportsman second, but any one of his friends would have said that the first had a very narrow win. In spring and summer his thoughts concerned his test tubes alone, but from August the 12th to January the 31st they had a serious rival in his brace of twelve-bores. Somehow or somewhere he contrived to get not fewer than two days' shooting a week, and many an important analysis had to wait while he enjoyed himself on manor or moor.

When in 1903 he went on his famous expedition to Bolivia in the interests of the Great Santa Fé Minerals Concession he gained to himself not only notoriety but a very considerable fee. Under the circumstances he decided that he deserved a thorough holiday, and the morning after his arrival in London betook himself to the offices of the well-known agents—Day, Teddy, and Grooving—full of sporting purpose. He would stand himself a four-hundred-brace moor if such a thing was left in the market.

Mr. Day interviewed him, and, as all agents in like case do, hummed and ha'd and shrugged his shoulders. July was hardly the month to take moors of the first class. Sir William would know that as well as Mr. Day's self. He would, however, consult Ledger A.

Ledger A being brought was drawn blank. Eight-hundred-guinea moors were there; eleven-hundred-guinea forests; magnificent rivers; tempting lochs. These were dangled before the eyes of the man of science in vain. What he wanted—and meant to get—was four hundred brace of grouse for four hundred pounds. A comfortable lodge—he was beyond the age that delights in roughing it—was also a *sine quâ non*. Mr. Day's jaw lengthened.

Suddenly he gave his forehead a melodramatic slap and plunged heavily for a note-book on the far side of his writing-table. He took it up, flipped the pages excitedly, and consulted an entry. After which he confronted his client with a beaming face.

"Sir William," he said, piously, "this seems almost like an intervention of Providence. But for my failing memory I need have given you no cause for hesitation. Yesterday—only yesterday—the thing you require came into the market."

"What name, where, and how much?" said the baronet, concisely.

Mr. Day tapped his notebook, as if the answers to these questions were concretely bound within its covers.

"Brothertap Moor, the property of Skene of Skene," he replied. "In Aberdeenshire, within four miles of a station, in lovely country, with two miles of burn which gives excellent trout."

"And the bag?" asked Sir William.

Mr. Day hesitated, but only momentarily.

"The bag is estimated to be four hundred and fifty brace," he said.

Sir William examined him steadily. There had been a queer inflection in the agent's voice.

"I suppose they will show the game registers for the last five years?" he submitted.

Mr. Day made a funny little gesture of deprecation by turning his palms upward.

"Yes and no," he answered. "I will be quite explicit. Mr. Skene came in yesterday and saw our Mr. Grooving. It appears that for reasons that are private to himself he has sudden need of augmenting his income. He is accordingly going to divide the best-known of his moors into two portions, retaining one half—the smaller—for himself, and letting the rest with his house. He himself will take up his abode in a farmhouse which has become vacant, the land attached to it having been added to another holding. The moor has always been good for eight hundred brace as a whole. He thinks he is doing himself no more than justice by apportioning four hundred and fifty brace to the moiety which he proposes to let, or rather to lease."

"Oh," said the client, "we aren't discussing leases. I want a yearly agreement."

Mr. Day assumed a courteously persuasive air.

" Sir William," he implored, earnestly, " pray go and look at it. And understand that no difficulty will be put in the way of subletting if by any chance you can bring yourself to such a course in succeeding years."

The other considered. " I have yet to hear the rent," he said, coldly.

" Three hundred and fifty—only three hundred and fifty pounds for nine hundred grouse," said Mr. Day. " You are well aware how much below the market value this is—due, no doubt, to the fact that Mr. Skene's necessities are pressing. It is a bargain, Sir William—I assure you it is a most unquestionable bargain."

The baronet, by no means convinced of this, took himself off after vainly endeavouring to get Mr. Day to suggest to his client a compromise. This was that if, on inspection, the moor realised its prospectus, Mr. Skene should take four hundred pounds for the one season's let. No, said the agent ; Mr. Skene's terms were specific. Nothing less than a seven years' lease would suffice, but subletting would be permitted.

After a very unprofitable forenoon spent at various agencies the would-be tenant found himself back with Mr. Day again, and five hours later in the Scotch Express *en route* for Aberdeen. Nothing else suitable had turned up, and the more the vision of the baronet's desire receded, the more desirable it loomed in his eyes. There could be no harm, he told himself, in merely going to have a look, and settled himself into his sleeping berth with the very comfortable conviction that no Scotch laird would persuade him into taking a moor unless it showed signs of due return for rent. He sent Mr. Skene a hasty telegram from Aberdeen, and three hours later was deposited at Mernay station, on the Great North of Scotland line.

He realised at once that the man who sat in the trap awaiting him was no groom. He was a tall, thin-faced, fair-moustached Scot, who greeted his guest with what the baronet inwardly stigmatised as an " overdone " smile. He was full of his pleasure at meeting the eminent traveller, and of hopes that the journey had not been found over-fatiguing. He introduced himself as the Master of Skene, eldest son of the owner of Brothertap Moor, and of the Skene lands generally.

Sir William, all for business, began his cross-examination at once. The bag, the health of the birds, the quantity of heather burnt the previous year, the wages usually paid to beaters, the staff of gillies necessary, the basket of trout possible in an evening's whipping of the stream—these were all passed in review. The young man was most willing to oblige.

The moor, he averred, was in first-class condition, and so were the birds. There was no disease, a large breeding stock had been left after last season, and the extraordinarily dry summer was no doubt partly responsible for the health of the broods. But the best plan would be for Sir William to accompany him over the moor after he had breakfasted. He would rather let his guest's own eyes be witness to the truth of his statements. They would take a few sandwiches and have a long morning in the heather. If Sir William could only see his way to staying the night he could also investigate the stream for himself.

The baronet made a hearty meal, filled his flask and sandwich box, and in due course set forth with his entertainer.

The moor, it appeared, covered two sides of a mountain, which ran for three miles east and west in a long ridge. It was grooved across the middle by a sort of shallow gully, and this was almost precipitous on one side. The rocks which faced it had a scored and splintered appearance, making it look in places as if stone had been recently quarried. Sir William remarked on the strange effect.

Young Skene did not seem to respond to the idea.

"It is very perishable, weathering stone," he answered, carelessly, "and liable to break off in masses after frost. This gut is known as the Cow's Mouth Gap."

The morning was a warm one, and they had had two hours of fairly heavy going by the time they reached the gully. Sir William looked at his watch.

"If you will excuse my Southron want of training," he remarked, "I must say that a little whisky and water would be most acceptable. Is there a spring handy? I don't care to take my whisky neat in this temperature."

Skene laughed pleasantly.

"I didn't bring you out to perish of thirst," he said. "I provided for the emergency." As he spoke he produced a couple of bottles of Schweppe from his capacious pockets. "Suppose we sit down and peck a bit, too?" he suggested.

Nothing loth, the baronet accepted the situation, and for the next ten minutes munched sandwiches and chewed the cud of his meditation in silence. So far there was no doubt that the moor had impressed him favourably. Broods had been frequent, and strong on the wing. Cheepers, considering that July was scarcely half over, were not greatly in evidence. The lodge had appeared decently furnished. Things had seemed to be as represented.

Young Skene was the first to speak.

"Well, and what do you think of it?" he asked, gaily.

The other hesitated.

"I see nothing to cavil at," he said at last. "I notice, of course, that the heather is wonderfully parched; but the season, I am aware, has been one of exceptional drought. There are plenty of birds. One rather peculiar thing about them I have noticed. Those we have disturbed have invariably winged westward, sometimes going over our heads, sometimes going forward and making a sweep back. Yet the wind is behind us."

Was it his fancy, or did Skene's tanned skin grow faintly crimson?

"There is no accounting for the flight of the broods at this time of year," he said, hastily, and took rather a deep suck at his flask.

Sir William shook his head.

"My experience doesn't lead me to agree with you," he said, rather drily. "Perhaps you haven't noticed how very regularly the thing occurs."

"I'll watch next time we raise a brood," said the other. "Shall we be getting along now?"

The baronet nodded.

"We might make for a spring if you don't mind," he said. "I should like to fill up my flask with water, and in this heat that is where we shall find birds. Then I can point out to you what I mean."

For a moment young Skene looked undecided.

"The nearest one is about a quarter of a mile the other side of this gully," he said. "A little out of the way if you wish to see the rest of the moor, but such beautifully cool water that it is almost worth the detour."

Sir William said that a few hundred yards here or there made no difference to him. They accordingly climbed the steep rock-face on the westward side of the dip, and after a few minutes' striding through deeper heather than any they had yet encountered, walked out on to the squashy "sag" which surrounds the mouth of moorland springs. A large brood got up, scattering right and left.

Skene looked at his guest and laughed.

"I saw no peculiarity in their flight," he said. "They went south if they went anywhere."

Sir William shrugged his shoulders.

"The exception which proves the rule," he answered, and stooped to fill his flask. The pool was still and mirror-like, and reflected, among other things, the young man's face. It also reflected the fact that the Master of Skene was grimacing at his companion behind that companion's back.

Sir William pondered the matter somewhat deeply during the next two hours. Broods were not so plentiful as the day wore on, but that they were in good quantity was not to be denied. The heather was deep, if dry, and an adequate quantity had been burnt. The young heather of the last two years' burning had not made good progress, but this was doubtless due to the inordinate drought. But why had Skene grimaced?

After debating the matter in his own mind the baronet could find no explanation beyond the fact that a young man might be very much bored by having to drag an old fossil like himself across interminable acres of moor for no better purpose than bargain-hunting. There seemed no other explanation, and he resolved to accept it. He also accepted the invitation to stay the evening and whip the stream.

This last gave undoubted results. A nice little basket of half-pounders was evidence that could not be gainsaid. After a cosy little dinner and a decent cigar, Sir William took up his candle on his way to bed, fully decided in his own mind to take the moor on its merits.

" By the way," he said, suddenly, with his foot on the first stair, " I don't think you pointed out the boundaries to me after all."

" I don't think really that I did," said Skene, glibly. " There is no division line marked out yet. But we mean to place a set of cairns marking a straight border from the lodge to the Cow's Mouth on this side, and from the Cow's Mouth to the pine wood I showed you on the other. We shan't prosecute you if you make a furlong's mistake now and then," he added, laughing.

Sir William paused.

" Then that spring where I filled my flask is on the part you mean to keep? " he inquired.

Skene made a careless gesture of assent.

" Yes," he answered. " Can I give you a light? " He put a match to his guest's candle.

Sir William took the hint, and, nodding his thanks, betook himself to his room.

He left the next morning without having committed himself to any definite statement of his intentions, but while the train thundered south set himself carefully to weigh the evidence of his eyes. He had seen the moor. That was perhaps poorly heathered, but the season had been a dry one. He had seen the grouse, and there were without any sort of doubt plenty of healthy birds. He had seen the burn and the lodge, and both were certainly excellent of their kind. Summary: no reason for not taking what practically fulfilled his desires. But why the devil had young Skene made that peculiar grimace behind his back?

Much pondering failed to elucidate an answer, or, at the same time, any valid reason for failing to agree with his prospective landlord while he was in the way with him. Before he was forty-eight hours older he had made up his mind, visited Mr. Day, and left his office the tenant of Brothertap Moor for the ensuing seven years.

Then Fate launched her bolt at him, and no later than the same evening. As he was sitting in the smoking-room of the Scientists' Club smoking his after-dinner cigar and meditating his deal with growing satisfaction, there entered to him his nephew, Arthur Challoner, a young engineer, who possessed talents, a capacity for hard work, and a by no means poor opinion of himself. By dint of these three qualities he was already being talked of as that rather nebulous quantity, "a rising man."

Uncle and nephew exchanged greetings and family gossip for some minutes before Sir William casually imparted the information that he had just returned from the North—Aberdeenshire to wit.

" Business ? " said Challoner, who was lighting a cigarette; and Sir William assented.

" Business of a sort," he agreed.

" Where ? " said Challoner, tersely inquisitive.

Sir William mentioned the neighbourhood of Mernay.

Challoner became suddenly interested.

" Nothing to do with that earthquake job ? " he asked. " Have you been called in as geological expert? Rum thing it is, to be sure."

The baronet experienced a sudden qualm of discomfort. Funny the Skenes should not have mentioned such a local portent.

" No," he said, quietly. " I went to take a moor; and, as I hope for the pleasure of your company when we shoot it next month, Arthur, you'll be glad to hear that it's a good one."

" You've taken a moor near Mernay ? " cried his nephew.

" Within four miles," assented Sir William.

" Not——? "

" Brothertap Moor," interrupted the baronet, composedly; but Challoner gave a most disquieting yell and sat heavily down.

" O Lord! O Lord! O Lord!" he wailed. " Uncle, if ever a man was done you're the very article. It's the most shameful swindle that ever was, and only a man who has been three months out of England could have been taken in by it. D'you mean to say you haven't heard a word about the great Mernay earthquake ? "

" Not a syllable," said Sir William, still calm outwardly; " and

76

how it can affect my moor I utterly fail to understand. The grouse are there, and so is the heather. What's your quarrel with it?"

" The *grouse* are there?" repeated his nephew, incredulously.

"Certainly. I saw them myself."

For a moment Challoner hesitated. Then he gave an emphatic nod.

"Of course," he agreed. "I should have thought of that. He knew you were coming, and had them driven on to it."

Sir William gave a sudden start. The birds—for July—had certainly been wild, and they *had* on rising invariably made back in one and the same direction—except that one brood at the spring, and that was not on his portion of the moor.

"Look here, Arthur," he said, "I haven't a notion what you're driving at. I've got the moor for seven years. Just explain as concisely as you can what—on earth—is wrong—with it!"

Young Challoner groaned again.

"Seven years!" he bemoaned, "seven years! And you don't know where you have been had! You're the only man in England who wouldn't."

The baronet's temper burst its bounds. He thumped his fist upon the arm of his chair.

"Damn it, speak out, can't you?" he cried, and Challoner made haste to obey.

" It is strange, and yet as simple as tossing ha'pennies," he began. " There was a strong seismic disturbance that took in Aberdeenshire, Ross-shire, Sutherlandshire—in fact, half the North of Scotland —in May. Among other freaks it played was a stratum cleavage— it can be nothing else—under Brothertap Moor. From being one of the best watered moors in Scotland it became an arid desert. Every one of the springs dried up on the eastern end—the half to the east of the Cow's Mouth—while those on the west give double supply. As the peat is absolutely shallow above the rock the heather is dying and the grouse won't harbour in it. Next year it will be like the desert of Sahara, and this year you won't get forty brace off it. That's the long and the short of it."

For a moment Sir William sat absolutely silent. The completeness—and the neatness—with which he had been sold palsied him. It was the first real defeat of his very well-ordered existence. Then something weird in the way of anathema—acquired, doubtless, in the Bolivian solitudes—rolled from between his lips.

" I wonder now——" he presently said, quite sedately.

Challoner skipped in his chair.

" What?" he cried.

Sir William had assumed a lamb-like air of composure.

"There may be a remedy," he submitted, with a very queer smile about his lips.

"In law?" asked Challoner. "There's none elsewhere."

"You may be mistaken," said the baronet. "Stratum cleavages are rummy things."

Sir William looked carefully about him. There was no one in the smoking-room, but a couple of men stood very near the glass doors in the billiard-room beyond. He drew his chair alongside his nephew's, and began to whisper intensely.

The various changes that passed over the youth's ingenuous visage while his avuncular relative expounded his views might have been of immense value to a student of expression. From pure surprise they passed through periods of growing amazement to stupor, followed by excitement, and ending in abundant laughter. Soon he lay back in his chair and kicked under the goad of his emotions. He made himself so remarkable that an intruding waiter, who happened to hold an ambulance certificate, began to probe his memory seriously for the cure of apoplectic hysteria. Finally, Challoner left with the avowed intention of obtaining a three months' holiday from his firm—one which he explained had been due to him for the last five years. Uncle and nephew arranged to travel north within a week to take up their residence in the former's new-leased dwelling.

Ten days later the two were installed at Brothertap Lodge, wearing to the world an aspect of extreme innocence, and on the best of terms with Sir William's landlord. The parching heather, the evasive grouse, the dried-up springs, were as if they were not. And yet the pair were continually upon the moor, though they confined their expeditions to the Cow's Mouth Gully, and that alone. Skene hugged himself in the recesses of his farmhouse. Of all the flats he had ever encountered he told himself that these were the flattest. Even now the fools didn't know how they had been done. Sir William actually discussed the late earthquake with him.

"A most interesting phenomenon in our own land," purred he; "in Bolivia, of course, matters of almost daily occurrence. I wonder if we shall have another. What?"

Skene politely hoped not, and withdrew stifling his merriment and thanking his stars that such an egregious old innocent had fallen into hands capable of dealing with him. He went on later to show his tenant a horse—a bad case of navicular. He suggested that he would take £40 for him, and that he would be most useful in connection with a trap—unvarnished, with loose felloes, and costing only another £20—to run up and down from the station. Sir William thanked him warmly, but explained that a motor car would shortly make its appearance, or otherwise he would have been glad to make him an offer for both. The two parted with mutual—admiration.

Ten days later Challoner went south, and while he was away a strange thing happened. Sir William, who by no means confined his visits to Cow's Mouth Gully to daylight, returned from a midnight expedition thereto white-faced, breathing hard, and much disturbed. He said nothing to his old housekeeper, but the latter reported the portents to the rest of the establishment, and when Macdonald, the head keeper, was summoned the next morning, he was prepared for *dénouements*. The man was a creature of Skene's. The silly old gomeril, he told himself, had at last realised the situation.

The truth was far from what he had expected. Sir William's manner was solemn, but by no means testy.

"Macdonald," he asked, ponderously, "has anyone, to your knowledge, ever come to—to a bad end in Cow's Mouth Gully?"

Macdonald's eyebrows lifted.

"I'm no recollectin' it, Sirr Wulliam," he answered.

"Think," said the baronet, persuasively. "Angus, the gilly, alluded, if I remember right, to some story of a snow-bound shepherd who——"

"Losh me! but y'r right, Sirr Wulliam. But it'll be five-and-forrty years gone by——"

"Macdonald," said his master, lugubriously, "last night I *saw* him!"

The keeper skipped.

"Preserv' 's a'!" he muttered, piously. "Y'r no jokin', sirr?"

The baronet rolled his eyes.

"Joking!" he exclaimed, grimly, and then sank his voice to a blood-curdling whisper.

"Last night, shortly before midnight, I passed down the gap on my way home from my after-dinner stroll. I give you my word of honour that as I did so a tall figure, clad in what looked like a winding sheet, with dark stains upon its forehead, showed up in the moonlight, following silently the same track as myself. The thing was distinct for over half a minute. The next instant the moon was veiled by a passing cloud. When it reappeared I was alone!"

Sir William Crundal was an eminently truthful man, and to allow him to continue to merit this description I must interpolate a slight explanation. *He himself* had walked down Cow's Mouth Gap as described for purposes of his own. If these were to make the gully a place avoided after dark his device was marvellously successful. Macdonald, superstitious as most rascals are, carried the story far and wide. The baronet was able to inform his nephew, on the latter's return, that the local shepherds, poachers, and gillies were more likely to visit a small-pox hospital after dark than the Cow's Mouth. Its reputation as a harbourage of ghostly visitants was assured. The uncle and nephew seemed callous to these spiritual portents. Their nightly expeditions into the heather continued, and if anyone had had the courage to follow them they would have found that they invariably had a definite end in the very home of the spectral manifestation.

A week, in fact, after Challoner's return north the two might have been dimly descried facing each other in the darkness at the foot of the rent rocks of the gully. Sir William was speaking with every accent of content.

"There is absolutely no sort of doubt about it now," he was saying. "The stratum 'tilt' is not ten yards inside this crag," he added, laying his hand upon the weathered stone. "Our work is practically done, Arthur."

"About time, too," complained his nephew, wearily. "What with the digging, and the carting the mould away and scattering it so as to show as little sign of what we are at as possible, I'm getting about beat. The stone drilling that has been your part of the business is boy's work compared with mine. You keep a straight back to it. Mine is half broken."

Sir William clapped the broken back admiringly.

"I'm not forgetting it, my boy," he said, cheerily, "and perhaps after I'm gone you'll realise as much. For the present let's fill up the mouth of our tunnel and get off. One more night— and then——" He made a significant gesture. Challoner gave a chuckle as he began to fit boulders with a certain careless precision into the mouth of what looked rather like a badger's earth in the rocks.

The next morning, as the two lounged lazily in basket chairs upon the lawn, young Skene came riding by. He stopped beside the hedge, peered at them doubtfully, and then hailed them good morning. Uncle and nephew strolled up to the railings and chatted with him across the privet.

"How are the birds looking your side?" asked the baronet, with an air of babelike innocence. "Macdonald seems doubtful about ours. In spite of the storms we have had our springs don't seem to fill up as you were inclined to think they would."

The Master of Skene passed his hand across his moustache.

"It's a *very* dry year," he submitted, in a rather gasping voice.

"The little runnels fill up for a few hours after rain," rambled on Sir William in a garrulous, confidential sort of way, "but the springs are hopeless. It almost seems as if there was something geologically wrong with the water supply. Eh?"

"Almost," agreed young Skene, chokingly. "The heather *does* look parched."

Sir William looked up at him with innocently pleading eyes.

"Nothing you can suggest to help us?" he asked.

Skene looked down with an air of amused contempt. He was feeling reckless. After all, they had the old fool quite completely and tightly bound by the terms of the lease, and there was no particular reason to keep him in the dark any longer.

"Could the earthquake possibly have had anything to do with it?" said Skene, with the air of one hazarding an original notion.

Sir William looked gently surprised.

"The earthquake?" he repeated, "The earthquake?"

"We had one about three months back, you know," said Skene.

Sir William stared at him with meditative amazement.

"Of course you did," he pondered, slowly. "That explains a lot, doesn't it?"

Skene flushed.

"Does it?" he answered, with a sort of non-committal surliness.

"Of course it does," said Sir William, brightly. "And if that is the true cause of our dryness——"

"Yes?" said Skene, interrogatively.

"Suggests a remedy," continued Sir William, thoughtfully.

Skene's eyes grew wide. He examined the man of science almost timorously. He glanced at Challoner, whose expression told about as much as an English journal that has been passed by a Russian censor.

Sir William seemed lost in thought.

"A remedy," he repeated, purringly, "a remedy," dwelling on the words in a sort of contemplative rapture.

Skene echoed the word inquiringly.

"A remedy?" he debated. There seemed a tinge of exasperation in his tones. Now the murder was out this silly old man and his stony-faced nephew did not yet realise that they had been badly sold. "I see no remedy short of another earthquake," said Skene, with a sour laugh.

The baronet looked up at him silently. Then for a moment he turned and confronted Challoner.

"Mr. Skene puts his finger on the spot, Arthur," he said. "Mr. Skene is a very clever man, let me tell you."

The very clever man looked from one to the other of them with the growing conviction that he was in the presence of what is locally termed "a pair of naturals." The situation was growing beyond him, and he cut it short—with his spurs. " I'm late for an appointment as it is," he cried, suddenly. " You must let me hear your notion another day." He went cantering up the moor track firmly convinced that his tenant was, to say the least, childish. " Old Man Innocent from Innocentville," said Skene, and laughed aloud. On the lawn before the lodge the old man in question was looking after him with smiling eyes.

"On his own head be it now, Arthur," he was saying. " The swindling hound! He has said the word himself."

That same evening, if Macdonald or any of his clan had had the courage to peer over the precipitous edges of the Cow's Mouth they would have seen an instructive sight. Out of a narrow entrance between two rocks emerged Sir William Crundal, Bart., into the moonlight, followed by that rising scientist his nephew. The latter trailed delicately behind him a wire. The two brushed the dirt from their skirts, and turned to confront each other, smiling lavishly.

Sir William suddenly put out his hand.

"Shake a paw, Arthur," he said. " You've worked like a Trojan. I shan't forget it."

" That's all right," said Challoner, a little shyly. " You're quite convinced the thing is going to work?"

" If it doesn't," said his uncle, solemnly, " I'll return all my degrees, British and foreign, to every university that has done me the honour of calling me a geologist. Come along."

Silently they strolled down into the heather a couple of hundred yards, Challoner still trailing his wire. On a knoll they seated themselves, while the baronet produced a small wooden box. The end of the wire was deftly inserted into an armature in this.

Sir William looked at his nephew. " Nothing to wait for?" he hazarded, and the other nodded—with a tiny gasp.

The scientist turned a small brass handle rapidly.

There was a roar like thunder from the direction of the gully. Lumps of heather flew through the air. Boulders crashed, stones whizzed abroad like shells. One, indeed, whistled over the heads of the two on the knoll, making them duck like recruits in their first engagement. As the uproar died, and the loosened crags finished rolling into new resting places, a new sound was distinct through the after quiet. A burn could be heard splashing and tinkling through the gully. Moonlit gleams shone on pools. A sudden tiny spate came bursting through the parched heather, and purled past the very feet of the watchers. Challoner leaped up and flung his cap into the air.

" Victory!" he yelled excitedly, " Victory!"

His uncle showed a quieter but none the less solid satisfaction.

"I told you so!" he remarked, solemnly. "That hill beyond the gully was a cistern—practically speaking. When that stratum tilted it raised the outflow by thirty feet. We have simply blown in the side of the tank, and—I rather gather—lowered the level of the water pretty considerably under our landlord's side of the gully. The next thing is—bed!"

And in spite of Challoner's protests bed it was. The morrow was time enough for investigation, said his uncle.

*   *   *   *   *

"What!" exclaimed Sir William, wonderingly. "What!"

The hour was ten the following morning. The place was the Cow's Mouth. On one side of the new-made stream which ran two feet deep from the gully stood the man of science and his nephew. On the other, young Skene, his face absolutely mottled with his passion.

"*Outrage* was the word I used," cried the latter, passionately. "Outrage! This is the result of—of artifice!"

"Artifice?" repeated Sir William, in horror-stricken accents. "Artifice? My dear Mr. Skene, what extraordinary notion has taken you? I see no signs of any forces having been at work here save Nature's self."

He pointed around him. There was a great rent in the side of the gully. Rocks were flung awry—turf and peat were scattered in heaps. But of explosion no sign was to be seen. The secret miners had dug well into the clay, and the friendly water had washed out any tiniest blackening that might have been left.

Young Skene snarled an oath.

"Nature!" he gobbled. "Nature be damned! What could mere Nature do?"

Sir William looked at him with his wide and compassionate eyes.

"You suggested it yourself," he said, plaintively. "Another earthquake. Could Nature have been listening?"

Skene stood silent, but his throat muscles worked as if he fought for breath. Challoner smiled at him pleasantly.

"Good old girl is Nature," said he, cheerily. "She only needs one thing."

Skene stared at him malignantly. The other returned the gaze with a glance of concentrated content.

"What does Nature need?" asked Skene at last.

Challoner smiled.

"A nudge," he said.

STRANGE STORIES OF SPORT

VII.—FLETCHER'S MAD HAGGARD

A TRUE AND WEIRD TALE OF MODERN FALCONRY

BY MAJOR CHARLTON ANNE

" It's no good, gentlemen, we must give it up! Feed all the birds, Jim, we shan't fly to-day. The only thing that we can do is to go and eat our luncheon."

There was no possibility of our seeing any falconry that afternoon. The wind, which when we had started on our fifteen-mile ride over the fells that morning was but a bracing breeze, had gradually increased in force as we progressed, and had by the time we reached Blenshope Castle developed into a regular gale accompanied by a blinding rain. There was no question of it; it was the autumn equinox that had begun, and with a vengeance. It was a cruel and unlooked-for disappointment. We had given up a whole day's shooting on the moor we had rented that year, and a large party of us had come over on the invitation of the owner of Blenshope to see what to most of us was indeed a novelty—an afternoon's grouse hawking.

Colonel A. cordially welcomed us on our arrival; but, alas! with a dubious shake of his head. With a tap on the barometer he remarked :

" You don't know the falconer's old couplet,

" If the wind be high,
Do not fly,

or I should not have had the pleasure of seeing you all here to-day. Falconry is, *par excellence*, a fine-weather sport, and if I were to put up one of my birds on the wing in such a hurricane as this I should stand a very poor chance of ever seeing it again, and indeed should richly deserve to lose it. But come along, I see we've an hour yet before lunch; the unexpected may happen before two o'clock even now! We'll go to the mews and have a look at the birds, and we'll hear what my gamekeeper has to say about the weather, although I always find the local weather prophet most unwilling to commit himself. When he does do so he is, as a rule, entirely wrong."

We had smoked many cigarettes and had admired the half-dozen peregrines sitting in a row on the screen in the mews, looking smart and alert in spite of the hoods they all wore. We had noticed the beauty and perfection of their plumage—had been told of the mysteries of the imping and sewing-in of feathers; had discoursed with our host and his falconer, James Hare, on the difference between eyesses and passage hawks, red hawks, and haggards—had learnt something about bewits, jesses, "waiting on" and "raking out," and had heard many other technical terms which the modern exponents of that delightful old-time sport of our fore-elders still make use of, when the luncheon gong sounded in the castle, and Colonel A.'s orders to his falconer put a death-blow to our hopes for the day.

We departed to derive such consolation as could be obtained from a good lunch, in which some of the grouse previously killed by the hawks of course found a place in the *menu*. We soon determined to make the best of it. Champagne and conversation flowed, and by the time that coffee and cigarettes made their appearance we had almost forgotten our disappointment.

Colonel A. was an excellent host, and also, we soon found out, an admirable *raconteur*. The conversation, from shooting, hunting, and sports of all kind, presently turned to the subject of Blenshope Castle itself—its antiquity, and the legend of the ghost of a certain white lady which was still reputed to walk on the battlements. One of us, who belonged to the Psychical Research Society, and who therefore took the greatest interest in anything to do with the supernatural, plied Colonel A. with questions as to whether he had, during his residence at Blenshope, ever come across its ghostly inhabitant.

"No, I can honestly confess I never have," replied the Colonel. "At the same time, that such things may be I am quite willing to admit. Nay, I will go further. I believe as firmly as I am sure that I am sitting here now that I once saw a ghost myself. But it was a long way from here, where nothing of the sort has ever occurred to my knowledge sufficient to upset the nerves of a neurotic patient."

"Tell us all about it," "Where was it?" "Never believed in anything of that sort in my life!" was echoed about the table; and very soon, with very little pressing, Colonel A. began:

"It was in the early seventies—in fact, the first year that I came up here after having taken this place on a long lease—and uncommonly lucky I looked upon myself, when everything was signed and settled, in having got hold of a nice house in the very centre of the best bit of moor in the North of England for my purpose. Nothing could be better from a falconer's point of view. It lies away sufficiently from any other big shootings, and I can pursue my favourite sport without fear of having any disagreeables with the votaries of the gun, who are apt, in this twentieth century, to look upon a falconer as a nuisance, and somewhat of a pariah amongst the other sportsmen. You see these two thousand acres or so, besides being exceptionally well heathered, are to all intents and purposes practically flat—a great advantage in grouse-hawking; and then, the castle being exactly in the middle of the moor, I can slip out and be on my ground in a moment—a great pull in such an uncertain climate. Well, I spared no pains in getting together a likely lot of hawks for my first season—eyesses most of them; that is, birds from the nest, and these were from the best nests, for I may tell you that some eyries have the reputation of always providing good birds, whilst there are others whose young I would not have at a gift. Old Jack Martin was my falconer in those days, with my present one, then a mere lad, as his underling. I hurried up to take possession as soon as everything was settled, as time was getting on and we had a lot of work to get through before our young birds could be trained and fit for the Twelfth. Everything went smoothly for the first few days, when a nasty accident happened which at first looked like spoiling our whole season. Jack Martin, in climbing over a loose stone wall one morning, slipped, and in his fall brought half a hundredweight of stones on the top of him, with the result that one of his legs was badly fractured, and I had to send him to the Newcastle Infirmary, where the poor fellow lay for a couple of months. I was thus left, almost at the beginning of the season, with a mews full of likely hawks, which required far more personal attention at that critical moment than I could possibly give them myself, a moor well stocked with grouse, and no falconer—for Jim knew nothing in those days.

"There were very few professional falconers then, nor for the matter of that are there many more now, and I wrote in vain to all my friends who, like myself, 'followed the bells,' asking them if they knew of any good man that would be likely to suit. I might have saved my notepaper and stamps—I could hear of no one—and I was in despair until one day I received an envelope bearing on its flap a gaudy crest with the words 'Magnolia Club' in huge gilt letters underneath! I had heard of the Magnolia as being one of those cheap, fifth-rate, flash West-end clubs situated in some by-street off Regent Circus, and frequented chiefly by small professional men, young artists, and budding authors and actors. On opening the letter I found that it was from one Tom Fletcher—I suppose none of you ever met him, poor fellow, in his palmy days, when he was by way of being somewhat of a celebrity on account of his strange magnetism and dealings in the occult, and anything in fact to do with the supernatural? He had picked it all up in India, where he had spent his youth, his father having been the European manager, or something of the sort, to a native Rajah. In fact, I always thought that there was something more than just a touch of the tar-brush in Fletcher himself, and that he had a large half of a Hindoo in him. I had heard vague rumours of there being some dark mystery about his birth, and that his mother had been a Ranee or Indian Princess; anyway, the man, both in appearance and manner, was a born gentleman to the tips of his finger nails. It was at the Rajah's Court, too, that he had gotten his wonderful knowledge of falconry, at which he was an expert and an authority, and I am sure that I am right in saying that he had forgotten more about the art of training hawks than any of us ever knew.

"But he was an unsatisfactory customer in many ways. He was thriftless and happy-go-lucky, and a regular devil-may-care Bohemian at the best, always out at elbows, and he hardly ever had a penny in his pocket. He was also the oddest fellow in the world—used to make sudden disappearances, and go off on the tramp, living as best he could. He had grown to be too fond of this, too"—tapping the whisky decanter—"and occasionally had terrible bouts.

"His letter was short and to the point. He had been very ill but was now convalescent, and his doctor had said all he wanted was a bracing air to set him right again—that he had heard casually from Lord L. of my dilemma, and that, provided I would send him the wherewithal for his travelling expenses, he would be only too happy to come down and do *locum tenens* for Jack Martin and help me in every way that he possibly cou'd with my birds. Here was a chance indeed. I had already met Fletcher once or twice and had rather liked him. A better falconer I knew did not exist. I recollected his failing, but as Blenshope is so out of the way (quite ten miles from the nearest public-house) and I always keep the key of my own cellar, I felt pretty easy on that score. He had been ill, and had most likely had a lesson and would keep straight in future, or anyhow for some time. I wrote to him by return, enclosing a fiver, and asking him to come down as soon as he possibly could. He arrived here on the morrow of his getting my letter, and set to work at once with a will. I was delighted with him, found him a capital sort, and we speedily became great friends. We soon had my young hawks fit, on the wing, and well entered. The weather was propitious, grouse plentiful, and we enjoyed excellent sport throughout that month of August.

"And now I must hark back a bit, and tell you that a few days before Tom Fletcher's arrival a wild peregrine falcon, which had previously been doing much mischief, had been trapped, luckily unhurt, on the estate of a friend of mine in Scotland. He, knowing something about falconry and thinking to do me a good turn, had at once sent it to me carefully packed in a poultry basket. It thus arrived in good condition and without a feather broken. The bird proved to be a young haggard; that is, a falcon over its first moult— the most valuable kind of hawk, providing that the falconer has the time to spare and sufficient patience to train it. This one was the most magnificent specimen that I ever clapped eyes on, with a small, well-bred head. She had the bloom of a ripe peach upon her plumage; her chest was flat; her shoulders broad, while her wings crossed with a rare rake behind her. In the mews amongst my eyesses she was like a Derby winner amidst a crowd of Argentine South African remounts!

"But we soon discovered that my friend had indeed caught a Tartar in this bird—we could make nothing of her! At the mere sound of one's footsteps she would fall backwards, almost tumbling from the pole, hissing like a cobra! She bit, she struck with her feet, she fought with her jesses and battered her bells to pieces. She refused to eat anything beyond making a few ravenous snatches in the dark at her food. The men called her the 'mad haggard,' and well she deserved her name, for a bigger devil I never wish to tackle. I soon gave up all hopes of trying to reclaim her, and had made up my mind to have her knocked on the head, when Fletcher came upon the scene. He begged of me to spare her yet awhile, and allow him to try and see what he could do with her. I made him a present of her there and then. And henceforth she became 'Fletcher's mad haggard.'

"Straightaway he carried her out of the mews up to his bedroom. I did not see her again for some days, and in fact had almost forgotten all about her—being so much engrossed with my own sport—when one night over our pipes Fletcher astonished me by calmly announcing that to the best of his belief the 'mad haggard' was thoroughly 'made,' and that he intended, there being no objection on my part, to fly her at a grouse the following day. I roared with laughter at the bare idea of any haggard, and least of all such a one as this she-devil, being put on the wing without at least a couple of months' preparation. Any man would be mad to think of such a thing, and I made that remark to Fletcher. His reply was to leave the room. I heard him go up the stairs, and presently he returned. Sitting unhooded, quietly and serenely on his fist, was the 'mad haggard'! Fletcher sat down again. The hawk looked inquiringly around her, as they all are wont to do when coming into a strange room and strange company. Otherwise she might have been carved out of a stone, and she never so much as flapped a wing or jingled a bell.

" I felt utterly amazed at this most extraordinary metamorphosis. 'There is something uncanny about this, Fletcher,' I exclaimed, as soon as I had sufficiently recovered from my astonishment. 'How on earth did you manage to reclaim what I considered to be quite untamable—in so short a time, too? Tell me the secret of your success.'

" 'My secret,' replied Fletcher, 'belongs to Khooroo Khan (the Rajah's old falconer), and is not mine to give away. But I can tell you this much—that I have sat up for nights with the bird without either of us getting a wink of sleep ; and—by Jove !—it has taken it out of me, I can tell you. I took her out at daylight this morning and flew her to the lure. She is all right now, and I am sure will give a good account of herself to-morrow. We shall both have a good night's rest to-night, I can promise !' And helping himself to a stiff whisky and soda Fletcher departed, bearing the hawk on one hand, and his old enemy the glass in the other.

" I sat up late that night over my pipe, thinking about Fletcher, of whose marvellous power over dumb creatures I had so often heard, and of which I had just seen such an example. I ran over in my head the many yarns he had told me of himself, which I had certainly received *cum grano*—of serpents charmed, wild boars arrested in the act of charging home, and man-eating tigers turning tail by the power of his will. Then I wondered at so delicate and frail a creature as he possessing all that occult force, and I also got to thinking of how his hand shook when he poured out that whisky and soda, and that I must not leave so much of it about in future. The man, who since his arrival had been most abstemious, had evidently found the work of hawking on the moor all the afternoon, and sitting up all night with the 'mad haggard,' too much for him, and had had recourse to stimulants again. I sighed as I thought of the wasted career, lit my candle, turned out the lamp, and went to bed ; but I heard Fletcher, for long after I had retired, restlessly walking up and down his room and talking to himself or his falcon in Hindustani, till at last I fell asleep.

"Next day we flew the 'mad haggard,' and I will not weary you with a description of what followed on that first and on every subsequent occasion that we put her on the wing. Suffice it to say that I have never seen her equal on this moor or on any other, and never do I expect to see such another. With a few rapid beats of her powerful wings she would gain her pitch amongst the clouds, looking no bigger than a swallow once up there; backwards and forwards she would rattle over our heads, and then woe betide any game that we put up, no matter at what distance they rose or at what speed they went. There was a rush of wings. Like a bolt shot from the blue the 'mad haggard' fell from the sky, and amidst a whirl of small feathers another grouse lay stone dead amongst the heather. Every day it was the same thing, and she never seemed to tire, killing half-a-dozen head herself in an afternoon. She never failed us, and I am afraid that we sadly neglected the other hawks for her.

"She had only one fault, and that was—after a kill—she would never suffer any person but Fletcher to approach and take her up. As a rule, when once a falcon is trained and has overcome its fear of man, one man is much the same as another to her; but it was not so with the 'mad haggard.'

"Three weeks of splendid sport with this unique bird, the finest falconry one could possibly see, did we enjoy, when one morning on coming downstairs I found a note lying on the breakfast table. It was from Fletcher, dated on the previous night, saying that he had been feeling very slack for some time past, and that it was only out of gratitude to me for my kindness and hospitality that he had continued working against the collar for so long; that he had not had a real night's rest for a month; that he felt most restless and depressed, more so than I could possibly believe; and that he thought the only way to work off the fit was to go on the tramp at once and walk it off, as he had so often done before. He asked if I would send his portmanteau to an address given in London, and, thanking me a thousand times for his very pleasant visit, he wound up by saying, 'Keep the "mad haggard" until I come back and take her from you myself.'

"On inquiring, I found that Fletcher's bed had not been slept in, and that he had evidently left the house directly after writing the letter. I was very much shocked and grieved, but not surprised, at this abrupt departure. For some time past his behaviour had been, to say the least of it, erratic. He had been alternately lively and gay, sullen and morose, changing from one mood to another with startling rapidity. There was no doubt that he had by some means or other got hold of a private supply of drink, and the day before he left I remember well, when walking on the moor behind him, that the air smelt as if the heather had been literally watered with whisky.

"I sent off his portmanteau, also forwarding him a letter in which I enclosed, and begged of him to accept, a small cheque in recognition of the services he had rendered me. I also promised to take every care of the 'mad haggard' until we met again.

*   *   *   *   *   *

"I spent the following winter abroad, returning to England in February, when I took my falcons to Tynshed, a secluded little hamlet on the outskirts of Salisbury Plain, where it was my custom invariably to betake myself and my hawks every spring for rook-hawking.

"Of course the 'mad haggard' came along with the rest of the birds, and we took her out with us on the very first day, together with Minerva and Guinevere, two red falcons of that year. I was, of course, mounted on my old cob Punch. We had followed the bells together for many seasons. Jack Martin was on foot, and Jim followed with the hawks in a covered pony cart—a very necessary precaution on the plain against the bitter north-easterly winds. We had had three or four very successful flights with the young hawks, and as the short February afternoon was already beginning to show signs of waning, I determined to fly the 'mad haggard' and then return home. We had by this time worked our way a very fair distance from Tynshed, and were well out upon the wild, open downs, in as bleak a bit of country as the plain could produce. The wind had grown perceptibly colder, and now and then brought stray flakes of snow with it. I felt chilled to the marrow and anxious for a gallop. A 'budget' of rooks were feeding, unconscious of any danger, some hundred yards up wind over the low rolling downs. I rode slowly towards them, my falconer on foot, crouching behind my cob's shoulder, ready to slip the 'mad haggard' the instant the crows stirred. At length the crucial moment arrived, and with a hoarse caw or two the whole rose en masse. In a second the 'mad haggard' was tearing into the teeth of the gale and in pursuit, climbing up and up into the wind so as to gain her pitch over her quarries. These soon dispersed in all directions amidst a chorus of indignant caws. She at once singled out a sable victim from amongst the many, and swinging round went away in full chase. She rapidly gained upon it; and, although missing her first stoup through the rook making a sudden shift, she quickly threw up into the wind, and getting higher than ever, with one headlong downward rush she

hurled the doomed creature to the ground. I had followed the flight
at full gallop, and both the birds were now close to me. I waited,
fully expecting to see the 'mad haggard' descend upon and begin to
plume her prey, as invariably was the case after a kill. Imagine
my astonishment on seeing her instead mount higher and higher, as
if disdaining to come down upon her lowly quarry. Up, up, and
up she went, and finally, when she had become almost a speck in
the grey sky above, she turned, and tore away up wind as hard as
she could go ! In vain did we swing our lures and show our live
pigeons ; she would have none of them, but had evidently sighted
something better further afield. There was nothing for it but to
follow as fast as my cob could lay legs to the ground, and so keep
the truant in sight until she tired and treed, or, what was more
probable, killed what she was after. So away we rattled as hard as
we could go, I keeping my eye steadily on the now distant hawk,
and my old cob going at his best pace. Thus we must have covered
some miles, the 'mad haggard' never once pausing in its wild career
nor swerving from her bee-line course.

"Suddenly my mount stumbled, but recovered himself cleverly,
only, however, after a faltering step or two, to pull up dead lame. I
dismounted at once, and found that he had contrived by some means
or other to strain a back sinew. He was, of course, done for that
day, at all events. Being well trained to his work, I had only to
throw the reins over his head, knowing that the patient animal
would remain on that spot until either I returned or else Jack
Martin came up. There was nothing for it now but to continue
the chase on foot. I was a good sprinter in those days, and thought
nothing of running a mile or so. I had, of course, now lost sight of
the haggard, but I knew that when last I saw her she was
going straight up wind, and in the direction of a small clump of
trees which stood out about a mile ahead in bold relief upon the lonely
plain. There was every chance, as I knew from experience, that
the hawk would light on one of these to roost, especially now that
daylight was fading fast and the shades of night rapidly closing o'er
the dreary waste. And so I put my best foot forward and ran and
ran on. By this time I had reached a part of the plain to which I
was an entire stranger ; but as I trotted along I came upon a cart
track going in my direction, which gradually improved as I proceeded into a road of a better class, with ragged unkempt hedges on
either side. I presently became aware that I was not alone, but
that there was the figure of a man in front of me, going at a good
pace, too, in the same direction as myself, and keeping steadily
about thirty yards ahead of me. Seeing him, I put on a spurt, and
diminished the distance that divided us by a half. I called out as

loud as I could so as to attract his attention, thinking it most probable that by the sound of her bells he could not have failed to have noticed the 'mad haggard' when she passed over his head.

"To my intense surprise the man neither turned his head nor took the slightest notice of me. Was he deaf? I was now only about ten yards behind him, and yelled again : ' I say, sir, have you seen one of my birds—a trained hawk, with bells on it—fly past here just now ? '

"He paid no attention, but continued on his way just ahead of me. Had my words failed to reach him ? Was he stone deaf, or only stupid ? You may not know it, but there are few things so irritating to a falconer's nerves as losing a good hawk, so you may guess that I was not in the best of humours when I first caught sight of my friend, and his imperturbability and insolent behaviour had now thoroughly roused my dander. I ran my hardest, shouting, and I am afraid vituperating loudly, but for all my running I was unable to come up to the figure in front. It did not dawn upon me then as strange that, in spite of all my efforts to catch up with him, the man still maintained his lead, apparently without any exertion on his part. So we continued along the road, I calling out, ' Can't you hear, you dunderhead ? Hi, there ! Hi ! Surely a civil question deserves a civil answer ? ' One side of the road was now bordered by a wall built of white stone and of a goodly height, such as usually surrounds the kitchen gardens of country houses ; on the other side the hedge had gone, and there stretched only a lone, wild expanse of common, thickly patched with furze, and dotted here and there with a few sheep. We both went down the side of the wall at a great pace, and as we went I was pleased to find that I was at last gaining upon the figure, which somehow or other now struck me as strangely familiar. By heavens !—yes, it *was* Fletcher !

"It *was* Fletcher ! But Fletcher deaf and dumb ! What could be the meaning of it all ? As I followed him at my best pace I was able to notice that he wore the same old clothes that he had habitually done when out hawking with me, only they looked much older and shabbier, and there was a damp, stained look about them. But what was he doing there at this time of day ? Perhaps he had sighted the ' mad haggard ' and was after her, too. Anyway, I determined to come up with him, and, though feeling pretty well at the end of my tether, I made a final effort, and really thought I had caught him up. I was actually reaching out my hands to grab him by the coat when what I grasped at vanished into thin air, and I saw he had turned a sharp corner !

"Like a knife I was round it too; but Fletcher was not there —only the path running along by the newly-made road and wall to the right, and to the left wide, open, flat country.

"I stopped dead, half paralysed, and a cold shiver ran down my back. What had become of Fletcher? Why, of course, he had leaped the wall to the right. My mind was instantly made up. I crossed the road, and, taking a quick run, I landed on the top; but, alas! I had miscalculated my pace or the height, for when I got there I could not get my balance. I slipped, or rather rolled off, fell heavily what seemed to be rather a long way, and, my head striking something hard as I reached the ground, I lost consciousness. As I sank into the unknown, as in a dream I heard the bells and the wild shriek of the 'mad haggard' as she rose and flew away.

*   *   *   *   *   *   *

"When I came to, night had fallen; but a bright moon was shining, and as I sat up and tried to look round me I only saw four very narrow walls.

"I had strained one of my feet badly, and it was paining me a good bit; but I hobbled along till I got out on to the road once more, and then saw in the distance the twinkling lights of a small town. A minute or two later I heard wheels, and it was with a distinct feeling of relief that I hailed the driver of the dogcart and induced him to stop.

"'Hallo!' called out a hearty voice. 'Can I be of any use? You seem to be a bit lame; will you have a lift to the town?'

"I thanked him, and was quickly up and seated by his side.

"Dr. S. introduced himself to me and asked if he could be of any service in a professional way. I thanked him, but said that all I wanted was a lift and to be told where I could hire a conveyance to take me home. The doctor was very hospitable, and I expect I was looking pretty bad, for he insisted on taking me to his own house and on giving me some light refreshment. I was really so done that I accepted his kindness. Seated opposite me in his little study I saw him eying with some curiosity my falconer's glove which hung from my left wrist, and after a few moments' silence he exclaimed:

"'You will excuse me, but I cannot help remarking your glove, for it is a very uncommon one. But the strange thing about it is that it is the second of its sort I have seen this week. Only a few days ago I was called to the cottage hospital to attend to a poor fellow who had been picked up on the plain a mile or two from here in an unconscious and dying condition. He was very shabbily dressed, but his clothes had been made by a good tailor, and he

94

looked like a foreigner—a gentleman. I could do little for him—double pneumonia and other complications were evident. He never became conscious, but rambled a bit at times and gradually sank. We don't in the least know who he was, as his linen was not marked. The only distinctive thing he had about him was a glove the counterpart of yours.'

"I started forward in my chair and exclaimed excitedly: 'A rather tall, thin man—dark, clean-shaved, curly black hair, slightly grey—a scar over the left eyebrow?'

"The doctor also showed excitement.

"'Yes, yes!' he exclaimed. 'And all we could make out from his ravings was that his name might be Flasher or Fletcher, or something of that sort! We buried him this morning, poor fellow, in the new cemetery close to where I picked you up, and his is the first grave there, just in the far corner under the wall.'

"I was shaking like a palsy. Everything was revealing itself to my mind. . . . Fletcher was dead and his ghost had been walking the plain. It was his melancholy wraith that the faithful 'mad haggard' had sighted and followed—it was the same restless shade that had decoyed me to his grave . . . And to what end? The whole thing came to me in a moment. Fletcher's proud spirit could not rest in a nameless—a pauper's grave! The man who doubtless had the blood of kings in his veins, though he had lived a reckless and, latterly, a miserable life, had always had great pride of his forebears, and his spirit had made an effort—not in vain—to retrieve the final follies of his life.

"I bought the ground where the grave was. There stands a modest monument to his memory. Fletcher's spirit may rest now —anyway it has been seen no more. The 'mad haggard' was never brought to the lure again. She haunted the place for weeks, so Dr. S. told me some time after, and was found dead by some keepers. They recognised her by the bells she still carried. I expect they shot her. . . .

"That is my ghost story—with no embellishments."

STRANGE STORIES OF SPORT

VIII.—NABOTH'S VINEYARD

BY FRANK SAVILE

John Osborne's face was illuminated with a great content. He sat back in his chair, puffing at his after-dinner cigar with the quiet enjoyment of a man whose to-morrow holds out every prospect of pleasure, after a virtuous to-day spent in winding up business toils to make that to-morrow a possibility. Bluntly he was a busy man of affairs, whose infrequent holidays had to be carved out of his strenuous life with foresight and precision, and of these few weeks of relaxation he valued none more than those he spent with his lifelong friend Alfred Warburton, Squire of Blakesea, and the owner of the manor of that name. He took a pull at his whisky-and-soda and nodded to his companion beamingly.

"Here's to to-morrow's sport!" he said, as he drank.

Warburton nodded back cordially, but a doubtful little frown clouded his face as he put his lips to his own glass. "You mustn't expect too much, old chap," he answered, with a tiny shrug.

Osborne showed surprise.

"What?" he cried. "Aren't we going to shoot the Arenside beat?"

"Certainly," said Warburton. "We've done that every year when you come as a matter of course. But——" He concluded with another silent lift of his big shoulders.

"We got forty-six brace to our own two guns last year," persisted his companion, "and you told me yourself that birds had nested well and come on splendidly. It will be quite good enough for me if we can repeat last year's record."

Warburton made a gesture of agreement.

"And for me too," he replied. "But things were very different last year."

"Different? Of course they were—it wasn't anything like such a good season—we ought to add fifty per cent. to our bag by my calculation," said his friend. "It must be something deuced queer to spoil *that* beat in the best year for the last ten."

"Not so very queer, after all, in these days of agricultural depression. This countryside isn't what it was, old boy. You forget that Buckleigh was sold last autumn."

"Buckleigh—Buckleigh sold! You mean to tell me that Lord Layne has parted with a property which his ancestors have held for six centuries or more?"

"He couldn't help himself. What with mortgages and charges for younger sons there was nothing to be done but break the entail and realise. My neighbour is *not* Layne any longer," said Warburton, with a significant inflection.

"Who is it?" cried Osborne. "Not some infernal——"

"It's Mr. Esmond Maurice," interrupted Warburton. "At least that is the name that appears on his visiting cards. But I believe there's a register of births in Whitechapel referring to a son of Ezra Morris who was called after his father. I have every reason to think that the owner of Buckleigh is the same man."

Osborne set down his glass with a thud.

"Good heavens!" he lamented, heavily. "Buckleigh in such hands! *Buckleigh* of all places—a house that's never so much as seen one of these modern millionaires inside its doors, if all one's heard of Layne is true! But what in the name of wonder has that got to do with you and Arenside?"

"Maurice is not a sportsman," said Warburton, tersely.

"Doesn't he *try?*" demanded Osborne. "After all, though there are bad hats enough among his kind, it's no more than justice to say that there are also dozens of decent self-made men who——"

"He tries—after his own fashion," interrupted Warburton, "but that merely consists in seeing how high the Buckleigh bags can figure in the papers. I take it that he considers all things fair in love, war, and—shooting."

"The insufferable beast!" sniffed Osborne. "But now you haven't told how that affects *you*. He isn't the owner of Arenside."

"But would very much like to be," retorted Warburton, "and that's where the trouble begins. I suppose I'm an old fogey; but certainly the methods of the modern business man are a revelation to me. He came—he settled down—and I—didn't call. There was that affair of the National and Universal Corporation in which he was mixed up only a year ago, and not less than three of my own personal friends had been hard hit and half ruined by it. I thought I saw no reason to cultivate such a neighbour. He wasn't put about by *that*. He came and called on *me*,"

"What an excellent Christian spirit!" commented Osborne. "Well?"

"He came in with what I suppose he considered an air of hearty bluffness, said he had been considering a letter to me for over a week, and had come to the conclusion that an ounce of talk was worth a pound of ink. He believed, so it appears, in straight business between man and man, and, if you wanted a thing, to ask for it. Would I sell Arenside because it cut in between his hill spinneys and the Welton farms? He was prepared to give a shade over the market price for a quick sale."

Osborne chuckled. "The artless soul!" he said, sarcastically. "Of course you immediately offered to close the bargain over a sound glass of sherry wine."

Warburton smiled.

"I explained as succinctly as I could that Arenside had belonged to my forbears since Henry VIII. sat upon the throne, and that I was likely to be as tenacious as any of my ancestors. He was by no means disconcerted—he merely doubled his terms. He said frankly that he *must* have it and that he looked to my gentlemanly feeling not to overcharge him, though he admired my commercial tact. It was only when I finally convinced him that nothing on earth would induce me to sell a foot of land that the veneer warped in places and showed the hooligan beneath. I was edging him gently towards the door.

"'Look here, Mr. Warburton,' he said, as I got him on to the step, 'that Arenside land between Buckleigh and Welton is like a small nut in the jaws of a big pair of crackers. And I own the crackers.'

"'And I the nut,' said I, quietly. 'I'm sorry it inconveniences you.'

"He hoisted himself up into his mail phaeton, and gave me a very ugly look.

"'I don't often pose as a prophet,' he said, 'but I think you'll be sorrier.'

"'Indeed,' said I politely. 'When?'

"'When I *crack* it,' he answered, and gave the horses a flick.

"That is the last I have seen of the gentleman; but he hasn't by any means forgotten me."

The look of interest was growing keen on Osborne's face. He leaned forward. "He's begun to hit below the belt?" he hazarded.

Warburton nodded.

"Exactly," he agreed. "Money can do pretty well everything if you want queer things done. He began in the nesting season. Every egg-stealer in the district seemed suddenly to concentrate his energies upon my land. We caught one or two. They paid their fines complacently, and within two weeks were caught again. They were prettily heavily docked by the bench the second time, and warned that the third occasion would mean gaol. They retired elsewhere, but others took their places. It grew such a scandal that the magistrates trebled the penalties. The grinning rascals paid up without a murmur, and every respectable man in the countryside knew where the cash came from as certainly as if he had seen Maurice hand it over; but there was nothing to be done. In June he tried other tactics. Two confounded village loafers, who notoriously had not a penny to bless themselves with, claimed a right of way across Arenside, tore up my fence, and when I prosecuted, carried the matter, on appeal, to a higher court. I had to spend quite as much as I regained in costs to win my case, and the beggars managed to get an injunction to prevent my closing what they called the road while the action was pending. So for six weeks any villager who chose—and to their honour I'll say that hardly a respectable man took advantage of it—could wander across Arenside with his dog while the young coveys were feeding. How many were given half-a-crown to do so I don't know, but there were sufficient of them to scare half the young birds over the border. Finally, he set his keepers in relays to haunt the surrounding marshes before the pheasants were turned into his own spinneys, and they had instructions to blaze away at vermin with black powder all day and every day. Most of the time they were firing royal salutes at the open sky, but the consequences were what he calculated they would be—namely, that the few birds left on Arenside refuse to go within a mile of the gorse beside the woodlands, and in that way two of our best beats have become empty and useless to us. So for the present I think I may say that my ingenious neighbour has gone far to fulfil his own prophecy."

Osborne's face had grown longer and longer as the recital proceeded. As Warburton concluded, his friend's expression exhibited wrath at its extremest tension. He swore resoundingly.

"The outrageous scoundrel!" he spluttered. "And you mean to tell me that nothing can be done to dish him—that you're going to sit down under it and smile?"

For the third time that evening Warburton answered his friend with a shrug.

"What *is* to be done?" he answered, pessimistically. "He's cut by the neighbourhood; for that he cares not a snap of his thick fingers. Beyond publishing the story of his misdeeds as widely as possible I see no penalty that will reach him. He has his own friends, and the opinion of the countryside simply doesn't affect him,"

"Then you mean to tell me that you are doing—nothing ? " exploded Osborne.

Warburton answered with his rueful smile and a little nod.

Osborne flung the end of his cigar in the grate. He finished his whisky at a gulp, and reached for his bedroom candle.

"If I hadn't more resolution and pluck than that," he declared, " I'd burn all my briefs and turn navvy ! If _I_ don't think of a way of settling the brute before I'm twenty-four hours older, write me down 'Idiot' with a capital 'I.' And now for bed, my boy. Good-night ! "

*   *   *   *

The next morning, about eleven o'clock, the two friends, attended by the two keepers and a couple of spaniels, approached the broad dip between the slopes of Welton on one side and Buckleigh Spinneys on the other. So far matters had gone satisfactorily. Partridges had not been plentiful, but had lain fairly well. Both guns were in good form. The bag, after two hours, amounted to fifteen brace, while the best beat lay untouched before them. But Warburton's cheery face began to cloud as they approached the debatable land.

"The beggar's been so uncommon quiet lately," he confided to his companion, " that I can't help suspecting trouble is brewing. Two of my men watched here all night, or I daresay he would have hired some of his poaching protégés to drive it."

"Humph," grunted Osborne, and would have proceeded to other remarks, but a covey suddenly arose and claimed his attention. Four shots rang out in the quiet, and four birds were summarily retrieved by the eager spaniels. But in the act of reloading Warburton made a sudden exclamation.

"Good Lord ! look at that ! " he shouted.

Osborne, following the direction of his friend's gaze, saw a dark object rising smartly upon the breeze from the direction of the Buckleigh Woods. He echoed Warburton's surprise.

"The beggar's kiting—actually kiting on the first of September," he declaimed. " The unmitigated ruffian ! "

"Yes," agreed Warburton, quietly. " And do you observe that the kite is strung out to float over my land, not his."

"I don't quite follow his object there," said Osborne. " The kite will only make your birds lie till we flush them."

"Possibly—for to-day," said his companion ; " but think of the future. What is to prevent his flying his kite to-morrow, and the next day, and so on _ad infinitum_. I don't need to remind you that even at the end of the season you can't kite any land more than twice without making birds shy of it for months."

Osborne was still staring at the dark object which swung against the sky. He was muttering below his breath. Suddenly, out of the distance, came the sound of half-a-dozen shots—from the Welton side of the valley this time.

The two friends were standing upon a knoll which commanded the mile of narrow meadows which flanked the Aren brook. As the shots were fired they could see a covey rise and burst into terrified flight, the birds making singly for the cover of the hedges. The floating kite rose and fell jerkily upon the breeze as if a derisive finger controlled the string.

"Now do you understand?" said Warburton, significantly. "He is flying his kite from one side of the valley; he has posted his guns on the other. As soon as the coveys cower he gets as near them as he can, and from his own land shoots in their direction. Before an hour is over he will have every bird on the place scared out of its senses and as wild as a hawk; not to mention that the half of them will have run and skulked up the valley on to his own pastures beyond!"

Osborne's honest face was crimson with rage.

"It's an outrage!" he stormed. "It's misdemeanour—it's trespass—there must be *some* law against it—I tell you I——"

"And I tell *you* that, for the present at any rate, there is nothing to be done," said Warburton, calmly. "But for goodness' sake don't let us look as if we were dished. Come on and take no notice."

Osborne gave a gulp and pulled himself together. The two friends continued to walk in line as if such a thing as a kite did not exist within the United Kingdom. Here and there they flushed single birds which rose with the quick, snipe-like dash of the kited partridge; but Osborne's feelings worked disastrously upon his shooting. Before they reached the end of the valley he had missed five decent chances out of ten, and his feelings were by no means ameliorated as the sound of a laugh echoed from behind the hedge.

"Turn here," said Warburton, tersely, as they reached a huge, uncut ox-fence; and the two faced about the way they had come. Suddenly a hail came from behind the thick barrier of quicks.

"Mornin,' Warburton, mornin'," cried a voice. "How's sport your side of the bed?"

Osborne looked round. A thick-framed, coarse-looking man in violent tweeds was standing peering over the fence, while round him a group of keepers stood and sniggered a little shamefacedly behind their fingers. A look of beaming content was upon the big man's features. He cocked his eye upward and winked derisively towards the soaring kite above their heads.

Warburton's reply held no inflection of wrath.

"Good morning," he said, sedately. "We are doing fairly well, thank you. I should be much obliged if you would try to float your kite over your own land."

The big man laughed hoarsely.

"Sorry," he gurgled, "awfully sorry. It's impossible to control the wind, isn't it? I'm new to this sort of thing, you see, but I think it's a deuced fine way of getting birds to lie. What?"

"It's a device I have never seen employed at this time of year by *gentlemen*," interposed Osborne, "but it appears to give *you* satisfaction."

Maurice stared at him insolently.

"Perhaps not, Mr.—er—What's-your-name," he replied. "But I can tell you this—it's thundering fine sport!" Emitting another throaty chuckle, he turned to give the pair a direct view of his tweed-covered back. Yielding to an admonitory twitch upon his elbow from Warburton, Osborne suffered himself to be edged away without giving vent to the words which were burning his tongue. But as they drew out of earshot he boiled over into a perfect flood of entirely indefensible language.

"It's incredible—it's monstrous!" he concluded, as his catalogue of expletives failed him. "I didn't believe such absolute bounders existed outside Pentonville. But look here, old man—you *must* best him. Give me a free hand, and I'll promise you he shall have such a surprise later on as will make the little account between you show such a credit on your side the ledger as will entirely wipe out the few brace he's robbed you of to-day!"

Warburton looked a little incredulous.

"How?" he said, bluntly.

"For the present that's my affair," said his friend, "but you shall know all in good time. The principal thing I wish to know now is if these spinneys on our left are the ones where they get the big rise of the season—if that isn't the famous Collier's clump that we've all heard of?"

Warburton nodded.

"Yes—that's the one they drive to by progressive beats all day," he said. "Last time I shot with Layne we got eight hundred birds there in five and twenty minutes."

"Exactly," said Osborne. "And now, if you don't mind, we'll leave further discussion of an unpleasant subject till evening. My plans are as good as complete. Let's get away from the land this scoundrel has poisoned with his villainies, and see what we can do where we're fairly out of his reach."

Late that evening the two friends were contemplating each other over the rims of their respective glasses. For ten minutes Osborne had been speaking with entire satisfaction to himself, but on Warburton's face there was a distinct tinge of doubt coupled with amusement.

"It's most ingenious," he admitted. "Most original. But it's hardly playing the game, is it?"

"Original! Playing the game!" echoed Osborne. "Why, the beggar himself suggested it!"

Warburton shrugged his shoulders with an air of indecision.

"Well, I suppose he did," he allowed, grinning. "But——"

"There are no buts," contradicted Osborne, stoutly. "The facts are too well known to the countryside for any of your neighbours to put any blame on you. And, if you like, go away and leave me to bear the brunt of it. I don't think *my* reputation is likely to suffer in dealing with human vermin like this creature."

Warburton shook his head.

"I don't think I should care to go away," he said, slowly.

"Why not?"

The Squire's grin broadened.

"Well, to tell you the truth, old man," he said, guiltily, "I wouldn't miss it—if you *do* bring it off—for half my yearly income."

* * * *

Seven weeks later the two friends were contemplating each other in much the same positions as they had occupied on the evening of the first of September. But the smoking-room wore the aspect of a haunt of commerce. Brown paper was littered about in rolls. Huge thin packing cases were stacked against each other and against the walls. Thick balls of stout twine were heaped upon the table. And in the middle of this varied assortment of articles, which was the personal property of Mr. John Osborne, that gentleman sat exuding complacent content from every feature.

"Your note only gave me the bare announcement that he was to shoot the spinneys to-morrow," he was saying, "but I've had all these arrangements ready for the last fortnight. Just as well I have. He's early enough—the leaf's not half off most of the trees yet."

"He's managed to get hold of the Duke of Musselbuck," explained Warburton, "and, as His most graceful Grace is off to South Africa in a week, it was a case of now or never. Fancy a man of Musselbuck's name allowing himself to be mixed up with such a beast as Maurice!"

"Musselbuck? Why, he's our friend's prime draw—his leading guinea-pig," said Osborne. "All the city knows *that*. Well, his ducal life has been a fairly eventful one, but I'll dare swear that the surprise he'll get to-morrow will beat anything he's confronted yet."

Warburton sniggered.

"I don't know now that it isn't a bit too thick," he wavered.

"Thick!" exploded Osborne;" "it's not a quarter as thick as that bloated brute's hide or his conceit. He'll be the laughing-stock of sporting England!"

"Possibly; but——"

"And I its admiration," added Osborne, complacently, as he rose to his feet and made the first move for bed.

*   *   *   *

Buckleigh Woods wore an air of great animation. The white-smocked beaters were gathered at the far end of the long copse, and the guns and their loaders were being lined out on its western edge. Spaniels and retrievers stood in leash or wandered humbly at their masters' heels, and not too far away the game-cart—and that very modern innovation, the refreshment-van—made an appearance. The master of all this display was in high feather and good humour.

"If we don't beat all old Layne's records by a thousand head to-day," he said, as he left the Duke of Musselbuck in position, "call me a Dutchman!"

His grace smiled cordially, and reflected that he might have done so without deviating very far from facts, the late Ezra Morris, in spite of his son's British patriotism, having laid the foundations of his commercial success in a rag-and-bone shop in Amsterdam. But the guest amiably kept his thoughts to himself as he watched his host souse himself upon his shooting-stool fifty yards away and raise the starting whistle to his mouth.

At the signal, the line of beaters rocked forward. The under-growth crashed: the rattle of two score sticks rapped upon the saplings; heated injunctions from the head keeper to keep rank were passed from mouth to mouth in forceful undertones. Rabbits showed white scuts as they twisted from tussock to tussock, and the patter of birds legging it hastily towards the spinney's end came gratefully to the listening guns. An old cock swung up through the branches, turned a glossy breast to the sun, and came sliding across the ride thirty feet up. Musselbuck's gun flipped to his shoulder. Almost before the report sank into the echoes the bird turned, making a graceful parabola, and crashed into the bracken at his back.

Another followed and another. The brown hens began to imitate the example of their more reckless lords. They whirred up by twos, by fours, by fives, by tens, and by twenties. The intermittent rattle of shots became a continual fusillade. But few fell as neatly as that first bold champion, save, indeed, to his

104

executioner. Musselbuck was the only man present to whom shooting had not come as a hard-earned experience, but as a life-long recreation. Mr. Maurice's City friends, thick in the neck and broad in the waist, turned watery eyes to the sky. They banged and banged again. Profanity was loud : execrations followed the missed or tailored birds—and they were many. But in such a cloud of targets it was impossible to miss utterly. Apart from Mussel-buck's well-killed contribution, a good few birds were added to the bag by dint of dog or keeper. And Maurice was still quite content.

"The beggars are only going on to the clump," he remarked, calmly, as a huge rise split over the heads of two incompetent guns almost unharmed. "We shall see them all again."

Ten minutes later the hurried pick-up was over, the guns had been moved forward to new positions, and the next drive was in full progress. In its details it presented few variations from the first one, save that the City Fathers, warming to their work, grew more sarcastic over their friends' misses and more expletive over their own. And at the end of it the host's face was not quite so com-placent. Unless the slaughter grew more deadly by at least fifty per cent., any hope of a record was out of the question. But the thought of the clump rise animated his hopes. If the birds only rose in the solid battalions which his keeper—and the amount of his egg bills—led him to expect, the biggest duffers on earth could scarcely help doing adequate damage in the browning of them. Through five similar beats the morning drew on to its much-anticipated close. Flight after flight of uninjured birds had gone forward, and the head keeper's face was crimson, and his *sotto-voce* anathemas almost blood-curdling in their intensity. But he, too, was telling himself that the clump *must* make up in some degree for the first few disappointments. Leaving his master, he hurried forward to interrogate the stops who encircled the far side of the famous spinney, and to hear their reports. He came back, his lowering visage a shade or two less frowning.

"There's a matter of fifteen hundred birds at least in them few acres," he announced. "The men say they never saw them run in sweeter, sir. If only the gentlemen will contrive to *hit* 'em, I'll promise you as there will be such a rise as Lord Layne never saw in 'is life."

Maurice nodded importantly.

"Now, you fellows," he announced to his assembled friends, "you've simply *got* to make the best of this next spinney. My expenses for this shoot ain't one penny under five thousand pounds, and if you're going to do no better than you have done, I might as well have chucked the money down a sewer."

There was a subdued murmur from the financial magnates which finally ended by simply swelling into a chorus of approval of a suggestion from Mr. Moses Backstein, the well-known outside broker. This, it need hardly be explained, consisted in directing their attention to the conveniently situated luncheon van. In a body, all the guns save Musselbuck and his host moved off to obtain such tonics as would " clear " their faulty vision. Ogden, the head keeper, watched their departure with a certain doubtfulness.

"I *do* hope as they'll do better, sir," he said, wistfully. "There's Squire Warburton and half a dozen men down on Arenside, looking on."

Maurice's face deepened in colour.

" No ? " he said, eagerly. " Well, we'll show them what'll turn their envious visages green, I hope."

He turned to his guest and began to give him a somewhat fantastic account of the prowess with which he had dished " that selfish old fossil from Blakesea." The duke listened imperturbably, but annoyed his host by entirely failing to laugh where Maurice considered that his brightest points were made." " Monstrous amusin' ? What ? " concluded the master of Buckleigh ; and Musselbuck agreed with stony calm.

" Oh, monstrous," he echoed, blandly, and wheeled to greet the returning carousers.

They all wore an air of grim confidence born of their libations. With renewed instructions—one might also say threats—from their leader, they were conducted to their stations, where their loaders, it was noticeable, greeted them with a deference not altogether untinged with anxiety. Maurice gave a last look round. Suddenly Musselbuck, who was next him, gave him a hail.

" What game is your friend in the valley playing ? " he queried, and made a gesture in the direction of the foot of the slope.

Maurice trotted forward and stared in his turn. His eyes grew rounder and his cheeks redder as he looked.

A balloon was rising gaily upon the wind, but such a one! Its great wings stretched twenty feet from tip to tip. Its tail swung out illimitably. Its great head, garnished with a fiercely curved beak, showed a wicked eye, which even at that distance was red and menacing. And the thing was rising rapidly, soaring upon the faint breeze into a position which would bring it directly over the clump!

Maurice broke out into a passion of blasphemy which nearly choked him. The Duke, viewing developments with an impartial eye, was pleased to show signs of intense amusement.

" That's not all ! " he cried, suddenly. " There's another one ! "

It was too true. The semblance of another feathered monster was arising, not far from the first, and this was quickly followed by a third. Before the situation had been prolonged another three minutes half a dozen of the hawk-like objects had taken the air and were straining at the cords which gently insinuated them into position. They practically surrounded the clump. Musselbuck handed his gun to his loader, sat down, and laughed till the tears came.

"Oh, it's neat! It's damned neat!" he chuckled. "Maurice, my boy, your famous rise is bust up—diddled—done for! He's utterly queered your pitch!"

Maurice poured blasphemy upon blasphemy till he was hoarse. He shouted, he called gods and men to witness the disgraceful, unsportsmanlike, ungentlemanlike, un-British outrage which was being perpetrated upon him. He called wildly upon his friends to shoot at the hideous monsters in the wild hope of bursting the bags; he denounced the abject inaction of his keepers; he called upon them to sally forth and fall upon his adversaries if they had to go to gaol for it. He promised a pension to the man who would shoot Warburton on the spot!

And through it all Musselbuck continued to laugh with a wholehearted enjoyment in which Maurice's own friends, thinking a Duke no mean source to take a cue from, were soon prevailed upon to join. At last His Grace managed to pull himself together.

"Look here!" he said, "the more you storm and rave the more your neighbours in the valley are hugging themselves. Drive the clump—drive it and make no sign. The birds won't rise into the open—you can't expect it, but at least we shall get a little shooting on those that fly low to the next cover, and if these gentlemen like to massacre a few runners—why, they'll have every opportunity."

It took ten minutes of profuse argument to get the heated Maurice to see reason, but it was finally allowed to prevail. The guns returned to their stations, the beaters were whistled in, and the drive began. It is probable that a beat like it has never taken place in the British Isles before. A fine old cock was the first to get up. His shrill call of affright as he viewed the hovering monsters intent upon his blood echoed down to the clustering hens below. He dived swiftly into the foliage, wheeled like a woodcock, and plunged back whence he had come. The mob of pheasants skulked and scuttled into the tussocks, clucking wildly.

A grinning beater stuck his pole under a bird and levered it into the air. It fluttered squawking through the branches, and fell upon another beater's head! Knowing old cocks, the experience of years at fault in the face of this entirely new and horrible development, flew low through the undergrowth like shuttles through a loom. Prodded hens, refusing to get forward, broke back between the beater's very feet! Here and there a bird or two, crazed into recklessness, burst into the open and skimmed frantically towards the cover from which they had been originally driven, but these exceptions were few and far between. The main mass of pheasants ran and scrambled to and fro like cornered rats on a barn floor, and the orderly rank of beaters was broken into the semblance of a disordered riot. The men lost control of themselves. They shouted their amusement: they laughed, they struck wildly at the flustered birds: they exchanged rustic witticisms of the bluntest as they thrust and hammered through the bush and bracken. Finally, with a frantic bolt, a dozen cocks raced upon their feet into the open.

And that was the beginning of the end.

Following this bold lead, by dozens and scores the birds took to their heels, and with fearful eyes cocked at the menacing sky fairly legged it across the open, squeaking their terrors like cat-hunted mice. Men or dogs could not stem the torrent or induce them to rise a yard. For minutes the ceaseless stream of traffic continued, and by the end of it fifty scared birds, crouching in tussocks and rabbit holes, were all that were left of the fifteen hundred which had aroused Maurice's fond aspirations of half-an-hour before. Less than two score were brought to bag, and of these twenty had been shamelessly shot as they ran. The famous *rise* at Collier's Clump was over!

As the last of the scanty bag was laid in the meagre rows of slain Maurice flung down his gun. He looked round the circle of his friends. From Musselbuck to Backstein he stared, and met no sign of sympathy, save what was almost entirely smothered by unfettered amusement. The grins which confronted him were wide and liberal.

A sudden resolution seemed to stiffen him. He turned and walked off down the slope into the valley, in spite of admonitory calls which earnestly advised his return.

Osborne turned from the string he was manipulating deftly to see him coming. He handed it to a keeper and lounged forward. Maurice glared at him.

"I want Mr. Warburton," he said, curtly.

"Sorry," explained Osborne. "A few minutes ago pressing business took him home."

Maurice's bosom heaved.

"Then I suppose I'm to thank you for this—this outrage?" he demanded.

"Eh?" said Osborne, with stolid surprise. "I hardly follow you. I'm new to this sort of thing, of course; but I think it's a deuced fine way of getting birds to lie. What?"

The veins swelled beneath Maurice's thick hide.

"I tell you what it is," he shouted; "it's the most damnable, ruffianlike, unsportsmanlike proceeding that ever disgraced a country-side! That's what it is!"

Osborne nodded his head with an air of cordial agreement.

"Perhaps it is, Mr.—er—What's-your-name," he drawled, pleasantly; "but I have your word for it that it's also *thundering fine sport*," and so stood with folded arms, a picture of satisfaction incarnate, as the other turned away panting, and breasted slowly up the hill into his empty wood.

*   *   *   *

Six hours later Osborne was standing in the smoking-room, examining certain parcels with a regretful eye. As Warburton came in he looked up and sighed.

"I'm almost sorry there was no wind for the kites to-day," he complained. "If there had been they would have helped to astonish his weak mind and his pheasants even more!"

Warburton laughed.

"John, my boy, I don't know which has triumphed most to-day—your malice or your ingenuity. If the former, then you will not be as gratified as I am by this," and he waved a note towards him.

Osborne looked at it.

"Who's it from?" he demanded.

"Musselbuck," replied Warburton. "Listen:

"'MY DEAR WARBURTON,

At Eton we were not unfriendly, and I am sorry that later years have taken us very far apart. I look, however, to the memory of schoolboy days to smooth the path of mediator, a *rôle* which to-day's events have thrust upon me. Maurice is a passionate man, but not unbusinesslike. He realises that you have the whip hand of him. Will you take his apology for former unpleasantness, his assurance that it shall not be repeated, and agree to call the battle drawn? If you can you will earn the gratitude of one who would still like to subscribe himself

Your friend,
MUSSELBUCK.'"

Warburton looked at his friend.

"Is that satisfactory?" he said, cheerily.

"Humph," grunted Osborne.

STRANGE STORIES OF SPORT
IX.—A DEAD MAN'S JOKE

BY H. KNIGHT HORSFIELD

I HAD been working late, and I felt tired. The problem I had set myself to solve still baffled me. Earlier in the day a distinct ray of light had fallen upon my mind. Patiently, for many hours, I tried to trace it to its source, but at length I found myself at the end of my clue with nothing tangible in my hand. And it is the tangible, the definite, that I determined to have. Vague illumination is the property of the man in the street. The true worker in the domain of the so-called occult must be known by his results.

I was not altogether sorry when I heard a faint knock at the outer door. I felt that I needed companionship. I glanced at the clock: it was 2 a.m.—a black October morning—wet, too, for I had heard the rain at intervals beating against the panes. It was late, of course, for a casual caller; but my friends do not, as a rule, tie themselves to the conventional divisions of time. My visitor made no reference to the hour as he entered and took an accustomed seat.

He was an old friend. In days gone by we had worked together, but as time went on we had drifted apart, each to follow his own mental bent.

Stewart—George Andrew Gordon Stewart, to give him his full title—was a fair biologist and chemist, who later had taken up electricity. Now he was engaged in training it to ring new kinds of bells, and to drive more or less complicated machines. I, on the other hand, had discovered that I was surrounded by occult mysteries, occult in the sense that they are partly hidden, and mysterious inasmuch as they are imperfectly understood; and I wanted, if possible, to make one or two of the simpler of these clear to science before I died.

So my friend always described himself as a practical man, and myself as hopelessly impractical.

" Been working late ? " he said, as he lighted his pipe.

" Yes," I replied.

Then I waited for one of the old friendly gibes on the vanity of hunting the supernatural—an absurd word which even educated men still use when they plainly mean the super-physical. To my surprise the gibe was not forthcoming.

As I glanced across at Stewart I recalled in a mental flash his somewhat picturesque history. The only son of a Scottish laird, he had been at one time heir to great possessions. But a deep temperamental gulf had been fixed between the father and son from the very outset. The laird was a man of giant frame, a keen sportsman, a dead shot, a hard rider, and a harder drinker, drawing his nature, as his son expressed it, direct without a tincture of intervening civilisation from his fierce cattle-lifting ancestors. Andrew, on the other hand, following on the lines of his dead mother, was a gentle creature without a trace of sport in him, a bookworm from his cradle, living altogether in a small mental kingdom of his own. The father and son stood at opposite poles, and it would have been hard to say which regarded the other with the more settled contempt. Things had gone badly with Andrew whilst the laird remained a widower; when he met and married the strange woman —a countess in her own right, said to have been divorced—a lady who rode with him, shot with him, and, unless rumour lied, drank with him on perfectly level terms—home life for the son became frankly impossible. So Andrew withdrew to a narrow circle of his own, and within six weeks of his marriage the laird was hurled into eternity by the intervention of a rabbit-hole and a stumbling horse. Then the pale student learnt that the whole of his father's possessions had gone to the interloper, and that save for the small deer forest of Bala-huie, which he derived from his mother, he was left acreless and penniless.

I don't think this condition of affairs worried Stewart much, but it unquestionably surprised him.

"I cannot bring myself to believe that the old man had sufficient independence of character to do it," he once said to me. "I am the next link in the chain that goes back through the centuries. He hated me, of course, but he would naturally argue that I must have something of the primeval ruffian latent in my system, and that the chances of marriage might bring the old line of cattle-lifters back again. To break this chain, by which through long tracts of time we have been enabled to cheat our fellows out of their fair share of the earth, argues an amount of enlightenment of which I feel sure he was incapable."

And this view was strengthened by certain oblique hints which reached Andrew from the office of the family solicitors. The entail had been broken by consent, generations, back; but, notwithstanding family feuds, the land had always gone by will from father to son. Now Andrew learnt that great efforts had been made to divert it; but in the end, as ever, the strong race-instinct had asserted itself, and the final will on a single sheet of parchment had been drawn up to keep the old hills in the old line.

The question now arose, where was that single sheet of parchment? Andrew firmly believed that the countess had destroyed it; a most natural thing, in the circumstances, he said.

There was, of course, no proof of this. The fact remained that an earlier will was proved leaving her ladyship in full possession, and that the one known to have been made later had disappeared, destroyed probably by the laird himself.

As I looked across at Andrew, I saw that he had something on his mind. His thin, almost colourless face wore a look of uneasiness; it was the face of a man who has a difficult subject to broach, and is in doubt as to how he shall approach it. We spoke of passing things, but I soon saw that he was shaping the conversation to some definite end.

"I myself, as you know, am not drawn to this so-called occultism," he said, at length. "In fact, its vagueness repels me. At the same time, things occur which are not easily explained on purely scientific lines."

He looked up guiltily; he was plainly horribly afraid of being chaffed.

I had no desire to chaff him. I was growing intensely interested. I had seen that look on a sceptic's face before.

"That, of course, is a commonplace," I said. "Such occurrences are perfectly well known. The rare thing is to find them approached in a scientific temper."

I saw his face lighten. "I can talk to you freely, I know," he said; "without fear that the matter will be repeated. I have a reputation for critical common-sense to lose, and I don't want it to go lightly," he added, with a touch of his old humour.

I threw my pouch across to him. "Smoke," I said, "and speak freely. I daresay I shall understand."

"Well, you remember my father's will. I know, from the solicitors themselves, that it was duly signed, sealed, and witnessed, very shortly before his death. It has disappeared, and an earlier will altogether in favour of my stepmother has taken effect. I believed that my stepmother had destroyed the later will. That is not true. It is still in existence."

"How do you come to know that?" I asked.

He looked confused. "That is the strange part of the story," he said. "I dare not name it to anyone but you." Then he lowered his tone impressively. "*I have seen my father.*"

There was no mistaking the earnestness in his voice. I took a turn up and down the room. What luck some fellows had! Why will these wayward forms persist in appearing to rank outsiders, when so many trained psychical observers are waiting to take accurate notes and data. The momentary annoyance made me unjust. The astral laird had obvious reason for preferring his own son to myself.

"You are certain of your facts?" I said, at length. "Late suppers, alcohol, and so on, all out of the question, I suppose?"

He was visibly put out "Don't rot about it," he said, irritably. "It was in broad daylight. I was sitting in my own room engaged in intricate calculations. To prevent interruption, I had turned the key in the door. My brain was at its clearest and soberest. I chanced to look up, and my father was standing before me, leaning against the mantelpiece."

"You had no sense of fear?" I asked.

"Not the slightest. Not even of surprise. That seems odd now I reflect upon it. At the time, the appearance seemed quite natural."

"It *was* quite natural. A little reading will assure you that this occurs in all ages and in all countries in the world. It was merely supernormal, which is quite a different thing."

"Well, to cut it short, the old man spoke to me. Now I think of it, that again is an odd thing. Death had failed to improve his manners in the least degree."

I offered no comment, but why a casual trip in a rabbit hole should be supposed to change on the instant an irascible old gentleman into a silvery-tongued angel I have never been able to see. So far as manners and morals were concerned, the old laird would be precisely the same upon the astral plane as upon the physical.

"He spoke to me," Stewart went on, "sneered at me, gibed at me. Every physical and mental demerit of mine came in for its due share of abuse. But it was as I believed: he could not rest in the thought that the old hills were to go out of the old line. He said he had come to give me another chance. The will leaving me sole heir, save for a reasonable jointure for the wife, was still in existence. He said that I must hunt for it. Those were his words. 'Pluck up some of the old Gordon Stewart spirit, and hunt for it. Remember you must hunt—hunt literally.' And he grinned as though it were some occult joke. Even as he spoke, I lost sight of him. It seemed rather that the mantelpiece behind him became plain than that he disappeared."

"Did he give you any clue to the hunting ground?" I asked.

"Yes; he spoke of Bala-huie, that God-forsaken wilderness of rock and heather which I have from my mother. He said that the will was there."

"You must go to Bala-huie at once," I said. "The clue, faint as it is, is worth following."

He reflected. "Yes," he said, "it will be well to go. There is only one trouble. The countess is there. My father, as you know, died at Bala-huie, and his widow on one pretext or another has not yet seen fit to leave. Still, the place is my own. I will telegraph to the housekeeper at once that we are coming."

"We!"

Stewart looked up quickly. "Oh, you won't leave me in the lurch, I know. I shall need you badly."

So it was decided after some little discussion that Stewart and I should take train as early as possible for the far north.

*   *   *   *   *

It is a far cry to Bala-huie from King's Cross, mainly because the last sixty miles have to be done by road. It was late at night when we reached the little white shooting-box lost in the hills in the wildest corner of the West Highlands.

The furniture was of the barest; a few scattered deerskins served as carpets, and many rifles, mostly of a bygone pattern, rested on rude wooden racks; a place meet enough for a few hardy stalkers, but badly suited for the residence of a lady. Yet here the countess had lived, practically in solitude, for many months.

We were not destined to meet her ladyship that night, but in the morning she awaited us in the barren reception-room. I am bound to say I was agreeably disappointed by her appearance. Instead of the strong masculine figure I had pictured, I found myself in the presence of a slight, blue-eyed girl dressed in dainty mourning, and barely the age of Stewart himself. Later, I spoke to Andrew, referring to the inadequacy of his description.

"Wait till you know her better, my friend," he replied. "See her handle a rod or a rifle. Then she rides over precipitous places as though she were possessed by a whole colony of restless devils."

I remembered my friend's hatred of the athletic woman in all her forms, and I saw that it was necessary to make due allowance for his prejudice.

Certain it is that from the first the young countess showed us all consideration and courtesy.

I, at times, felt something like dismay at the vigour with which the usually philosophic Andrew prosecuted his search for the missing will. The scanty furniture was overhauled, boards were torn from their places, even the walls were dismantled in the bootless hunt. Yet the countess gave no sign of either surprise or annoyance.

At length we both grew rather weary of the chase. To vary the monotony, I suggested that we should take a rifle and try for a deer on the hills, but Andrew was hopelessly unsympathetic. So it was settled that I should go alone with old Angus, the gaunt stalker, for an escort.

I found a Winchester, somewhat out of date, which fitted me; and early on the following morning, without waiting for the tardy breakfast, I prepared to set out. But, early as I was, the countess was before me. She met me in the hall, and with a faint smile wished me success. " There is one thing I want to ask you," she said, as we parted. " There is an old stag on the hill with a broken horn. If you chance to see it, may I ask you to spare it? It had once a narrow escape from death, and my dear husband promised that it should be held sacred. It seems childish, I know, but you will forgive me for naming it. His last wishes now seem to grow into laws."

She sighed involuntarily. I began to feel that the countess was a misjudged woman, and I promised readily.

    *   *   *   *   *

It was a glorious morning. Before us stretched the vast expanse of heather and rock, and the great mountains reared their serried crests on every hand. The note of a wandering curlew fell fitfully on the ear, and a golden eagle, the last it might be of a noble line, swept across the sky. Truly, Andrew's God-forsaken wilderness promised well for a man with a drop of sportsman's blood in him. Intuitively I felt a touch of sympathy with the old laird regarding from these sunlit heights his degenerate heir.

Old Angus, too, was a man after my own heart. He was a keen naturalist as well as a sportsman, and had ears and eyes for everything that moved in the heather or in the sky. So we fared forward, making for the brow of one of the loftier hills. Here the telescope was withdrawn from its brown weather-stained case, and the old man lay down to make his careful observations. In the meantime I swept with my eye the intervening valley and the great slopes beyond, but although they seemed devoid of cover, I could make out no living thing. Now the slowly-moving telescope stopped. I saw that Angus was concentrating his gaze upon a bare stony ridge to the right.

" The deer are there," he said at length, slowly. " It's a bad place, whateffer."

I took the glass and turned it in the direction indicated. At first I saw nothing, but at length a faint greyish-red form came within my ken. Then suddenly I made out several; some lying down, and others slowly feeding on the sparse herbage between the stones.

It was indeed, as Angus said, a bad place. There seemed to be no vestige of cover in any direction from which the beasts could be approached.

"We will just gang awa' to yon far ridge and lie doon," said Angus, rather hopelessly. "It's nae gude trying to get near them the noo."

"Yon far ridge" involved a long detour. After a hard scramble "o'er moor and fen, o'er crag and torrent" we at length lay down in the shelter of a great barrier of rudely-heaped rocks, to await developments. The deer were still resting where we had at first seen them, and our hope depended on their movement to more broken ground where our approach would be hidden. The day was fortunately nearly windless, so we were able to beguile the long waiting with whispered conversation and a pipe.

By degrees I turned the chat in the direction of the countess. I found she had a warm adherent in old Angus.

"No finer leddy ever stepped the hulls," he said. "With her rifle on her shoulder, she was ever on the mountain with the old laird, and no day was too long for her."

"I suppose it was mainly for the company of her husband that she came?" I suggested. "She was still almost a bride, you remember, at his death."

Angus gave a decisive puff from his pipe, as he lay face downward on the rock.

"It wass no the company at a'," he said; "nae, nae, it wass just the sport. She would gang on all the day and all the nicht for just a chance of a shot at Auld One-horn."

"Auld One-horn," I exclaimed, in surprise. "Why, did she wish to kill him?"

"She did indeed, just that," said Angus, chuckling as though at some amusing reminiscence. "Once when the two were alone on the hull (I was awa' with the sheep) the laird broke off the horn of a royal with his bullet, and never again could they get a chance at him. He wass a strange mon, the laird, full of wild ways, but on the hull there wass no better. He would tease the leddy, and promise her some fine thing (I would hear them talking) if she would but get Auld One-horn roped down on the pony's back."

I smoked reflectively. There was a marked discrepancy somewhere between the countess's pleading words and the strange statement of Angus.

"Oh, it wass no just the company that brought the leddy to the hull," the old man went on, still chuckling. "It wass just the sport. Why, on the very day after the laird was taken to his buryin' at Glenisla, she wass out on the hull again."

"Do you mean to tell me that on the very day following her husband's funeral this lady was out on the hills trying to shoot a stag?" I spoke incredulously, but Angus was firm.

"Ay, she was that—and me with her. And every day since," he added, "up till just when Maister Andrew and yoursel' came to the lodge. An' aye it wass just Auld One-horn she wanted. She cared for no other, whateffer."

I began to see the countess in a new light. There was a mystery here which I was quite unable to fathom. Why was she so keen herself to kill this one-horned stag? Why so anxious for me to spare it? Why had she lied——? But my musings were cut short abruptly. Old Angus had raised his head like a setter who winds game. His quick ear had caught something.

"Hoot, mon!" he hissed; "your rifle—quick. The deer are coming doon the glen."

The Winchester was at my side. In a moment I was ready, but I was barely in time. I peered over the rocks and saw the deer, probably alarmed by something beyond, trooping in a hurried mass in the narrow gully just below. I had little time for discrimination, for the great boulders blocked my view on every hand, but I marked what I took to be a decent beast, and fired just as he disappeared beyond the brow.

"I missed him!" I exclaimed, as I remembered that I had caught the barest glimpse of him as he vanished; but the old stalker did not reply. Already he was climbing down the steep side of the gully, whither I followed him with more cautious steps. When I reached the brow, I saw the flying herd far below in the valley.

"A clean miss," I said, and I was cursing my luck, when I heard a low whistle. In a moment more I was standing by the side of Angus. In a hollow at his feet a great stag lay quite dead, and I saw that one antler had been cut off as with a bullet, within six inches of the skull.

*   *   *   *   *

As we drew near the lodge, with Auld One-horn slung on the hill-pony, my feelings were not easy to analyse. I knew I had made a most singular discovery, yet I could not be quite certain whether I felt elated or depressed. As I expected, the countess was waiting. She offered me no recognition at first, save one bitter glance; but as I entered the hall she turned upon me.

"You lied, then?" she said, drily.

I steeled myself for the coming scene. I wondered how she would take it.

"Not altogether," I replied. "The killing of the stag was the merest accident; yet it may be that, in the circumstances, I owe you an apology. And now, on your side, what have you to say? It may save time if I tell you what you have already guessed, namely, that I have found the last will and testament of your late husband. I found it, as you know, bound round the remaining horn of the stag I have just shot, and protected by some webbing, which appears to have been hastily torn from the lining of a shooting coat."

*　　　*　　　*　　　*　　　*

And so, to end the matter, she told me the whole story, and I believed every word of it.

After the marriage, the laird had made a will leaving his whole estate to his wife. Later, Andrew's absence having, it may be, a softening influence upon him, he wavered, and taunted her ladyship with his intention of reinstating his son. She never credited it, but at length she found that a new will had been actually prepared. In one of his most tantalising whimsical moods, when the matter was still held in the balance, the laird fired at a stag, the bullet cutting off the horn. The animal was completely stunned, and appeared to be inanimate. But the laird, drawing upon similar experiences, believed that it might recover. Thereupon, he amused himself by carefully binding the will upon the remaining antler.

"There," he said to the countess, "if it goes away, it will give you each a fine sporting chance. If you can kill it, I give you full leave to destroy the will, and I swear never to make another. If Andrew can pluck up spirit enough to bring it to bag, the prize, of course, goes to him. If it escapes permanently, you win; if it is bagged by an outsider, and the will is found, you lose. Nothing can be fairer."

Then the eccentric old gentleman sat on a rock and watched the stag. Soon it showed signs of returning life, then it raised its head, and at last, to the disgust of the anxious lady, it cantered off as though untouched.

"Good," said the laird. "Now I'll notify Andrew at once as to the terms of our arrangement."

Andrew never got his letter, the rabbit hole intervening; but, as we have seen, the old laird was too good a sportsman to forget his promise.

*　　　*　　　*　　　*　　　*

It is good to see my old friend a large landed proprietor, especially as I have the run of his domains. Still, I always feel a little sorry for the countess.

STRANGE STORIES OF SPORT

X.—THE BACKNEY HUNT POULTRY FUND

BY FRANK SAVILE

"Yes," said Lord Terence Searle, as he cantered easily along, "I like the country, the hunt servants know their business, subscribers pay up what they promise, and there's next to no wire. There's only one drawback: the tenants—or perhaps I should say, some tenants—are the biggest graspers for poultry damage in the three kingdoms. They are all my near neighbours, too, and good fellows on the whole; but the number of geese and fowls, not to mention turkeys, that they profess to lose in a twelvemonth is simply miraculous; and, considering how decent they are in all other points, I hate to be 'scrapy' with them. But it's almost past a joke."

Charley Sneyd, his bosom friend, raised his eyebrows.

"You are a new man to the country—it's your first season. I expect they are getting at you," he hazarded.

Searle shook his head.

"No," he answered. "I went into the matter thoroughly with Elgar, the manager of the poultry fund. He says it has been so for the last three seasons; and all the claimants being, as I say, most reputable people in every way, he sees no reason to doubt their word. The absurd part of it is that it is immediately round this district, within a mile or two of the kennels, that the damage is done and five-sixths of the claims are made."

"Is the country absolutely littered with foxes then?" asked Sneyd.

"Quite the contrary," said Lord Terence. "There's not too much cover between here and Essington, and in a good deal of what there is I am not allowed to cub. None of the shooting tenants are absolute blackguards, but I wouldn't trust half a dozen of their keepers in the same spinney with a fox till, at any rate, the first shoot of the season was over. At least, I wouldn't insure the fox except at extra-hazardous risks."

"And yet it is round here that all the damage is done?"

"Within a three-mile circle of my own door," said Lord Terence. "We are on our way to interview one of the claimants now."

"Farmer?"

"A poultry farmer, who rents a bit of land I took with the lodge—a woman. She has another grudge against me besides the fox damage."

"Women tenants are the very deuce at times," said Sneyd, feelingly. "What is the trouble?"

Searle laughed.

"It arose from my being an Irishman, and she the most British of British matrons, I suppose," he answered. "I tried a mild joke upon her. She came to tell me that one of her breeding pens had been unroofed in the last gale, and that the rain had collected on the floor—which was in a bad state I'll own—and drowned the half of a young brood of chickens. I asked her what was to prevent her keeping ducks? She went away fuming!"

"Never jest with the English agriculturist," said Sneyd. "Is this a journey of penitence and propitiation you've dragged me out upon?"

"Well, I felt I should like a little backing under the circumstances," grinned Searle. "Here we are."

Sneyd looked up to see a long, low, thatched building, confronted by a gravelled yard, which was filled with pens and wired-in runs. In these fowls and turkeys of various sizes and ages disported themselves, while in the adjoining field a mob of hens scratched and pecked at some weedy-looking stubbles. A very tucked-up looking old nag mare gazed solemnly over the gate of an orchard, and under a lean-to stood a rickety market-cart. The horse, and a lurcher chained up in a barrel beside the door, seemed all the live stock in evidence besides the feathered folk.

"Signs of a great prosperity are not exactly thick upon the ground," said Sneyd. "Is this all she has for a livelihood?"

"And a dashed good one she gets," retorted his friend. "Her poultry is known far and wide. She goes into Hollerton behind

120

that old mare every market day and sets up a stall in the market place. She drives a roaring trade. Report has it that she is worth her hundreds."

Sneyd looked round him a trifle incredulously.

"Then she must be an exceedingly wily old bird herself," he vouchsafed. "I suppose that is the good lady, getting up steam to receive you?"

A woman, clad in a somewhat dirty print gown and a sun-bonnet, had come out on to the doorstep, and was looking at the two riders from beneath a shading hand. The afternoon sunlight beat upon a very weather-beaten face and two rather aggressive black eyes. The chained lurcher began to bark furiously.

She sent it back into its kennel with a hearty cuff before she remarked, with a distinctly distant and huffy air—

"Good afternoon, me lord."

"Ah, good afternoon to you—good afternoon, Mrs. Grimes," said his lordship, cheerily. "I've just come to see you about that poultry pen and one or two other little matters."

"It's not too soon, either, me lord," said Mrs. Grimes, sourly. "There's enough rain collects on that pen floor to water a herd of bullocks."

"Quite so, quite so," agreed Lord Terence, hastily. "I'll take your word for it, my dear madam. I've already told the Hollerton mason to come and put it right for you. I assure you I've every desire to give you satisfaction."

"Then you'll have the lean-to thatched at the same time, me lord," interposed the good lady, quickly. "It's a disgrace to have to put my good cart under such a contraption."

"Well, well, if you'll provide the straw, Mrs. Grimes, we'll——"

"How could I have straw, me lord, me being but a poor woman with nothing but my two hands between me and the workhouse?"

"Tut, tut! I suppose I shall have to see if I can get a load from Farmer Gooch."

"Farmer Gooch hasn't any straw to be called straw, me lord. It's all twitch, and charlock, and——"

"Very well, very well," said his lordship, desperately. "It *shall* be thatched with *good* straw *not* from Farmer Gooch's; but I just want a word with you about your poultry claim. You have sent in an application for fox damage for sixty-eight pounds fourteen and six! Now, my very dear Mrs. Grimes, I put it to you frankly—isn't that just a bit too thick?"

The good lady drew back a step with a snort of indignation.

"Thick?" she said, blinking her black eyes at her questioner.

"Does your lordship mean too much? I'll tell your lordship this: it's very nigh to beggary your foxes have brought me with their thieveries. If I had me rights, it's *one hundred* and sixty-eight pounds I'd be asking, and not less than the half of it!"

Lord Terence laughed uneasily.

"Now come, come, my dear Mrs. Grimes," he expostulated. "I only want to be reasonable, but I like fair treatment myself." He made an expressive gesture towards the paddocks and feeding pens. "Do you honestly mean to tell me that there's the worth of anything like sixty-eight pounds in that!"

Mrs. Grimes's eyes blazed.

"I'd have your lordship know that there is not a week in the year that a hundred pounds would buy my stock!" she cried. "My black Minorcas alone are worth the money; my geese can't be bought under ten shillings apiece!"

Sneyd pointed his whip to a rusty-black rooster which was pacing meditatively down the yard. Like not a few of its brethren its feathers drooped; a melancholy glint was in its eye. Its aspect spoke most convincingly of "pip."

"Is that one of your *guinea* fowls, then?" japed Sneyd, flying in the face of his own lately expressed convictions.

Mrs. Grimes rose at the poor attempt at a joke like a trout at a may-fly.

"It's all very well for you and the likes of you to come here flinging your insults at a widder woman what can't protect herself!" she declaimed. "I'm asking no more than my rights, and them I'll have, if I have to write to every paper in the country. I'll see as people know how you treat your own tenants, me lord, not to mention the scores of others that are robbed of their living by your mangy foxes. There's not a poultry yard in the district that hasn't lost a five-pound-note's worth nigh every month of the year. There's *lambs* gone as well as chickens, and my neighbour, Farmer Long, will take his affidavit to your lordship that he surprised a vixen and six cubs chasing his best foal to death in the long paddock if he hadn't happened along to—— "

Lord Terence held up a propitiatory hand before he hastily climbed back into the saddle.

"My good Mrs. Grimes—my dear Mrs. Grimes," he interrupted, "that will do; and the less you see of Farmer Long the better. The fever in his imagination might be contagious, and things are bad enough as they are. I'll get the Poultry Fund Committee to investigate your claim thoroughly, and you may be sure you shall be justly dealt with, though I cannot promise you that you will receive all you think you are entitled to. Er—good morning!"

Mrs. Grimes's reply was voluble and emphatic, but the two friends had put spurs to their horses and fled out of ear-shot in disordered rout. The victory of the afternoon lay most certainly with the lady. Sneyd having forcibly refused to be taken to interview any other plaintiffs of Mrs. Grimes's calibre, their horses' heads were set towards Essington Hall, the residence of Mr. John Elgar, Lord Terence's principal supporter and loyal right-hand man in the Backney Country. But here, though they received sympathy, they got little consolation. Over the poultry claims Elgar could only shake his head.

"Mrs. Grimes is a regular Tartar, I know," he acknowledged. "Her recriminatory powers are notorious through the country-side, but I have never heard her honesty impugned, nor that of any of the other claimants. James Farrow, of this parish, keeps a deal of poultry, and I would stake my life upon his honesty. He came to me almost shamefacedly with his claim, which he told me didn't represent anything like his real loss, and yet it amounted to five-and-thirty pounds!"

Sneyd made an exclamation of incredulous amazement. Lord Terence threw up his hands with a gesture of despair.

"But where, in the name of all that's preposterous, are the *foxes?*" he cried. "There isn't a cover within five miles that we don't draw blank three times in four. If it was over beyond Essington I shouldn't be quite so staggered at it—the country there is rank with foxes. But here—here in Backney parish! it's monstrous—it's unbelievable."

Elgar shrugged his shoulders.

"I have my own testimony to the truth of the matter to give," he said, ruefully. "Twice when coming home from cubbing early have I seen a great dog-fox loping across these very meadows, and on each occasion with a fine cochin-china from Farrow's farm— apparently—in his mouth!"

"I wish to goodness I could get fifteen couple on the rascal's trail," said Lord Terence. "As likely as not it's one and the same great savage that's doing all the harm. We must live in hopes. Let me get him in the open, a mile or two from his own cover, and I'll give him more to think about than poultry stealing."

Little encouraged by this interlude the two set off home. As they rode out of Elgar's hospitable gate Lord Terence turned in the saddle. "It's only a kennel meet to-morrow, as you know," he shouted; "but if the frost *should* give I'll let hounds have a breather. Come over on the chance!"

From the doorstep Elgar waved his hand in acceptance of the invitation.

As luck would have it the following morning the stiff north wind which had held the country frost-bound for over ten days backed to the west and south. The sun shone brilliantly, and the M.F.H. and his friend, as they dug inquisitive heels into the lawn before the door, agreed that in another hour—or say by two o'clock—the country would be not too murderous for either pad or hoof. They agreed to see what ten or twelve couple could find in some of the home covers. Soon after midday Elgar arrived to buttress this good resolution with enthusiasm.

No other member of the hunt had appeared by the time they started, so it was a small enough field which turned up the lane which led upon Buntington Gorse. Butcher boots and bowlers, and for the hunt servants the third best pinks, were the order of the day, and no one had the aspect of taking matters seriously. Tom Slick, the whip, cantered off to take up his position at the far side of the cover where the gorse dwindled out among the scattered firs of a young plantation. Hounds went feathering in.

Sneyd brought out his cigar-case.

The next instant he had slipped it back into the pocket with a snap. A piercing yell had come from the direction in which Slick had disappeared. He pranced into view, his cap whirled up on the end of his whip. Almost at the same moment a burst of melody came from the hounds as they closed up upon what was evidently a minute-old scent. Led by old Galloper, nose to stern they threaded smartly through the rabbit paths in the gorse and bracken and burst in full cry into the open.

Elgar and Sneyd followed them in time to see Lord Terence charging the first fence, a stake-and-bound, side by side with the huntsman, Dick Donovan. Elgar gave a whoop of gratified excitement as he saw them. "It's going to be a run and a half!" he exclaimed. "Not more than twice in the last five years has a fox taken that line by Buntington Ford. Once over the brook there is no chance for him for six miles or more. He must make for Portsell earths, and those were stopped the week before last, and it's ten to one they are stopped still. We're in for a fifteen-mile point, my friend!"

Sneyd gave a nod of satisfaction, though he felt a piercing qualm of regret that he had mounted himself on one of his "three-leggers" for the afternoon, keeping his two brightest and best for the first official meet after the thaw. However, the nag under him, if not absolutely sound, was warm and willing. For the next two miles he sailed along in great style, going great guns over sound pasture and quick fences or post-and-rails. It was not till they had passed a strong field of plough that the hounds began to make ground from the horses and Sneyd's old warrior started grunting his distress. And then Chance, who many people think is over-kind to the "late division," smiled upon him benignantly. There was a check.

But not for long. Donovan's first cast picked up the scent beside a fence. Galloper whimpered, faltered, whimpered again, and finally hit off the line with a deep-throated joy. Clustering to him the eager pack echoed the one long note into a chorus. Off went hounds, spreading, but not spreading over-wide, upon the scent, and Elgar's chuckles were ecstatic. "The run of the season!" Sneyd heard him muttering to himself. "Poor beggars! poor beggars!" Sneyd did not find it hard to understand that this commiseration was directed to the address of all the keen hands in the hunt who were missing such opportunities of bliss. He galloped along musing on the contrariety of things in general. Fancy a kennel meet providing the most sensational of spins, from a country, too, where blank draws, it was evident, were the rule and not the exception! "The run of the season!" He wondered if that was really likely to be a true bill.

It proved so, though not exactly in the sense in which Sneyd imagined. Hounds ran, checked again twice, recovered their line with marvellous quickness, and finally ran from scent to view. There was a strenuous ten minutes at the last in which Sneyd's aged though indomitable champion failed to live with the others. He cantered up ten minutes after the kill to find Lord Terence and Elgar congratulating themselves and Donovan with beaming faces.

"An hour and ten minutes. Three checks and a kill. A good old-fashioned hunting run," he commented. "What's the distance?"

The huntsman looked at the Master. Then he cocked his eye at the sky, which was rosy from the sunset.

"It's only five miles home from here, m'lord," he submitted. "But there's a frost coming up. We'd better hurry if we're going to save hounds' feet."

Lord Terence nodded.

"We'll go the road. There's plenty of good grass edging all the way," he decided. "I don't care to get pounded, and to have to smash half a dozen fences in the dark."

Donovan nodded his approval, collected his hounds, and jogged for the nearest gate. The whips followed, expatiating to each other on the unexpected glories of the day. Searle and his two friends halted to put a match to their cigars. Sneyd got off to ease his horse. The light of the moon-rise shone pale over the horizon.

The horses of the huntsmen and whips clattered out on to the road, the ring of the iron telling that the prophesied frost was well on its way. Suddenly Donovan's voice was uplifted in a vehement exclamation.

"Lord ha' mercy on us!" cried he, his words carrying distinctly in the crispness of the evening.

"Hulloa!" cried his master; "Hulloa! What's the trouble?"

He cantered on towards the gate. Sneyd mounted hurriedly, and followed with Elgar. The three hunt servants had come to a halt in the middle of the road, the hounds clustering unconcernedly around them. Sneyd meditated that what he saw might be accounted for by the wan light of the half-risen moon but he confessed that he had seldom looked upon a face as white as that of the usually ruddy huntsman. Lord Terence had evidently marked it too. He bustled towards his man demanding explanations, excitedly.

"What's the matter—what's the matter?" he shouted. "You look as if you'd seen a ghost!"

Donovan swallowed and choked, apparently incapable of reply.

It was Slick's voice, high-pitched and faltering, which answered:

"If you please, m'lord, *we have!*"

Lord Terence turned towards him wrathfully.

"You great blockhead!" he thundered. "What the devil d'you mean?"

The whip touched his cap sullenly.

"We all three seen it with our own six eyes, m'lord," he said. "You can ask Mr. Donovan or Sam here. There weren't any mistake about it, I'll take my solemn oath."

"Oh, you very egregious asses!" bawled his master, crimson with exasperation. "Any mistake about *what!*"

"About that there fox," said Slick, doggedly.

"A fox—a fox? There's no mistake we've just killed a dashed fine one," joined in Elgar. "What's wrong with it?"

Donovan had found his voice again.

"There's n-n-nothing wrong with that one, m'lord," he stammered. "Here I have his mask and brush all right," he added, touching his saddle. "But it's the other one—the one that jumped into the road just now, and went padding off down it *with a great white ball in his mouth!*"

"What!" chorussed all three gentlemen—"What!"

Donovan nodded his head decisively.

"It's just as I tell you, m'lord," he continued. "We just got into the road. I was here, Slick he was 'gentling' the hounds through the gate which Sam was a-holding open. Something turned out of that there field opposite and bounced into the road. I ain't telling no sort of lie. We could all see it as plain as plain. It was a fox, but no sort or kind of ordinary fox, *for the hounds never took the leastest, tiniest piece of notice of it!*"

Searle stared at him as if the man was a new and startling specimen of the human freak.

"Oh, get out, you idiot!" he snorted.

Donovan touched his cap in his turn.

"Very well, m'lord," he said, morosely.

"If there was a public-house within six miles I'd swear you were all three drunk," declared his lordship, forcibly. "As it is I suppose you're dreaming."

The three men sat in their saddles with wooden, offended faces, without attempting any reply.

"Eh?" said their master, fiercely.

"I didn't speak, m'lord," said Donovan, icily.

"Then why didn't you?" cried his lordship. "Do you think I'm going to swallow an impudent yarn like that without worrying the truth out of you. What d'you think I'm made of?"

A new voice broke into the silence. Sam, the second whip, was moved by the desperation of his colleagues' needs into speech.

"If you p-p-please, m'lord," he stuttered, "d-d-down to W-w-warwickshire, where I was born, there was an old party, Betty Mucksy by name, as could change herself into any sort of cat or dog or what-not. A witch, she were, and a proper wicked 'un. I'd allow as this is summut o' the same sort."

"Oh, you very preposterous lunatic!" foamed Lord Terence; "you'll tell me the brute flew off on a broomstick next!"

"No, m'lord. She didn't do no such thing," continued Sam, stolidly. "She trotted off a-down the road as proper as could be."

"The *fox!*" screamed his master.

"Yes, m'lord."

"And these hounds—these hounds of *mine*, with some of the best noses in England—didn't so much as whimper, you dare to tell me?"

"Never twitched, m'lord. That's what's the witchery of it."

Lord Terence's cheeks swelled. He gasped. Then he shook his head sorrowfully.

"It's no good," he confessed. "There are no words in the dictionary to tell you what I think of you. But we'll put this matter to the test quick enough. The line is down the hard, high road, is it?" He cantered forward along the grass edge, blowing his horn. "We'll put hounds along it," he cried, "and if I'm not mad, and you haven't been having mightmare, and the hounds haven't become Maltese terriers, they'll own to a fox that has passed not three minutes back. Come along!"

The procession started. Sam, indeed, was heard to mutter that they'd all be doited, like as not, if they meddled with such a customer as a witch vixen, and Donovan's expression vouched for the fact that he more or less shared his underling's opinion. But the three servants could hardly disobey their master's explicit orders, and they took a certain comfort from the fact that they were not being hustled into the adventure alone. They had, they mused, three of the gentry to share with them the perils of the unknown.

Hounds gambolled along cheerily. The horses had their second wind and had got over their distress. The pace warmed up, but the hounds were obstinately dumb. Lord Terence cantered upon the crisp grass, glaring ahead along the white riband of the road, his two friends close behind him. For several minutes there was no sound but the thud of hoof, jingle of curb, and the slight noise which Sam's cob, a whistler, always made.

Suddenly the leader surprised his followers by an emphatic oath.

" There *is* something padding down the road!" he added.

The two behind looked up.

The moonlight was vivid upon the macadam. They rubbed their eyes. Yes—there was no sort of doubt about it. A small, dark object was scudding swiftly and silently along, eighty yards ahead. And—they rubbed their eyes—was it—no, it couldn't be— but the fact remained that there *was* a very evident white lump where the thing's head should have been!

Lord Terence gave a mighty view holloa and sent the spurs into his horse's flanks. Hounds, surprised out of their apathy, lifted up their heads and gave an unconvincing yowl or two. The whole concourse sped along with increasing animation.

They gained upon their quarry hand over fist. They were only fifty yards away by now, then thirty, then only twenty. They had a view of it that put all doubts out of the question. They were pursuing a fox, and one which carried an Aylesbury duck in its mouth! And hounds were as unmoved as if they were on the kennel benches!

Finally old Galloper put the gilded roof upon the mystery. He sidled up alongside his natural enemy and made a half-hearted snatch at the burden which it carried. The brute simply made a cur-like vicious snarl between its closed teeth and trotted unconcernedly on, Galloper drew aside with a crestfallen, shamefaced air.

Lord Terence put up his hand to his head and looked wildly about him. The rest of the pack had closed up by now, and the quarry was padding along in the midst of the hounds, who made a sort of a circle around it, yet without offering to draw nearer than a yard or two! The M.F.H. absolutely pinched himself to see if he was alive! Then, with a sort of desperate air of incredulity, he released the thong from around his whip-stock and lashed at the mysterious apparition! The brute flinched, squealed in a sort of muffled way through the feathers in its mouth, and then, darting through the hounds, leaped upon the low wall to the right and dropped into the pasture. It made a bee-line across it.

Lord Terence reined in his horse, put him at the wall without a word, and bucked over. Hounds, after a moment's hesitation, answered to the horn, and bundled over in their turn. The servants followed, Sam keeping most obviously to the rear. The gleam of the white duck led them directly for a big ox-fence at the far side of the meadow. The next moment it had disappeared as its bearer slipped through a gap. Still without a word, Lord Terence turned his horse, came back eighty yards to get steam, and thundered at the obstacle in the best Leicestershire style. Sneyd, careful of his wearied mount, sidled along the ditch till he came to a negotiably thin place beneath a tree. Hounds, horses, and men reassembled by various methods on the far side of the massed thorn bushes. The field in which they found themselves was dotted about with trees.

A loose horse cantered up to them. Sneyd looked at it with a spasm of doubtful recognition. He stared around him. Suddenly, wide to the left, he caught the gleam of whitewash. Yes—he told himself that there could be no doubt about it—it was from this paddock that the old horse had contemplated them on the previous day. This was Mrs. Grimes's orchard, and that long, low, white-washed edifice was her dwelling.

For an absurd instant Sam's gloomy prognostications were vivid in his memory. Was it possible—no, his common sense swiftly assured him that it was not. But, all the same, it was in a state closely resembling stupefaction that he saw the white gleam of the duck's breast pass on into the gravelled yard.

Close behind this most audacious fox Lord Terence flung open the orchard gate. The brute wheeled round the corner of the house, halted, shook itself, dropped the duck upon the threshold, and then deliberately disappeared into the barrel which stood beside the doorstep. Sneyd waited with conviction for the battle royal which surely must ensue between invader and invaded. Nothing was heard save the rustle of an animal settling itself down into a lair of straw.

Lord Terence, muttering strange and inaudible things, flung himself from his horse. He marched up to the barrel—he stooped. A low growl greeted him from within.

He drew back, searched his pockets, and produced a match-box. He struck a vesta and held it flaming in the kennel mouth. He put out his gloved hand towards the inmate.

A snarl and a baring of white teeth followed, then the brute flew out at him !

With a quick instinctive motion Lord Terence whirled round the crop in his hand and brought the heavy top smartly down upon the fox's head.

It gave a squeal and rolled over. Its limbs moved spasmodically once or twice and grew still. There was a panting breath, and then silence. The five other men felt a sort of stupefaction. It was as if priests condoned a sacrilege. Under their very eyes a fox had been foully done to death, and its executioner was no less a wretch than a Master of Foxhounds ! They gasped as they realised it !

Lord Terence stooped, gathered up the corpse, and began to examine it with a sort of remorseful wonder. At least, thus the watchers explained his action to themselves. But his next words rather destroyed this illusion.

" Sam," he said, peremptorily, " bring your knife ! "

Sam tottered forward. His master pressed the body into his hands. Sam leaped back as if he was stung !

" You fool ! " said the M.F.H. forcibly—" Skin it ! "

" S-s-s-kin it ! " gurgled the second whip. " M'lord, I d-d-daren't ! "

Lord Terence threw back his head, and his laughter echoed and re-echoed among the breeding-pens.

" Then *unbutton it !* " he shouted, holding his sides and rocking to and fro with emotion. " It's the *lurcher !*—Mrs. Grimes's damned, thieving, roost-robbing *lurcher ! In its new foxskin suit !* " His emotion overpowered him. He leaned against the wall of the house. His mirth found vent in peal upon peal.

" That old woman ! " he cried. " That old hag with her woes and her sixty-eight pounds damage, and her thatch, and her lean-to —and *she's* at the bottom of it all with her confounded gipsy tricks. She trained the brute, stuck him in this disguise, and sent him out raiding. No wonder hounds wouldn't own to the scent. She smothered the pelt in carbolic ! "

Sam snatched up the body. He turned it this way and that ; he probed into the draggled fur. Along the belly and chest he quickly discovered a neat row of hooks and eyes. With trembling fingers he loosened them, held up the empty skin, and flung the limp body of the lurcher upon the ground.

There was a clang of bolts from the door. Suddenly it was drawn open, and the prosperous figure of Mrs. Grimes stood outlined by the lamplight.

Sam gave a strangled cry, stooped, picked up the corpse, and flung it straight at its mistress's head.

Mrs. Grimes slipped as the body struck the doorpost. She stooped, peered at it, and then cast a swiftly apprehensive glance at the men and horses in her yard. One look was sufficient. Stepping back into the passage she slammed the door and crashed the bolts into the sockets most emphatically. The game, as a much weaker intelligence than hers could understand, was most decidedly up.

Lord Terence, still panting under the stress of his emotions, beat upon the panels with the butt of his whip.

"All right, my dear madam," he admonished her, "all right for to-night! But I'm coming round to settle that little poultry claim of yours in the morning."

"Well," said Elgar, as he climbed upon his horse and followed the Master out of the yard, "I said it would be the run of the season! I don't think I made a bad guess."

       *   *   *   *   *

But the satisfaction which Lord Terence had promised himself in interviewing Mrs. Grimes on the following day was denied him. He was early at her door, but not quite early enough. In the hours of darkness she had taken herself, and her horse, and her cart, and her poultry, into regions unknown. She has never been traced. A policeman in a neighbouring county, indeed, made note of the fact that a gipsy camp had received recruits in the shape of one old woman and one old horse, but did not make report of this insignificant piece of intelligence in time for the fact to receive weight in the quarters where Mrs. Grimes was being sought. She has departed and taken her peculiar methods with her. Poultry damage is an insignificant item in the debit column of the Backney Hunt Funds once more. But to every M.F.H. let me close with a word of warning :

If complaints of poultry-eating foxes in your district become too extravagant, make search diligently in your midst. And if you find a round, leathern-faced, black-eyed, aggressive looking old lady who keeps lurchers, if possible annihilate her!—she is Mrs. Grimes.

STRANGE STORIES OF SPORT

XI.—MR. BURKINGTON'S BEAGLES

BY FRANK SAVILE

Mr. Phineas Burkington wore a frown of extreme dissatisfaction on his fat and somewhat foolish face. He gnawed his short sandy moustache and poked the fire with unnecessary fierceness. It wasn't his own fire, and the fact that he poked it showed extreme tension of mind. For he was quoted as a pattern of politeness by many ladies who owned marriageable daughters, and he must surely have been aware of the adage which permits such familiarity in a house where you have been welcomed for seven consecutive years, but under no other circumstances.

But his companion and host, Mr. Connor O'Connor, showed no signs of resentment. His acquaintance with his guest had not, indeed, endured for the period prescribed—not even for as many weeks—but his respect for the young man, and for his shekels, was limitless. He was prepared to endure much at the hands of the sole proprietor of Burkington's Boot Beautifier, a concern which employed its thousands and had made its owner one of the most prominent men in all Ireland. Mr. O'Connor, in fact, viewed the young millionaire through very rose-tinted glasses—imaginative lenses which swelled his financial virtues to the exclusion of any small defects of face or form. In Moyle and the surrounding district he posed as Mr. Burkington's social godfather. Many of his neighbours accused him of hankering after a closer connection.

He looked at the frowning face and the fiercely-brandished poker, and spoke smoothly.

"Ah now, Phineas," he pleaded, "don't be after disturbing yourself."

"I *do* disturb myself," retorted Mr. Burkington, defiantly. "It is the most disturbing thing that has ever happened to me. After all your encouragements to be refused with—with *ignominy*. She said she'd as soon marry Flitty Boyle, the travelling knacker!"

The ghost of a smile dinted old O'Connor's lips and fled unseen —of Mr. Burkington.

"'Tis but her wild way of speakin'—the unbridled filly that she is," declared the father of the lady under discussion. "For a penny I'd lend her a slap—the colleen; but as likely as may be she'd return it, and 'tis no small fist she has. Take time, me bhoy, take time!"

"My patience has its bounds," remarked the young man, importantly.

"Of course it has," said the old man, suavely; "but you're a terror for resolution—many's the time I've marked that in your eye. You'd not be allowing yourself to be bested by a shlip of a girl?"

Mr. Burkington's features relaxed.

"If I had the rights of a husband I have no doubt I could—er—tame her," he allowed. "At present I'm at a disadvantage."

Mr. O'Connor remembered that he himself had possessed the rights of a father for twenty-one years and some months. At no period did he recollect relations existing between himself and his offspring in which he could be regarded as tamer and she as tamed. But these reminiscences he kept to himself. He nodded propitiatingly.

"That's your own self that's talking now!" he assented, eagerly. "In six months you'll be riding her on the snaffle."

"I have yet to get her bitted," Mr. Burkington reminded him, with ponderous joviality.

"And that you'll not do with one finger or two," remarked his host. "It comes to this—you must be always at her. She has to get accustomed to the idea of you—you must be there always—slap in her eye. Once she understands that you're the bhoy for her— the only one I'll let her live and marry—she'll take you at a gulp!"

Mr. Burkington hardly seemed to relish this metaphor. The old gentleman, however, failed to notice his frown and continued the parable.

"Don't let her out of your sight, Phineas," he admonished him. "Ride with her, run with her, sit with her! Put another meet a week on to your beagling fixtures and show her sport. I'll see that she attends them. She'll come with all her heart. She adores running, the light foot that she has."

In spite of the stimulating nature of this address the young man's frown deepened.

"She's fond enough of beagling," he agreed, "but so is that weedy lad from the barracks—Gaisford. She's always a great deal more in his company than mine."

"Him?" sneered the old man, contemptuously. "The fathom of pump water! A sound man like y'rself could throw him up and catch him in y'r mouth! Oust him—shouldher him out of the way! Show spirit, me lad! Cut in between them!"

"I have to attend to my hounds," said the Master of Beagles, with the manner of one who directed the destinies of the Pytchley or the Quorn.

"You'll have all your married life before you to demonstrate upon them," argued his would-be father-in-law. "Leave them be temporarily. Huggins, your whip, will cast and yoick if your attentions to Nora keep you lagging. For this season you've but the one hare to hunt, and that's my daughter, bad scran to her obstinate sowl!"

Mr. Burkington still looked doubtful. The old gentleman's parchmenty face took on a flush of exasperation.

"See here—you!" he cried, wrathfully, "must I in my sixty-sixth gouty year come on me old shooting pony to show you that's health and strength and full nourishment how to bridle a filly that's yours for the asking? She's mine, and now I've said she's yours! Go you and take her. And if any red-jacketed stick of an Army captain stands between you, into the first ditch with him! I've given you the sole right to the girl's company. Keep it!"

The Army captain's rival nodded.

"There's a good deal in what you say," he admitted. "You'll impress this—this arrangement upon Miss Nora?"

"I'll impress that and a birch-rod on her sleek, deceptive skin!" declared the irate parent, "if she so much as squeaks under your hand. But do you do your own part with the hardest heart in you. Stick to her—cling to her, me lad, and if by March she isn't Mrs. Burkington, I'll eat every hare you'll have caught, skin and teeth!"

Mr. Burkington's lips relaxed into smiles. As one who seals a bargain, he suddenly shook his Mentor by the hand.

＊　　＊　　＊　　＊　　＊

The little beagles tailed out across country with shrill melodies of joy which demonstrated that scent lay warm. They had found early, in an unlikely spot, and after many misgivings on the part of the field that sport would dally. But luck had been with them. The pack had not frittered away its energies in useless manœuvrings for a find. A stout old jack hare had sprung up almost under their noses in a sedgy pasture, and was scudding across the open towards the distant moorland as straight as a dart. For the first three fields the hounds had run in view. Now their noses were well to the ground, but on a scent which—as old Larry Pike, the Moyle Hunt earthstopper, was wont to express it—" rose and shtruck thim in the eyeball."

The field was long and straggling. Tim Huggins, the whip, pranced gaily at the tail of the hounds, taking the ditches with springing leaps which none but a born bog-trotter could emulate. A little behind him came a resolute line of boys, ardent sportsmen every one, running with breathless jealousy, each with his own pet theory of a likely line, but each with an inquisitive glint of the eye towards any neighbour who showed signs of improving on it. Back of these again ran one or two striplings of slightly maturer years, panting more than their younger rivals, but wearing down by degrees into their second wind, and covering the ground with long and regular strides which spoke of experience as much as ardour. In an irregular patch followed the main body of the field.

There were several girls among the followers—bright complexioned, grey-eyed daughters of Erin, each with an attendant train of cavaliers. It was noticeable that of these Miss Nora O'Connor held the largest court.

A detachment of subalterns and a junior captain or two from Moyle barracks made up a majority of it, but among these dapper youths Mr. Burkington's massive form was bulking largely. He ran doggedly at Miss O'Connor's shoulder, towering over her like a battleship over a sloop. The military cruisers—to complete the metaphor—invariably found the wind taken out of their sails if they attempted to run alongside. Now and again Miss Nora looked up at him curiously. The Master was displaying the agility of one of his own hares. Several times she endeavoured to disembarrass herself of his proximity, but turn and twist as she would he invariably kept within armsbreadth of her. He made no remark—he never tried to emulate the breathless repartees which the young warriors exchanged—he reserved the powers of his lungs for the business of running. But he was *there*.

Suddenly the full chorus from the hounds died to a whimper. The runners looked up gratefully to recognise a check. The pack went feathering across a pasture under Tim's able directions, casting for the line. Miss O'Connor mopped her brow and dropped into a stroll.

"Praise Heaven for *that!*" she ejaculated, piously. She looked up at Burkington again. "Won't you be giving them a cast?" she inquired.

The young man eyed his pack indifferently.

"I'll not improve on Huggins's line," he answered, and stood watching the feathering sterns without enthusiasm. He remained steadfastly at his captivator's side.

She turned and raised her eyebrows ever so slightly at the young man who had been sharing the duties of escort with Burkington. He stood as near her on the right as her other admirer did on the left. She had a comically bewildered air as she gazed at him.

He smiled back. He was a tall, bronzed, supple-looking man of about eight or nine and twenty, and he and Miss Nora contemplated each other with every sign of mutual satisfaction.

"Ah, me!" she deplored suddenly, "they've hit it off—they'll be running for Hennessy's Flat. I'll not be able to keep the line any longer. I'll make a cut for the bridge below Shan's Paddock, and with luck catch up to you there."

"Now—now, Miss Nora!" objected one of the youngsters, "with your limbs and talents you've no call to run cunning. And 'tis as likely as the next thing that she'll make another swerve and evade you and y'r cut entirely."

One of his companions pinched his arm and frowned. A sudden look of intelligence pervaded the youngster's features. He sidled off with his friend. "Sure, I forgot," he apologised under his breath. "'Tis not the hare she'll be after catchin'."

By twos and threes the little crowd took up the running and followed the disappearing pack. Gaisford stayed where he was.

"Yours is a wise decision, Miss O'Connor," he remarked, "but there is a good deal of water out in the river meadows below Shan's. If you'll permit me I'll be your guide in avoiding it. The old sheep lane will be our way, won't it?" he added, turning to Burkington, who still stood doggedly at his elbow.

A frown was creasing the Master's fat face. He hesitated.

"Ay," he said at last, "I'll show it you."

The other two made a simultaneous protest.

"Oh, we couldn't possibly take *you* away," they began; but their unsolicited guide interrupted grimly.

"Oh, but you *could*," he affirmed, resolutely. "*I'm coming.*"

They looked at him blankly—they made several somewhat incoherent protests. Mr. Burkington answered with no more than monosyllables or silence, and began to lead the way towards the sheep lane. They toiled up it at his heels, exchanging glances which pictured wrath, surprise, and a musement, as different points of view in their companion's conduct suggested themselves. He, on his part, offered no further explanation of this sudden desertion of his pack than a still more aggressive proximity to his lady-love.

They had passed out of the lane, crossed the bridge, and reached the Moyle high road, when Miss O'Connor complained of weariness. No sign of hounds had rewarded their attempt to cut in, and without the goad of excitement she explained that her energies weakened. She looked up hopefully as the sound of wheels drew attention to a pony-cart which was trotting down the road.

"Is it you yourself, Flitty Boyle!" she addressed the driver, a dark-eyed, clean-shaved youth who touched his hat to her with great respect. "Would it be within the powers of the good cob there to give me a lift on the way home?"

"'Twud be iverlastin' honour to me poor contrapshun of a car, miss, if you'll enthrust y'rsilf to me," said the man, grinning cheerfully. "Sure, I'll have ivry plisure in life in takin' the whole three of ye."

Miss O'Connor shook her head hastily.

"No, no," she dissented. "I'd not allow any such cruelty to your little nag. Besides, Mr. Burkington and Captain Gaisford will be only too glad to be rid of me. They want to find hounds again."

Gaisford's face showed a trace of astonishment—almost annoyance. Then it suddenly cleared into intelligence. As she passed close to him to mount upon the step of the car, Miss O'Connor had covertly pressed a small object—her empty purse, to be explicit—into his hand.

Mr. Burkington stood with his mouth open, the picture of indecision. She seated herself and made an impartial farewell to both with a very pretty smile. Flitty flourished his whip and brought it down smartly upon the pony's back. The car went off at a gallop, leaving the two men staring after it with envious eyes.

They turned at last to scan the country for the vanished hunt. Suddenly Gaisford heard his own name called in distinct but dulcet tones.

A couple of hundred yards away the car had stopped. Miss Nora was waving energetically. "I've forgotten my purse!" she shrilled, and Gaisford made a melodramatic gesture of self-reproach.

"How forgetful of me!" he cried. "She gave it me to carry for fear she should lose it!"

He darted down the road holding the missing piece of property conspicuously in his hand. Mr. Burkington sullenly awaited his return. Gaisford held out the purse. Miss Nora took it with a demure smile of thanks.

"Captain Gaisford," she remarked, "Flitty here thinks the pony could manage *one* more conveniently."

"Without cruelty?" grinned the Captain, and upon the word leaped up and perched behind her. Again the whip descended upon the little nag's flanks.

There was a shout from behind. The Master of Beagles had broken into a hand gallop and was pursuing frantically down the road, making a sporting attempt to win a race in which the odds against him were something like a bank to a button. Gaisford waved him a cheery hand; but Miss O'Connor, in view of subsequent explanations, forebore to look round. The distance increased. In a little while even the semblance of pursuit was given up. Mr. Burkington stood panting, a dark blot upon the dusty highway, while the lovers drove on in pleasant converse with the grinning Flitty. They were dropped five miles further down the road at the back of the coverts which fringed the O'Connor demesne.

*   *   *   *   *

"It's been worth it," remarked Miss Nora half an hour later, "but they'll never forgive it me. Father or Phineas—the one or the other of them—will never let me out of their sight after this."

Gaisford smiled confidently.

"It all comes round to what I've tried to persuade you of a hundred times, my darling," he said. "In blunt English, you've got to elope with me—there's no other way out of it."

"Must I now?" said the girl, with dancing eyes. "It's easy talked of, but not so easy done. I'll be under the eyes of the pair of them every hour of the day."

"Just look the situation squarely in the face," urged her lover. "Do you want to marry Phineas Burkington?"

"I'd sooner take in washing for my living," said Miss O'Connor, with great decision.

"And you've no insuperable objections to marrying me?"

"For the moment I can't recall them," allowed Nora. "But how? That's the question."

"It's as easy as kissing," said Gaisford, illustrating his remark with warmth and conviction. "We'll be married in Moyle parish church in the light of the open day. Jim Lascelles, the vicar, has been my pal since schooldays. The barracks are in his parish, so I'm a parishioner. A special licence and his affection for me are all the goads he needs, and he'll keep a shut mouth about it till it's over."

Miss O'Connor's eyes opened very wide indeed.

138

"And how am I going to get to Moyle parish church without a
'Yes' or a 'No' or a 'By your leave' from my father?" she asked.
"What will I say at all—'Excuse me, dad, for half an hour; I've
just remembered I've got to run into Moyle to be married to Jack
Gaisford'?"

Gaisford grinned.

"Not quite that," he agreed. "It's not by leave of your father
at all that you'll get the chance, but by the goodwill of Tim
Huggins."

If the girl had shown amazement before, her emotions on hearing this remark can only be described as stupefaction.

"Tim Huggins—Phineas's whip?" she cried.

"There's no other Tim Huggins," said Gaisford, "and he, I'm
glad to say, is my very good friend. He'll arrange it—under my
supervision—so that you'll have no fuss, no trouble, no explanation
of any kind. All you have got to do is to attend next Monday's
meet of the Beagles. It's at Allonby. You'll get a straight run
away to the river—a four-mile point—and very likely without a
check. The hare will cross the river, and there's no bridge."

His lady-love stared at him as if he had gone suddenly daft.

"My dear boy," she deprecated, "are you dreaming or wandering, or what? Who are you to say how and where and whence
next Monday's run is going to take place. Have you trained your
private hare and put him in Tim Huggins's bag?"

"I'm prophesying," said Gaisford, with a laugh, "but I'm on a
certainty. I had the luck to pick Huggins's youngest out of that
same river when she fell in, in flood time, last March, and her father
would do more than I'm going to ask him to do, out of gratitude.
It's all quite simple. The run will end at the river bank, and the
river will pound the hunt. There's no bridge, as I impressed on
you before."

A sudden gleam of intelligence lit Miss O'Connor's features.

"And no boat?" she inquired, meditatively.

Gaisford nodded.

"One," he said. "Mine."

*   *   *   *   *

A strange procession was passing across the fields from Allonby
towards the marshland and the river in the small hours of Monday
morning. Huggins led by a string an object which seemed to have
all the agility of a grasshopper and the elasticity of an indiarubber
ball. Flitty Boyle, walking a yard or two to the rear, stirred up the
unwilling captive whenever it substituted passive resistance for
active, admonishing it with an ash rod or the toe of his dilapidated
boot as circumstances seemed to advise. The deep dusk, which is

deepest just before dawn, shrouded both escort and prisoner, and a passer-by, if there had been one at that hour, would have been puzzled to discover the details of what was toward. As a matter of fact it was an extremely robust jack hare which the whip was tugging by a cord wound round the unfortunate animal's neck and withers, and which Flitty goaded from behind.

"Ah, get along wid ye—get along!" expostulated Flitty, thrusting at the hare as it turned a complete somersault after an energetic effort to tie its tether into a true-lover's knot. " 'Tis possessed the cratur is—as full of its fal-las as a—a gymnasium! What for will ye not walk demurely wid two gintlemin that's expandin' wid nothin' but kindness towards ye?"

" 'Tis poor atin' he'll be," said Tim, tugging remorselessly at the cord. "His blood will be that fevered and his muscle that drawn! I'll let him loose to recover himself when the line's once laid. There won't be enough sound mate on him to feed a chickun! Howiver—he's spreadin' the scent like a water cart."

"He is so," agreed his colleague. " 'Tis time we were thinkin' of the first check. We've come a full mile, or the best part of two."

Tim nodded. With a turn of the wrist he suddenly jerked the animal towards him and grasped it in his arms. Holding it tight he walked solemnly across the pasture for a hundred yards or more before he released it.

"That'll give us all a breather," he remarked, as he set it down again. "I'll not make me cast this way till I see Miss Nora gettin' her own breath back again. Come you now! We'll give them a touch of deep goin' in Packy McKeough's potato patch. Be this and be that! 'tis the most artistic run they'll be havin' laid out be a master hand, though 'tis mesilf that declares it!"

From these fragments of conversation it will be seen that Gaisford's plan was in full process of foundation. Mr. Huggins's gratitude had not been worked on in vain. He and his bosom friend the knacker were leading a line across country for the subsequent benefit of the beagles, and were using no half measures to ensure success to their undertaking. By slow and dogged degrees the procession proceeded upon its way, the hare's terror gradually fading into apathy, and its acrobatic performances deteriorating sadly in its fatigue. Other artistically placed checks were engineered, and the hare, instead of resisting, lay inert in Tim's arms, worn with its emotions. Pasture, plough, and moorland were each in turn insinuated deftly into the trail, till at last men and hare brought their arduous duties to a close upon the banks of the Lycke, the well-known salmon-infested river, which has given the town of Moyle more importance in the eyes of the outside world than its citizens altogether appreciate. It was in full spate, foaming a fathom deep between its clay banks, its waters touching pollards and thickets which were generally far back from its encroachments.

The two men heaved a sigh of relief as they sank upon convenient boulders and instinctively fingered in their vest pockets for pipes. The hare panted in a comatose state at their feet. For a few minutes they smoked restfully without moving or speaking. Then Flitty rose. He beckoned his companion forward.

The two sidled along the bank for a few yards till they reached a clump of brambles at the water's edge. Within its recesses lay a coracle, the tiny wicker skiff which the professional fishers use.

"There 'tis," said Flitty, tersely; "and do you, Tim Huggins, disthract ivrybody's attintions from prying in this direction by any manes short of assassinatin' thim. When once the captin's got her launched, and Miss Nora in it—why thin, let thim swim who will."

"And they'll not be many," said Mr. Huggins, significantly, as he strolled back to his captive and resumed charge of the cord which he had tied to a tree. "The water's as cold as Miss Nora's silf when Phineas is passagin' about her, and you'll not find much that's colder. I'll carry this unfortunit baste a furlong down the bank and let it deliver itsilf where it will. Sure it's had its Purgathory, the cratur; let it make its own Paradise."

*   *   *   *   *

The Allonby meet had proved an early success. The usual tuft-flicking and bush-punching which precedes a run from a moorland find had been short enough. Huggins, as he made a wide beat to circle the gorse which edged the moor, was suddenly heard to holloa loudly; the next instant his battered cap was whirled aloft upon his stick, while the whimper of the hounds swelled from doubt into full-throated certainty. Young men and maidens drew their elbows down to their sides and set their caps firmly upon their heads. At a swinging trot the field followed the whip, who was already bounding over a dyke at the far side of an arable enclosure.

The Master did not lead his field. If the previous week he had closely accompanied Miss O'Connor, on this present occasion he could only be described as shadowing her. Step by step he dogged her twinkling heels, turning as she turned, slowing as she slowed, sprinting as she sprinted. And in the background, "unstiffening his limbs and easing the cob's wind," as he expressed it, trotted Mr. Connor O'Connor on horseback, watching his daughter with grim determination. The young lady's self-appointed directors had evidently been more than a little alarmed by the previous week's escapade, and were taking no chances. Each of them had addressed the blackest of black looks to the imperturbable Gaisford when he and half a dozen of his colleagues had turned up in due course from barracks.

The captain had shown no signs of being impressed by the want of cordiality extended to him. He had wished the Master and his desired father-in-law good morning with unabashed good humour, and had offered Miss Nora a bow and a smile which she very naturally acknowledged. But he had not pressed into her company. Indeed, the find had come so quick upon the meet that the usual few minutes' dalliance, which as a rule accompanies all such encounters of young men and maidens, had been lacking. Everybody jostled forward at best pace—one which left little enough breath for compliments.

The well-manufactured check came in its appointed place. Miss O'Connor threw herself down upon a dyke and fanned herself violently, expressing her conviction that one more minute of such going would have seen her a purple-visaged corpse. Mr. O'Connor's cob whistled like a blackbird. Mr. Burkington paced up and down before his charmer pantingly; want of wind, however, not depriving him of one wrinkle of his aspect of determination. Huggins seemed to make his casts somewhat perfunctorily, casting an eye at the group as if he waited more for the convenience of his field than to the mere chance of the hour. As Miss Nora stood up, and found breath enough to offer a remark to her nearest neighbour, Huggins strode away with an air of satisfaction. The next minute his holloa apprised them that the scent had been taken up in McKeough's potato patch. With feet that gradually assumed elephantine proportions as the heavy soil clung to them, the runners proceeded upon their way.

About an hour had gone by. There had been another check or two. Nearly four miles had been covered. Suddenly Gaisford supplied a note of tragedy to dilute the morning's cheerfulness. Crossing a dyke he stumbled, and fell with his foot doubled under him. There were many offers of assistance, but none from Messrs. Burkington or O'Connor, when it seemed that the gallant captain had slightly sprained his ankle. Large grins, indeed, suffused these gentlemen's faces, and Miss Nora's father relentlessly prevented her stopping to offer more sympathy than could be compressed into three words and shouted from a distance. Doggedly he and Burkington urged her on. Not that the sufferer permitted anyone to lose sport by staying with him. The hurt was a mere nothing, he declared, and he could limp after them quite easily and take up running again when the first bruised stiffness had gone out of the joint.

And so the whole field passed on. Gaisford watched them out of sight round a convenient spinney and then took to his heels and sprinted across country, following a course parallel to the one they had taken. As a recovery, this incident came positively near to the miraculous. As a side light on the deceits practised by the military profession it has other aspects.

Meanwhile the field had come full stop upon the brim of the foaming Lycke, gazing blankly at its turbid floods. A rich, full-brogued voice hailed them from the opposite side. Flitty Boyle was to be seen waving an excited hand from the seat of his car.

" 'Tis right over, swimmin' like an allygaytar, the baste came ! " he declared. " He's gone down the Moyle road, drippin' and layin' the dust like a sprinklin' cart ! "

The breathless hunt looked disconsolately at him. There was no bridge within five miles.

" Where will we find a boat, Flitty ? " cried the whip. The knacker stood up and pointed eagerly down the river to the right.

" There should be one at Duveen's house, Mr. Burkington, y'r honnour, sorr. If Mr. O'Connor wud take it upon him to give a canter down and see, 'twud perhaps save the bulk of you a useless matter of manœuvring."

Old O'Connor looked round. Gaisford had disappeared and Mr. Burkington still maintained his rigid proximity to Miss Nora. He gave a nod and flicked his nag. In another minute he was out of sight.

Huggins was kneeling twenty or thirty yards away, examining one of the hounds which he held upon its back between his knees. He called to the Master.

" Wud you come here, sorr ? I mislike the look of Fanciful's foot. She's limpin' sadly."

Burkington made an impulsive step forward, and then hesitated. Nora O'Connor held her breath.

He stared round him. Gaisford was not in sight and the girl was standing beside the water, idly watching the eddies. He stepped quickly towards Tim and stooped over the hound.

Nora edged a pace or two up stream. Burkington's broad back was towards her, and his gaze fixed upon the pad between his fingers. Silently, quickly she glided behind an intervening bush and fled through the pollards to the left.

A minute later Burkington dropped the dog's limb, expressing the opinion that nothing ailed it except the application of his whip's too easily roused misgivings. Something splashed on the surface of the stream.

A coracle had shot out from the bushes on the left, skimming across the ripples towards the opposite shore.

Burkington stared at it in incredulous wrath.

Whatever injury Gaisford might have experienced to his foot, his arms were certainly in the best of trim. He was working the paddles most lustily. Nora O'Connor, kneeling and facing him, was wearing a smile of demure satisfaction.

Burkington lifted his arm and shook his fist at them.

"Come back!" he demanded, imperiously. "Come back this very instant!"

Miss Nora raised her eyebrows.

"There's no room for more than two at a time, Mr. Burkington," she answered, with mild surprise; "but if you'll put hounds to me I'll get them on the line. Make them swim it."

Burkington danced with rage.

"You'll be sorry for this, you—you hussey!" he cried, as the coracle grounded against the far bank. "Your father will take satisfaction from you if he has to do it with a stick!"

Miss O'Connor shrugged her shoulders.

"I think you hardly know what you're saying," she deprecated, and turned to Flitty, who beamed upon her graciously.

"If you're on the way to Moyle, perhaps you'd give me a cast so far in your trap?" she asked.

Flitty gave a duck and a smirk.

"With ivry plisure in life, miss," said he. "Give me y'r hand an' I'll drag ye up."

He suited the action to the word.

Gaisford looked solemnly at his watch.

"Sorry I've no time to bring the boat to ferry the lot of you," he informed the grinning field. "I've an important engagement in Moyle myself."

Burkington poured forth a flood of imprecation. "You—you scoundrel!" he roared. "I'll have the law of you—I'll—I'll——" His rage made him inarticulate. He spluttered incoherently.

Gaisford nodded.

"You'll tell me all about it next time," he answered, genially. "Right away, Flitty!"

He skipped up and occupied the same seat which he had used to such advantage the week before. The whip fell upon the pony's back. Flitty, his trap, and his friends flew off down the road in a cloud of dust. As they disappeared round a distant corner Miss O'Connor's handkerchief was seen to flutter over her shoulder in ironical farewell.

For an instant Burkington made a motion as if he would throw off his coat. He looked at the surging ripples and hesitated. He was a poor swimmer at the best of times, and what sort of pursuit he could make upon his own feet with his clothes sogging full of water, even if he gained the opposite side in safety, was hard to tell. He relinquished his notion, and instead began to run furiously in the direction which Mr. O'Connor had taken five minutes before. With the sporting instinct that the end of *this* run, at any rate, should not escape them, the field followed valiantly.

Half an hour later Mr. O'Connor turned in great amazement from superintending a temporary caulk of Pat Duveen's very leaky punt, to see the whole hunt—minus his daughter—sweep into the boatyard and confront him.

It was another five minutes before he gathered the true inwardness of the situation, so rabid were Phineas's denunciations. But when he understood the many explanations which everybody seemed anxious to supply, he fairly emulated the Master of Beagles' fury. He seized upon tow and mallet and hammered and caulked like one possessed. His anathemas were brilliantly inventive : his energy sublime.

In spite of both another twenty minutes went by before the most reckless adventurer present suggested that a launch was possible, and even then Mr. Burkington eyed the gaping seams askance. But the old gentleman was beyond the restraints of mere prudence. He hustled his cob and his would-be son-in-law aboard.

Pat Duveen took the pole, and leaned forward to shove off. Suddenly he paused, and, like all the others present, turned his eyes in the direction of the town. A sort of incredulous hush fell upon the assembly. It was followed by an instinctive shout of amazement, of glee, and of unrestrained laughter.

The wind was fair from Moyle, and gleefully upon the gusts rang out the peal of wedding bells !

STRANGE STORIES OF SPORT

XII.—THE SATYR MAN

BY H. KNIGHT HORSFIELD

THE great museum was closed for the day. In the dim galleries many skeletons stood: whitened bones of man and ape and mammoth; grinning masks and fleshless limbs; weird relics of things which had once wandered in long-forgotten forests, or browsed on plains now hidden by the sea.

The subordinates had departed, and Mr. Sugg, the assistant curator, accompanied by a friend, alone remained. Mr. Sugg was young—young and untravelled enough to have eliminated all mystery from the universe. For him poetry was merely an elevated form of ignorance, and wonder a matter of imperfect education. He smiled at the word "Soul," knowing that Life is a process pretty much akin to combustion, and for the weaker brethren, including religionists of all denominations, his contempt, even if genial, was none the less thorough. In the spectral light, and surrounded by the jetsam of the dead ages, he was engaged in arranging certain bones on a rough table for the delectation of his friend.

"Now, these are what beat us," he said, when he had concluded the arrangement to his satisfaction. "We have never been able to determine with certainty the species to which they belong."

His friend, no mean zoologist by the way, examined them with keen interest.

"Gorilla!" he said, at length, rather decisively.

Mr. Sugg appeared to be amused. "Before we travel quite so fast we may at least take it that the remains are those of a true anthropoid ape."

His friend assented. "Certainly," he replied.

" Well, wait a moment. In the first place we may, of course, pass by the gibbons. Apart from the question of size, the extreme relative length of hand and arm so characteristic of the gibbons (*Hylobates*) is too conspicuous by its absence here "—indicating the skeleton—"to make further inquiry on that head necessary. Now we come to the orang. The length of the entire foot of the orang, as compared with that of the backbone, is strikingly great. In the present case the length is not remarkable. Again, take the hand; there is no marked discrepancy in the relative lengths of thumb and fingers. The orang has the shortest thumb as compared with the forefingers of all the anthropoids."

The friend reflected. " That is true," he said. " As I told you, there is nothing for it but the gorilla, or possibly the chimpanzee."

Again Mr. Sugg smiled.

" But the ribs," he said ; " there are only twelve pairs, as in man. No gorilla or chimpanzee has ever been discovered with fewer than thirteen. Then the wrist-bones; there are only eight. In a chimpanzee or gorilla there would be nine."

The friend looked utterly blank. " Still, the skeleton is not that of a man," he said, reflectively. " Apart from the abnormal length of limb, the bones of the feet alone make such a hypothesis untenable. You see that the hallux is so constructed as to oppose the other toes (much as our thumb can oppose the fingers), instead of being parallel with the other toes and exclusively adapted for supporting the body on the ground. The prehensile character of the hallux, in fact, is fully developed, and renders the foot a distinct and tremendously muscular hand. By the way, what does Stacpoole say of it ? "

Mr. Sugg toyed with the bones a moment without speaking.

" That is the really strange part of the business," he said, at length. " Stacpoole says never a word."

    *   *   *   *   *

But although Professor Henry Stacpoole, whose name rings at short intervals through the whole scientific world, has systematically refused to enlighten the curiosity of Mr. Sugg and his like, it by no means follows that he has nothing to say.

The unclassified bones which Mr. Sugg handles with professional carelessness are closely linked with an episode in his career which he is never likely to forget. Incidentally they may be said to have discovered for him a very charming wife, but their associations have none the less a distinctly painful side. The skeleton has never been articulated in the ordinary way ; usually the bones are stored in one of the vast drawers which line the workroom. For whenever the Professor's glance falls upon them he sees a dim vista in a West African jungle. The ground is slippery with blood, and a girl, newly snatched from death, is at his side. However, here is the story :—

With his reputation still in the future, Henry Stacpoole, like most young zoologists, was avid of discovery. He was also a keen sportsman, and the spirit of adventure was strong within him. When, therefore, a letter came from the Rev. Dr. Stirling, a missionary settled at Bakéli, hinting at mystery and sport, Stacpoole read it with unusual interest. Bakéli is a small station on a tributary of the Gaboon River, and Stirling wrote of a tradition current amongst the natives, that certain large ape-like animals differing from all recognised species exist in the dense jungles thereabouts. These animals were named indifferently, Gina, Qugeena, and M'wiri, the latter a term signifying "Satyr Man." The higher caste Fans, Stirling went on, had a superstitious reverence for these strange creatures, and refused in any way to molest them, believing that the souls of their dead ancestors had entered their bodies. This belief had given rise to a Fantee saying: "He who kills M'wiri kills a Soul." A further safeguard from offence lay in the fact that M'wiri was credited with altogether supernatural knowledge and power : that his long arm could reach his adversary irrespective of place or distance, at any time, no matter how far he might flee, nor howsoever cunningly he might hide himself. Stirling concluded by saying that notwithstanding his long residence, he had never seen one in the flesh, but that recently certain unidentified bones, which he forwarded, had been brought to the mission house. He was interested to know what Stacpoole would make of the matter.

Now Stacpoole recalled certain words of Winwood Reade's : he remembered Wallace had predicted that new forms akin to the gorilla might still be found in the dense, unexplored forests of Western Africa. And here was a remote spot practically on the Equator, the mystic line which all the giant anthropoids love; and here was the legend—widely spread, whatever might be its base— that the new form actually existed. Besides, there were the bones.

After a very brief delay for the procuring of suitable arms and accoutrements, the West Coast mail steamer bore Henry Stacpoole down the Southampton Water on his way to the Gaboon.

The mission house at Bakéli was of bare wood, thatched with fan palms, with a wide veranda in front. It had been originally occupied by the native catechist and his wife, and fell far below any

European standard of comfort. Still, it contrasted favourably with the irregular rows of huts which surrounded it, and Stacpoole was well content.

The road of beaten red dust, strewn with unnamed *débris*, ended in the rude market-place, where the butchers sold their reeking goats' flesh. To the left the silent river ran, almost hidden in places by the dense tangle of creepers and lianas which lined its banks, and behind grew clumps of wild ginger and stately groups of date palms. Here William Stirling lived his simple life amidst the savages, the monotony of which was alone broken by the stray visit of some official from the distant railway on a hunting-trip, or of a drunken half-caste Portuguese rum-dealer. Here Stirling's devoted wife lived and died, and the little stone which marked her grave could be seen gleaming white at the foot of the palms.

Stacpoole found himself welcomed warmly, and it was only on his arrival that he learnt that the old missionary had a daughter. Later, she entered the little bungalow where the two men were seated.

"A strange child, Stacpoole!" said the old man, as he stretched out his gnarled and knotted hand to clasp the little white one at his side. "She wanders where she will in this Heaven-forsaken country. She has no fear."

Stacpoole glanced at the slight figure and fair, delicate face of the girl as she stood stroking her father's hand.

"It strikes one as being rather a wild life for a young lady," he said. "Miss Stirling should at least avoid some of the errors of conventionality."

When they were alone the old man again spoke of his daughter.

"Yes," he said, reflectively, "I sometimes wonder if I am acting fairly to Enid in permitting her to remain here. But she is so happy—and—and so strangely good. Even to me she appears like a spirit. She passes through the foulest scenes, the most devil-like orgies, but she touches them exactly as pure sunlight might. Darkness, sin, disease—even in this death-dealing climate she has never known ache or pain—seem to shrink from her as though she were something of an essentially different nature. As I said, she knows nothing of fear. When the plague decimated half the country-side, she was out alone in the blackest night on her errands of mercy. The lowest savages, even the wild animals, seem to recognise something which they cannot understand, but which they instantly give way to. She is a strange child!"

Stacpoole assented. Even he had been touched by the sense of radiant power which this girl, who was little more than a child, seemed to possess. But for the keen sportsman and naturalist there was something more important afoot than missionary capacity, however sublime. He unstrapped the cases where the rifles were carefully packed, and he noted with satisfaction that his host ran over their fine lines with a practised eye, and that his hands lingered on the barrels with the pleasure which betokens the old sportsman.

Already the conversation had turned many times on M'wiri, the mysterious ape-like creature of which Stirling had written. The old man was deeply interested in the matter, but he had little of personal knowledge to impart.

"Since the day of my first coming here many years ago," he said, "I have heard rumours of this strange beast. They were usually accompanied by wild tales plainly apocryphal, and I dismissed them from my mind. In this weird country anything seems possible. A touch of fever in the blood, and dark forms may arise in the brain which it is hard to distinguish from realities. It is best to be on one's guard."

"Is it not possible to interview anyone here who has really seen the apparition, god or brute, as it may be?" asked Stacpoole.

The old man looked troubled.

"Few state that they have actually seen it," he said; "and it is hard to get them to speak. As I told you in my letter, I had doubt of its existence, but——"

He paused, and the troubled look deepened on his face. Stacpoole looked up quickly.

"The fact is Enid now claims to have encountered it. I can hardly believe it to be pure hallucination—but—the circumstances are so strange. You know well the timidity of all the gorilla tribe; how it takes most careful tracking to get a sight of them at all. Well, here is a monster, vaster in girth and length of limb than any known man, moving in the midst of the street at broad midday, passing her within three feet."

"It must have been seen by many others besides Miss Stirling?" said Stacpoole, quickly.

"No; the street chanced to be empty—that is not unusual. It is strange—very strange—but something of the Fantee feeling, which I have hitherto held to be blank superstition, appears to have affected the child's mind. There is no fear; not even shrinking. She has nothing of these in common with the Fans. It is rather a sense— how shall I express it?—a sense almost of reverence; a feeling that it would be a terrible, even an impious, thing to offer it injury. We must beware how we discuss any murderous scheme in Enid's presence, Stackpoole!"

That night Stacpoole smiled a little in self-derision. His hope of adding a new anthropoid to the meagre list already known to science was growing remote. It occurred to him again that the bones might be merely some abnormal example of a known type after all. The evidence of the existence of a new species became more and more shadowy—the half-dreamy babblings of a few superstitious savages, most of which were demonstrably absurd ; the " vision " of a neurotic girl, seen amid circumstances in the highest degree improbable—upon these rested his hopes, lately so rosy.

He looked from the low veranda. The African moon had risen. It touched the snaky lianas and other monstrous growths with unearthly radiance. A white gleam lay upon the river, and dim forms rose, or seemed to rise, in the water, appearing to dissolve rather than to sink, leaving the mind restless. Strange perfumes were in the dead air, and sometimes a low, wailing cry came from the woods. Above, towering far into the gloom, rose the funereal plumes of the date palms.

Stacpoole turned aside impatiently. In this devils-land anything seemed possible. Given but a touch of the omnipresent fever, and the strongest brain might see trees as men walking.

He took out the rifles and began to oil the locks. Even if M'wiri was a myth, there were deer in the woods, and hippo and crocodiles in the river.

In the morning two scantily attired savages, Kanga and Salombo, stood stolidly in the veranda ; mighty hunters and professional trackers who knew the jungles as snake or tiger might, and who could subsist for many days on a cassava ball or mere handful of plantain paste.

Yet, keen sportsman as he was, Stacpoole showed no undue eagerness for the fray. The fact was he had become rather interested in Miss Stirling. At first psychologically, and subsequently for reasons which hardly came within the domain of true science.

Anything apparently less neurotic, or more winsome, than this daughter of the forest he had never met. She was so utterly free from the artifice usually inseparable from feminine civilisation that Stacpoole had come to look upon her as a child. Yet her knowledge was extraordinary. In the matter of the intricate fauna and flora of the region he found himself sitting at her feet, drinking from deep and original wells of information. Plainly she owed nothing to the text-books : she had an instinct for birds and beasts and flowers, and she saw them in new and interesting lights, always at first hand. A saving grace of humour destroyed all trace of the bluestocking, and the little caressing ways which she had never been taught to hide were delightful to behold.

Stacpoole refrained from referring to M'wiri. If the girl were the victim of hallucination, as he firmly believed, the matter were better left. Still, she was a most interesting companion.

As the little hunting party passed through the village, Stacpoole's attention was attracted by a hideous and extremely old savage sitting in the red dust of the roadside. He was attired in the uncouth garb of a native priest or witch-doctor. His mouth was partly open, and his eyes had the fixed piercing quality not infrequently seen in the insane or the dying. He appeared to look through the group to some distant vista beyond, but he gave no sign of being aware of their presence.

Stirling touched Stacpoole's arm. " Come ! " he said. " Don't speak to him. We may have trouble.—That is Mongulamba," he added later. " Mainly mad, I think, but with some method in it. Why he is here, I don't know. He belongs to another tribe— cannibalistic devil-worshippers, if rumour is true. They have learnt, however, to keep their proceedings carefully secret. So much of civilisation has at least reached them. But why that half-witted monstrosity is hanging about here, so far from his own people, it is difficult to imagine."

But Stacpoole soon forgot the loathsome figure squatting in the dust. A new world seemed opening around him. The wonders of tropical vegetation, the giant ferns, the trees which were each a towering mass of flowers, the brilliantly dyed birds and butterflies— all these brought a new delight to the soul of the naturalist. In its lower reaches the river broadened into a lagoon, and here the keen eye of Salombo, peering through the tangled greenery, marked a dull grey object lying like driftwood on the water. Here Stacpoole got his first shot at a crocodile ; but, although the bullet was true, the grey driftwood merely sank from sight, and appeared no more.

That night the young naturalist felt at peace with the world. The bag might be nil, M'wiri might be the mere phantom of a fever-striken imagination, but at least he had gained a near intimacy with a tropical forest, a thing worth many journeys, and one which surely no man can ever forget. As Stacpoole lighted a cigar he heard Kanga and the stalwart Salombo busy in the small bamboo enclosure where they cleaned the rifles and prepared the gear ready for the morrow.

Within the little bungalow Miss Stirling was still seated at the table. Her father had risen and had moved towards the door. Outside, the moon made little pools of light, their outlines sharply defined by the black shadows of the trees. The girl had been chatting merrily with Stacpoole. Suddenly she fell back, her eyes fixed strangely on the little blindless window,

"*There! There! It is there!*" she said, in a low, breathless voice.

Instantly Stirling turned and seized her in his arms. "Enid—Enid—my darling," he whispered, soothingly, "you forget yourself. You are dreaming—dreaming!"

But Stacpoole had leapt to his feet, his face pallid with excitement.

"By Heaven, she was right; I—I saw it myself. There was a weird, unearthly face pressed to the glass."

In a second more he was outside. "Kanga—Salombo," he whispered, "the guns—quick, and not a sound!"

The hunters knew many words of English, and handed the rifles silently, wondering what game was afoot. Then, armed themselves, they passed out quietly with Stacpoole into the blackness of the trees.

The ground here was fairly free from undergrowth, and Stacpoole lined out his men with orders to shoot if anything moved. In the stillness of the night the crackle of a dry twig could be heard. Every second Stacpoole expected to hear a mighty rush, but nothing stirred. They were now nearing the edge of the belt of timber. The pale light began to filter through the trees and to illuminate the wide open space beyond. Sometimes a faint breath of wind moved the boughs, and again all was silent. Stacpoole leaned against a tree and waited listening.

Suddenly a sound came—a half-cry choked in its utterance. A noise of crushing, followed by the fall as of some heavy body from a height. Then again all was silent, save for the faint rustling of the boughs.

On the instant Stacpoole had rushed to the spot whence the sounds had come, barely twenty yards away; but Kanga had reached it first. For one moment he crouched over the shattered corpse of Salombo, whining like a dog. Then with a terrified cry of "M'wiri! M'wiri!" he bolted through the wood like a gun-shy setter.

*   *   *   *   *

For many days the death of Salombo spread consternation through the village. The natives feared to leave their huts. Stacpoole, alone, rifle in hand, worked the nearer woods day by day, but without result. A sense of gloom descended upon the little bungalow, and Miss Stirling's face grew white and strained. Even Stirling himself appeared to be uneasy.

One day he took Stacpoole aside. "I wish you would cease to hunt for this accursed thing," he said, somewhat abruptly. "It is affecting Enid's mind. Do you know she claims to have seen this weird beast again?"

Stacpoole started. " She must not venture out," he exclaimed. " The thing is too dangerous."

Stirling passed his hand with a distressed movement across his brow. " It is not that," he said. " I begin to fear for her reason. She contends now she has not only seen it, she has touched it, held some uncanny communion with it, and she asserts vehemently that we are in the presence of some Power, some Intelligence which we do not understand."

In his turn Stacpoole looked distressed. " Poor child," he thought; " pray heaven it is only a touch of fever. In this land of shadows dreams thicken into realities. I have felt it myself. I will speak to her. Surely her mind cannot have gone hopelessly astray."

He was standing in a clearing in the wood where Stirling had left him. It was still early to return to the bungalow. He knew some of the better-marked tracks in the forest fairly well now, and he turned down one of these which led to the river.

He rested for some time hoping to see the grey motionless streak which marked the head of a waiting crocodile, but the black waters were empty of living things. It was growing dark when he came to the village again, with the plumes of the date palms hovering far above him in the gloom like ominous wings.

Near to the spot where he had seen Mongulamba hunched up in the dust he met the Kruboy, Kanga, breathless and scared. Stacpoole spoke to him sharply.

" It iss Missy Enid ! " he panted—" Gone away—lost ! "

Stacpoole turned in sudden fear. " What new devil's business was this ? " he asked himself.

Kanga's vocabulary was of the sparsest, but he made himself clear. Enid had disappeared, leaving no trace behind, and Stirling was already away with a hastily mustered search party.

It was long after midnight when the two white men met at the bungalow, each having taken his own line of search after the missing girl. They recognised the folly of wearing their strength out in the blackness of the jungle, so they had come back for food and water. Now they lay down with their rifles at their side to await the tardy dawn.

When the first streak touched the little window they were ready, talking in hoarse whispers. Their hope rested largely on the sagacity of the Kruboy, Kanga. In many broken words he had already communicated to Stirling his summing up of the situation. It was the eve of the great sacrificial feast of the devil-worshipping crew to which Mongulamba belonged. And Mongulamba had gone too. Stirling's face took on a dull greyish hue in the early light. He fingered the trigger of his rifle a little nervously. If that and all

154

which lay behind it were true, he would gladly have compromised the matter by putting a bullet through the little one's heart with his own hand.

A bitter disappointment was in store for the searchers. The men whom they had relied upon as scouts and guides had all disappeared. In their cooler moments the terror of the M'wiri had reasserted itself, and their accustomed haunts knew them no more. Kanga alone stood firm. For the moment he had forgotten the godbeast in his honest solicitude for the little White Lady whom he loved. With his rifle slung on his shoulder he would go out to meet mortal foes, though he knew them to be in numbers which would render his life not worth a pin's fee, without one single backward glance.

Seeing that it was idle to attempt to get together a stronger gathering, Stacpoole and Stirling took a plentiful supply of cartridges and set their faces to their task. It was a heart-breaking thing to follow the Kruboy through the thorny tangle, the dark lithe form holding on its way unwaveringly, following some unseen track. There was consolation in this. Kanga, at least, knew where he was going. Many times the two lay down from sheer exhaustion, but the nameless terror in their hearts forced them to rise almost instantly. So, torn and bleeding, they went on for what appeared to be days, when suddenly Kanga dropped on his breast and lay still. Stacpoole seized his older companion and helped him forward, and together they lay by the side of the Kruboy, choking back their sobbing breath and watching the sweat drop from their faces upon the grass.

A sense of dreaminess oppressed Stacpoole. Peering through a vista in the dense growth he could only make out the scene before him little by little. In a darkened corner of the jungle where the strong sun left its traces only in the dimmest twilight, he saw figures sitting. They appeared to be grouped about a circle of rude stones heaped in strange devices. On every side the vegetation made a wall, and a dense canopy of interlaced branches stretched above their heads. The figures were so motionless that it was sometimes hard to detach them from the grey up-heaped stones.

In the centre of the circle there appeared to be a stake or bare tree-trunk from which a slim pale form depended.

Stacpoole wiped the moisture from his eyes. In the dimness and utter silence the feeling of unreality deepened. He heard Stirling fumbling uneasily with the lock of his rifle. The old man leaned heavily close to Stacpoole's ear—

"Can you see to shoot her?" he said, hoarsely. "We can't leave the child alive,"

Stacpoole assented. It was plain the girl must not be left. At the first shot he knew there would be a straight rush for their hiding-place. The three, back to back, might hold their own for a little while, but the end could not be long delayed. Then the girl would be left alive, and that plainly must never be. He must wait a little for his trigger finger to grow steady; he was still breathless with the run. And when at length he knew the little one to be safe in death, then—oh, then to let hell loose for so long as the living hand could cram the cartridge into the breech!

As he waited the savage ranks swayed as though stirred by the wind. A new figure appeared and bent before the altar. At a glance Stacpoole saw him to be the mad priest Mongulamba whom he had last seen crouched in the village dust. He appeared to be muttering some incantation to which the surrounding group responded by a swaying motion of their heads. One hand was extended, and in the other Stacpoole caught the dim gleam of a knife.

As the priest knelt murmuring his monotonous chant, something moved in the leaves above his head. One or two of the worshippers turned their listless gaze upwards. The restless stirring came again. Then unreality closed in upon Stacpoole, and he lost belief in his eyes. From the matted mass of lianas a great hairy foot slowly protruded—slowly and silently like some hideous piece of mechanism it descended, and gathering around the throat of the kneeling man drew him swiftly upwards. Stacpoole saw the livid face and heard the crushing bones, and in a moment more a shapeless mass fell on the stones below.

The whole scene was enacted with incredible celerity. For a while the savages never moved; then one stretched out his hand and took up a broken twig, examining it curiously. In a second more the spell suddenly dissolved, wild cries filled the air, and the brushwood was torn aside by a hundred flying feet.

*   *   *   *   *

Stacpoole and his wife rarely speak of the matter now. Sometimes the Professor half deludes himself that he was the victim of some fever-engendered hallucination, but he has still two dead men to account for.

Enid, on the other hand, stands to her guns. She thinks, rightly or wrongly, that the British Association have not yet succeeded in plucking out the whole heart of nature's mystery; that there are domains, especially in West Africa, for the feet of science yet to tread.

STRANGE STORIES OF SPORT

XIII.—HIGH STAKES

BY ALMA SCRIVEN

BENEATH a cloudless sky, intensely blue, Peter Gordon was leading the way across the upper end of the Eigisch Glacier which divides the peaks of the Eigischhorn and the Schneeberg. Peter was a strong, cheery-faced boy of two or three and twenty, with honest grey eyes, and pluck and determination written in every feature. With his porter, Kauffmann, he had just accomplished the transit of the Eigischhorn, ascending by the precipitous rocky southern slope, and they were now making the descent by the glacier and the Wildig Arête.

The glacier in this region, far above the line of perpetual snow, presented many dangers. The vast mass of ice was split up into numberless seracs, many of them covered with treacherous snow roofs, where a single careless step might at any moment precipitate the climber into the depths beneath. Some of the seracs were of such dimensions as to necessitate the skirting of them, while others could be traversed by means of narrow snow bridges. In the latter case Peter would venture first on hands and knees, the better to divide the weight, while Kauffmann, standing firmly on solid ice, held the rope tightly between them, prepared for Peter's sudden disappearance beneath his perilous path; then Peter would perform the same office for Kauffmann.

It was a risky, perhaps a foolhardy, experiment to travel on a glacier of this character accompanied only by a porter; a slip or a false step on the part of either threw the whole weight on the other. But Peter's adventurous spirit rejoiced in danger; the glorious views, the wonderful air, the almost unbroken solitude of these lofty regions, touched his spirit in a way he could not have described, while his narrow purse forbade him the enjoyment of his favourite pursuit in a safer or more luxurious manner. Kauffmann, too, had all the rashness of youth; but though he was ready to face anything, his nerve had been known to fail at a critical moment.

Suddenly Kauffmann pointed to the cleft in the mountains towards the east, and uttered the monosyllable, "Schnee!"

Peter, who was cutting a step in the ice, looked up. His small knowledge of German was unnecessary in helping him to understand Kauffmann's exclamation, as he saw the heavy clouds which were rapidly moving towards them. In their present position a snowstorm would be fraught with grave danger, for they were still a good four hours from the Schneeberg hut. In ten minutes they were enveloped in a blinding snowstorm.

The fresh loose snow on the frozen surface was an additional source of danger to every step, and moreover the blinding storm deprived them of all sense of direction. For some time they plodded wearily on, till at length Peter halted. They were standing on the brink of a chasm, on the further side of which protruded an overhanging cornice of snow.

"Do you think this crevasse has a bottom, eh, Kauffmann?" asked Peter.

Kauffmann's English was on a par with Peter's German, but his eyes brightened with assent as they followed the direction of Peter's finger, pointing down the serac.

"It's our only chance," thought Peter; and they both proceeded to untie the ropes from their waists. Peter fastened one end to his ice axe and lowered it over the edge and down the almost perpendicular wall of ice to plumb the depth. At about forty feet it touched bottom. They then drew it up, and firmly fixing their axes in a crevice, securely knotted the rope round them. Peter made the descent first. With his face to the wall of ice he swarmed down the rope hand under hand, and at length found solid ground beneath him. At this depth the lower side of the crevasse sloped towards the other almost horizontally, and allowed standing room about four feet in width. Just a glimpse of the scurrying storm was visible above.

"By Jove, we're in luck," thought Peter, and shouted to Kauffmann to follow him, which he did immediately.

It was late in the season; the storm was not unlikely to last for two or three days, and, in addition to the danger of frost-bite and the difficulty of keeping awake, their provisions would not last long.

Enveloping themselves in such wraps as they had, they seated themselves on their knapsacks.

"Now, old fellow," said Peter, "we must not go to sleep; *nicht schlafen*, you know."

Kauffmann's teeth were chattering; Peter looked at him curiously, and it struck him that it was something besides the cold that was blanching his face.

After about half an hour they heard something that sounded like a shout from above.

"There's somebody else lost," said Peter; "up you go, Kauffmann, and see what it is."

Kauffmann obediently swarmed up the rope, and when he reached the mouth of the crevasse found three men: an English tourist whom Peter had seen at the hotel below, Ringwood by name; Brawant, one of the guides of the Eigisch Valley; and a porter, Brawant's son.

In a few minutes Peter was joined by them all.

"Very glad to see you," said Peter, cheerily; "more chance of our being able to keep ourselves warm."

"Goot idea," said Brawant approvingly to Peter. "I thought also of crevasse—and then—I see the rope."

Peter and the half-frozen Englishman looked at each other. Ringwood was a tall, strong, clean-shaven man of four or five and thirty, with a pleasant if somewhat too keen expression in his eyes.

"Rather a queer experience this," remarked Peter.

"Well, it's a new one to me," replied the new-comer.

"Have you done much climbing?" asked Peter.

"First time," he answered.

Peter looked at him in surprise. "And you came over the Wildig Arête?"

Ringwood laughed. "I've kept a cool head in worse places than that," he answered, carelessly. "Now, I expect you know more about mountains than I do; how long do you think we can stand this?"

Peter shook his head. "I can't say at all," he replied. "It's better not to think about it. My fellow is rather a rotter, unluckily; I'm afraid he may give in."

"Well, I'll answer for mine," remarked the other, "though I met them to-day for the first time."

"Oh, the Brawants are splendid chaps!" said Peter.

Ringwood produced a flask out of his pocket.

"Have some?" he said, offering it to Peter.

Peter shook his head.

"I've got my own," he said, "but I'm saving it up."

Ringwood laughed and took a pull.

"'Sufficient unto the day,'" he remarked, and replaced it in his pocket.

There was a short silence. The three Germans were talking together in low voices in their own language, while Peter drummed his feet on the ice to keep the numbness out of them. Night was approaching, and with it the dreaded snow-sleepiness was beginning to dull their senses. As they sat, their eyes wide open and unnaturally bright, Kauffmann was the first to succumb to the fatal influence. His head fell suddenly forward; Peter and Brawant each seized him by a shoulder and shook him into wakefulness. Ringwood turned to Peter.

"I'm feeling rather like that myself, aren't you?" he said. "It wouldn't be a bad idea to have a game of cards, if we had a light, would it?"

Peter laughed. "It would be a very good one," he replied; "but where are the cards? I've got a light."

Ringwood, without a word, produced a pack from his pocket.

"That's ripping," said Peter. "I've got a lantern and a couple of candles."

"Do you know écarté?" asked Ringwood.

"I know something about it," said Peter, putting one of the candles into the lantern and lighting it as he spoke.

Ringwood, with practised hand, threw the low cards out of the pack, while Peter balanced the lantern between his knee and the side of the crevasse.

"What about stakes?" asked Ringwood.

"Oh, anything you like," replied Peter, carelessly. "Shall we play sixpenny points?"

Ringwood gave him a lightning glance.

"Oh, all right," he said, in a tone of indifference.

They began to play. At the end of the first deal, Ringwood cast a discontented glance at the lantern.

"I can't see anything by this infernal flicker," he said. "Can't we do better than this?"

"Brawant has another lantern," responded Peter. "Eh, Brawant?"

Brawant, who had drawn close, and was watching the game with interest, nodded and lighted a second lantern.

Peter won the first two games, and at the end of the second Ringwood yawned palpably.

" Don't go to sleep, man," said Peter, who was beginning to feel very wide awake.

" I don't think these stakes will keep me awake long," replied Ringwood, with a smile.

" What do you want to play ? " asked Peter.

" I don't mind in the least," replied Ringwood, cheerfully ; " but I should think we might raise the stakes to half-a-crown. You see, I generally play for fivers even when I haven't got to keep myself awake."

Peter's face lengthened.

" I'm afraid I can't do anything like that," he said ; " but we'll play for half-crowns, by all means."

Peter won the two following games, and again Ringwood yawned. The next suggestion that the stakes should be raised came from Peter, and Ringwood began to play with more interest.

Young Brawant and Kauffmann were now also watching the play. The elder Brawant, who had grasped the principles of the game at once, explained them to the other onlookers in a few low, guttural words. Again Peter won.

" You have the devil's own luck," remarked Ringwood, as he shuffled the cards.

Peter made no answer; he was in the first stages of the gambler's fever, and he picked up the cards with hands trembling with an excitement altogether new to him. By the end of the next game he had won £50; and then the luck turned. His excitement increased as his winnings disappeared. Again and yet again the stakes were raised, each time the suggestion coming from him. Brawant suddenly laid his hand on Peter's arm.

" He play too goot for you," he said, slowly.

Ringwood's face flushed a little.

" We'll stop if you like," he said, watching Peter as he spoke.

Peter turned his excited eyes on Brawant.

" Nonsense, man," he said, " I shall win it back; it's all a question of cards."

Brawant said no more, and the game went on in tense silence. It was a strange scene—the five men buried in the depths of the ice, all kept from the sleep that must have been death by the excitement of the man who was losing all, and more than all, he possessed. The first rays of the grey autumn dawn found them still playing.

Suddenly there was a shout from Brawant. Peter was dealing

with shaking hands and took no notice, but the others looked up hastily. Through the crack that intervened between the lower side of the crevasse and the cornice of snow, a glimpse of blue sky was to be seen. Ringwood rose stiffly to his feet, looking at his score as he did so.

"You owe me £2,250," he said. "I'll give you your revenge another time if you like."

Peter gazed at him with scared eyes; the fever was already gone, leaving him with a sudden strange sickness at heart.

£2,250! It meant ruin; nay, it meant more than ruin, for he could never pay such a sum; it meant disgrace! With a great effort he pulled himself together, scrawled I O U on the paper which recorded his losses, signed his name, and handed it to Ringwood, who pocketed it in silence. Then, one by one, they scrambled slowly and painfully out of the crevasse.

*   *   *   *   *

The storm had passed; the rays of the sun, not yet visible above the mountains, had just reached the highest peak of the Schneeberg range, and were bathing it in crimson splendour. Save for that one spot of burning colour the whole world looked utterly desolate. Brawant turned to Peter, who was staring before him with unseeing eyes.

"It would be safer," Brawant said, "one rope for all to use."

Peter started, and nodded assent. As soon as the rope was tied round them—an operation which in their benumbed state took some time to perform—they moved slowly and stiffly towards the edge of the glacier. Every motion caused them intense pain as the blood began to course freely in their veins, but Peter welcomed the physical discomfort as a relief to the mental agony which tortured him. Nearly a foot of fresh snow had fallen. Brawant, who was leading the way, sounded the ground with his ice-axe before every step, and the party, plunging nearly up to their knees, progressed very slowly. When they reached the edge of the glacier the sun was already high in the heavens, and they rested a minute or two to put on their smoked glasses before continuing their route. A steep snow slope had next to be crossed before they reached the Wildig Arête.

Brawant examined the state of the ground anxiously. Only about six inches of the new soft snow rested on this slope.

"We shall have to cut steps in the lower hard surface," remarked Peter. "There is not enough fresh snow to provide foothold. I think I'll go in front here, Brawant."

Brawant glanced doubtfully at him; but Peter had apparently recovered himself; his mouth looked firm, and his voice was steady.

162

"I must be doing something," he muttered. "You don't object, do you?" he asked Ringwood.

Ringwood shrugged his shoulders. "You know your work, I suppose," he said.

"Oh, he knows," Brawant said, and the change was made.

Peter was certainly steady enough, and cut the deep, safe steps with a sure hand. Ringwood watched him with a feeling of vague surprise. The excitable boy, who had so completely lost his head in the past night, was not to be recognised in the firm, active figure before him, whose every movement showed courage and self-possession. Ringwood, though the word "fear" had no meaning to him, was gifted with a vivid imagination, and pictured the effect of a single false step: the first slip, the slide at lightning speed down the smooth slope, and finally the crash from precipice to precipice beneath.

At length the snow slope was passed and they reached the Wildig Arête. This arête was a razor-like ridge of rock; on the western side, a long, steep slope of solid ice ran down to meet the precipices of the Schneeberg, while on the eastern side there was a sheer drop of several thousand feet on to a glacier. The ridge was level—given a steady head, there was no particular risk in crossing it under ordinary circumstances, but now as they emerged from the shelter of the mountain they encountered a terrific hurricane raging from the east at right angles to the ridge.

"Are we going to cross it in this?" Ringwood asked.

"It's all right," Peter explained. "We shall have to lean against the wind and we shall be as safe as on a calm day."

Peter had resolutely put from his mind all recollection of the night's experience—it was in the past, and it lay like a dark shadow over the future; but the present was his to enjoy with all the young, healthy vitality that found an additional zest in every danger. They again changed their order on the rope to that in which they had crossed the glacier. Brawant led the way, followed by Ringwood; then came Kauffmann, Peter, young Brawant bringing up the rear. The wind was so strong that only by leaning over the abyss at an angle of some forty-five degrees could they keep their balance.

The knife-like ridge was almost crossed—indeed, Brawant's hand was already on the solid rock of the Schneeberg slope—when suddenly, without any warning, the wind dropped. Peter and the three Germans were at once instinctively erect. Not so Ringwood! Failing to adjust himself to the new conditions, he fell headlong over the precipice. Kauffmann, instead of holding tight the short coil of the rope which he was carrying in his hand, let it go; Brawant, though in an absolutely insecure position, managed to sustain the sudden weight of Ringwood, and literally before the jerk of the rope, which would undoubtedly have been fatal to the whole party, came on Kauffmann, Peter flung himself over the other side of the ridge, trusting entirely to the strength of the hemp. Kauffmann was thrown violently to his face, and young Brawant was dragged over the edge by Peter; but they both had their axes in a moment into the surface of the icy slope, and regained the ridge without assistance, while the elder Brawant drew Ringwood back into safety.

Ringwood's face was rather white, but in a moment or two his colour returned. He walked steadily forward to the rocks and then spoke to Brawant with his usual easy laugh.

" By Jove, that was a close shave! How was it that we didn't all go over ? "

Brawant, with a keen glance at Ringwood, pointed to Peter.

" He threw himself over the other side," he said. " He saved your life—he saved us all."

Ringwood's cheeks flushed, and he looked at Peter's white set face.

Peter took no notice of him; the danger over, shame and despair were once more laying their grip on him. As his eye roved over the landscape of dazzling whiteness, he strove in vain to see some escape from the darkness that held his spirit. It seemed to him that there was but one way of eluding it. For a moment he closed his eyes to shut out the beauty of the world he loved, and something like a groan broke from his lips.

The rest of the way presented little difficulty; the party descended in almost complete silence ; in a couple of hours' time they gained the Schneeberg hut, where they unroped, and by three o'clock in the afternoon were nearing Eigischwald.

Ringwood suddenly addressed Peter :

" Look here, perhaps you have some difficulty in paying that money ? You saved my life and——" As he spoke he drew the I O U from his pocket and handed it to Peter.

Peter did not take it; he started and laughed harshly.

" What difference do you think that makes ? " he said. " Do you think I am going to live without paying my debts of honour ? "

The words were boyish, but the glint in Peter's eyes was not.

" Don't be a fool! " said Ringwood, with a half-contemptuous smile on his lips.

Peter made no reply, but walked on in silence. There was a shadow on Ringwood's face.

" Curse the young fool! " he muttered. " What is he going to do ? Sell up all his people, or shoot himself ? "

Peter gave him no further opportunity of speaking to him, but as soon as he reached the hotel went straight up to his room. He locked the door, and flinging himself on a chair, buried his haggard face in his hands. £2,250! He tried to think—to find some way out of the net that bound him; but there was none! He rose slowly, unlocked his dressing case, and drew out a small revolver.

Still he paused. His thoughts turned to his mother; he must write to her; she should know that in spite of his miserable weakness he had nevertheless in his last adventure played a man's part. It might comfort her a little; and he sat down and wrote her a long letter. There was nothing more to do. He closed the letter, and quietly raised the revolver.

At that moment there was a knock at the door.

" Who's there ? " he cried, impatiently.

" A letter for M'sieur."

Peter crossed the room, took the letter, and relocked the door.

He tore open the envelope, drew out the contents, and then stood very still.

They consisted of his I O U, and a single card—the king of hearts.

On the back of the card a broad red line had been drawn in a circle. It surrounded a small, almost imperceptible cross, and below were the words, " I was cheating."

STRANGE STORIES OF SPORT

XIV.—THE PARSON'S BARGAIN

BY C. C. AND E. M. MOTT

THERE were once two men who lived near a chalk stream. Both were men of means, of middle age, and of some local importance. One was a baronet and a director of the Great Mudland Railway, the other was a parson. Both were fishermen— No. The Rev. the Hon. Philip Harington Foljambe was a fisherman; Sir Hardman Testie, of Red Knights, was just a man who fished.

He had four miles of the Twist to fish in: the Twist, beloved of all dry-fly artists who can buy, rent, or—or contrive the delights of casting in its dappled reaches, its slumberous pools where the "pounders" lie darkling below the tumult of the lasher. Four miles of the Twist to fish in, and the haughty privilege of ordering off any fellow-creature whom he caught doing likewise. He might have been happy, one would think?

But oh! as the song says—"If it wasn't for the man next door!"

The fishing rights of the glebe meadows belonged to Canon Foljambe (he was an honorary canon among other things). And when he was not pounding about the parish of Slapper (which was most of it comprised in the estate of Red Knights)—when, I say, he was not hastening to comfort the stricken and to urge the backslider —hastening on a bicycle in an apostolic undress that included suitably austere knickerbockers, and what ladies call "a black sailor hat"—the canon was fishing. Fishing with an airy touch, with a supple control, as of a grass-widow on the affections of a wary admirer. Fishing with a second-hand rod tied up at the joints with bits of string. Fishing—confound his priestcraft!—with a success faintly praised, bitterly grudged, by his neighbour, whose bills from Hardy were distracting merely to read (and would have been more distracting to pay); whose fly went in with a plop and a flump, and came out with a fluther and a scrape. Well, well! We cannot be great executants in all directions. Sir Hardman was a pillar, or say a sandbag, in the fabric of commerce: he had made a fortune, and a name, and a handle to it. The Hon. Philip didn't sweat and pant after these prizes. He had loafed and dandered on till his charm of manner and a cousinly viscount had foisted him into this soft sinecure—and there subsided on his luck.

Well might he rest and be thankful and ask no more of fortune. He had only a mile of water, true; but the best on the river—clear of weed—abundantly stocked—too close to the rectory windows for poachers. They poached Sir Hardman's four-mile beat instead! (The baronet was thrifty—a Hunks, if you like—and would not pay a river-watcher's wages.) In all ways the trend of circumstance favoured the parson, and accounted for his triumphs: luck, all luck, Sir Hardman was ready to swear. Indeed, he was ready to swear without any further defined grounds for the proceeding, as, much embarrassed by his sumptuous tackle, he clambered over the riverside stile one evening. The time was spring, the fly was up, his creel was almost empty, and the canon was coming over the bridge, bulging with satisfaction as usual, thought the baronet, who himself bulged unalterably and with no satisfaction at all—some outworks of his figure always would protrude from behind the ambush whence he endeavoured to stalk an astute "two-pounder."

"What luck?" said the layman, with a snarl.

"What sport?" said the priest, with a smile, as they advanced towards each other, and met in the middle of the bridge—neutral territory that divided their fishing grounds.

"No luck at all," said Sir Hardman bitterly.

"Nor I," said the bland canon, "but I've got fourteen all the same—beauties, six or seven of them"—and he displayed his creel. They *were* beauties! "Let's look at yours," he suggested.

The miserable magnate complied.

"Ha!" said the rector, cheerily, "you've had a lot of practice to-day, I see."

"Dashed sight too much," snapped the baronet.

"Not *quite* enough, I think," the rector suavely corrected him.

"Enough what?" cried Sir Hardman.

"Fish," said Mr. Foljambe, getting over the stile.

"What for?" shouted the other.

"Dinner," said the Rev. Philip, over his shoulder as he walked away. Then he relented and called behind him, "Did you get a bow from the Archdeacon to-day, Sir Hardman?"

"No," said the baronet, seemingly mollified. "He cut me dead."

"Try him with a 'Fisherman's Curse,'" advised the rector.

"I have," said Sir Hardman. "All I knew, at least!"

And on this pleasantry they parted. Sir Hardman felt better; he had capped the parson's joke, and the point was at his own expense—to be able to get a laugh against himself makes a man feel magnanimous. He wasn't really a bad sort, Sir Hardman.

The baronet stood on the bridge to light a cigar; he paused, and puffed, and his anger rankled and rose again as he watched his rival's satisfied back diminishing across the rectory meadows. A man's back expresses so much more than his face. There he strode, with the gait of ownership, along his goodly heritage, and his neighbour sat on the bridge breaking the Tenth Commandment, and (what is a deal worse) breaking it all in vain.

Sir Hardman had hinted that he would enjoy fishing the glebe water. The rector appeared unaware that any suggestion had been made to him. The baronet said cordially, "Look here, Foljambe: take a day on my beat—next week; say Tuesday—I've a board meeting. Dine with me when I come back from town."

Foljambe courteously accepted the sport, and declined the dinner; made a tremendous basket and sent the best of it to Red Knights—came in the evening to thank his host and was all wit and affability over his cigar. And returned the invitation? Not he! covetous old squarson.

Then Sir Hardman spoke out like a man of the world for neighbourly accommodation and exchange. But the canon was a man of both worlds, and he smiled and rebuked the greed of the railway director by quoting Scripture about ewe lambs and Naboth's vineyard. Smug hireling of a State-pampered Church! Confound his selfish heart, his cunning hand!

But the ingenuous reader is all this while asking, " Who was the Archdeacon ? "

He may have been venerable—his age was unknown—but he wore no gaiters. He was a gigantic trout, who had his habitat just above the stone bridge. The rector had nicknamed him after a brother of the cloth. " Just old Maudsley's evasive manner," he said pensively, " and very much his expression and figure too."

The trout dwelt between two large stones, and Sir Hardman had got to know him well by sight—knew the two white marks on his brown shoulders caused by the attrition of the stones. He had often and often tried to catch him—with every lawful kind of dry-fly when the canon watched sardonically from the bridge ; with other and less legal lures (I blush to say it) when he was alone and unobserved.

But in vain. The Archdeacon was not to be tempted. To tell the truth, he was a fish with a sense of humour. Alone all day, Sir Hardman's evening visits appeared to cheer him. He would sometimes flirt and toy with the badly-presented fly—just to amuse the angler. Sir Hardman's baser lures he scorned. He saw them out of the tail of his cunning old eye, but let them pass by. He put up with a good deal of splashing (when Sir Hardman's wrist grew tired with casting, or his temper gave out), but stood it all good-humouredly for a spell. When he, too, grew tired of it or felt bored, lazily moving his fins he would drop majestically out of sight under the arch of the bridge, or would deliberately, being too self-contained a trout to hurry, seek the seclusion of a patch of duckweed higher up the stream ; and Sir Hardman, sighing, would reel in his line and go in to dinner.

*　　　*　　　*　　　*　　　*

It was a beautiful Sunday evening, and Sir Hardman was out for a riverside stroll, at peace in his innermost, soothed by the bland influences of Nature. And the scent of tobacco assailed his nostrils, and he beheld the rector, in a layman's garb—not even a priestly collar to sanctify his mufti.

" Thought you were off for a holiday ! " said the baronet, this phrase being the politest he could frame for " What the dickens are *you* doing here ? "

" I am, to-morrow. Rayne, my *locum tenens*, hospitably insisted that I should stay as a guest in my own house for the week-end. I *did* enjoy hearing him preach this morning ! " said the canon.

" Is he a sportsman—a fisherman ? " was the director's jealous inquiry.

" Rayne ? Not he ! " said the canon ; " he's a married missionary with a brace of daughters." Foljambe was a bachelor—the polite sort that never succumbs. "So I've given him leave to fish in my water. He'll do no harm. Keep the poachers away."

Sir Hardman uttered something between a groan and a grunt. He leant over the bridge parapet. The Archdeacon, at large leisure, hung fanning himself in mid-stream. The Rev. Philip followed the magnate's eye, and—moved by what springs, who knows? —perhaps in a mere luxury of holiday benevolence—he put a sudden challenge.

"Testie!" said he, "here's an offer. If you can land that fellow this season, we'll 'pool our water'—that's an appropriate phrase, what?—we'll share the five-mile stretch, and fish it between us. What d'ye say?"

The baronet, after all, was a business man.

"Not I," quoth he. "That's one for me and four for yourself, rector. But, suppose I creel the Archdeacon by a given date, I'll *let* you, at an easy rent, the mile of my water that's next your own, and you shall fish my three miles and I'll fish your two, separately or in company——"

"Not more than twice a week," inserted the parson.

"Mf." The baronet paused—considered—agreed. "Not more than twice a week without special leave from either side. Yes. Well, Foljambe?"

The canon reflected in his turn. "If you basket the Archdeacon (I'd like you to produce him—mere formality, of course) before August, I consent. The arrangement to be binding *in sæcula sæculorum*."

"Dissoluble only by mutual consent," subjoined Sir Hardman. "Is it a bargain? Shake hands on it!"

They shook. The baronet looked over the bridge at the witness and subject of the treaty, who still wavered, unconscious of this conspiracy, above the pebbles. "Er—any stipulations about what tackle I may use?"

"My dear sir," declared the canon, "to make any would be to insult a fellow sportsman!"

And the curtain drops upon the Rev. Philip making his exit with a bag of golf clubs in the direction of St. Crambo's. From the train windows he regarded the shining stretches of the Twist. "*He* won't catch the Archdeacon. Let him try any dodge he likes. Might as well fish for him with his hat!"

    *   *   *   *   *

Sir Hardman angled for the Archdeacon with hope, with patience, with desperation, for the weeks were dwindling, and so was the **water**. Then, realising that his intemperate whipping of the river was likely to defeat his ends, he gave the pool by the bridge a long rest and fished elsewhere.

During this abstinence there came a dreadful evening when he only saw one fish, and lost that, and lost his cast, and his flies, and his temper, and nearly lost his balance on the bank and fell in—not his balance *at* the bank : that was more stable. After that he savagely dislocated his rod and stumped homewards.

En route something caught his eye—a fragment of gut floating from a bush. He paused. " I didn't get hung up just here." He clawed at the bough with the handle of his landing-net, and secured the drifting strand.

He scowled. He had lost a lot of tackle that day, but this was none of his. Coarse Marana—a regular cart-rope—revolting to a trout of sensibility. No wonder the fish were all sulking !

Who—who was the scoundrel ? Almost Sir Hardman repented his thrift—wished he had a gang of river-watchers patrolling the banks, instead of being left to play the detective alone. Alone ? Why, there was his young nephew, Horace Lyster (Magdalen, Oxon :) coming next week. He would find the young shaver some scope for his assumed smartness !

Sir Hardman passed the bridge with a shudder. The poachers might have caught the Archdeacon ! " They may catch him yet, if I don't catch *them !* " thought he.

In a few days Horace arrived, a youth of muscular build and sedate manners. He smoked his uncle's cigars with apparent gusto, and listened to his uncle's grievances with what looked like respectful sympathy.

" I'll come with you," he said, " and if we come across any poaching rascals I'll try and shove 'em into the river."

On this agreement they sallied out next morning, Horace as gillie, with a pipe and the landing-net.

" Hereabouts, Horace," said the baronet, coming to a solemn pause, " was where I found the broken cast on Tuesday night. On that bush, Horace."

Horace regarded the bush, regarded the baronet, with unfaltering eye, and said, " Sure it wasn't one of your own ? "

Sir Hardman gave vent to that indescribable noise peculiar to old gentlemen in their scorn. Horace did not wince ; he only stood at ease with the landing-net and stoppered his pipe with his little finger and watched attentively the movements of his uncle, who had got his fly hooked up in some grass.

" *Come* along," said the irritated baronet jerking out the fly and the command at the same instant. Followed by his lieutenant he lowered himself with ponderous precautions down a steep bank.

The angler here could cast from the convenient screen of a black-thorn bush. The bulky magnate disposed himself for action, and then—

"Hullo!" he breathed, in a stertorous *sotto voce*. "What's THAT?"

It was a pair of legs, long and slim, and visible nearly to the knee, in brown hose and tan shoes with square toes. The owner, out of sight, recumbent on the high bank opposite, seemed at ease; the legs swung to and fro in sheer abandon, to the rhythm of a tunefully-whistled air.

The baronet glared and blew. "It's some beast of a boy!"

"*Quis puer gracilis—*" murmured Horace, who flirted, of course, with his irresponsible old namesake's muse. He recognised the sex of the phenomenon well enough, young dog; and so did Sir Hardman next minute.

"It's a girl—why, there are some more!"

"Are there? How many?" inquired his junior in a stage whisper and with distinct interest.

Peering further from their covert, uncle and nephew observed another pair—of boots this time; brown boots laced trimly, thoroughbred ankles, a glimpse of a serge skirt.

"Girls—two girls!" Sir Hardman gurgled and choked. "D'you see, Horace?"

"Yes," said the Oxford man, demurely. Then, in a tone of detached criticism, and, as the French say, *pour soi*, "I should think the girls are pretty."

The enraged uncle neither heard nor heeded his nephew's comment. He climbed a step backwards up the bank, with a view to dealing with the situation from the top of it. He could now see both the intruders quite plain, though neither of them was plain to see. Tan Shoes was long-limbed and freckled and fifteen, and going to make a beauty by-and-by, but not worrying herself about the matter at present. She lay on her back whistling in ragamuffin content. Brown Boots was some three years older; she had no hat on, her hair was the curly sort that doesn't flop and go limp in the rain, and she was eating jam sandwiches

with keen dispatch
Of real hunger,

like the angel who dropped in to luncheon with Adam and Eve. At her elbow was propped a rusty and archaic trout-rod, the top dapping into the water. Between the precious pair lay a creel fit to carry a Spey salmon. So plainly this apparatus declared the tiro, contempt almost smothered the baronet's wrath. Probably they had not done much harm! But just then the younger damozel rolled over with a laugh and said audibly, "Oh, I must take another look at them!"

"Baby!" replied the elder sister with indulgent mockery, biting into another jam sandwich—oh, such *dents de jeune chien!*

The basket opened, and out of it tumbled a cascade of trout, and trout, and more trout, some stark already, the first of the catch, some agape and twisting yet, glistening and sleek, creamy belly and crimson dot, all sizes, here a bulky pounder, a finger-long skipjack there—a couple of dozen at least. A pretty kettle of fish!

Seething, impotent, hypnotised, the baronet stood at gaze.

"That's all, I think," remarked the graceless hoyden, and she turned the creel upside down and shook it, and the outraged proprietor's fury burst.

Reckless of the tender age and the fragile sex of the intruders, he bellowed as through a megaphone, "Hi!"

With this apostrophe his foot slipped. The Lord of Red Knights plunged headlong, flourished his arms like a callow seraph learning to fly, sat down wildly on a grassy promontory, scrambled on end with a blaspheming splutter, and remained rooted mid-leg deep in the cold water with the collar-stud loose at the back of his neck and his top joint jammed in a tree. Horace put out his pipe, and stood at attention on the bank. He had expected to be bored; but fishing with his uncle was developing picturesquely.

The splash had cooled Sir Hardman, and from his Triton posture he continued the interview thus, with icy suavity:

"I trust you have enjoyed your sport, ladies?"

He said ladies. These wretched girls must have seen him fall in, but he had not heard a giggle, and both looked quite composed now. The young beauty with the sandwiches suspended her luncheon, and said with pleasant ease—

"I think you must be Sir Hardman Testie, aren't you? Don't you live quite close to us?"

"I hope you did not hurt yourself just now?" the junior added, gravely.

("Not bad for the flapper," Horace criticised.)

These inquiries after his identity and his welfare flustered Sir Hardman. *He* wanted to find out who the deuce *they* were! He replied in surly confusion, "Yes—no, thank you," and automatically he lifted his cap in answer to the salute of the fair unknown; and Horace, of course, followed suit, which altered the relations of things, and made it difficult to be frankly brutal. Resuming the ironic method Sir Hardman began again.

"Nice stream, isn't it?"

"Nice bwambly stweam," the 'flapper' gurgled with infantine candour.

At this moment Horace, who still stood taking notes, addressed the elder fisher-maiden with earnest politeness, as his manner was. "I think your cast's got hooked fast over here," he remarked. "Can't I get it loose for you?"

She responded, "Oh, would you be so kind?"

Young Oxford, *ventre à terre* on the edge of a beetling bank, at the risk of his life, or at any rate of his beautiful grey flannels, made a bold and victorious grab at the gut. Piscatrix whisked it across within a few inches of Sir Hardman's nose. The baronet caught at it in self-defence, and then in amaze, almost in horror, cried—

"Why, you're fishing with wet fly!"

Piscatrix looked puzzled. "Wet?" said she. "Oh, yes, I suppose they are rather."

Mystery thickened round the baronet. Could such ignorance be? More staggering still, could ignorance have such results as that pile of silver plunder heaped and stiffening on the grass? At that his anger boiled up again. Grimly he inquired—

"Don't you know that you are trespassing here?"

"But we have leave to fish!" "But the rector gave us leave to fish!" they exclaimed in a reproachful duet, and the baronet exploded. A-ah, that perjured priest!

"But it's *my* water!" he thundered. "My water! My fish! I can prosecute you both for poaching!"

The girls for the first time looked taken aback. Then the younger hurled herself into the gulf of silence. Pulling at her long pigtail as if it gave her confidence, she declared—

"I only caught one little baby one, and Gwacie only caught thwee. John caught the w'est. Of course John didn't know either!"

John! John didn't know! Very possibly he didn't, but the baronet didn't care. Who was John? Some rascally brother, some blackguard cousin; anyhow, something male to vent his rage upon.

"Where is John?" he inquired, now bland and deadly; Horace reflecting, with mixed feelings, that it might be his part to pitch John into the river. "Where is John?"

The girls looked up stream and down stream, and the younger one exclaimed brightly, "Here he comes!"

Sir Hardman splashed out of the pool and stood ankle-deep in a shallow, breathing fury against the new-comer. He expected a pert thirteen-year-old, all impudence and knickerbockers. Horace

174

looked out for something of his own calibre, and awaited orders to collar the ruffian.

John was barely five feet high, and his age might have been anything up to three hundred years. He was lemon-coloured, with the impassive eye of the Sphinx. His European trousers were turned up over bare legs that moved with the padding tread of the coolie; he wore a vast hat, more like a straw beehive than anything else. In one arm he was cherishing a large brown sack.

"Jap?" Horace asked himself. "No; looks too sleepy," he decided. "Chinee. Heathen Chinee. He *is* peculiar. And what the dickens has he got in that bag?"

Something alive inside the bag was fidgeting about. Horace conjectured wildly, "He can't have been fishing with a ferret!"

The baronet simply gaped, and Miss Gracie, with tact, seized this moment of calm to explain things. Decidedly some explanation was wanted, but up to now Sir Hardman had appeared too much heated to listen to any.

"I am Miss Rayne, and this is my sister Sydney, Sir Hardman," she began. "We are at the rectory, and Canon Foljambe gave us leave to fish in his part of the river, and we thought this was it. I hope you won't blame our Chinese boy John. It was our fault that he caught all your fish, and of course we will give them all back; and will you please show us where we *may* fish? We are so sorry for the mistake!"

"So so'wy," Sydney echoed.

The baronet partly melted. Who would not have done so at fair words from a fair speaker? They were the parson's daughters, neighbours and new-comers—manners must be considered. No doubt they had been mistaken; but—he looked at the overpowering results of the mistake!

"Perhaps your boy John hasn't caught *all* my fish even yet!" he drily remarked. "But oblige me, Miss Rayne, by explaining how he managed to catch so many?"—the sportsman's eagerness getting the upper hand. "What fly has he been using?"

The younger Miss Rayne chimed into the dialogue. "Oh, John doesn't fish with flies nor a w'od," remarked she.

"Then what *has* he been fishing with?" Sir Hardman demanded at large, blazing. What indeed? What unholy contrivance?

"John caught them all with his bird," Miss Sydney asserted.

"His *what*?" Sir Hardman turned on the young creature; she met him unflinchingly and repeated—

"His bird." Then she addressed herself in a foreign tongue to John, who was sitting on the ground like an image of Buddha, embracing his unexplained bag. What she said seemed equivalent to " Show this gentleman, John." The heathen thrust in a yellow hand, and from the mouth of the bag protruded a sleek head, two shrewd fiery eyes, a powerful bill. " It's a cormo'want, you see," Sydney superfluously explained.

Cormorant, Corvorant, *Pelicanus carbo !* Across the baronet's mind came the look and smell of library shelves, of a calf-bound Bewick adorned with woodcuts—with charming and totally irrelevant woodcuts—and printed with long " s's " like " ʃ's," so that to his mind's eye the page read somewhat thus: ". . . The Corvorant as before obſerved is found in every climate . . . Among the Chineſe it is ſaid that they have frequently been trained to fiſh . . ."

The memory passed, and in a flash came hard upon it a wild, a grand, a desperate idea !

At the same second Horace lifted up his voice with quite a perceptible shade of *empressement.* " It's all right enough, Uncle Hardman. There was a chap exhibiting with some birds like that last winter in town. I went and saw it."

" Oh, the deuce you did ! " Sir Hardman was elated beyond all propriety of speech. " Then it's more than likely, my lad, that you'll see it again ! " he chuckled in a jubilant aside ; and Horace stared uncomprehending at his relative's altered cheer. All smiles now, the baronet pursued—

" Miss Rayne, would you oblige me by ordering your boy John to catch one more of my fish ? "

Gracie showed surprise. The baronet overruled it. " One more fish ? " said she, in wonder.

" One only," he replied. " I'll show you which one ! " And with this masterful utterance he waded across a shallow of the Twist, scaled the farther shore, and motioned imperiously to Horace to follow him.

The baronet was on the top of the bank and of the situation too. Horace shouldered the net and walked through the river, flannels and all, without protest. Possibly he thought his uncle had developed sudden lunacy, and had better not be left. In a pregnant silence Sir Hardman led on to within ten yards of the bridge ; stopped his personally-conducted party here with a gesture and a scowl ; grovelled like an Indian scout along the bank, peered with the stealth of an otter from behind an alder-stump, and from this position commanded in a blood-curdling whisper, " Miss Rayne, come here ! "

Gracie advanced.

" John, too, and the bag ! "

John followed Gracie.

"On your hands and knees—crawl!" the baronet ordered.

Humble as we all are when at the mercy of justice, Gracie dropped on all-fours, and John dragged himself like a wounded snake, the cormorant flapping and kicking in the bag. Sydney in the rear pulled nervously at her pigtail; things were getting beyond her. Horace reassuringly smiled, "Hold on, we shall see some fun in a minute."

There was a colloquy, the conspirators squatting on the ground, the baronet instructing in undertones hoarse with suppressed emotion; Gracie's eyes brightening—the mishap was turning out an adventure—translating to John. The cormorant, making savage grabs, was unloosed, a leather thong fastened round its neck, and John manœuvred it softly overside into the glassy reach.

Sir Hardman, puffing from his exertions (he wasn't of the build that enjoys stooping, even to conquer), stationed himself as near the water as he dared. Gracie retired a yard or two, Sydney let go her plait and stood with her mouth open, Horace shortened his grip of the landing-net. So disposed, the band held their breath in a silence only broken by John, who from time to time addressed the cormorant in a kind of yap.

Pelicanus Carbo looked superciliously about him; dived beneath the gin-clear surface, and swam upstream under water at an amazing rate. Sir Hardman held his gaze fixed at a point where under the big stone, his accustomed shelter, the Archdeacon hung at ease—lazy, arrogant, picturesque. The cormorant eyed him—darted—snapped short; the great indignant trout rushed for the covert of the weed-bed. The baronet trembled, and something like a pang of remorse shot through him. Too late for him to repent, or for the Archdeacon to escape! He was already in the grip of those ruthless mandibles. *Now* the baronet gloated over his scandalous triumph. "If only the beast doesn't bruise him!" he panted. The 'beast' emerged and swam for land, the prey across his beak. Sir Hardman already saw him dished up, saw the canon's dumbfoundered expression—ah! he would have dished Foljambe, too!—when, in act to waddle ashore, the cormorant tossed the trout aloft—missed the catch—the Archdeacon, a game fish to the last, made a desperate twist in mid-air, and fell among the ooze and pebbles within six inches of the river, of life and liberty!

With a yell the baronet flung himself flat and grabbed the vanishing quarry at the extreme reach of both his arms; his cap fell off, and the cormorant snapped at that under a natural mistake; Sir Hardman lay in a sprawl transfixed, rolling like a walrus in the death flurry, and Horace, inspired by beauty's eyes, leapt like Quintus Curtius from the bank above, and thrusting the net under the baronet's hands still clenched upon his victim, shouted aloud : " I've got him, Uncle Hardman ; let go ! "

And thus, even thus, the Archdeacon was grassed. Mobbed and hustled to his death, he fell to the base lure of an undesirable alien—he who had mocked the arts of half a hundred fishermen— O miserable end ! *infandum ! infandum !*

He lay among the buttercups at Sir Hardman's feet ; the baronet had collapsed on the lowest step of the stile, and I believe he shed tears. The girls clapped wildly : Horace waved the landing-net round his head and cheered. What the cormorant's feelings were nobody knows, for John crammed him back in the bag, snapping like a turtle.

" By Jove ! " said the baronet, getting up and wiping the drops of agony from his brow.

And the last tableau of this amazing drama presents a back view of the baronet, of Sydney's pigtail swinging cheerfully beside him, of Horace following, flirting with Gracie with the same staid and resolute attack that marked his methods in the football field ; the whole quartet making for the rectory, John having been dispatched as advance courier—how he reported the adventure I don't know. Mrs. Rayne, a cheerful matron who had consorted with heathen potentates, was not at all flustered when her offspring turned up with the baronet in tow ; Horace discovered that the Rev. James Rayne had in his day rowed in the Magdalen boat ; there was a lively tea in the canon's bachelor sanctum. The Rayne family lived on poached trout all next day, and the cormorant was (as heralds describe it) "royally gorged " on the same.

The Hon. Philip Foljambe, at St. Crambo's, received this remarkable telegram :

" *Archdeacon goes by parcel post to-night.*"

*   *   *   *   *

Rector and baronet still live side by side, and still fish their joint property in peace and comradeship. I met the canon at a fishing-inn up in the Shetlands, and he told me this tale. So I know it is fact and not fable. Besides, a fable always has a moral, and I am sure this hasn't any.

STRANGE STORIES OF SPORT

XV.—MR. LYNCARGO'S PROFESSIONAL

BY FRANK SAVILE

"LYNCARGO?" said Carruthers. "I don't think there can be more than one. You mean the millionaire—the man who's just settled down in our part of the world. He bought poor Sackville's place after the smash."

Halbeigh nodded.

"The man, without a doubt," he agreed. "What sort?"

Carruthers laughed.

"Unique!" he cried. "There's no other word for it. To begin with, he wouldn't desire the honour of *your* acquaintance," he said. "Why? Because you're a peer, which in *his* alliterative vocabulary becomes 'parasite.' He's death on the leisured classes; 'The drones must die,' is his favourite quotation."

Halbeigh whistled ruefully.

"So that's his line, is it?" he commented. "Genial old boy he must be. Has he *any* redeeming qualities?"

"Two," said Carruthers. "His golf links and his daughter. The first are about the best private ones in Great Britain. The second's a great deal prettier and nicer than the daughter of such an old ogre has any right to be. Haven't you ever met her?"

"Yes," said Halbeigh, curtly. "I met her last week at the Braids'."

Carruthers laughed.

"I see," he said; "and your admiration is serious enough to cause you to take an interest in a possible father-in-law. You'll find him rather more interesting than you bargain for, I expect."

"I suppose he's accessible to ordinary politeness?"

"It depends what you call 'ordinary.' The neighbourhood called. He has returned few of those calls, or rather permitted his daughter to return them. The ordinary landed proprietor, living or starving on his meagre rents, is anathema to him. If a man owns land he says he should make it his business to work that land, and not sit at home while others work it for him. His temperature rises so high in the presence of a mere squire that he has to forego the pleasure of that sort of company—or so he gives out. He is the antithesis of the usual *nouveau riche:* he doesn't care a hang for titles or social prestige. He entertains 'captains of industry' now and again, Americans as often as not. He has made a golf course along the foreshore of the firth which is supposed to be a vision of delight for completeness. He has hired Alastair, the ex-champion, for his professional."

"No!" said Halbeigh. "Jack Alastair worked in our gardens years ago. He and I learned our rudiments of golf together as boys. I used to hear from him occasionally. I think I shall drop him a line."

"I dare say you'll find him an interesting correspondent on the subject of his employer," said Carruthers. "He ought to have had some amusing experiences. Well, I must be moving!"

He gave his companion a nod, and strolled away, leaving Halbeigh before the club smoking-room fire, apparently wrapped in a brown study.

He came out of it in time to return to his rooms, and there change his town attire for the flannels of the country-seeker. An hour later he was at Euston, parading down a platform in search of that desideratum of the travelling Britisher, an empty smoking compartment.

Suddenly he came to a halt opposite a first-class carriage which was by no means empty. A lady bowed and smiled from its open window. Halbeigh bowed, wrenched open the door, and sat down.

"Now, what stupendous luck!" he exclaimed. "Where are *you* off to, Miss Lyncargo?"

"To Leame, to spend a week with the Frobishers; and you, Lord Halbeigh?"

He gave a boyish shout of delight.

"To do the very same thing!" he cried. "My word! what ripping games of golf we'll have together. I'll put another forty yards on to your drive, if you'll stick to what I tell you, see if I don't!"

She smiled at his enthusiasm.

"You seem to take my desire to learn for granted," she replied. "Life isn't all golf. There are other duties, sometimes."

"I know," he agreed; "Bridge and that sort of thing. But I always refuse to play before dinner; I think it's simply rotten to stuff indoors when you can be out; and if you *are* out—why, naturally, you play golf!"

She laughed, but she viewed the young man with very sympathetic eyes.

"I know you're not really such a monomaniac as you make yourself out," she said. "I hear you're a crack shot, and Mr. Carruthers says he'd rather trust to your advice on a horse than to the best vet. in London. Why haven't you done something with all your knowledge, Lord Halbeigh? You were talking farming to Captain Graves the other day like an expert, and yet——" She shrugged her shoulders.

"And yet?" he repeated.

"And yet you're so idle," she answered, simply.

"Idle!" He looked at her reproachfully. "Why, I'm busy every hour of the day. Didn't I spend whole strenuous afternoons over your golf education at the Braids'? I'm afraid you're not a very grateful young person."

She shook her head.

"I'm very grateful," she answered, "and that's why I'd like to see you doing work one could respect you for. Couldn't you earn your own living?"

He grinned, but not very mirthfully.

"As a matter of fact I suppose I *do* earn it, such as it is, by acting as my own agent. Not that the land really brings me in anything—it's mortgaged up to the hilt."

"And yet you spend your life as you do?" she reproached him.

They were off by now, and Halbeigh realised with joy that they could not be interrupted for another hour. He leaned forward with a confidential air.

"It's delightful to be lectured by you," he said, cheerily. "Please go on!"

Perhaps it could hardly be described as a lecture, but certainly the lady's conversation claimed his very closest attention till they both arrived at Leame station.

Five days later Lord Halbeigh could be seen escorting Miss Lyncargo from the golf links by way of the Frobishers' garden. The afternoon was uncommonly hot, and they had played thirty-six holes. His lordship proposed a halt and a rest under one of the famous Leame cedar trees.

"I've let you over-tire yourself," he said.

There was a distinct heightening of colour in the girl's cheeks at the obvious tenderness in his tones. She sat down silently.

On the distant terrace a footman appeared, scanned the prospect keenly, departed, and reappeared almost instantly with a salver. He approached the pair and handed Miss Lyncargo a telegram.

"It came an hour ago, miss," he informed her, "but we didn't know where to find you."

She tore the envelope, read, and then, almost involuntarily, uttered an inarticulate exclamation of annoyance.

"I've got to go home at once," she announced.

"No!" he remonstrated. "Why, you came for the week, as I did."

"My father's orders," she said, curtly; "I must go and find my maid and see about packing."

"But—but, hang it all!" cried Halbeigh, "if you're going right off like this, when—when am *I* going to see you again?"

The prospect seemed to have suddenly sapped his mental vigour. He stood before her the picture of consternation.

"I—I don't know, Lord Halbeigh," she said, with something which sounded suspiciously like the echo of a sob.

The young man seemed to find this sign of weakness strangely encouraging, or so his action proved. For he gave a hasty glance behind him and then fairly took Miss Lyncargo in his arms.

"I know I'm a pauper and a rotter, my darling!" he said, with conviction, "but 'pon my soul I love you to distraction. I can't let you go!"

The girl gave him one glance which began in protest but ended in surrender, and then allowed her head to rest very comfortably against the lapels of his coat.

In the shadow of the verandah the footman—whose body, but not whose eyes, had been obscured by the creepers—hastened to descend with stirring news to the pantry.

*   *   *   *   *

Five minutes latter the new-made *fiancée* was vouchsafing her admirer some unpalatable tidings.

"Someone has been talking—or writing," she told him. "Yesterday I got a letter asking if you were staying in this house. I answered 'yes.' This wire is the result. He hates a lord like poison, dear. He'll be simply furious!"

"I'm the least of all the lords, and not worthy to be called a lord," cried Halbeigh, "considering that I haven't two thousand a year to bless myself with. Won't that melt his heart? I'll drop the title as soon as look, and save a lot by it."

She shook her head dismally.

"Nothing will melt his heart except to prove to him that you're a working man, and a successful one," she answered. "Well— we'll have to wait two years. I'll be of age then."

182

"*Two years!*" vociferated her lover, in horror-stricken accents. "Two years! You talk as if they ended the day after to-morrow!"

She looked at him demurely.

"Of course, if you can't wait——" she began, but Halbeigh hastened to close her lips by drastic methods.

This interlude having been satisfactorily terminated, the point of Mr. Lyncargo's consent again came up for discussion. Somewhat gloomily Halbeigh confessed that the prospects of success in obtaining it were not alluring.

"I don't think any reasonable business man would appraise my talents at more than a pound a week—as a navvy," he confessed. "I could be a gamekeeper or the secretary of a golf club. Which would you prefer?"

She shook her head.

"Father doesn't approve of preserving, and he wouldn't consider a secretaryship *work*."

"My handicap is plus four," he argued. "I should be as good as a professional."

"You could hardly combine the posts," she smiled.

For a moment he stared at her—silently. Then the light of a most illuminating reflection began to shine in his eyes. His face grew suffused with excitement. He drew his lady love towards him and began to speak with intense rapidity and animation.

At first her features expressed amazement, then protest, next abundant mirth, and finally assent. She looked at her beaming cavalier with undisguised admiration.

"It's—it's really rather romantic," she allowed.

"Romantic! It'll be simply heavenly!" declared the enamoured youth, and again gave dramatic proof of the intensity of his feelings—to the great satisfaction of the butler, who had been moved to occupy a dominant if inconspicuous point of vantage in the verandah as the result of the ungrudging report of his lieutenant.

*　　　*　　　*　　　*　　　*

"I'd do pretty well everything to serve your lordship," admitted Jack Alastair, "but this is just awful!"

He was sitting in his little shop, surrounded by the tools of his craft, and eyeing Lord Halbeigh with an expression of undiluted awe.

The latter would scarcely have been recognised by his friends. He wore a suit of neat but distinctly *passé* tweeds, a cap which had seen better days, and a more than dingy pair of boots. His enthusiasm for disguise had carried him over far. Alastair was distinctly the better dressed man of the two.

"You're not to call me 'your lordship,'" said Halbeigh, severely. "I'm Reginald Smith, your old playmate, and a fine golfer."

"Well, but, sir——" compromised the other.

"There are no 'buts' and no 'sirs,'" was the retort. "I'm surprised at you, Alastair. Here is your old mother getting very frail and shaky, and all alone, yearning to have her boy within reach in her declining years. The Club at Fulkington, not ten miles from your old home, needs a professional. The obvious thing is for you to apply for the post—at once. I'll see that you get it, and I make you an offer of a pound a week above and beyond your salary. With your talents you're burying yourself on a private course."

"It's the master I'm thinking of," pleaded the other. "I've no right to disappoint him."

"Disappoint him!" cried his tempter, "when right here to your hand is a colleague whom you can recommend with confidence to take over your post—the friend of your childhood, trustworthy, and playing at plus four! What more could he want?"

"Nothing, your lor'—I mean, sir—I should say, *Smith*," answered Alastair, desperately. "But the week after next he's entertaining Mr. Plunderbilt Flash, the American. The jealousy between them two about their golf courses is something to frighten ye, and Mr. Flash is bringing his own professional, Willie Beck, with him. If I leave him in the lurch at a week's notice with *them* coming, he'll be like to assassinate me!"

"In the lurch—in the lurch!" retorted Halbeigh. "You'll be leaving him in as safe hands as your own. Didn't I get to the sixth round in the Amateur Championship the year before last? I'll give Willie Beck a third and a beating, or never touch a golf club again. Now get off and find your employer, and tell him how you are situated. Pull up a tear or two in your eyes, and remember your old mother's dying."

"When I had a letter from her, this very morning, saying she'd walked eight miles and killed a pig!" said Alastair, simply. "It makes me feel like a murderer to tell such havers."

He made a motion to touch his cap—met Halbeigh's frowning eye—and followed his guest into the road.

"Wire me at once!" said the latter, impressively, and faded away in the direction of the town.

With pursed-up lips, and a particularly scared expression, Alastair trudged towards the house.

* * * * *

Mr. Lyncargo, somewhat tightly filling a knicker-bocker golfing suit, sat behind his study table and inspected Halbeigh minutely. The latter and Alastair had just been ushered in.

"So this is your friend?" said the millionaire, and the professional nervously made the somewhat obvious reply that it was.

184

Mr. Lyncargo rose, walked primly round the table, and shook Halbeigh by the hand. As he resumed his seat the aspirant cast an inquiring gaze at his companion.

"Whisht!" whispered Alastair, hasily. "He does that to all— it's part of his system!"

Somewhat reassured, Halbeigh endeavoured to assume a Social-Democratic expression, and awaited developments.

"You have had considerable experience of golf?" demanded Mr. Lyncargo. "You have the right to consider yourself first-class?"

"I hope so," said Halbeigh, modestly.

"Humph!" snorted the millionaire. "Of that I will judge presently. You have credentials from your last place?"

Halbeigh produced a couple of envelopes.

"These are from the secretaries of my last two clubs," he said, passing them over the table. They were taken, scanned deliberately, and laid down.

"They seem satisfactory," said the reader. "Are you sober or married?"

The unexpectedness of the question became somewhat entangling to Halbeigh's intelligence.

"Neither, sir," he said, wildly. "At least—I mean I don't drink."

"And are single?"

"Yes—for the present. I'm—I'm *walking out*," said Halbeigh.

Mr. Lyncargo made no comment save a nod. He rose and motioned the pair towards the door.

"Bring your clubs," he said, curtly, and led out through the gardens to the first tee. He pointed to the first green about 350 yards away. "Drive!" he said, monosyllabically.

Halbeigh took his club with a greater sense of nervousness than any Championship had called forth. With an effort he pulled himself together and swung. The ball rose straight and true, seemed to pick up the little extra impulse which a well-hit ball assumes half way in its career, and fell, to slip onwards another thirty yards before it stopped. Alastair gave a sigh of great content.

"Just the neat furlong!" he breathed. "Ye've not forgotten y'r lessons, me—*Reggie*."

Mr. Lyncargo gave a little nod which expressed approval. He led up to the ball.

"Approach!" he remarked, tersely, as before.

Halbeigh took his iron. It could hardly be described as anything but a lucky fluke, but the fact remains that the ball, dropping just over the edge of the green, ran unerringly upon the pin and lay dead. With a matter-of-fact air Halbeigh walked up to it and ran it down. Alastair bubbled with excitement.

"A three!" he gasped. "Losh me—a three! And there's many a one that's played here has said we should make it a bogey six. A three! Think of that now!"

Mr. Lyncargo permitted himself to smile.

"A very good performance," he allowed. "I have pleasure in engaging you, Mr. Smith, to replace Mr. Alastair. Your wages you know. I shall hope to have a round with you this afternoon, when I think you may allow me—say twelve bisques!"

* * * * *

"I think the new professional is—in some ways—a better teacher than the last," said Miss Lyncargo, with a judicial air. "I had a lesson from him yesterday."

"I'm glad to think you're taking up a rational amusement at last," said her father, looking at her across the breakfast table. "I am quite satisfied with Smith—the greens are wonderful—and I think he has discovered what is my proper stance. Alastair never did."

"What *is* it?" asked his daughter, curiously.

"Six inches further away from the ball, and two and a half further behind it," said Mr. Lyncargo, with the serious air of one discussing matters of world-wide import.

"When I've had a few more lessons we'll have a game," she suggested, "and you can give me a stroke a hole?"

"Possibly," agreed the old gentleman. "At present I am training for my match next week against Plunderbilt Flash."

"What does *he* give you?" asked the girl.

He snorted with indignation.

"*Give* me!" he replied. "My dear Hilda, that remark shows how little real interest you take in your father's pursuits. I have played Flash dozens of times, and always at evens. So far I have not beaten him because the fellow has such stupendous luck, but I have twice squared the match. Owing to Smith's alteration of my stance I drive at least another forty yards. Next week I shall win."

"I hope so," she said. "Which day do you play?"

"This day week—the singles in the morning; the doubles— Smith and Beck being our partners—in the afternoon. Unfortunately I am unable to practise to-day, so you can make use of Smith's services if you desire."

"I think I will," said Hilda, sedately. "I never thought I should get the golf fever, but I rather fancy I have."

Half an hour later the lovers had met upon the course, Halbeigh touching his hat with great deference as he received his mistress's clubs. He made a scrupulous tee, showed anxiety about the position of her feet, exhorted her to seclude her left thumb further within the grip of her right hand, and permitted her to drive. The ball went a fair hundred and forty yards.

"Very good, miss," said Smith, respectfully, and led on. A couple of gardeners were within earshot, and it was not till they had reached the first green that the pair permitted themselves the luxury of untrammelled conversation.

"Do you know that father is under the impression that he can give me a stroke?" smiled Hilda, after the usual protestations of undying affection had been exchanged. "What do *you* think?"

"I wish he'd back himself for a hundred thousand," said Halbeigh. "I'd be a taker—every time. Not but what he's improved," he allowed. "I think Alastair was too frightened of him to do himself justice."

"You know about this match next week?"

"I don't think it's ever out of his mind," he said, simply. "It certainly is seldom off his lips. He takes his pleasure uncommon seriously."

"It's his view of life," answered Hilda. "When this story of ours comes out—as it must do in time—I'm afraid he won't see the humour of it at all."

"If he sees the logic of it, that's all I care for," said Halbeigh. "He declares that for him there is neither caste nor creed. So he can't refuse his daughter to a man who is honestly making his living by the work of his hands as a golf professional—can he?"

And yet by the fateful morning when the great Flash-Lyncargo Match was to come off Halbeigh had begun to acknowledge to himself that his life was by no means an absolutely alluring one. The work he did not mind. The hours he spent with his lady-love made him forget everything. But the evenings in his lodgings—and these had to be humble ones to avoid exciting suspicion—the food, the want of society, the little petty annoyances to which he was subject, had begun to grate upon him. He was dogged to show his employer that he was a man who could work, and work well, but he had begun to wonder if the time of his probation could not be shortened.

He eyed Mr. Flash, as that worthy appeared clad for the contest in wonderful checks, with an instinctive dislike. The latter was in boisterous spirits.

"Well, Miss Hilda," he cried, as the girl appeared. "Here's your Pop up against me for the six and twentieth time, and as usual he'll go down the shute! To-day I'm just the Giant Golfer from Golfville. No holding me—if I get a new ball for every hole I win it'll amount to more than a box!"

The girl smiled.

" We'll see ! " she remarked, and watched him narrowly as he took the honour. He stood carelessly, smothering the ball. She gave Halbeigh a quick look of inquiry, and from behind the American's back he nodded with great satisfaction. With a quick stabbing shot Mr. Flash half-topped.

He was not abashed.

" The way I always begin," he explained, and stood aside to let his adversary address the ball.

Mr. Lyncargo swung short but steadily, and sent his ball straight as a die if not very far. But he was practically a stroke ahead of Mr. Flash, who took five to reach the green and two to run down. He lost the hole by two strokes.

The next hole was but a replica of the first. Flash, viewing his opponent's drive of a hundred and thirty yards with unconcealed scorn, pressed, topped again, and got into the rough. He smote the ball unavailingly for four more strokes, and then surrendered the hole. Two up to the leader.

At the third—a short one—Flash fluked a good drive. The ball, really half-topped, just cleared the bunker, and sailed low, to finish with a good run against the wind. Mr. Lyncargo got under his a mite too much, lifted it into the wind, and had the mortification of seeing it carried away into sand. He arrived on the green two strokes behind, and had the additional mortification of seeing his adversary fluke a putt, the ball, really far too strong, encountering a new-made worm-cast which actually swerved it into the hole. Flash was down in three, and in correspondingly high feather.

"The Golf Terror from Golfville—that's what I am !" he repeated, and smote with hideous force at his next drive. Willie Beck, his professional, who was caddying for him, groaned aloud.

The ball actually landed behind his back ! In his careless excitement he had driven it against the sand box, and it had rebounded !

From that moment dated his downfall. He got hot—he muttered—unmindful of a lady's presence, he began to swear—he pressed violently—he sliced—he topped. An hour later, at the thirteenth, Mr. Lyncargo stood in the happy position of dormy six.

And then a most unfortunate thing happened. The leader took his stance unconsciously upon one of the tin markers, swung, slipped, and fell, his leg doubled under him. He scrambled to his feet, but his face was twisted with pain.

They were within a short distance of one of the avenues. Hilda suggested that the carriage should be summoned to take her father home. He refused with scorn.

188

"As if I should give up my match at a moment like this!" he cried, and insisted on continuing. He limped valiantly after his ball, supporting himself on Halbeigh's arm. "I wouldn't give up if my leg was *broken!*" he muttered, under his breath.

As an evidence of pluck, such valiant exhibitions may have their uses. As far as golf is concerned they are totally out of place. A man cannot swing if he has to keep his feet immovable—he cannot keep his eye upon the ball when every motion causes him stabs of pain. The result of Mr. Lyncargo's persistence might have been predicted. The American squared the match on the last green!

He didn't conceal his triumph.

"A-ho, a-ho! A narrow squeak for P. F. *that* time," he cried, "but the Eagle isn't always dead when you see him stretched and panting! I pulled it out of the fire, my boy—I pulled it out of the fire!"

Lyncargo simply *looked* at him. Words failed. This loud-voiced boaster actually had the effrontery to imply that he had evaded defeat on equal terms!

Relief came from an unexpected quarter. Hilda Lyncargo stepped forward with a flushed face and shining eyes.

"I'm sorry you should not get a match this afternoon owing to my father's unfortunate accident," she said, sweetly. "You must let me take his place."

Flash stared at her as if she was a beetle.

"You!" he said, with amazement, and then laughed genially. "In the foursome, you mean? But—what shall we give you?"

"You needn't trouble about odds," she answered, quietly. "We shall do our best to give you a match at evens—Smith and myself."

Halbeigh, as he watched his employer, saw a look of pride pass into his face, though the old gentleman shook his head doubtfully. Flash laughed again—louder.

"Well—well!" he answered, "there's no getting away from a direct challenge like that; but—but you'll excuse me if I say I hardly think it will be a game, Miss Hilda—hardly a game."

Which words were in the nature of a prophecy, as the events of the afternoon proved.

Compared with his afternoon's play his morning's performance was Championship form. He couldn't drive—he couldn't approach —he couldn't putt. Whether anxiety or lunch was responsible for a complete breakdown it is impossible to say, but as the winning ball rolled into the twelfth hole the American realised that for the second time that day his adversary was dormy six.

It was Hilda's drive. Mr. Lyncargo, who had insisted on

following throughout in a bath chair, watched her advance to the tee with eyes of almost devout admiration.

Before she took her stance she happened to catch Halbeigh's adoring glance, and this, in addition to its usual fervour, was quickened by a master's pride in a pupil. Had she not done his lessons justice and more than justice? He forgot his usual caution. He beamed upon her with all a lover's tenderness.

With the same inadvertence she returned this silent message, and then—was suddenly aware by her father's astonished features that he had intercepted and had understood the glance.

She blushed—she swung hastily—she topped! Surprise and sorrow completed Halbeigh's downfall.

" *Oh, my dear !* " he expostulated, in all-unconscious reproach.

For a moment there was an oppressive silence, broken at last by a tiny snigger from the American as he advanced to the tee. He swung, and—wonder of wonders!—brought off a stupendous drive. The ball lay within twenty yards of the green, from whence Beck could be trusted to toss it up dead to the hole. Hilda's ball had travelled scarcely twenty feet.

Mr. Flash's whoop of triumph was overpowering.

"Gee-whiz!" he cried. "Again at the crucial moment P. F. chases his enemies into the long grass! I'll take you six to one we don't pull it off as I did this morning, Miss Hilda—if you'll agree to play an extra hole, I take you ten to one we don't win!"

Halbeigh gritted his teeth as he took his brassey.

"And I'll bet you evens we halve this hole!" he retorted, recklessly.

Flash looked him over.

"I don't bet with—professionals!" he remarked, loftily, and, as Halbeigh made the stroke, changed colour considerably. It is doubtful if a better-played ball had ever been hit upon that course before. Straight, low, and true it sped away, rising to describe a graceful parabola, and come at last to rest two hundred yards away upon the green at the very lip of the hole!

In silence Willie Beck led the party as he strode up to play second, and in silence he dropped his ball within a yard of the pin. And in a stillness which could be felt Mr. Flash putted—and missed!

His imprecations were sonorous, but they could not drown his host's very distinct remark. Mr. Lyncargo neither indulged in triumph nor offered congratulations.

"That is the match!" he said, as his daughter tapped the ball into the hole. "I prefer that there should be no bye!"

Hilda looked at him inquiringly.

" Have the goodness to accompany me ho me ! " he said, coldly.

*   *   *   *   *

" A preposterous proposal ! " said Mr. Lyncargo, an hour later. The scene was his smoking-room. The company his professional.

" Preposterous ! " Halbeigh repeated the word with scornful rancour. " Permit me to remind you of your own frequently expressed opinions that *all* social grades stand—in *your* estimation— upon an equality. I'm honest, hardworking, and—in my special line—successful. If your daughter returns my love, why should I not confidently ask you for her hand ? "

A grim smile curved Mr. Lyncargo's lips.

" Honest, did you say ? " he asked. " Have you been honest with me, *Lord Halbeigh* ? "

The other started and winced.

" Who told you ? " he cried.

" My daughter," said the old man. " She decided to deceive me no longer. Do you understand me *now* ? "

" No ! " said Halbeigh, valiantly. " I can't help my title. You can't get over the fact that I've made myself a working man. I persist in my request."

Lyncargo looked at him meditatively.

" If I consent, then, you remain here as my professional ? " he said, suddenly.

Halbeigh started. This was an unconsidered point of view. He remembered his lodgings—his food—many things. And *how* people would grin ! Then the other and most important side of the question came to him with a rush. His face cleared.

" With Hilda as my wife ? Why, certainly," he agreed.

Lyncargo gave him a piercing stare.

" You swear that ? " he demanded.

Halbeigh laughed cheerily.

" My word has generally been considered as good as my oath," he said, " but I'll swear—if you make a point of it."

The old man rose, wearing a curious and rather inscrutable expression.

" Then we call that settled, I suppose," he said, slowly. " By the way, I was thinking of combining the post with that of my agency, which will be worth two thousand a year. In that case I should have to give you an assistant on the links. Are you agreeable ? "

Halbeigh seized his would-be father-in-law's hand.

" I say," he said, heartily and ingenuously, " you're no end of a good chap—*really*."

STRANGE STORIES OF SPORT

XVI.—THE LANTERN

BY "DALESMAN"

I.

"IF the fishing is as good as the house is quaint," remarked my wife to the agent, "we shall have no cause of complaint."

The house-agent—a despondent individual—smiled an enigmatical smile.

"You will not," he said, dryly, "be complainin' of the fishing, I'm thinkin'."

I must say I thought we were lucky to get that house and its eight miles of river and moor for the very moderate rent we were asked to pay. High on the mountain side it stood, sheltered from the winds sweeping down the dale by firs and larches, the river churning brown and foamy among mighty boulders below. It was a very ancient mansion of grey rough-cast, with the squat round chimneys so familiar in the Cumberland and Westmorland dales, large, low and rambling, with big, odd-shaped panelled rooms, open hearths, and black oak floors. At one end stood a massive square tower of weather-beaten red stone, known as "the Pele," containing a spiral staircase and three rooms, which, however, as we had plenty of other and more convenient accommodation, we decided not to use.

Salmon and sea-trout came up the brown river in autumn, grouse dwelt among the heather, while high among the fells lay a big wild tarn known as Lyke Water, in which, according to the agent, trout swarmed, trout which the tenancy of Swayne Keld Pele gave me the right of fishing for. Altogether, though we were rather beyond civilisation, we felt distinctly pleased with our bargain when we came into residence in time for the autumn fishing, which fishing we discovered fully bore out the grudging commendation of the gloomy agent.

"Charles," said Eva, one wild October evening, charging into the gun-room with that inconsequence which is very characteristic of her happy-go-lucky manner of tumbling through life generally, "I've found something."

I laid down the gun I was cleaning, with the sweet resignation of the six-months-married husband, and asked what it was now. It was comforting to find that her incursion was not due to the cook having been discovered in a state of intoxication or the bath-room hot-water supply diverting its course *via* the drawing-room ceiling.

My wife turned up the lamp and held her find out in my direction. "It was in the old lumber-room in the pele tower," she explained.

I took "it" from her gingerly. It was very dusty and rusty, and cob-webby. "What is it?" I asked, viewing it from every possible aspect. "It *looks* like a mediæval stable lantern."

"That's just what it is," said Eva, excitedly. "It's been stuck in that mouldy old tower for—oh, centuries, Charles! I am certain it is a genuine old thing this time."

Triumph rang in her voice. Eva's finds in the antiquity line had previously been very far removed from the period assigned to them, which made the unquestionable venerableness of her present discovery doubly attractive, and I peered at it with slowly awakening interest.

It was evidently of great age, made of solid wrought iron, the spaces between the ironwork filled in with horn. The ironwork was very well designed, rusty in places, but still strong, and the design was good.

I put the lantern down on the bench along with the cleaning rods and gun oil. The fire was low and the room seemed to have suddenly become bitterly cold.

"Come along," I said to Eva, "we'll look at that thing by daylight and clean it up. It must be getting on for dinner-time."

Thus was the lantern once more brought to the scene of its activity. I saw it standing out in dark relief on the bench as we made for the door, the ruddy embers of the wood fire throwing weird shadows on and around it as they flickered up before dying down and going out.

"I don't believe that beastly thing is canny," I said, with a shiver, as a sudden gust of wind banged the door after us.

"You are a superstitious donkey!" returned my wife, elegantly, slipping a small, strong hand protectingly into mine. I felt bound to lift it to my lips, and in the agitation of being thus discovered by the butler I for the moment quite forgot Eva's find. Not for long, though. It took good care of that.

II.

"Charles," said Eva to me next morning as I cut her a slice of ham at the sideboard, "I didn't sleep well last night."

I turned round and looked at her. I had slept abominably myself.

"Two of the servants have given notice," she went on, gloomily. "The kitchenmaid is a native"—she waved an explanatory hand in the direction of the hamlet below—"and she has been telling them that the house is haunted, and they—fools—think they have heard footsteps and doors opening and shutting all night, so they won't stay."

I sympathised with them, though I daren't say so. I, too, had heard things which I ought not to have heard during the silent watches of the night, though I knew Eva would crush me if I acknowledged the fact.

"Did the kitchenmaid happen to mention what the history of this mansion may be?" I asked, cautiously.

"There was a scandal and a murder, I believe," replied Eva, lowering her voice decorously as the butler with a countenance of funereal gloom brought in some fresh toast. I wondered—from his face—if he, too, had passed a disturbed night.

I began to comprehend why the agent who let us the house had appeared so unenthusiastic over our prospects connected therewith, and my reflections as I went to the gun-room to unearth rods, etc., for a contemplated day's sport were not very pleasant. On the bench Eva's find still stood. It was evidently a really remarkable curiosity seen by daylight, and before I went out I locked it carefully into my safe, the key of which I invariably keep about me.

It was bitterly cold coming home over the moor that night. Sport had been exceptionally good, and we had stayed much later than usual, consequently by the time we finally reeled up it was very nearly dark—the dreary darkness of a moonless night with a sky heavily overcast with clouds.

"Ugh!" grumbled Eva, as she stumbled heavily against the boulders with which the so-called pony track was thickly strewn. "Charles, are you sure we are going right?"

I wasn't at all sure; in fact, I was almost certain we were wrong. The situation was really unpleasant, and a stinging whirl of snowflakes by no means improved it. I was extremely relieved to see, dancing away to the left of us, a swinging, moving light. Evidently some statesman (yeoman farmer) or shepherd was out late, seeking perhaps stray sheep before the threatening storm broke.

We hastened our lagging footsteps after the flickering light, and hope again dawned that we might reach our pele that night.

"He's leading a horse!" said Eva, in a curious voice, as we came closer—close enough to make out the figure of a slightly-built man wrapped in a heavy cloak, leading a big grey horse, on the back of which was strapped a dark, shapeless bundle. In his left hand he held a lantern, constructed on lines very similar to those of Eva's find in an embrasure of the disused pele tower at Swayne Keld.

We shouted to him, but the wind howling past us carried the sound behind us, and he evidently did not hear, for he held steadily on his way, and try as we would we could not catch him up.

"Never mind," said Eva, "we shall land somewhere."

As she spoke, with appalling suddenness horse, man, and light disappeared utterly and completely, and we were left in the darkness and the blinding snow. I threw myself backwards, wildly clutching Eva as I did so, for my foot had stepped into nothingness. It was as by a miracle we had escaped walking over a precipice five hundred feet sheer down to the valley in which the river thundered. I knew where we were now though, and going slowly and cautiously we at last struck the track again, and so wound down the mountain-side to Swayne Keld.

Before I went to bed I unlocked my safe to look again at the lantern and compare it with the one which so silently and terribly had vanished over the crag. It was not there! Considerably startled, I lighted my big hurricane lamp and hurried to the disused pele tower. The clumsy keys grated in the rusty locks, and an icy air swept past me as I scrambled up the spiral staircase from room to room. In the top room of the three—a mere lumber-room now, light and air admitted only by deeply-embrasured loopholes—I found the lantern back again in its old haunt from which Eva had taken it; high up the wall on the deep sill of one of the narrow loopholes it stood, as doubtless it had stood undisturbed for centuries. On the rude stone floor beneath it a big, dark stain stood out with startling vividness in the flickering light of my lamp. For a moment I stared, then I bolted, locking the doors behind me.

Next day I went over to the county town and interviewed the agent. He did not seem at all surprised to see me.

III.

"Ah, Sir Charles," he said; "I thought I should be seein' you before long. Been turnin' out in the pele tower perhaps?"

I looked at him angrily; but, reflecting that if I wished to get to the bottom of things I had better not quarrel with the fellow, I swallowed my wrath and asked point-blank what he was driving at, telling him about our misadventure on Grey Crag, without, however, mentioning Eva's find in the pele tower. He listened attentively.

"Ye'll have been finding the lantern, Sir Charles," he remarked, quietly, as I finished.

I stared. "My wife did," I said, helplessly.

"An' doubtless moved it from its appointed place," he went on, more as if speaking his own deductions aloud than addressing me.

I took the bull by the horns.

"Mr. Wilson," I said, "I do not wish to throw up Swayne Keld, but I want to know the rights of the mystery upon which we seem to have stumbled. Unless we do know it we cannot stay on. You shall not be the loser by telling me the truth."

"Maybe I will then," returned Mr. Wilson, imperturbably; "ye appear to be a gentleman of sense, Sir Charles, but then ye are both a good sportsman and of this country. Previous gentlemen and ladies have mostly run away—scairt away, one might conclude. The truth of it is this, sir: leave the lantern alone in its appointed place, and all will go well. Ye canna' get rid of it. It has bided in yon niche nigh on three hundred years folks tell, and 'twill bide there till as close on the judgment day as the pele stands. Folks have put it in a furnace, droppit it i' the river, but always it is back next day, and always they are disturbed for their pains. Nay, nay, leave it alone and it 'll leave you alone."

I stared at him. Was I living in the twentieth century, or was I back in the superstitions of the middle ages?

"But why?" I asked, in blank astonishment. "What is the story of it?"

And this is the legend of the dales that Mr. Wilson—a solid hard-headed North-country man of business—poured into my astonished ears:

"There lived at Swayne Keld some centuries ago a family called Wilson—no relation of mine," my informant hurriedly told me. "They were a bit wild, and one of the daughters, 'twas said, made a foolish marriage in her youth. However, the man went off and disappeared, and later on she succeeded to the estates and married a neighbouring squire, also a Wilson, whose serving-man, a lad of nineteen, was devotedly attached to both master and mistress. He was the young brother of the man Dame Wilson had been reported to have wedded in her youth, whom Dick had not seen since he was a child of eight years.

"One wild day, however, a half-starved beggar-man came over the fell and implored shelter for the night. Squire Wilson, with northern hospitality, took him in, and he was to sleep in the top room of the pele; but next morning it was found that he had rewarded his host's kindness by making off with his host's favourite grey horse, taking young Dick with him. This was all that was ever definitely known."

"Well," I said, as old Wilson paused. "Where does the lantern come into this very sordid story?"

"We guess at the rest from the lantern's behaviour," old Wilson went on. "Gradually ugly whispers went about the country-side. Occasionally travellers over Grey Craig moor would meet a man leading a grey horse, carrying a lantern in his left hand. Once or twice storm-stayed folk followed the lantern light and fell over Grey Crag."

I shuddered. The memory of that footstep into space came tumbling into my mind with unpleasant vividness.

"What was surmised and pieced together was this," the old man went on. "Dick recognised in the beggar-man his lost brother, who had doubtless come to threaten the happiness of master and mistress; perhaps, indeed, the elder brother attempted to induce the younger to throw in his lot with him. At any rate, Dick is supposed to have killed the elder man as he lay asleep in the tower room, by the light of the lantern. He then carried the body of his victim down to the stables, which were then on the ground floor of the pele, and strapping it on the grey horse, started over Grey Crag moor with his gruesome burden, which he probably intended to dispose of in the depths of Lyke Water tarn. Some disaster may, however, have overtaken him. At any rate he was never seen or heard of again, and the only thing remaining was the lantern. The dalesfolk say that Dick, the grey mare, and its load, are doomed to roam the moor till the Last Day dawns. On that I cannot express an opinion: such matters are beyond a plain man. Now, Sir Charles, you know all that I can tell you."

I thanked Mr. Wilson, and thoughtfully descended into the street. It was something to be thankful for that the pele tower only was concerned in that bygone tragedy.

I had the entrance to the upper room in the pele tower walled up, with the lantern in its niche still keeping watch and ward over the dark stain on the rude stone floor. For all I know it is there still, except when occasionally lost travellers over Grey Crag moor meet a great grey horse with a dark burden on its back, led by a slim man carrying a lantern in his left hand.

I do not attempt to explain these things. As Mr. Wilson said, I am a plain man: but I have bought Swayne Keld, and we have not again been disturbed o' nights.

197

STRANGE STORIES OF SPORT

XVII.—THE CATACOMB FOX

BY DANIELE B. VARÉ

HE is old, and lean, and cunning, and he lives in the catacombs near the Cecchignola, ten miles out of Rome. These are not the catacombs that tourists visit as a rule; in fact, I very much doubt if anyone has thoroughly explored them; but they evidently extend for miles, for I have noticed at least a dozen openings into underground passages, and should you ever drive along the Cecchignola road on your way to a meet you will often hear the ground ring hollow under the wheels of your carriage.

He has given us many a good run, and may give us a few more before he goes where the good foxes go, for I have not heard of his decease up till now, and a faster-going fox I never knew; also you cannot stop up a catacomb as you would an ordinary burrow or drain, to cut off his retreat. He is generally known as the " volpe della Cecchignola," but I prefer to call him the " catacomb fox," if only for the part he plays in this same story.

The finest run he gave us was just two years ago, when we caught him in the open far from home—thirty-five minutes by my watch, and without a check. It was a run to remember all one's life, and to tell of in the evenings in the firelight, when sporting memories come back thick and fast, and you see through clouds of tobacco-smoke the big timber fences and green pasture land with its background of blue hills. What a pace he went that day! Disdaining the tricks with which he had thrown off the hounds many times before, over hill and valley, straight for his home. And how we followed! With hats crammed over our ears, racing over the flat stretches of pasture, plunging into the hollows and through the big ditches that drain off the valleys, bending forward as we topped each steep hill, slowing down a little before each fence or wall, then to dash forward harder than before as the obstacle was safely taken and left behind. It was a run to make your blood tingle in your veins, your breath come quick, and your eyes sparkle with the very joy of living! We were a big field when the run began, but there were barely eight of us when we sprang off our panting horses before the large black opening in the hill-side where the fox had gone to ground, and I think that I was prouder of being among those eight than of anything that I had ever done.

The hounds disappeared underground for a second or two, but came out again almost immediately, and stood round the opening with heaving sides and tongues out, their drooping tails expressive of their disgust and righteous indignation.

The first to come up was Colonel Barletta on a thoroughbred mare; he and the Master and huntsman stood mopping their faces with their pocket-handkerchiefs and alternately praising and cursing the fox who had given them such a run only to escape. Only one lady kept up with us to the end, an American, Miss Dalton, from New York. She was a pretty girl, with fair hair and a fresh, clear complexion just a little tanned by the Italian sun. She rode splendidly on hunters that her father had bought in Milan. She sprang down from her saddle, and giving me her horse to hold went and peered into the catacomb; then she came back to me.

"You don't happen to know what's become of Gino, do you?" she asked.

She was engaged to an Italian by the name of Gino Velardi, a young man who had taken to fox-hunting only a few months before, his fondness for the sport of kings being merely accessory to the deeper passion that he bore for Miss Dalton.

"He was all right when I saw him last," I answered; "he was giving pennies to a *contadino* who had opened a gate for him."

"Think of stopping in the middle of a run to give pennies to a *contadino!*" exclaimed Miss Dalton.

"Eet is a goot zing zat somebody stop to pay," said Barletta; "we all not too excited to wait till him open ze gate, but we too excited to give him somezing!"

The Colonel stood with a large sandwich in one hand and a saddle-flask of marsala in the other, his horse's reins hanging loosely over one arm. Never very fluent, his English was rendered worse than usual by the fact that he spoke with his mouth full. "'Ere 'e com'. 'E all right! Keep still, you fool, can't you?" This last was in Italian and addressed to his horse.

Young Velardi rode up at that moment. He was mounted on a big roan hunter and dressed in black, with a broad-brimmed hat like those worn by the *buttari* or cattle-drivers on the Campagna; he made no secret of the fact that it was the pleasure of Miss Dalton's company more than any keenness for sport that brought him out hunting, so he modestly left pink coats and sporting attire to the men who were in reality or in their own estimation better sportsmen than himself. He rode very fairly nevertheless, and looked well on horseback, being thin and wiry, with a rather pale, clean-shaven face, and wonderful eyes of the kind one reads of in books, black as ink, restless, everchanging, with a latent fire in them which to his friends spoke of an intelligence beyond the ordinary, and reminded his enemies, who were not a few, of the insanity which had once or twice shown itself in members of his family. His intelligence manifested itself in many ways, but principally in his researches and experiments in electrical engineering and chemistry; his insanity, if such it could be called, in occasional paroxysms of anger, to which he was subject if roused or thwarted in any way.

He cantered up in a leisurely way, and asked what had become of the fox. The situation having been explained to him, he got off his horse and, giving the reins to the huntsman to hold, went and peered into the tunnel.

"Why didn't the hounds follow?" he asked next.

"They did go in a few yards," answered the Master, "but there is a spring of water in there somewhere; the ground is all wet. I suppose there is no scent, and they were afraid of the darkness."

"I wonder how far it extends," said Velardi. "Lend me a match-box, will you? I should like to see what it looks like inside."

Barletta handed him a match-box.

"Don't go in far, Gino," said Miss Dalton, "or you'll get lost or fall down a hole. One catacomb is much the same as another, I suppose; there cannot be anything very interesting in this one."

"All right," said Velardi, "I won't go in far." And stooping down, for the passage was very low at the opening, he stepped in and disappeared. Two of the hounds started to follow him, but the Master called them back.

"I wish he wouldn't be so foolish," said Miss Dalton; "even if he doesn't get lost he'll probably catch a chill going into that damp cellar of a place after such a run."

"Oh, him all right!" said Barletta, who was sitting on the grass near the opening. "Him no fool! Eet is quite warm in zere, and I can see his light in ze passage."

In a minute or two Velardi's face reappeared at the opening, and he scrambled out and began dusting his clothes.

"This passage is evidently a side entrance," he said; "there is quite a broad tunnel a little further down that runs at right angles to it; probably there is a big chapel or hall somewhere near. I daresay the early Christians managed to make themselves pretty comfortable in their time. I can imagine life being very pleasant even in a catacomb under certain circumstances;" and he looked at Miss Dalton.

"I am afraid that if you intend to set up house in a catacomb," said his fiancée, "that I could have nothing more to say to you; think of the bats and the damp!"

"Fair lady, you are so practical! Think of the memories and the silence. You would look so pretty, too, by candle-light—like some fair-haired Christian martyr ready to face the lions in the Colosseum rather than betray her faith!"

"Thanks! I'd rather do the Colosseum with a Baedeker and safety, though I guess I would have received a more lasting impression in the old way!"

The Master had mounted and was moving off with the pack. Miss Dalton and Velardi followed his example. Old Barletta stared after them as he finished his sandwich. "Those two are always chaffing each other," he said to me in Italian. "It seems a funny way of making love; it usen't to be mine, I remember!"

"But it leads to the altar, Colonel," I said, "which your methods did not apparently, as you are still a bachelor."

"That, my dear young man, only proves their superiority!" And mounting his mare the Colonel trotted off after the hounds.

That run was the finest we have ever had after the catacomb fox. As a rule he keeps too near home to give us much sport, and he invariably succeeds in reaching one of the many openings to his own special residence. It was about a year after the run I have just described that he again gave us a gallop, and this time he nearly lost his brush. Several things had, however, happened in the mean-time. First of all Miss Dalton fell ill of typhoid fever, and her marriage, which was to have taken place in the spring, had to be put off indefinitely in consequence. In the first week of November, however, just before the beginning of the hunting season, a more tragic incident occurred, which we all thought at the time must inevitably put an end to all poor Velardi's or Miss Dalton's hopes of conjugal happiness.

Velardi, as I think I mentioned before, was an electrician of considerable talent, and though barely twenty-two years old had already made a name for himself in the world of science by some discoveries concerning the transmission of electric currents through liquids. He used to conduct his experiments in a large laboratory built over the stables of his father's house in Rome, and at the time of his engagement he was at work (so it was understood among his friends) on a discovery which was, if all went well, to place him on a level with the greatest electricians of our days. He passed most of his time in his laboratory either alone or with one assistant, a boy of about nineteen whom he had found almost starving in the streets, having been out of work a long time. Gino had taken him home and educated him, and made him his assistant, and the boy worshipped the very ground his master trod on. Gino would work for long spells at a time, a short nap on a divan in the laboratory often serving him as a night's rest. So one morning, or, to be more precise, on the 12th of November, when his valet Mariano, entering his bedroom to call him, found that the bed had not been slept in, he naturally supposed that his master had passed the night at work, and took his breakfast of coffee and rolls over to the laboratory; but he found the door locked, and though he knocked several times received no answer.

Still he was not alarmed; young Velardi had all the eccentric habits of genius, and might have gone out early in the morning and breakfasted in some café or restaurant. At about twelve o'clock, however, the coachman, coming in and out of the stables, noticed with surprise the behaviour of his dogs, a couple of fox-terriers, who stood alternately whining and growling outside the laboratory door, and would not come away when he called them. He mentioned the fact casually to Mariano, who, beginning to fear some misfortune, went to Gino's father and asked permission to force the door. Old Velardi hurried at once to the laboratory, and setting Mariano and the coachman to work with an old flint-lock gun that hung in the saddlery, used as a battering-ram, they soon broke in the lock and opened the door. What he expected and feared to find I do not know, probably he did not know himself. As he entered the room, he saw the body of a man lying on the floor by the window, and he ran forward with a sob, thinking that it must be his son. But as he came nearer he saw that he was mistaken: the man was not Gino, but of shorter and heavier build, with fair hair and beard. The bright winter sunshine shone down pitilessly on the huddled form and black distorted features, and old Velardi realised that the man was unknown to him, and that he had been strangled.

There is no need to enumerate the thousand and one conjectures and inquiries that followed the discovery of the man's body and young Velardi's subsequent disappearance. There was never any doubt as to who was guilty, nor did the police have great difficulty in discovering the motives of the crime. The murdered man was identified as one Giovanni Lezzani, an engineer of doubtful reputation, and from some sheets of letter paper covered with notes in the defunct's handwriting it became evident that Lezzani had entered the laboratory, probably by means of false keys, in the hopes of obtaining information about young Velardi's discoveries. He had most likely been discovered by Gino himself, and the scene that must have followed can easily be imagined. Public opinion, which had been very much against Gino at the first discovery of the crime, soon veered round so as to be almost entirely in his favour, and much sympathy was felt for him among his friends when it was discovered that the murdered man had not been unarmed, as it had been said at first, but had even succeeded in wounding his adversary with a peculiarly deadly-looking knife. This was deduced from the fact of the knife being found in the courtyard opposite the laboratory window, where young Velardi had probably thrown it before his fingers, nerved by one of those sudden paroxysms of anger to which he was subject, closed round his opponent's throat. That he had been wounded himself was apparent, the towels in the laboratory wash-hand stand having evidently been used to stanch a wound; and as the body of Lezzani had no scratch on it, one could only suppose that Gino himself had received a cut in the struggle. He was not even blamed for having fled from justice instead of facing the consequences of his act, and this because of a rumour that originated with his father, that Gino was not hiding merely to escape imprisonment but in order that he might bring his experiments, which were then at a critical stage, to a successful termination. To prove that his theory was not unfounded old Velardi declared that several of the more important batteries and instruments were missing from the laboratory, though, to tell the truth, nobody believed the old gentleman.

This only was certain: that Gino had disappeared, and with him his assistant, notwithstanding that the former could have made almost sure of his acquittal by claiming that he had acted in self-defence, and the assistant, except for the fact of his disappearance, would never have incurred even the suspicion of being accessory to the crime. The police in the meanwhile had not obtained a single clue to indicate the whereabouts of the fugitives.

Such was the state of affairs when the hunting began as usual on the 15th of November. Much to everybody's surprise, Miss Dalton, who we all supposed to be in a state of nervous agitation over her lover's fate, appeared regularly at the meets and followed the hounds with all her former keenness, a constant pallor and a suspicion of suppressed excitement in her manner being the only signs that she felt her strange position in the least, and even these might have been the consequences of her recent illness.

It was December before we caught a glimpse of the Cecchignola fox, and when one evening after a long and blank day our friend suddenly got up a few yards in front of the hounds and started off home like a streak of red lightning, there was a general chorus of laughing approval from the old hands who caught a glimpse of the long white line across his back, probably the scar of some old wound, by which we, who had seen him often, used to recognise him.

" Good old fox ! " exclaimed Barletta as we started off ; " he is always ready to oblige ! Seems to me he will lose his brush to-day, though ! "

This certainly appeared probable, as the hounds were barely forty yards behind him when the run began, and seemed at first to be gaining ground. But the old fox was wily and his home very near ; knowing that their heavier weight would put his pursuers at a disadvantage running up hill, as he entered the valley into which the catacombs opened he did not make straight for the entrance to his lair, but kept rather to the right of it, going full speed to the top of a neighbouring hill ; then, having gained fully ten or twelve yards by this dodge, he turned sharply to the left and made straight for home, disappearing underground just as the hounds began to gain on him once more. In all former runs, when the fox had escaped down a catacomb the hounds had never followed him in for more than a few yards, so that when we saw the pack dash into the opening after their prey we expected them to reappear almost immediately. This, however, they failed to do, having penetrated, probably because the scent was stronger than usual, deep down into the passages of the catacombs, so that on reaching the opening the Master and huntsman could only hear a distant confused baying, but could not be sure from which direction it proceeded. During the run, which had been a very short one, I had ridden alongside of Miss Dalton, and had noticed that she was even paler than usual ; and thinking that perhaps she might be tired, for we had been many hours in the saddle, as soon as I pulled up I offered her some brandy and water from my flask. But she shook her head without answering, and kept her eyes on the opening to the underground passage, where the huntsman was standing blowing his horn to recall his hounds. I remembered then the almost identical scene of just ten months before, when Gino Velardi had explored the nearer passages of the catacomb with the aid of Barletta's match-box. "Poor girl!" I thought, "she remembers it too!" and I walked away, leading my horse.

The hounds were beginning to come out one by one, and soon the pack was almost complete; yet two were still missing, and though the huntsman blew his horn and called them by name they failed to appear. A catacomb is a dangerous place to enter without many precautions, and I believe that the huntsman added to the very natural fear of getting lost a superstitious terror of the tomb-lined passages through which he would have had to grope his way.

Barletta suggested that some one should go in with a ball of string to let out as he moved forward, but as no string was forthcoming he did not help us much with his advice.

We were still discussing what should be done when Miss Dalton suddenly called me, and as I went up to her bent down in the saddle and whispered to me: "For pity's sake don't let anyone go in!"

I stared at her in amazement; her face was drawn and haggard, and her voice shook as if she was afraid. "There is no danger, Miss Dalton," I assured her, "nobody will go in without taking every precaution."

"Oh, you do not understand! You do not understand," she repeated, and her eyes were full of tears. "Nobody must go in! For my sake see that nobody goes in!"

I remained silent with my hand on her saddle-bow, looking down at the grass and wondering what all this could mean and what I should do (I could hear the Master declaring that he would not go home till his hounds were found), and then suddenly I understood.

"Would it matter if I went in?" I asked, looking up.

Her eyes met mine for a moment, and then her face cleared.

"Oh! If you would!" she answered.

So I turned and went up to the Master. I do not take any credit to myself for having guessed the truth at that moment, though I hope I am not more dense than my neighbours; but, as I stood there by Miss Dalton's horse, looking down my glance had rested for an instant on something that gave me a clue; it was indeed merely the stub of a half-smoked cigarette lying in the grass, but was of a peculiar brand, tipped with straw—a brand that I remember Gino Velardi always used to smoke. So I went to the Master and offered to go in and look for his two missing hounds.

"But you'll get lost, man!" he said; "the whip has fetched a piece of candle from a shepherd's hut near by, but he says he cannot get a ball of string anywhere. How are you to find your way out?"

"I could scratch a line along the ground or on the sides of the passages as I walked forwards," I answered, "that is if one of you could lend me a pen-knife or some pointed instrument, and then I could follow the line when I turned to come back."

"Yes, that's not such a bad idea," commented the Master; "but are you sure you don't mind going in alone? Hadn't one of us better come with you?"

I declared my preference for going in alone, and soon I was furnished with a candle and a corkscrew belonging to Barletta (what he wanted with a corkscrew out hunting I cannot conceive), no more suitable instrument being obtainable wherewith to mark out my way. I glanced at Miss Dalton's face; it was still pale, but calmer; then I stooped down and entered the passage.

As long as the aperture by which I had entered remained in sight I did not trouble to use the corkscrew, but when the passage, which was narrow and hollowed out of the hard red earth or tufa, opened out into a broader and loftier tunnel I began to mark my further progress by scratching a line on the wall as I moved forwards. For the first twenty yards or so this was easy enough, but as I got further in the passages began to intersect each other more frequently, and their sides were, in places, honeycombed with tombs similar to those in the catacombs of St. Calixtus, which the tourists visit; this made the drawing of the line, as I had begun it, very difficult, so that I decided at last, though it was not so comfortable a process, to scratch the line on the ground. I had been moving all the time in the direction whence proceeded a low, continuous murmur, which at the time I took to be the distant baying of hounds. As I stooped down to mark the ground with my corkscrew I noticed low down on the side of the passage a small arrow roughly drawn in chalk pointing in the direction I was following. I stood up and peered along the passage. A few yards further down a similar arrow was drawn at the same height from the ground, and further on another; after that came the darkness. Suddenly the sound I had been following died away, giving place to absolute silence. A large bat, disturbed by the light of my candle, flashed past me and disappeared. I confess that for a moment I felt a strong desire to turn and leave the hounds to their fate and the mystery of Miss Dalton's strange agitation unsolved; for although I would have taken any odds that Gino Velardi lay hidden somewhere among those passages and tombs, and though I no more feared poor Gino when in his normal condition of sanity than I feared Miss Dalton herself, yet as I stood there alone in the darkness the sinister rumours of my poor friend's latent madness occurred to me, I remembered how only a few days before he had killed an armed man with his bare hands, and I reasoned that his surprise at my appearance, should I come upon him unawares, and his fear of capture might well raise the devil in the man, whose control over his passions could never be entirely relied upon. Yet I did him an injustice, for even as I stood hesitating whether to proceed or not a quiet voice at my elbow made me turn with a start, and I saw the well-known figure close beside me, smiling at my discomfiture.

"Oh! it's you, is it?" said Gino. "Did she tell you to come and see me?"

He was wearing a workman's blouse over a dark serge suit, and held a lighted cigarette in his hand; he looked much as usual, and spoke as if it were the most natural thing in the world for me to come upon him in the passages of an unexplored catacomb.

"She did not want any of us to come in," I answered; "but the Master said he wouldn't go home without his hounds, and she did not seem to mind *me* going in as much as the others, so I came."

"Others! What others?" said Gino, looking grave. "Does all Rome know of my being here?"

I explained the situation hurriedly, adding: "You had better help me to find the hounds, or you will have half the field in soon to look for me."

He nodded, and turning down a side passage beckoned me to follow him. "This is more serious than I thought," he said. "I supposed on seeing you that my fiancée had told you of my whereabouts and that you had merely come to see how I was getting on. But I think I know where the hounds are, and if we can find them and get them out again there will be no harm done. If you will come in here a minute I can get a lantern and go with you."

We emerged as he spoke into a small vaulted room, which had evidently been a chapel when the early Christians had used the catacombs, for on the walls were the remains of old frescoes, and at one end there rose a broad marble altar, blackened with time. From this altar a petroleum lamp shed its light on a collection of various electrical appliances, a small battery, two electroscopes, and several rows of bottles and glass jars containing chemicals and salts. These articles were distributed, some on the floor, some on two collapsible card-tables of English make, and some on the altar. Comfort had evidently been sacrificed to science, for though the room boasted only two camp-stools there was a large mortar in one corner with a pestle and some blue salts beside it, and I guessed that the noise I had mistaken for the baying of hounds had really been made by Gino pounding some salts in the mortar.

"This is only our laboratory," he said, taking up a lantern from the floor and proceeding to light it; "if I had more time I would show you our bedrooms."

"You are not alone, then, down here?" I asked.

"Oh dear no! I have my assistant; he is at Frascati just now, disguised as a shepherd; he always goes up there to get provisions: it is nearer than Rome, and there is less danger of his being recognised." He took up the lantern as he spoke, and led the way down several passages, turning now to the right, now to the left, till we came to a place where the ground seemed to have given way so that the passage was nearly blocked up, and we had to creep over mounds of fallen earth on our hands and knees—a most uncomfortable proceeding when you are carrying a lighted candle in your hand.

"You seem to know the way about very well," I remarked; "but where are you taking me to?"

"To the fox's lair," he answered, "it's just round the corner here; I found it one day by accident, when I was exploring the catacombs. Phew! I can smell the brute already!"

We took a few more steps forward, stumbling over the broken ground, and found ourselves in a room very similar to the one used by Gino as a laboratory, except that here the walls were lined with tombs, hollowed out of the earth and closed with slabs of marble; one of these was open at one end, the marble being broken, and before this tomb were the two hounds. As we came up to them they began to display the greatest excitement, under the impression that we had come to help them reach their prey. There was the fox, right enough, glaring at me from a corner of the empty tomb, his eyes shining red and green and his white teeth flashing in the candle-light as he snarled at us. The aperture was far too small for the hounds to pass through, so he was safe enough as far as they were concerned, and as I did not feel inclined to molest him we left him master of the situation and retired, Gino preceding me as before, while I dragged the unwilling hounds after me by the scuff of the neck.

When we came to the place where he had first found me, Gino stopped and held out his hand. "Good bye, old man," he said, "and good luck; you can find your way out easily now, you have only to follow the arrows!"

"Good bye," I answered, and we shook hands. His face stood out clear and pale in the candle-light against the dark of the passages —he was smiling. I felt very sorry for him, and tried to say so; after all, the man he had killed had been a scoundrel, and had tried to rob him. "Why don't you come out, Gino?" I said; "it was only manslaughter all told. There is no dishonour attached—it only makes it worse, your hiding in here!"

Gino laughed. "You take for granted that it was I who killed the little beast!" he said.

"Well, didn't you?" I asked in amazement.

"Oh dear no! It was my assistant, Gianni. We went into the laboratory together and found the man copying out my notes. He tried to rush past us to the door, and struck at me with his knife; it was a mere scratch, but I staggered against the wall, and before I knew what was happening Gianni had him by the throat, and was choking the life out of him. He is a strong little beggar, and devoted to me. I called out to him to let go, but it was too late."

"Then why in Heaven's name are you in hiding?" I asked.

"Oh, I could not afford to have my work interrupted by the police just now," he answered; "my experiments are at a critical stage, and I need Gianni to help me; but we shall not be very long now—a few more experiments, a few months of work, and I shall be back among my friends. In a year's time, at most, you will see me again."

"A year!" I exclaimed; "you don't mean to say you are going to remain buried in this place a whole year!"

"No," he answered, "I shall leave this, if all goes well, in a day or two, and I think you will be able to guess my whereabouts. So good bye, once more. You must hurry off, or we shall have the whole field in here in a minute or two."

"Good bye," I said, and I turned down the passage, and following the line on the wall, soon came to the opening where I had entered, and where my friends were waiting anxiously for my return.

The sun was just beginning to go down as I stepped out into the thyme-scented air of the Campagna; from some little village on the Alban Hills a few miles away there floated over the plain the sound of church bells. I was dimly conscious, as I stood there dazzled by the unaccustomed light, that old Barletta and Miss Dalton were looking at me curiously; but neither spoke, and the Master and huntsman were busy calling off the hounds. So we mounted and rode off, each occupied with his own thoughts.

When we got back to the place where we had met, I helped Miss Dalton into the brougham that was to drive her back to the town.

"I want to thank you for your kindness," she said as we shook hands, "and to say good bye!"

"Good bye?" I echoed in astonishment. "Are you leaving Rome, then?"

"Yes," she answered; "my father is coming to Civitavecchia the day after to-morrow in his yacht, and we are to go on a cruise round the world together." Her glance met mine, and to the unspoken question in my eyes she answered in a whisper, " Yes, he comes too."

Old Barletta and I drove home together as usual ; we always share a cab out to the meets, and as a rule it's the Colonel who does most of the talking. That evening, however, he seemed thoughtful ; he wrapped himself up in his blue cloak, lit a cigar, and sat staring out over the Campagna. The sun had set behind the hills, and the air was growing cold ; in the distance the town, with its many domes and steeples, rose up clear and dark against the deep red of the sky, and already a few lights were shining here and there among the houses. On the road in front of us was Miss Dalton's brougham, trotting homewards at a smart pace.

" Nice girl, that ! " said the Colonel at last.

" Very," I answered, and I glanced at the brown face beside me, wondering how much this old cynic had guessed of Miss Dalton's story.

" It must be very nice," he added after a pause, " to have some-one like that to be fond of you and true to you, come what may ! "

" You were not always of that opinion, Colonel," I answered ; " what has converted you ? "

But the Colonel was not listening.

" Gino is a lucky beggar ! " he said.

210

STRANGE STORIES OF SPORT
XVIII.—HAZLETON'S SHIKAR

BY FRANK SAVILE

" Poor old Hazleton! I'm afraid his nose has been put out of joint!"

The words were not spoken loudly, but in the evening quiet they carried distinctly. They reached the ears of a man who sat by himself in the shadow of the great deodars which fringed the camp clearing. His shoulders twitched slightly; he frowned.

The speaker was Colonel Traske, late of the Bengal Tail-twisters, but for the present of no permanent address save the rather spacious one of Baltistan. The spot was the Colonel's shikar camp on the spurs of the Latayun Hills. The time—after dinner

There were four men in camp and two women. The Colonel, his wife, and his bosom friend Robert Eads, Commissioner of Jileyl, sat apart, and the two cronies, wonderful to relate, had deserted the eternal subject of shikar, to indulge in a little mild gossip. Admonishment came from Mrs. Traske.

" Hush!" she reproved. " He's somewhere near."

Hazleton stirred again—uneasily, and his lips parted to show a tiny glimpse of his white teeth. It was an unpleasant smile—the sort of grin with which a bayed wolf bares its fangs.

He looked across the dusk of the clearing to where a patch of white indicated the position of Maurice Bryan's shirt-front. Within a couple of feet of it a tiny red spark was evidence that Mary Haldane was enjoying, with her coffee, a cigarette. Hazleton's eyes dilated as he marked the shortness of the interval between the white and the red.

His mind wandered back over the last six weeks. He pondered the many attentions he had shown Miss Haldane—the assiduous pains he had been at to win her regard—his fears, his doubts, and latterly his dawning hopes. And now?

A week ago Bryan had joined them, and in a single day had ruined Hazleton's patiently-built fabric of months. The latter's dogged adoration had become a mere background to show up the more brilliantly the Irishman's ardent, reckless wooing. Already Hazleton knew that Mary Haldane was lost to him. Without the passing of a word he read it in her face, saw it in the eyes which she turned upon his rival. He ground his teeth as her laugh rang out into the quiet. In that moment he could have killed Bryan— shot him—stabbed him—bludgeoned him into shapelessness!

Very silently he rose and slipped back into the deeper shadows of the jungle to wrestle with his rage alone. To hear—to suspect what the dusk hid from him was more than his passion could bear. He found the path and strode towards the little Balti village where the daily supplies were obtained.

He halted before the first hut he came to. There was a stirring inside. A man appeared through the opening—half trench, half doorway—which was the only aperture.

"Salaam, sahib!" he said, respectfully. "The sahib desires— what?"

Hazleton looked at him curiously.

"You knew, then, through this darkness, that it was I?" he said.

The man smiled.

"Could I mistake the footfall of a sahib?" he answered. "Do our people go shod so?" He pointed to the Englishman's rubber soles.

Hazleton nodded.

"You have made your preparations?" he asked. "We start at dawn?"

"If the Presence so wills," said the Balti, meekly. "Word has been brought me that the Captain sahib—Bryan sahib—claims to have taken a head in these hills of 44-inch horns? Is it the truth?"

"He claims to have so done," agreed Hazleton, dryly.

The tracker made a quaint gesture.

"It remains to show him that there are other heads as big, or bigger. We must shoot with discrimination to-morrow, sahib,

212

Nothing that gives promise of less than five-and-forty inches—or more."

Hazleton laughed grimly.

"Considering that for five days we have not so much as seen hoof or horn of ibex—" he began.

But the Balti interrupted eagerly.

"Nay, sahib," he cried, "*this* time there is no talk of failure. *I have made preparation.*"

There was a curious emphasis on the last four words which made Hazleton inspect the speaker steadily.

"Fine words!" he sneered, with a shrug of his shoulders. "Let us hope for deeds as fine. You have my leave to go!" and so turned again to the jungle path and paced thoughtfully back to the camp as the tracker made obeisance and slid into his burrow.

Twelve hours later the two had gained the heights, far above the woodland camp, where snow and forest are divided by a broad frontier of arid rock. The shadows had already left the higher peaks, and were drifting across the valleys. Carrying the rifle the tracker stepped noiselessly from boulder to boulder, keeping carefully below the level of a ridge which cut off the view of the further slope. Once or twice he halted, motioned his master to be seated, and then slid with infinite caution to peer over the knife-like edge above him. After each inspection he shook his head gravely, pointed forward, and resumed his dogged, swinging step.

Half an hour later a dip of the rock showed a vista of gullies framed as if in a picture by the grey crags on either side. The Balti came to a sudden halt.

Slowly, with infinite care, he sank to the ground; and Hazleton, accustomed shikari as he was, silently followed his example. Under cover of a heaped mass of rubble he drew out his telescope and focussed it.

The Balti whispered some half-articulate words. Hazleton directed his gaze towards a distant declivity where half a dozen dark specks were distinct in the increasing sunlight. The glass revealed them as a herd of ibex, wandering slowly across the face of the hill.

Hazleton made a tiny gesture of disappointment.

"Out of shot and absolutely no cover for a stalk," he whispered. "They are beyond our harming."

The tracker smiled.

"Nay," he contradicted, "they shall be our easy prey. You shall have your choice of them, sahib!"

Hazleton frowned.

"A stupid jest," he answered. "How should we approach them—can we make ourselves invisible?"

The Balti's retort was an indirect one. He merely pointed in another direction.

" Look, sahib ! " he murmured. " Look well ! "

For the second time the telescope revealed a herd—a larger one this time, and pacing from one of the more distant ridges in a direction which would bring it face to face with its half-dozen first-seen fellows. Hazleton gave a little gasp of wonder.

His companion nodded with a self-satisfied air.

" And outside our seeing are other herds, sahib," he breathed slowly. " Of that I have assurance. As surely as I am Sitka, tracker of Latayun, all the ibex within miles are afoot, and all ambling in the one direction."

Hazleton eyed him narrowly. The Balti met his stare unflinchingly.

" And where does this miracle take place ? " inquired the Englishman.

Sitka chuckled and pointed into the distance.

" Where the sahib shall have no chance to mistake it," he averred. " With your own eyes you shall have proof. Follow ! "

He slipped behind a rugged stone, sank into a crevice between a couple of boulders, and so, keeping well under cover, led the way down the centre of the ravine.

For half an hour they kept within the valley. Next they breasted a steep slope, crossed a rugged table-land, and came finally to the brink of a jutting cliff. Sitka dropped upon his breast and wormed noiselessly to the verge. Hazleton followed.

His astonishment almost betrayed him into an exclamation. No fewer than *six* herds of ibex were in view. The gorge seemed brimmed with them—buck, doe, and fawn were collected in groups which advanced towards a common centre as if they meditated merging into one immense drove. Sitka's glance roved over the leaders of the different files in keen speculation. With scarcely perceptible gestures he indicated the most conspicuous heads.

A few moments later he slid the rifle into his master's hand.

" To the left, sahib," he breathed. " Between the two does, flanked by the playing fawns. A noble beast ! "

Hazleton looked and experienced a mighty pulsation of the heart. Those branching horns could scarcely stretch less than fifty inches from brow to point.

Slowly, carefully, he took aim. The unconscious buck paced on. Hazleton followed the mighty shoulder with the muzzle, hesitated, took confidence again, dwelled upon it, experienced all the multitudinous terrors which crowd upon a sportsman at such

214

a moment, and at last—*squeezed* the trigger. The echoes of the shot went leaping from crag to crag.

The sudden frenzy of fear descended upon the beasts. In a turmoil of flying pebbles they raced for the safety of the hills, and despair filled Hazleton's heart as he recognised that their leader was the patriarch of the stupendous horns. Frantically he demanded another cartridge.

None was pressed into his twitching fingers. Instead came the answer of the Balti's triumphant laugh.

"No need, sahib—no need!" he cried. "Watch—watch!"

The great buck was no longer leading—the following herd was sweeping past him—had left him behind. His canter slowed to a stumbling trot—to a walk—to a halt. For a moment he stood motionless, his great eyes searching the ravine with a sort of piteous wonder. Then his knees bent beneath him. He rolled upon his side—stone dead.

Three minutes later the tape was being carefully pressed round the arc of the mighty horns. Sitka laughed again gleefully as he read the verdict—forty-six inches from skull to tip!

And then, in the sudden revulsion after the tense emotions of the last few minutes, Hazleton found that a devouring curiosity was the feeling uppermost in his mind. He sat down upon a boulder and stared at the tracker, who was whetting his flensing-knife upon a stone. He called him by name.

Sitka looked up.

"Sahib?" he answered inquiringly.

"What is the meaning of it?" said Hazleton, bluntly. "Why were they there—why did we, who have seen no ibex for five days or more, find over fifty awaiting us in this ravine?"

Sitka shrugged his shoulders.

"The Presence would not accept my explanation," he answered, quietly.

"But desires to hear it," retorted Hazleton. "Is there a salt-lick below? Is that what they sought?"

"A salt-lick?" The tracker's tones were full of scorn. "By ones and twos they might seek such a thing, but not by tens and twenties. Nay, this was a matter outside your knowledge, sahib—and outside your belief."

"That remains to be proved," said Hazleton. "Say on!"

The Balti stood silent for a moment, twisting the knife-handle between his fingers. He smiled, hesitated, and then spoke.

"Sahib," he said, "the matter of the ibex had begun to touch mine honour. A week we had scoured the hills and seen not so much as one. I betook me last night, therefore, to Malik La."

Hazleton's eyes conveyed the fact that the name told him nothing.

"Malik La," repeated Sitka, "the Wonder-worker of Sangan. I stand in his favours. He gave me a potion. I came hither, smeared it on these rocks, and—the sahib has seen. As the fisher-folk of Srinagar fill their nets by the lures they pour into the river, so can Malik La seduce every beast upon the hills whither he will. Ibex, I told him—ibex we desire, and—so it came about. Had it been wolf—bear—tahr—the result would have been the same. None can resist potions of Malik La!"

For nearly a minute Hazleton sat silent, looking at the tracker, his brain working furiously behind his impassive features. He laughed.

"And I am to believe this?" he said at last.

"Have I not given proof?" said the tracker, gently.

Hazleton shrugged his shoulders.

"Allah knows!" he answered. "This Wonder-worker of yours—what is his price?"

Sitka laughed.

"Price? He has none, sahib. To whom he wills he gives his favours, and for pride in his own skill. But for money! No!"

"For pride? If you return to him, then, saying that your sahib still lacks conviction, will he repeat his miracle? Is that the nature of his pride?"

"Possibly, sahib. He desires no fame, but his honour is dear to him. I could find words to persuade him—of that I have little doubt."

Again Hazleton was silent, but a light of eagerness was growing in his eyes as he debated upon his words. With a sudden passionate gesture he smote his fist upon the rock.

"Say this to him then," he cried. "Say that I have seen the ibex cooped into a gully as chicken are cooped within a pen, but that I doubt him still, for ibex, as we all know, have their moods when they will travel far, and in one direction, for reasons no man can probe. Let him show me other beasts held by his wiles. Let him give me what will tether the wolves of the jungle to one spot—let me see the packs drawn from their hunting!"

The Balti was silent.

"That is no matter to play with, sahib," he said at last, and gravely. "The wolf pack! They can be stirred to passions far above their normal cowardice."

"Ay," sneered Hazleton, "they may not be driven as ibex are, by concealed watchers on the hill. I thought your Wonder-worker would fail at such a test!"

A sort of mask of impassivity fell over Sitka's features.

"It can be as the Presence wills," he said, quietly. "Yet—I have warned him. Explain your test, sahib!"

"I ask this much," said Hazleton. "Bring to me—to *me*, mark you—what will draw the jungle wolves as the ibex were drawn. Place it in *my* hands. Let *me* use the bait—let *me* fix the trap! Then, if I see the miracle, as you claim it to be, performed at *my* hands and by *my* choosing, I will own myself a believer. I will proclaim in all lands the wonders of the skill of Malik La."

Sitka nodded.

"As the Presence wills," he said, indifferently, and turned to his work upon the pelt and head.

*　　*　　*　　*　　*

Mrs. Traske gave a little shiver.

"I don't like ghost stories," she said. "Who started the conversation? I believe it was you, Captain Hazleton."

Hazleton smiled apologetically. The moonless night was over the clearing, and the sole illumination was the sparkle of four well-lit cheroots. The little company was more sociably inclined than on the previous evening; all six of the campers were gathered in an after-dinner group.

"Sorry, Mrs. Traske," he said. "The mystic has always rather an attraction for me—especially up here. One hears—and for that matter occasionally sees—some very strange things."

"When I'm alone I'm rather inclined to agree with you," said Mary Haldane to her hostess, "but when I'm with other people I think it's rather delicious to be thrilled."

"But, of course, it's all rot," said Bryan, taking his cheroot out of his mouth and sending a long streak of smoke into the night. "These Balti beggars are eaten up with superstition."

Hazleton turned towards him.

"You have absolutely no belief in the supernatural?" he hazarded.

"None," said the other, tersely.

"You'd pit your nerves against any sort of bogey—even in Baltistan?"

"Any djinn or afreet the devil-doctors like to conjure up," said Bryan. "I suppose my Irish birthright includes a belief in spooks, but, as a matter of fact, I haven't a vestige of it. I've no pronounced objection to spirits, but they must be intimate with soda-water before I begin to take an interest in them."

Hazleton laughed—a laugh which held a faint but unmistakable tinge of a sneer.

"Is your incredulity so stalwart that it would disdain a test?" he asked.

Bryan straightened himself in his chair.

"What's that?" he said, with sudden interest.

Hazleton laughed again.

"Have you heard of the Lgi Dras gorge?" he asked. "It's scarcely more than three-quarters of an hour's walk from here."

"No. Why?"

"No native of these parts would walk through it at midnight for any sum you liked to offer him. The ghost-wolves hunt there— the spirits of those who have lost their lives in frontier vendetta and remain unavenged. They take their own vengeance on those they meet—now."

"The illogical divils!" said Bryan. "Would you have me go and reason with them? Is that what you're driving at?"

"I'd like you to walk through the gorge in a couple of hours' time," said Hazleton, "and I'd like you to come back and give us your word of honour that your heart hasn't beaten an extra pulse to the minute while you were doing it. Then I'll be satisfied that your courage is—superior to a Balti's."

"I've no stethoscope," chuckled Bryan, "so the matter of me heart's pulses must be left out of the question. But I'll bet you a month's pay, me boy, that I'll do it and come back without having quivered an eyelash from fear. Will that satisfy you?"

"Done with you," said Hazleton, tersely, and got upon his feet. "I'll be up to see you start, but I'll ask you all to excuse me now if I take a bit of a snooze. I've had a long day." He gave a nod which included all the company, and disappeared into his tent.

A minute later he was worming upon his face beneath the far side of the canvas, a grey shooting coat covering his evening dress, and a tiny jar clasped in his hand. He rose to his feet, passed noiselessly into the jungle, and ran up the forest path with a vigour which went far to discount his statement about his fatigue. At the end of half an hour's hard going he found himself at the entrance of a narrow defile.

He pushed his way down it till he reached the centre, a narrow gut enclosed by precipitous crags. He halted and drew out a cork-screw. He laughed grimly as he used it.

"Hardly the weapons of true romance!" he muttered to himself, "but the result, I trust, will be worthier than the means." He began to trickle a dark, oily liquid upon the leaves and stones.

He had emptied half the jar when he replaced the cork. "If at first you don't succeed, it's just as well to leave the means of trying again," he soliloquised, and turned in his tracks. Avoiding with infinite care the touching of leaf or stone where the liquid had fallen, he hastened back down the path up which he had come, diverging from it soon after he had re-entered the jungle. He was not the sort of man to overlook trifles, and was well aware that a chance meeting with a native might be reported later and give rise to inquiries which might be difficult to meet. So he took a round-about route which landed him in his tent again within the hour. Ten minutes later he walked out into the clearing, yawning and stretching his arms.

"Where's Bryan?" he inquired of two shadows who revealed themselves as Colonel Traske and the Commissioner.

"Gone quarter of an hour ago," said the former, laconically. "Miss Haldane and my wife got to wrangling about ghosts after you'd gone to bed, and the upshot of it was that the girl asked Bryan to let her accompany him. I needn't tell you it was an offer he jumped at. I expect it will clench the affair—I'll bet you a peg they come back engaged?"

Hazleton gave a terrible cry.

"What!" he thundered. "Miss Haldane—gone—with—with Bryan!"

The Colonel showed real concern.

"I say, old man," he said, "I'm sorry you should take it like that. But you must have seen how things were going lately. You really hadn't a chance."

But Hazleton was clutching at his collar as if it choked him. He reeled—he made inarticulate noises. With an indescribable gesture he swung round and fled into the jungle as a man flees for his life. With wondering ears the two heard the crash of the underwood bursting open to let him through.

He ran with great strides which devoured the ground, smiting against the shrubs with his clenched fists. Creeping vines tripped him, thorns tore his clothes, night birds fluttered with shriekings from each side of his path. He scarcely looked where he went, making a bee-line in the desired direction with animal instinct rather than by any reasoned plan. And his ears strained for hearing into the blackness of the night. He heard nothing but the rush and rustle of his own going. Fancy, indeed, bore other sounds to him—fierce baying yells, the snap of teeth, the pad of innumerable feet. He gasped—he cried aloud—and imagined answering outcry which eluded him in greater distance as he ran. Fearful pictures limned themselves against the darkness. The perspiration of his fear rained into his eyes.

Ten minutes later, reeling, sobbing, panting, he raced into an open glade and came to a sudden halt. No picture of his disordered fancy, this which met his eyes; the quickness of his jealousy told him that what he saw was real beyond all doubting.

Half in the shadow, half in the moonlight, they stood, those whom he sought, and Mary Haldane's forehead was against Bryan's shoulder, and his arm was about her waist. The moonbeams shone on the man's face, illumined with a great triumph. The girl's hands were white upon her lover's sleeve.

As the jungle grass parted to let Hazleton through into this new-made Eden the two started and sprang apart. They stared at him as he fled towards them—they half drew back with a sense of un-explained terror.

He made a furious gesture towards the direction of the camp.

"Come back!" he cried, hoarsely. "Come back!"

For a moment they were silent—with the silence of surprise. And then Bryan laughed.

"What!" he cried. "And lose a month's pay when it's as good as won? Not much, my boy! Not for all the ghosts in Baltistan!"

Hazleton grew almost inarticulate in his passion. He waved his arms wildly.

"You're in danger—horrible danger!" he shouted. "I thought I was too late! My God! I thought I was too late!"

Mary Haldane's face paled. She shrank back towards her lover, and stood looking at Hazleton with scared and wondering eyes.

"What is it?" she stammered. To her, at least, Hazleton's emotion was convincing enough.

But not to the Irishman. He burst into an uproarious laugh.

"As if I didn't see through him and his devices!" he cried. "He's trying to frighten us, mavourneen—he sees his money as good as lost unless he can work on our poor fluttering little hearts with another tale of his bogles. 'Tis a fine actor ye are, Hazleton, me boy, but we'll neither of us play Ophelia to y'r Hamlet. The trick's lost; ye'll have to pay forfeit."

Hazleton fairly danced with rage.

"It's true—it's true!" he yelled, fiercely. "I can't show you—I can't explain, but you're walking to your death—your *death!* Man! can't you see I'm in earnest? Can't you—*won't* you—understand?"

Bryan still wore a smile of great content.

"I can understand this much," he said, serenely, "that I'm within ten minutes of winning what'll keep me in cheroots till Christmas. That's good enough for me. Come along, Mary, dear, and see me win it."

Hazleton stepped forward and laid his hand upon the girl's arm. "You shan't take her!" he thundered. "Go to your death if you will, you fool! Miss Haldane comes back with me!"

The smile died out of Maurice Bryan's eyes, and was succeeded by a very ugly frown.

"Take your hand away, Hazleton!" he commanded, shortly. "And take yourself off, once and for all!"

"I won't!" cried the other. "I won't! Her life's at stake—her very life, you madman!"

"If there's any madman in this vicinity," said Bryan, "he's inside your skin, my boy. For the last time—will you leave Miss Haldane alone?"

"No!" shouted the other. "No!"

"Then, b' Gad, I'll have to make you!" cried Bryan, shooting out his fist.

It caught Hazleton squarely between the eyes.

With a crash he went down across a boulder. There was a grating sound of broken earthenware as he fell.

He rolled over. A thick stain was growing upon the breast of his tunic where an oily liquid seemed to be oozing through. A sweet, pungent odour rose, grew upon the breeze, and seemed to fill the whole ravine.

Hazleton rose gasping. Bryan faced him, standing in front of Mary Haldane with clenched fists.

The other made no attempt to renew his attack. He stood motionless through a long moment, his face turned up the gorge, his whole attitude that of one who listens. The two watched him with a sort of wondering stupor.

And then—

Far, faint at first, but growing in intensity, came a sound out of the distance—a sound utterly unmistakable. The bay of a wolf pack a-hunt.

Hazleton turned to his companions, and a light of despair shone in his eyes—his features were transformed—he made a gesture which seemed to imply that all hope was lost.

"For God's sake come—come!" he screamed, and fled back into the thicket direction from which he had emerged. The infection of his terror was overmastering. Unquestioning, fleeing from they knew not what, Mary Haldane and her lover found themselves racing at his heels.

Blindly they followed Hazleton as he parted the jungle before them. The bushes ripped and crashed—huge leaves and twigs battered their faces. Once Hazleton stopped with a jerk as a great branch shot out athwart his path. He seized it between his hands and snapped it, great limb though it was, as if it had the thickness of a mere walking cane. He rushed through the undergrowth like a human engine of destruction, mowing a path for those behind.

So they fled, tearing the forest silences to tatters with the uproar of their passing, but the noise of broken saplings and sundered shrubs did not smother that other growing sound behind. It increased, doubled itself, rose to a deep chorus nearer—nearer—nearer—till it seemed to echo at their very heels. The great deodars seemed to toss it from trunk to trunk.

And then, with a little cry, Mary Haldane sank down.

With a heave and a jerk Bryan swung her to her feet again and drew her on. She gasped with pain.

"My ankle!" she panted. "I can't run—Oh! I can't!"

Her lover shouted after Hazleton.

"Come back!" he cried. "Come back and help me carry her!"

The other stopped, wheeled, and came racing back. Then with a shudder he hesitated, standing before them in a sort of agony of indecision.

"I daren't touch her," he faltered. "I daren't."

Surprise held Bryan speechless at first.

"You—you daren't!" he cried. "Are you mad?"

"No!" shrieked Hazleton. "No!—but I *daren't*. She—she will get the — *infection* — they will hunt her as they are hunting me — *me*— if she touches the stain—*the stain upon my coat!*" As he spoke the bush behind them parted.

Wide-eyed, white-fanged, a huge dog-wolf leaped upon him, the red jaws gaping for his throat.

He shrieked again while his fingers gripped and sank into the thick fur below the brute's jowl. Man and beast rolled over, fighting rapidly.

Stunned for the moment, Bryan's presence of mind was not long at fault. As the huge hind feet whirled up out of the *mêlée* the Irishman caught them, dragged them across a trunk, and bent them downwards with all his weight and force. There was a crack, and that fight at least was over. Hazleton scrambled to his feet.

"Run!" he commanded, shortly. "Run!" and waved the two down the path. He himself stood motionless and upright, facing away from the camp. They hesitated—they looked at him. He waved his hand again—fiercely, insistently.

"Run!" he yelled, "Run! It's your only chance."

Bryan started and then half turned.

"And you?" he cried. "And you?"

"This is *my* only chance—to go cleanly!" came back the answer in a voice which they hardly knew as Hazleton's, and smothering his last words was the snarl and rush of half a dozen wolves leaping upon him out of the night.

Bryan caught Mary Haldane up in his arms and stumbled down the path with her, reeling like a drunken man, half crazed by suddenly realised but undefined fear.

And she?

She cried aloud and then stopped her ears. But for all that the sounds which seemed to fill the forest rang in them—rang in them till she and her lover blundered into the camp unharmed—will ring in them, indeed, whenever Hazleton's name is mentioned, until her dying day.

*   *   *   *   *

Not long ago another Englishman stood in the glade where a white stone cross tells how " John Hazleton gave his life for his friends."

Sitka, the tracker, stood behind him.

" He was buried here ? " said the Englishman, carefully picking the lichen which had begun to deface the stone.

The Balti shook his head.

" Nay, sahib," he answered, gravely ; " here he died. The grey wolves give no chance for burial."

The other shuddered.

" What infinite—what incredible—self-sacrifice he showed ! "

The tracker smiled—an enigmatic little smile.

" He had a man's passions and he died the death—of a man ! " he said. Of the two epitaphs Sitka's is, perhaps, the nearer to the truth.

STRANGE STORIES OF SPORT
XIX.—THE SALMON WITH THE WHITE TRIANGLE

BY H. KNIGHT HORSFIELD

TORRID weather in town. The steady glare on the hot pavement: the ceaseless beat of the traffic: the very leaves of the city-bred trees as they hang motionless in the dead air, all make for weariness. I feel that I cannot remain here much longer. The spirit of migration—the primal instinct of the birds—moves within me. Pictures, books—the glories of a vast metropolis—what are they? Let me turn to this little spray of heather fading in the garish light of a boot-shop window! It will help me to remember something at any rate of the mountains and the lochs and the sea, and it will add not a little to the impulse which is bidding me to fly. Then I have work to do which I feel I cannot do here.

*   *   *   *   *

Away on the sea at last. Oban with its white-fronted hotels and busy quay is already left far behind, and London lies reeking in the heat at some immeasurable distance, punctuated by the innumerable trees and meadows which we passed in the night. Here the tropical sun-rays evoke no discontent. They touch with silver the little wavelets which break from the steamer's bows and glisten on the breast of the wheeling herring-gull, but all sense of their oppression disappears in the keen fresh breeze. As the hours go by, Mull is lost in the haze, and the islands of Barra and South Uist cease to be mere dark lines on the horizon and take on more definite features. In the early morning, when one comes on deck to breathe again the sharp eager air, the coast-line of the Lews is barely a cable's length away. Soon we draw near to the little landing-stage, and now the birds are all about us—guillemots and puffins riding on the water, and lesser blackbacks and kittiwakes, screaming amidst the shipping, or about the dark sheds where the cured fish are stacked.

Then the long rod-cases and the baggage are borne to the quay and bestowed with some difficulty in the ancient "machine" which awaits me, and I leave the screaming gulls and the hamlet of grim grey stone behind. And so I take my solitary way through this land of heather and of rock, driving for hours on a road which looks like a tape thrown down loosely on the landscape, and which winds on, mile after mile, far into the heart of the hills.

*   *   *   *   *

Solitude. For a man who delights in sharp contrasts my present quarters are unique. Anything less like the baking motor-reeking city from which I have escaped, my imagination fails to picture. Stand with me at the little white porch of this little white house perched on the rounded green of the hill and look around !

Behind and far to the left a battlement of broken rock extends, with the white thread of a waterfall creeping down its sides and a tiny bird-of-prey—a golden eagle maybe—hovering motionless against the blue, above its uppermost edge. Away to the right, through the clefts in the hills, you may see the changing white lines of the distant sea. And nearer home, just at the foot of the hill upon which this tiny fir-guarded lodge stands, you will gain a brief glimpse of the river—the little Oikel, where the salmon are, or rather where they will be when the first decent fresh gives them water enough to get up from the lower reaches. Furthermore, you have merely to go down that little mountain track through the stiff squares of potatoes and wheat, to find yourself on the best pool on the whole river—the Devil's Punch-bowl of the sporting guidebooks, but spoken of by the gillies hereabouts by a name much less easy to be pronounced.

Now we must perforce rest awhile. Longing for action we yet lie—" with half-shut eyes, hearing the downward stream." But the time is coming. The weather has already broken. At last, after a long dry spell, the flood-gates are opened. When I look from the little porch late at night the rain is still descending steadily, and there is every sign of its continuance. There will be plenty of water to-morrow.

      *   *   *   *   *

Daybreak. The higher peaks are hidden in a cloud and stray wisps drift across the lower slopes. The volume of the waterfall has visibly increased. The rocky ravine through which the Oikel takes its course is lost beneath a level bed of mist. It is still raining a little, but as I take my early tub I hear the short corn-crake-like cries of the reel, as Duncan—most silent and worthy of gillies—draws the line through the successive rings. Clearly he is satisfied with the outlook. From the tiny window I can just catch a glimpse of his checked cap—a legacy from some departed sportsman—and of his grey beard moving in the wind. Now for a scone or two and a cup of the hot coffee which Duncan can make to a marvel, and we are ready for work.

Duncan is the most charming companion whom a recluse or anchorite could desire. He never vouchsafes a remark on his own initiative. One may brood for hours in silence without the slightest fear that he will consider himself neglected. But his wits are always at hand. Like the hackneyed Bourbon, he forgets nothing, but he is always ready to learn. As I take my way down the little mountain road I know that nothing has been left behind. Now, through the mirk and mist, we reach the low-lying rocks at the tail of the great pool. The water has very perceptibly risen. Even if newly-run fish have not yet ascended, the fresh will have awakened to life those which already lie in the erst-languid deeps. A few preliminary casts give me the right length of line. A little higher, near the opposite shore, is a holt in the submerged rocks, where a good fish usually lies. Why this should be so I have never been able to determine—there are many lurking-places which seem equally promising—but the fact remains as a matter of experience. It is borne out to-day. No sooner has the fly alighted on the swirl beneath the little ledge than a great rush comes and the torrent is torn across by a swiftly-moving force. The silvery mass turns and descends, but there is no answering pull on the line. Yet before the great spade-like tail lashes the water into foam, I have seen the fish fairly. Near its head is a curious mark—a whitish patch, triangular in shape. I turn eagerly to Duncan. Has he too noticed the vast bulk of the lost one? He has. Usually cynical in regard to the weight of fish which refuse to be tested by the spring-balance, he is now plainly impressed. He even grows enthusiastic. Never before have his eyes beheld such a salmon in the Oikel River, and he has seen it fished, man and boy, for a span which is well-nigh patriarchal. With this I am content. We will leave this place for a little time. Then we will come back and catch this fish of fish—this giant with the white triangle.

So, in a very brief space, we return. I cast carefully, expecting every moment to see the mighty rush. Then with shortened line I try all the likely water at hand. But nothing comes.

Possibly I have pricked him : in any case I appear to have put him down effectually. After many changes of fly, I leave him with a saddened heart.

After-events are in the nature of an anti-climax. I land two freshly-run fish, clean and silvery, with the sea-lice still adhering to their sides—7 and 8 lb. respectively. At any other time these would have more than fulfilled my usually modest hope. But all the way from the river, through the squares of potatoes and wheat, the vision of the White Triangle still haunts me. I even turn a little im-patiently into the house without waiting the announcement of the weight of our captures. In the evening, when the blazing sun descends behind the western crests, I will try my luck again.

There is something in isolation—in the sense of having a world entirely to oneself—which appeals to me. Duncan is well able to attend to my simple wants. He has sown the scanty crops below us with his own hand, and no alien form lingers about the place. He understands my moods, and never obtrudes himself, though where, in the narrow limits of this house on the hill, he contrives to hide all day when we are not fishing, I have never yet been able to determine. His household duties performed, he weaves fishing nets, I believe, in a dark rat-hole which is also the kitchen ; but the main thing is that he never disturbs me. So it comes that I may smoke on this green summit and survey the valley from the rocky escarpment on the west, to the east, where the sea dances between the hills, with little fear that the solitude will be broken by anything worse than a raven or a hawk. For I have things to think of—to arrange slowly and carefully in my mind—memories which seemed to be forgotten to collect ; dreams to examine in the cold light of reason, and to fit into their place. And all this needs solitude and tobacco. The presence of what is called a companionable man would spell madness. But all sublimity has been knocked clean out of me to-day by that confounded fish with the white triangle.

Forgetting my work, which in town I had persuaded myself was far more important than salmon-fishing, I essay the river in the evening. The sky has clouded over. The air is cooler, and the level reaches of the stream are curled by a gentle breeze. The conditions are ideal. But now a cruel disappointment awaits me. What has become of my vaunted solitude—my sole kingship of this happy valley ? On the opposite shore, over against my cherished pool, a man is standing. He is fishing carefully. I recognise at once the practised hand as his fly goes straight out slightly against the wind, to fall light as thistle-down, on the swirl just beneath the rocky ledge. He too has marked my friend with the white triangle. Why else does he shorten his line and fish so persistently every eddy and backwater at this particular spot ? Black hate arises in my heart, modified a little by the fact that, time after time, his fly comes back fruitlessly. From a hidden recess in the rocks I watch him at work, and my prism glasses bring him almost to my side. Not an ill-favoured fellow, I am bound reluctantly to admit, were he seen in less prejudicial circumstances. He is an old man, surely ; yet his calmly gentle face bears little sign of the fret and turmoil of years. It is the kind of face one sees so often in monastery and convent, and so rarely in town, especially in the vicinity of the Stock Exchange. On the whole, I am compelled to like him, and this gives a new and unwholesome turn to my annoyance, for Hate, like any other active force, is the more satisfactory when it has a strong and definite objective.

Still the fact remains with me as I gloomily lash the lower reaches. Even on this distant acquaintance I find myself summing him up in the brief and only speech of a friend who was suddenly called upon to toast the health of a brother sportsman:—"He's a good sort and a real good fisherman."

But how does he come here? I examine my friend Duncan McQuat upon this point. The answer is so common-place that I am ashamed to have made even a temporary mystery of the matter. Away in the hills at the other side of the river is a shooting lodge with some fishing rights on the Oikel, concurrent with mine. I have heard of them, but have never known them to be exercised, for the distance is great and the lodge itself stands on the banks of a river of far greater repute. It is strange, therefore, that my friend and enemy should have ventured so far, but his right is indisputable. It appears that he is "a learned man" of some kind, seeking solitude, perhaps—a man of cranks and dreams, a little after my own kidney, it may be, barring the "learning," which is a thing I can never be righteously accused of. If so, this may account for the curiously well-defined sense of sympathy which I felt when I first saw him, notwithstanding his unholy occupation. But be this as it may, the glory of the White Triangle must never be his. To-morrow, long before the first sun-rays touch the eastern peaks, I will be down at the river trying that swirl by the ledge.

*   *   *   *   *

Faint dawn. The mist lies sea-like in the ravine, and there is no sign of the Interloper. With slow care, holding my impatience by the throat, I get out the requisite length of line, and my little Jock Scott drops just where I would have it. And this time the great salmon comes. As the torrent lifts, I see his whole shining bulk. This time surely he means business! No: he has missed it . . . the fly comes slackly back, and I curse him for his carelessness with an inconsistency which would be disgraceful even in a schoolboy. All my after-efforts are unavailing. No glimpse of silvery sheen, bearing about it the radiance of the unattainable, greets my vision. One consolation alone the gods vouchsafe to me. The man from the distant lodge—the poor chap must have walked miles—suddenly presents himself on the opposite bank. He draws back instantly, but I am glad to note the malediction in his eyes. Thank heaven, he is mortal after all. But how swiftly the evil leaves him; vanishing from his face like breath from a mirror. Just as he draws back, he smiles a little and slightly raises his cap. The gesture is an infinitely small thing, but I find myself pausing to calculate how much it embraces. A recognition of rivalry, with a full expression of a desire to play the game. Some natural disappointment, of course, but how much real good-will and good sportsmanship! He certainly *is* a good chap. If it were not for the torrent I would cross, and together we would compare notes on the nature of this thrice accursed and illusive Triangle.

So I go back to the white house on the hill. Something in the stranger's face has certainly impressed me. I am an indifferent recluse after all, for I am conscious of a deep desire to see him more nearly. Questions rise in my mind to which I think, unreasonably enough, that this calm-faced man would find pertinent replies. But this I set aside as mere idle fancy. One thing, however, is clear. He is a sportsman and a gentleman, and I also will play the game. For this day at least he shall have the river to himself. We will fight for the White Triangle fairly : or at least as fairly as circumstances will permit. For, after all, his chance is not so good as mine. From my platform of low rocks I can reach the salmon's resting-place without an effort. On his side, the cast is most difficult. The sheer declivity makes a straight approach impossible. He can only command the pool by wading up-stream through a chaos of huge submerged stones, and this is an arduous, and, in view of the coloured water, even a dangerous task. As I smoke my pipe, after my frugal lunch, I wonder how he will fare.

*   *   *   *   *

Midnight. Here, as in Norway, one never keeps very regular hours; day and night are too much alike. Personally, as a rule, I sleep when the sun is hottest or when I have nothing better to do. To-night I have been working and trying at the same time to get rid of a trivial sense of irritation. For earlier in the night I have had an altercation with my sole retainer—Duncan McQuat—a difference ending in bitter words on my part, and in a respectful but mulishly obstinate resistance on his. The matter is still inexplicable to me, and there is nothing much to tell. In the earlier part of the evening Duncan had been down to the river, possibly to observe the movements of the stranger, and later he had come to me, as I thought, for his usual instructions. These instructions were briefly that we should fish the stream early on the following morning. Then, to my surprise, he definitely and flatly refused to accompany me. I asked him why; and, looking back, I saw that the old man was strangely moved. *There was something abroad in the glen : something that moved silently and that the eye saw not.* It was not lawful—(I am trying to give a rough translation of his words, for they were partly in Gaelic)—that he "should go doon tae the feshin' while yet a speerit wass seekin' its rest." And so on indefinitely.

Much of my work happens to lie in the direction of popular superstitions and of the so-called occult, so I pressed for further information. As usual I could get nothing concrete; no fact that the scientific mind could rest upon. The Highland ghost-seer is always an unsatisfactory personage. Just when he becomes interesting, he drifts into intangibility, and ekes out his story with the vaguest references, mostly biblical, and obviously borrowed from the nearest conventicle. Yet on one point the old man had something definite to offer. He had seen the salmon with the White Triangle: it was moving in the pool in eccentric circles; swimming as no right-minded salmon should. "Oppressed by some speerit influence," I had suggested, but Duncan had fallen back into a solemn silence. Still, the incident has given me food for thought. I am sorry that I spoke so sneeringly. There is always the off-chance that there may be something in the Universe outside the limits of my intelligence. I will take a few hours' sleep, and in the early morning I will go down to the river by myself.

Before I turn in, however, I go to the little porch to look at the weather.

  ✻   ✻   ✻   ✻   ✻

I take up my pen to record a strange experience. I shall set down the facts as simply and as briefly as I can. I have said that at about midnight I went to the door of the little porch. In these latitudes, in late summer, it never grows really dark, and in the wan light the mountains and glen and river were clearly visible. Then suddenly I saw my friend of the water-side, ascending the hill. He was walking easily, taking the rise without any apparent effort. Soon he came near. On reflection I see that his manner was peculiar, but at the time it occasioned me no surprise. He came near, but he offered no greeting. I was conscious at once of the sympathetic feeling which exists between old and familiar friends, and which dispenses so easily with all the smaller formalities. It seemed to be the most natural thing in the world that I should be leaning against the little whitewashed porch, smoking a reflective pipe, and glancing from time to time at the pleasant, kindly face of my uninvited guest. Yet we had, at this time, exchanged no word. Something in the outlook, in the spectral mountains and the vale sleeping in the pallid light, gave a cause for conversation. I touched upon a matter of common observation: the unfamiliarity of familiar things when seen at night.

He smiled slightly.

"Yet the mountains are the same," he said quietly. "Science will tell you that their chemical constituents are unaltered. Any apparent difference must arise from some imperfection of the senses, which forbids a man to see things as they are."

I assented; the remark was of course a platitude.

He paused for a little time. "Have you ever been conscious," he went on at length, "when looking on the ordinary phenomena of Nature—the setting of the sun, for example—of a keen sense of disappointment?"

"Many, many times," I replied.

"You have felt, I take it, that there must be something—something wonderful—which you just fail to see."

I shook my head. "My disappointment goes deeper, I fear. The setting sun suggests unimagined glories just beyond my ken; but reflection, and a rudimentary knowledge of atmospheric conditions, warn me that no such glories exist. Hence, I think, arises the depth of the disappointment."

He listened thoughtfully, resting his arm on the little ledge. The day was breaking. In the east, the broken crests of the mountains lay like golden islands in a sea of rose. The pale, delicate face of my unbidden guest seemed almost transparent as he turned, with eager expectancy, to the new light. The thought struck me that his æsthetic perceptions must be abnormally developed; his whole form seemed to be transfigured. A dreamer might well have thought him a fitting inhabitant of these realms of azure and of pearl, so soon, alas! to resolve themselves into common rock and cloud. At length he turned. There was nothing patronising in his manner, yet I felt he was trying to mould unusual thoughts into words suited to my comprehension.

"Has it ever occurred to you," he said, "that you have only five senses? Why five? An arbitrary number, surely?"

I relighted my pipe in silence. I knew instinctively that the mere commonplaces of dialogue were unnecessary.

"You have noted, too, that one sense may corroborate another in some particular. For instance, a blind man may know that an object is round, and sight would merely confirm this impression. But other senses stand entirely alone. No inkling of music can reach you through the channel of the eye. The most exquisite touch fails to reveal the fragrance of the rose."

I acquiesced in silence.

"Imagine, then, a sixth sense—any number of additional senses. Why chain yourself down to this purely arbitrary five? Ah, you cannot! To think of a new sense and of what it might reveal—a sense as distinct from the known five as hearing, let us say, is from seeing, is an impossible feat. Well, well! (He spoke tolerantly as though to a child.) Let us fall back upon the known. If you cannot imagine a sixth sense, you can at least picture the condition of mankind, if they had been deprived of any one of the familiar five. We will cheat the human race of hearing, for example, leaving this channel open to the lower animals, including, if you like, your dull-witted gillie, Duncan McQuat. Now, at least, we shall get a clear view of what your philosophers call the occult. You are out with your dog and suddenly you see that the animal's attention is arrested. His ears prick, his whole attitude is strained. 'That dog *sees* something!' you exclaim. Yet your own eyes survey the long stretch of road, which is clearly void. Soon a wagon turns the distant corner. Now, you ask yourself, how came that dull brute thus to peer into the future? to foreknow this coming event? What mystery is here? No mystery at all, my friend. The dog merely *heard* the rumbling of the distant wheels."

I smoked on quietly. The stranger, as before, seemed to reply to my thoughts.

"But the fact remains that you have no sixth sense. You still live in a world of vague conjecture. Well? Piece together, at any rate, the hints of the unseen which have already reached you—

> The sunset touch,
> The fancy from a flower bell: some one's death,
> A chorus ending from Euripides.

and assure yourself that here at least you have a problem, the solution of which cannot be far away."

He spoke gravely; then quickly he gave a gay little gesture as though he were throwing something aside.

"But I am boring you," he said. "We will abandon abstract philosophy for a while. I want you to catch the salmon with the White Triangle. *You will only need a gaff.*"

I passed with him down the hillside. I felt that I was on the edge of a discovery.

"This is merely a whim of mine," he said. "You will, of course, make no unnecessary fuss about what you will see. It is merely an everyday incident. Try that shallow flat."

We had now reached the side of the Devil's Punch-bowl, where the dark torrent raged beneath the rocks. He did not descend the steep. When I saw him last, he was standing on the upper bank, with a genial, half-whimsical smile playing on his lips.

Armed with the gaff alone, I descended to the flat at the tail of the pool. Soon I saw the salmon, moving in eccentric rings, as Duncan had described. I gaffed it, and found it to be hooked. When I traced the line to its source, I found, held by the weedy rocks, the dead body of the man, still grasping his submerged rod. He must have been already dead when Duncan first saw the strangely moving fish.

STRANGE STORIES OF SPORT

XX.—CANAVAUN

BY M. ALEXANDER

THEY were driving across Kilgurney Bog after an afternoon's fishing —Nugent Sugrue, the Englishman, and old Desmond O'Neill, who, in spite of his seventy odd years, was the keenest sportsman of the three.

He and Sugrue had been talking for the Englishman's benefit, for it was back in the early seventies before Ireland became the hackneyed hunting-ground of the tourist. Moreover, the "Sassenach" had but lately arrived, with his head full of Lever's novels and visionary forty-pounders. The comparative smallness of the salmon and the absence of Leveresque characters inclined him to scepticism about all things Irish. He looked with an eye of suspicion on the "fairy doctor"; he insinuated that Lever exaggerated, that his types were fictitious creations.

"There you're mistaken," said old O'Neill, "he merely caricatured the truth. Pity you didn't know the Antonys of Castle Antony. This place we're crossing now—Kilgurney Bog—always reminds me of 'em. There was never a scrape in the whole of Munster or Connaught but one of them was safe to be in it. They gambled away two big fortunes, and in the year I'm talking of—1827—they were finally and irretrievably broke.

"The family by this time had dwindled down to three—old Morgan Antony, his grandson Jack, and Jack's sister Claire.

"It was the fashion in those days to put children out to nurse. The two young Antonys spent the first four or five years of their

lives with the wife of Phelim Duane, the local 'whisperer'—
'Phelim of the Fairies,' the country people called him—a man who
possessed extraordinary powers of healing. He was the seventh
son of a seventh son and a queer beggar in many ways. I, myself,
have seen him stop the blood from a severed artery. How did he
do it? That's more than I can tell you, but it was the work of a
minute. Ask Sugrue there, he's seen a fairy doctor at work."

Sugrue laughed and shook his head.

"Some secret passed on from father to son, I believe," he
answered; "but it beats any vet. to fathom how they do it."

"Just so," said old O'Neill. "Well, Phelim Duane knew
things that passed all explaining. He could do just what he
pleased with anything that went on four legs: draw rats out of
their holes in broad daylight, whistle a fox to him, catch and handle
a hill pony that had been running wild and untouched on the
mountain since the day he was foaled.

"He wouldn't take money, so people paid him in kind for his
services. Many's the goose and boneen my father's sent him in the
days when he did all the veterinary work of a big stable for us! He
had no children, and for that reason he grew as fond of his foster-
son, Jack Antony, as if he had been his own. He taught them both
some of his secrets, but neither Claire nor Jack would ever divulge
them.

"Now, when Phelim died he had in his possession a black mare
which Walter O'Sullivan gave him, half in payment for something
he did, but chiefly because she'd the devil's own temper, and the
stable-lads were afraid of her. Though she wasn't much to look at,
hardly showed her breeding and carried too short a rein, Phelim
valued her highly, and when he was dying he left her to Jack Antony.

"You know what an Irish county is; everybody takes the
greatest possible interest in the things which concern some other
person, and if there's a horse in the matter they are not to have or
to hold. As soon as it was definitely known that Jack had got the
black mare Canavaun, everybody hastened to tell him how utterly
unmanageable she was: how she had run away with Lady O'Sullivan and backed Walter into the big drain at Castle Sullivan, and
goodness knows what besides; not that any of us believed these
yarns, for we had all seen her carrying old Phelim Duane, but out
of a friendly desire to annoy Jack. In this we failed signally. Jack
returned, in the coolest manner, that he believed the mare *was*
possessed by the devil, and that he would give her to the first man
who could ride her over two fences. A nice challenge for the
county! The worst of it was that Jack scored so heavily in the
long run, for the mare wouldn't let anyone get on her back.

Directly you put your foot in the stirrup the fun began. No one could hold her.

" When John Costello vaulted straight into the saddle, Canavaun bucked herself clear of him and all the tackle as well, inside of two minutes. At his next trial she flung herself down, ironed him out flat, and bolted. They found her the following day near Phelim's old cottage, but after that no one did more than advise Jack to shoot her.

" Jack laughed. ' She carries me and Claire,' he said, ' which is all I want;' and the provoking thing was that he only spoke the truth, for both he and Claire could do what they pleased with her.

" Hands? No, there were several pairs of good hands in the county. Possibly Phelim the Fairy passed on that secret to them among others.

" We had a good season that year, and during November and December Canavaun made many people break the Tenth Commandment. She was as fast as a greyhound and as clever as a cat—a combination I've seen since in just such another weedy little mare. You couldn't throw her down. We all admitted that. The thing we wouldn't admit was her turn of speed. No one denied it more obdurately than I, and no one paid more heavily for being pigheaded.

" It came about in this way. I rode back from hunting one December afternoon with Claire Antony. We had had a blank day, and as my shortest route lay past her hall-door I escorted her home. Castle Antony was one of those houses which some people think are common in Ireland to this day—a great tumble-down barrack of a place, begun forty years earlier by Jack's great-grandfather, and never finished for lack of funds.

" The main staircase was marble. The drawing-room had an acre of parquet floor. The mahogany for the doors had been shipped specially from Honduras, but the third story remained unplastered; the sunset shone straight through its unglazed windows with an extraordinary effect, and the slateless rafters of the roof suggested the skeleton of a dead whale.

" Originally, the building stood in a finely timbered demesne, now, thanks to old Morgan and Jack, every tree had disappeared and 'The Park,' as the country people called it, was bare as the Curragh of Kildare—and grand galloping ground.

" As Claire and I rode into the demesne, through a gap in what had once been a high wall, we were greeted from behind by the shouts of Mr. Antony, who, too delicate to ride, always drove after hounds in a cabriolet.

" ' Hullo, O'Neill! What do you think of the mare?' he cried,

" 'She seems a good sort,' I answered   'Fine fencer, but not exactly a flyer on the flat.'

"Hah! Is that your opinion? Take her up the gallop to the house, Claire; the horses have done nothing to-day. She'd give that bay of yours, O'Neill, two stone, and win as she pleased over any distance."

" 'I doubt it,' I exclaimed, rather nettled.

" 'Try! Try!' said Mr. Antony, with a wave of his hand. 'It is over two miles from here to the house, and no finer galloping ground in Ireland!'

" I laughed, for the suggestion seemed to me utterly ridiculous. Foolish as the old man admittedly was, he could hardly suppose that this weedy little cast-off of Walter Sullivan's could hold her own against Patriot, who was by Waxy, and had won a couple of races in his three-year-old days.

" 'I shouldn't say Canavaun had a turn of speed, looking at her,' I returned; 'but if Miss Antony wants a gallop I'm ready.'

" 'Very well,' said Claire, and as we brought the two horses into line her grandfather added :—

" 'Don't let her get too far ahead of you at first, O'Neill; I want to see what sort of show Patriot will make against the mare.'

" I was young, silly, irritated by Mr. Antony's suggestion, and inclined to look on the whole thing as a piece of tomfoolery; so, just to prove to them what nonsense they were talking, I let Patriot out from the start, intending when he drew away from Canavaun to ease him and finish the performance at a trot.

" Judge then of my surprise and mortification when I found that to shake the mare off was apparently more than Patriot could do. I sent him along as if he'd been going for his life, getting more and more vexed as Canavaun swung beside me, stride for stride.

" After a bit I began to realize that instead of struggling to hold her own and failing, as I had expected, the mare was actually forcing the pace. Presently she passed Patriot without apparent effort.

" 'You wouldn't say Canavaun had a turn of speed, looking at her, would you?' quoted Claire, maliciously, when I at last overtook her, pulled up at the end of the two-mile gallop, having beaten me by nearly two furlongs.

" I was too cross to respond amiably. Patriot's reputation as the fastest horse of his class in the county, a source of great gratification to my youthful pride, must be upheld at all costs, but as the mare had undoubtedly beaten him it was a difficult task.

" 'Look at the difference in the weights,' I protested feebly, to stop Miss Antony's gibes.

"'Oh, a stone isn't much,' she responded.

"'A stone! Why it must be nearer three.'

"'It isn't then. You ride twelve stone. I stand nine, and my saddle weighs two. I really doubt if there's more than eleven pounds between us. There's grandpapa, triumphant, no doubt.'

"Triumphant, old Antony certainly was; offensively so, I should have said.

"I began to think my various elderly relatives, who had cemented my friendship with Jack Antony by warning me solemnly and repeatedly against the whole family, were nearer right than might have been expected, considering their age.

"When the old man remarked, 'A stone won't bring those two together,' it proved the last straw.

"'I'll run my horse against your mare at even weights, over any distance you please, and for any sum you like to name a side, Mr. Antony,' I said.

"'Gad, I'll take you!' he cried. 'Once round the Bog of Kilgurney—that's four miles and a bit—for a thou. a side. Are you on?'

"The Bog of Kilgurney was then the stiffest fenced bit of country in four baronies; reclaimed land, green as an emerald in the hottest summer, and unrideable after heavy rain.

"'Oh, yes,' said I, rather taken aback, and remembering reluctantly that Patriot had once or twice refused the big Kilgurney gripes when hounds were running. There were many courses in the county I would have preferred to Kilgurney, but this, I need scarcely say, I had no intention of admitting. All the same, I honestly believed I should win, and though I felt pretty sure that in that case old Antony's thousand wouldn't be forthcoming, I didn't care about the money as long as Patriot made a show of Canavaun.

"So we settled the match. Once round the Bog of Kilgurney for a thousand pounds a side, each horse to carry 12 stone 7.

"I might either ride Patriot myself or find someone else to do it, and Mr. Antony was at liberty to put whom he pleased on the mare. It was to be a case of play or pay, with the usual condition that if either owner died the match would be off.

"I at first inclined to look upon the whole thing as a joke, but the Antonys soon proved that they took it seriously by producing the thousand pounds in hard cash and nominating old Morgan's nephew—his only respectable relative—stakeholder.

"This surprising feature excited the county nearly as much as the prospective match. Many were the speculations as to where and how old Antony had raised that thou., for even in those·days of innumerable extraordinary wagers, when the average Irishman was ready to fling any money he possessed about like gravel, a thousand commanded respect.

"Of course people began to back me at once, partly on Patriot's reputation, partly on the chance of something happening to Jack, for everyone knew the impossibility of finding a substitute who could ride Canavaun. Well, six weeks or so before the date fixed for the match things took a most unexpected turn.

The O'Dynors of Ballydynor had given a dance, I remember, and the following day the hounds were to meet at Ballydynor cross-roads.

"I was getting into my hunting things about eight o'clock in the morning, when word was brought that Jack Antony wanted to see me in the stable-yard. Down I went, feeling rather cross. Jack, still in his evening clothes, was waiting near the gate on a four-year-old bay colt belonging to Brian O'Dynor.

"'Desmond, I'm in the devil's own mess,' he said, as I came up; 'I've shot George Hicksworth.' I suppose I stared at him open-mouthed, for he went on irritably: 'It was bound to happen sooner or later, no one could have stood the fellow's insolence; but it about settles me. My day's work's done—in this country any way.'

"I understood him then. Duelling wasn't a dead letter, except in theory, at that time, and when I asked a few questions the whole story came out.

"They had started playing hazard at Ballydynor after the dance was over, and apparently George Hicksworth insulted Jack. Now, Hicksworth, whom we all hated, was a cantankerous, quarrelsome fellow, the only son of rich people newly come to the county. When I had last seen him in the small hours of that morning he had been far from sober, and possibly, if Jack had refrained from throwing a glass of claret in his face, things might have adjusted themselves. All that, however, mattered little now, since they had fought on the lawn at Ballydynor by the first grey light of dawn, and Jack's bullet had gone through Hicksworth's brain.

"'I'm off to France,' said Jack, in conclusion, 'following in the footsteps of my cousin, Jim Luttrell. He made Ireland too hot for him seventeen years ago! And unless I run now the Hicksworths will hang me as high as Haman. I only looked in to say good-bye to you, Desmond.'

"What could I say? I was genuinely sorry about the whole wretched business, but it was obvious that Jack must go. I watched him canter away across the lawn. The morning was extremely stormy, with a wild, rising wind which rushed screaming out of the west and, even as I looked, a bunch of flying twigs slapped Brian's colt on the hocks, making him plunge like the devil. Among a medley of other thoughts it struck me that Jack would have a lively ride home.

"You can fancy what a hullabaloo there was all that morning. Hounds were taken back from the meet, and everybody rode to everybody else's house to waggle their heads over the affair and abuse Jack. But by evening the excitement redoubled itself, for it transpired that Jack had been killed on his way home. He was found doubled up under a fallen tree in the demesne at Castle Antony. I shall never forget the shock I got when old Flaghertie, the Castle Antony head man, came in floods of tears to tell me. He brought a letter from Jack's grandfather, asking me to come to him.

"Jack and I had been good friends enough, and I was desperately sorry. I rode off straight to Castle Antony, though it was seven o'clock in the evening. Would you believe it? The old chapel beside the house was all lit up, and through the open door I saw a crowd of country people standing round a coffin on the altar steps. No need to ask the reason! The Antonys were notorious for their bad taste, but I remember wondering how Claire could countenance this vulgar display of poor Jack's body to all the idle gossips of the county.

"I went into the library so disgusted by the atrocious vulgarity of the thing, that when Mr. Antony began his lamentations I couldn't second them.

"And then, quite suddenly, the old reprobate changed the subject and spoke about the match.

"'The match!' I said. 'Surely that's off?'

"'Not at all, not at all!' he exclaimed. 'The mare's mine, I bought her from Jack. Of course I meant to put him up, but I'll get another man now. I thought you'd be thinking that, O'Neill, and so I sent for you.'

"What was I to say? If Jack's death made no difference to his grandfather, I could hardly consider it. The conditions of the match were pay or play—unless of course either owner died.

"I shrugged my shoulders, therefore, took my hat and went out, utterly disgusted by the old man's heartlessness. It was not my business to remind him of the utter impossibility of getting any one to ride the mare. He knew that better than I did; he had in fact seen the useless efforts of every man in the county to get the better of her.

"Jack was buried next day in presence of the whole neighbourhood, including George Hicksworth's father, who came to make certain of the death of his son's 'murderer.'

"No one, of course, troubled about either an inquest or a

doctor's certificate. We were agreeably lax about such matters in Ireland in the year '27. The nearest medical man lived forty miles off, and the coroner had not sufficiently recovered from his latest attack of delirium tremens to do more than catch purple snakes on his bed.

"I avoided the funeral. I avoided the Antonys for the next month. I even avoided the comments of my neighbours who now, to a man, were backing Patriot.

"Claire Antony took to riding Canavaun, but otherwise the mare apparently had no exercise, and the match seemed absolutely certain to degenerate into a farce.

"One day I went to see Claire's grandfather about it. I was quite ready, if he wished, to consider Jack the owner of Canavaun and the match consequently off.

"Old Morgan, however, would not hear of this. I found him admiring the new, handsome, and unpaid-for headstone on Jack's grave; but his demeanour, for all that, bordered on the jocose. He wanted to lay five to one against Patriot in hundreds.

"After that I made some inquiries, and found that Morgan Antony had been raising and borrowing money to right and left to back Canavaun. Those were the days of big gambling, when men smashed themselves in one day at Newmarket or the Curragh, or in one night as the spirit moved them. I began to think old Morgan was playing a deep game, but for the life of me, I couldn't find it out. Every afternoon Canavaun paraded solemnly about the least frequented roads with Claire, draped in black, on her back. She rarely went out of a walk and she never saw a fence. On the face of things, it was any odds against her getting the first mile of the match.

"As it wasn't in human nature to let the matter rest, all kinds of wild rumours began to fly about the county; one that a horse had several times been seen doing a school near Castle Antony in the first grey glimmer of daylight.

"I never gave this tale a thought until one day, a fortnight or so before the match, when hounds ran across the road where Claire and Canavaun were taking their usual walking exercise. Up went the mare's head, she whipped round, flew the low bank, and was off after them like a streak of wind. Claire did her best to pull her up at first, but when she realized who was mistress, she dropped her hands and let Canavaun sail away close to hounds for as grand a fifty minutes as any man ever rode. During that hunt I recalled the story of the early school: no horse as short of work as Canavaun apparently was could have kept a lead and finished comparatively unblown, as the mare did.

240

"But what, in the name of common sense, could old Antony be driving at? That was what I wanted to know.

"The day of the match was grey and misty, and up to the time of starting to Kilgurney I had no idea who was to ride Canavaun.

"In the stables I learnt that a disreputable nephew of Morgan Antony—a certain Jim Luttrell, who had made Ireland too hot to hold him seventeen years earlier—had arrived the previous night from France to ride in the match. I knew Jim Luttrell by repute—most people did! Knew him as a wrong 'un in every way, except on a horse, where he was bad to beat; but I felt pretty certain Canavaun wouldn't have him, for I had seen two of the best men in Ireland tackle her, and the best man to ride in Ireland takes some beating.

"I never felt more confident in my life than I did that morning, as I rode down to the Bog of Kilgurney. You can see how it lies, a great strip of flat green reclaimed land between two ridges of hill. Sugrue here can tell you what it means to get into a Kilgurney gripe!

"That February morning the bog was black with people come to see the match. You know how, even now, a day's racing will gather a big audience in the loneliest part of the island, and in '27 the population doubled its present number.

"Canavaun, who was being walked round in a small ring, took things very quietly, but Patriot resented the crowd, and when I slipped off my hack and walked up to him, I found him sweating as if he had done a hard gallop.

"'He has the heart fretted out of him, sir,' said his lad, Patsey Duane, turning the horse's head in to a high bank. 'Sure I'm after travelling the bog wid him to see would I come at a quiet place he could rest aisy, but every field is throng, and ye'd think he lose his life the way he does be trembling if any of them offers to come near him.'

"This was annoying, but I had anticipated it, for Patriot was one of those nervous, excitable brutes who go literally mad on the slightest provocation, and a crowd always upset him.

"Just at this moment, I saw Jim Luttrell drive up to the potato scales in which we were to weigh. He took no notice of anyone, 'gentle or simple,' and no one quite knew how to greet him after seventeen years' absence under a cloud. In height and build he reminded me of Jack Antony, but he was as dark as Jack had been red. He had a short black beard up to his eyes, black hair, and a strong foreign accent.

"Old Morgan, who was in great fettle, went round informing every one, as an original and exquisite joke, that his nephew 'felt shy,' a remark which finished people already hopelessly embarrassed by the prodigal's return!

241

" As you probably can imagine, we all watched Luttrell with intense interest when he first walked up to the mare. To my dismay and to the horror of most of the county, who had backed Patriot heavily, Canavaun stood like the wooden horse of Troy. People gaped open-mouthed at this phenomenon, remembering her tactics with John Costello and others. Old Morgan suppressed his satisfaction manfully, only informing me in a stage whisper that the mare would go for anyone with ' the family hands,' a piece of nonsense that put the finishing touch to my annoyance.

" Jim Luttrell kept watching me out of the corner of his eye as we rode down to the start, but when I made some remark to him he did not answer.

" I got off badly, but as the start doesn't count for a great deal in four miles, and as I rather wanted a lead over some of the gripes, I didn't much care.

" Patriot was not exactly the horse one would have picked for the job on hand, particularly when he had previously been thoroughly frightened and excited. He pulled pretty hard for the first mile or so, and he jumped as badly as a two-year-old.

" Now, Kilgurney Bog takes some doing. The fields are big, mostly flat as a billiard table, and divided either by a gripe or a wide double with a thorn hedge on the top of the bank, and very often a devil of a drop on the further side, as well as the ditch. A horse can't take liberties with them, and Patriot did—or tried to. He got half way up the banks; he dropped his hind legs twice in a way which involved a desperate scramble, and altogether his rotten fencing took more out of him than he could at all afford.

" Before we'd done much over a mile I realised what an incredible fool I had been—not that I had much time to think about it, for Patriot fought me at every jump. He always wanted to rake his head away and rush the thing sideways, and I knew what that would mean.

" Canavaun, meanwhile, was going like a clock. I can promise you I cursed Jim Luttrell inwardly!

" Patriot came into my hands more after the first mile and a half, and we pegged away steadily, the mare leading by about three lengths.

" There were a lot of people riding, and a lot more running along the hillside, and the country people, of course, clustered like bees on all the banks, yelling encouragement. You know the sort of thing, Sugrue. Well, we were pretty equal when we took the turn for home.

" The finish was all uphill, through four long fields, and Luttrell began to shove his mare along from the bend. My fool had used himself so much at the start that now, when I wanted him, he commenced to hang.

" The last two fences were stone gaps, but between them there was one of those straight-up, narrow, high banks you may see in Duhallow. I had forgotten the bank, and when I saw it confronting me I swore. It was the one fence of all others Patriot was certain to boggle over.

" There were two courses open to me : to steady him and take him at it at the proper pace, in which case it was any odds he refused, or to rush it and chance his falling. I knew Patriot wouldn't face the thing at all unless hustled. He'd had a bad fright as a youngster at just such a place.

" I decided on the fall, got him short by the head, and shoved him at it. He tried to fly the whole thing, changed his mind, and landed on top of it on the girths.

" For a moment I hoped he was going to lurch forward into the next field, and if he had I might have got him on to his legs again and made a fight for it still; but unfortunately he fell back. I slipped off when I felt him going, and hauled him up, for he showed an inclination to lie where he was.

" By this time Canavaun was half-way across the next field.

" I flung myself on to Patriot and shoved him at the bank again. Of course he refused.

" Two or three dozen country people came up, all yelling advice of the most exasperating kind.

" ' Will I have a couple of skelps on him, sir ? ' ' It 'd be as well for yer honour to get over quickly the way the other haarse wouldn't have, ye bet ! ' ' Take care ! Is he tired, sir ? He'd be apt to fall on ye ! ' And last, but certainly not least, ' Slip off, yer honour, till we try could we entice him over. Sure, he has the cross look about him—'tis what he'd distroy ye, av ye went to lep him at it ! '

" I cursed them all impartially as I took Patriot back five yards, and sent him once more full tilt at that confounded bank.

" This time he jumped wildly, hit it with his chest, and went over, head first, like a shot pheasant.

" The country boys followed gleefully, dragged us both seven ways at once, and put the last touch to my annoyance by imploring me to walk the remaining three fields and let them lead the horse.

" ' His honour does be very handy with his talk ! ' I heard one remark, as I galloped off.

" Canavaun passed the ' post '—a certain stunted Scotch fir— before I reached the next fence.

"To say old Antony was jubilant is to describe things most inadequately.

"'Ha, ha! my dear O'Neill, the old 'uns sometimes know something—I'm not such a bad judge of a horse after all!' he kept repeating again and again, and he went round, pursuing all the people who had cut Jim Luttrell twenty years before, and calling on them to admire his nephew's riding.

"I wanted to have a few words with Luttrell, but, having weighed in, he disappeared immediately, which seemed natural enough under the circumstances.

"Only one point about the proceeding puzzled us all. Why had Canavaun gone so kindly for Jim Luttrell?

"That mystery was elucidated about a year later.

"Morgan Antony died in the interval, and there was a great sale at Castle Antony—a mighty gathering of the creditors.

"The evening before the old place was put up for auction, Claire Antony, to my great surprise, came and asked to see me.

"Directly the drawing-room door shut behind the man, she said—

"'Sir Desmond, I've come to tell you that Jack is alive—his death and funeral were all a sham!'

"I stared at her open-mouthed, and she went on.

"'Grandpapa arranged it all, when he heard how Jack had killed George Hicksworth—he said it was the only way to settle matters, for no one else could ride the mare.

"'We spread the report that Jack had been killed in the park, and he lay in the chapel, as you saw. He was under a sheet in the coffin, with flowers and things over him; and, as nobody touched him, there was very little chance of his being detected. He did it splendidly; lay so quiet that even Mr. Hicksworth had no suspicion.

"'Grandpapa and I were to screw the coffin down—it is a family custom, you know.' She paused, shivered slightly, and then went on. 'We filled it with books, and we hid Jack in the upper story.'

"'But the servants?' I interrupted.

"'Oh, they knew—at least, old Cassidy and Mary Regan knew—but they were safe. Grandfather said Jack must ride the mare—so——!'

"'Then Jim Luttrell,' I cried, bursting in on her narrative ruthlessly, 'was Jack?'

"She nodded. 'Yes. Hair dye and a beard altered him out of all recognition. He used to ride the mare in her gallops very early in the morning—my exercise was only a blind. We sent him away three nights before the match, so that he might come back on the Dublin coach. You see, no one else could ride Canavaun!'

"'So I thought!' I exclaimed. 'Where's Jack? I must see him.'

"'On, no, no! He mustn't know that I ever told you. He's abroad, and I'm going to join him; but I—I—hated myself for the trick we played on you. If there'd been any real fraud about the match, I'd have told you beforehand in spite of them—but the mare won fair and square, on her merits. She ran fair and was ridden fair.'

"Claire paused again, and added: 'Jim Luttrell died six years ago. I think that's all I had to say—except to beg your forgiveness.'

"Of course, I reassured her on that point; I think I even told her I'd have helped if I had known what was going forward.

"On the whole, when I came to think things over, I was not so much surprised as you might suppose—it was just what one might have expected from an Antony."

STRANGE STORIES OF SPORT

XXI.—THE CATASTROPHE OF THE "FEATHER"

BY C. EDWARDES

I.

THE balloon rose and the lady said, "Oh, we're off!" But the balloon's captain and lord didn't heed his companion's primary emotions. He had emotions enough of his own. He was looking down upon a pair of dark eyes, the mirthless smile of which faded for him all too soon: the atmosphere claimed him, his associate, and his steedless chariot with an insidious celerity which soon reduced the loved face to little more, for him, than one tiny white upturned oval among others.

"How enchanting, Mr. Capell!" exclaimed the lady, with a sigh as of rapture.

"Y-es," said he. He tossed his straw hat into the car's basket, glanced up and round about him, and then looked straight at Miss Jessamine Rodd, with a smile as devoid of levity as the girl's beneath him—she was already three hundred feet beneath.

"And you *must* forgive me, Mr. Capell," the lady went on. She was evidently a prey to conflicting desires. The supreme one was to make the most of the sights and sensations incident to the adventure. But she held this in check, and now met her companion's gaze with an expression in which sympathy of a sort and iron-plated conscientiousness might have been discovered. "I could not possibly permit Dorothy to come with you. I'm an old-fashioned woman, and, besides, her heart—its valves—are not very strong. It *is* a strain on the heart, is it not, in the rarefied air?"

"We shouldn't have gone that high," said he.

"Ah! but you know the chief reason, Mr. Capell: you must know it. How exquisite it all is! Motion without effort or sound. A suspension of earthly trials and a foretaste of—— "

"Heaven's bliss!" said he. "I'm glad you like it. Tell me when you've had enough."

She craned her head earthwards, and Nigel permitted himself the indulgence of a sardonic curl of the lip as he contemplated the slab of purple cheek and the large ear of his enemy. No one could at any rate have acted so inimical a part towards him. She had a straw thing on her head shaped like an oyster shell, bandaged to her chin by a grey dust-veil; and in her hands were the notebook and pencil with which she proposed to record her impressions. They should be few, those impressions. Dorothy's Aunt Jessamine, though not tall, was built on heavy lines. Neither the "Feather" (his car) nor the "Feather's" lord would submit for many minutes to so unwelcome a burden. And then, with a gasp and a plain (very plain indeed), wide-eyed stare at him, Miss Jessamine Rodd confessed that she was unnerved.

"I shouldn't have thought it possible, Mr. Capell," she whispered, "but I—I feel—I declare I feel *frightened*. The thought of so much space—empty space—under the very soles of my feet, and of what would happen if—— '

"Oh, but it won't," he interrupted. "The conditions are perfect. I should not otherwise have arranged to take Dot."

Unnerved or not, Miss Jessamine Rodd started and set herself squarely towards the aeronaut on her camp stool.

"You must not call her by her Christian name, Mr. Capell," she said.

He folded his arms. The car caught a more positive puff of wind than hitherto, and swayed to it. He swayed with it, like an old salt on a rolling ship. His companion uttered a little cry and grasped the rim of the basket as if her life were at stake. And then all was serene and vertical again, with nothing but the blue ether about them. The old feeling of contempt for commonplace human existence on that mud spot they had left recurred in Nigel. He was as free as any bird. The glorious blue air was nectar and ambrosia to him. He was less man than god. And she—this one unpleasant link which connected him with the earth he despised and pitied at such times—she presumed to enunciate laws of conduct for him!

"I happen to love your niece, Miss Rodd," he said, calmly, "and she loves me. We have every intention of marrying, and neither you nor any absurd *ex parte* matrimonial arrangement of her late father's shall stand in the way. I'm afraid that sounds theatrical, but it conveys my sentiments."

"You speak like a Capell, Mr. Capell," said the lady, "but I am sure you will also act like one. A Capell of Moss Court has a reputation to maintain. Poor Sir Barker Brown——"

"Oh," cried Nigel, lifting a clenched fist, "I don't care *that* for Barker Brown." He brought the fist into his other palm with a whack. "Neither does Dot. The fellow must find someone to teach him sense if he hasn't got any of his own. Does he think, and do you, that girls grow up like—er—asparagus, to be cropped without more voice in the matter than that?"

"It is an honourable obligation, Mr. Capell. Families like ours are bound by their birthright to take broader views of life than ordinary persons. Dorothy herself, from her thirteenth year, has fully understood the advantages of her destiny. But—this is all very painful to me. Such a waste of my opportunities too, Mr. Capell."

He controlled himself well.

With the words "What ancient stuff!" breaking from his lips, and his brain aboil with impatience, he could yet remember the lady's natural interest in the adventure upon which she had foisted herself.

"Let us change the subject then," he said, courteously. "I'm sorry I can't take you to the sun or the moon, but we'll see what we can do. If you want to write, don't mind me."

He tossed out sand. Miss Rodd said "O-h!" as she watched the grains scatter into apparent nothingness. She gazed with agitated breath at the blurring medley of patches and lines now nearly a mile beneath her; then at the blue sky, and then at Nigel himself. Nigel was busy with his instruments.

"It's wonderful," she whispered.

"Wind's shifting nicely to the south," said he. "We might run a whole day or so before a south wind. That's the worry of living on an island. You've always to be thinking of the sea. But a south's all right. Those chimneys down there are Chesterfield, I believe. We've gone up like the feather we are because we're a couple of ethereal individuals, I suppose; but there isn't much driving power in the wind."

He sat down, and it was as if already he had cast overboard his trouble about Dorothy as easily as that sand. His smile was one of good fellowship. Dorothy's objectionable aunt seemed displaced by someone else—a colleague in his own enthusiasms.

" It's a record afternoon for this kind of thing," he added.

" And it's so enchanting, Mr. Capell!" said Miss Rodd, as if she also were only too willing to leave earthly cares to the earth. "I'm not in the least afraid now. Please to smoke if you wish— Oh, I forgot ! How inconsiderate of me ! (He had pointed cheerily to the " Feather's " great gas bag above them.) I ought to shudder at the thought of such a danger, but I—I feel only as if I could live on like this for ever."

" Yes ? " said he, and he couldn't help it if it flashed to him that this was the very sensation he had hoped to evoke in Dorothy her-self. Being involuntary, there was nothing ungenerous in the flash. " That's the beauty of the sport, Miss Rodd. It transfigures a man, and is death on brain cobwebs. But I'm sure you want to be writing. I'll read the paper while you're at work."

Someone had pitched a newspaper into the car when it was about to be released. He had had no time to devote to terrestrial news all the morning. The gas people had bothered him. Social responsibilities and Dorothy were also in his way. Chief of all, there had been the stirring anticipation of the afternoon's pleasure, when he and Dorothy were to be alone far above the heads of the world for so long as he chose. But this aunt (Dot's guardian) had suddenly turned up and—well, things were as they were. Instead of a foretaste of the joys of honeymoon in a sublime solitude of two, there sat Dorothy's determined aunt, and here sat he ! Miss Jessamine's pencil began to plunge ; and, over his paper, the aero-naut watched her.

Was that, he asked himself, how she manufactured the novels which had made her so passably famous ? She wrote and wrote. Now and then her eyes turned upon him, only to revert promptly to her note-book. Her mind was evidently teeming. He interrupted her once.

" Do you know, Miss Rodd," he said, gently, " I think you ought to be rather grateful to me."

" Yes," she said, " I am. It's perfection. I never dreamed I should be so fortunate. But I—I mustn't talk. I have so much to visualise with my *mind's* eye, Mr. Capell."

Her business-like smile with the words interested him. On earth it had seemed to him that she seldom troubled to take him into serious consideration. He began to understand. That mind's eye of hers had perhaps stood in the way of her fleshly pair of eyes, spectacles included. Any other girl's guardian would surely have perceived the developing, if not the very birth-moment, of his love for Dorothy. She, preoccupied soul, had assumed that Dorothy's future was as precisely mapped out as the vicissitudes of her own paper puppets. From Dorothy's report of her aunt's fiction, it was impossibly romantic stuff. And this was the woman to whom was committed the charge of steering Dorothy's sweet life to the haven which best befitted it !

He dropped the paper and put his foot on it; welcomed the freshening air current, jettisoned more sand, and yet more, and marked the westering of the sun in that hot white blue of its own particular environment. And still the lady remained in thrall to her inspirations.

"I'm afraid I'm disgracefully unsociable, Mr. Capell," she glanced up suddenly to remark, her eyes sparkling now with an electricity of exultation. But he read their appeal aright and humoured her.

"Not at all; my time's yours," he said.

"One's perspective of things is so marvellously altered, I find, when one is outside them—above them, I mean."

"I'm glad," he said, smiling, "you agree with me to that extent. Off the earth like this, its little bothers and cantrips don't seem worth fussing about, do they?"

"Ah!" she exclaimed. "So you have made *that* discovery also. How very extraordinary!"

"Yes, it's much like discovering a chop or a steak under one's nose when one has ordered it from the waiter, you know. Is that rude? I hope not. This is about my fortieth ascent. I want you to realise that I'm seasoned to the jokes of skyflying."

She nodded her acquiescence in his point of view and resumed her scribbling. He caught himself yawning twice in a minute or two. Well, who could wonder? It had been an exciting day, with a certain flatness in its outcome, and Nature was reminding him that he could well afford to feel tired. It wasn't as if Dorothy were opposite to him. At the third yawning fit he made an effort.

"Pardon me, Miss Rodd, but if I drop off to sleep, will you wake me?" he asked.

She gazed at him with sphinx-like solemnity.

"Yes, of course," she replied.

"It's a day in a hundred, with every promise of a night to match it, but I don't suppose you'd care to make Iceland by breakfast time."

"Iceland!" she murmured. She looked over the basket and then at him. "*Could* we do that?"

"Not at this rate. Pretty well if we sighted Inverness. But (he yawned again)—oh dear, pray excuse me—I'm wondering what scandal would get into the newspapers if we did chance to be benighted."

The lady's sphinx-like calm broke all to pieces.

"Don't be so monstrous," she laughed.

"Very well," he said, giving her laugh for laugh. "I repeat, I'm in your hands and—Ah! another rush of beautiful thoughts. I'm a dumb dog, Miss Rodd."

She was writing anew as if her salvation depended upon her pencil's speed when he yawned again; this time with eyes shut, bent head, and folded arms. A very little later he nodded and nodded and nodded.

The "Feather" sailed on, and the sun began already to draw its bedtime gold around it.

II.

When he opened his eyes darkness reigned. He had been dreaming strangely. It was a steeplechase, and his mount's antics were something incredible. He had a passion for horses as well as ballooning, and was known as a daring and successful rider. But this horse! *Was* it a horse or an intoxicated sea serpent? So far as he could judge, he was leading in the race; at least there was no one else in front of him; but the thing's gyrations and undulations discomposed him so that there was no room in him for triumph of the familiar kind. It had got out of hand. The more he pulled to restrain it, the worse it heaved; and it was at the crest of one of its most astounding bounds when he awoke.

Darkness reigned. Nevertheless, there was a faint silvery light nearly overhead where the masses of inky cloud were lothe to coalesce; and by this momentary gleam he saw the balloon's bag dart forward as if it were trying to shake free of the encumbrance of its car. The car swung after it with a jerk that almost sickened him.

Without even an exclamation, he reached for the cord and opened the valve. Then he remembered.

"Miss Rodd," he shouted, "what's the matter?"

She lay in the well of the basket at his feet. A regiment of anxieties charged at him. They had struck a hurricane, or something like it. The "Feather's" caracolling was simply awful. The wind above the basket threatened to blow his head off and fought with the escaping gas to drive it back. He understood this risk and let the cord go. The "Feather" was a fine-weather lady. Her silk was not meant to be a battlefield for contesting vapours in a temper. He had never been in such an unholy mess. And—was the lady dead? He dropped on his knees by her.

"Miss Rodd!" he cried. That silvery gleam had gone and all was dark now. But he found her neck and supported her head on his arm, laid his ear to her mouth, and was comforted to find breath in her. A little brandy did wonders. She struggled against it, but he forced some between her teeth, and presently she could speak.

"What *have* I done, Mr. Capell?" she wailed, when he had roused her mind by a more or less jocose report on the situation.

"Fainted, I expect," he said. "There!" He propped her against the sandbags. "Don't get up. I—haven't the smallest idea where we are, or what time it is, or anything. Can you help me? What happened to you?"

He felt her tremble violently in the curve of his still-supporting arm.

"Oh, Mr. Capell!" she sobbed.

"Pray don't distress yourself," he said, soothingly. "Try and drink another spot or two."

"I'm an abstainer—a total abstainer," she exclaimed, reproachfully. "I—but I deserve it all. I—this darkness terrifies me. I remember now. I overtaxed my strength. It occurs sometimes when I write for long without a rest. I felt it coming over me and tried to call out to you, and before I could touch your arm I must have fallen. Oh, Mr. Capell, how ashamed of myself I am!"

"I see," he said. "Never mind. We must wait till the clouds roll by, as the song bids us. It's something to go on with that you're not dead. Do you know, you gave me one of the worst quarter-minutes or so I've ever had. I wish I knew what the wind was doing with us. What an ass I was to tumble off like that! Oh, it's no good; we *must* get down a bit."

He stood up and, clutching the stays and rim of the basket, strained his eyes and ears towards the nether void; then, seizing his chances in the lulls of the storm, managed to part with a few hundred cubic feet of gas.

"It's an experience anyway—something for you to write about for those dear stay-at-home souls asleep in their warm beds!" he shouted in an interval of his toil.

His tone was quite blithe now. He was no coward at any time, and face to face with his responsibilities he nerved himself for the duel with circumstances. No doubt his nap had done him good, untimely though it was. If Miss Rodd had been dead, he would have felt in a very bad way; but, as it was, the main thing he wanted to know was where they were. If the wind had shifted and swept them out to sea—— But he wouldn't contemplate that calamity until it was forced upon him.

Miss Rodd among the sandbags interjected penitent words off and on. Later, her remorse gave way to admiration.

" How splendid men are in emergencies ! " she said.

" We're meant to be. We're not much good if we can't be," he laughingly replied to that.

She even had a mild attack of philosophy.

" At least, Mr. Capell," she said, hoarsely, when he had just proclaimed his belief that the dawn would soon break, " I can assure myself that I am dying in brave company, if we are meant to die together. I had no idea your character was so full of resources and—nobility."

"Nobility be bothered ! " said he. "Any fool would cling to a straw to save his life. I'm doing the only thing there is to do : letting off steam and—hoping."

" Yes, hoping," she echoed.

" They're feather-weight hopes, you know, Miss Rodd, but I daresay they'll be enough for us. I don't know how you feel, but I could eat some breakfast. We've missed a dinner as it is, but it is quite permissible for weak human flesh to long for—breakfast."

" Yes," said Miss Rodd.

Then, for a spell, there was silence between them, and Nigel's thoughts flew to Dorothy. He did not know it, of course, not being accomplished in thought-reading, but Miss Rodd's own mind was also engaged with her niece. If she had not thus come upon the scene, Dorothy's little pleasure-trip would have ended with all conventional seemliness, and she—she herself—would be asleep in bed. Well, it was her own fault. She deserved all that had come upon her and was to come. But he, Nigel Capell—supposing his death were to lie upon her conscience, whether in this world or the next !

The wind, though fierce, was not now so vicious as an hour ago ; and day was at hand. They were lowering in the atmospheric world. This was certain. While he carefully paid out gas, Nigel again and again endeavoured to see things. His watch had stopped, and so had Miss Rodd's. He was quite prepared therefore for surprises when his eyes could do their work. They might have travelled hundreds of miles. At any moment he was ready now for the rhythmic voice of the sea, to hint of doom or salvation, as Fate pleased. But it was, in his opinion, very like Fate to spring the least expected of surprises upon him. In the stealing greyness, he suddenly beheld a dark something loom, if he might guess, not a hundred yards ahead of the car, almost in line with it. He dashed at a sandbag, heaved it over, and then another. The mysterious something was just avoided, and, looking back at it, he proclaimed his news.

"We're in the land of mountains, Miss Rodd. That was a near shave. A cairn on the top too. It would have knocked us silly. But we're all right now. It's Scotland, I'll warrant. And I'm going to land first chance."

They could see each other now. Miss Rodd ventured to rise to her feet.

"Thank God!" said she. "Thank God, Mr. Capell."

And then, almost ere the words were out of her mouth, there was a startling commotion above them. A dull explosion, followed by a hissing sound, and a sudden oblique movement of the "Feather" which made Miss Rodd scream in fear, as she collapsed into the car's well again.

"A rip, by all that's unlucky!" cried Nigel. "Never mind; stay where you are and trust our stars. We mayn't have far to fall anyway, and ——"

But it was no time for talk. The "Feather's" movements became increasingly erratic and alarming. Nigel clung to the braces, ready for anything. Glimpses of other mountain-tops were showing to the left—the left one moment, the right the next, the next after that in front—no, behind. Reckonings and anticipations were futile in the midst of these mad whirling kicks and capers of the balloon.

The speed of the fall became greater. Miss Rodd shrieked and shrieked. Nigel cried, "Don't do that!" and then felt sorry. The poor woman was being tumbled about among the four or five remaining sandbags. He also, as touching his legs. But this was nothing. The end would soon come now, whatever it was.

And then the earth seemed suddenly to rise up and butt at the poor "Feather." The shock tossed them all high—balloon, inmates, and sandbags. For a few earnest seconds everything seemed indeterminate again. There was water, dark water, underneath; a spot of land with trees on it; more water; and then, with a crash, the "Feather" brought up in the midst of trees, and Nigel found himself gripping the bough of a Scotch fir with one hand, resolved that nothing should make him loose it, while with the other he was still fast to a brace of the balloon. He watched the detached remains of the "Feather's" bag sail away, and realised that they were saved.

The car was on the whole quite handsomely forked into this particular tree, which was very strong and not so very high. Yet though they were not more than twenty feet from the ground the task of getting Miss Rodd comfortably to the heather and granite of the surface was both long and arduous. Tokens of the risen sun had shown crimson on a mountain-top ere he could cry, "There, Miss Rodd, that's something to be thankful for."

He had lowered her with the poor " Feather's " ropes as carefully as if she were Dorothy herself. She looked very anguished throughout the ceremony. As for her weight, it was of the dead kind.

"Here ends a jolly bad business!" mused Nigel. He wiped his face and prepared to follow Miss Rodd in much more haphazard fashion.

III.

"Well, Miss Rodd, I'm sorry I can't do better for you than this."

It was two hours or so after their fortunate escape with sound limbs from the perils of the night, and the sun's radiance was all over the lake. A hot day had begun. Miss Rodd was nested among heather and bracken under a thin wisp of a birch tree, with the placid water close to her boots. She had recovered her presence of mind and even something of her spirits, and was looking much less haggard and ancient than in the first half-hour of her sojourn on the island. Nigel offered her about ten bleaberries in the trough of a leaf. He felt pretty fit, considering. While Miss Rodd was composing her nerves, he had bathed on the other side of the island. This over, and a first survey of their surroundings giving no promise of immediate rescue, he had taken chivalrous thought of the lady's necessities. The berries among the granite were the result of his investigation. She smiled the smile of a convalescing invalid and accepted his gift.

"It is more than I merit," she said. Her voice was still tremulous, but her eyes were kind.

"By no means," he demurred. " Few women would have gone through it so well. But it's a shameful poor breakfast to offer to a lady; especially remembering that yesterday's luncheon was your last square meal. I sincerely hope it *was* a square meal, Miss Rodd."

She seemed to wince at the words, and her smile vanished.

"Was it, Miss Rodd?" he insisted.

"No," she said. "I was too anxious to put a stop to—you know what, Mr. Capell. You are heaping coals of fire upon my poor head. But I will be quite candid with you and tell you that the moment I got home and learnt what Dorothy was going to do, I—drove straight to Moss Court."

"Good heavens! Without luncheon?"

"I snatched a sandwich and a glass of wine."

"And that is all you have had since breakfast this time yesterday! Oh! It's worse than I thought. I must go on Robinson Crusoeing."

"Mr. Capell!" she exclaimed, when he was climbing afresh into the upper scrub of the island.

"Yes?"

"Do eat one or two of them yourself."

"Not for worlds," he laughed. "Who can say when you will get your next berry? Besides, I have a gill or so of cognac left. Only fancy my making you break the pledge last night! You haven't forgiven me that, I expect. Well, *au revoir*. I can't be long."

Miss Rodd shook her head at him and watched him scramble out of sight. But instead of looking for berries, Nigel sat on the highest rock-point of the island and renewed his scrutiny of the lake's shores. It was a charming lake, as a lake. Perhaps three miles long by from a mile to a few yards in breadth. There were four islets to it, and they were on the largest. But—and this was the fact that annoyed him—their island was in the middle of the lake, at its widest part. Unfortunately he could not swim. Not that this ought to matter in a civilised and well-peopled country like Great Britain. Rescue could surely be a question only of hours. Nevertheless, supposing no one came to the lake! It was compassed by very picturesque mountains, with the suggestion of lower lands only in one direction, where its waterway narrowed towards a parting in the hills; but there was not a sign of human habitation. Heather and grass and bracken patches, some shading of birch trees in two places, pinkish sand to the lake's shore; but not the ghost of a cottage.

Nigel knew quite enough of the wilds of the Highlands to know that there were such lochs as this, bedded in the mountains, on which for days in succession no human being set eye.

Now supposing——

But he had no patience to contemplate such a supposition. It had been an absurd last day or so, plus an element of the tragic which now in retrospect seemed only an added strain of the ridiculous. The situation of himself and Miss Jessamine Rodd marooned indefinitely on a Scottish loch, with nothing to eat and unable to help themselves, might become tragic in real earnest; but just at present the thought of its farcical side most affected him. It irritated him exceedingly. Why in the world hadn't he learnt to swim? Scanning his horizon with bent brows, he now discerned something. Four—no, five shapes outlined on one of the hills, the leader with a branch to its head! A stag and hinds, of course. Well, there was no comfort in them. They only proved that the island, like the mountains, was part of somebody's deer forest. The stalking season hadn't begun, and—why, it worsened the odds against a speedy rescue! The deer were an assurance of the dearth of human beings in the neighbourhood. His and Miss Rodd's lives might depend on the mere mood of a gamekeeper. If the man were a lazy fellow neglectful of his march, in a fortnight's time there would be two corpses on this wretched little island, unless of course in the meantime they decided that it were better to commit suicide by drowning.

He found a few more berries and returned with them to his fellow sufferer. She was writing ; her straw dish-cover hat was laid aside, and her long grey hair, spread upon her shoulders, stirred in the gentle breeze which had crept to the lake.

" Well ? " she said, greeting him with a very pleasant smile.

" Well ! " said he. " What a comfort a ruling passion must be, Miss Rodd ! "

She nodded and smiled still more pleasantly. " Yes, Mr. Capell. The work I did yesterday in the balloon was—though I say it— very good. Excitement stimulates the brain. Even the want of food, in moderation, is no bad thing intellectually. I never remember being so full of ideas."

" Really ! " said he. " Then I am perhaps in the way ? "

Her smile now became as sunny as the lake itself.

" I'm not," she whispered, " likely to be so ungracious as to say so, but if you *could* let me write for half an hour alone, Mr. Capell. You don't know what it means to an author : the pride and animation of feeling—as I do at this moment."

" I can guess," he said. " And I obey."

Again he betook himself to the island's summit. This time he had a practical inspiration. What more easy than to build a bonfire and light it ?

In less than Miss Rodd's prescribed half-hour, the island smoked like a sacrifice. The supply of half-rotten wood—alder, birch, and fir—was ample, and the last year's bracken fronds were as tinder to the pile.

He rejoined his companion. She welcomed him with all the goodwill imaginable, pocketed her note-book, and asked about the smoke.

" A distress signal," he told her.

" Oh, I see. But isn't there anyone in sight, anywhere ? "

" Judge for yourself," he replied, with a shrug and a wave of the hand.

"But there soon will be—surely ? "

" Who can say ? " said he.

Then, sitting by her, he gave her the other berries, and told her how sorry he was that his education, physically, had been neglected. He hoped she believed, he said, that he was ready to do anything in the world that was possible to get her out of the scrape, but it were worse than useless for a man unable to swim to attempt to swim. The only ally he could think of was the balloon's basket in the tree. By caulking that somehow he might make it lakeworthy, paddle ashore, and then hunt for help. Meanwhile, they must simply hope.

She seemed much more interested than alarmed by his gravity and the hints conveyed in his words.

"I wonder—" she said, and then stopped and looked at him, archly.

"Yes?" said he, still heavy with anxiety.

"—if I should shock you very much, Mr. Capell. You think no one may come for hours and hours. Well, we should get weak, shouldn't we, fasting so long a time? I feel quite strong now, and I'm sure I could swim the distance."

"You!" he cried.

"Yes. I have always been fond of swimming. Oh, it would be nothing for me to undertake, I assure you. Don't look so concerned. But, of course, there are inconveniences which—well, they would have to be made the best of. Mr. Capell, you are in command of this expedition; shall I do it?"

He was about to protest against such a step; but, turning his head, leaped to his feet instead, and pointed.

"*What* have I done?" he gasped.

Tongues of flame were springing amid the tree-trunks above them. There was no need for Miss Rodd to tell him what he had done. He rushed at the mischief, only to rush back and bewail his carelessness. And with him came a cloud of smoke, telling of a change of wind which would soon make that side of the island untenable.

"Miss Rodd, I'm a fool!" he declared. "With this breeze we shall be burnt out to a certainty. The water's shallower on the other side. Come. We may have to take to it in self-defence."

But Miss Rodd's mind was now made up.

"Go away, Mr. Capell," she said, "for two or three minutes. I mean to swim it. I wish I could feel sure of being able to take you with me, but it would be unwise to run that risk perhaps. You understand?"

She offered him her hand and he accepted it humbly.

"I shall be all right," he said. "But you have *no* doubt about yourself?"

"None, Mr. Capell. And you?"

"I can get twenty yards into the water on that other side. It's a shoal."

" Then, if you please, Mr. Capell, give me my directions, and say good-bye."

" You *will* ? " he asked, still holding her hand.

" My dear man, it is no more to me than walking a mile. Do believe that. What shall I do when I am on shore ? "

He pointed to the end of the loch and the nether valley there suggested, and with a lively nod and a last smile (replete with friendliness) Miss Rodd released her hand.

" There's no time to lose," she said. " Be as brave as you were last night, and all will be well. Run away, Mr. Capell, and don't get roasted."

With a parting word of advice and caution, Nigel began to work round the island's coastline, as far as possible from the heat and smoke of the conflagration. But Miss Rodd had something more to say to him.

" Mr. Capell," she called. " Don't look round, please, but I want you to know that I—I have altered my mind about Dorothy's future. You deserve her. Good-bye for the present. That's all."

" Thank you," he shouted. " Thank you, Miss Rodd."

Another quarter of an hour, and from the western cape of the island he watched her cleaving the water with strong strokes. She had a bundle on her head, and was in all respects a figure such as the lake had probably never before seen in its midst. But there was no doubt about her powers as a swimmer.

He watched her to the mainland, roared a " Well done ! " which did not reach her, and then changed his standpoint. The flames were licking all over the body of the island, with greedy noises. It was time for him to take to the water on its shallow side and there stand like a hot and otiose cow, knee deep or so, until the island had burnt itself out.

IV.

He was thus in the water, smoking his pipe and very far indeed from miserable, when the final stage in the adventures of the last day and night opened to him. Miss Rodd had been absent about four hours. Now he saw her returning, accompanied by two men, curiously burdened. The men looked like walking mushrooms as they climbed into full view by that evident waterway from the foot of the loch. Their mushroom heads were in fact a couple of Berthon boats, and with these Nigel's rescue was easily managed.

Only three miles down the valley Miss Rodd had come upon a fine shooting lodge, with another and larger lake below it ; and every necessary help was soon procured. From the shore she watched the man in one boat towing the other, even as Nigel had watched her earlier in the day. She was in such gay spirits that the other man, who stayed with her, didn't know what to make of her. If her tale was to be believed, she ought to be an exhausted woman instead of what she was. She laughed and wrote in her little book; but her eyes were never for long off that short procession across the water. That Nigel was no cinder she knew, of course, full well. The waving of his pocket-handkerchief from the edge of the island ash-heap had been her best sensation of the last hour.

"Good morning," said Nigel to the boatman when they were alongside. "I'm in luck."

The man assented, with raised eyebrows at the charred island.

"I was to give you this from the lady, sir," he then said, "for she is sure you will be gey hungry." It was a neat little packet of sandwiches, garnered at the lodge. But there was more than that. A sprig of white heather was thrust between the string and the paper of the packet.

"Ah!" said Nigel, with a sigh of happiness, as he put the heather in his buttonhole. "I *am* in luck. I'm the luckiest beggar on this earth. As for eating, I don't want anything yet."

They made careful haste to the shore, and Miss Rodd's own hand helped Nigel from the boat.

"What do you think of me?" she asked him, looking almost handsome in her honest womanly pride. "But there, I'm not fishing for compliments. You may (and she whispered this) tell Dorothy if you think I'm worthy to be her aunt and—yours, Mr. Capell."

Nigel kissed Miss Rodd's hand by the side of the loch in token of his esteem and gratitude.

"I'm truly glad," he said, "that *you* were my passenger yesterday."

STRANGE STORIES OF SPORT

* XXII.—THE CLAN OF THE FOOTLESS

A Tale of Kashmir Shikar

BY FRANK SAVILE

MAINWARING stirred uneasily in his sleeping bag. A pebble was grooving a hollow beneath his shoulder-blade and chafed him into wakefulness. His eyes blinked up at the mighty cliffs, and on beyond them to the shine of eternal snows. The first glint of sunrise was touching the great ridge which closed the valley, and its rays outlined half a dozen dark objects against the dazzling white. Mainwaring blinked again, for the dark objects appeared to move. He slipped out of his bag and reached for his binoculars. He focussed them and breathed an ecstatic sigh. He turned to nudge Sitka, his Balti tracker. The man was already alert. He stood up, shading his eyes and following the direction of Mainwaring's gesture.

He nodded.

"Ibex!" he announced, and for a moment was silent. He gave a peculiar shrug of the shoulders. "They will give us no chance, sahib!"

Mainwaring showed surprise.

"Why?" he asked. "If they follow that direction——"

"*If,*" agreed Sitka, with emphatic intonation. "Watch, sahib! In five minutes—or less—it will be all over."

The Englishman seized his glasses again and concentrated his gaze upon the herd. Suddenly the buck, trotting gallantly at the head of the file, stumbled. The doe behind followed suit. Within a second all six were down, sliding helplessly and with stupendous swiftness towards the brink below. As they slid the snow ridged up round them—half-buried them—mounted in layer upon layer—grew to huge bulk—doubled and redoubled its mass at every yard.

With a thunderous roar thousands of tons of snow and ice poured over the verge into the ravine below. The herd was slain and buried by the one resistless stroke—Nature their undertaker as well as their assassin!

Mainwaring looked at the Balti.

"I have seen it so again and again!" said the man, simply. "Even from here I could mark the break in the smoothness of the slope—the cleavage which showed how the old snow was shifting. A herd of passing ibex—nay, even the settling of a bird has sufficed—and the avalanche starts. How it ends you have seen."

Mainwaring gave a little shudder.

"I have seen," he said, "and have lost the desire for sleep. We will breakfast and start while the drifts are hard."

Sitka gave one of his taciturn little nods. He found the spirit lamp, lit it, packed the saucepan with snow, and set it to boil. Meanwhile he busied himself in rolling the sleeping bags into a neat bundle.

Mainwaring watched idly. As he watched he told himself that this suddenly improvised shooting expedition had already done for him what he asked. It was detaching him from all but the vivid interests of the moment. Up in these great hills of Baltistan the emotions—the passions—which had dominated him in the plains could be viewed from a perspective which was more dispassionate. Five days ago Violet Markham had—jilted him? No; that put the case harshly. But she had made it evident that he was no longer supreme in her regard—that others shared what he considered should have been a pedestal—that one man, indeed, had come near to displacing him. And so—he had come away for reflection. And he had learned to reflect. The snows, the crags, the interests of shikar were anodynes to his unrest. In another two days he would go back and Violet should choose. He had gained strength to meet that choice unflinchingly.

The silence and his abstraction were suddenly shattered. Sitka gave a violent cry.

"Drop!" he thundered. "Drop, sahib! Behind the boulder!"

Mainwaring's experience of hill-shooting had already made it clear to him that obedience to your tracker is of all things necessary. He slipped down. Sitka was extinguishing the lamp and thrusting the pack into a cleft. He beckoned his master towards him.

"In here, sahib!" he commanded, pointing to a crevice between two boulders. Mainwaring crept in and then turned for an explanation.

The Balti's face was grey with fear.

"You have seen—what?" asked his master.

"What no sahib has seen—and lived!" faltered the man. "Tell me! Did we cross snow yesterday in coming here?"

Mainwaring reflected.

"No," he said, at last. "We were on rock all day."

The tracker sighed in his relief.

"So I thought," he answered, "but my brain whirls. There will be no trail, then, for them to trace."

Mainwaring stared.

"Them?" he repeated. "Them?"

Sitka pointed to the narrow slit between the boulders. He made a gesture towards the valley on the south.

Mainwaring searched the foreground, discovering at first nothing but the endless vista of rubble and crag. Then it appeared as if some of the boulders themselves moved. Finally he discerned that a company of men, clad in garments of dusky grey which matched the rocks, came hurrying up the centre of the ravine.

He looked round at his companion.

"May Allah in His mercy grant that we have not been seen!" prayed Sitka. "Dawn must have surprised them—they are miles from their fastness. It is the Clan of the Footless, hot from a raid!"

For one wild moment Mainwaring told himself that his shikari raved. Perhaps Sitka read something of this in his master's face.

"Watch them, sahib," he whispered, "but for your life's sake do not move. Need of haste goads them. They may pass us yet."

Gluing his eyes to the tiny cleft, Mainwaring stared again. He noted suddenly that the men walked with a high-stepping action which gave to their stride a most curious appearance. The last four bore between them something slung from a couple of poles—a sort of rough palanquin. So swift was their advance that within five minutes they were abreast of the two watchers behind the stones. Then the mystery of their stilted stride was a mystery no longer. Each man was shod with stout cloth slippers, poised upon a wooden sole, and this last tapered almost to a point. The termination of this point was a cloven hoof.

Leaning upon staves which had for ferrule the same device as the footgear, they swept by with such a clatter as a herd of ibex would have made, and, as they crossed a patch of drifted snow, left just such a track. They did not speak among themselves as they passed, but each, from beneath a crown of matted hair, darted keen glances around him. One sound alone broke the patter of hoof on stone—a sound from the palanquin as of weeping.

Not till they had paced on a full furlong did Sitka venture to break silence. His voice, when it came, was intense; filled with a sort of wondering anguish.

263

"They have taken a woman!" he breathed. "A memsahib!"

Mainwaring whirled round.

"An Englishwoman?" he cried. "An Englishwoman in their hands?"

Sitka made a significant gesture.

"Ay—assuredly a woman of your race. Our daughters do not sob. They cry from the throat, shrilling their grief. Nay, sahib—do not move. They have the eyes of eagles—keep hid!"

Mainwaring shook him savagely.

"In Allah's name why should they seize a memsahib—why?" he cried. "What proofs have you?"

For a moment the tracker was silent. Then a sudden inspiration shone in his eyes.

"You ask me why?" he cried. "A moment back I could not have told, but now an instinct whispers to me. They are the revengers of Malik Kel, these men. Think, sahib. You remember the taking of that outlaw in the marches of Kashmir?"

"For brigandage," said Mainwaring. "What have these men and their captive to do with that?"

"This much. The cateran was doubtless a brother of the clan; one of these men whom no man tracks, who work in the night alone, upon whom the sun shines but once—as now—in a span of years. As djinns and afreets they go about their lawless work—unseen. They have captured one of your kin to hold her against the freeing of Malik Kel!"

Something told Mainwaring that he was hearing the truth. He fought against the intuition.

"Mere empty words!" he cried. "You give me no proofs that a woman was there at all!"

The tracker glanced keenly up the valley. The men were passing out of sight round an angle of the cliff. As the last one disappeared he drew his master forward.

"Come!" he said, curtly, and in the centre of the ravine began to search the ground.

Suddenly he gave a cry. He held up a tiny shred of amber silk.

"Twice—thrice—I saw such a thing fall from the litter. The prisoner hoped for rescue and so left a sign for those who followed."

He pressed the thing into Mainwaring's hand.

The other looked and—his heart seemed to stand still!

Two letters flared upon the silk, traced with the crimson of the writer's blood—'V. M.' Who else in the distant hill station owned those initials save Violet Markham, his promised wife! And had he not seen her wear—and admired—a sash of that amber hue!

He wheeled upon his companion.

" We follow ! " he cried.   " We follow—upon the instant ! "

The Balti laughed—a high-pitched, nervous laugh.

" Sahib ! " he cried, " who are we to match ourselves against—the Clan—the Clan which holds all the mountain peoples in its thrall ? There is no talk of rescue here. Ransom or exchange—yes, but that is a Government matter, outside our handling. Let us thank the Almighty for our own escape."

Mainwaring shook him as a terrier shakes a rat.

" We follow ! " he insisted. " She whom they have taken was to be my wife—my wife ! "

The tracker's limbs grew rigid with surprise.

" Nay ! " he protested. " Nay, sahib, you deceive yourself——"

Mainwaring struck at him. The Balti crouched, looking up with dog-like, unresentful eyes.

" Sahib ! " he pleaded, " strike me not ! If thou goest I go, but—but, is it indeed the truth ? "

Mainwaring's passion made him incoherent—he stormed, he issued vehement commands. He lifted his rifle and strode forward a dozen steps before the other could grip his elbow and stay him.

The incredulity had left the tracker's face.

" Listen ! " he cried, earnestly. " All my powers shall serve you, but here is need for infinite caution. By daylight we walk to certain death. Night alone can give us our chance."

" Have we no rifles ? " cried Mainwaring, furiously. " We carry the lives of sixty hill dogs in our bandoliers ! "

" And they ? " asked the Balti, quietly. " Have they no knives ? Will they leave her whom you seek unharmed for your rescuing. If we won a way to her side, what should we find ? Think, Sahib—think well ! "

With a groan Mainwaring sat down and covered his face. It was all too true—Sitka's arguments were unanswerable—force could carve no road to Violet Markham's rescue. And yet ? How could he wait the long twelve hours till dusk, bearing his anguish through a whole inactive day ?

Sitka watched him anxiously, and then, as if struck with a sudden impulse, unpacked the spirit lamp and for the second time set the water a-boil. Ten minutes later he pressed a steaming cup into his master's hand.

" Drink, sahib ! " he entreated. " Drink and gain strength to bear your sorrow. The event is with Allah—who is merciful ! "

Mechanically Mainwaring put his lips to the cup and drained it. A sudden drowsiness stole upon him. He shifted his position, tried to rise, and finally rocked back to stretch himself at full length upon the pebbles. With careful, kindly hands the tracker slipped the sleeping bags beneath him and then sat down at his side. Mainwaring slept dreamlessly.

When he woke the dusk enshrouded him. He started to his feet.

"You used opium—you drugged me!" he cried, menacingly.

Sitka nodded.

"Even so, sahib!" he answered, quietly, "and so saved for you the strength which you would have wasted in sorrow. Here is food. Eat!"

Mainwaring took the bowl of rice and stew. He swallowed the contents with great gulps. Within a minute he set it down, seized his rifle, and pointed up the ravine.

"Forward!" he cried. "Already we have wasted hours!"

"Nay, not a minute," replied Sitka, meekly, as he stuffed the pannakin in his pack and followed. "Even now the darkness barely hides us, though it deepens."

In the centre of the ravine they picked up the track, and Mainwaring, trained to hill shikar though he was, realised how the trail would have deceived him. It was absolutely as if a herd of ibex had passed. On the patched snow, on the infrequent outcrops of soil, the hoof-marks were defined into distinctness, a distinctness which might have duped the keenest eye. Yet Sitka was never in doubt. Through six hours he traced it, lost it, found it again on snow or rubble, speeding steadily on through the gorges at their darkest. They saw nothing, heard nothing. The silence of the crags was unbroken. Once, as the tracker halted to shift his pack from shoulder to shoulder, Mainwaring took the lead. For a furlong or two they kept this order. Then the earth seemed to open at the Englishman's feet! He toppled forward, to be dragged back into safety by the Balti's sinewy hand. A snarl echoed up from the pit which had nearly engulfed him.

"A wolf trap!" explained Sitka, curtly. "We approach dwellings."

Mainwaring peered into the hole. Two pairs of green iridescent pupils glared back at him as the caged brutes pawed at the over-hanging walls. He shuddered at the narrowness of his escape.

"With infinite silence now!" whispered Sitka. "These pit-falls often protect the outskirts of a village."

The trail failed upon a patch of rock. A long, sloping snow field stretched beyond it, but they searched the edge of this in vain.

Sitka sighed wearily.

"Fresh fallen!" he breathed. "We must go on, trusting to chance." For twenty minutes they ploughed steadily upwards. This time it was the tracker who came to a sudden halt, gasping.

"In Allah's Name!" he panted wonderingly, and pointed downwards.

The perspiration of sudden fear bathed Mainwaring's forehead. The slope broke off into a sheer, an overhanging, crag!

They looked down. A hundred feet below a huge shelf cut deep into the face of the cliff, a plateau, many acres wide, carved in the rock as if by the action of a gigantic punch. Black shadows dotted it here and there, and it was not their eyes alone which told them that these were the habitations of men. The faint reek of smoke hung in the still, crisp, mountain air.

Mainwaring searched the cliff side keenly. The moonlight lit it into distinctness, but look where he would he could discover no access to the stronghold. The tracker twitched at his sleeve.

He made a significant gesture towards the far side of the ringing crags, to a point where a thin shadow, as it seemed, was flung across the stone. Mainwaring, as he gazed, realised that it was down this narrow foothold that they must go.

"There is a watcher, leaning against the boulder where the path sinks over the edge," whispered Sitka.

Gazing keenly, Mainwaring at last marked how now and again a darker dot among the shadows moved. How could they approach across the last bare furlong of snowfield unseen? He whispered his doubts in his companion's ear. The Balti nodded silently and drew him back down the trail up which they had climbed. He did not speak till they halted beside the wolf trap.

"There is but one way, sahib!" he said simply, and leaning over the pit, snarled with an uncouth, mocking sound.

With an answering snarl a wolf leaped up, its jaws snapping in unavailing effort to reach its enemy. The tracker's knife darted down. With a thick cough the brute fell back and lay still.

Again the tracker voiced his beast-like challenge, and again it was accepted. The second wolf shared its comrade's fate. Sitka slid into the hole and passed the bleeding carcases out to his master. He scrambled back and began to strip the pelts from the bodies.

"Let us learn wisdom from those we seek!" he explained. "As men we have no chance. As wolves Allah's Will may favour us!"

A quarter of an hour later Mainwaring stood up, eased himself of his outer clothing, and with Sitka's deft assistance bound the raw hide about his body and limbs. The grinning mask fell over his forehead to the level of his eyes. He helped to disguise the tracker in his turn. Leaving their packs and rifles beside the pit and taking only their revolvers they climbed the snow-slope for the second time. As they came within view of the cliff head they sank upon knees and elbows. They were half way across the open patch which lay between them and the boulders which crowned the crag before they were observed. Then a stone came whizzing through the air.

"A-r-ré!" growled a hoarse voice, following the execration with another stone. With all the speed they could devise the sham wolves padded into the shadow of the rocks and were lost to sight among the crevices.

Silently they neared the verge. At a sign from his companion Mainwaring dropped behind.

Sitka crept forward inch by inch till his face overhung the drop. Mainwaring saw his body suddenly stiffen, as the cat stiffens when she is within leaping distance of the unconscious bird. The tracker's limbs were drawn in beneath his body, his muscles tautened, He sprang out into the air! There was a thud, a faint scuffling sound, a smothered, whimpering cry. Mainwaring drew himself forward to the brink. A dark mass lay upon the footway below him. As he stared it divided into two parts. The tracker stood up; the stark body of the hill man lay stretched at his feet.

"So it befalls a watcher who does not watch!" whispered Sitka, grimly. "Those eyes were cast down which should have ceaselessly looked up. Come, sahib! We are but at the beginning. May Allah's Protections follow us! We need them!"

Without another glance at the corpse he led the way carefully down the succession of narrow ledges which was the only path.

The moon was sinking by now and the velvet shadow of the cliff was falling aslant the collection of stone-built, earth-roofed huts. In this thicker darkness Sitka moved with confidence, dropping from hold to hold with the lithe grace of the animal he simulated. Mainwaring followed, his knees and palms bruised and aching from contact with the stone. The pair sidled softly up to the first of the huts. Sitka tried the door. It gave smoothly under his touch. He relinquished it, shaking his head.

"We have to find one barred—*on the outside*," he explained softly, and led on. Half a dozen latches were examined and passed by. A sense of keen anxiety began to fill Mainwaring's heart. Were they on the right track—was this the lair of the Clan at all?

Suddenly Sitka halted with a significant gesture. They had reached a small, stone-built circular tower. The one entrance was near the roof, ten feet from the ground. Access was gained by a ladder—a ladder which lay upon the ground at its foot. A sound sank down to them through the night—the same which they had heard as the raiders passed them in the dawning—the sound of a woman's weeping.

Silently they raised the ladder and poised it against the wall.

Mainwaring waved his companion back. He climbed, tapped softly, and breathed the prisoner's name.

" Violet ! "

The sound of weeping ceased. There came a tiny incredulous gasp.

Whispering a caution, Mainwaring laid his hand upon the rude bars and drew them from the sockets. The door swung back. His hand groped into the darkness. From within it was seized, pressed, passionately kissed. With a sigh that told of weariness and pain and hope all too long deferred, Violet Markham crept into her lover's arms. He held her to him. For a moment he halted as his lips sank down and touched her brow, her eyes, her hair. The next instant he had lifted her and was stepping delicately from rung to rung. Her face was pressed against his shoulder. She raised it as he dropped from the ladder. She saw Sitka—the wolf! Her self-control deserted her. Suddenly, too, she saw the grim mask which dropped over the eyes of the man who carried her. She made a little inarticulate cry.

There was a stirring in the nearest hut. With a wild gesture which expressed the very limits of despair Sitka led the way towards the ledges at a run. They gained the lowest step. Mainwaring drew Violet after him from hold to hold, while the tracker, revolver in hand, crouched upon the narrow way. A voice pealed into the stillness. The cry was answered from twenty different points. The first faint streak of dawn filtered over the ridge to show a hundred ghost-like forms break from the huts and join concourse at the foot of the empty tower. Then the rush swept headlong for the cliff.

Mainwaring, as he dragged Violet over the topmost shelf on to the safety of the slope, turned to see the crouching figure rise. A red flame streamed across the morning dusk, and the leader of the charge fell prone. The hill men halted. Another shot filled the echoes and a second cateran fell. The pursuers broke and fled to cover. Imperturbable as ever Sitka turned and sped up the pathway like a cat. As he reached the summit his voice rang down to the pair who were flying down the slope.

" Take the rifles, sahib, but leave the packs ! Then to the right—to the right ! I can hold them, but have haste, sahib— have haste ! "

Mainwaring heard. He paused beside the wolf-pit to snatch up the rifles and the bandoliers. He looked towards the right. A succession of snow-covered terraces rose, tier on tier, to the shoulder of a knife-edged ridge. Below were cliffs, sheer and ledgeless. The way led up and ever up towards dizzy heights. For a moment he hesitated. Would they not cut themselves off from

269

every avenue of escape? So it seemed, if they climbed thus higher and higher into the very heart of the hills. He half halted, looking round.

The Balti saw.

"To the right, sahib!" he reiterated. "Climb! Climb! It is our only chance!"

Mainwaring hesitated no longer. Gripping Violet's hand he set off at a slow, dogged run across the slope and gained the first of the terraces. Here the snow crust was weaker than on the wind-pressed slope. Their feet sank into it. Try as she would the girl staggered, gasped, showed her distress. Grimly Mainwaring linked his arm through hers and drew her on. They passed the second terrace and panted up the ascent which led up to the third. As they gained it Mainwaring looked round. The tracker was speeding towards them, and motioned them to halt. With incredible strength he raced up the steep to their side, and took his rifle from Mainwaring's grasp. He waved them on and up.

"Here again I hold them!" he explained, pointing to the crowd of dark figures which suddenly appeared upon the brink of the snow-field far behind. He shook the rifle. "For half an hour I will bar their path with this before I again join you. The top of the ridge is our goal, sahib—the very top!"

Again the two dragged themselves at the slope, ploughed the yielding snow, stumbled desperately on. Leaning over the edge of the terrace behind them the tracker covered the leader of the pursuit and fired. The man fell, and for the second time the hill men wavered and fled to the cover of the boulders, not daring to tempt that unerring aim. For another half-hour the Balti waited and then looked round. The fugitives had passed the terraces and gained the ultimate slope—the one which led upon the summit of the ridge. He leaped to his feet and raced after them. He took his final stand behind a boulder which rose grey and naked from the surrounding snow. Above him the two climbed doggedly on. Violet had reached the limits of her strength. Mainwaring saw it in her white face and glazing eyes, heard it in the short, quick gasps which burst from her parted lips. The end came suddenly. With a groan she sank upon the snow and lay helpless.

"I'm finished!" she cried, despairingly; "I'm finished!"

Mainwaring looked keenly ahead. The crest seemed little more than a hundred feet above them. He stooped, swept Violet up into his arms, and stumbled on.

She sobbed—she protested.

"No!" she cried, weakly. "You have done your utmost! You are throwing away your life for me—in vain—in vain!"

He laughed fiercely—scornfully. He set his teeth in grim determination—step by step he climbed—fought through the yielding drift—and won! With a satisfied gasp he laid his burden down upon the very summit of the ridge. She rose—she locked her hands about his neck—she whispered in his ear.

"This is the end!" she panted, but not despairingly—almost, indeed, with a kind of triumph. "Together—with you—I can bear it. And to think that I doubted you—played with your love—persuaded myself that you did not care! Forgive me—forgive me!"

His hand caressed her hair.

"My darling!" he said, quietly. "My darling!"

She still clung to him, averting her face.

"And he—that other one," she went on. "Do you know what his admiration was worth? I was riding with him—alone. Then these men rose out of the dusk like phantoms—snatched me from my horse—bound me! Did *he* stay—did *he* risk his life to save me? He put spurs to his horse and galloped—galloped, shouting for assistance! And I had fancied him your equal—*yours!*"

A great joy was shining in Mainwaring's eyes. How little other matters loomed—how the import of life or death dwindled in the light of that confession. He had found his love—he had found her again!

The sound of a voice rang up to him. Sitka was climbing towards them, while over the brow of the lowest terrace the hill men scrambled into view. The Balti flung himself down beside them at last, panting.

"And now to crush them!" he cried, shaking his fist at the dark dots which swarmed upon his track. "Hide below the crest, sahib, and then—watch!"

A sudden hope grew in Mainwaring's breast. There was confidence—even elation—in the tracker's tones.

"How?" he cried, incredulously. "You have a plan?"

Sitka showed his teeth in a grim smile.

"One that will not fail, sahib!" he replied. "They will reach this open slope below, thinking us already flying down the far side of the hill. Then we shoot. What protections will they have from our bullets?"

Mainwaring shook his head.

"You mean that we shall destroy them all?" he asked. "That is beyond our powers, even if each bullet accounted for a man. We have but fifty cartridges left."

The Balti laughed.

"Would the cowards remain in the open to be shot down?" he replied. "Nay—when we begin our fire they will break for the

271

nearest cover—for that patch of boulders far to the right, *and immediately below us.*"

He laid a curious stress on the last four words.

Mainwaring looked at him.

" Well ? " he asked.

Sitka laughed again.

" Watch, sahib ! " he said, curtly.

The men were off the last terrace by now, and breasting out on to the slope. They shouted fiercely, waving their muskets and encouraging each other along the trail which the fugitives had left. They drew up at last within four or five hundred yards.

The Balti brought up his rifle to his shoulder. As the report rang out a hill man pitched upon his face and lay still.

The others halted.

" Shoot, sahib ! " cried Sitka, and fired again. This time two bullets found a billet.

The hill men looked wildly round for cover. With one accord they made a rush for stones which the tracker had indicated.

As they reached them Sitka flung himself forward upon the snow and swept a mass of it together. In the form of a roll he set it moving.

He repeated the process—he did it a third time.

The lumps whirled down the slope, gathering bulk—doubling themselves yard by yard.

And then Mainwaring *knew*—knew what would happen even before he had marked the huge crevice which seamed the slope—the ragged breakage which told of the cleft below. The first of the huge snowballs lumbered into it. The whole hillside below that point seemed to shake. A moaning, quivering sound echoed up among the peaks. And then the other two monstrous missiles joined the first. The snow moved—slid forward, gained speed and bulk— crested up ridge by ridge till vast acres of it were in motion. It thundered down into the ravine irresistible!

Shrieks rung out from among the boulders in its course. The hidden men rose—leaped wildly right and left—flung helpless, gesticu- lating hands towards the sky. And then were gone—blotted out— sucked down ! Buried beneath unnumbered tons of ice and snow, the avalanche carried them over the brink of the final drop and poured into the depths of the valley below.

Up on the summit Violet Markham hid her face upon her lover's breast, while Sitka laughed again fiercely, triumphantly, the wild mirth echoing from crag to crag.

" The Clan of the Footless " would raid no more.

THE HAUNTED HUNT

BY RALPH JOHN

THE smoke-room of the Haycester and County Club looked cheerful enough in the firelight which was slowly getting the better of the dreary winter's day, and the white-haired man lay back in his chair, and, stretching out his slight, neatly-gaitered legs to the blaze, pulled thoughtfully at his cigar.

"As you all probably know," he said at length, "Anthony Nunn took the hounds close on fifty years ago, and hunted them himself for eleven seasons until his death."

He paused with a grim, short laugh.

"'*Until*,' did I say? Well, be that as it may, it is thirty-nine years since Anthony Nunn met with his death, and the Haycester lost the keenest huntsman that ever cheered a hound. The man was born to hunt hounds, he lived to hunt hounds, he died hunting hounds—and then came that ghastly day which I can never recall without a shudder.

"He was too keen; he thought of nothing but the hounds from year's end to year's end. In fact, whether he was always so, or whether it grew upon him, there is not a shadow of doubt that at the last he was a monomaniac on the subject of fox-hunting.

"He always killed a May fox; and there were strange tales about his having been seen cub-hunting by himself with a few couple of hounds in out-of-the-way parts of the country before the end of June. Of course he always denied it, and said that he was merely exercising the hounds; but, knowing the man, I can well believe that rumour, for once, was no liar. It was just the sort of thing he would do. Indeed, as he himself said, only lack of sufficient means prevented him from hunting seven days a week.

"He was very far from being an ideal Master of Hounds. He never considered the field in the least; and time and time again he slipped out of cover without so much as a touch on the horn, leaving the entire field, and sometimes even the whips, too, behind.

It was not selfishness; only that in the hunting field he was practically a hound himself.

"Many considered him bloodthirsty; and certainly he would go to extraordinary lengths to kill his fox, often digging him out of what had seemed the most impregnable places at all hours of the night. The more trouble a fox gave him, the more bent on killing him he became; and if he and his hounds were baffled he used to get beside himself with rage. With him, hunting was not a sport, it was an obsession.

"Fortunately the fox supply in the Haycester country has always been exceptionally good, and fortunately they take a good deal of killing; he would have well-nigh exhausted most countries in a very short time. As it was the show of foxes in some of the more open parts was not what it should have been for several years after Nunn's *régime*.

"He was no society man. He cut an awkward little figure on foot, with his bandy legs and wizened, scowling face like a monkey's. He was a bachelor, and lived by himself in the huntsman's cottage at the kennels, acting as his own kennel-huntsman. He never entertained, and rarely went out anywhere. Away from the hounds he was impossible, curt and morose almost to rudeness; but the Haycester people forgave him all his faults for the sake of the sport he showed.

"The way Anthony Nunn hunted hounds was Fine Art: to watch and listen to him was the most exquisite pleasure I have ever enjoyed. He had a voice like a bell, and the cleverness of the fox himself. I verily believe that people preferred the bad-scenting days to the good in his time, it was such a delight to watch him help hounds. The sheer inspiration of some of his casts was enough to take away one's breath.

"With the hounds he was on the best of terms, and going to cover or returning home used to talk to them as if they were human beings, keeping up a continual prattle, after this style: 'Shall we find a fox in Coney Rough, my lads, think ye? Old Challenger there thinks not. Didn't find there last time, says Challenger.—And which of you boys is going to cut out old Marksman to-day? You, Primate? Primate thinks he'll have a try.—Well, Sympathy, are you going to let us hear your voice to-day, Sympathy? You and I will have to part if you don't find your voice, you know, Sympathy;'—and so on, addressing not a word to any of the field; and even in answer to a question only growling a monosyllable over his shoulder. To ride over hounds would have been as much as anyone's life was worth. I once saw him thrash a man, whose horse had kicked a hound, till he had to be dragged off him. Although he looked such a shrivelled-up little fellow, Nunn could box like Nat Langham and hit like a kicking horse.

"There was one hound in particular that was the apple of his eye; an ugly hare-pied brute called Marksman, in his eighth season and still running to head when Nunn's death took place. This hound was so savage that none of the men at the kennels dared handle him, but with Nunn he was as gentle as a lamb. He was a wonderful working hound with a curious deep voice, and a marvel at holding a cold line. We used to say that Nunn's 'For-ard to Marksman!' was as good as a view-hallo, and that the two were sufficient to account for any fox. Anthony Nunn and the Haycester Marksman were renowned all over England.

"I have dwelt somewhat on Nunn's peculiarities because, to my mind, when it is realised what manner of man he was, the experiences which I am about to relate become so much more credible. Looking back with a calm mind, the whole thing seems to me in perfect accord.

"I have told you how the killing of his fox was the be-all and end-all with him, how he looked upon the hunted fox as his natural and most deadly enemy, and how he would rage if Reynard managed to save his brush. To lose a fox affected him like a mortal insult, and he would brood over it until he was satisfied that he had brought the offender to book.

"That last fox was a typical instance. Twelve days before Nunn's death the hounds met at Yewbarrow Mill, then as now in the Monday country. We found a fox in Canonby Whin, and he broke close to where I was standing. He was good to know, that fox, and I could have sworn to him again among hundreds: a great raking, grey dog-fox, with most of his brush missing. Details of the run are immaterial; it is enough to tell you that after a clinker of eighty minutes we lost him the other side of Hareham, and, try as he might, Anthony Nunn with all his craft was beaten. Of course it upset him as usual, and he took hounds home there and then.

"No one acquainted with Nunn's idiosyncrasies was surprised when the following Monday's meet was changed from Wingley to Yewbarrow Mill. Again we found the big grey fox in Canonby Whin; and he gave us an even better run than before: by Hareham, Owland Banks, and Buckfield; over Priestland Park and Shepley Down; past Hindholt to Windleby, where, after two hours and thirty minutes, we lost him again. This time Nunn's fury was a sight to behold. He raved and cursed, and screamed out, '*I'll kill that —— bobtail if I have to jump the gates of Hell to do it!*' He tried forward and back, round and round, every place that could possibly hold a fox. Long after the last remnant of the field had gone home he was at it, until pitch darkness forced him to give it up.

"Eccentric as we thought him, no one was prepared for his next move. The next day messengers and telegrams were flying about the country to say that Wednesday's meet was abandoned, and that hounds would meet next on Friday at Yewbarrow Mill *at 9 a.m.* The telegrams bore the cryptic addition, '*Cub-hunting.*'

"Naturally the people, especially those on the Wednesday and Friday sides, were furious, and the weight of their wrath fell on the Secretary, a mild person, very much in awe of Nunn, who could throw no light on the enigma. Many indignation meetings were held, and feeling ran so high that the Mastership of the Haycester Hounds would certainly have become vacant at the end of the season, even had the event not been precipitated as it was.

"Under the circumstances a very small field turned out at Yewbarrow Mill on the Friday. There were not half a dozen of us, besides the remarkable cavalcade that arrived with hounds. Nunn had with him not only the whips and second horseman, but every man and boy in any way connected with the kennels; all his own and the hunt servants' horses were out, ridden by stablemen, feeders, and what not; and he had brought every hound that had a leg to stand on: dogs and bitches, forty-seven couple in all.

"Nunn himself looked as if he had been out of bed for a week; and we heard afterwards that, having spent all the preceding days in destroying every earth and stopping every place where the fox could get in between Canonby Whin and Ridgeweather Hill, he had been out with the earthstopper the night before the meet, had gone carefully over all his work again to make sure that it was intact, and had then returned to Canonby Whin, watched the grey fox out, and made all safe behind him.

"He never even stopped his horse at the meet, ignored our salutations, and went straight on to cover.

"When we got to the Whin he turned round and addressed us; and then we understood the meaning of the strange telegram and of his miscellaneous following. 'Get all round it,' he said, 'and hold him up like a cub.' I think it had dawned upon all of us by this time that the man was insane, so, thinking it best to humour him, we spread ourselves out round the Whin.

"However, you know what a wild, straggling place it is, even now; and we were not nearly numerous enough to invest every corner of it, especially with a bold, enterprising customer like the grey fox inside. And sure enough, hounds were barely in when he broke at the far end and went away like a greyhound.

"Nunn came tearing out to the hallo, black in the face with

passion, and blowing the gone-away note as if he would burst his lips. The forty-seven couple swept out like a great breaking wave and opened on the line with a crash of music that I have never heard the like of. I could hear old Marksman throwing his tongue like an organ above them all, and Nunn's beautiful voice blaspheming and cheering them on.

"THE HORSE WENT INTO THE BANK LIKE A SHOT FROM A GUN, AND
TURNED A COMPLETE SOMERSAULT"

"I can shut my eyes and think I see him now, with his eyes glaring out of his ape face with madness. Driving his horse along and 'forrarding' to the hounds, he never seemed to realise that there was a bank just in front of him, and was within two strides of it when he awoke to his danger. He tried to collect his

277

horse, but the impetus was too great; the horse went into it like a shot from a gun, turned a complete somersault, and came down on the other side with a *thud* that could have been heard fields away. When we got over, there were two things to be done at once: to send for a gun to finish the horse, and the whips after the hounds to stop them if possible. One look at Nunn as we turned him over was enough. The full weight of the horse must have come on his head with tremendous force, smashing his skull and driving his face into the ground.

"It was the middle of January when Nunn was killed; and a fortnight after the funeral we hunted again, the first whip carrying the horn, under a temporary committee, for a couple of months.

"Next season Furlong, from the Burstover, took the mastership, bringing his own whips and engaging a professional huntsman. This huntsman was one of the slow, 'try-back,' family-coachman sort, and although, thanks to a succession of good-scenting days in the early part of the season, we had fair sport, the proceedings seemed very dull after Nunn's brilliance.

"Furlong brought a few hounds of his own, but took over the greater part of Nunn's pack, and even these seemed affected by the changed spirit of things. Old Marksman in particular was not like the same animal: from being the oracle of the pack he became a mute, listless shirker; so markedly so that Furlong talked of putting him down, and the huntsman remarked with a grin, 'So this is the famous Marksman!'

"The hounds had not been in Canonby Whin at all that season until one day late in December, nearly a year after Nunn's death, when they met at the 'Black Bull,' which, as you know, is a very few miles from there. There was no scent in the morning, and we had done nothing but potter about until we came to the Whin in the afternoon. There I got on to my second horse, a brown, five-year-old thoroughbred called Pride of Tyrone, which I had bought out of Ireland for a longer price than I could really afford, but which I confidently expected him to recover with interest as a steeplechaser: I even cherished golden dreams of future Grand Nationals. My young horse was rather a handful in a crowd, so I went on to the whip at the far end of the cover.

"We had not long to wait before there was a whimper; and half a minute later, there, stealing away, was my old acquaintance the big, grey, bobtailed fox. Away he went on his familiar line; and I, with the thoughtlessness of youth, and in the excitement of getting well away with hounds, never recked that I was riding at the very part of the bank which had been fatal to Anthony Nunn. I was coming nicely at it, when suddenly Pride of Tyrone swerved, crossed his legs and fell, shooting me out of the saddle. Quite unhurt, I picked myself up at once. Pride of Tyrone was already on his feet some yards away, drenched with sweat and plunging back towards the Whin. As I started to go after him, he circled round at a canter and went at the bank exactly as if he had been ridden at it. I was too late to intercept him, and he popped on and off like a bird, and strode away over the rise of the next field.

"I remember noticing as he went past me that the reins had somehow got caught on the saddle.

"By this time the field were galloping by me, some going over the bank as the shortest way, others following the huntsman through a gap a hundred yards or more to the right.

"Running across the next field and climbing on to the next bank for a better view, I could see the hounds fairly racing, and close up with them, served by his great speed, was the runaway Pride of Tyrone; a widening space between him and the rapidly tailing field.

"Pursuit on foot and in riding boots was out of the question, and as there was no probability of anyone stopping him my anxiety was great lest he should manage to injure himself.

"I was at my wits' end what to do until it occurred to me that my first horse might still be within hail. I ran back as fast as I could across the two fields and on to the road at the top of the Whin, where I came upon a group of second horsemen just turning away from watching the disappearing hounds, and among them was my man. Fortunately we had done nothing to speak of before I changed on to Pride of Tyrone, so the horse was quite fresh, and I galloped down the line in pursuit of the fugitive.

"Hounds and Pride of Tyrone and all were out of sight and earshot by this time, but the tracks of the horses led straight away over the line the grey fox knew so well. It was not long before I began to meet people coming back, thrown out by falling or beaten by the pace, among them the first whip with his horse badly staked. But of Pride of Tyrone there was not a sign, and the tale of casualties did not tend to lessen my uneasiness on his account.

"The tracks became fewer and fewer, and at length between Humbleby Farm and Buckfield I encountered a man leading his horse back. From him I learnt that the pace, terrific for the first few miles, had slackened to a slow hunting run, when he, alone of all the field anywhere within sight of the hounds, had come to grief. He said that when he last saw the hounds they were running straight ahead, more slowly now, but in full cry ; and right up alongside them, moving like a machine, as though he revelled in the game, was my embryo racehorse.

"Wasting no time, I followed Pride of Tyrone's trail. For the greater part of the way it was plain enough, and I was able to travel at a good pace; but in places, especially on the Downs and higher-lying grass lands, it was only with the greatest difficulty that I could find anything to guide me at all.

"The tracks went straight over Priestland Park and Shepley Down to just below Hindholt, where the fox had evidently been headed and had swung left-handed along Kelton Bottom. I saw the tracks of the hounds in the soft ground there, and knew that Pride of Tyrone was still with them.

"Coming up by Checkley on to the high land again the line lay to the right over Anyman's Down to Cockover Wood, where the hoof-prints were a puzzle that took me some time to unravel. From what I could make of it, Pride of Tyrone had galloped into the wood, had turned back half way down the ride, had walked and trotted back, standing still more than once, and had broken into a gallop again before leaving the wood by the way he had entered it, going away in the direction of Swingstone.

"In another hour or so it would be too dark to see any tracks at all, and as I seemed to be no nearer to Pride of Tyrone than when I started, my chance of catching him before nightfall appeared remote in the extreme; but I was determined to persevere while I could, and kept plodding along on the trail.

"From Swingstone it led right on by High Firs and Kyte Common, as straight as a die past Ridgeweather Hill, and on to the Teal Valley. Sinking the valley, I followed it on through Frogbere plantations and across the water-meadows straight to the Teal.

"'Surely,' I thought, 'the water would stop him.' But no; I saw the marks where he had taken off. 'What a horse!' I thought, 'what a horse!' The Teal at that point was 30 ft. across.

"I knew the horse I was riding could not jump it, so going round by the bridge, quarter of a mile higher up towards the village, I came along the opposite bank till I found the tracks again. As the valley was already in twilight this was no easy matter, but I struck them at length and discovered that Pride of Tyrone had landed with a yard to spare, and gone straight on without hesitating.

"By this time my mount had had quite enough of it, and as I had more and more difficulty every minute in tracking my way along, I came to the conclusion that further pursuit was hopeless, and was just turning my horse's head in the direction of home when the sound of a hoof on a road caught my ear.

"I rode quickly towards the sound, and, sitting on his horse in the lane which leads up out of the valley by the edge of Baron's Wood, came upon the new huntsman listening intently with his hand behind his ear. Though how he, who never jumped a stick if he could help it, and almost a stranger in the country, had managed to get so far, I could not imagine. Certainly he had a marvellous knack of picking his way about by lanes and gates, and this was the only direction in which I ever knew him to exhibit the least intelligence.

" ' Hark! ' he said, when he caught sight of me, ' Hark! they're in there,' and pointed up to where Baron's Wood, lying along the top of the valley side, loomed against the sunset sky. I stopped my horse and listened, but the bellringers were practising in Frogbere Church, and the sound, echoing from both sides of the valley, lent itself to any construction the imagination liked to put upon it.

" ' They're in there,' said the huntsman, ' I heard them before the bells began. And there's someone hunting them! '

" Someone hunting them! At this piece of information the notion flashed across me that I had come all this way on a wild-goose chase. What more likely than that someone had nicked in with them, probably when the fox had swung out to Checkley and back to Cockover Wood? And had I read aright the riddle of the returning tracks in Cockover Wood? I was convinced that I had been following a single line of tracks and that those belonged to Pride of Tyrone. ' But,' I said to myself, ' I am not a Red Indian, and it is quite possible that I have made a mistake somewhere in spite of all my care.' After all, was it probable that any horse, least of all a young one who had that season seen hounds for the first time, would, of his own free will and riderless, stick to them all through a run like that, jumping everything as it came and the Teal as well? The more I reasoned the more absurd did the idea seem.

" As we sat there straining our ears, a labourer came down the lane from the direction of the wood. ' The Hounds? ' he said in answer to our questions. ' Yes, they've been up there hunting about in the big wood this half-hour. Yes, there's someone with them, I heard him. No, I didn't see him; I saw some of the dogs; and there's a horse that's lost his master.'

" We rode up the lane and turned into the wood. ' Now,' said the huntsman, ' we shall see who is meddling with my hounds.'

" We had gone some way along the main ride before we heard the hounds running towards us from the left. They came nearer and nearer, and presently burst out of the undergrowth about eighty yards ahead of us, turned sharp left-handed, and went straight up the ride in full cry. Just as they passed a branch ride leading from the left, an object dashed out of it and followed in their wake. It was Pride of Tyrone in full career.

" Both our horses were dead beat, so, bucket along as we might, we could not keep the hounds in view, and the cry was getting fainter and fainter when the huntsman's horse behind me came down with a squelch and a clatter. I never even stopped—I am afraid I set more value on Pride of Tyrone—but sent my horse along for all he was worth to the end of the wood. There I found that the hounds had crossed the road into Oxlow Wood, Pride of Tyrone with them.

"As you know, Oxlow Wood is an irregular crescent in shape, with only one ride through it lengthways, and a horse can therefore only get in or out at the ends, or horns, of the crescent. It was just the same in those days; so, having made sure that Pride of Tyrone had entered, I cut across to the far end, thinking to intercept him. There were no tracks leading out of the wood, and the chances were against his turning back, so I awaited developments.

"The sun was just setting blood-red. The sky in the west was like a sheet of flame. Not a breath of wind stirred the woods, and behind them the mist was creeping out of the Teal Valley. The bells of Frogbere Church were still faintly audible, mingling with the intermittent cry of hounds, which, now on one side of the wood, now on the other, was gradually coming towards me.

"At length the cry ceased altogether, and then from the wood came a sound that made my spine crawl.

"It was a voice.

"A voice that never had a like: the voice of *Anthony Nunn* !

"' *Yeu-eup !* ' it went, ' *Try for-ard !* '

"With the cold sweat dripping off me I sat there paralysed; and the beautiful voice came on:

"' *Eu, Marksman !—Yooi, my lads !— Yooi, wind him !* ' Nearer and nearer it came, ringing and echoing through the wood like a bell. And still I sat there. My limbs were lead and my brain was numb, and I sat there waiting, for what unspeakable apparition I had no conception.

"Louder and louder it grew: ' *Yeu-eup !—Push him up !— Yooi, my lads !—Yeu, try in there !* '

"Then from the wood there crept the dim form of the grey bobtailed fox. With one foot raised he stood listening a moment, and stole away towards the sunset.

"In cover a hound spoke, then another: a deep note like an otter-hound.

"The voice cheered him till the air throbbed, ' *Huic !—Huic !— Huic ! to Marksman !—Ho-o-o-o-ick !* '

"The old hound crashed through the brushwood, alert and eager—the Marksman of yore. Throwing that sonorous tongue of his, with his nose on the line he drove along. Scoring to cry the hounds poured out. And then, every muscle on my body literally twitching, I heard the voice close at hand, and an approaching horse.

" It seemed hours that I stared with aching eyes that I dared not blink at the end of the ride where the Thing must appear.

" What I saw burnt into my brain.

" Out of the wood came—*Pride of Tyrone* !

" Pride of Tyrone, white with lather, eyes wild and nostrils

"OUT OF THE WOOD CAME PRIDE OF TYRONE"

distended. The bit was pressing on his mouth; the reins extended stiffly back from the bit to empty air above the withers. They were held in a grasp, and they were held by—*nothing* !

" And from the empty air above the saddle, from on a level with my own head, pealed and cheered that clarion voice.

" Pride of Tyrone passed close by me : I could have touched

him. And as he passed a sense of unutterable, nameless horror and doom swept over me. And the voice blared like a trumpet right in my ear: '*For-ard. Awa-ay!*'

" Blind with terror, I drove the spurs into my horse and rode for my life.

" My recollection of the journey home is a blurred jumble of furious galloping and weary leading of a foundered horse.

" Next morning I went to the kennels. I found the huntsman, scared and shaken, big with news. After the fall his horse was dead lame, and as he could not hear a sound of the hounds he went home. It was after nine o'clock when he got to the kennels; the whips were already there, having collected four and a half couple of lost hounds—all new hounds of Furlong's. Of the rest of the eighteen couple taken out in the morning there was not a trace.

" He got his supper and went to bed ; and had been asleep some time when he was aroused by a violent knocking at the door, which continued until his hand was on the latch to open it. He looked out. In the yard, which was as light as day with brilliant moonlight, stood six couple of hounds. Not a sign of anything else. He was about to call out, when such a feeling of utter horror came over him as he had no words to describe. Something was hurled past his head into the house. And out of nothing, right in his face rang yells and shrieks of unearthly laughter.

" How he even managed to bang the door to, and how long he crouched there sick with fright, he had no idea. He left the six couple outside to shift for themselves till daylight.

" He showed me the object thrown through the door. Still lying where it had fallen was the mangled, wolfish mask of a great dog-fox, and crammed into the mouth were the four pads and a grey fragment of a brush.

" During the next few days tidings came in.

" Pride of Tyrone was found, stiff and dead, in a lonely by-road within five miles of the kennels.

" Singly and in twos and threes the rest of the hounds came back, led, in carts, and limping home alone on weary bleeding feet.

" By the end of the week there was only one hound unaccounted for. Then we had the story of the doctor at Stoatswold, in the heart of the Oaklands country.

" Driving home late on the night of the run, he heard hounds killing a fox on the moor above the village, and someone whooping and whooping till the whole countryside resounded.

" The doctor said it was gruesome and turned him cold. The villagers heard it, broad awake, and shivered in their beds.

" Next day on the moor, surrounded by the remains and fragments of a fox, they found a hound, dead. It was old Marksman. They must have run nearly forty miles.

"Nothing of a like nature ever occurred again," said the white-haired man, after a pause. "For years there were rumours among the country people of a deep-voiced hound being heard at night,

"HOUNDS WERE KILLING A FOX ON THE MOORS ABOVE THE VILLAGE."

particularly in one part, and of a man's voice cheering him. But the evidence was never at first hand."

The white-haired man lit a fresh cigar.

"Yes," he said, "it is strange that we never find a fox in Canonby Whin."

STRANGE STORIES OF SPORT

XXIV.—THE CHARMED BULLET

A Tiger Story

BY J. NUGENT

THERE are people who find no difficulty in accepting the supernatural as the natural solution, so to speak, of any event at all out of the common, without caring to satisfy themselves whether in the first place it ever really took place at all, or if it did whether it cannot be accounted for much more easily in some more rational way. Now as to the occult I am a complete sceptic, yet I once met with an experience that I cannot persuade myself to look upon as a mere ordinary occurrence.

I was Assistant Magistrate in Ajabpoor in the North-West Provinces, as they used to be called in those days, and was spending three months' shooting through the wild country to the north of that district along the borders of Nepal. I had just two tents and an elephant and the few servants absolutely necessary in an expedition of the kind.

One day a native came to my camp with a long story, only part of which I understood, for he spoke the patois of the jungle; but the gist of it was that a tiger had harassed his village the whole cold weather and he wanted me to shoot him. At first, as well as I could make out, only cattle had been molested, but of late he had taken to men and killed regularly every three days. They had sacrificed to half the gods in the pantheon, but two days before he had claimed his usual victim. The people were in terror of their lives, and hearing a sahib had come with an elephant they had sent the man to me to beg me to come. The shikari, for so he described himself, struck me as confused; and Khuda Baksh, who was acting as my interpreter, evidently thought so too, for he commenced a cross-examination in the truculent style invariably adopted by a sahib's servant to any native who will allow himself to be bullied.

"A lame tiger and ye have to send for a sahib! Are ye all afraid?" he began, and proceeded to deliver a tirade about things in general.

"He is a gaon war!" [a yokel], he exclaimed at last, contemptuously, after a long and excited controversy, turning to me. "These jungle folk believe anything!"

"Why, what does he say?" I asked.

"He saith there is an Aghori about the place, whom all the people dread. They think the tiger is his servant and obeyeth his orders. It is only since his coming that the trouble hath been."

I asked him what an Aghori was, and he explained that he was a kind of Hindu fakir that had given up everything, houses, clothes, even caste, and went about wandering in wild places naked, feeding on whatever he could pick up, however unclean—even the corpses of dead men dug up from their graves. "It is said," he ended up, "that their god sometimes giveth them power to change themselves into beasts of prey, but these jungle folk are ignorant and superstitious, they read no books, sahib, and believe what their fathers and grandfathers believed before them."

Khuda Baksh was a bit of a character in his way. He was an old and well-known mahout, and he and his elephant Bara Kallie were well known as the staunchest shikaris in the province. He measured everybody by his own knowledge of woodcraft; it was perhaps because he had initiated a couple of generations of bigwigs into the mysteries of sport that he had such a poor opinion of the intelligence of sahibs in general. To me as a mere griff he used to lay down the law as befitted my ignorance. He was a Mussulman, yet with all the ways of thinking of the Hindus of his class, for he had been born and bred in the jungle, and for all his lofty scorn for the ignorance of the rustics, as he called them, he was in reality as superstitious as any of them. In fact, there was certainly a tentative note in his last sentence, as if he was putting out a feeler to see whether I, too, had any leanings that way.

"Oh, of course," I said, "an educated Mahommedan would laugh at such silliness as that."

He could not write his name, as I knew very well, and the sarcasm told. Besides, to be chaffed by a chota sahib was too much. He shrugged his shoulders sulkily and kept strictly to business for days, whatever I might do to draw him out.

The shikari appeared disappointed that we were not going to start there and then. Next day a kill was due, he said, and perhaps by going at once we might prevent it. It was not very far, we could get there before night, and so on. He was obviously afraid and wanted our escort, but I could not go at once, and at last he set out to return alone, praying me to tell no one he had come.

Shikarpoor, the tiger's happy hunting-ground, was twenty miles off, and it was late next evening by the time we reached it. It was one of the wretched fever-stricken villages that one comes across in those parts buried away in the forest, and so palpably a product of it that it emphasized rather than dispelled the loneliness of the scene. As we passed through it we could not see a soul, and an air of eerie desolation seemed to pervade the place.

The next morning, after breakfast, Bara Kallie was got ready and we rode over from the camp to the village to make inquiries; but nobody would tell us anything. One would have thought they had never heard of such a thing as a tiger in their lives.

"Why, what do you mean?" I asked the little crowd that had gathered around the elephant. "You sent to fetch me the day before yesterday, and now none of you will speak!"

They stared at one another uncomfortably with open mouths, then began eagerly protesting that they had sent no one and knew nothing at all about the matter.

"Where is Tulsi Ray," I asked, "the man who came to my camp? Send for him and let me ask him."

Then it came out that he was dead. He had been waylaid and killed by the tiger as he was returning the evening before, and his death was evidently looked upon as a warning.

Try as I might I could get no one to come with me, and it was not till next morning that the offer of unprecedented baksheesh at last induced another so-called shikari to act as guide, and even he nearly cried off at the last moment under a volley of vituperation from his wife. An extra rupee, however, finally closured the debate, the enemy retired routed though noisy still, while her husband climbed into the back seat of the howdah behind me, and we set off.

We bumped and scrambled through the thick wood for hours, till at last we came to the river. It being the beginning of the hot weather this had shrunk to a single stream, which flowed in the centre far away in a waste of sand, while between it and us lay an island cut off from the main bank by the bed of what in the rains was one of the channels into which the river spreads itself, but which was now dry and sandy. Along this Ram Din, who now rejoined us, led me for some distance till under an overhanging tree he stopped.

"Look, sahib!" he said, pointing to a mark in the sand below, "This is where he jumped down. He has gone across to the island.

It is the lame tiger." He spoke in a whisper as if afraid of being overheard, though the channel was eighty yards across; and when I proposed that we should return to the elephant he flatly refused to accompany me. He would climb into the tree, he said, and watch; so leaving him carefully concealed in its branches, I hurried back myself, and we got the elephant across.

The island was densely wooded, and should have been full of game; but it was empty as though swept by a pack of wild dogs, and not even an old boar broke cover.

"The animals have fled through fear," whispered Khuda Baksh. "Without doubt it is the home of the tiger," and as he spoke we came upon a lair. Whitening bones were scattered around, and from the dark shadow of a cane brake grinned a bleaching human skull.

Roofed in as it was by overhanging boughs, and floored with rushes trampled into what at first sight looked like a rough mat, it suggested a rude hut rather than a wild beast's den. A ghostly uncomfortable atmosphere hung about, and even Bara Kallie seemed to scent danger, for she thumped her trunk against the ground with a warning tung. Suddenly a monkey chattered in a tree ahead, then another further off; in a moment the whole forest was in full cry. The beast was on foot, and following the chorus we pressed on till we came to the edge of the channel that separated us from the mainland. It was a wide open space, but neither could we find pugs, nor was there any sign of Ram Din, though we got off to search. We could not imagine what had become of him till just under the tree in which he had been perched we found the footmarks of a man.

"Confound the fool!" I cried, "he must have got down out of the tree and the tiger saw him and went back. Why couldn't he sit still instead of spoiling a shot like that!"

But the mahout, who was bending down examining the ground attentively, was muttering to himself. "Far be the evil eye," I heard him exclaim, in an awe-struck tone. Then standing up he said, mysteriously, "These are not Ram Din's footprints, Huzur (sir). See, there is no toe."

"Nonsense!" I cried, irritably. "Whose else could they possibly be? If they were not his, why should he have run away? Of course they're his, and he has spoilt my sport. Do you think a man came down from the skies?"

He shrugged his shoulders resignedly and climbed up the elephant's trunk into his seat in silence. Then, when he had arranged his feet in the stirrups, he said, oracularly, "We shall see, sahib; but it was not Ram Din who stood here." And all the way back to camp he was silent and meditative : nor could I manage to extract from him what he meant.

Next morning, when we went to the village, the whole place seemed deserted. The mat doors were fastened down tight as for a siege, and the only creature to be seen was a woman with dishevelled hair sitting on the ground and crooning distractedly. " Hai, hai," she wailed. " Did I not warn thee not to go ? But when would a husband listen to his wife ? Alas, unhappy one ! that thou shouldst have meddled with a bhoot " [demon].

It took some time before we could make out what had happened, but at last we discovered that her husband had been killed by the tiger. At nightfall, she told us, he had run back from the forest speechless with terror, and at midnight the lame man-eater had come to the house, dragged him out of his hut, and torn him limb from limb in front of his own door.

I was beginning to feel uncomfortable.

" And who was your husband ? " asked Khuda Baksh, who was carrying on the conversation.

" Why, sahib," she said, " Ram Din Goojar, the young man you took with you on the elephant yesterday."

And at the name the old mahout's face turned, I will not call it pale, but the colour of the whitey-brown mottled patch on Bara Kallie's trunk between her two little twinkling eyes.

" Allah re ! " he cried, in consternation. " Ram Din killed ! It is true she wanted to keep him back." Then after a pause he added inconsequently, still speaking to himself, " He must have seen him in the tree."

Whatever fear had overtaken the woman, it was obvious that it was shared by her neighbours. Panic reigned, no man dared venture into the forest, for he felt as though the sword of Damocles were hanging over his head. The herds were afraid to take their cattle to graze, and those who had come from places around were driving off their beasts to safer grazing grounds. Shikarpoor was being deserted as a plague-stricken spot.

The worst of it was that the scare quickly spread to my servants. A sudden slump seemed to have set in among their relatives, and one after the other came to me for leave on urgent private affairs to marry his daughter or bury his great-aunt, till at last my establishment was reduced to the cook and Khuda Baksh himself, my invaluable factotum, who, with the quiet self-confidence of conscious genius, had constituted himself my bearer and table servant combined.

He had changed of late, and in place of the haughtiness of his former demeanour, he now treated me with a deference almost embarrassing by contrast.

"What is the meaning of all this?" I asked him, the second day after I had tried in vain to get some of the natives to give assistance. "Why should they all be so terrified of this beast?"

He hesitated, looking at the ground, till I encouraged him. Then he spoke.

"Your honour will remember about the Aghori?" he said, diffidently. "It is him they fear. They say he can do magic, and that to vex him is to die. It is by the tiger that he wreaketh vengeance on those against whom he hath a grudge."

I had suspected something of the kind before, though nobody but the old man himself had ever yet said a word about this wonderful personage who I was beginning to think was a fiction of his own brain.

"But you," I said, "who fear neither man nor beast. You don't mean to say you believe this old woman's tale?"

I suppose he suspected me of sarcasm, for he answered deprecatingly, "Your honour must not laugh. This country is not like Wilayat, nor is the forest like the town. Strange things happen in the jungle, strange things such as are not written of by the wise men of the West. Men do change into beasts, sahib; I have known it myself. When I was a boy there was a fakir in the village, and anyone who refused him alms was sure to lose a cow or a bullock by a tiger, till at last he could take what pleased him, like a Brahmanee bull in a bazaar. One day a Colonel Sahib came shooting and hit a tiger. He followed him till he came to a stream where a man was sitting washing a wound in his leg. The Colonel Sahib asked what was the matter, and the man said, ‘Why dost thou ask when it was by thee that I was shot?’ Then the sahib, growing angry, said it was a tiger he had fired at, not a man; but the other answered, ‘I, the fakir, am that tiger.’ Everyone knew," he wound up, "and it is true, for my wife's first cousin on the mother's side was the sahib's mahout."

He then set to work to induce me to leave the place and go on a march or so to Baghpattee, the best jungle in the district, he declared, where there was game under every bush and no bullet was wasted. Besides, Mozuffer Hussain was the head constable in charge of the police-station. I had no doubt heard of Mozuffer Hussain, who used always to show sport to the Commissioner Sahib, and had even been out with the Jungee Lat Sahib himself (the commissioner-in-chief). He knew all the country for twenty miles around, and would of a surety give us shikar.

As a matter of fact, were it not that it would have looked like running away, I should gladly have taken his advice, for there did not seem much chance of doing much where we were; but I had spotted a likely place which I wanted to try, going alone on foot. So I told him that he was to send for Mozuffer Hussain and that we would march to Baghpattee when he came, but meanwhile I was going to have a hunt on my own account next day.

He held up his hands in horror. It was certain death, he declared. To go alone even after a common man-eater was fool-hardy; but this was no common beast, but a *bhoot*, as all the villagers knew. Besides, I had only the *Paree dam*.

My Express had got jammed and I was reduced to a curious kind of gun I had picked up somewhere. It was a muzzle-loader built for shot or ball, like the well-known Paradox, the progenitor of which it may have been. "The Paradigm" its makers had christened it, *Paree dam* (Fairy's breath) was the mahout's poetical translation, and for this weapon he had the greatest contempt. I urged that a fairy's breath was just the thing for a magic foe, but the matter was too grave for levity and the joke fell flat. Again and again he tried to dissuade me, and when at last he saw that I had made up my mind he solemnly produced a bullet which he besought me to be sure to use, as in it lay my only hope of salvation. He had made it on purpose from the prescription of an ancient Pir (saint). Lead was useless against a spirit, but this was of silver, and inscribed with a word so potent that no demon could turn it aside. With this, if I loaded with it, I might prevail if I would not be wise and give up the attempt altogether. I accepted the compromise, amused at his pertinacity, and promised what he asked.

Next evening, after beating about all day without success, I was nearing camp on my way home when the bushes beside me rustled and a man stood before me in the path. He was stark naked but for a necklace of bones, and his fierce animal eyes and white fang-like teeth might have been those of a wild beast.

" Baksheesh, sahib bahadoor (brave sahib)," he cried, stretching out his bony hand, " baksheesh for the poor fakir."

He had come upon me so suddenly, and there was such a tone of menace in the professional whine, that involuntarily I stepped back, gripping the gun.

He laughed mockingly.

" Thou startest at a man, Farangi " (foreigner—a contemptuous term for Englishman), he sneered, " thou that huntest after tigers ! Yet the tiger thou pursuest is more terrible than a man. Thou hast seen what came to those that helped thee. Beware lest it be thy turn next."

Hideous and repulsive as he was, the voice, the fair skin, were not those of a low-caste criminal or of one born a savage ; yet, though the extravagance of bitterness in his voice savoured of madness, there was no madness in his eyes, only deep implacable hate.

"Sahib bahadoor," he said again, and the sarcastic emphasis on the adjective was unmistakable, "go hence. Leave the jungles to us. Towns and cities are safer for ye, and women the game for the white man. Ask in the village who I am; I am the man tiger, and take warning, brave sahib!"

There was a depth of scorn, a studied insolence in his manner that maddened me. Clearly the filthy apparition meant mischief, or at least thought to bully me with his absurd threats; or it might be he was trying to extort alms perhaps with violence.

"Out of the way, swine!" I cried, a sudden fit of passion seizing me. "Do you take me for one of your wretched dupes? There, there is my baksheesh!" and I struck him full on the head with the barrel of the gun. In my rage I could have killed him where he stood.

He reeled back half stunned, but recovered himself at once, and for a moment I thought he was going to spring, but the blood blinded him, and bending down with a curse that sounded like an angry growl he glided into the brushwood as noiselessly and as lithely as a leopard, and in an instant was gone.

The camp was almost in sight, and Khuda Baksh, who had been on the look-out, came towards me with a lantern in his hand to take the gun.

"I've just met a madman," I said, and told him what had occurred.

"Alhamd il illah!" [Praise be to God], he ejaculated aghast, when I had finished, and without a word went back with the lantern, searching the path by which I had come.

"You struck him, sahib?" he asked, when he returned, his face of the unwholesome colour I had seen before. "Wa! wa! It was not well to strike a fakir. It was the Aghori," he whispered, drawing close and sinking his voice. "Allah guard us from harm this night!"

I used to dine outside the tent as the weather was getting warm, Khuda Baksh, as I have said, acting of late as khidmatgar. That evening, as he was laying the table, he smoothed and resmoothed the cloth, arranged and rearranged each spoon and fork with mathematical and irritating precision. It was obvious he had something on his mind and was waiting for an opportunity to speak. At last out it came. The cook and he wanted to sleep in the village, and as Mozuffer Hussain would probably arrive in the morning, and we were to march that day, he proposed that I too should "convey my honour" to the headman's new cowshed, where my bed could be made up comfortably.

"What!" I cried, "you afraid, too! Why, what has come over you all—you who fear neither man nor beast?" (for this had been his boast).

"Ah, Huzur," he said, shaking his head, "of a truth this thing is neither man nor beast: there is magic abroad. The Aghori is the tiger, and none may escape his wrath. Was not Tulsi Rai killed who brought khabbar [news], and Ram Din Goojar who for greed of pice showed the lair? Consider. In truth I marvelled at the island, for the tiger's pug wanted a toe, the same toe as was missing in the man's footstep; but your honour would not listen. But now what doubt is left? There on the path near the stream are the marks of the man that stopped you. It is the same man, the second toe of the left foot is gone."

"And you think there is magic in that?" I said, chaffingly. "Well, you are certainly all bewitched. But you have slept in a tent every day for a week and nothing has happened. Why should you be frightened now?"

"Your honour struck him," he answered, "and of a surety will he be revenged. And to-day is the third day. He always kills on the third day."

It was useless to argue: that I could see at once. So panic-stricken had the old man become that, faithful servant as he was, one thing was evident—he had made up his mind that for no earthly consideration would he pass the night in the forest. I was his father and mother, he protested, but it was madness to stay, and kneeling and clasping my feet he besought me again to go with him; but I refused, making game of his alarm.

Nevertheless it was with a pang, I confess, that after dinner I saw the last glimmer of the lantern that lighted him and the cook on their way, till it was lost among the trees. I lit a pipe to pretend that I was at ease, trying to persuade myself that I was enjoying the picturesqueness of the scene. But the old mahout's terror had infected me. I could not laugh it off as I had tried to when he was there.

"What if there is real danger?" I began to think. The ghoul-like fakir's evil scowl haunted me. It spoke revenge or the yearning for it. But what could he do, a naked unarmed man, unless indeed he was mad? There was that, no doubt, to reckon with. I knew that he believed in his own threats, I felt certain that he had managed to persuade himself of the possession of the supernatural powers he was credited with; but that was monomania at the most: he was not mad. There was nothing to fear, therefore, on that score. So far I might rest in peace.

All the same I was uncomfortable, the vast loneliness oppressed me as it had never done before. I longed to be among men, even the headman's cowhouse would have been a palace and a pye-dog's bark music.

The smell of the hot weather was in the air : not a leaf stirred ; an occasional sambhur's far-off call only accentuated the silence. The empty cooking tent shone white like a sheeted ghost ; there was no sign of life but a solitary vulture on a tree, its uncouth outline silhouetted against the starry sky. Doré might have taken the scene for an illustration for " Paradise Lost."

The stillness got on my nerves. In those gloomy woods all that was uncanny, all that was ghost-like and unearthly, seemed to brood, and thoughts crowded up tinged with the darkness that begot them. Do what I would I could not get rid of the notion that some weird, unhallowed drama was stealthily working itself out.

" Can there be really some mysterious connection between this revolting man and the tiger ? " was the question that kept asking itself in spite of me. It was certainly odd about the man at the island. Where had he come from, and was he the Aghori ? Whatever it was that had stood under Ram Din's tree, it must have been that which paralysed him with fear, as his wife described. That night, too, he was killed, the third day after Tulsi Rai, and he the third day after the previous victim—and to-night was the third night after Ram Din.

" Strange things happen in the jungle," Khuda Baksh had said, and surely these things were strange ? Here was a widespread belief accepted by generations of people concerning a matter of their daily life. Was the whole thing superstition pure and simple, or was there observation in it ? Might a man, sunk already to the level of the beasts—— Great Scot ! What was I coming to ? This confounded solitude was telling on my mind. The sooner I got out of it the better. I stood up and knocked the ashes out of my pipe with a rat-tat that woke the echoes like shots. Bed was ready in the tent, and bed was obviously the best place for so nervous a sportsman. I turned in, and had soon forgotten my metaphysics in the deep sleep of the tired shikari.

Towards two o'clock I awoke with a start ; a creepy feeling was upon me. I listened, but the only sound was the clank of the chain with which Bara Kallie was tied, and a roaming jackal's howl of mocking laughter. I lit a candle and propped the rifle handy, still loaded with the wonderful bullet.

Gradually, however, I persuaded myself I must have been dreaming, and was just dozing off again when the tent shook as something brushed against a stay-rope. This time there was no doubt. I started up and grabbed the gun. It must be the Aghori— with a knife, no doubt. Then the purdah at the door was slowly pushed aside, and as I covered the place with the barrel a tiger looked in.

For a second I sat numb with terror, while he paused as if enjoying my fear. Then, as gathering himself for a spring he hurled himself upon me, I fired wildly.

*   *   *   *   *

But the curious part of the story is to come.

I was carried the sixty odd miles into the station unconscious, Mozuffer Hussain, as I afterwards learnt, arriving just in time to take charge of the arrangements. Then I was sent home, and it was a long time before I was able to return to India.

Sometimes, generally when I was shaving, that shoot used to come back to me; but though I grew to think that my imagination might have been responsible perhaps for part of the impression it had left upon my mind, still I could never bring myself to think of it as an ordinary sporting adventure.

Seven years after I met Mozuffer Hussain. He had retired from the police and had settled down in Allahabad, where I held an appointment at the time. He had written to me once or twice about some trouble he had got into, but I had not seen him since the Ajabpoor days till he came one afternoon to call.

"Your honour remembers Shikarpoor?" he asked presently. " I have often wished to see you since."

"I am hardly likely to forget it while I have this to remind me," I said, laughing, pointing to the great scar across my forehead. " Did you ever find out anything afterwards?"

"Allah be praised that your honour escaped," he exclaimed. " They still bless your name in the village. They told me when I went back how you had destroyed their enemy, and they and their cattle were at peace." Then he dropped his voice, as he whispered confidentially: "I found him in the jungle, Huzur, that is what I wanted to say."

"You found him," I said, interested in the fate of my only man-eater. " Tell me about it."

"I lost my way in the forest," he went on, "as I was going back to the outpost, and wandered about till at last I came to the river, and there in an island I found him dying. He was skin and bone, and I could see the bullet under the skin. Having some skill as a hakim [native doctor] I extracted it, but he died."

"In the name of goodness, what foolishness is this?" I asked, thinking he was mad. "What or whom are you talking about?"

"Why, the Aghori, sahib," he answered, puzzled; "the fakir of Shikarpoor who tried to murder you in your tent."

"The fakir who tried to murder me," I repeated, bewildered. "No one tried to murder me. It was a tiger that attacked me."

He looked at me inquiringly for a moment. "Your honour can trust me," he said, a note of disappointment in his voice, and evidently mistaking the cause of my excitement. "You have always been my patron, my father and mother. Was it not through your recommendation that I won my case, and do I not owe my promotion to you? I told no one, sahib. No one knows to this day that the man is dead or that I found him, no one but I and the vultures."

I was beginning to see light, I thought. The villagers must have told him a garbled tale, or could they have shot the Aghori themselves, I wondered, and fastened it upon me? I suggested something of the kind.

He shook his head. "I have the bullet here," he said, commencing to untie the corner of his waistband. "I brought it to show."

I stretched out my hand. "Give it me," I cried, eagerly, and he put it on my palm.

I gazed at the little lump of metal in helpless amazement. Old and dinted as it was, there could be no mistake. It was a Paradigm bullet, and I fancy mine was the only gun of the kind that ever found its way to India. It was silver, too, and roughly scarred upon the base I could just make out an almost illegible "Allah."

My visitor sat watching me while I examined it. "Huzur," he said at last, "why should you fear to tell me? It was you that shot the man?"

I have no notion what I answered: I cannot answer yet. It is a riddle I have given up long ago as insoluble.

If the whole thing was some strange freak of chance, some extraordinary, inexplicable coincidence, then all I can say is that the coincidence is as astounding as magic itself. But be that as it may, to this I can swear—that the bullet Mozuffer Hussain gave me that day, as found in the body of a man, was the identical one made for me by Khuda Baksh and which I fired at the tiger. It was the charmed bullet.

STRANGE STORIES OF SPORT

XXV.—GORMAN'S FEUD [1]

BY FRANK SAVILE

They had been at Eton together—in the same house. They shared the same proclivities—both were dry bobs. In form they were lumped upon the same levels of learning. Both were sons of squires of reputable name, and held the same traditions. Every tendency of their lives, you would think, made for harmony and comradeship; in spite of which they cordially hated one another, and their aspects in approaching any given subject were the aspects of two dogs confronting one bone. Wilfred Heyford inevitably swore by codes which John Gorman held anathema. Gorman made no secret of the fact that he considered his enemy's tastes those of a vulgarian, and his performances those of a fool.

They left for Oxford together—one for Balliol, the other for New. As athletes they came into frequent collision. It was currently reported that upon the occasion when Heyford as three-quarter eluded Gorman as full back and gained the try which won the match for Balliol, the latter retired to his bed with *angina pectoris* induced by suppressed rage; while the malignant glee with which the New man—who bowled as well as full-backed—uprooted Heyford's middle stump and sent him back for a duck's-egg will not soon be forgotten where college batsmen congregate.

Both lived in the same county, and both, by Death's decree, entered on their inheritance at an early age. Fortunately for the peace of mind of two easy-going M.F.H. they were members of different hunts, but even here their antagonism found occasional opportunities to sprout. Heyford hunted—*and* shot. Gorman shot —*and* hunted. The first would hack fifteen miles when his foe's coverts were cubbed for the express pleasure of sniffing at the sport and impugning the character of his head keeper. Gorman would go to any lengths to be included in a day's shooting where he was likely to meet Heyford, for a single chance to wipe the eye of his *bête noire* or to feign alarm at his dangerous handling of his gun.

In spite of which they were the best of fellows and held in high esteem by a wide circle of acquaintance. But this little preface is necessary if you are to understand what follows.

Gorman took a Norway shooting one autumn. It included ten miles of shore with a wide hinterland, two good streams, and a few islands, the resort of many wild-fowl, dotted along the coast. The name of the place was Hjorunfjord, and it was accessible from Aalsund by pony or boat, with difficulty. The accommodation was simple—it was provided by a farmer and his wife at a saeter about a mile inland. Guns and rods were the chief caterers.

Gorman and his son Thomas installed themselves here at the beginning of August, and prepared to live the simple life with the zest of the true British countryman. The fact that sport left small margin in their lives for other matters at home did not prevent its brimming their days in Norway to the exclusion of all other interests.

" It's worth all the money to have no silly fools interrupting one," said the elder Gorman, genially ; and Thomas, a taciturn young man of four and twenty, nodded agreement.

Fate must have been listening, for a week later this Nimrod's Eden was raided by the serpent in a guise which was as unexpected as it was unwelcome.

When the weekly post came in—the first after their arrival—the head of the family lit his pipe and prepared for ten minutes of domestic enjoyment in perusing a budget of news from home. He expected no more than the serene annals of a well-conducted house, home farm, and stable. Judge then of Thomas's astonishment when the second page of rustling foreign paper produced from his father's lips a full-flavoured oath.

" Hallo ! " said the son, anxiously.

Gorman waggled his correspondence with a furious hand.

" Of all the cursed bits of luck ! " he bellowed. " I simply can't get away from the fellow ! "

" Who ? " demanded Thomas, who was nothing if not terse.

" Heyford ! " thundered his parent. " It's not enough that he poisons the air in our own neighbourhood, but he's had the confounded impudence to follow us here. Your mother met his wife at a garden party last week, and after the usual cackle found out that he and the boys and his girl have taken the lodge six miles to the west of us—Stuyflaaten—and are actually coming—come by now, no doubt—to be the bane of our lives where we can't get away from them ! "

" Oh ? " said Thomas.

His father threw him a most unpaternal scowl.

"Oh?" he mimicked, wrathfully. "Is that all you've got to say about it?"

The son tucked the ash into his pipe with a careful forefinger. "What *is* your quarrel with old Heyford?" he submitted. "I can't say I've ever got to the bottom of it."

Gorman apostrophised the deal ceiling with outstretched arms. "I'm fifty-two years of age," he confessed, "and ever since I was twelve the sight of Wilfred Heyford has soured my blood. And the fact has only just reached my son's intelligence!"

The young man shook his head. "Naturally I know you hate him," he rejoined. "All I ask is —why?"

For a moment or two his father regarded him with a sort of bewildered wonder. His dislike of his enemy had been a fact so intimately bound up with his own existence that he had never probed for the foundations of it. The baldness of the question staggered him.

"Why—why?" he bubbled, angrily. "You'll be asking reasons for the Prayer Book next, you young—radical! I hate him. That's enough."

"I thought him rather a decent old cock," said Thomas, calmly.

The squire flushed the colour of the best red lead. "You—*you* dared to think him d-d-decent!" he stuttered.

"I've never spoken to him before this summer," went on Heyford's defender, stolidly, "but I got to talking to him at the Allingham Tennis Tournament, and found we'd lots in common. The daughter plays a ripping game."

"You talked to *her?*"

"Drew as partners; worried through into the semi-finals," said the laconic Thomas.

"And this is the first I hear of it!" cried his father. "And I suppose you've made it your business to meet her again?"

Thomas flushed a little, but grinned. "Once or twice," he confessed, cheerfully; "but not often enough by a lot."

Gorman stood up and menaced his son with his fist. "If you think you're going to philander after this girl here, there, and everywhere, under my very nose, you'll find yourself most egregiously mistaken. I forbid you to have anything to do with the family—father, sons, *or* daughter!"

The unfilial Thomas laughed. "Come, dad," he suggested; "this ain't the Middle Ages, and I'm not fifteen!"

" You young puppy ! I tell you I'll keep you out of the hands of this girl, if I have to leave the place to-morrow ! "

Modern youth is not apt to put upon the fifth commandment too rigid an interpretation. Thomas chuckled again, and edged to the door.

" Be a man, dad ! " he urged, pleasantly. " Be a man—and remember that I'm one, too ! " and so took himself and his pipe out into the starlit evening.

The squire was left to finish his letter in an atmosphere which excluded all possibility of peace of mind.

If the above conversation introduced into Gorman's soul a certain passionate animation, what can be said of the state in which his son found him eight-and-forty hours later ! The two days had been passed by both with thrills of anticipation—thrills, it need scarcely be explained, born of widely different sources; but as yet no Heyford, male or female, had appeared to make a target for their emotions. On the third evening, however, Fate launched her bolt at them.

Coming home wet but jubilant, with five brace of ryper and a leash of duck, Thomas encountered his father stalking up and down before the saeter door, rage incarnate. He was quite carried above his usual bucolic planes of wrath—he gesticulated—he raved—he swore. For a minute or two he was scarcely coherent.

His story, when it did come, was quite explicit. He had been fishing on Dimōn, a little island of about fifty acres, with a small tarn in the middle of it which supplied incredibly game and tooth-some trout.

" I had just put up my rod," gurgled the squire, " I was taking a pull at my flask before I turned to the boat, when I heard a shot close to me. The next moment a ryper flew towards me, towered, and nearly fell upon my head ! What do I see next but three men walking towards me, bold as brass ! They came strutting up, staring at me as if I was a limpet—Heyford, his son, and ' Bully ' Blades."

Thomas started.

" No—not—not ' Bully ' Blades ? " he pleaded.

His father laughed grimly.

" That touches you on the raw, does it ? Yes—' Bully ' Blades, the millionaire, and the biggest scoundrel unhung. They've noosed him for Miss Nora, you may bet—got him away here on the quiet to tame him into a husband, and I think you may take my two to one that *your* nose is pretty considerably out of joint ! "

The young man was noticeably pale.

" They—they can't *know* about him ? " he protested.

" What Wilfred Heyford knows or doesn't know," snarled the

squire, "is a matter that doesn't concern me or you either—except in one respect, and that's the ownership of this shooting. He's had the impudence to tell me that Dimōn—*Dimōn*, the best island we've got—is on his side of the marches!"

Thomas's eyebrows rose.

"No!" he deprecated.

"He did!" cried his father, "and no two words about it. Though my very gorge rose at the sight of the fellow, I was as civil as a shopwalker. I merely suggested that even in Norway it was supposed to be commonly courteous to ask leave before you shot another man's land, when the brute began to roll his eyes at me and pant like a bullock. '*Your* land!' says he. 'Why, it's *my* land—scheduled in my lease as plain as ink and a pen can put it. You're fishing *my* waters!'

"Well, you can hardly suppose I took that sitting down. I told him that it was in my lease considerably plainer than I'd any reason to think it was in his, and that I could get twenty local witnesses to prove it. The beggar's a lunatic! He wouldn't hear reason—he roared at me like a tiger—he anticked like a baboon. And through it all 'Bully' stood there, laughing his disgusting, sneering laugh as if the two of us were a couple of pantaloons in a pantomime, capering for his benefit!"

A peculiar expression flickered over Thomas Gorman's face in which students of physiognomy might have found a tinge of sympathy—for Mr. Blades.

"And what's the upshot?" he demanded.

"Just this much," said his father. "I told them that I had an indisputable lease of the ground I was standing on, and that they were trespassing—in ignorance, perhaps. I said that it wasn't a plea they could advance again, because now they had had their warning. And I finished by remarking that if I found them or any of their party on Dimōn a second time I'd prosecute them for poaching as sure as there is a law in Norway. 'Bully' and young Heyford had practically to drag the old man to their boat. I believe he wanted to go for me, he was in such a rage, and begad I only wish they'd let him!"

"It would have been an interesting spectacle—two old gentlemen of your age getting to fisticuffs about a five-pound note's-worth of shooting," said Thomas, dryly.

"You young jackanapes!" returned his father, hotly. "Just because you're sweet on that girl of his I suppose you'd have liked me to lick his boots and retire in good order?"

"I don't see why you shouldn't have offered to share it with him pending inquiries," suggested the enamoured youth.

"Oh, you don't—don't you?" sneered the squire. "Well, I'll just tell you what I do mean to do. I'm going to put a notice up on Dimōn first thing to-morrow announcing that it's private land— I'm going to spend the day there with my rod and gun—and I'm going to take steps to prosecute the first man that lands on it without my leave if he has the whole Norwegian Fleet to back his landing. That's what I'm going to do. Any remarks?"

The young man shrugged his shoulders with a superior air.

"The whole thing appears to me exceedingly silly," he said, and escaped into the house, leaving his father to pollute the evening airs with anathemas which impartially condemned the stupendous insolence of rapacious neighbours and undutiful sons.

Not quite such an early riser as his parent, Thomas strode out from breakfast the following morning to find the squire's preparations already complete. In addition to the impedimenta of sport he bore a long pole adorned with a cross-piece on which appeared the following legend in magnificent letters of white : —

ADVARSEL ! PRIVAT !

INGEN ADGANG FOR UVEDKOMMEDE !

The youth examined it critically.

"Think they understand Norwegian?" he suggested.

Gorman shrugged his shoulders.

"That's their affair," he said. "If this thing has to be fought out in Norwegian courts it's got to be conducted according to Norwegian law. I'm off."

"Don't be in a hurry. I'm going your way," said his son.

"Where?" said his parent, suspiciously.

"The fjords beyond Dimōn. Sea trout," explained Thomas, brief as usual, and went to fetch his rod. Father and son presently strode down toward the shore in a silence which a novelist might describe as "brooding." Trofast, a nondescript retriever, borrowed from the farmer, accompanied them.

Arrived at the little landing-stage the elder man arranged his paraphernalia in the stern of the sea-going boat which he usually used. Thomas busied himself in bailing out his canoe, which had filled with the rain of the previous night. The former was ready first, and whistled up Trofast. The dog came bounding towards him, stopped, snarled, and then trotted up to Thomas and licked his hand in an excited, eager sort of way. After which he seized a pebble, bit at it, and began to roll like a puppy.

"What's the matter with the brute?" demanded Gorman, irritably, and whistled again. Trofast cantered up obediently and took his place in the boat.

Thomas looked at him keenly.

"He's been a bit off his feed the last day or two," he said. "Want's a powder, I expect."

"Been fed rankly," said his father. "I found him with his nose stuck in an empty potted-meat tin only yesterday."

The young man nodded.

"A morning's work will straighten him out," he said, and launched his bark. With long steady sweeps of his paddle he soon left the heavier boat behind, and disappeared round a headland while his father pulled out into the bay towards the island where he meant to keep his sentinelship over his threatened rights.

Dimōn was certainly a model of what a sporting island should be. Its sparse vegetation was the haunt of not a few ryper. Plover and oyster-catchers shrilled from every tuft. The shallows of its foreshore were alive with duck and dotterel, in addition to which the tarn in its centre teemed with trout. Reflecting on these matter a smile of grim determination broadened upon the squire's lips. "I'll bankrupt myself before the beggar shall rob me of it," he told himself, and cast a keen glance in the direction of Stuyflaaten as he landed.

No hostile expedition was in sight, and slipping a couple of cartridges into his gun he prepared for enjoyment.

He had not gone thirty yards before a brood rose, and a neat right and left put him on the best of terms with himself. Marking the birds down, he succeeded in flushing them again and repeating the performance. Before half an hour was over he had made a bag of half a dozen brace. A couple of teal whirred in from the sea and were downed—three oyster-catchers rose in succession and sounded their last whistle. Gorman began to forget his wrongs in the excitement of the chase. So far there were only two flies in his ointment: first that he had not brought sufficient cartridges to cope with the situation, secondly that Trofast was retrieving shamefully. He mouthed the birds badly, and practically tore one to pieces before he relinquished it. Gorman admonished him savagely with his boot, and Trofast snapped angrily back.

Finding that no more than five cartridges remained to him, he decided to expend them cautiously. Shy after so much shooting, the duck had left the shallows, but after an interval of quiet would soon return. Gorman concealed himself behind a boulder upon the foreshore and waited.

His confidence was not misplaced. With a rush and a whizz a great flock passed over his head and splashed among the weed, well within range. A couple of barrels among them sitting accounted for five. He was able to reload and get two more from the flock as, unable to locate their enemy, they swung past him on rising.

His last shot was a "cripple stopper" directed at a mallard which was threshing out to sea with a broken wing. Gorman rose from his ambush with a well-satisfied expression.

Trofast was already swimming. He gathered a couple into his capacious jaws, laid them on the sand, swam out after another, brought it back, produced three from the weeds by wading, and then sat down stolidly. He refused to take any notice of the last, which was rocking upon the ripples twenty yards out. Gorman motioned him towards it. The dog did not budge. His master flung a stone at the bird to direct his attention. Trofast rose, made a circular motion, howled, and began to bite savagely at the seaweed. A little rope of viscous saliva hung from his lips.

" Good Lord!" said Gorman, and drew back a pace.

He eyed the animal keenly. It howled again, snapped at an imaginary fly in the air, ran round another little circle, and sat down, panting.

" They say there is no such thing as rabies in Scandinavia," soliloquised Gorman, " but I'm hanged if I like the looks of this!"

Suddenly Trofast rose and galloped towards him. Instinctively Gorman cocked his gun, forgetting that the chambers were empty. But as he ran a tuft of ling brushed the dog's face. He stopped on the instant and tore at it fiercely, lying down at last and rolling upon the shreds. Gorman was no coward, so it is no reflection upon him to say that he used this interval to make the best time towards the boat that his legs had compassed since he was in his teens. He pushed off a yard or two and stared at Trofast as the latter pattered down towards the shore. He had left off snapping, but howled pitifully. The stringy saliva was thick upon his jaws.

"Not good enough," decided Gorman, setting to his oars. " I'll leave him here and go for Halvorsen. If the brute is given to these capers the farmer will know and we can fetch him away. If not "—he shrugged his shoulders—" nothing for it but a charge of No. 5."

For a quarter of an hour he rowed steadily, meditating over the incidents of the morning, the matter of Heyford and his aggressions completely planed from his mind. It was restored to his memory with dramatic suddenness. The sound of oars broke into the stillness. He looked round. Passing him was a boat, rowed by " Bully " Blades and steered by his enemy's daughter.

Nora Heyford blushed and bowed. " Bully " gave him a patronising little nod. " Good sport on Dimōn? " he questioned, with a little snigger.

Gorman stared at him.

" Excellent," he said, tersely, and " Bully " sniggered again.

305

"Glad to hear it. We're just going to try our luck," he answered, with another nod towards the fishing-rod beside him.

Gorman's eyes gleamed.

"I've already warned you that I don't allow trespassing," he said, wrathfully. "I forbid your landing on my island."

"Bully" laughed.

"Now, my very dear Mr. Gorman," he rejoined, "Mr. Heyford, who is unfortunately too seedy to come himself this morning, has shown me his lease. Dimōn Island is expressly scheduled in it. From inquiries we have made, it appears that there are two Dimōns —the Big and the Little. We are not inclined to think that ours is the little one."

"That settles it," said Gorman. "My island *is* Store Dimōn —is so called in my list. Yours is the rock in Stuyflaaten Bay."

"*Of* course," sneered the other, "you're to have fifty acres of the best shooting on the coast, while we're to have a rock a gull can hardly perch on. We'll see!"

Gorman commanded himself, though he felt that if a lady had not been present a boarding expedition, in which Mr. Blades would have been cast for the part of the defeated, would have inevitably terminated the interview.

"Look here," he said; "I warn you that if you land on Dimōn I shall prosecute you for trespass. I also warn you that I have left on the island a dog which I strongly suspect to be suffering from rabies. If you go, you go at your own peril!"

"Bully" shouted with laughter.

"That's won it!" he derided. "A mad dog in Norway! There hasn't been such a thing known since the creation of the world!"

Then the devil entered into John Gorman.

For a long instant he stared at the two opposite him, seeing not the distressed expression on the girl's face, but only the mocking smile her companion was directing at him. Without another word he rowed stolidly away.

He rowed on and on, the sound of "Bully's" derision dying into the distance. He saw that the other boat was pointing straight for Dimōn, but he made no sign. He reached the shore, moored, took up his gun, and walked with long steady strides up to the farm, thinking, thinking, thinking. Certain words were ringing in his head—words casually heard in a train when a doctor had been describing to a friend the death of a patient under hydrophobia.

"His people weren't allowed to see him till quite the end, and he didn't know them," the medical man had said. "Poor chap, he was simply wrapped up in his wife and kids!"

He gasped—his brow grew darker and darker—he began to realise just what a thing John Gorman had done. At the door of the farm a sudden tension seemed to break in his mind. With an incoherent exclamation he darted into his room, stuffed a dozen cartridges in his pocket, and went flying back to the shore again like a man possessed. He rowed out into the bay with tremendous wrenching strokes.

Meanwhile the boat which bore Nora Heyford and her companion was grating its keel on Dimon's beach. As " Bully " looked round him he sighed with satisfaction.

" No wonder that old sinner wants to keep this to himself," he said. " It's a little sporting Paradise—that's what it is. Look at the duck in those shallows ! "

" Other people seem to have been of your opinion in times past," said the girl. " There was a house or castle here once."

She pointed to some tottering ruins built of beach cobbles from which the mortar had been weather-worn for centuries.

" They knew a bit—those old sea-kings," said " Bully." " No end of times here once, I daresay. Wassails and what not."

They strolled along a couple of hundred yards and stood at the foot of the wall. It had evidently once enclosed a peninsula, but the seaward end had rotted under the influence of storm and tide. Nora produced her camera.

" Lucky I brought this," she remarked. " It's well worth a picture."

" Bully" watched her admiringly. Suddenly he gave a start.

" What's that ? " he cried, anxiously, and started again. A wild and piercing howl came from the far side of the island, and was obviously drawing nearer. " Great Scot, perhaps old Gorman wasn't rotting us after all ! " suggested Mr. Blades, suddenly very pale of face.

The next instant there was no room for doubt. A dog, openmouthed and wild-eyed, appeared about a furlong distant, galloping towards them. His yell of rage as he discovered them made them shiver.

With a simultaneous rush they started towards the boat, "Bully" running as he had probably never run in his life before. But Nora Heyford dropped her camera. The strap caught her foot. She blundered upon her knees.

She gave a cry. " Bully " looked round, hesitated, and in that moment the dog howled again. Without another glance the man continued his maddened rush towards the boat, leaped upon it, and pushed out into the open. Nora rocked up to her feet again dizzily to see the dog bearing down upon her not a hundred yards away.

Mere instinct saved her. Escape to the boat was obviously beyond her powers. She rushed at the wall, got her fingers in one crevice and her foot in another, and—she scarcely knew how—dragged herself to the top. She lay upon her breast panting as the dog lumbered up to the wall and flung himself against it. The cobbles shook beneath his weight. He scrambled and bit at the stones only a little way below her.

She looked round. Her gallant cavalier had manœuvred the boat to within a few yards of the seaward end of the wall, and was watching her with an expression of shame-faced terror.

" Come in ! Attract his attention ! " shouted the girl. " He'll have the wall down directly. The stones are so much rubble."

" Bully " made a reluctant stroke or two. The dog rushed down to the water's edge, snarled at him, and then made another attack upon the wall. Several stones fell from its face.

" Come in with the oar and beat at him ! " cried Nora. " Hit him ! Stun him ! You can do it easily if you come close enough ! "

" Bully " made another stroke gingerly, feinted with his weapon, but missed by a matter of yards.

" Closer—closer ! " shouted the girl ; but the prudent Mr. Blades shook his head.

" It's no manner of use," he argued. " If I come any nearer he'll spring aboard. There's nothing for it but to row off for a gun. You'll be all right up there till I get back."

Nora made a piteous gesture.

" I shan't—I shan't ! " she cried. " He'll have the wall down long before then." But " Bully " had already made a bee line for Stuyflaaten.

She fell upon her knees in an agony of despair. " The coward—the coward ! " she sobbed, and watched with desperate eyes how her enemy was sapping her defences with rush on rush.

Ten minutes later Thomas Gorman was paddling solemnly homeward in by no means the best of tempers. A regular sea monster—or at any rate he liked to think it such—had taken his line into a pool, fouled it with drift weed, tangled it upon the rocks, and finally returned half of it sawn asunder. The imprudent youth had omitted to take a " spare," and was in consequence despoiled of a morning's sport. He eyed Dimōn keenly as he rounded the headland, wondering whether hostilities had already commenced.

He rubbed his eyes. Had his father erected a pillar upon the old ruined masonry at the seaward side ?

No pillar this. It moved—it fluttered a handkerchief—faintly across the surface it was sending him appeals for help. The cries were mingled with the howlings of a dog.

Thomas sent his canoe bounding over the ripples at a most meritorious speed. In response to frantic gestures of warning he brought it to a halt a few yards from the shore. He stared at the occupant of the castle wall with unmixed surprise.

"Nora—Miss Heyford!" he stammerd. "Why, it's *our* dog—Trofast!"

"He's mad—he's mad!" panted Nora, "and the wall's crumbling!"

In another instant Thomas would have been ashore, but the girl's shriek of dismay stopped him.

"No!" she cried. "He *is* mad—your father warned us. Have you got a revolver—any sort of weapon?"

"No," said Thomas, stolidly. "Except my gaff," he added, looking at the great barb of steel. With a sudden inspiration he took it up.

"Throw a stone towards me!" he cried.

Without understanding, but with feminine obedience, the girl complied.

She plucked a pebble from the wall and flung it. It was not a great shot, but the missile reached the shore. Instinctively following the retrieving instinct with his poor clouded brain Trofast pursued, and, as it splashed into the water, bit furiously at the weed round the point of its disappearance. The canoe shot forward, and the next instant the gaff was firmly fixed in the dog's collar. He was jerked into the sea. He snarled and snapped savagely. The canoe rocked, shipped water, settled, and finally sank. Thomas was left standing in a four-foot-deep pool, straining every muscle in his arms to drag his enemy under.

In the fury of his mania the dog fought with incredible strength. He swam with great panting strokes, mouthing at his antagonist, forced under every instant only to reappear again more furious than before. The ripples widened from the struggle and lashed the shore as man and beast strove, and the little pool was white with foam. Round and round they whirled, Thomas's arms taut as wire hawsers, his fingers gripping the handle of the gaff as a man only grips when his life depends on the hold. For five minutes they swung and gasped, the dog still held off a full yard at the gaff's end, and then Trofast began to weaken.

After each immersion he coughed and choked more deeply. A glaze began to grow upon the maddened eyes—his strokes were feebler. Steadily, relentlessly, Thomas thrust him down. Another minute—another few seconds, and the struggle would have inevitably ended.

Then, in very sight of victory, fortune deserted the youth. His foot slipped upon a bank of weed! With a most resounding splash he went completely under, while Trofast, after a wild stare round, began to paddle weakly to the shore. The gaff trailed from his collar.

The dog climbed upon the rocks and shook himself. His breathing grew easier—savage lights began to glitter again in his eyes, and at that moment Thomas Gorman staggered up to his feet. For a tense instant man and brute glared at each other. Then Trofast's limbs strung themselves for a spring.

Nora Heyford shrieked despairingly. Then she gave another cry—one filled with amazement—with hope.

There was a crash of pebbles, and like a bull at the charge John Gorman came racing across the beach, gun in hand. His eyes were bloodshot—his breath came in great gasps. Trofast whirled round to confront this new enemy.

Gorman pulled himself up twenty yards away, still panting. The butt of his gun sprang to his shoulder.

Trofast lumbered forward—there was a flash—a report. The dog sprang with a curious headlong motion into the air, rolled back, kicked, and lay still. There was no need for the second charge which Gorman poured into his inanimate carcase.

Then a tension seemed to break in the squire's body. He sat down suddenly and covered his face with his hands. Thomas looked at him queerly, hesitated, and then walked up to the foot of the wall. He held out his arms.

With a little gesture which seemed to imply infinite content and surrender, Nora Heyford slipped down into them. Thomas held her very tight.

He looked into her eyes.

" Eh ? " he questioned, tersely, and seemed to read an answer, for there was none in words.

With imperturbable practicality Thomas kissed his lady-love.

Twenty yards away John Gorman raised his head and gazed at the pair. They faced him, awaiting explosions.

None came.

" Thank God ! " said Thomas's father as he rose to his feet. " Thank God ! "

*   *   *   *   *

And so ended the feud between the houses of Heyford and Gorman—a feud which had such flimsy foundations that the present historian has never, even with earnest probing, discovered them; but the reconciliation to which it gave rise has very solid buttresses.

STRANGE STORIES OF SPORT

XXVI.—THE WINDS

BY GEOFFREY WILLIAMS

"I REALLY shouldn't wonder if there were something in the story," observed Dick Redwood.

"Stuff and nonsense," I snapped, crossly, for I was not in a good temper at the moment.

I had come up a fortnight ago to spend a few hard-earned weeks at my pet fishing-place in Western Ross, and the Fates had been adverse. Day after day had slipped by, and still the rain held off and the clear low water ridiculed my most skilful piscatorial efforts. My long-looked-for holiday was turning out a dismal failure, and I think that sufficient excuse for a good deal of irritation.

"In spite of your highly impressive arguments," went on Dick, imperturbably, "I am of the same opinion still. Let's go and investigate for ourselves."

"Really you're very obstinate," I said; "if you are going to believe every strange yarn you hear up in these parts you'll find your credulity is put to a pretty severe test. Every glen and every tarn has its mystery."

"Yes, I know all that; but the story seems to me to have a basis of the truth in it, and I want to know more about it. I shall certainly go. Will you come?"

I picked up my rod, balanced it thoughtfully for a moment, and then looked up at the sky. Clear and brazen, it cast a glare on everything, even at this early hour, that betokened ill for fishing prospects. Not a breath of air disturbed the seeding grasses in the little field across the road. Reluctantly I accepted the decision of Fate, and, turning with a sigh, I said, "Very well, I will come," and so it is the weather I have to thank for embarking me upon an expedition which has more than satisfied my exploring instincts.

Should I have gone if I had known what was to come? I wonder?

The story which had fired Dick's curiosity to such an unusual interest was in essentials pretty much the same as many others I had heard in my frequent wanderings in the wilder parts of Ross and Sutherland. In fact I think it was more the convincing manner of the teller than the story itself which had impressed us. The surroundings at the time also doubtless heightened the effect, for the story was told by one of our gillies, an ancient person answering to the name of Dugald, as we were walking back from our unsuccessful fishing the previous evening. We were very late coming home, having stayed on by a promising little tarn in the mountains in the hopes of an evening rise, which desire of our hearts was, I need hardly say, denied us. The sun had gone well down behind the hills before we knew, and the twilight was already peopled with the mysterious shadows that ever shift and wander by night among the Scottish moorlands.

Our homeward way was wild and desolate, passing over rocky heather-clad slopes from the crests of which, from time to time, we looked down on the still grey sea with its craggy barren coast. The place seemed different somehow from when we had crossed it in the morning. Then the rocks gleamed and sparkled in the sun, and the glistening white gulls swooped and wheeled over the shimmering bays, while each little tarn and burn was set in a bright frame of purple heather. But the cheerfulness of the scene had passed with the sunlight, and all was now a gloomy expanse in grey, shapeless and undefined. The path was rough, and we scrambled along in silence, feeling that talk was out of place, while the stillness grew about us till the sudden mournful call of a curlew protesting against unwonted disturbance of its usually peaceful haunts seemed like the cry of a spirit of despair.

Presently we came to the edge of a rugged hill from which the country sloped down to the rock-bound coast, and old Dugald, pointing to a particularly imposing cliff that jutted out into the distant sea below, broke the long silence.

"In that rock," he said, "dwell the little men."

Dick pricked up his ears: he was new to this kind of thing. "Tell me the story," he asked, eagerly.

312

And Dugald, wishing nothing better, plunged into his yarn in the hushed tone suitable to the time and the subject. He told of strange sights seen around the cliff at night, of weird cries heard in the surrounding glens, and of women whose experiences had bereft them of their reason. Many and horrible were the details he gave, and when finished he stopped suddenly and whispered " Listen ! " He had so wrought upon my imagination that I could have sworn I heard something that one does not look to hear in a barren heath— a dry, low chuckle passing simply over the moors ; the old man knew how to produce a good effect, and was a born *raconteur*.

He went on to tell how in days gone by various bold persons had set out to solve the mystery of the cave in the cliff whence all these strange happenings sprang, and how their hearts had failed them at the last, and they had fled from the mouth of the cave with their inquiring spirit effectually quenched. All this I had heard often before, but he finished up in an unexpectedly definite manner, declaring that when he was a boy of fifteen or so, which would be some fifty years ago, two men had set out to examine the cave, had been seen by friends accompanying them to enter it, and had never come out. No one dared go in to look for them, and there, according to Dugald, they must be still.

It may seem impossible that two men could disappear in this way without a proper search being made, but in the wild country old superstitions die hard, and to anybody who knows it and its people it will not be hard to believe that no one was found hardy enough to tempt the fate that every soul in the district was convinced had befallen the two unfortunates.

The whole story, especially the end, had profoundly impressed my companion, and the result was that I had bound myself to join him in exploring the cave in question. When once I had agreed to go he was for starting immediately, and I had some trouble to induce him to wait while I made a few preparations. If you decide to set off on a wild-goose chase at all you may as well be ready for the wild goose should you chance to find it, and I accordingly provided myself with a supply of rope and candles, a lantern, and a revolver, the last-mentioned article being a satisfying thing to have by one, though I confess I did not expect to use it.

The cave could only be reached by sea, and we started off from the little pier below the inn with the prospect of a good three hours' pull before us, as there was no breeze and sails were merely a useless encumbrance. We had intended to go alone, and had said nothing of our intentions to anyone ; but just as we were starting we found that our second gillie, Ronald, a smart and intelligent young fellow of about twenty, wished to accompany us. I had noticed that he was a good deal moved when Dugald had told his story the night before, and he now explained that one of the missing men had been his grandfather, so that, guessing our intention and being either less superstitious or more daring than his fellows, he meant to try to solve the mystery of his ancestor's fate. We were only too glad of another pair of arms to help pull the heavy boat, and accepted him and his filial affection with alacrity, at which he expressed himself grateful, though I must confess that his set expression and the obvious way in which he had steeled himself to go through with what he considered an excessively dangerous quest did not strike me as likely to enliven us during the journey or strengthen our nerves if anything startling did happen in the cave.

It was a glorious day, and as I sat lazily in the stern pretending to steer, watching Dick, who was rowing with admirable energy if with a slight lack of skill, I felt that I was enjoying myself considerably. Dick's cheerful grin and obvious delight in his little adventure should have been enough to put anyone in good spirits.

But my beatitude of mind did not last, and as we passed point after point that marked the succession of bays that indent this coast I felt my spirits sinking lower and lower. A glance at Ronald tended little to raise them, and I wondered whether by some form of telepathy he was transferring his own feelings to me through the wide grey eyes that were fixed on mine with that peculiar unseeing stare which is so characteristic of an oarsman.

A sensation of impending evil grew on me as we neared our goal, and at last I found myself admitting in my own mind that I was not the sceptic I gave myself out to be, and that in my heart of hearts I was by no means sure that our investigation would be attended only by the purely scientific interest of ordinary cave exploration. I am practically a pure Celt, and I suppose superstition is in the blood and can never be rooted out through education, though education and environment may cover it with a crust which takes a good deal of breaking. However that may be, I found myself thinking that these weird Highland stories must have some foundation and that I was about to do an exceedingly foolish thing; but caution had come too late, and realising that it was impossible to draw back now, I resolutely put my forebodings behind me, though with something of an effort, I confess. Time had slipped by while I had been struggling with depression, and when I pulled myself together I found that we were already approaching the mouth of our cave.

The opening was a great arch about fifty feet across, the dark grey rock walls sloping sheer down into the sea floor which ran

314

straight in as far as the eye could see. We halted at the entrance for a rest, and while Dick lit a pipe and Ronald prepared the lantern, I gazed thoughtfully down the deep shadows beyond and wondered how things would be with us in another hour or two. As I looked it suddenly struck me that there was no possible path from the cave to the land except by water, for nothing could have found foothold on the precipitous walls that shut us in as we drifted slowly forward. At the thought my spirits rose considerably, for if this were the case no dwellers in the cave could get ashore, since it was hardly likely they would be provided with boats, and therefore the stories of the deeds perpetrated by them on the moors behind must be totally without foundation.

I pointed this out to the other two, who took it differently, Dick showing only disappointment, while Ronald looked decidedly relieved, and cheered up sufficiently to relapse into a smile. But it soon faded, and his superstitious feelings evidently got the better of him again. In his view the inhabitants of such a place, if any, would not be hampered by mortal disabilities. In fact, it was evident to me that our delay at the entrance was only telling on his nerves and setting his Highland imagination to work; so, seeing that the lights were ready, I gave the word to go ahead.

We rowed slowly for fear of sunken rocks, and it must have been some ten minutes after we left the sun behind us before we saw any possible landing place. The sea floor ran in for an unusual distance, and the precipitous walls showed no break in their smooth steep slopes. At length the arched entrance began to change in character, the width decreased rapidly, and the sides grew rugged and broken, while from every ledge and cranny rock pigeons flew angrily forth, clapping their strong wings in protest. The roof became higher and the walls showed an increasing slope away from the water. After a hundred yards or so of this, a spit of rock loomed up unexpectedly out of the floor ahead, and in another instant our keel was grating on a gravelly beach beside it. Our voyage was at an end.

The passage had so far been very nearly straight, and a faint streak of light was still visible from the way we had come. I think we all felt a disinclination to see the last of it and lose our communion with the outside world, and when I suggested lunch and whisky before going on, the idea met with instant approval.

Although I was glad of the chance to watch the tiny streak of light for a few minutes more, suggestive as it was of life and sun and brightness, I confess that it seemed to me rather uncanny to eat in such a place. Dick, however, had no such qualms, and devoured ham sandwiches and marmalade scones with the untroubled appetite of two and twenty. I am not exactly a centenarian myself, but a few years makes a difference in these little matters.

I was tempted to waste more time over a pipe, but thought better of it, realising that if it was undesirable to hang about outside the cave, it was still worse to stand upon the order of our going now we were well embarked on our enterprise; so I seized the lantern, and led the way up the beach with the others close behind me carrying candles. The spit of rock by the side of which we had lunched ran straight along on our right, the top of it being some four feet above the water's edge. But the beach sloped steeply, and a few yards brought us to the level of it. It was about two feet broad, and flat, making a good smooth path with shingly gravel on either side, and along it we marched in single file for some distance, when I noticed to my surprise that the beach on either side sloped down again to water, the rock path running through it like a jetty. Soon after reaching the water again, the cave took a sharp turn, so sharp that I, in front, as nearly as possible fell over the edge. Had I done so I might have had an exceedingly unpleasant time, as the path was now a good eight feet above the water, and to climb up the steep sides would have been impossible, while I am not a sufficiently good swimmer to regard a swim of some two hundred yards back to the beach in my clothes as within the region of practical politics.

Another two or three hundred yards round the corner brought us to the end of the path and the water together, and we found ourselves standing once more on shingles and gravel. At this point the place again altered its character, and the light of the lantern showed black murky passages in the walls leading away in every direction. The main passage was, however, still quite definite, and we pursued our way along it, though not before I had fastened the end of the ball of string with which I had come provided to a projecting spur of rock. I had no desire to be lost in the labyrinth around us, and meant to make sure of one retreat. The darkness was now, of course, complete, and the feeble glimmer of the candles seemed merely to accentuate it, swallowed up as it was in the passages on either side that grew more numerous at every step. We walked carefully, fearing pitfalls or a sudden descent of the roof, and I was beginning to feel that we should wander for ever in these dark places of the earth when a sudden cry from Dick, a few paces behind me, brought me to a standstill, in a surprise that nearly made me drop the lantern.

"What on earth is the matter?" I called, my voice echoing weirdly through the vaults of rock; "I wish you wouldn't startle me like that."

"Startle, indeed!" cried Dick, indignantly, "small wonder if I did. What blew my candle out?"

I had not noticed it before, but I now saw the red end of the wick glowing dimly before me.

"There isn't a breath of air in here," he went on, "and yet just now a bitterly cold gust came down one of these passages and blew the candle out and left me shivering."

He certainly was; but before I could answer, Ronald's light went out before my eyes, while an icy blast that cut through me till I felt like an iceberg shook the lantern in my hand, swinging it violently to and fro on its jointed handles.

"Merciful heavens!" I ejaculated, while Ronald groaned dismally, evidently half scared. "What can it mean? Gusts like this don't——"

But Dick had impressed silence on me. "Listen," he whispered. In an instant we stood hardly breathing, waiting I knew not what, and there came a chuckle—a horrible, dry, crackling chuckle—from the passage nearest me. I jumped back with an exclamation, nearly knocking the others down, and stood with my back against the wall, breathing uneasily, while that infernal travesty of laughter went on, coming apparently from just beyond the circle of light thrown by the lantern.

Pulling myself together, I dashed forward up the side passage towards the sound, but another of those awful blasts met me and swept by, while, as I staggered back, shattered with cold, the chuckle came again, this time from behind me.

I would have given anything to have run back at full speed towards the boat; but I knew that to give way to panic in that place would be fatal, and walking as casually as I could up to the others, I said in a voice I strove vainly to render steady, "Come here against the wall away from the passage, and we'll think what to do." They came, and we talked it over, pretending to treat it as a joke, a pretence that deceived no one, but helped to steady our nerves, which were badly jangled. Dick was for returning, feeling he had had enough of it; but the obstinate side of me was now uppermost, and I voted for going on. To my surprise, Ronald voted with me; I believe he felt, and rightly, that to go back would be harder than to go forward, and that if we ever gave in to the impression against which we were now struggling it would make bad worse. So Dick, entreated, came round to our view, and we relit the candles and went on.

We soon found that we must rely solely upon our lantern for light. The blasts of air—were they merely blasts of air? I did not feel very sure about it—continued from time to time to issue from

317

the narrow ways on either side of the main tunnel, and finally our
stock of matches grew so low that we dared not relight the candles,
which went out every few seconds. The constant chill resulting
from the perpetual shocks of cold air, together with the malevolent
and uncanny chuckles which accompanied them, began gradually to
tell upon us seriously, and I think we should have all soon turned
back in despair had we not, on turning a corner, seen a gleam of red
light ahead of us. It wavered and rose and fell like a fire, and the
flickering beams cast varied shadows on the rock walls and down the
mysterious passage, while to our excited imagination the labyrinth
became of a sudden peopled with indefinite forms, and watching,
eager eyes seemed to gaze at us as though they were lit up by the
reflection of the strange light. How much of this we really saw and
how much we fancied I should hardly like to say, writing now in
cold blood; but if I shut my eyes I can see those malevolent orbs
glittering once more against the background of unfathomable black
that rolled away behind the rays of light like the folds of a gigantic
curtain.

Intense curiosity rendered us for the moment oblivious of aught
else, and we hurried forward with renewed energy towards the light.
A few moments brought us to the spot, and the mystery of the fire
at least was explained. It was merely a small escape of natural gas
which had in some way become ignited. The flame was small and
far from steady, but though it rose and fell it never quite went out.
We stood awhile in silence, watching the flame rise and fall, and
the strange phenomenon so invited attention that the sudden grip of
Dick's hand upon my arm made me jump as if I had been shot.

"What's the matter now?" I ejaculated, snappishly; but Dick
made no answer and only gripped my arm tighter. I looked up at
him in surprise, and saw that he was pointing with arm outstretched
down the tunnel beyond the flame, his usually cheery face set in an
expression of horrified incredulity.

Following the direction of his gaze, I stared curiously into the
darkness beyond, wondering what had created such a powerful impression upon him. At first I could distinguish nothing but twin
points of brightness glowing like stars in the gloom; but as my eyes
grew accustomed to the faint and flickering light something gradually
seemed to shape itself out of the wavering shadows where the red
beams merged with and were lost in the deep fall of blackness
beyond. The twin stars grew in strength and brightness, till a conviction grew and strengthened upon me that they were eyes—eyes
glittering with cruel mischief and malevolent enjoyment. As the
light twinkled and danced in their evil depths, I appeared dimly to
make out that they were set in a small brown face, below which the

shifting shadows slowly formed themselves into the vague, indefinite semblance of a miniature figure, which began to sway gently to and fro and chuckle to itself as though at some hidden joke which gave it intense satisfaction.

On a sudden my nerves went with a snap, and turning swiftly I started to make my way at a run down the tunnel. The others followed me, but before we had gone a dozen yards we were met by blast after blast of frozen wind which beat us back as we struggled madly and unavailingly, till, shattered with cold and exhausted by new efforts, we found ourselves standing once more beside the flame, while I strained my eyes to see if the shape existed only in my imagination. As I gazed the sound of diabolical mirth was repeated, a wave of blind rage surged within me, and, hardly realising what I was about, I snatched my revolver from my pocket and fired twice.

As the bullet sped, the chuckle changed to a shriek which battled with the report of the pistol, then died slowly away up the countless passages, and as the last echo ceased a new sound became audible. Around us the air filled rapidly with long-drawn wailing murmurs that grew in volume as they approached from out the vistas of black darkness. Swiftly they were borne down upon us by the winds that swept past. At the first onset I was hurled back into a recess in the wall, and the lantern dropped from my hand, extinguishing itself as it reached the rock floor, and the strange flame was put out in an instant as the winds passed furiously by.

For hours it seemed to me that I stood cowering in my recess, protected by the projecting wall, and listening to the cries wailing and sobbing up the tunnel; but I suppose the whole thing did not last more than a few moments. At length the last wailing sped soughing away through the impenetrable gloom, and I was left alone with the two unconscious figures before me in the darkness, absolutely alone. For I seemed to know, though how the knowledge came to me I cannot tell, that the powers, spirits, influences, whatever they may have been that had followed us in our wanderings, had left us, at any rate for the time.

The relief was intense, and I felt more myself as I picked up the lantern which lay at my feet and relit it. The faint light fell across the narrow passage, and showed up the crack in the rock flooring through which the flame had found its way until extinguished by the rush of winds, and at the sight I remembered that the gas must even now be escaping and vitiating the air. Hurriedly I stepped forward and set a match to it, forgetting in my anxiety that enough gas might already have escaped to produce something in the nature of an explosion. But fortunately the flow was slight, no harm came of my somewhat rash experiment, and I turned to find my companions, silent and awe-stricken, close to me.   I had not thought of them.   Our one desire now was to be out of the vault that hemmed us in, and I looked for the string which was to lead us back to our boat, and which I had dropped in my battle against the Winds. To my horror it was gone.   In vain I searched for it.   By some unknown agency it had been removed.   The only thing to be done was to try to retrace our steps as best we could without guidance. I supposed that, as the tunnel along which we had come had been quite distinct from the side passages, we should find it equally easy to follow when returning, and it was not till we had gone some two hundred yards that it dawned upon me we were traversing a different tunnel.

The situation was an awful one, and we were for a time too overcome to do aught but look at each other in horror, not daring to put our thoughts into words.   We soon saw, however, that there was nothing for it but to try passage after passage in the hope of finding the right one, and wearily we traversed those endless tunnels with steadily diminishing hope of escape.

At length a thought came to me.   Possibly the cave had an outlet on the land side, and unless the passages on the other side of the flame led also to a common centre, we might stand a better chance by going straight ahead instead of trying vainly to find our way through that hopeless maze.   With doubt and trembling lest we should meet with another disappointment we passed forward beyond the zone of flickering light, and to our inexpressible relief found that the tunnel pursued its way as before, the branching passages still tending onward, and not back as we had feared.   At last we discerned a ray of faint grey light, striking through from above, which spoke to us joyfully of the fresh open air. A few more strides brought us to the entrance, a narrow crack in the rocks, and with a squeeze and a struggle we were through and sitting on a clump of flowering heather with the twinkling stars shining a welcome to us from the deep vault of the evening sky. Thankfully we sat there and rested, fanned by the light air that blew softly past us, charged with the scent of bog myrtle and heather, and wondering what were the mysteries we had heard and felt and dimly seen, and what had been the fate of those unfortunates who had last attempted to brave the terrors of the Winds.

STRANGE STORIES OF SPORT

XXVII.—A MISSFIRE

A Tale of Monte Carlo

BY PEYTON WREY

"Trente-six, trente-deux. *Rouge gagne et couleur.*" So says the croupier, out comes the rake, and Morson's pile of louis is swept away with the rest. He rises from the table, a dark, clean-shaven man of thirty-five or so, at whom you glance twice, wondering, if you are a bit of a physiognomist, whether there is or is not a suggestion of furtive cunning in his eyes.

"Had enough? Shall we go?" inquired Wynne, a younger man, light complexioned, with a small upturned moustache, who had just come up and stood behind the other's chair watching the play as the last cards were dealt. "No luck?" he continued.

"Can't do right!" the other replied. "I was playing for runs, and never saw so many alternations. Then I tried for them, and there came a run of thirteen red. I shouldn't have had the pluck to leave it all down, but it would have been a lovely haul even if I'd watered it."

They passed through the Atrium, down the steps, and turned round to the terrace, where was the usual throng, strolling up and down, leaning on the balustrade gazing on to the bright blue waters of the Mediterranean, or seated and intent on their journals.

There is the shabby little old man who lives at a third-rate hotel on the Condamine and plays maximums. Some well-known English owners of racehorses are deep in conversation, not improbably about the runners for an approaching steeplechase at Nice; smartly and charmingly dressed women of all ages and countries—smartness and charm by no means always go together—are enjoying the sunshine.

A hawk-nosed croupier is talking to a chubby English youth who puffs out the smoke of his cigarette in thoughtful fashion as he listens; a smirking Frenchman marches along, taking careful stock of the pretty faces; a couple of young Englishmen pause in their walk to argue energetically over a coloured diagram of the roulette wheel which one of them has in his hand.

"They've got a system, poor beggars!" Wynne observed, with a nod at the argumentative couple. "I wonder what it will cost them before they have done with it?"

Just then the report of a gun came from the little green plateau towards which they were going.

"Some fellow practising at pigeons. Shall we see who it is?" Wynne suggested. "Are you going to shoot again?"

"I don't know; I expect I shall, but it's not a good game. I suppose I'm pretty useful, but so are many of these fellows, and some of them a bit more. It's difficult to find out what's going on, and quite easy to make mistakes and lose a lot of money. I've had a bad time lately; indeed, if it hadn't been for meeting that little ass Russington, who thought he could play cards, I should have been hard put to it to get on."

Wynne glanced at his companion. He was easy-going, rather weak, but thoroughly straight, and as Morson mentioned Russington's name he recalled a fleeting doubt which had crossed his mind one evening as he was looking on—he looked on at most things instead of taking a hand—as to whether the business was on the square? The two men were not intimate friends. They had met occasionally in England, and staying at the same hotel had got into the habit of going about together; for Wynne found Morson full of shrewdness and knowledge of the world, and perhaps it suited Morson to consort with such a man as Wynne, of good family, a member of clubs membership of which meant social position.

"*He* shoots well—George Heath," Wynne observed, indicating a well-groomed young Englishman with a pleasant face who was at the moment intent on lighting a cigarette. "Particularly well, considering that he says he doesn't care about it. You and he would make a good match. 'Pon my word I shouldn't know which of you to back! You are really a bit more than the 'useful' you call yourself. I should think you are steadier than he is, but I've seen him shoot quite brilliantly, at game as well as pigeons—we have met at two or three places in England."

Morson looked thoughtful and gently bit the end of his thumb, a habit of his when contemplative.

"I should rather fancy myself, I think. I've had more experience of it than he has, but it wouldn't be a good thing, of course.

I should be quite game to try it, though, all the same. I wonder whether he'd take it on? Who's that just joined him?"

"He's a chap called Sydney, a very good fellow. Rides; you must have seen him?" Wynne answered.

"I don't remember him. He doesn't look a genius," Morson said, in a low voice, for the men were now approaching each other, and perhaps there was a somewhat pronounced expression of innocence on Sydney's face.

"He's no fool, I can tell you!" Wynne had time to rejoin before the pairs met and exchanged casual greetings.

"Good morning!" Heath said. "We're all at our usual occupation, doing nothing! I love the place, wouldn't miss it on any account, but I do get rather bored all the same. There's nothing to do."

"Tables? You can generally do good to the shareholders," Sydney suggested.

"It's so beastly stuffy in the rooms, and I don't much care about a game that's all unmitigated chance," Heath replied.

"You haven't got a system?" Morson suggested.

"No, and I don't expect you have! I can't imagine harder and more exasperating work. I've got a cousin here who sits in that pestilential atmosphere all day long, labouring away at figures. He generally wins a little every time he tries, but now and then things go very wrong and he loses much more than he has carefully collected during the last ten days or so. The steady percentage against you must tell in the long run."

"I like the place, but I get bored, too," Sydney put in. "I always drive to Nice the first day, not because I want to go there but for the sake of something to do, and I must say for the sake of the drive and the scenery. That I never get tired of! Next day I go up to La Turbie and walk down; then I walk round Monaco, go to Mentone and walk back, see a little racing at Nice when there is any, a little pigeon-shooting, and the programme's exhausted."

"I was just saying," Wynne remarked to Heath, "that you and Morson would make a good match at pigeons. I should think from what I've seen you were about as nearly equal as two men well could be. My impression is that you're a trifle the better all-round shot, but that Morson has a slight pull to make up for that, because he's done more pigeon-shooting."

"Yes, the idea struck Wynne, and if you would care about it I'm willing. It would be something to do at any rate," Morson rejoined, "and I certainly do think that chances would be pretty equal."

"Well, I'm not keen about pigeons," Heath answered, "but

it would be something to do, as you say, and I've run through Sydney's programme twice. Some day when the ground's free I'm game if you like."

"Very well, then, that's settled! There's a ground at Eze, but we may as well have it here. What shall we say? 500 a side?" Morson said, "and five-and-twenty birds?"

"I don't mind a bit! Just as you like," Heath affably answered; 500 francs was only £20, and gaining or losing made practically no difference to him.

* * * * *

"I feel like winning this match," Morson observed to Wynne as three days later they strolled down the terrace to the shooting ground. "I suppose some of the men there will want to bet, and you might do worse than back me."

"I hope you'll score, my dear fellow; but I really don't know, and to be quite frank I shouldn't be inclined to risk much money about it. I saw Heath practising yesterday, as I told you, and he was wonderfully dead on them. Good birds they were, real rippers, and scarcely one got away. It will be a good fight, at any rate!"

"All the same I fancy myself; but don't bet if you don't like it," Morson rejoined, with something of a sneer: and they descended the steps, finding Heath, Sydney, and some dozen or more men who had come to look on.

"M. Morson for two hundred franc?" a little Frenchman exclaimed. "I bet M. Morson. Who will have?"

"I'll take you, sir," Sydney replied.

"You are all right, sir. You shall have. M. Sydney, I think? It is the Comte de Ronville, me," and with a bow he presented his card and entered the bet.

"Don't be too rash, my dear fellow. I think it is odds on Morson," Heath said.

"You underrate yourself," Morson put in, as he looked down the barrels of his gun and inserted the cartridges. "I fancy it is a shade of odds on you, and quite expect to have to pay my monkey."

"Monkey?" Heath exclaimed, with surprise. "I thought you suggested 500 francs?"

"Oh, my dear fellow," Morson replied, "I really shouldn't have bothered to shoot for that! When one says '500' one does not mean shillings or less. I've always understood that Englishmen betted in pounds."

Heath was a rich man and a generous one, but far from being a gambler. The money was of small consequence, only he did not care to lose or to win considerable sums. However, if Morson had meant a monkey he felt that perhaps he ought to let it stand so, since he had accepted the challenge.

"Oh, very well," he answered. "I thought you meant francs, simply because, so far as I know, the prizes here are always calculated in them; but just as you like!"

Wynne's face changed, and he looked at Morson with something between doubt and dissatisfaction, for the match had been mentioned between them, and he retained a strong idea that Morson had regretted the smallness of the stake. It certainly seemed as though the notion of expanding the francs into pounds had been an afterthought.

"Wait a minute!" Sydney suddenly observed to Morson. "You think it is a shade of odds on Heath? I think so, too, and I'll lay you 100 to 80—pounds."

"Oh, I can't resist odds! Yes. Twice?" Morson said.

"Three times if you like?" Sydney suggested.

"Very well, that's 300 to 240 you lay on Heath," and Morson wrote it down, while various other little bets, in francs, were taken and offered by adherents of either man.

Heath had lost the toss for choice of start and was to take the first bird. He walked to the mark, the trap fell, a grand rock darted out like an arrow, and a second afterwards was a little heap of motionless feathers.

"A good start, old boy!" Sydney exclaimed, as the dog brought back the bird.

Morson in turn took his place, raised his gun, the bird flew swiftly forward, to collapse immediately.

"And a good follow!" the little Count who had backed the shooter jubilantly cried.

Again Heath went out. This time the bird after darting forward low down rose and swung like lightning to the right just as the shooter pulled trigger; but a second barrel stopped him, after the pigeon had given one kick he lay motionless, and the dog cantered off to retrieve him. Morson's face was absolutely expressionless as he again prepared himself, and an easy bird gave him no trouble. Heath was less lucky. He hit his third very hard, but had not been quite quick enough in getting on it, and though it fell dead, it dropped just out of bounds. If Morson scored he would have the lead, which is always such a source of confidence to the player at any game; and he made no mistake. Three to two in Morson's favour the score stood, and a grim smile curled his lips.

Heath downed his No. 4, but so did the other; both dealt effectively with No. 5, and Heath's No. 6 looked as if, hard hit, it would repeat the proceeding of No. 3 and fall out of bounds, but it struck the netting and counted. Morson led by one as he once more stood ready, the trap fell, he fired with his accustomed rapidity and easy action at a fair bird, which flew away apparently untouched, to the shooter's evident astonishment.

"I felt certain I was dead on that one!" he muttered as he went to the balcony, while Heath knocked over his No. 7 before it had got three yards from the trap. As he returned Morson seemed to look at him with an expression of perplexity. They were level, six out of seven each, as Morson went out again and killed. Heath's No. 8 was a repetition of No. 7: the bird dropped almost before it had started on its last journey, and then the trap falling for Morson's shot a regular owl flopped out and seemed to hesitate which way he should go. Morson had snapped off his first barrel and missed; he had calculated that the bird would fly, and it simply fluttered; but he aimed carefully with the second, and the pigeon, apparently not at all disturbed by its novel situation, flew a little way out to sea, turned round, and quietly winged his course to the top of the casino. Heath was now one to the good, for though Morson looked wonderingly at the bird, that did not stop its flight, nor could anyone satisfactorily reply to M. de Ronville's query, "But 'ow come that to be?"

Heath missed his ninth, allowing Morson to catch him, but killed the next five, of which Morson let two escape, to the dismay of his supporters and the anguish of the Count. At twenty Heath led by four, and killing his next two, his opponent again missing, placed the issue beyond doubt.

Morson vainly strove to appear impassive. His lips trembled in spite of his best endeavours to be calm, and he had not been able to repress the looks, half wonderment, half malignity, which he had cast from time to time at the unconscious Heath. There was silence for a moment after he had ineffectually fired his last shot. Then Sydney spoke.

"That was not such a good thing for you as you imagined it to be, Mr. Morson, was it?" he asked, in a curiously significant tone, looking the other very straight in the face. He was either gratuitously offensive or there was a hidden shaft behind his words.

"What do you mean?" Morson angrily replied. "I never thought it a good thing."

"Oh," Sydney observed, as the other men stood round, puzzled at his tone and manner, "I rather thought you imagined that you had a bit up your sleeve—quite a big bit, in fact?"

Morson seemed about to make a furious rejoinder, but there was something in Sydney's steady look which stopped him. He paused, muttered that he would send cheques to the hotel, and turned away.

"Will you dine with us at the Paris this evening, Wynne?" Sydney asked, as Wynne was turning to go with the beaten man. "All right, eight o'clock! I'm very glad that you can come."

"You've been puzzling me a good deal, do you know?" Heath said to his friend as they walked away together down the Condamine, having decided that a quiet stroll round Monaco would be a good way of getting an appetite for dinner. "Why did you speak to Morson in that peculiar way, and why did you so pointedly ask Wynne to dine? I'm glad he's coming, for I like him, but he and Morson seem to go about together, and inviting one in that way is really snubbing the other. I don't think I do like Morson——"

"I'm sure I don't," Sydney replied. "He's a regular wrong 'un, plays a quaintly effective game at cards amongst other things, and had got a beautiful little plant on this afternoon that would have come off, my dear boy, at your expense if I hadn't tumbled to it. That's why I asked Wynne. I wanted him to know that I didn't suspect him of being in it. He's a trifle feeble, but quite straight."

Heath was listening eagerly.

"What do you mean by 'a plant'?" he inquired. "I couldn't help thinking that there was something odd when Morson told me that he had meant a monkey instead of five hundred francs. I thought the match was just to be an hour's amusement, and had no idea of winning or losing anything like money. The way you spoke to him——"

"My dear fellow, I'll tell you all about it," Sydney said. "What the brute meant was five hundred francs unless he imagined he had made it a safe thing, and a monkey if his little dodge came off. I tumbled to it in Nice on Wednesday, quite by a lucky accident. This is how it was: The evening before—Tuesday, that is—I chanced to be going to the station, and on the way through the grounds saw Morson in very earnest conversation with a man whose face I knew, though I couldn't recollect where I had seen him. Morson seemed to be persuading the man to do something—that's how it struck me, perhaps because he was offering the fellow a banknote and the other hesitated about taking it. Next day I went to Nice, as you remember, and at the door of the gunsmith's shop I saw the man—that's how I had known him, for I'd been in the shop once or twice. Something induced me to stop the car at the door and go in; and on the counter I saw two lots of cartridges, one addressed to you and the other to Morson. Then an idea struck me: What could Morson have been wanting our friend to do? Could it have been any dodging about cartridges, I thought! I glanced at the two packages, read the names, and said, 'Ah, I see you have been getting ready for the match. Which will win?' He had no idea, he replied; both were very good; it was impossible to choose. I wanted to get hold of those cartridges, so I said that I was a friend of yours, it was your car at the door, and if he liked I would take them, also I added while I was about it I might leave Mr. Morson's, he also being a friend—I didn't say 'of sorts.' It saved somebody a journey here, I suppose; at any rate he thanked me and said if I didn't mind the trouble M. Chose, his master, would be very grateful; so I took both lots and brought them to the hotel. I opened the boxes carefully; they were both the same to all appearance, and for the matter of that I had some more of the same, which was lucky, as I wanted to examine a few of those intended for you, and so could fill up from my own supply. Well, I opened a couple and found them all right, opened a third, all right too, a fourth that had seemed to be all right till I investigated, and discovered—no shot! Sawdust or something or other! I had suspected something of the sort. A proportion of stumers had been mixed with the good cartridges, how many of course I couldn't guess. It would not have done to have had too many wrong, you see, for then you would not have killed a bird, and that would have given the show away; but you and Morson were really a good match, all being square, and if he could arrange that a quarter or so of your cartridges were harmless, he had quite enough in hand to make it a certainty for him. I need hardly tell you what I did. A card with your name on it was nailed on your box, one with Morson's on his, and I just changed the cards before I very carefully left his—that is yours—at his hotel. I saw from the brute's face when he missed that easy bird that he began to suspect something, but was at his wits' end to find out what was wrong—he didn't know that I had left the cartridges for him, thought they had been brought straight from the shop by his pal, no doubt. It amused me to watch him picking and choosing afterwards, but of course there was nothing to tell him which was which, and I laid odds on you! I won't touch his beastly money, of course; at least, I'll take it, but I shall send it on to an old aunt of mine who's a whale at charities—if I ever get it, that's to say, for it won't surprise me if those cheques he talked of never come along."

After dinner Wynne heard the gist of the story, and was quite ready to believe it, for having gone to Morson's room before leaving the hotel, he had found him in the midst of a heap of cartridges, the contents of which he had evidently been investigating. His temper was diabolical, Wynne said, and his manner had been so offensive that they had parted on terms which gave Wynne a perfect excuse, had he needed one, for terminating the acquaintance; but next day Morson had disappeared.

STRANGE STORIES OF SPORT

XXVIII.—THE BOWLER WHO DISAPPEARED

BY "OSGOLDCROSS"

My friend Salter has now retired from journalism. He has a cottage which he calls "home" on the East Coast, where he and his wife live one month in the year. For the remaining eleven months they wander. At any given moment they might be peacefully sojourning with a Tasmanian apple-grower, or they might be rounding the Horn on a "wind-jammer," or, again, they might be partners in a claim on the Yukon.

*　　*　　*　　*　　*

This story is of one of Salter's greatest "scoops," and it is here set down for the first time. It has to do with the strange disappearance and yet stranger return of Walter Street, the famous Tykeshire cricketer.

As a matter of fact, I had had a long spell of illness and knew nothing of the affair till Salter came to see me when I was recovering; therefore I will give it as he told it to me.

"I've made a good score since last I saw you," said my friend, "and, as you've been stowed away all these months, I s'pose you've not heard?"

"No, what is it?" I asked, for I was thinking for the moment only of the joy of being alive, and of feeling the breeze blowing untainted on my face.

"Beaten the field, bagged the pool, and, in a sort of way, scraped a rival with his own potsherd."

Some men would say that Salter is a trifle vain of his exploits, but to my thinking there is a distinction between vanity and

329

legitimate pride—besides, my friend was not given to promiscuous bragging.

"You retired from the world," he went on, "about the beginning of March, and the last of the Test Matches between Macpherson's team and the Colonials was due to begin at Melbourne on the fifth."

"I remember; each side had won two; I heard only last Sunday how the victory went at the finish."

"Well, there was rain on the evening before the final match, and it was announced that the wicket was sure to be soft. So at home we rejoiced, for we knew that would suit Walter Street, who was in tremendous form. He'd taken fifteen wickets for 94 against South Australia, and eight for 40 against Victoria, and the Cornstalks were more than a little fearful of him. Our hopes were pinned on him, for the other bowlers had been far from deadly. You can imagine the sensation which was created when the cable brought word that on the morning of the game Street had been missing and that play had had to begin without him. He had simply disappeared."

"Disappeared?" said I. "What do you mean? Why on earth should he disappear?"

"Nevertheless, that was the size of it. It seemed that he and Haynes (they both come from the same West Riding village, you know) had been chatting in the hotel garden the night before, and that Haynes had left his chum and had gone to bed. Street said he'd finish his pipe and come up almost at once. Next morning he was absent from breakfast, and when they went to look, his bed had not been slept in. Search as they would, no sign of him came to light until ten days later, when his clothes were found in the Yarra River."

"Was he inside them, then? Suicide, impossible! Murder, or what?"

"Only his clothes, fortunately. He himself had simply vanished. As to the cricket, Australia made over 600, we replied with 460; Haynes in the second innings rose above his grief, for he was fearfully cut up, of course, and bowled like a demon. Colonials only made 87, and, thanks to a glorious innings by Cloudsley, the Red Rose man, we pulled it off by one wicket."

"Oh, gorgeous, great!" ejaculated I.

"But the Street mystery was unsolvable. The Australian police could find nothing like a real clue. A rich Bradford rag merchant sent out two of our finest detectives at his own expense, but they came back confessing themselves completely beaten. The public forgot the matter—something else turned up—peer in the

Divorce Court or an absconding banker—I forget which; but in his own shire, where "our Walter's" face was as well known as the King's, they remembered always. Why, in Halifax some of them tried a clairvoyant, who gave the usual hazy information and pocketed the usual prosaic fee.

"About the middle of May I was in town, and Mellin of the *Magnet* telephoned me one day to go down to him. When I got there, I found him talking to a big, bluff, red-faced chap whom I put down at once as a seaman of some sort.

"He was introduced to me as 'Captain Swallow, of the barque *White Wings.*'

"'Y'r servant, sir,' said the skipper, extending a paw about as big as a shovel.

"'Now, Captain,' said Mellin, 'will you be kind enough to explain to this gentleman what you've been telling me?'

"The chap was smoking some kind of filth in a short clay pipe, which he shifted to the other side of his mouth, and then he began:—

"'When I got inter London River yesterday week, I hears about that there young feller Street, the cricketer, 'ow he's been put away. Me and my mate, Robins, wuz talking it over day 'fore yest'day, and we says mebbe some chap has shanghaied the feller and run him off on to a wind-jammer to get 'im outer the way. I've sailed outer Melbourne myself, and it's not once nor twice, but often enough the boarding master has brought us down deadbeats as drunk as Davy's sow and shot 'em into the fo'c'stle as A.B.'s. And I won't deny,' added the Captain with a grin, 'as we've made some sort of seamen outer most of 'em. Now I says to Robins, "What's to 'inder someone as wants t' get this chap outer the way doing the same?"'

"Well, Mellin and I talked to the old boy for a good half-hour, and we concluded that, even if it was a long shot, it was not altogether an impossible one.

"'What's about a fair average passage for a sailing ship back to England?' said Mellin.

"'Depends,' replied Swallow. 'If anything like weather, say between 85 and 110 days to Falmouth, where a lot of 'em puts in for orders.'

"'Let's see, then,' I said. 'That match was begun on——'
Mellin looked it up and found March 5.

"'Supposin' the feller was put aboard ship on that date, ye can find easy enough what left Melbourne for home ports then, ye know. But if it's anything, I reckon it'll be sail, and a slow ship at that; the longer the trip the better.'

331

" ' Now look here,' said Mellin, when the big skipper had gone, ' it's worth trying, though as likely as not it won't come off. Suppose Street was hocussed and put aboard a ' lime-juicer,' it doesn't follow she'd be bound for home. Still, it's worth chancing.'

" On the 30th of May I was in Falmouth, where I chartered the sea-tug *Comrade*, owned and commanded by a man of whom Swallow had told us. I explained to him that I wanted to get into communication on the earliest possible occasion with each of five ships, a list of which I gave him. He didn't want to know more of the game, and promised to be ready for sea at noon next day. That evening, however, a telegram from Mellin informed me that Swallow and his mate had quarrelled, and that the latter had been to the *Daily Beacon* and given the show away. And, sure enough, next morning my captain told me that a rival tug, the *Comet*, had been chartered under similar conditions. He did not add, the old sinner, that this rival was at least three knots faster than his own boat.

" We put to sea at noon, and, as I heard afterwards, the *Comet* was an hour behind us. We cruised about for six days, waylaid two of the five we were after, and in each case found that we were behind our rival. Fortunately, neither vessel had on board the man we were looking for. It was clear that we must go farther afield if we were going to come out top.

" In the evening we picked up the *Comet* some three miles ahead of us, whereupon my skipper, to my astonishment, turned round and began to retrace his course. I expostulated, but he assured me that he knew what he was about, and when darkness fell we changed back to our old course and went ahead again, all lights covered. We made a big sweep and, keeping our enemy's lights in view, passed him in the first watch. I turned in before midnight, but about four they wakened me with news that a big four-master was close by. We showed our lights now and came up alongside her. There was a very gentle breeze, and she was not making more than four or five knots.

" Our skipper hailed her. She was the *Strathmore*, Melbourne to London River, and she didn't want a tow.

" ' Have you got a fellow aboard of the name of Street ?'

" The reply of the officer on watch told us that he didn't care the smallest iota if they had or not ; and if they had, it wasn't our business.

" ' But look here, Mr. Mate,' I sang out, ' it means good money for you and the Old Man if you have.'

" That seemed to touch him ; but he refused to parley further till he had consulted the captain, and he wasn't going to wake him for any etc., etc. tug in creation. So we hung round waiting till it should please the Old Man to wake up.

"Very soon, to our chagrin, daylight began to show, and we found the *Comet* about a mile astern of us. As soon as they spotted us it was full speed ahead; and when at half-past six the skipper of the *Strathmore* came on deck in his pyjamas, he found two tugs close by, each hailing him with the utmost urgency. The mate on watch told him what was in the wind, and, on the 'first come, first served' principle, he shouted over to me to come aboard. My rival's boat dropped down at the same instant; but while I was clambering over the port side the *Comet* man was vainly endeavouring to obtain admission on the starboard side where no ladder was slung.

"In a few words I explained matters; and, to my unutterable joy, found that the long shot had hit the target. Street was there.

"When I had suitably appeased the captain and officer on watch, I was allowed to interview the bowler, who looked very unlike his usual smart self in a blue dungaree suit and with a fine yellow beard. It was precisely as old Swallow had suggested: he had been sand-bagged in the hotel garden, and knew no more till he had awakened in the *Strathmore's* fo'c'stle off Port Phillip Heads.

"In an hour I had the whole story from him, but in the meantime found that the wily skipper had been bargaining overside with my rival. It was, as I felt certain, a *Beacon* man, one Platten, whom I knew by reputation. He smiled as we met on deck.

"'I may be a bit behind the fair at the start,' said he; 'but yon Noah's Ark of yours'll be an "also ran" when we get under way.'

"He went down to the fo'c'stle, whence I had come. By Jove, I was in a fix, I can tell you, for I knew that in the race home we should not be in it. My mind worked quickly; desperate diseases need cures to match; so I went down to the cabin where the skipper was dressing.

"'Cap.,' I said, 'if you can keep that other fellow six hours here—for the good of his health, say—there'll be a hundred pounds waiting for you when you put your mud-hook down.' But that line was no good, and I was bundled overboard by a couple of deck hands.

"So, sick at heart, I regained the *Comrade*, and the message went down to the engine-room to whack her up for all she was worth. We had ninety miles to go, and I knew that Platten's tug could give us two hours at least and a beating.

"Well, they did whack her up to such a tune that the bearings got hot and we had to slow. About eleven the other fellow came pounding past us, hell for leather, and signalling, if you please, 'Shall we give you a tow?' Can you imagine anything more utterly and perfectly diabolical? A grand summer morning, sea like glass, and my rival cutting away for Falmouth with the scoop of the season all fine and large.

"Just then, when I was feeling as if my back teeth were submerged in bile, a big P. and O. passenger boat was coming up behind us, doing her eighteen knots good. She was overhauling us fast, and my captain remarked sympathetically, for I had told him the trouble:

"'Now, if you was aboard *her*——'

"'Why, that would do me no good. *She* won't be home in time to cut him out.'

"'No, but what price yon wee spar on top of her foremast? Don't ye see she's got a Marconi apparatus?'

"'Skipper,' I shouted, 'you are an angel! Shove me as near as you can, and when you see me hit water, cut and run for home. I'll fix the rest.'

"He didn't tumble to it for the moment; but, after some persuasion, he agreed. He put the tug within thirty yards of the big black liner. Overboard I went, and promptly the *Comrade* sheered off and skedaddled as hard as she dared. In five minutes I was up on the high bridge hearing a choice oration from the captain of the *Hindu*.

"However, he proved to be a sportsman; and, after vowing to place me in irons forthwith, he sent me down to his cabin for a change of clothes. Then I sought the smooth-faced young man at whose will the air-waves struggle in space, and within half an hour I knew that from the slender installation pole a hundred feet above the deck my message was speeding home."

Salter finished speaking, and we sat in silence for a few minutes.

"Who's top of the bowling averages now?" I asked.

He took out a newspaper from his pocket, turned over the sheets, and then replied:

"Why, Street is."

STRANGE STORIES OF SPORT

XXIX.—THE SNAKE OF FIRE

BY J. L. HORNIBROOK

THE great cañon near which we were camped was lurid with the reflection of flames. Across the open, not more than a hundred yards away, the underbrush was blazing furiously, the devouring flames sweeping along with a crackle and roar that was well-nigh appalling.

It was in New Mexico, a good many years ago ; away back in the early seventies, as a matter of fact. We were a small party of young Englishmen, only three in number, with the usual retinue of mules and Mexican Indians, bound on a sporting expedition into the interior. How the fire had originated was a mystery, for this was a lonely spot, entirely uninhabited. My companions, Shaylor and MacKenzie, had some previous knowledge of the country, but neither could assign a cause for the outbreak or give any explanation of the matter.

"It's odd," Shaylor said, as we watched the sea of flame. " I cannot understand it. It could not have been caused by a neglected camp fire, for there's not a soul but ourselves for miles around—not even a stray Indian, I fancy. In that case I don't see——"

" Perhaps it was the *culebra de lumbre*, señors."

The interruption came from the background, where the Indians were squatted. All three of us turned in that direction. It was old Miguel, our guide and principal attendant, who had spoken.

" The snake of fire ? " I questioned in astonishment, for I had never heard of such a thing before. " What is that, Miguel ? "

The old Indian appeared reluctant to speak. He sat with his knees drawn up to his chin, his bony hands clasped around his shins, while his black hair fell in a tangled mass on his shoulders, framing a wrinkled, copper-coloured face. He was an old man, as I have said ; but how old exactly nobody could tell, not even himself. It is certain, however, that he had been acquainted with the wilds of Mexico before the eldest of those squatted around him was born.

" The señor has never heard of the *culebra de lumbre* ? " he said, in answer to my question.

" No," I answered, scenting one of the many curious Mexican legends, as I imagined it must be. " Tell us about it, Miguel. We all want to hear the story."

" Ah, señor," the old Indian broke out, " it has been the curse of the land, the terrible *culebra de lumbre ;* but the curse is passing away. Each year the number of these reptiles grows less. Soon they will die out altogether. When I was a boy they were plentiful. Many a time I have seen them, out in the grasses there, these fearful serpents that glow like fire and shoot out flame with their breath."

" Shoot out flame ! " I said. " Surely, Miguel, that is a little too much to expect us to believe."

" The señor doubts it ? " he replied, with a flash of his coal-black eyes. " Then let him look at this." He pushed back the tangled hair from his forehead, exhibiting a scar which had undoubtedly been caused by a severe burn. " That is the mark of the snake of fire," he said, in his grave, impressive manner, as he allowed the hair to fall back into its place.

We looked at each other, we three young fellows, scarcely knowing what to think. Little as we were disposed to credit this story of the snake of fire, there was something in the way the old Mexican spoke, in the mark of the burn on his forehead, which impressed us a good deal.

" How did you come by that scar ? " Shaylor asked, turning to Miguel again.

" It was years ago, many years ago," the Indian answered. " I was riding down this very cañon with some of my companions. We had a dog with us—a large, fierce dog that had killed many wild cats and coyotes in single fight. He was afraid of nothing, that dog. He was running on ahead of us when suddenly I heard him yelp, saw him spring into the air, and fall over sideways. He lay quite still. It was strange, I thought. He could not have been bitten by a rattlesnake, because they do not cause instant death.

I rode quickly on, dismounted, and laid my hand on the dog. He was limp and lifeless.

"As I rose up I was conscious of a peculiar and sickening smell all around the spot. It was so overpowering that I became faint and dizzy, and my strength seemed to be leaving me. Then, suddenly, I saw in the grass a few feet away what appeared to be a streak of fire. With a great effort I vaulted on my pony. Just as I got on its back the streak of fire sprang through the air towards me. Instantly my pony commenced to rear and snort with terror. Looking down I saw twined around one of its forelegs a large specimen of the terrible *culebra de lumbre*—the snake of fire! My terror was great, señores ; but I had little time to think. The pony plunged forward and I was thrown to the ground. As I touched the earth a blinding flash appeared before my eyes, and I felt a sensation as if a burning brand had been thrust into my face. Then my senses left me.

"It was many hours later when I awoke. My companions were standing around me. They had seen me thrown, and rode quickly up. They caught sight of the streak of fire disappearing through the grass, and knew I had been scorched by the deadly breath of the *culebra de lumbre*. Luckily for me the flame did not strike me in a vital part, and after a time they succeeded in restoring me fully. Then we examined the pony. Where the snake had twined itself around the creature's leg the flesh had been burnt away and the bone was exposed. That is the story, señores. Believe it or not, as you think fit."

Miguel relapsed into his usual grave silence, but we were by no means done with him yet. Legend or otherwise, this weird story of his interested us greatly. We questioned him each in turn, and succeeded in drawing further information from him regarding the snake of fire.

These luminous serpents, he told us, were more dreaded by the Mexicans than the rattlesnake itself. When full-grown the reptile measured some ten or twelve feet, and was wonderfully quick in all its movements. In colour it was bright scarlet ; and from its skin, when enraged, a yellowish glow seemed to be diffused, while long, lightning-like streaks of flame shot from its mouth. This fiery breath meant death to any human being whom it struck in a vital part.

Many people, Miguel further declared, had been scorched by the flame, and in nearly every instance with instantly fatal results. Moreover, when the reptile writhed its way along the ground it left a scorched trail behind it, and the flame from its mouth frequently set the herbage on fire. To this cause Miguel attributed the brush fire which was raging at present, as well as many other such fires on mountain and plain, the origin of which appeared a mystery.

When we had listened to all he had to tell us (and he mentioned several other occasions upon which he had seen the snake of fire), we continued to discuss the matter among ourselves.

"A queer story," remarked Shaylor. "I wonder if there is any truth in it, or if it is purely the outcome of the old fellow's vivid imagination."

"I don't know," replied MacKenzie, doubtfully. "I have heard something of the same kind of yarn before, though I took it to be merely a native legend. There is no doubt, however, that some such fiery serpent existed in the days of the ancient Mexicans, for many of the rocks in the interior bear rude representations of the reptile. I have seen them myself."

"In that case," I said, "Miguel's story may have more foundation than we are inclined to believe. These Mexican stone-pictures are generally records of fact, which would tend to show that the snake of fire was known to the ancient inhabitants. Whether it exists at the present day is another question."

"If these serpents were here in olden times, there is no reason why they should not be here still," returned MacKenzie. "Miguel says they are dying out. I wonder if there are any left?"

We put the question to our guide, but he shook his head doubtfully. He could not tell, he said. It was a long time since he had seen one. He appeared reluctant to discuss the matter further, for the fear of the terrible and mysterious *culebra de lumbre* was evidently very real to him.

"Well," said Shaylor, "it would be a rare sight to see one of these flaming fiery serpents, as one might call them; that is, of course, at a safe distance."

Our talk ended at this point, and we lay down for the night. The strange story we had heard dimly haunted my brain as I dropped off to sleep, and I am not sure that I did not dream of snakes of fire.

Next morning we were up early and continued our journey. Our way lay through the cañon before us, and Miguel pointed out to us the identical spot where he had the encounter with the snake of fire. He gave such precise details, and spoke with such quiet impressiveness, that it was almost impossible to doubt him. Yet the story, if true, was certainly a most extraordinary one.

Our attention, however, was soon diverted in another direction. As we emerged from the cañon a fine tract of wooded country opened before us, and here we had our first real taste of sport. The place abounded with game of all sorts. We had not proceeded far when something flashed across our path, with a grunt like that of a hog.

"A peccary!" cried Shaylor, swinging his rifle round.

"Wait!" said Miguel. "There are others."

We concealed ourselves behind the bushes, and waited. Soon we heard low grunts, and a small herd of peccaries appeared in sight, grubbing as they came. We fired right into them, bowling over three. The rest were off like a shot, scattering in all directions. Pheasants were as plentiful as in an English park. Shaylor brought down the first one, which dropped some little distance away. He dismounted and advanced leisurely to pick it up, but before he could reach the spot a tiger-cat bounded out, pounced upon the bird, and carried it off under his very nose. We added to our bag a number of flying squirrels, a black iguana, and a curious, ungainly creature known as the alligator tortoise. In the open we sighted some Mexican black-tailed deer, a good dozen or so, and worked cautiously round to get to windward of them. We were here followed by a number of coyotes, which skulked along behind us, stopping when we stopped, and sitting quietly on their haunches until we moved forward again. These coyotes always follow hunters in this way, and if a deer is killed they rush in and devour what is left of the carcase; if badly wounded, they pursue it in a body and pull it down. On this occasion, however, they were doomed to disappointment, for we were unable to get within range of the quarry.

Before halting at mid-day we killed a black sugar-cane snake, and this brought the conversation round again to the snake of fire. We questioned Miguel further on the subject. He informed us that the dreaded reptile was not always to be found on the ground. Once he had seen its scarlet body stretched along the bough of a tree, its brilliant colouring causing it to be visible from a distance. On another occasion, while pushing through a thick patch of chapparal, he had caught sight of it gliding over the top of the dense brush. It was at night-time, however, he told us, that its appearance was so terrible. Then it gave forth its yellowish glow, while at intervals a scorching flame shot from its mouth.

Of the three of us, Shaylor was the one who seemed most inclined to pooh-pooh the idea, if not to ridicule it altogether. "These Mexican Indians have powerful imaginations," he remarked, aside. "Old Miguel must certainly think us very gullible. For myself I'll believe in the existence of this fiery serpent when I see it."

We rode far that day, and at nightfall pitched our camp near a low hill. We had selected an open space, clear of bush or shrub; but further off the brush was thick all round us, while above it rose the Mexican oak and other stately trees. In the centre of this space we lit our fire; and Miguel, who was our cook, set about preparing supper.

While we sat and watched him, waiting like hungry men until the meal was ready, Shaylor glanced round towards the brush and up at the dark, silent trees. "This looks a likely place for your *culebra de lumbre*, Miguel," he said, with a slight laugh.

"The señor should not mock," returned the Mexican, gravely, and went on with his cooking.

Shaylor laughed again; but presently he became intent upon the preparations for supper, and the subject was dropped.

It was just then, when Miguel was about to lay the meal before us, that I fancied I caught a slight rustling sound amongst the underbrush. I looked round and saw a cottontail rabbit bolt out into the opening. The creature dodged about in the most curious manner. It seemed perfectly bewildered by fear, hardly knowing which way to turn. It ran hither and thither, darting forward, scurrying back again, and apparently quite heedless of our presence. Finally, in its confusion, it made a bolt for the spot whence it had emerged.

What happened next occurred with the quickness of a flash; and was so sudden, so startling, that it was all over before I could realise it. I can only relate exactly what passed before my eyes. Just as the rabbit reached the edge of the brush, I saw something like a streak of fire shoot along the ground. There was a squeal from the cottontail, a yellowish flash, and the fiery streak was gone again in an instant. The Mexicans, who had seen it also, raised a howl of terror.

"The *culebra de lumbre*! The *culebra de lumbre*!" they cried.

Shaylor, whose back was turned towards the spot, started up when he heard the cry. "What? Where?" he exclaimed, looking quickly round. "I did not notice anything. Where was it?"

One of the Mexicans pointed a trembling finger in the direction, but there was nothing to be seen by this time. The brush, below and above, was dark as pitch.

"Pooh!" said Shaylor, turning to me. "This is another of their fairy tales. They have heard so much talk of their wonderful *culebra* to-day that they imagine they see it everywhere."

"No," I answered. "You are wrong this time, at any rate. I saw it distinctly myself."

"You did!" he exclaimed. "What was it like, then?"

"Exactly what Miguel described: like a streak of fire shooting along the ground."

He stood for a moment gazing across towards the brush, as yet plainly only half convinced. "I'd like to catch a glimpse of it," he said. "It may be hanging around somewhere still. I'll go and have a look."

"You will do nothing of the kind," I interposed.

He laughed, and before I could rise to restrain him, strode away in the direction of the brush. He was young, younger than either MacKenzie or myself, and foolhardy into the bargain.

"Come back, Shaylor!" I called out after him. "Don't be a fool. You may meet your death."

"It's all right," he shouted back; "I'll take care."

I had risen to my feet, and stood there hesitating, scarcely knowing what to do. I felt half inclined to follow and drag him back by main force; but he had already reached the edge of the brush, and was craning his neck to peer into it.

He remained standing awhile in that position, moving his head up and down and from side to side. Then, as he evidently could see nothing, he pushed his way in among the brush, and for a moment or two we lost sight of him. The next second almost, while he was still hidden from sight, there came a terrible cry from the under-brush, a cry that told us something dreadful had happened. We ran to the spot, MacKenzie and myself. Paying little heed to our own danger, we pushed into the brush, and soon came upon the unfortunate Shaylor. He was lying there in a heap, dead—stone dead!

Between us we carried him back to the fire, and proceeded to examine the body. Over the region of the heart the clothing was scorched and burnt, while the flesh beneath was seared as if with a hot iron. How to account for it, save on the ground that he had been struck by the terrible snake of fire, we knew not; but there was no doubt whatever in the minds of the Mexicans. They were firmly convinced he had met his fate in this way.

That is the strange story I have to tell; and I can only add, in the words of old Miguel, the reader may believe it or not, as he thinks fit.

STRANGE STORIES OF SPORT

XXX.—THE ANT-LION

BY GEOFFREY WILLIAMS

BENEATH the cool stars of an East African night the Gascoignes and Jerome Harcourt sat round their camp fire and renewed the excitements of the day to an accompaniment of pipes and tea. That is to say, the men smoked and Mrs. Gascoigne drank tea, not because she wanted it, but because it seemed more companionable. Two months ago they had left Nairobi with a string of porters that stretched from one end of the straggling little town to the other, laden with a goodly supply of guns and ammunition, and, incidentally, with various other trifles; and ever since they had wandered in the wilds, adding to their store of heads and horns, utterly and completely content. At least the Gascoignes were. Jerome Harcourt's opinions were not so obvious, and he was wont to keep them to himself.

As soon as they had made up their minds to take a shooting trip to East Africa they had agreed with one accord to travel well out of the beaten track. The suggestion had come from Harcourt, who was, in fact, primarily responsible for the whole idea ; but Jack Gascoigne and his wife were so delighted with the plan that they could see no objections, and accepted every proposal without cavil. Consequently, after their two months' wandering, they found themselves a long way to the north in practically unknown country. For some days they had been passing through thick bush containing apparently very little game, but they were now just emerging from it ; and beyond, across the river that flowed silently past the camp, its deep pools undisturbed save by the splash of a feeding hippopotamus, lay the wide plains from which they hoped so much, and of which they had heard such wondrous stories from the natives.

" Isn't it jolly ! " murmured Jack, stretching himself lazily in his big folding chair. " I really think the evening is the best time in the whole day. Who wouldn't enjoy sitting under these stars, tired but comfortable, fighting the battles of the day over again ! I don't believe I enjoyed the shooting of that pig this morning half as much as I did going over the whole story to you just now."

"Of course it is the best time of the day," laughed Mrs. Gascoigne ; " you have the benefit of my society, that's why."

Jack looked remorseful. " It is too bad to leave you alone so much. It must be horribly dull."

"Nonsense ! Sympathy is entirely thrown away upon me. I have plenty to keep me occupied ; and your stories in the evening, though you are usually too sleepy to talk much, are worth looking forward to. Why is it, I wonder, that the effect of the stars always seems to be that you become sleepy or sentimental ? "

Jack sat up indignantly.

" I am never sentimental. Really, Molly, you are most insulting. But, I say, you two, just look at those dim plains over the river. Don't they seem full of big possibilities ? I can almost fancy I see strange forms of unknown game stalking among the shadows."

" I am afraid I have not your imagination, Jack," said Harcourt, sarcastically. " And I do not believe in those plains. You know what lies the natives tell about wonderful game, and how often we have been disappointed."

" I don't care : hope still springs within me. I am of a sanguine disposition, so you must not throw cold water on my harmless little enthusiasms," and Jack puffed contentedly at his pipe and gazed at the grey misty plains.

" By the way," cried Molly, suddenly, " have you heard of the latest marvel they say is to be found over there ? "

"No, we have not. Is it very terrible—like the ghost buffaloes we heard of last week ? If so, you had better not tell us till the sun is up. It might frighten us, told among these mysterious trees to the music of the grunting hippo."

" Don't be so silly, Jack. It really is rather interesting. Selebo told me this afternoon, and I felt quite nervous after it. Do you remember how, the other day, we spent half an hour watching an ant-lion catch ants, and agreed that we had never seen a more ghastly tragedy in miniature ? "

Jerome Harcourt leaned forward as though suddenly interested.

" Yes," he said, " I remember very well. I have often thought of it since. There is nothing like it in nature for fiendish ingenuity and horror."

" Well, Selebo says——" began Molly.

But Jack held up his hand in protest. " Stop a minute," he interrupted. " I was not with you when you saw the thing. What was it like ? "

" It is a small insect," explained Jerome, "that digs a hole in an ant run, and then, covering itself with sand, quietly awaits events. Presently an unsuspecting ant trips over the edge and rolls down the sloping sides of the hole to meet its doom at the bottom. The fight between the ant and its invisible enemy is a horrible thing to watch."

"Yes, it made me feel quite sick," chimed in Molly; "and yet I couldn't help looking on till the end. There was a fascination about it. But, as I was telling you, Selebo says that out on the plains there is a giant ant-lion that lies in wait for big game as the ordinary ones do for ants. It digs an immense pit with loose shelving sides, just like the tiny ones we saw, and remains secreted at the bottom, hidden beneath the loose sand. Men have fallen into the trap before now, according to old Selebo, and once in there is no escape; they are dragged down and are seen no more."

"My dear child," murmured Jack, indulgently, "you really are too credulous. You don't mean to say you believe that nonsense."

But Harcourt's face looked strangely excited in the gloom, and there was a curious ring in his voice as he asked, "Did Selebo tell you anything else about it?"

"Not much, he seemed too frightened of the thing to speak as freely as usual, but he wished to warn us. It seems that the tribes round here regard it as an evil spirit, and never dare attempt to kill the creature. It is rare, and there is seldom more than one in an area of many square miles. It does not stay long in one place, not more than a few days. After that it destroys the old pit and makes a new one several miles away, moving only on the darkest nights; at least so they say, for it appears that no one has actually seen the creature, which never emerges from its bed of sand, but remains invisible save when anything falls in. Then the sand heaves, a long grey claw shoots out, and the victim is dragged under, struggling and screaming. Ugh, I can't bear to talk of it. I have made myself quite nervous. But for pity's sake be careful to-morrow. I don't say I exactly believe the story, but Selebo says that it is never safe to go fast over the plains. The pits are hard to see, and the edges are soft and treacherous."

There was silence for a moment, and then Harcourt got up and knocked out his pipe. "I'm tired, and think I shall turn in," he remarked.

"You look rather white, old man, and your voice is shaky. Better take some quinine."

"No, it's nothing," returned the other, irritably, and disappeared in the direction of his tent.

Jack looked after him curiously. "Jerome doesn't seem himself to-night somehow," he said at last. "I wonder if there is anything wrong with him?"

Molly sighed, but made no reply.

"Why that sigh?" he went on. "You don't think he is really ill, do you?"

"N-no, it is hardly that." Molly's voice was doubtful.

"Out with it, dear. I know you have something on your mind."

"Well—yes, I have. Did you see Mr. Harcourt's face as he went off just now? He looked at you with an expression I did not understand. It frightened me."

"My dear girl," remonstrated Jack, "you really must not indulge in these fancies. It is unlike you, and is absurd. Why should you be frightened because Jerome looks at me?"

"It may be foolish, but I can't help it. The moonlight struck full on his face at the moment, and there was something there which he did not mean me to see. You know, dear," Molly hesitated for a moment, and then went on, "you know that he once asked me to marry him? Well, when I said I could not, and that I was engaged to you, I saw the same look on his face, and it frightened me then. He is a strange man, Jack, and who knows what may be going on behind that enigmatic smile he always wears?"

Jack heaved himself lazily out of his chair and, moving across to his wife, bent down and kissed her gently. "The loneliness is getting on your nerves, Molly; if you can't throw it off we must cut our trip short. I won't have you worried on any account."

"I will try and not be silly if you promise me to take care of yourself and not to run needless risks."

"Anything you wish, my dear. Now it is high time we followed Jerome's example," and Jack strolled off to his tent.

The next morning the camp was up early, and everyone stumbled about in the dark and fell over things, calling for lanterns and matches, in the blundering way people have when awakened before the sun has made his appearance. The great shoot on the plains was coming off at last, and the sportsman who would be successful does not lie abed, especially when he has a long walk before him. Shooting in the heat of the day in East Africa has its drawbacks, and the cool fresh air of the morning is soon sucked up as the swift tropic sun leaps from its bed in the east to its throne in the centre of the heavens. Tempers are usually short on these early morning starts, and the extraordinary manner in which essential articles of attire, socks, shirts, and boots, manage to get lost at such times, is calculated to try the patience of an angel. It is not until the big cups of boiling cocoa make their appearance that irritability gives way to peace and smiles take the place of scowls.

The first greyness of dawn had but just begun to spread over the dark plains when Jack and Jerome swallowed the last of the cocoa and set out to cross the river to the promised land beyond. Jerome looked a little pale in the dim light, and his face was strained and anxious ; but the suspicions of the night before seemed ridiculous in the day-time. Still, Jack had promised his wife to be careful, and he determined to keep his promise.

The crossing of the river was a simple matter, and the sun was but just rising above the horizon when they landed safely on the far side and began their march across the treeless miles that stretched away into the distance. They were guided by Selebo, the headman whose strange story had interested them all on the previous night, and the care with which he picked his way through the tall tussocky grass showed plainly that he fully believed his own tale and meant to run no unnecessary risks. There was something uncanny in the idea of being at any moment precipitated down a sandy slope into the jaws of some unseen horror below, and whenever Jack's foot slipped in the yielding sand he shuddered slightly as his imagination conjured up the picture Molly's words had drawn beneath the moonlit trees. He laughed and called himself a fool each time, but the shudder ran through him nevertheless again and again, till he began to conceive a distaste for the endless grass-clad wastes that seemed to grow ever wider and more extensive as the sun sucked up the mists that rolled away over the slopes, grey and gloomy. They sighted plenty of game, looming up vast and shadowy, but found nothing out of the common, and, not wishing to disturb the rarer specimens, they left in peace the great herds that stared after them with wide wondering eyes. At length they reached a broad shallow basin in which, according to Selebo, they might expect to find something to repay their trouble, and that excellent person announced his intention of proceeding to the far side in order to turn whatever game there was towards the guns. As soon as he was gone the two made their way towards a neck of land about a quarter of a mile off, which seemed to be a sort of exit from the basin, and along which it appeared likely that the game would pass.

"If we sit down here and wait," remarked Jack, as they approached the spot, "I think we ought to do pretty well." Then his voice changed suddenly. "Good Lord, Jerome !" he cried, sharply, "what is that ? " and he pointed towards the spot where they had intended to take up their position.

Jerome stopped and stared curiously before him. "I don't see anything special," he observed at last.

"Isn't there a depression in the sand over there ? "

"Now you say so, it does look rather like it. But what if there is ? " Jerome's voice was studiously uninterested.

"Nothing, only somehow I wondered if it was one of those pits Molly was talking about last night."

"What nonsense! You don't mean to say you were affected by that lie of Selebo's. But it's easily settled. We had better go and look, and he led the way to the bottom of the neck, Jack following with a sensation of nervousness most unusual with him.

Presently they stopped sharply and looked at each other in mute astonishment. Right before them, only a few yards away, lay a great sandpit, fully ten yards across and about the same depth, shaped like the depression which forms in an hour-glass.

The edges were sharply defined, but soft and crumbly, and from time to time a few grains of sand detached themselves and rolled slowly down the shelving sides. The place looked deserted and empty, yet Jack shivered as he gazed. Something must have been at work to excavate a hollow so symmetrically perfect, something endowed with intelligence.

It could not be chance which had set a trap so accurately in the very centre of a game-path. On either side the sand was trampled with the spoor of innumerable beasts. The trap was new and its object obvious, yet it showed no sign of life. If it were indeed a spider's web, where was the spider? Did a gigantic replica of the terrible little ant-lion lie in wait beneath the sand? The idea was too wildly grotesque.

"It is impossible," muttered Jack at length; "the pit must be empty. And yet—how did it come there?"

But Jerome did not seem to hear, and, his dark keen face alight with excitement, went down on his hands and knees and crawled to the edge.

"For Heaven's sake come away!" cried Jack, anxiously; "if the sand gives way you will fall in, and even if the pit is empty it will be no joke getting you out. It is like that horrible trap of which Kipling writes in the 'Strange Ride of Morrowbie Jukes.'"

Jerome made no answer; but, still staring into the depths below, drew a couple of cartridges from his bandolier and dropped them down the slope. As they struck the bottom there was a sudden movement in the sand, and a little cloud of dust flew up from below and covered them. Then all was still once more.

Jack, standing back from the edge, saw nothing of this, since the bottom of the pit was hidden from him, and Jerome's manner gave no sign of anything unusual. "Well," he inquired, "nothing happened, I suppose?"

Jerome drew back and rose slowly. "No," he answered, "the place is evidently empty; it is quite safe. Come and look over the edge."

Jack took a step forward, and then a sudden unaccountable suspicion seized him, and he glanced sharply at his friend. Jerome's face was white and set, and on it was stamped the strange expression of the night before. At the sight Molly's warnings rushed back upon Jack, and he sprang aside hastily.

"No," he cried, trying to keep his voice steady, "I don't think I want to look into that horrible place. Come away, Jerome."

Almost before the words were out of his mouth Jerome was upon him, madness glaring in his eyes. "You shall go down," he hissed; "you took from me the girl I loved, and from that moment I lived for revenge, only waiting my opportunity. But I never dreamed of such a chance as this," and with the strength of insanity he dragged Jack nearer and nearer yet to the edge of the pit that held he knew not what. Braced by despair, Jack fought gallantly for his life; but as they reeled to and fro on the warm sand he knew that he could not keep up the struggle many seconds more. Barely a yard now separated them from the edge, and as Jack felt the loose treacherous rim slipping beneath his feet he gathered all his energies into one convulsive spring for safety. The effort was successful, and he felt firm ground once more; but he had only managed to swing round as on a pivot, bringing his antagonist upon the very spot whereon he himself had stood an instant before. It was useless; another moment must see the end. But even as the thought passed through his brain Jerome suddenly flung his arms wide, staggering wildly in the effort to regain his balance. The crumbling edge, treacherous at any time, and further weakened by the shock of Jack's last spring, had given way and was sliding downwards, slowly at first, then faster and faster, till almost before Jack could realise what had happened his would-be murderer had vanished with a despairing cry down the loose yielding slope, snatching and clawing vainly in his descent. Breathless and exhausted, Jack sank down and lay gasping on the rim of the pit, unable to do aught but watch for the end.

At the instant when Jerome's body struck the bottom a cloud of sand shot up, impelled by some invisible force, covering him with gritty particles, a few of which even reached the horrified spectator. Half blinded by the sand and shaken by his fall, Jerome struggled to his feet and dashed frantically at the shelving sides of his prison in a desperate effort to escape. But the sand poured down in masses from above, and a fresh cloud flew up, in the midst of which the wretched man fell back to the bottom of the pit, now no longer quiet and still, but heaving and shifting with the excited movements of its invisible tenant.

Before he had time to rise again the restless sand parted to give passage to a great grey claw that groped blindly round for an instant, and then, seizing its prey in a vice-like clutch, began to drag him slowly down.

The struggle that followed was fearful and protracted. Jack felt his brain reel with the horror of it, and shudderingly put his hands before his face to shut out the scene, though nothing could shut out the cries that rent the still morning air.

Then suddenly his strength and wits returned, and springing up he sought with frenzied haste for his rifle. Alas! in that dread wrestle on the brink both of the combatants had dropped their weapons, and now they lay half buried in the sand, choked and useless. With a groan of despair Jack sank again to the ground and hid his face in agonised waiting till the cries died away and silence reigned once more. Then, compelled by some horrid fascination which drew him against his own will to the scene of the tragedy, he peered a second time over that pit of horror. All was still and quiet, the past few minutes might have been a dreadful nightmare. But just as he was turning away the sand became agitated as before, and with one last desperate effort Jerome Harcourt's head and shoulders burst out into the sunlight. The insanity was gone now from the great dark eyes, and the expression on the grey and ghastly face was but a hopeless appeal for help. It was visible for a moment only, but as the sand closed over it for the last time something snapped in Jack's overtaxed brain and he lost consciousness.

It was two hours later when Selebo returned to find his master lying motionless beside the pit, his head hanging loosely over the crumbling edge. Fearful and trembling, the hunter dragged him carefully into safety, and after a while life came back and with it memory.

The return to camp will stand out in Jack's mind for many a long day as an awful dream, but it was accomplished at last, and in time he recovered from the shock, though it was long before he could tell the story of that morning.

Though utterly unfit both in mind and body, Jack insisted on going the next day to revisit the spot where Jerome Harcourt had lost his life, feeling that he could not rest till he had slain the unseen horror in the pit. But when he reached the well-remembered neck of land the pit was gone! The sand was once more smooth and level, and nothing but the spoor of some unknown animal which Jack followed unavailingly till advancing darkness compelled him to return remained to show that the whole incident had not taken place in the fever of delirium.

STRANGE STORIES OF SPORT

XXXI.—HIS HIGHNESS'S DEER STALK

BY C. EDWARDES

THEY were at the Spartan Club in Lorton Street, one of those elegant new institutions where you ask in vain for a French dish, but may rely on a mutton chop of unsurpassed excellence. Major Bullock (or Tom B., as he was generally called) was entertaining. He had picked up Greenstone, the rich Australian, and Russell-May, the rising young secretary to a Cabinet Minister, and invited them to a modern luncheon. Some respectable barley broth, a grilled beef-steak, a morsel of the latest invention in cheese—the Hertfordshire self-digesting—and there you were. A magnificent haunch of venison had tempted Russell-May, but Tom B. had dissuaded him from the adventure.

"I don't know whose forest it comes from," Tom B. said, "but the rearing of such meat is too complex an interference with the economics of latter-day civilisation for simple-life Johnnies like us to have anything to do with it. Nice phrase, isn't it? Not my own, thank heaven!"

"Ha! ha!" laughed Greenstone, rather louder than was seemly in the dining-room of a simple-life club.

Just after that General Magrimmon came in, and passed Tom B. with a facial contortion which might mean "How are you, my boy?" or "What the devil brings *you* in my way?" according to the humour of the man it was aimed at.

Major Bullock, however, always went for the brighter side of things, and his "Good morning, Magrimmon!" in response was of the cheeriest.

The general wore about the most extraordinary pattern of tweeds then to be seen in London, or even, it was said, in the North of Scotland. A host of little squares, diamonds, and moons in heather-crimson, green, blue, yellow, and white spread all over him in kaleidoscopic confusion. The effect would have been striking upon any man, but the general was more than six feet tall, very broad, red-faced, white-haired, and with a white moustache. A cap like his coat completed his charms of exterior.

"Who on earth——" whispered Greenstone. But Tom B. checked him.

"Tell you directly," he whispered back. "Sure you won't take coffee or any bad thing like that, either of you? If you won't, I'll tell you about it now. Did you see him scowl at the haunch, Russell-May?"

"I truly did," replied the young politician, with a smile. "I expect it's a bit spoiled by this time."

"Ah!" said Tom B. "Come along!"

He took it for granted that his guests were, for the hour at least, not mere triflers with the simple-life scheme. Anything to drink were a mistake.

With a hand in an arm of either of them, the agreeable major steered them from the dining-room into the Spartan's smoking-room. He shut the door of the latter with a deft touch of his well-shod foot, and rejoiced that they were alone together.

"Poor old Hector! Poor old lad!" he then exclaimed, his eyes twinkling. He cast himself into a deep armchair and nodded several times. "And yet, I don't know, you know," he added, abruptly. "It ought to do him a world of good in time. But that's the rub. Will he live long enough to get the good of it, as they say? I'm afraid he won't. It's an awful business to be born a Magrimmon and the last male of the house, by Jove! The proudest chap that ever inherited a tartan of his own private pattern, Greenstone, that man! You can form an idea of the pattern from what you've just seen on him!"

"Can I?" said Greenstone. "Ha! ha! Then I am sorry for him. But what's the—mystery, or tale, or whatever it is?"

"I'm coming to that," said Tom B. "It happened last September. You haven't heard it, Russell-May, I hope?"

"No, but I'm on fire to," said the young secretary.

"Ah! That's all right then." Tom B. rubbed his hands and looked relieved. "I was there, so I know all its ins and outs. But I'm telling you both in the most absolute confidence. The old chap would kill me with one of his ancestors' claymores if he knew what I was up to. Well, I'll risk it anyhow.

351

" There was a great to-do at Castle Magrimmon last September —in Ross-shire, it is—and I was so fortunate as to be one of the old boy's house party. He'd chummed with a continental Highness the previous spring down at Cannes or somewhere, and this gentleman—the Prince of a place ending in ' stein '—had consented to honour him with a visit in autumn. He wanted to lay low a few deer in the Highland style, and Magrimmon's forest of Stob Alloch was placed at his disposal. He had only a couple of days to spare for Scotland, however, and the stalk on the second day was to be a mighty careful sort of function.

" The Highness, you must understand, was as testy an old boy in his way as Magrimmon in his. About Magrimmon's age, too— be kind and call him sixty. Stoutish and very tightly laced everywhere, as if to make full exhibition of his curves, and so forth. Complexion plum-purplish, due to temper and indiscreet living. I shan't tell you any more about him except that he had divorced his first wife and been divorced by his second, and was still very mad about the latter event, which hadn't ministered to his princely vanity.

" Well now, as I don't suppose either of you know The Magrimmon's district, let me first remark that its mountains are little fiends. They get up to sharp points and razor edges without any waste of time and space. There's a view from the windows on one side of the castle which would astonish you, I'll wager. They're like a pale red saw fifteen or sixteen miles long, with gaps in it—the toughest bit of forest in Scotland, I believe. Anyway, I'd say ' No, thank you,' at my time of life to anyone who invited me to follow his men into a land he claimed to be still rougher.

" Such a joke it was to see the Highness's bushy eyebrows go up in the air that morning when he understood that he was not to proceed to his sport on the back of anything, but just his own legs or nothing. The black clouds had rolled off the points of the hills quite nicely, as if on purpose to gratify a gentleman of his importance.

" ' You wish me to *walk* up there, Magrimmon? ' thundered the Prince in a pre-breakfast minute.

" ' It is impossible, general,' said the Highness's factotum, a Count Something. ' His Serene Highness has not walked three miles for several years.'

" We smiled at that, we others. There was Magrattan of that ilk, and his son, a fine lad, though a bit sentimental, the Duke of Alloa, Tounlaw, a big local laird, and two or three more, including myself. Some first-class shots and first-class men.

" Magrimmon seemed much taken aback. Naturally, he supposed the Prince had come to Scotland knowing what to expect. He had other irritations just then, and it was no end of a blow when it turned out that the Highness thought he was to be taken up the mountain in a motor car, then seated comfortably in a chair, with refreshments to his hand as well as a servant with a gun ; that was his notion how deer were stalked and shot in the Scottish Highlands.

"The stalk was for the next day, and all the first day there seemed a considerable doubt if his Highness would not shy altogether at the programme which had been prepared for him. He was pretty decent among the pheasants, I will say, thanks to the driving, which was very smart. We flattered the gentleman to the top of his throat about his shots, and that pleased him. The weather also was encouraging. Magrimmon's table cheer was most encouraging of all, and it was after an extensive indulgence in this that his Highness pulled himself together and declared he would go into the hills in the morning like a native-born Scot, and—dash the consequences.

"'You will guarantee that I get a royal, Magrimmon ? That is all I ask in return for my toil,' he said.

"The general and all of us guaranteed him that, at random or otherwise.

"'Very well then,' said he, casting brave defiance in the teeth of that pathetic Count of his. 'I go with you, my dear friends !' He puffed up his chest, and we all looked suitably delighted. Magrimmon, poor wretch, most of all.

"And there matters stood, when, with a great deal of ceremony, the general had escorted the Prince to his rooms, and wished him good night. The rest of us also retired betimes, for an early start.

"It was then that Magrimmon paid me a very special visit with a face as long as a Lurgan spade, and told me a little domestic history which would have interested me more if I hadn't wanted to get into bed.

"I knew before this that he had had a disagreement with his head stalker, a fellow named Rob Carter. It had to do with the man's religion. The Magrimmons have been Catholics since the time of Adam, and this Rob Carter set the general's back very much up by changing his faith, and renouncing the Pope in favour of some small sect—I'm sure I don't know what it was, but it was a very sociable and informal kind of religion which had got rather a footing in the county. It was just like a Magrimmon to take the matter with the gravity he did. His forefathers stuck to their privileges of hereditary jurisdiction, I've heard say, longer than any other heads of clans, and what must the general do but try to kick Mr. Robert

Carter back into the faith of his forefathers. Raised his foot to his knickerbockered body, and called him a low-minded scoundrel. Whereupon, and very right too, the man asked for his wages on the spot, threatened an action for personal assault, and left Magrimmon, warning him that he would be sorry ere long for what he had done.

" The general came to me in my room to gloom about this. It had happened five days before the Highness's coming, and he cherished forebodings about the result in the morning.

" ' My dear fellow,' I said to him, feeling rather out of patience with his palaver at that time of night, ' what silly nonsense ! '

" He agreed that it ought to be silly nonsense. His other keepers were experienced and good men, and the reports about the deer in the Corrie of the Spring were all that he would have wished. But the Highness had got on his nerves, and—supposing anything prevented the great man from bringing down a royal—supposing the weather turned impossible—chief of all, supposing the other men showed a lack of just those abilities which were so very pronounced in the delinquent Carter !

" And then he produced a letter which had come that evening by hand, and read some of it.

" Mr. Robert Carter seemed to know him pretty well in some ways, by the tone of that letter. Magrimmon was calmly invited to re-establish the man in his service that very night, apologise for kicking him, and so make sure of giving his distinguished guest the satisfaction he desired.

" He was, it appeared, engaged for a picnic with sundry local members of his new faith at Kinlochalloch on the morrow, but he would throw that all over if Magrimmon would do the straight and magnanimous thing with him. He would return to the castle by midnight and superintend the stalk in the morning. It struck me as very significant that a man like the general should give a moment's thought to such a screed.

" ' Surely,' I said, ' you don't want to eat a helping of that fellow's humble pie ? I never read such impudence ! '

" ' Ay,' said he, hoarsely, ' it's impudence. But I'm tempted, Bullock. I don't know what's the matter with me, but I do know that Carter hasn't his equal among stalkers, and I've set my heart on gratifying the Prince.'

" ' Oh, well,' said I, ' it's too late now, anyway.'

" ' Yes,' said he, ' it's too late. It's five hours over the hills to Kinlochalloch, and he couldn't do himself justice after a trudge like that if I were to send for him.'

" When it got to this, I could only laugh and try to cheer the old donkey out of his depression. He went to bed at length, but with a parting word or two which showed that it isn't more than half a blessing to be a Highland chief of the very old stock.

" 'The fellow's as vindictive as an elephant, Bullock. That's what upsets me. And I wish to heaven to-morrow was comfortably over, with all the good results we anticipate. Good night,' he said.

" Pack full of prejudices, autocratic fads, and little baby fears about bogies, and so on—that's what Hector Magrimmon was last September, and is to this day, I'll be bound; especially the prejudices. I wouldn't for a hundred pounds go to him, where he's sitting in that room yonder, and just say these trumpery words to him: ' Hullo, Magrimmon, remember the fun of that stalk at your place last year ? ' I really wouldn't.

" But to get along with the story ; for there's no knowing if he mayn't stride up else in the middle of it. The weather was all right next morning. We turned out with lively hopes after a breakfast for which the keen, but not too keen, air had given us a devouring appetite. The Highness, from what his indispensable Count said, was not usually in anything like spirits so early in the morning; but this great day he was as excited as a school-girl about a bun-feast. I can see him now, holding Magrimmon by his kilt, and making a weird jest after he had, for about the tenth time, invited the general to swear by his saints and ancestors that he should get a royal to his own gun.

" 'If *you* don't get one, sir,' Magrimmon had assured him, ' no one else shall.'

" A noble sight in a kilt and his own tartan the general made, believe me, Greenstone. All the same, his dignity didn't permit him to enjoy having his skirts toyed with, even by a gentleman as high up in the world as this Prince. Such red knees he had, I remember. But that's a trifle not worth mentioning, though the Highness did mention it, and, with some tempestuous laughter, suggest that he ought to use powder for them.

" Well now, away we went; and for the first four miles in the glen we were all mounted, so that we could relish our cigars in the crisp air while the mountains slowly threw off the lingering shreds of their silken veils. Yes, by Jove ! a morning like that's enough to make any one poetical. Magrattan's young hopeful tipped us a Gaelic song of his own composing as we moved up the glen, and very nice it sounded.

" No doubt we were a picturesque procession for the rabbits and birds we startled on our way. We should have been still more so if the men had worn the Magrimmon badge of a silver trout in their caps. But that was barred, of course, in the interests of the stalk. The Prince was sorry to miss that detail, but it was about the only thing he did regret until we began to climb. Then he mighty soon realised that he would have done well to have had a Turkish bath before tackling the Magrimmon deer in their haunts.

"The perch we aimed for was an *arête* where the Strath Alloch mountains are most alarming. Something between three thousand five hundred and four thousand feet up. The men led us in rather a roundabout way, to make things easier for the Highness, and there was no crawling necessary, just for the reason that the live venison was neatly boxed up in the corrie on the inside of our mountain, and there was only one upper way out for them. They couldn't come in our direction, and only when we broke out, so to speak, on the inside edge of the mass, were we obliged to take cover.

"From that point on to the post prepared for the Prince was another half-mile, and here you may imagine our gentleman seated, at last, in a little shelter of quartz blocks like a porter's lodge, which the obliging Magrimmon had had built for him the previous day. The rest of us scattered about on our stomachs or so, except Magrimmon and the stalker who had succeeded the conscientious Carter as the business-head of affairs. These two crouched at the Highness's feet among the rocks, and if they liked their job on that acute-edged carpet better than I did mine, they may be congratulated on the thickness of their hides.

"As I said, it was a wonderful day. The warmth of it and the unclouded blueness! There was a magnificent view and that kind of thing, and there was a devilish lot of midges. I'd no idea midges explored such heights in quest of blood, especially in September, but I suppose the uncommon heat and the stillness gave them their chance. It was just as if they meant to have a last good feed before the winter. And though they made things hum for the rest of us, for reasons best known to themselves and the quality of the Highness's blood, they paid most attention to our well-beloved prince on his marble throne. In spite of Magrimmon's whispers about the indiscretion of it, the Highness cursed audibly in quite three languages, including English.

"Alloa was some four lengths from me, and, like myself, heard most of our gentleman's objurgations. We both thought it a splendid joke. 'Serve the old fool right!' Alloa passed the word to me, and I agreed. Given another quarter of an hour of it, and I expected to see him dance a very-high-land reel of his own, and break up the show altogether.

"Poor old Magrimmon was a model of earnest solicitude all the time. I daresay he's midge-proof, thanks to his long line of local ancestors, but he had his other worry, and I admit he bore that well. The deer were a precious time coming up from the corrie, and it seemed quite possible something had interfered with the drivers down there. We could see nothing, however, because of the steepness, and could only wait and keep our eyes on that one ladder-way to the ridge, which was their regular thoroughfare from the waterbrook they loved to the cool heights they loved, I suppose, equally well.

"At last news crept up in the shape of one of the younger gillies. The way that chap wormed among the rocks to us without disturbing any one of them was a lesson in mechanics. But none of us thought of that. It was much more to the point that the Prince might now be saved from the death by spontaneous combustion to which the midges and his own impatience were inviting him. A royal was actually at the head of the herd, we were informed, so that, all going well, and the Highness's nerves being fairly under control, he couldn't help realising his ambition in a minute or two. We were only about a hundred and fifty yards from the spot where the animals were bound to climb to the sky-line, and—well, I'm not an envious fellow as a rule, but I envied the gentleman his first shot in such a situation.

"Yet even now he couldn't control his tongue about the midges. I gave him the corner of my eye during this interval of quite thrilling expectation, and could see his shining brows working and his lips twitching out more naughty words. He had the look of a man in an awful temper, only just managing to keep his stopper on.

"Magrimmon was still more interesting. To see his great carcase hugging the ground (and such ground!), and the appeal in his face as he kept it sideways up to the Prince!

"Never in all my days, and I've had a few, did I behold a more eloquent proof of the truth of that fellow's words who said we Britons take our pleasures sadly. By sadly I mean, you know, as if they were anything rather than an amusement.

"Alloa suddenly drew me to attention elsewhere.

"'Here they are!' he whispered, no louder than the chirp of a grasshopper; and, by Jove! it was a grand spectacle.

"About nine or ten of them were already on our eye-line, making up a slope that only just escaped being a precipice. Coming up as sharply, too, as if they had climbing irons on. Three or four superb stags in the leading company! It seemed safe betting that our Serenity would now have his reward, and in a few minutes be blooming like a rose in the sweetness of his triumph.

"But what do you think happened in about ten ticks later?

"When the royal at the head of them all was only some twenty steps from the crest, a human head showed up from the other, the Kinlochalloch side; and before we had got over our first gasp of stupefaction, hang me if six or seven women and a man were not already on the very spot to which the herd was scrambling for all it was worth. The women were oh-ing and ah-ing with delight—we could positively hear them ; and after that first burst of joy, what must they do but form a group and begin to sing a hymn !

" Magrimmon was sitting up looking like a petrified demon by this time ; glaring with about ten eyes.

" Of course there was no end of a stampede among the herd. One of the stags broke its neck over the crags, and they were all out of sight in two Jack Robinsons !

" The stalker who was at the prince's feet was the first to give tongue about the wicked truth of the matter. He did it with language after the Highness's own heart, though this mighty gentleman didn't seem to notice it.

" That one man with the women was Rob Carter, and loudly the gillie proclaimed the fact to his master and all the midges who had leisure to listen.

" ' It is Carter indeed, be tammed to him ! ' cried the Magrimmon's servant for his master's ear.

*   *   *   *   *

" There ! that's the history of the famous stalk of Stob Alloch last September which has put a permanent scowl on old Magrimmon's face, and, for all one can tell, almost broken his heart.

" The man Carter fitted in his picnic party to the precise minute to bring utter humiliation to the head of the clan Magrimmon. I must say, when we others grasped the situation, we didn't do much to soothe either Magrimmon or his guest. It really was sublime in a way, you know. Alloa started the laugh, and I don't imagine Magrimmon will ever forgive me for doing my share in backing him up.

" The poor old wretch had his hands full in explaining to his Highness that the game was up—and why.

" Those devout picnickers finished their carol of praise, notwithstanding the shouts and fist-shakings of the two stalkers, whose clan blood was evidently thicker than any water-tie of esteem they might have acquired for Carter as his subordinates.

" The funny thing was that no one could suitably interfere with Carter and his sectarian sisters in time. The route to them was exceedingly craggy, although in bee-line they were only those few score yards from us. They sang their hymn—there were eleven of them by this time—and went down on their side with all the honours of war. And Master Rob Carter was the last to withdraw from our sight, like the clever captain he was, protecting the rear of his forces. By the way, three or four of his company were young lassies, with scarlet skirts. As colour, the scarlet had a charming effect on the bleached mountain top under a cloudless blue sky, but it was only afterwards, I fancy, that any of us appreciated it.

"Our Highness was about the angriest prince in Europe when he understood that he had climbed that mountain and surrendered himself as a feast to the midges all to no purpose. It was no use Magrimmon talking of trying another corrie three miles farther. His Highness said he wouldn't dream of it, and his toady, the Count, agreed that it would be madness. Even as it was, he said, he wasn't sure his princely master hadn't ruined his constitution for life.

"And so down we went, Magrimmon and his Highness like folks at a funeral the corpse to which had behaved badly in the matter of legacies.

"And the next morning our gentleman made straight tracks for his principality, with no Highland trophy about him except the marks of the midges.

*   *   *   *   *

"That's the whole story, though you must get under Magrimmon's skin and look into his family archives thoroughly to understand what a thing like that can mean to a man.

"I believe he'd have killed Master Rob Carter if he could have laid hands on him within twenty-four hours of the tragedy. But that astute individual put many counties between him and The Magrimmon long ere twenty-four hours, and subsequently defied his late master from the heart of Glasgow. There was a warrant or something out against him for trespass, but I don't think it came to anything.

"Castle Magrimmon is to let this year, if you and your millions, Greenstone, have a taste for such luxuries."

STRANGE STORIES OF SPORT

XXXII.—THE CHARMED RING

BY PEYTON WREY

"WHAT a perfect place this is!" Lyght exclaimed, as he stepped from the motor at the door of Strathesk Castle, and was greeted by his host, Hugh Lumsden.

High up, on a green plateau surrounded by heathery hills, the castle stood, stone-built, rugged, with a round tower at each side rising above the roof, and yet, by reason of the flowers which adorned some of the sills and the bright curtains visible in most of the windows, possessing an air of comfort or even of gaiety. The hill-side on which the structure was built had accommodated itself to the formation of green terraces, set here and there with flights of stone steps, and it was evident that the gardeners took pride in their work, for the beds were radiant. The boundary of the grounds was formed by a stream which might almost be dignified by the name of river, over which a stone bridge led to the moor.

"I'm glad to be here again—for the last time!" Lyght remarked, as he gazed round at the prospect.

"Yes, we shall never see it again, that's pretty certain," Lumsden replied; "but come in and have something. I've got you a cold grouse and some ham to keep you going till dinner. We'll chat whilst you are eating."

He led the way into the dining-room, where his friend seated himself at the table, nothing loath after a long journey by rail and twenty miles in the motor from the station.

" How's your girl ? " Lyght asked.

" All right, thanks—out on the moor. They'll be back rather early, there are only three drives after lunch to-day, and she'll wait, I expect, and walk home with the guns."

" No good news, I suppose, or you'd have told me," Lyght continued. " It's awful to think of a brute like Dunstan having this dear old place. If testimony that Alleyn intended to leave it to Clive were any good there would be no want of it ! "

" Of course it was a perfectly well-understood thing. Dunstan has his own place and any amount of money ; but it is strange that though Alleyn so well knew his heart was wrong and he might go off at any moment, he never made a will and left Clive safe. I had a very strong affection for Alleyn, the kindest creature in the world, but I must say it is desperately hard on Clive. If I were a wise father I suppose I should break off this match with Edith, for I don't see how they are to get on. He has about £300 a year. I'm a poor man, and if I squeezed out another £500 for them it's as much as I could manage, with strict economies to make up for it. It's so hard for a fellow like Clive to make an income. What's he to do ? He might get an estate agency in time, for he knows country life, but there are lots of details he would have to learn, and those things aren't well paid. It's so different, too, when you have had every reason to expect to be a rich man. Alleyn allowed him £1,200 a year, and now of course that's gone."

" Yes," Lyght went on, " there's nothing harder than for a fellow like Clive to make money. He couldn't turn wine merchant —tout like Bob Capper, and bore people to buy some weird brand of champagne. When does Dunstan come in ? I do hate that fellow! I met him shooting last year, and I believe he only goes out for the sake of the excuse it gives him to thrash his dogs. They say he keeps his hand in by practising on his wife, a nice little woman, but evidently afraid of him."

" It'll be settled in a short time now," Lumsden answered. " There were some matters that couldn't be decided till the Courts sat again, and the Master said that I, as Alleyn's trustee, had better come here, and what he called administer the place. He happened to know something about sport, and understood that it would not be a good thing to leave the grouse alone for a year. Rather odd ! He knew Alleyn, and told me he had shot here himself years ago."

" Why aren't you shooting, by the way ? I expect the truth is you gave up your day just because I was coming, as if I couldn't have waited till you got home ! " Lyght said.

" No, I really had letters and business, and I thought perhaps you'd like to come and get some trout ? " Lumsden suggested.

"Nothing I should like better!" Lyght exclaimed, taking the glass of port which his friend had poured out for him. "It won't take me five minutes to change," and he went off for the purpose.

*   *   *   *   *

Meantime on the moor sport had been proceeding. Edith Lumsden and Lady Oswald, the wife of one of the other guests at Strathesk, had driven out as far as any road took them to the hut where the men were to lunch, had climbed the rest of the way, and waited the arrival of the party. Birds had been plentiful, and had come well in three of four drives, a heron hovering over the moor having played havoc with the fourth, as herons will. The proverb says "as hungry as a hunter," but there is surely no stronger incentive to appetite than a morning on the moor. The breeze with just a touch of autumn in it has its effect, and at Strathesk the guns had a considerable amount of exercise, for the butts were unusually long distances apart over particularly rugged country. The sportsmen who had done well said little, as they sat at their cheery meal, about the shooting; the duffer of the party, whose contribution to the bag had been infinitesimal, had long laments to make about the curious persistency with which the birds had evaded his neighbourhood, the extraordinary conglomeration of circumstances which had conspired to prevent him from accepting all his chances, the iniquity of his gun-maker in supplying ill-loaded cartridges, and the stupidity of his loader's dog which seemed to have no nose. He was confident he had nine down, if not ten—it was, he believed, eleven—at the first drive; but only three were gathered, and one of those his neighbour's loader claimed as his master's unquestionable spoil. The reader may have met this gentleman, who shoots in a great many different localities. Cold grouse, a succulent rabbit pie, some seductive patties, had been consumed with excellent appetite, the whisky and soda, corrected with apricot brandy, had gone down sweetly, and with tobacco in various forms alight the party set off to continue the sport, Edith accompanying her lover.

Clive's loader discreetly lagged behind, knowing it would be some time before his services were required.

"It isn't complimentary to me that you should look so sad, dear," Edith said, as she sat on the seat when they had reached the butt, Clive leaning gloomily against the side; "but no, dear," she continued, "I quite understand! It *is* cruel!" and she held out a kindly sympathetic hand, which he took and kissed.

"I've got you, and that's the only thing that really matters, darling," he replied; "but it's about you I'm thinking. I'm a pauper, and it seems selfish and wicked to drag you down to poverty.

362

I know what I ought to say and do, but I can't!" She made a gesture which eloquently protested. " My poor cousin knew that he could not live long, and—I never spoke of it to you—he told your father that he would give us at once enough to enable us to get on comfortably. He was so generous that his idea of comfort would have been luxury. When I asked you I was practically a rich man —there is no doubt he meant me to have the place. He was very fond of you, too, and we should have been so happy here! Now what am I to do ? "

" Something will turn up for us, dear. I have great confidence in the future, if we are only patient," she answered with a smile.

" I wish I could think your confidence was well based. I don't know where the luck can possibly come from," he said, sadly. " What's that ring, dear ? I don't remember seeing it before ? " he remarked, chiefly desirous of changing the subject, taking the ungloved hand which she had again consolingly stretched out to him.

" No, I've never worn it before to-day, and I don't know what whim made me put it on. I found it in my dressing bag, and thought I'd wear it," she replied.

" It isn't very pretty ! What's it made of ? Some green stone seems to be mixed up with the gold. What's the history of it, dear ? " he asked.

" It was given me by an old woman when we were living in Italy," Edith said. " She was a poor old thing, very poor and ill, and I used to take her a little wine and dainties. She gave me the ring a few days before she died. She said it was a wishing ring and would bring me luck," Edith went on, with a smile. " You know how superstitious those Italian peasants are."

" You were to put it on and wish, I suppose ? I'm afraid I should not have very much faith in such a talisman."

Before she replied the loader made his appearance with the guns. Edith rose and found a new resting-place on the heather at the mouth of the butt, where she could see what was going on ; Clive prepared for action, and in due time the birds began to come, he taking toll of them as they passed.

The other drives were accomplished, leaving the guns some two or three miles from the castle. A brake and a pony carriage were waiting not far off to convey the guns home, but Edith, a good walker, suggested that they should stroll quietly back; it was almost the last day they would have on the dear old moor which had been Clive's home all his life, and was to have been his own when his cousin Alleyn Vaux was gone. Of Alleyn's intentions in the matter there could be no shadow of doubt. He and his half-brother Dunstan had never been on cordial terms. Dunstan was rich, and did not want, that is to say had no reasonable need of, another estate. Alleyn had always felt the warmest affection for his cousin Clive, and had treated him as a son. When Alleyn perceived Clive's devotion to the daughter of his old friend Lumsden, he had encouraged him to speak, delicacy having prevented Clive from doing so; for though it was perfectly well understood that he would inherit Strathesk, the understanding was not binding, and did not absolutely ensure Clive's position. In the plainest terms Alleyn had told Lumsden, and had repeated to Clive, what his intentions were; but when the dreaded but always anticipated end had come, and Alleyn one evening was found dead in his chair, no will was discoverable, and it seemed inevitable that the property, with the rest of Alleyn's fortune, must pass to Dunstan as heir at law. Some details had to be examined, and, as already noted, the Master in Chancery had suggested that Lumsden, as Alleyn's trustee, should take charge of the estate till matters were finally settled.

The loader was about to pick up the guns when Clive took one of them.

"I'll carry this, I think, in case we happen on anything by the way," he said. "Come on, dear, and pick your path carefully. It's very bad going just about here."

Soon they came to firmer ground, to a spot from which they looked across to the castle on the side of the opposite hill. The same thought occurred to both as they stood and gazed over the expanse of heather at what was to have been their home. They were looking for almost the last time; the castle they had regarded as their own was to pass into the hands of a stranger; their future was dim; where their new home was to be they had no idea, but it must be a humble one.

Edith knew the moor well; Clive, of course, was familiar with every bit of it. Straight between them and the house was a large tarn with very boggy ground, full of peat holes, all round it. They must make a widish detour to left or right.

"Which way shall we go?" Clive asked.

"Whichever you like, dear. You know best," she said.

"No; I'm going to be entirely guided by you. You've got your lucky ring on, and perhaps we shall find a gold mine," he replied, trying hard to be bright and cheerful.

"I don't know much about such things," she answered, "but I should not suppose gold was found in this sort of country! Well; we'll go to the right. But I don't suppose the ring is likely to act immediately, you know. I'm sure the poor old woman believed in it, all the same."

"I wish I could share her faith," Clive said; and as he spoke a grouse rose some twenty yards in front of him. Unexpected as the bird was, he just had time to get his gun up, and a hasty shot brought it lifeless to the ground. They went forward to pick it up.

"What a curious bird!" Edith exclaimed. "It is quite silvery, isn't it? And look! the flight feathers—don't you call them?—are perfectly white!"

"Yes. I've never seen one so oddly marked and coloured," Clive rejoined. "Poor Alleyn would have been interested in it. He was a very keen naturalist, and had all sorts of theories about plumage. Lyght is an authority, too, and we shall find him at the castle when we get back. There are some more birds over there, see!" he exclaimed, pointing to the left. "I might get quite a bag, with luck!"

As it happened, however, no other chance presented itself for the rest of the journey, and they reached home to find the party at tea in the library; the two fishermen well pleased with themselves, Lyght having landed a handsome four-pounder.

"You know all about grouse," Clive said, taking the bird from his pocket and handing it to Lyght. "Have you ever seen one like that?"

"Why, it's an albino," somebody said.

"No, I think not," Lyght replied. 'I've never seen an albino grouse, and don't think such birds exist. Albinism is the correlation of white plumage and pink irides, and this bird's eyes are quite normal," he said, opening the closed lids. "This is more in the nature of leucotism."

"I dare say you are right, my dear fellow, but I must confess I don't quite know what leucotism is," the other rejoined. "You are getting a long way beyond me! In fact, I should have thought that albinism and leucotism were as nearly as possible the same thing?"

"I won't try to deliver a scientific lecture," Lyght replied, with a smile. "I know there is a learned disquisition on the subject in a book on birds on one of the shelves over there. It's really rather an interesting point."

Going to the shelf he took down a large volume with coloured illustrations of birds, and turned over the pages to find the section relating to grouse. As he did so a paper fell to the floor. Lumsden picked it up, and was about to replace it on the table when the writing attracted his attention. He looked at it with care, an expression of surprise spread over his face, and he began to read.

"Good heavens!" he ejaculated, in a tone of amazement. "This is most marvellous!"

"What is it?" Clive inquired.

"It's what we've searched for high and low in vain," Lumsden replied. "A letter from poor Alleyn to Marston, his solicitor, about his will."

"This is thrilling!" Lady Oswald exclaimed. "May we know what it says and what it means?"

"I'll read it," Lumsden continued, after having himself first mastered the contents. "It is dated May 3—a week before his death. 'Dear Marston,—I know it is an absurd superstition that induces a man to suppose that if he makes his will he is likely to die, but somehow or other I have put off what I know I ought to have done, and perhaps I have been influenced by this stupidity. I won't delay any longer, and am having a shot on my own account at what I want done. I remember reading my grandfather's will. It was quite a volume of parchment, and puzzled me utterly; the legal jargon was incomprehensible. Somewhere I have read of a big lawyer who wrote his will in the plainest possible language on half a sheet of note-paper, and that's what I am doing, for now that I have started I want to get it over. I know it has to be signed by two witnesses, and I'm seeing that that is all right. Here it is. All I want you kindly to tell me is whether this is in form and binding, and if not please put it straight. Yours most sincerely, Alleyn Vaux.' And here is the will on the other half-sheet: 'I, Alleyn Vaux of Strathesk Castle, leave everything of which I die possessed to my cousin Clive Wentworth for his absolute use. I do not ask him to treat with kindness and consideration dependents who have served me well, as I know he will do so.' That is all. It is signed and witnessed by Gregory the butler and McHuish the head gardiner. They both told me that they had witnessed a will, but knew no more."

"And it is good—all right?" Lady Oswald asked, while Clive and Edith gazed at each other speechlessly.

"A perfectly sound and legal instrument. Short as it is, it ensures the possession of the property to Clive," Lumsden stated.

A chorus of congratulations resounded from all sides.

"But why on earth was the letter not posted, and how did it get into the book?" Oswald asked.

"That I don't suppose we shall ever find out," Lumsden answered.

"But the one thing certain seems to be that we should never have found these papers if it had not been for Edith's ring," Clive continued.

Curiosity was forcibly aroused. "What do you mean?" and "What ring?" were the questions asked.

Edith took it off, it was handed round, and she told the simple history of how she obtained it.

"I don't understand how the charm worked?" Lady Oswald said, interrogatively. "How do you make out that the ring helped you?"

"It was perhaps indirectly and rather roundabout," Clive replied, "but nevertheless it was the ring that has led to all this. When I come down from the Higher butts I always go by the path to the left of the tarn—I don't know why, habit I dare say—but when we reached the division of the ways this afternoon I asked Edith which we should take—said, in fun, that we would be guided by the ring and that it might lead us to a gold mine. If we had not taken the path to the right I should not have shot that grouse, if I had not done so the discussion would not have arisen, the book would not have been taken down—most likely no one would have looked into it for years—and there the will would have lain!"

"And if Dunstan had found it, the chances of his disclosing the facts and producing it would, I fancy from what I know of him, have been exceedingly remote," Lyght cut in.

"If any one had told me this story twenty-four hours back I should have derided the idea of it," Clive said. "As things happened there is no shadow of doubt that the ring led to the discovery. I'm not superstitious, but it may be that 'There are more things in heaven and earth, Horatio'—you know the rest."

The story is told, for it need not be said with what wrath and vexation Dunstan Vaux heard of the discovery, or how Clive and Edith settled down to enjoy their own. The ring never leaves her finger.

Of course the hard-headed man of the world will desire to know how a dead Italian peasant woman could influence the flight of a grouse on a Scottish moor, and there is plenty of satirical humour to be derived from the idea of such a thing. The fact was, however, as Clive stated. Had she not been wearing the ring in all human probability the discovery would never have been made.

STRANGE STORIES OF SPORT

XXXIII.—THE WARNING

BY PEYTON WREY

A TRUISM constantly impressed upon us is that no one can guess what is going to happen to him. There are, of course, those who plod on in the same path from year to year, fulfilling the same round of daily duties, receiving the same reward; there are others who in their wildest dreams have never imagined that they could possibly find themselves in the circumstances which surround them.

Raymond Hetherington was a case in point. His father had died leaving the remains of a property which just sufficed to pay his debts; Raymond had been called to the Bar, for which profession he had no great aptitude, and though he added to his income by ill-paid casual journalism, an occasional article on some subject connected with sport, his future had been sadly dubious. Yet here he was, at the head of a perfectly appointed table, in a dining-room which would have afforded the most fastidious of painters a model of a " baronial hall," sending priceless vintages on tour round the board. It was a hall rather than a room, panelled in oak, with a carved roof, just such a chamber as that in which the occupants centuries since might have been pictured, except that now electric lights shone down on the china dishes which held the choice fruit, on the glass and antique silver. Only half a dozen people were seated at the small table in a room which, as the phrase goes, would have " dined " sixty—Raymond, a man of thirty or thereabouts, brown-eyed, clean-shaven, a thoughtful expression, which nevertheless broke at once into a kindly smile; on his right a pretty girl, Ethel Daunce, whose brown hair gleamed almost golden where the lamps caught it; on his left an elderly lady, Ethel's mother, the thoughtful lines on whose pleasant face disappeared as she talked cheerily to her host. Facing Raymond was a dark-visaged man, his stern mouth partially covered by a moustache, which, however, did not quite disguise a certain sinister and bitter curl of the lip—Raymond's cousin, Dunstan Gawthorpe.

" I must have another glass of this port," Captain Berford, who sat at Mrs. Daunce's left hand, remarked as the decanter reached him. " You must have a little, too," he said to his wife, an amiable, good-looking, but rather commonplace girl opposite to him. " It is extraordinarily good, a wonderful wine! Do you know what it is ? " he asked his host.

"I've no idea, but I'm very glad you like it," Raymond answered. "Do have some, Mrs. Berford, though I was going to recommend this madeira."

"I must experiment on that some other evening if you kindly give me a chance," Berford said. "What a cellar you must have!"

"These are beautiful grapes. Are they from your own houses?" Mrs. Berford asked.

"Oh no. Covent Garden, I expect, or the fruiterer's in Abbotston; we are not nearly in going order yet—the green-houses are a desert."

It seems strange that a man should know nothing of the wines he is offering to his guests, but everything that had lately happened to Raymond was strange.

His prospects of making anything like an income at his profession were small, his pen was a poor supplement, and his possessions apart from these aids under a couple of hundred a year. Being thus impecunious he had, of course, fallen devotedly in love with Ethel Daunce, daughter of an old brother officer of his father. A modest annuity was nearly all Mrs. Daunce had to depend on, and Raymond's marriage, if it were ever to take place, was contingent on his "getting something to do," a phrase which never shaped itself into definite meaning. He had influential friends, for his father had been distinguished and popular; but in these days there are few if any of those snug sinecures which men of high rank and position were formerly able to bestow. The outlook was gloomy in the extreme, till one morning it grew suddenly radiant. Raymond had scarcely a relative in the world, except his cousin Dunstan, who as it chanced lived in the same building in the Temple. He was supposed to he an engineer and was a clever mechanician, but idle, thoughtless, and extravagant, indeed several times Raymond's scanty resources had been drawn upon to supply his cousin's wants. On the memorable morning referred to, however, a letter had come from a firm of solicitors to inform Raymond that as next of kin to an old uncle of his mother's he had inherited the Manor House, Whitmere, and a fortune which represented some £14,000 a year, together with a large sum of ready money.

Raymond had forgotten the old man's very existence. As a boy he just recollected being taken by his father to the big gloomy house in Bloomsbury where Mr. Cathcart lived; since then the old man had evinced no desire to see Raymond. The heir, as he proved to be, had not known whether his relative was alive or dead, as it seemed a matter of no interest or importance to him. As for the manor house, Raymond had never heard of such a place, and went to see it with much curiosity. It was a really magnificent sixteenth-century structure, but had been shut up for years. When light was at length let into the long-shuttered windows cobwebs, dust, and mildew were found to be the prevailing features. To make the place habitable everything had to be done to it; but, money being no object, an Abbotston firm had devoted themselves assiduously to the work, renovated and refurnished, installed electric light, and while maintaining as much as possible the character of the mansion, had made it a model of comfort and luxury. The pictures had suffered comparatively little, it was discovered, when they had passed through competent hands, and the cellars were bountifully stocked with wines of all descriptions, though much of the champagne and claret had become undrinkable.

The men soon followed the ladies to the hall which it appeared was likely to do duty for a drawing-room, a huge apartment with a minstrels' gallery at the end of it. Ethel and her mother had only arrived on this visit the day before, and had not nearly made acquaintance with the place of which she was soon to be mistress. Dunstan and Berford started a game of billiards, Mrs. Daunce and Mrs. Berford talked, giving Raymond and Ethel the welcome opportunity for a chat.

"We seem quite lost in this great room," she remarked, as he seated himself beside her.

"There will be a house full next week," he said. "The Kenyons can come, with them there'll be fourteen altogether. It's lucky that the shooting has been regularly let and the game well kept up. Fourteen, you and your mother, myself, seventeen. Isn't there some nice girl you could ask to make up an even number?"

"Then he'll be gone?" Ethel said, glancing towards the billiard table where Dunstan was standing, and speaking in tones which expressed much satisfaction.

"Yes, dear, he's going on Monday. I wish you didn't dislike him so much! I feel bound to be considerate to him, you know; if I had not been in the way the property would be his. We've seen a good deal of each other, and I should be a brute if I cut him now that things have happened as they have—and he's been very useful, too, down here getting the place in order."

"I do dislike him, and it's no good pretending I don't," Ethel said. "I have a sort of instinctive horror of him. I hate cruelty, and I can't forget his face the day the motor ran over that poor dog, the absolutely diabolical grin with which he looked back at the unfortunate creature. I hear its scream of agony now," and she shuddered as she spoke.

"You must have misjudged, dear. No one could be such a brute as that," Raymond answered; but she merely shook her head.

"We won't talk about it," she rejoined. "Has the lady been smiling at you? I must go and make her acquaintance to-morrow, but I'm rather jealous!"

"She smiled sweetly. She's a darling and I'm extremely fond of her!" Raymond replied.

"You don't know who she was?"

"No, I've found out nothing, and don't know how to do so. Some ancestress, I suppose. It's really a beautiful face, gentle, tender, and womanly, and as I tell you the eyes seem to follow you about and watch you kindly in whatever part of the room you may be. She seems quite a companion."

"And you intend to desert me to-morrow?" Ethel inquired.

"Yes, dear. Dunstan and I are just going to shoot the hedge-rows and little spinneys, and it's an excuse to get a bit acquainted with the property. But look, Mrs. Berford's saying good-night. I must see them off."

The game of billiards was over, the motor which was to take the Berfords to their home, some eight miles distant, was heard panting outside, and Raymond went to perform the—to him—un-accustomed duties of host. Ethel and her mother retired, and Raymond went up the broad staircase to the half study, half dressing-room, where he proposed to master the contents of a long report from his lately-appointed agent. Switching on the light the first thing he did was to look at the portrait of which he and Ethel had been talking. The eyes were apparently seeking his with a glance of welcome which had something of mournfulness and something of love in it.

He read the report. The farms were all let to substantial tenants, every one of whom, however, seemed to want something done which he thought the landlord was the proper person to do. Raymond replied to the letters, put away the papers, opened the door of his bedroom adjoining, switching off the light. His head was full of business, recalling what he had just written, wondering whether he had done wisely in agreeing so readily to all the requests that had been made to him; when of a sudden he seemed to be conscious of a presence, to feel that he was not alone. It was strange, for certainly no one could possibly be there. He listened intently, his hand raised to turn the light on again, when near his ear a soft voice whispered, "*Do not cross the stream.*"

In a moment he had flooded the room with light and glanced hastily round. He was alone; the picture returned his gaze with its unfailing sympathy and sweetness; no one could have spoken, for there was no one there to speak; and yet he had never in his life heard words more distinctly uttered! What could they signify? What stream was he not to cross? The tones had seemed to convey warning—affectionate, almost entreating. He was utterly bewildered, and stood irresolute. Would the mystic voice speak again? Overcoming a tremor of the heart, he turned off the light and stood where he had stood before; but all was silence. For perhaps two minutes he waited motionless in the dark, straining his ears to catch the faintest murmur; none came, and passing into his bedroom he was soon lying and still listening till presently he fell into a sound and dreamless sleep.

Raymond rose next morning still dwelling on the inexplicable occurrence. Assuredly it had not been imagination. He had heard the words and could recall the cadence and expression of the voice, but of course it was not a thing to be spoken of, and he endeavoured to maintain conversation brightly at breakfast, though Ethel did not respond with her usual gaiety, seeming indeed anxious and depressed.

" What's the matter, dear? " he quietly asked when the meal was over, and the others had risen. " Come in here and tell me about it. I'm sure something has upset you? " and he led the way through a door into a little drawing-room.

" I had such a horrible dream. I can't get over it," she replied.

" Tell me about it, darling," he said, recalling his own experience. " Why, what is it? " he asked with keen anxiety, for she had suddenly raised her hand, and with a look of horror on her face was pointing to a water-colour drawing on the wall just behind where her lover was standing.

" Why, that's the very place! Oh, tell me where it is? " she cried.

He turned and looked. The scene represented was a landscape without figures. A small building, something between a summer-house and a cottage as it appeared, stood on the borders of a wood; on the other side of the building was a brook fed by a tiny waterfall, close to which was a rustic bridge; in the distance was another wood—a pretty sketch, but certainly with nothing about it to create emotion.

" I have not the remotest notion! " Raymond replied. " I've not looked at it before, and have no idea whether it is near by or a hundred miles away, or merely a fancy sketch. Do tell me all about it, dear. You are almost fainting! "

" It's the very place I saw in my dream, and you—I'm sure it was you—were lying dead in the field there! " she answered in a faint voice, sinking into a chair.

" But, my dear little girl, I'm not lying dead in the field there, you see! I'm alive and particularly well," he said, cheerily, endeavouring to raise her spirits. "Don't they say dreams go by the rule of contraries? That means that if ever I find the field—supposing it exists—I shall have a good time there, you see! It's odd, but you must have got that view unconsciously into your mind, and so recalled it as you slept!"

"That is impossible," Ethel said, solemnly. "I have never been into this room before, so I could not have seen the drawing; and yet in my dream I saw every detail of it—and you dead," and she shuddered at the recollection.

"I'm so grieved, darling," he said, kissing her; "but you know you mustn't let a dream make you miserable. You are going to Abbotston shopping, aren't you? Find some pretty ornaments and knick-knacks and things for the rooms, and forget all about it! There's the keeper; I must be getting ready."

"Wait one minute, Raymond," she rejoined. "That picture may be a view on the estate. If it is, promise me solemnly that you will never go into that field. Yes, promise!" she said, seeing that he was about to make a light reply.

"Very well, dear, I promise you then!" and with an affectionate farewell he went towards the gun-room.

Jackson, the keeper, was there already, and his boy, a bright-eyed, merry-faced urchin of twelve or thirteen, gazing at and evidently longing to touch Raymond's gun, which was lying on the table. His fingers, indeed, were furtively approaching the safety-bolt.

"Leave that alone, youngster," his father said. "He be quite wild about guns, that boy," Jackson added. "Quite happy if he's sitting and looking at one. I'm thinking you and Mr. Gawthorpe must have your 'nitials or something put on your guns or you'll never know 'em apart, sir, and get 'em mixed."

"Yes, they are exactly alike. My guns suited Mr. Gawthorpe so well that I had a pair made for him just the same. What's the matter with this lock, I wonder?" Raymond said, vainly trying to open the gun-case. "The thing seems to have gone wrong. I was just going to look at the other gun, but it doesn't matter now. I hope they'll both be busy next week. Ah! there's Mr. Gawthorpe. We'll get on."

In the yard they found little Ben Jackson earnestly struggling to stand on his head, to the apparent surprise of the two spaniels he was supposed to be in charge of, who were gazing at him, slowly and thoughtfully wagging their tails.

The manor house itself was almost at the easterly end of the estate, which projected for some three miles in a species of oblong shape in a westerly direction. A fair number of pheasants were

373

found in the outlying coppices, hedgerows, and spinneys. The energetic little spaniels worked indefatigably to push them out. Raymond, who had studied the map with care, learned much of the general lie of the land, the position of woods, &c., which to most people look so differently on a map from what they look in reality. He had been brought up in the country, was a decidedly good shot, as was Gawthorpe, and few of the birds that gave chances got away. Time had passed so quickly that Raymond was surprised to find it well past one o'clock. He was decidedly hungry.

"Gentlemen always lunch in the Cot, sir; and I thought as how you'd like to have it there," Jackson said. "We be best to go 'long the ride through the wood, if you be pleased, sir."

"I shall be glad to go the shortest road, for I'm deuced dry," Gawthorpe said. "This way, isn't it?"

"Yes, sir. Guess you know your way 'bout already near as well as I do? Funny thing, I thought I saw you down here last night, seven o'clock or so?"

"Saw me? No, not here, surely," Gawthorpe said. "I went out for a stroll last evening, but I couldn't have been within a mile of here I should think."

Jackson looked doubtful.

"Perhaps I was mistaken, sir; but I thought I saw you, to be sure!" he rejoined. "There, sir," he said to Raymond, "that be the Cot."

They had come to the end of the ride and passed into the open. Raymond looked where Jackson pointed, and started back in amazement. This was the scene of the picture which Ethel had recognised on the wall! The Cot was the building half summer-house, half cottage, the corner of the wood through which they had just walked was shown in the drawing; there to the left was the little waterfall, the plank bridge, the trunk of a sapling for hand-rail, the rushing brook, the meadow—in which she had seen him lying dead!

"Pretty bit of country this, sir!" Jackson said, noting Raymond's rapt gaze. "I recklect when I was a boy a lady as was staying in the house coming down and painting of it. The water seems to liven it up; don't it, sir?"

Raymond was too much moved to reply, but he and Gawthorpe went forward. The Cot consisted of two rooms, in one of which the lunch was laid; and, contrary to all his usual habits, Raymond poured out and drank a wineglassful of brandy to steady his nerves. His appetite, too, had gone, and he could only pick at the succulent partridge pie which had been provided. This was assuredly the spot of which Ethel had dreamed—and yes! "*Do not cross the stream!*" the mysterious voice had said; here the stream sparkled and rippled on its way!

"You seem dull?" Gawthorpe said, as Raymond ate, or affected to eat, speechlessly. "What's wrong?"

"Nothing, my dear fellow. I was only thinking—trying to remember the lie of the land, you know," Raymond answered.

"We're about two-thirds through now," Gawthorpe said; "and Jackson thinks there will be a lot of birds over the brook there. The partridges generally do well, he says. Wake up, Raymond! You're asleep!"

What should he do? He had promised Ethel not to go into the field, but he had done so merely to ease her mind. It was absurd to avoid a part of his own property; and as for the warning voice, to give way to superstitious fears was culpable weakness, a really serious thing, which, encouraged too far, might unhinge a man's mind. What could happen to harm him in a quiet stroll with a gun over a quiet part of his estate? There was not a mad bull in the field, nothing more alarming than a possible covey of partridges or a hare.

At this moment a knock came to the door. Jackson was there, the modest bag was laid out, and he was anxious to arrange the little programme for the afternoon. Raymond wanted to think, to be alone.

"Go and talk to him, Dunstan, will you? I want to jot down a few ideas that have been occurring to me before I forget them. It's a biggish job taking on a place like this," Raymond remarked.

Gawthorpe, unobserved, glanced at him half viciously, half superciliously, and with an "All right!" went out.

Raymond pondered. Should he go on? Yes! It was folly to be deterred, a mental feebleness to which he must not give way; and he looked again out of the window towards the field across the stream.

All was placid and still, and he was about to rise from his chair and go into the next room for his gun, which Jackson had taken to rub through and had put on the table while they talked, when his attention was forcibly arrested. A moment before the field had been untenanted. Now as he watched he saw a woman, little more than a girl, approaching the bridge. She must have sprung from the earth! He could have sworn that there was nothing human, nothing bigger than a possible rabbit, within sight when he looked last; but there *she* was, approaching, reaching, the bridge; and as he gazed awe-stricken he was stupefied to see that the face resembled—*was*—that of the portrait with the watchful eyes! Now she stood on the bridge. She turned her face, looked full at the window where he was seated, and raising both her hands, palms outwards, thrice made a gesture as of pushing someone back.

He rose to go to meet her, to see what the marvel might be, spellbound, keeping his eyes fixed on her; and as he looked she vanished!

"Not dreaming still? Come on, man! Quite a nice little bag," Gawthorpe said, standing at the door. "Seven brace of pheasants, four and a half of partridges, a hare and a couple of rabbits, and Jackson says with luck we shall do much better this afternoon. Come on!"

"No, I don't feel like shooting this afternoon. I have a lot of things to do," Raymond replied.

"Nonsense!" the other rejoined, an accent of persuasion in his voice. "You don't want to spoil my day? Come on! This is glorious!"

"It won't spoil your day. I've heard you say more than once that you'd sooner shoot by yourself than with other people."

"Yes, but I didn't mean that I wanted to be quite alone; I meant that I didn't care for big days," Gawthorpe said, a strange look of earnestness and anxiety on his face. "Let us be off!"

"No, I simply don't feel up to it. You go on. I really shan't."

"Well, as you like. You are master," Gawthorpe answered, sullenly, and with a malignant glance went out, spoke to Jackson, and strided off.

Raymond watched him cross the stream, and going into the next room to fetch his gun, strolled homewards.

Ethel and her mother were sitting in the hall after a late lunch, for the visit to Abbotston had been prolonged. When ladies with a taste for pretty things, and unlimited money to buy them, go to a town where shops are well stocked with fascinating articles, time passes quickly. All that was necessary in the way of furniture the firm entrusted with the renovation of the manor house had supplied almost in excess, as was to have been expected when a free hand was given to enterprising tradesmen; but ornaments for chimney-pieces, trifles for the writing-tables, and such-like little conveniences Raymond had asked Mrs. Daunce to find and order, and it was a task in which she and Ethel delighted.

They were talking of trivialities when the butler entered suddenly with a white, scared face.

"This is a dreadful thing, sir," he burst out; "Mr. Gawthorpe is shot!"

Raymond started up in dismay.

"Shot?" he exclaimed. "Who shot him? What do you mean? Where is he?"

"Oh, sir, Jackson's at the door. You'll see him, won't you? Shall I bring him in?" the unhappy old man inquired. He had led a placid life into which no tragedies had entered, and it was late to begin. Ethel and her mother were looking on and listening in wonder and distress.

"No, I'll go and see him. Don't worry yourself, dear Mrs. Daunce. It's very likely an exaggeration—a trifle. Perhaps he's not really hurt, it's merely an accident. I'll come back and relieve your minds directly, I hope," and he went to the gun-room where Jackson was waiting.

"What's this?" he inquired. "Is Mr. Gawthorpe badly hurt? How did it happen?"

"He was quite dead when we picked him up, sir," Jackson solemnly answered, his face showing that he had not nearly recovered from the shock. "It was all so dreadful sudden," he continued, in reply to Raymond's request for details. "When you had gone, sir, we just ran through that spinney by the brook. A cock pheasant broke out wide, out of reach. Mr. Gawthorpe he never got a shot at it, but as we was going across the field—we was nearly over, just by the far hedge—a partridge got up, Mr. Gawthorpe fired, there was a loud sort of bursting noise, and he fell down. The gun had smashed to bits, and a piece of the barrel had hit him on the side of the head. He scarcely moved, just seemed to be trying to stretch himself once or twice, and then lay quite still—dead. My boy ran to Fanfield for the doctor, and he came just after we'd got him to the Cot; but he had been killed on the spot, doctor said. It's an awful thing, sir!"

"Awful indeed!" Raymond replied. "One of the very best guns that could be bought for money from one of the best makers in the world, and used for about the first time! If that is not to be trusted, what is? Poor fellow! The doctor was quite certain, of course?"

"Yes, sir. You could see without a doctor. The side of his head was all smashed in. What's to be done, sir?" the bewildered gamekeeper asked. This was all hopelessly outside his duty and cognisance.

"There must be an inquest, I'm afraid, but the first thing is to write to those miserable gun-makers. The doctor will know what steps to take about my poor cousin. I'll have an account of this massacre in every paper in the kingdom, with the full name and address of the men who are responsible," and Raymond went off to write a letter which contained more than reproach and indignation.

The missive brought down next day one of the firm—a practical expert who carefully examined the pieces of the shattered weapon which had been diligently sought and collected.

"The fault is not with us, sir," he said, in low, earnest tones, when at length he emerged from seclusion. "I was convinced, indeed, that it could not possibly be, and that your condemnation was entirely unmerited. The left-hand barrel of the gun has been tampered with, and it is not, as you stated, the gun we made for Mr. Gawthorpe. It was one of the first pair we made for you—I can readily identify it, and also his, which your keeper has shown me. I will point out the marks by which we know them, if you care for me to do so. The barrel of the broken gun has been thinned—there is a mere film of metal like a sheet of paper—and a piece of steel has been welded on so as almost to block the muzzle. It was inevitable that it must explode the first time it was fired."

"But what do you mean?" Raymond asked. "You must be mistaken! It was Mr. Gawthorpe's gun. I have used mine several times—three or four times at least—and I must say found them all I could wish. The gun was one of the new ones I bought for my poor cousin."

"I assure you it was not, sir; and everyone connected with our firm will bear me out. We keep most careful record of every gun we make. There is some mystery here, sir. You have an enemy!" the gunmaker said, with conviction.

"There's two or three things that wants explaining, sir," Jackson, who had been present at the interview, interjected. "You remember you were trying to open your gun-case yesterday morning, sir, to look at the gun you were not going to take out? I picked the lock last night and there was no gun in it at all. The one you brought back was one of Mr. Gawthorpe's; and your own, sir, the one that isn't burst, was locked in a cupboard up at the Cot."

This information perplexed Raymond.

"Can you tell me just what happened?" the maker inquired.

"I took one of my pair, and my cousin took one of his," Raymond explained. "I of course thought that my second one was in the case, which I tried to open yesterday morning before I started. I did not want it—merely a whim to handle it. We shot all the morning, went in to lunch at a little building called the Cot. I gave my gun to Jackson here."

"I took it, sir," Jackson went on, "wiped it whilst I was talking to my master, and put it on the table in the back room. Mr. Gawthorpe was with us, and he wiped his own barrels and stood his gun in the corner; but," he continued, with some hesitation, "I'm afraid my boy Ben went into the room when nobody was there and he did get playing with them. I don't see that that makes things more simple. He took up the gun from the table, he says, thought he heard someone coming whilst he was looking at it, and in his hurry not to be caught put it down in the corner with the other one. Then he remembered, when he found he wasn't disturbed, that one of them had been on the table, and he must have taken the wrong one, Mr. Gawthorpe's, which the master carried home."

"Leaving Mr. Hetherington's gun, that which beyond doubt has been maliciously injured?" the gunsmith said.

"You are making a most serious charge against someone," Raymond observed.

"As serious as attempted murder. I am aware of it, and say it deliberately," was the reply. "You know best, sir, who would benefit by your death and might seek to bring it about. I can only state hard facts, that our gun which would have borne hard work with fair treatment for generations had been wilfully made into a sort of infernal machine by some deft mechanician."

Then for the first time suspicion of his cousin took hold of Raymond. By his death Dunstan would have benefited; he, too, had the technical skill to render the gun murderous to whoever fired it. Raymond recalled Ethel's instinctive horror of Dunstan. Could it be, Raymond thought, that the man who had plotted his death was now lying dead in the very room which was to bring the plot to fruition? Supposing Dunstan had taken the second gun out of the case, so manipulating the lock that Raymond could not readily open it and miss the weapon, that he had worked his wicked will on the gun, hidden it at the Cot, put it on the table in place of the sound weapon? Jackson's mischievous son had evidently changed the positions of the two guns. What Gawthorpe anticipated was—supposing the sudden chain of suspicion to be well founded—that after lunch Raymond would take his gun from the table and at the first discharge blow out his brains. Certainly Gawthorpe had been much irritated or disappointed at Raymond's refusal to continue the sport after lunch. Could it be that he had snatched up the gun he had prepared for Raymond, and not observing the difference, been hoist with his own petard? So it seemed, for there was no one else in the world who could have the faintest interest in injuring Raymond.

It was not till long after, till the horror of the occurrence had died away, that Raymond spoke of the subject to his wife.

"But you see that in any case, if what I was driven to suspect is true, he might have taken the wrong gun, as he did?" Raymond said.

But Ethel would not agree to this. Unless deadly danger had threatened imminently they would never have received the warnings.

The picture still smiles consolingly and protectingly upon them.

STRANGE STORIES OF SPORT

XXXIV.—THE STAIRCASE OF CHÂTEAU LOUBIÈRES

BY H. A. BRYDEN

Author of Tales of South Africa, etc., etc.

FRANK BULLINGTON rode home with his harriers on a soft November afternoon, after an excellent day's hunting. His hounds, a beautiful little pack, all of the old, light-coloured, West-country breed, followed sedately at his horse's heels, and Jim Woolcombe, his whip and kennel-huntsman, brought up the rear. They passed down the quiet village street, gleaning admiring glances, while every now and again Bullington greeted with a nod and a cheery smile some familiar face. Hounds were taken to kennel, and then, riding up a drive, the Master of Harriers halted before the old-fashioned, roomy, white house that was his home, gave up his horse to a groom, and went indoors.

It was just tea-time, a pleasant wood fire blazed on the hearth, and two ladies welcomed the hunter. One of these, a dark, handsome young woman, was his wife; the other, a white-haired old lady, to whom Bullington bore a strong resemblance, was his mother, just now staying at Pexton House on a month's visit.

"Well, Frank," asked his wife, "and what sort of a day's sport?"

"First-rate, my dear," was the reply. "You missed a lot of fun, but that's mother's fault for keeping you at home. We had quite a field out—five and thirty all told; killed three hares, after first-rate runs, the last of them a real clinker of fifty-five minutes. Scent was splendid and hounds ran like smoke—never made a mistake."

"Excellent," said his mother. "And who were out?"

"Oh, the usual crowd. A score of farmers, the Blencowes, Charlie Knight, Tom Hathaway and his sister, Mrs. Symons—who, as usual, over-rode hounds: I shall do that woman an injury some day—a man from Dunster, and Grenby, who brought with him a very nice Frenchman, a Count de Lalande, who keeps a pack of hounds somewhere in the west of France—Vienne, I fancy."

"I remember him," chimed in Mrs. Bullington junior. "He was out with the staghounds last week, and rode very well—a spare man, rather good-looking, with a high colour and black hair."

"That's the man. He's a real nice chap and speaks good English—which saves me a lot of trouble—and understands hunting thoroughly. He's been all over the world, shooting big game, mostly in British territory. I've asked him here for a few days next week. He fancies my harriers amazingly; says he's got a lot of light-coloured hounds himself, white and badger-pie, and white and hare-pie, and perhaps we may do a swop. I want fresh blood badly; these old light-coloured hounds are very hard to come by nowadays."

"That will be charming, Frank," said his wife. "We're rather dull down here till Christmas, when the boys come home. The Count can have the bachelor's room. Does he bring horses?"

"Yes, a couple of hirelings. I can help him out with others. We'll have three days with the harriers, and two with the staghounds."

"De Lalande!" echoed the elder Mrs. Bullington, musingly. "That name seems familiar to me. Where have I heard it?"

"Haven't the least idea, mother," rejoined her son. "Give me some more tea, Helen; I am dying of thirst."

A week later, in the same room at the same hour, the French Count made his appearance and was introduced to the two ladies. He was a pleasant man of the world, cultured, not too horsy and houndy, and, having travelled much abroad and seen a great deal of English folk, was quickly at home with the Bullington ladies. The talk presently shifted to France and the Count's home. He lived, he told them, in an old rambling château of Louis XIII's time, and hunted chiefly roe-deer in the neighbouring woodlands.

"What is the name of your place, Count?" asked old Mrs. Bullington.

"Château Loubières, in Vienne, madam, where I hope after Christmas to see your son here, if he will do me the honour to pay me a visit and look at my hounds."

"It would be delightful, Count," rejoined Frank, "if it could be managed. If I do go, Helen, you will have to whip in to Jim and look after the harriers."

"The Château Loubières!" repeated Mrs. Bullington senior. "Now I remember all about it. Do you know, Count de Lalande, my son's great-grandfather, who had a pack of foxhounds, knew one of your kinsfolk very well and used to stay with him as a young man. That would be before 1789. I think I have heard of some tragedy in your family during the Revolution."

"I am delighted, madam," responded the Count, "to hear that our families have been acquainted. It is quite like coming among old friends, especially in this charming and most English home of yours. Yes, there was a tragedy in my family. In 1791, during the Revolutionary troubles, the peasants attacked the château; there were terrible scenes, and my great-great-grand-father, who must have been the Count de Lalande whom your son's ancestor stayed with, was murdered under circumstances of shock-ing barbarity."

They had some friends to meet the Count that night at Pexton House, and, after the departure of the guests and a final cigar and whisky-and-soda, the two men went to their respective bedrooms. That night Frank Bullington, whose slumbers were usually of the most untroubled kind, had a curious dream. He dreamt that he stood in the great hall of an old-fashioned mansion, a hall hung with family portraits and garnished with heads of deer, wild boar, and other trophies of the chase. Two broad staircases descended from the upper rooms to this hall, in the centre of which Frank seemed to be standing. Some hideous sensation of dread held possession of him. He looked around for something that should answer for the horror that imbued him. There was nothing. Yet he remained there, rooted to the spot, numbed with an unaccount-able fear; then, suddenly, he awoke, streaming with perspiration, his heart beating thickly. It was a condition to which he was entirely unaccustomed. Well! It was but a nightmare, such as he remembered as a child. Presently he sank to quiet sleep again, and woke at his usual hour.

Count de Lalande had a capital week's sport with his English friend. They hunted wild red deer with the Devon and Somerset Staghounds, and enjoyed three first-rate days with the Pexton

Harriers. The Count was charmed with his visit, and extracted from Frank Bullington a promise that he, in turn, would visit Château Loubières and see how French hunting was conducted. The Count offered, moreover, to exchange a couple or two of his light-coloured hounds against some of the Pexton; and as Frank was seriously in need of fresh blood with which to recruit his pack, and would gladly have travelled to the other end of Europe to obtain it, he cordially accepted the invitation.

Rather more than two months later—to be precise, in the middle of the following January—Bullington, having made his way to France, found himself on a dark winter evening at the entrance to the Château Loubières. The Count had met him at the station in a dog-cart, and after a drive of four miles over good French roads they pulled up before the door of a big rambling building. The groom jumped down, rang loudly at a huge bell, and presently the door opened and the Count and his guest entered a great hall well lit by electricity. Frank Bullington looked round, and saw instantly before him the hall of his nightmare. It was an odd sensation, such as he had never before experienced. Here were the two great oak staircases, facing one another on either side of the apartment, with doors opening out to various chambers and passages. Above was a long gallery, which led to other parts of the mansion, and round about him hung the very pictures and trophies which he remembered quite well in his dream. There was, however, no sense of fear upon him now. Everything looked cheerful and homelike under the excellent illumination of the electric light.

" Do you know, Count," he said, " it's an odd thing, but this hall is perfectly familiar to me. I saw it all in a dream I had at Pexton on the night of the day you first came to us; I never had such a curiously unaccountable sensation before ! "

" That's very strange, my friend," remarked de Lalande. " I don't understand it. Thought transference, I suppose. The question is, ' From whose inner consciousness emanated the picture ? ' "

" Well, one can only suppose from yours," rejoined Bullington, with a cheery laugh. " But how and why the thing happened I can't for the life of me understand."

" Come here for a second, Bullington," said the Count, taking him by the arm and leading him to a large old picture. " There is my ancestor, the Count de Lalande of Louis XVI's time and the Revolution, whom your great-grandfather visited here in 1788. He looks what you call a good old ' sport,' eh ? "

Frank Bullington gazed earnestly at the picture, an equestrian one, showing the Count on his prick-eared, close-docked hunter, with his pack of hounds in front of him and two mounted hunt servants filling in the background. The Count wore a cocked hat, a white wig and queue, a blue coat laced with silver, breeches, and heavy boots. It was a hard, shrewd, cynical face that looked out of the well-painted picture. The servants were dressed, like their master, in blue uniforms, and had, to English eyes, with their huge French horns encircling their bodies, a somewhat grotesque aspect. Still, it was a most interesting picture, the more fascinating to Bullington from the fact that here in the pack of hounds before him he saw precisely the stamp of hunting dog from which to recruit his own pack.

"Got any hounds left like those, Count?" he queried.

"Yes, I have, Bullington," replied his host, with a well-pleased look. "I knew you would spot that pack at once. My hounds are lineally descended from those before you, and although the sort— the type you call it, don't you?—has somewhat altered, perhaps I may say improved, my hounds are, in nose and sound hunting characteristics, pretty much what those were like. To-morrow you shall see them. Now come and have a vermouth, and then we'll dress for dinner. As you know, I'm a bachelor, and to-night you and I shall be alone. I thought you would prefer it on your first arrival, and we can talk over hounds and hunting as much as you please. Then a game of billiards if you are agreeable, and to bed. To-morrow we hunt five miles away, in some forest where we have plenty of roedeer, and I hope to show you sport."

For ten days Frank Bullington stayed at the château, enjoying some first-rate sport, and watching with the keenest interest the work of de Lalande's old-fashioned pack of hounds. Although bigger and somewhat heavier than his own harriers, they were of much the same stamp, and the Count had promised to spare him two couples of the least in size to take back to England with him for the purpose of breeding with his own hounds. These, with another couple which, thanks to de Lalande's exertions, they had been able to pick up in La Vendée, which they had visited for the purpose, would be amply sufficient to give him the change of blood he required for the strengthening of his own kennel.

On a fine January morning they rode out to hunt a roebuck which harboured four miles away in a certain piece of woodland, and which had already given the Count's pack three or four good runs and remained undefeated. By this time Frank had grown accustomed to the pomp and panoply of French hunting, the *piqueur* and *valet de chiens* in green coats laced with gold, the hunting caps heavy with bullion, the huge horns encompassing the men's chests, and the methods of hunting so different from those to be found in an English countryside. At the meet were gathered a company of forty or fifty sportsmen and women, for the most part neighbouring landowners and personal friends of the Count. With most of these Bullington had already made acquaintance, and, although his knowledge of French was somewhat lacking, the cheery Englishman, already a great favourite among these polite people, was willingly helped out in any difficulties of the language which he found confronting him. In ten minutes a move was made for the covert, a wood of some twenty acres, in which the *chevreuil* was known to be couching. The services of the *valet de chiens à pied* and his tufters were on this occasion dispensed with, and the Count's harbourer having marked down the buck at dawn, the whole pack of eighteen couples was taken straight to the deer's resting-place. In complete silence the normally voluble field followed at the heels of the pack; presently, after ten minutes of breathless suspense, the deep voices of some of the most trusty hounds proclaimed that they had found traces of the buck; the clamour swelled to a magnificent chorus, and then, from a bed of russet fern, right in front of the pack, sprang a gallant roebuck and cantered away. Horns blew, enthusiastic sportsmen cheered and yelled, the hunt was fairly up.

Roedeer are often very difficult to force from covert, and the handsome buck in front of them offered no exception to this habit. For half an hour the clever little beast threaded the mazes of the woodland. Twice other deer were roused and followed, and twice the pack were skilfully brought back to the line of the hunted quarry. The roe began to find himself hard put to it; the baying pack clamoured with fierce chorus ever closer at his heels; and now, leaping a ditch and bank with one magnificent bound, the deer broke covert and was away for the open country. The run that ensued was one of the greatest ever seen with Count de Lalande's hounds, a run that will always be spoken of with enthusiasm by hunting folk and country people in that part of Vienne. Frank Bullington got well away with the pack, and, with the Count, the huntsman, and eight or ten of the most determined riders of the hunt, galloped, tingling with the most joyous excitement in the world, over a magnificent line of country. For two miles the chase lay over the wild heath of Charrière, where the going was on the whole pretty sound, with here and there deep and treacherous patches of bog, which reminded Bullington of his own beloved Exmoor. Then came some enclosed country, where hedges and ditches took severe toll of the field, and reduced somewhat the enthusiasm of all but the boldest and keenest riders. Over the wooded hill of Bazelle streamed the hunt; here the buck would willingly have lingered, but scent was amazingly good, the pack were running dangerously close, and after a half circuit the deer quitted the covert and was away again. As they descended the hill, the Count, streaming with perspiration, was riding stride for stride with Bullington. He pointed with his whip to a dark stretch of woodland lying on a hillside far away in front.

"The wood of Orbigny," he ejaculated, "seven miles away, that is the deer's point. Alas, we shall never get our second horses!"

And, in truth, they never did get them. The run was so straight and so fast that the second horsemen were clean thrown out, and could never get near their masters.

Now they passed the hamlet of Falandre, and a mile beyond that of Fatrissac. The field had by this time become reduced to four riders who were anywhere near hounds. Bullington and the *piqueur*, Georges Monfray, were nearest the pack, now some two hundred yards in front of them. De Lalande, whose horse was beginning to show some signs of distress, came next, a furlong behind them, and near him again rode Colonel de Guinfrey, a bold and a good horseman, whose heavy weight—he rode over 14 stone—was now telling upon his willing hunter. Before them stretched the wide grassy champaign of Mareuil la Haye, severed about its middle by a widish stream. As they approached the water, Bullington, who had been nursing his horse, pulled it together, gave the good beast a sharp touch of the spur, and, flying the brook—here some eighteen feet across—just landed on the other bank. It was a good performance for a horse that had already compassed nine miles of rough country. As he landed, he drew rein for a second and turned in the saddle. The huntsman had suddenly pulled up short on the brink of the stream.

"Allons, Monfray!" cried Bullington, with a cheery laugh. "Allons! sautez-vous!"

But the *piqueur* was not for it. "Non, non!" he cried, with a speaking grimace. "Pardi! je ne saute pas les grandes rivières," and, turning his horse's head, he galloped hard for a ford half a mile down stream.

Frank Bullington was now left alone with the pack. There was a momentary check half a mile further on, but hounds hit it off again unaided, and away again raved the chase. Two miles ahead Frank now saw in front of him the great wood of Orbigny, darkening the side of a lofty hill. If the deer reached that sanctuary it might yet escape the pack. But the gallant roebuck had shot its last bolt. The pack were now running from scent to view; they drew rapidly upon their game, and six hundred yards from the nearest limit of Orbigny they pulled down their quarry on a piece of gorse-clad common. Frank was up with them in two minutes, and, driving off the hounds, whipped out his knife, seized the buck by the horns, and with one deft thrust at the junction of neck and chest had given the *coup de grâce*. It was an ecstatic moment, one of those that the sportsman never forgets.

Presently the " field " came flickering in. The *piqueur* was first up after Frank; after him came de Lalande, wild with delight at the success of his English friend and the finish of so great a run; after him again half a dozen others. The hunt servants, ranging themselves by the dead deer, blew loud fanfares, the " Hallali " of French hunting, and the obsequies were duly performed, Bullington being presented with the head of the buck instead of the usual slot.

It was, all agreed, the greatest run of the *Rallye* (hunt) *de Lalande* for a generation—for many generations. Nine miles as the crow flies was the point, and the entire distance fourteen miles as hounds ran. The time very fast, considering the state of the country—1 hour 35 minutes from the moment the buck quitted the covert, close on two hours from the find.

That night Frank Bullington slept the sleep of the healthy hunter, made thoroughly happy by success. Half a dozen other friends of the Count were staying in the house, but they had retired early after a most cheery evening, and 11.30 saw them all in their bedrooms, most of them deep in slumber.

Two hours later, or thereabouts, Frank Bullington woke with a strange, vague sense of horror upon him. He never could explain why, but some overwhelming force impelled him to get up, put on some clothes, and go down to the hall. With beating heart he made his way down the long corridor. As he approached the hall he saw with amazement that it was full of light. He crept, with a hideous feeling of suspense and dread—to which he was entirely unaccustomed—down the left-hand staircase. At the bottom he halted with his hand on the broad oak baluster, and gazed across apprehensively at the other staircase. Something at the back of his mind told him what was going to happen, and this is what he saw : From the very topmost of the dark, ancient, polished stairway, always uncarpeted, there rolled the severed head of a man—a head bleeding and clean-shaven ; a head which, nathless the fact that it was lacking a wig, Frank knew instantly to be that of the old hunting Count de Lalande, whose pictured semblance hung there in the hall. The face was pinched into a hideous grin of pain and rage ; the grey eyes were open, and occasionally, as it seemed to Frank's tortured mind, they looked straight into his own.

The Englishman's heart, hitherto beating so vehemently, seemed to stand still during those hideous moments that followed.

Slowly the terrible head fell from stair to stair. It reached the bottom and rolled like a football across the hall. Then, in an instant, the light vanished and all was dark.

In that last unforeseen moment of horror some portion of Bullington's frozen energies seemed to come back to him. He turned, climbed the staircase, as it seemed to himself, at one bound, fled down the corridor, and reached his room—how, he never quite knew. Here his courage returned to him; he gathered breath, his pulses beat more evenly; he began to debate whether or no he should go to his friend, rouse him, and tell him what he had seen. But what was the use? De Lalande would not, could not, believe his tale, and would ridicule the idea of the apparition, which indubitably he himself had just seen. No; he would speak of it in the morning. Lighting a candle and stirring up the dying embers of his fire, he sought his bed again, and dozed fitfully till the valet brought his coffee and hot water in the morning.

Frank and the Count were the first assembled in the dining-room. De Lalande rallied his friend upon his appearance.

"You do not look very fit this morning, *mon ami*," he said, kindly. "After so glorious a day, and so moderate an evening, I expected to behold your usual cheerful self."

"Well, Count," responded Frank, "I have had a very bad night. I saw something in the hall yonder which I hope never to see again. I'll admit freely I was terrified; and I still feel a good deal upset."

"What! You saw——?" ejaculated the Count, his face becoming suddenly grave.

"Yes, I saw it!" And Bullington at once told his friend the history of his night adventure.

"My dear fellow," said the Count, after the Englishman had finished, "I'm shocked, terribly, about this. I would not that it should have happened for the world. You have seen the spectre of Loubières, a thing that has not appeared to my knowledge these eighteen years. I saw it myself once, more than twenty years since, and, like yourself, was horrified. But of late the thing has never appeared, and I had nursed myself into the belief that it had finally vanished. I never came near the château for five years after my own hideous experience. But, after all, the place is my home, and I took the risk and came back to it."

"But why should I have seen it?" asked Bullington, musingly.

"One can scarcely find a reason," rejoined the Count. "But it is an odd coincidence that your ancestor and mine foregathered in these old rooms more than a hundred years ago, and that yesterday, the 18th January, was the anniversary of the storming of this place by the peasants in 1791 and the murder of my great-great-grandfather. I had completely forgotten the matter in the excitement of the hunt. Even then it is difficult to see why *you* should have been dragged forth to witness that horrible spectacle. My friend, we know, happily for ourselves, nothing of the spirit world; nor can we account, any of us, for the apparitions that are occasionally vouchsafed to us. I am deeply sorry for this occurrence."

"Tell me, de Lalande," said Bullington, "what was the origin of this frightful thing?"

"It is a very short story," said the Count. "When the Revolution broke out, the peasants rose, stormed Loubières, caught the old Count upstairs and killed him, hacked off his head, and kicked it brutally down the staircase. I gather that my ancestor, like many of the *noblesse* of that time, was not a good man, nor had he been well disposed to his tenants. But let us dismiss this painful subject. Here come our friends. Say no more about the matter in their presence."

Frank Bullington stayed two more nights at the château and then took his departure. He slept with apprehension, but nothing occurred to disturb his rest. It is some years since these events happened, but Bullington can never forget them. Nor for the finest pack of hounds in Europe would he venture to visit Château Loubières again, much as he esteems its sporting and hospitable owner.

STRANGE STORIES OF SPORT

XXXV.—TOMMY PIPPS'S WINNING MOUNT

BY "RAPIER"

If, forty-eight hours before the thing happened, anybody had told Tommy Pipps that he was going to ride a hurdle race, and win it, moreover, against one of the best jockeys of the day and other competent and indeed skilful riders, he would have entertained the poorest opinion of that body's form as a prophet. Good, cheery little soul that he was, Tommy Pipps had never in the least fancied himself as a horseman, his performances in that capacity having been limited to an occasional sedate jog when he was at his father's place without anything better to do, and to a rare visit to a meet—home again when the fun began, for Tommy had no sort of enthusiasm for the chase; and as for jumping fences, did not think he should like that kind of thing if he tried it—which he had no intention of doing.

But then neither had he any intention of falling in love, a proceeding which makes a lot of difference. Miss Amelia Brumpley had entirely subjugated him; he worshipped the ground on which she trod, and there was good deal of it, for she was a large lady, and the superficial area of her boot soles was considerable. She must have weighed some thirty per cent. more than her admirer, but was arch and kittenish withal—he called it "charmingly naïve and full of adorable simplicity."

Tommy had taken to racing chiefly for want of other occupation, had got into the habit of attending the principal meetings near town, and was as ready as the next man to criticise a horse or a jockey; for one speaks so confidently when one is not hampered by a little knowledge.

The scene was Kemfield with a jump race meeting on, and Tommy had escorted the adorable Amelia and her friend Mrs. Naskett. They liked racing because they always won, the polite Tommy explaining away their losses by some ingenious fiction, so that if they did not get some money they never had to pay any; but it was more satisfactory, of course, if there were an air of legitimacy about the transaction, if they could see the animal they were on really come in first; and Tommy, who knew very little about it, was accustomed to seek counsel of his friends. Jack Hawbridge was one of these, and he conveniently hove in sight as the horses were going to the post for the Thames Selling Hurdle Race.

"I think it's good for the favourite, Bounding Wave," Jack replied to Tommy's question. "Beautiful jumper, isn't he?" he exclaimed with admiration as the horse slid easily over the preliminary hurdle. "I only wish I had some money! I'd buy him if he wins, put him in the seller to-morrow, and have a ripping ride! It will take a smartish plater to beat him just now, but I can't possibly afford it!"

Tommy had invested Amelia's two sovereigns at evens and told her it was 5 to 2, so she watched the red-striped jockey on the favourite with enhanced interest, saw him come to the front two hurdles from home, and win as he liked.

"That's delightful!" Amelia exclaimed, "and what a pretty creature he is, isn't he? Oh, Mr. Pipps, why don't *you* buy him if he has to be sold? It seems cruel to take away the poor man's horse just because it's won, I never can understand why they should, but if it must be sold *do* buy it? I should *love* to see you ride a race. You have ridden races, haven't you?"

"Not for some time," Tommy answered, and he was strictly truthful, the "some time" extending back to the period of his birth.

"Well, it's quite time you began again! You ought not to neglect these things, they are so interesting," Amelia continued. "Mr. Hawbridge, can't *you* persuade Mr. Pipps to buy this winner?" and she looked at her slave, pretending to believe that her influence was not sufficient.

"But of course he will," Hawbridge said. "Money doesn't matter to him; and besides, he'll get this for about half its worth. It always had a turn of speed, and you couldn't find a smoother jumper. He swings along over his hurdles as if they weren't there—you wouldn't know you were jumping them if you didn't see them."

This last sentence ensured the immediate destination of Bounding Wave. Ridden by Mr. Ventry, the famous gentleman jockey

391

two miles over eight hurdles had seemed a childishly simple performance. Tommy had jumped only a very few very small fences,
and had found it distinctly unpleasant—a disconcerting shake as the
animal rose, and a perfectly horrible jar, with some mysterious pro-
pelling power that seemed to be trying to knock you out of the
saddle over the animal's head, on landing. But he detected nothing
of this in the race just finished. Some of the riders lay back rather
over their horses' quarters, others seemed to take no notice of the
obstacles—took them as they came—and he pictured himself as he
rode off to weigh in after winning in a canter : likewise he pictured
Amelia's—might he call her Milly ? he thought he might after such
an exploit, and he certainly should !—admiring reception of her
hero.

Bounding Wave was being led round when they reached the
sale ring. What should the auctioneer say for this useful young
jumper, an improving four-year-old, really too good to be run in a
selling race ? Any advance on 150 ? Thank you, sir, 155, 160,
165, 170—200, thank you, sir.

The 200 was Tommy's bid. Hawbridge had told him to jump
to that amount, as it would show he meant business and frighten
the others off; but they were not frightened, for this was a useful
beast, and someone bid 210. "Go it !" murmured Hawbridge.
Tommy went it, and turned to receive an approving smile from
Amelia which made him cap the late owner's 230 without any
prompting. "250," said the auctioneer. "Any advance on 250 ?
Certain to get the money back with a nice profit ! Going at 250 ?
Yours, sir !" and Tommy was the proud possessor.

"Is it *really* yours ?" Amelia asked. "I *am* so glad ! What
do you do next ?"

Tommy had no idea, but did not propose to say so. One
thing he had to do was to pay; he recognised the necessity of
that, and as the auctioneer was evidently anxious for an interview,
murmured that he had better give him a cheque ; so, following on to
the Clerk of the Course's office, he wrote the document.

To his vast relief Hawbridge came on the scene.

"I think you've got a deuced cheap horse," he said. "Now,
what are you going to do with him ?"

"Well——" Tommy began.

"If I were you I should ask Downs to take charge of him."
Downs was his former trainer. "You can't have a better man,
and, of course, you are going to put him in to-morrow ? There's
the entry form," he went on, pointing to a sheet of paper on the
table. "That's it," as Tommy began to fill in particulars, "but
what about colours ? Have you got any ?"

This was a staggerer. Pretty colours would have been, if not half, a not inconsiderable portion of the battle, and Amelia might have views.

"Not got any?" Hawbridge continued. "Well, put 'green, red hoops'—Downs's colours those are—he's sure to have a jacket here to lend you till you settle on some of your own. That's it, 'quartered cap.' That's all right! You'll have 10.7, and that'll mean a comfortable saddle for you."

Downs expressed the utmost readiness to take the horse—possibly this might be a new employer who would go in for the game, and where is the trainer of jumpers who doesn't want horses? Tommy, who had always held owners in extreme reverence, was now actually one himself, and he felt at least two inches taller—which brought him up to Amelia's ear—as he joined the ladies in the enclosure and heard his charmer's "Oh, I do hope you'll win to-morrow," with Mrs. Naskett's "Yes, indeed!"—she always agreed with everybody: it saved the trouble of thinking.

Tommy had never before found the last edition of the *Evening News* so interesting. "The winner was sold to Mr. Thomas Pipps for 250 guineas," the principal paragraph in the journal read, and next morning there it was in all the papers with "Mr. Thomas Pipps's Bounding Wave, four years," one of nine entries for the Riverside Selling Hurdle Race.

No members' special for him. He and the ladies, with Hawbridge in attendance by particular request, went down by an early train, and found Downs also early on the scene.

"How's the horse?" was naturally the first question.

"Couldn't be better, sir," its trainer said. "Didn't leave an oat. I just sent him a gentle five furlongs."

"Will he win?" Hawbridge inquired. "There's nothing to beat that I can see, except Top Flat?"

"Yes, that was the one I picked as dangerous, and Mr. Ventry rides; but our horse is wonderfully well just now, and ought, I make out, just about to do it. He's quite quiet, miss," he went on, for Amelia was calling the horse endearing names, and evidently wanted to pat him, an aspiration which she gratified.

That Downs was anxious to know what sort of a figure his new employer was likely to cut on a horse need scarcely be said, but this was a subject about which he could not well inquire. He had been told that Mr. Pipps had bought the horse in order to ride it, and wanted to borrow a jacket, which, however, was not instructive. Hawbridge felt that he could be less reticent, notwithstanding that he was a comparatively recent acquaintance.

"Have you ridden much?" he asked, for though the name of

Pipps was strange to him in racing returns, the new owner of Bounding Wave might have called himself something else.

"Oh, in the country, you know!" Pipps answered, with a gesture of the hand that might have meant anything—only it didn't.

"I see. Point-to-Points, and that sort of thing? I wish Ventry wasn't up on Top Flat to-day. He's in wonderful form, and has an extraordinary average; besides, he doesn't often ride for the Top Flat people, and that looks as if it was supposed to be good. If you are out of practice he's likely to do you in a finish, I'm afraid."

Out of practice! Tommy had never been *in* practice—had never worn a silk jacket, and only put on racing boots and breeches for the first time the night before, when by great good luck he found some ready-made ones to fit him—more or less.

That all this time he was a prey to considerable nervousness and anxiety need scarcely be said. He well remembered the extraordinarily violent and distressing sensation of jumping fences, small as had been his experience, but for some reason or other he had persuaded himself that jumping hurdles must be a far simpler business, a notion inspired by the aforesaid ease with which the operation was accomplished. Hawbridge, too, was a particularly stupid fellow off a racecourse; anything he could do Tommy felt he would be able to do much better, and Hawbridge was always eager to ride anything. Bounding Wave knew his part of the business, that was certain; all his new owner had to do was to sit on his back and let him do it. And there was compensation for the anxiety. Tommy dressed early, returned to the stand in boots and breeches, an object of keen admiration to Amelia. Then, too, it was an intense delight to him when friends and acquaintances—acquaintances believe they are dear friends on these occasions—came up to him and said: "You're riding your own, I see, in the next race! Do you fancy it much? I think you ought to win if you can beat Top Flat."

Up went the numbers, five runners:

3.	Vent Peg	... ...	(Gilliam)
4.	Top Flat	... ...	(Mr. Ventry)
6.	Bounding Wave	... ...	(Owner)
7.	Nora	... ...	(Malone)
9.	Lady Jane	... ...	(Harker)

Tommy had never been into a weighing-room, but he was no fool, took note of how the others sat in the scale, with their saddle and cloths, and seated himself in his turn.

It was a proud procession across the paddock—Downs, carrying the saddle, Tommy, Amelia, the faithful Mrs. Naskett, and Hawbridge—to see the horse got ready. Tommy felt that he was qualifying for the position of hero.

"You know how much I hope you'll win, dear, don't you?" she said, and the "dear" was worth anything to the enamoured youth.

"What about backing you?" Hawbridge asked, anxious for a lead from Downs.

"I don't know how you bet, sir," Downs replied, "but the horse has a great chance on form. Of course, Top Flat's the danger."

"Oh, put us fifty on," Tommy said; "no, make it a hundred—there'll be a tenner for you, Downs. I'm backing it for you—dear," he murmured to Amelia, "and putting a little on for Mrs. Naskett if she will let me."

The moment had arrived! Tommy crooked his knee as if he had been through the business constantly for years, and was hoisted into the saddle.

"He gets the course well, sir," Downs remarked, "and has a nice turn of speed. I should lay up with the leaders and come away two hurdles from home."

"Good luck—dear," Amelia murmured, giving the horse a sort of half proprietary pat on the neck, and Tommy rode out on to the course.

How the brute did take hold! Tommy had never felt anything like it in all his mild equestrian experiences. There was a vigour, energy, dash about this the like of which he had never imagined. The preliminary hurdle was in front of him, an offshoot, apparently, from Jack's immortal beanstalk; at least, it had doubled its height since he looked at it from the enclosure; but Lady Jane was in advance, she never rose an inch, smashed through it, and Bounding Wave flew through the gap she had made, having no occasion to rise. All the same, poor Tommy, in no condition for riding, was hot and out of breath when he arrived at the post, and mightily envied the calmness and quietude with which Mr. Ventry cantered up, turned round, and took his place. Nora was fretting and jumping about, the other three were eminently business-like, Bounding Wave yawed and reached at his bit because Tommy was pulling at him, and just as he thought they would soon be getting into line, the rest being two or three lengths in front of him—they were off!

Bounding Wave's first stride shot Tommy forward on to his neck, and never had he felt so utterly helpless. For all he could do he might as well have had the reins round the funnel of a railway engine. If he had guessed what it would have been like, not even for Amelia would he have ventured on this whirlwind. A rattle in front vaguely struck his ears and sounded awful, the next moment the obstacle had apparently flown back to meet him, he was launched into the air, sent flying through space, and found himself on the ground, clutching fast hold of something which he slowly perceived to be his reins. Somebody leaned over him and told him it was "all right," a fact he would certainly never have suspected; somebody else appeared, two men, with an amiable intention of helping him, and before he knew what was happening he was in the saddle again, once more flying along on his wild career. More hurdles! But there was a gap in them where Lady Jane had smashed through, and his horse had not to jump. On they flew; he drew a long breath and faintly began to "take notice." More rattle and smash in front, Lady Jane was not rising an inch, crashing through every line of "sticks," leaving a clear path behind her. "Lay up with the leaders," had been Downs's instructions. How easily said! His arms were nearly out of their sockets, he was blowing like a school of grampuses; what was happening a couple of hundred yards in front he had no idea, but he had reached the stands, was borne past them, doubtless past the judge too, and then his horse, slackening speed, turned round and cantered into the paddock of its own accord. Since the first jump he had at least "remained."

He became conscious of Amelia and her friend as, after sitting a few moments in his saddle to get a little breath, he slid to the ground, just making out that Downs had hold of the horse's head.

"I hope you are not hurt!" she exclaimed. "It *was* brave of you to get on again after he had made that dreadful mistake!"

This was consoling, at any rate, for it would never have occurred to him that there had been any mistake but his own. He was about to ask what had won, when a cry of "Objection!" was heard at the weighing-room door.

"Nora came in first, sir, but she's sure to be disqualified. I never saw a more disgraceful piece of foul riding. Her jockey deliberately went for Mr. Ventry. He's sure to get the race," Downs explained.

Tommy staggered to the weighing-room, caring little what had won—he had not, and now that he knew what race-riding was to the unaccustomed aspirant, was fully aware that he never should win—or so he supposed.

"You'd better get into the scales, sir," someone at the table said, and Tommy did so, making his way to the dressing-room. Hawbridge followed him in.

"I didn't quite see what happened to you at that hurdle. Something cannoned you, I suppose? Funny, isn't it?" he said.

"What's funny?" Tommy inquired.

"Why, the stewards have disqualified Nora—they were bound to do so—and now there's an objection to the second. His late owner's in the Irish forfeit list, someone has just found out, and they say that there's something wrong about the entry of the third, Vent Peg, partnership not registered. I believe you'll be placed second!"

As Hawbridge spoke a very bandy-legged little man of distinctly horsey aspect appeared at the door.

"Beg pardon, sir, you're Mr. Pipps?" he said. "Well, sir, they say outside that Lady Jane will get the race, but I can tell you something about her that you'll like to know. She's a little mare that used to be called Cruiskeen, and she's run at all sorts of flapping meetings; this man Harker who was riding her has been taking her round."

"Are you sure?" Hawbridge inquired; Tommy did not know enough about the rules to grasp the significance of the situation.

"I can prove it, sir, easy; there's another man here that know's her well, and Harker too, but he knows he's found out and he's slipped away."

"My dear fellow, if this is true you've actually won after all!" Hawbridge exclaimed, with a laugh. "You'll have to object to Lady Jane. Come on!"

Tommy came on, that is to say returned to the weighing-room and objected to Lady Jane on the grounds given. Proof was speedily forthcoming, the race was awarded to Bounding Wave, which Amelia and Mrs. Naskett accepted as only fair, being convinced that Tommy *would* have won had he not been "knocked over" at the first hurdle. He has an average never surpassed by any jockey, amateur or professional, no less than 100 per cent., and nothing is more improbable than that he will ever lose it.

STRANGE STORIES OF SPORT

XXXVI.—"BOTH WAYS" SMITH[1]

BY FRANK SAVILE

TRANTER said it was disgraceful. Onslow couldn't think what the stewards were dreaming of. Half a dozen wrathful voices joined in to approve both sentiments and stiffen them with lurid adjectives. All the speakers were young—all, therefore, brimming with experience. Each had a story to tell of Turf villainy culled from an omniscience which would have cowed the collective wisdom of the Jockey Club. Yarn after yarn of shady transactions was trotted forth: poor old Running Rein even was not allowed to rest in his dishonoured grave. The future of the British Turf rocked uneasily on its pedestal.

What was all the trouble?

Simply this: John Mowbray, after his usual kindly custom, had collected a house party for the Hunt Point-to-point. The course, in a wide Midland district, far from a very large town, did not attract any considerable crowd, and—cause and effect—no considerable bookmakers. Our young friends, venturing a modest sovereign or two with men of no local reputation and in the face of their host's warning, had been pleasantly welshed. The favourite,

Hugo, had won the Hunt Cup. Backers, going to collect, were solemnly informed by the three white-hatted layers present that their wagers had been booked about No Go, an unfancied outsider who had fallen at the second fence. Hence these tears.

A man who sat silently puffing at a cigar in an alcove listened to the torrent of vituperation with a smile. He was a man of a certain age—the many wrinkles which seamed his kindly face told that. He was brown and hard-bitten, square of chin and steady of eye; and he seemed to enjoy listening. The boys were so very, very young, and their exasperation so very, very real. The portentousness of their wrath would have befitted the loss of thousands, while to the veteran's certain knowledge the collective gains of the peculant ring would not have made a large hole in a ten-pound note. But what refreshing enthusiasm the youngsters evinced!

A lull was filled by the eighteen-year-old Onslow's final dictum. "The Turf is going to the devil—the devil!" he decided. "In no other country in the world are there such red-hot scoundrels!"

At that the listener stirred—showed real interest—sat up.

"My dear sir!" he remonstrated.

The youth looked at him with the complacent cocksureness with which a terrier contemplates a Newfoundland.

"I beg your pardon?" he answered, interrogatively.

The other smiled.

"Aren't you a little hard on poor old England?" he asked. "I have seen a bit of racing in my time, and I assure you that the gentlemen who earned your thirst for vengeance to-day are a very mild form of desperado—their methods were so bluntly obvious, and—if you had listened to our friend Mowbray's warning—so patently to be expected. I can only say that if that is your idea of red-hot I have encountered sinners of the same kidney who could only be described as incandescent. And the cream of them are not to be found within the British Isles at all."

"Where then?" truculently demanded Pat Armstrong, who hailed from Connaught. "Not in Ireland, I'll go bail."

The man in the alcove made a cheery gesture of assent.

"Certainly not," he agreed. "In a place some few thousand miles further west—or east—according to your point of view. Australia, to be explicit."

Onslow grinned impudently.

"Aren't you an Australian yourself, Mr. Baillie?" he asked.

Baillie laughed.

"I'd be proud to call myself one," he answered; "but as a matter of fact I merely passed twenty years of my life there—I'm not a real Cornstalk at all. But don't mistake me. There are no finer sportsmen on God's earth than the Australians; but, from the very keenness with which sport is treated over there, extremes go both ways. Their scoundrels have reached loftier heights of scoundrelism. And I think they can give us a shade of odds in ingenuity. One of them could, anyway."

"Who and how?" cried the chorus.

Baillie shrugged his shoulders.

"That would be quite a yarn," he deprecated, "and I think I heard the clock strike twelve some few minutes back."

There were shouts of protest.

"Hang the clock—stop it—smash it!" demanded the assembly. "The yarn—the yarn!"

Baillie held up his hand.

"The women will all be getting up with the idea that the house is on fire if you make that uproar," he complained. "I'll tell you what I consider the best swindle I ever came across, if you absolutely insist; but I must warn you I'm no professional *raconteur*. And the thing's twenty years old or more—it happened quite in my early days in the colony. I must think a bit."

He helped himself slowly to a small half-tumbler of Scotch and siphon, filled a pipe, and then grinned round upon his audience—broadly.

"You mightn't think it, but I was young—once," he confessed. "So very young that I was under the impression that I knew as much about a horse as most vets and considerably more than many owners. I fancied myself hugely on the subject. As I happened to be the fourth of six sons and my father's income was derived wholly from land—and not very good land at that—the capital to enable me to start life as a breeder and runner of blood stock was far to seek. I failed for the army, shied at a desk, and had the common honesty to decline to qualify through Oxford for the family living. My old dad put the issue to me squarely. 'There's three thousand pounds coming to you, Gerald,' he told me; 'and, as things are at present, no sort of likelihood that it will ever be any more. What about the Colonies?'

"I didn't know anything about the Colonies except that you snowshoed in Canada, shot big game in Africa, and spent your days upon a horse in Victoria or Queensland—or, at any rate, I thought you did. With my proclivities I chose Queensland. I went out there with my cash, as verdant a young tenderfoot as ever crossed the ocean.

"There's no good bothering you with my early struggles. I got a run in time—or, perhaps, it would be fairer to say the run got me. I was had—badly had—by a scoundrelly land-jobber, handed him over one thousand of the three, dropped fifteen hundred into sheep, and settled down to shepherd them with a man or two, a Chinese cook, and half a dozen horses. It's what many a young fellow has done both before and since. Nine in every ten, I suppose, have had to buy their experience as I bought it."

He hesitated a moment, took a sip at his tumbler, and gave a queer little laugh.

" I purchased it in odd markets at times, as my story proves. The thing began with a letter I received one morning, just before the great drought which disillusioned and ruined me had set in. My correspondent went straight to the point.

" ' Dear Sir,' he wrote. ' I hear you have come to be my neighbour. Do you require a horse or two? I have some young stock which might suit you. Drop in some time, and look them over.—Yours truly, Charles E. Smith.'

" Not being aware that I possessed such a thing as a neighbour in the English sense, I called up my foreman, George Bean.

" ' Who is Mr. C. E. Smith?' said I, ' and what sort of cattle does he raise?'

" Bean scratched his head and looked puzzled. Then a sudden light shone in his eyes.

" ' Why, that's old " Both Ways," ' he said. ' He's called that because he's never been known to back a horse except to win *and* a place. His run's down beyond the Stalerib, about fifty miles from here. His nags are pretty fair, boss.'

" I was a horse or two short at the time, and pretty considerably tired of station company. I thought it would be a good way of brightening my wits to go and have a deal with a native, and I need hardly assure you that I had every confidence of being able to take care of my twenty-five-year-old self.

" Fifty miles is not thought much of down under—nor even here in these latter days of motors—and starting at sun-up I got over to the run beyond the Stalerib by late breakfast time. I was not greatly impressed by the look of the station. There was no attempt at tidiness ; bone-heaps and kerosene cans lay within a few yards of the front entrance : there was a sort of fly-blown effect over the buildings. I remembered with smug satisfaction my own small but spic-and-span dwelling.

" One or two mangy mongrels set up a barking as I loped up, and a man appeared on the verandah—a tall but scraggy old party with an iron grey moustache and hair. I spotted him for the proprietor.

" ' Mr. Smith?' I said, inquiringly. ' I'm Baillie, your new neighbour. I got your letter a few days back.'

"His face, which had been pretty glum up till that minute, relaxed into something like a grin. He welcomed me almost effusively, found a whisky and siphon, and shouted to an unseen cook to serve breakfast. He began to swap sheep news and other local items of interest till the food came in, and then fed me like a mother. He certainly was excessively cordial.

"It wasn't till we had adjourned to the verandah with cigars that I came to the object of my expedition.

"'What about these young horses, Mr. Smith?' said I.

"He gave me a glint out of one eye which made him look like an old magpie.

"'I reckon I can find you what you want, if you want *good* stuff,' he said, 'just about as well as, and a trifle better than, most. But I can't get them in till evening.'

"I was politely expressing the hope that I should not be in his way when he interrupted me.

"'Look here,' he said, suddenly, 'I haven't had a spree for months. What do you say to a kangaroo run? I'll mount you with pleasure.'

"I dare say you may think that a man who had just been fifty miles in the saddle would jib at another twenty or thirty almost on the top of them, but even I had been out long enough to be pretty case-hardened. I jumped at the offer. Twenty minutes later we were out in the scrub, with half a dozen kangaroo hounds running in full view of a regular 'old man' as they call them, and I enjoying myself as I hadn't done since I last followed hounds in my own country. We had a couple of ripping runs with a kill.

"My yarn doesn't include a description of that sort of thing, or I should keep you here all night. Mr. Smith's ingenious dealings with me began as we were ambling comfortably home.

"'How did she carry you?' he asked, pointing at the mare he had lent me, and I owned that she had never made a mistake. I began to wonder if she was included in the 'young stock' for sale, though she was obviously past mark of mouth, so I tried a gentle crab.

"'Steady, but not a great flyer,' I answered. 'Not what you'd call full of fire.'

"He gave a peculiar little laugh.

"'My good sir,' he said, 'I wouldn't take five hundred sovereigns for Bessie. At eight to ten miles there isn't her equal in Australia.'

"'Eight miles *at speed*?' I cried. 'Why, I never got her *racing* once this morning; she hasn't got it in her! I'd back almost any horse I own to beat her!'

"He gave me another of those magpie looks of his.

" ' Now would you ? ' he said. ' And how would you back your opinion ? '

" You must remember I was young, excessively young, and that I had no idea of being treated as a tenderfoot. I had ridden the mare through a whole morning, and fancied I knew just as much about her performance as her owner. I said that if he'd allow me to give the horse I had ridden over forty-eight hours' rest I'd match it against his mare for fifty pounds, distance anything from five miles to ten, owners up!

" Of course I was the worst kind of fool—the cocksure kind. Old ' Both Ways ' shook in his saddle.

" ' If you're as confident as all that,' he said, ' why not make it a hundred ; fifty is neither here nor there ? '

" A hundred pounds was as much loose cash as I had left me in the world then, but I was not going to be browbeaten, and I had an idea that the price of sheep was going up. I took him, anyhow. He nodded.

" ' All right,' he said, coolly, and pointed out into the scrub. We were just coming into sight of the station again. ' You see that building there beside the old dead gum ? ' he asked. ' I reckon that's about four miles out. I'll race my mare against your nag out and home to make an eight-mile stretch. It's sound going all the way.'

" I looked at the country. It was as flat as one's hand with the exception of one scrub-filled hollow beside the iron shearing shed which he had pointed out. It seemed to me that it was made for the long-reaching stride of the six-year-old Billy Boy which I had ridden over. I almost felt that hundred pounds in my pocket.

" ' Done ! ' said I, as confidently as you please, and ' Done ! ' said he, looking no less cock-a-hoop. ' The day after to-morrow, after sun-up ? ' I nodded acceptance, and that was all there was to it.

" Well, two mornings after that, just in the first dawn light, you might have seen me and my host climbing into the saddle. Billy Boy looked a picture. He was a bright chestnut, full of fire, but easy to handle as a donkey with any one who knew him. As I passed my hand over his barrel, looked into the gleam of his eye, and listened to his breathing, I felt my confidence swelling in me, for I don't mind owning that I half wondered if Mr. ' Both Ways ' might not have tried a gentle dose of drugs to settle the matter his way. One good look at my horse made my mind easy on that head. He was jumping out of his skin with condition.

" Bessie, on the other hand, looked neither the one thing nor the other. She stood like a rock for her owner to climb into the saddle, just the same steady-going, sheep-faced old hack I had found her throughout the hunt. Smith's half-dozen hands had turned out to see the fun, and made up the entire audience.

"The foreman started us, and when the flag fell Billy Boy went off like a shot from a catapult. I had to take a steady at him or he'd have run himself to a standstill in the first few furlongs; but when I had taken hold and sat down he fell into his great reaching canter that fairly ate up the ground. Half-way to the turn I looked over my shoulder. I almost laughed.

"Bessie was a full hundred yards in the rear, the old man sitting like a sack, flicking the reins upon her neck like a butcher boy. He hadn't got out his whip, but he was reaching for it, and a minute or two later I heard it come down on the mare's flanks like a flail. We were a full mile from the buildings, but 'Both Ways' had begun to flog already. I chuckled loudly. Where in the world did he expect to get the next five miles from if he was beginning forcing tactics at this point! I looked round again as I flew past the shearing shed. My antagonist was somewhere near half a furlong back!

"I regarded the match as over, and took another steady at Billy Boy, reflecting that he had to carry me another fifty miles the following day. I also began to meditate where that hundred pounds would be most usefully employed on my holding. I felt in a particularly pleasant frame of mind.

"It was suddenly borne upon me that the sound of following hoofs which had died away five minutes back was again in my ears. In great astonishment I stared for the third time over my shoulder.

"Mr. 'Both Ways' seemed almost at my elbow! In the intensity of my astonishment I nearly fell off. I rolled so in the saddle that the indignant Billy Boy changed step, half blundered, and as near as a toucher came down! My antagonist was overhauling me hand over fist!

"I turned, pulled myself together, and sat down to ride. Billy Boy let himself out, but thirty seconds later the mare was racing beside me. I was stupefied as I looked at her. Her nostrils arched, her eyes were alert and flashing, she thundered along, pulling at her bit and evidently taking every ounce out of 'Both Ways'' arms to control her. She seemed to have been re-incarnated! There was no question of flogging her home here—indeed, her rider had dropped his whip. She tore along neck and neck with Billy Boy for a few strides, and then absolutely left him standing. 'Both Ways' romped home a winner by twenty lengths!

"I don't suppose there was a more crestfallen man in Australia than I was when I dismounted, nor a more amazed one. I was so

404

utterly nonplussed that for a moment or so I did nothing but stare. Old Smith gave me a triumphant laugh.

" ' Well, my boy,' he chuckled, ' you can't always tell by looks, can you? There's a bit of horsemanship left in us old fellows yet. The stuff was there, you see, but it takes a bit of experience to get it out of her.'

" What I said I can hardly remember. Something incoherent and foolish, no doubt, for the old man was taken with another fit of chuckles which seemed to be shared by everyone present. The grin on the face of the man who took Billy Boy's reins from me seemed to endanger the permanency of his ears. Every one of the helpers simply rocked with amusement.

" Well, I wrote ' Both Ways ' his cheque, and left the next morning, feeling about as limp as chewed string. All through the fifty miles home I meditated upon the matter, and the more I puzzled the less I could make head or tail of it. I had ridden that mare, mind you, and I thought I had got to the bottom of her in ten miles' easy cantering. Two days later she had been transformed into a sort of equine whirlwind. What was the meaning of it— where, in the name of wonder, could an explanation lie?

" There *was* an explanation, and I suppose if I hadn't shortly afterwards become a—temporarily—ruined man I should never have arrived at it. I lost all my stock with the drought, got swindled again over the sale of my run, and finally enlisted penniless in the police. For three years I left that district and heard no more of ' Both Ways ' in any connection at all.

" Then my official duties took me to Bunderoo Races. There, seated in a brake with half a dozen friends, and surrounded by empty bottles, I beheld my former neighbour in all his glory.

" I saw something else a few minutes later—something which surprised me more by a lot than the sight of my old friend. For as the finish of the Bunderoo Cup flashed past me half a furlong from home I rubbed my eyes in sheer amazement. Coming away from her field to win in a common canter was the famous mare of our wager, Bessie, snatching at her bit and romping in as she had done on the Stalerib flats three years before!

" I turned for a race card. Not having anything to bet with beyond my wages, I had sensibly decided to leave the ring alone, and had not concerned myself with the list of runners. I ran my eye down the column.

" There it was, right enough. Mr. C. E. Smith's bay mare Bessie. *Six years* old! And three years before that she had been, to the best of my knowledge and belief, *aged!*

" I was bewildered—absolutely at a loss, and being on duty

could take no steps to verify my impression ; but that night, as I was reporting to my inspector, Glendinning, I couldn't help giving him the gist of my story. I ended by asking him if there could be any question of fake about the horse's age or description.

" He laughed. 'Mr. " Both Ways " is capable of a good deal, Baillie,' he said, 'but he has a wholesome fear of a vet. Our local man is no fool, and can spot a file on a tooth as well as most. Besides, what object could there be in it, now ? '

" That argument seemed sound enough, and I turned in without discussing the matter further—indeed, as the races, as usual, ended in something which in England would be called a riot, but which in Queensland is merely a spree, I had other things to think of. Four days later, however, Glendinning sent for me.

" He greeted me with a grin.

" ' That was an interesting story you told me the other evening,' he began. ' I've reason to think, Baillie, that there's a continuation to it.'

" I suppose I looked more than commonly interested, for he laughed.

" ' Yes,' he went on, 'you may stare, but it's so. You know that wealthy young ass Sanson, who's not been out six months? Mr. " Both Ways " is taking a great interest in him.'

" ' He isn't making *him* an eight-mile match out and home against Bessie, is he, sir ? ' said I, sarcastically ; but Glendinning wagged his head at me quite seriously.

" ' Not against Bessie, Baillie,' he answered, 'but it's not a bad shot of yours. The match is the same, but he's pinning his faith this time on a brown horse which was near leader in the brake team he drove down here. He's told Sanson he can bring up any of his nags he likes to Stalerib, and match them against him ! '

" I was fairly knocked out of time.

" ' For an eight-mile stretch round the shearing shed—like that match of—of *mine ?* ' I cried.

" Old Glendinning nodded.

" ' Precisely,' he answered. ' Odd, isn't it ? for young Sanson notoriously possesses some of the best racing blood in this hemisphere. I think we'd better attend the event.'

" He was grinning, as he spoke, like a Chinese idol, and I knew there was something more to come. He went on in his purring, matter-of-fact voice, which was never so soft as when he was professionally dangerous.

" ' The way I came to know it,' he said, 'was this : I happened to be in the snug of Simpson's bar yesterday, waiting for an explanation of a slight infringement of the terms of his licence. Simpson was in the house, making up the explanation, which, I may observe, turned out to be a remarkably poor one. The bar was empty. Suddenly two men came in and called for drinks. Simpson came out, served them, and went back to his brain work. I suppose they thought they had the place to themselves. I recognised one by his voice as "Both Ways'" foreman. He was speaking low, but, as you know, I've good ears. "The old man's got another *double* match on, George," he said. "What d'you think of that?" George gave a whistle. "No-o-o!" he said, in evident astonishment. "Not another shearing-shed stretch? Who's the mug this time?" I don't know that I should have paid much attention if I hadn't heard *your* story, but at that I pricked up my ears. "Young Sanson!" said the other. "It's the bay horse." I heard George gurgle into his mug and then set it down with a slam. "Well," he said, "I suppose there'll be a quid or two as usual for all hands, but blow me if I shouldn't like to see the game given away for the pure joke of it! Supposing somebody got up against the horse with a pot of paint and *marked it!*" And at that the two got up and left, laughing.'

"I looked at Glendinning and Glendinning looked at me. He was rubbing his chin with a very rum look on his face.

"'Well,' he said at last, 'what do you make of that, eh?'

"I shook my head.

"'I don't make anything of it, sir,' I said. 'It sounds to me pure nonsense.'

"He gave a little grunt.

"'Well, there I can't agree with you, Baillie,' he said; 'and the more I reflect upon the matter the more I think we'd better attend—unofficially. And don't forget to bring the essential article.'

"I stared at him without a notion of what he was talking of.

"'The essential article,' I repeated. 'What's that, sir?'

"He shook his head at me.

"'Dear me, Baillie,' he remonstrated, 'I'm afraid you're not very sharp. A pot of paint, of course!' And with that he stepped into the inner office and shut the door. I could hear him chuckling like a jay.

"Well, a week later Glendinning and I might have been seen ambling along together in the direction of the Stalerib. The inspector hadn't said a word more on the subject of our expedition, and it wasn't my place to begin conversation, but I was bursting with curiosity. I looked at him anxiously once or twice, and now and then caught him smiling very pleasantly to himself, but he never got beyond the smile till we were camping that evening about twenty miles short of the station. Then he looked up at me.

"'The match is at sun-up, as usual, Baillie,' he said. 'I'm going to slide in unostentatiouslike and ask for breakfast. But *you* mustn't.'

"'Not ask for breakfast!' I protested. 'Why not, sir?'

"'Because you'll not come as far as the station with me,' he said. 'You will stop in that bit of scrub near the shearing shed which is the turn for home in the race. You'll keep yourself very completely hid, if you please, and you'll keep your eyes very completely open. Those are your orders.'

"'Very well, sir,' said I, mystified, but not willing to show it. 'Am I to look at anything in particular?'

"'Prevail on yourself to glue your eyes on Mr. "Both Ways" from start to finish,' he answered, 'and I think you'll do all that I require of you. Good-night.' Without another word he curled himself up and snored.

"I was awakened by his hand digging me in the ribs. It was about two o'clock when we saddled up, and the first rays of sunrise were glowing over the scrub as we came in sight of the station. Glendinning turned and grinned at me.

"'I'll trouble you for that paint,' he said.

"I gave it him—it was only a tiny phial in reality by his own directions—and he pocketed it. Then he pointed to a dip in the ground behind us.

"'Hobble your horse there,' he ordered me, 'and then get as near the shed as you can unseen. Directly the race is over come in and report to me.'

"I saluted and he turned away. As I came out of the dip after hobbling my horse, I saw him cantering down the last slope into the station. I dropped on hands and knees and wormed my way up to the shed.

"For at least half an hour nothing happened to take my attention. There appeared to be a certain amount of animation down at the buildings, but even in Australia it isn't the easiest thing in the world to distinguish details across four miles of country. I saw one or two people moving to and fro—I saw horses being led out—I thought I caught the echo of a cheer. But against the shadowy background of the house the start must have escaped me. It wasn't till they were within a couple of miles of me that I realised that the race was actually in progress. The riders were only two dots upon the waste, and as they were coming towards me it was impossible to tell whether the interval which separated them was wide or narrow. I got out my binoculars.

"Then the matter was plain enough. One led by twenty lengths and was going great guns. The other, in the rear, was riding his horse out as if he was within a furlong of the finish. The event was coming off exactly as it had occurred in my own case three years before. As they drew nearer I could almost fancy that I could read the same confident smile on young Sanson's face as had adorned my own countenance; but this, I have no doubt, was merely the effect of a stimulated imagination. He swept past the shearing shed and turned for home a good couple of hundred yards in front of his antagonist. And he was sitting *anyhow*, not making an attempt to ride, but enjoying, as it were, a complacent before-breakfast canter.

" I drew in my breath and turned to stare at ' Both Ways.' His cutter was out and he was flailing his horse's flanks. As Sanson turned the old man brought his horse along with a rush which seemed to take every last ounce out of it, and it was with only a moderate shock of surprise that I saw it stop and prop with all four legs out just in front of the shearing-shed door. I gave a whistle of glee.

" ' There's the end of you and your wager *this time*, my boy,' I cried. ' Lord, how you must be swearing ! '

" The words were scarcely out of my lips before it was I myself who had let fly an oath—of pure amazement. As the horse propped, the door of the shearing shed flew open, and a man and *another horse* appeared—and it might have been the twin of the one ' Both Ways ' was riding. In height, span, and colour it was exactly the same ! It was reaching at its bridle and straining to be off !

" Mr. ' Both Ways ' didn't keep it waiting long. The performance, for a man of his age, was simply marvellous. He seemed to fly from one saddle to the other. I give you my word of honour three ticks of a clock had not passed while he changed seats, got going, and flew out into the open in pursuit of Sanson. And he was overhauling him with every stride !

" I can tell you that stupefaction nearly floored me—for the minute. The next instant it came home to me with overwhelming force that I had got to see the end of this performance to get the full enjoyment out of it, and I went racing down into the hollow for my horse. I had unhobbled and was tearing off after ' Both Ways ' a couple of minutes after he had passed.

" My nag being fairly fresh again after his rest, I wasn't such a very bad third to the race, all things considered. I heard the cheers and the shouts of applauding laughter as old ' Both Ways ' romped in, but they seemed to die down into a queer sort of hush as I cantered up, saluted, and dropped off my horse. I said nothing. A wink at Glendinning told him all he wanted to know, I expect, and he asked me no questions. He was standing by ' Both Ways,' patting the winner's neck, and the old chap was eyeing him with a very queer expression. The station hands were looking at me.

" Glendinning's hand stole down off the horse's neck at last and stroked his barrel. From there I saw the Inspector's fingers pass under the stifle joint and give a sort of little probing motion. Then he laughed.

" ' Both Ways ' glared at him.

" ' What's the joke ? ' he asked, and Glendinning laughed again.

" ' There's something funny to me about such a hollow race as that,' he said. ' I suppose Mr. Sanson must have won by as much as four miles. It's almost a record, isn't it ? '

" Young Sanson gave a jump.

" ' What's that ? ' he cried, excitedly. ' What's that ? '

" Glendinning rubbed his chin in his slow, meditative way.

" ' Just a mere statement of fact,' he drawled. ' Perhaps you didn't notice that he stopped, dead beat, by the shearing shed. You didn't actually think he was racing you home ? '

" I don't think I realised before how like a boiled cod a human being could look till I saw young Sanson gape. His eyes rolled— his mouth fell open. He gurgled.

" ' But—but——' he begain to stammer.

" Glendinning interrupted him.

" ' If you require proof,' he said, slowly, ' I may as well tell you that I marked the horse Mr. Smith started on, here, under the stifle joint, with a little blob of white enamel paint. You'll find both horse and paint in the shearing shed yonder. Eh, Baillie ? '

" I saluted.

" ' Yes, sir,' I answered. ' Mr. Smith changed horses at the turn.'

" And then—it was the queerest sort of noise—a sort of wondering moan went up from the station hands gathered round. Each man looked at his pal, looked at me, looked at Glendinning, and, last of all, looked at Smith. I was looking that way myself.

" The old man's face had gone a sort of parchment yellow. The skin was fluttering in and out under the cheek bones as the nerves twitched and strung. There was a sort of glaze upon his eyes —the saliva was trickling from the corners of his mouth. Suddenly he staggered.

" Before anyone could catch him he flung up his arms and shot forward, to fall at the Inspector's feet ! He was in a fit !

    *   *   *   *   *   *

" No—he didn't recover. He went out before evening and never spoke again. But his foreman gave the whole game away.

" It appears the old man had the most extraordinary talent for horse-faking that ever was known. With his dyes and scissors and clippers he could alter a horse so that his own breeder wouldn't know him. He'd a mania for the thing, using it in the first instance for making perfect team pairs, which, naturally, sold better than the same horses single. He'd made many a hundred guineas that way, selling them in open auction under different names and then clearing before the game could be blown. Of course he took good care to do these tricks a good few hundred miles from home.

" His first match, using this device, was something of an inspiration, and half by way of a joke. When he found out how easily the thing was carried through he did it again and again, squaring his few hands with a few sovereigns out of what he netted, and they, blackguards every one of them, were only too glad to keep mum. I, it appeared, was the third young fool he'd sold in the same way."

The speaker looked round on the circle of his audience with a paternal smile as he finished ; there was a twinkle in his eye.

" I met other scoundrels afterwards—more especially when fortune found me in the days of the gold boom. There were ingenious knaves among them, but when I talk of a *red hot* 'un— well, I don't think I know anything to beat Mr. ' Both Ways ' Smith."

THE HEAD OF THE ROSEG VALLEY (THE MONK'S DOMAIN)

STRANGE STORIES OF SPORT

XXXVII.—THE MONK'S FACE

BY JOHN SANDERSON

THE elder Reuss was coiling up the gleaming white rope through the centre of which the scarlet thread of the Alpine Club ran from end to end. André Reuss, his son, was solemnly lighting his great-bowled Swiss pipe, and their two "Herren," John Walden, landed proprietor in the county of Hertford, and John Duncan, barrister-at-law, were luxuriating once more in that peculiar sense of lightness and freedom which follows the untying of the rope when a climb is over. They had now only the side moraine of the glacier to cross in order to reach the woodland track leading down the side of the Roseg Valley to the village of Pontresina. They had finished just in time, for already in the narrow valley evening was falling rapidly. On the highest peaks the fugitive pink after-glow of the sunken sun was dying away, and the great array of snow-covered giants was beginning to assume the hard cold aspect of aloofness which comes with approach of night. The crossing of a moraine is always a tedious process, and by the time the party had reached the path they sought, the moon had risen, and, amid a world of gigantic shadows, the great peaks stood out, clear-cut and gleaming—a vast amphitheatre of rock and snow and ice.

John Walden and John Duncan walked together in silence along the path some distance ahead of the two guides. They were comparatively old friends, having become acquainted six years before when climbing in the Alps. Duncan had attached himself enthusiastically to the man who had taken him upon his first little rock climb, and who during the weeks they had there spent together had guided him in many a scramble on rock and snow. Since then they had not met till the present summer, and it was a mere chance that Walden had encountered his old acquaintance, who had come with his *fiancée* and her mother to Pontresina for the summer months. For Duncan was now engaged, and his life was almost too full of the marvel of the first love of woman. His attitude was one of perpetual open-mouthed wonder at his own incredible good fortune. He was given to long bursts of confidence and to equally long spells of silent reflection which found their sole expression at intervals in the two words " By gum ! " spoken in a tone of rapturous astonishment. And so with his back to the mountains and his face to the village where Honoria awaited them, he marched along in silence.

As for Walden, he too was sunk in silence, for the shadow of his life had again descended upon his soul, and his mind had entered once more into that eternal round of argument from which no stable conclusion was ever to be drawn, and which for him darkened the whole world. Why, he thought, had he come again to the neighbourhood of the Monk ? There it stood on his left, one of the circle of great snow-clad mountains. Shaped like the cowled head of a monk, but with a face hideous in its malignity—a cruel grin on his bearded lips. What dark power had carved out of rock and snow and ice that evil visage and planted it there for all time as a symbol of the power and eternity of evil on earth ? In his hollow changeless eyes one seemed to read inexorable law—on his lips the derision of those who struggle to evade such law. It seemed to be placed there amid these everlasting mountains to reverse the holy mission of the priest, and to proclaim derisively to Walden's very soul : " Nature is inexorable. For the weak there is no salvation." It was true, he thought, as he plodded onwards. There were things which men never forgave in others, things which men who were men never forgave themselves. And that was the cardinal thing—that a man should be able to forgive himself. In comparison with that nothing else mattered. How sick he was of the eternal argument ! Was what he had done years ago an act of this hopeless kind ? No living man could convince him either the one way or the other. He could

not convince himself. Men whispered about him. And this intermittent self-contempt and sense of dishonour were ruining his
whole life. The aspect of that hideous and cruel face clothed in
the garb of a Christian monk gave to his mind a sense of despair
which made all attempt at self-justification a mere writhing of the
soul under the car of irrevocable destiny.

Suddenly, as he raised his eyes, the gleaming lights of the great
hotels in the village sprang into view, and his train of thought
stopped dead, as if something had been cast into the wheels of his
mind and arrested its motion. This something was the image of a
woman—one of the many, and the latest, he had drifted into contact
with in the course of his solitary wanderings over Europe. A mere
acquaintance of one of the great tourist establishments of the village
below. It was Honoria Fleming. She was the woman his friend
loved and was brooding over in awed wonder at that very moment
by his side—the woman who loved his friend. What a miracle was
this love of man by woman! It had never been brought home
to him till now. It had created a new heaven and a new earth, for
in Duncan's case he had seen the old earth and the old heaven pass
away. To Duncan this wonder had happened whose old earth and
heaven were goodly places to dwell in, whereas his own past was
almost uninhabitable. God, how he longed for some such transformation! A noble woman who loved would not only condone but
justify and convince and make amends a thousandfold for all the
rest. And love capable of so much would receive from him in like
measure. For he knew that in spite of what had happened eight
years ago he had courage. And he possessed the capacity to love
intensely and lastingly. He could make it worth a woman's while.

Then his imagination carried him to the Enchanted Valley, that
sunny little recess in the lower folds of the mountains where a week
ago Honoria and he had spent one whole day together—Duncan
having gone for a climb. A secluded little valley it was, clothed
thick with fern and dotted with birch, above the main valley of the
Roseg and scarcely known. "Their kingdom for a day," he had
called it, as they came upon it in the morning and stood survey-
ing it from end to end. A radiant kingdom it was, brimming with
sunshine and happiness. And as they sat eating their "butter bröde"
by the trickling fall where the little rivulet entered the valley, they
had peopled their little kingdom with happy and devoted subjects
from the fairy books of their respective childhoods, and had composed for them all their difficulties and arranged their future fairy
destinies. They had retold many of the quaint old fairy tales to
each other with appropriate additions and grave absurdities. Of
their own destinies beyond that single day of fairy sovereignty no

mention had been made. It was as if it had been tacitly agreed that that day must be a day rounded off and disconnected from everything before or after—that nothing that day was to happen which should or could be extended into their ordinary lives or which might require them to think of the future which lay beyond. And then suddenly with a rush which made him stagger on the narrow path, the thought seized him that this particular woman alone could save him. He was in the clutch of the world's evil power, and she was the only one—his only chance—the one being to whom he could confess and be shriven—who represented

PONTRESINA

for him the power of good. Impetuously he stopped and turned to Duncan following behind, and, even as he turned, his eyes once more met the hideous face of the Monk, shining coldly in the moonlight, malignant, impassive, and evil. "For you and all such as you there is no redemption," it seemed to say once more in cold derision. Of course it was hopeless and unthinkable!

"Hallo, old chap," said Duncan, "you tear along like a tiro. What about the guide's pace you so persistently exhorted me to imitate in the old days? I say, the weather looks gloriously settled at last for Friday's climb. Won't Honoria be delighted, and won't it be ripping to have her with us! And what a shame the holiday is almost over. Heigh-ho for London and the Temple! Whatever shall I do then without Honoria!" he added mournfully.

"Just what I was wondering myself, old chap," said Walden grimly. "I was thinking you would get on all right after you once settled down."

"By gad!" began Duncan. "Oh, I say," and there once more began a burst of confidence which ended only with the arrival of the two climbers in the hall of the Kronenhof very late for dinner.

*   *   *   *   *

The Hotel zur Krone is a modern structure having as one of its wings a small old-fashioned building from which it grew. From its windows can be viewed at the far end of the Roseg Valley the great circle of snow mountains which constitutes the eastern portion of the Bernina range. In contrast to this scene of grandeur and solitude the central lounge of the hotel presents during the season a spectacle of somewhat garish frivolity. Life in such an hotel is the life of Kensington or of the neighbourhood of the Alster touched with emotion. For, though the crowd does not change, their altitude of 6,000 ft. above the sea level cannot fail to have its effect upon the human organism, and every feeling or sensation which at the level of Hyde Park maintains a comparatively frail and precarious existence, is here correspondingly heightened, and occasionally produces effects at which no one is subsequently more surprised than those naturally conventional persons who experience them under such conditions.

The prevailing scorched complexions acquired on the safe parts of the glaciers, mitigated though they are by lanoline and blue spectacles, heighten for these town-dwellers their sense of being someone else for the time being, and in the good old phrase applied to persons under the influence of liquor, they are all more or less "disguised." One's judgment upon one's own conduct becomes more charitable, and the naturally censorious even extend this charity to the conduct of others. It is only Pontresina! That is why Mrs. Wilmot-Hill always came to Pontresina. It suited her admirably. Cautious men liked her too, because they knew she could always be relied upon vividly to appreciate and studiously ignore any undue warmth of sentiment towards her handsome person to which they might give expression. That, too, was why her daughter Cicely and her niece Honoria Fleming were allowed to behave exactly as they chose without interference from their complacent mother and aunt. And—to resume the thread of this story—perhaps that was how it happened that Honoria Fleming came to be standing near the glass-doors leading into the entrance hall of the hotel, donning a cloak and shawl, whilst John Walden instead of John Duncan assisted in the process. The smiles of knowledge and amusement upon the lips of a few well-dined loungers holding cups of coffee and smoking cigarettes in the neighbourhood of the hall door were certainly attributable to no other causes. After all, there was an excellent excuse, for John Walden had just informed Honoria that the guides Reuss, father and son, were at the front door, having come to make the final arrangements for the climb of the Piz Aarlatz on the following day, and what is more exciting and interesting than to talk German to the big bearded good-natured men in homespun and to hear their answers, mostly monosyllabic and affirmative, and expressed in tones at once so respectful and parental? And then it was so natural to stroll a little farther. When Honoria Fleming and John Walden turned out of the busy little village street into the steep roadway leading down to the bridge over the foaming Inn, it was just nine o'clock. The moon shone fitfully, but every now and again with a hard radiance which illumined the whole valley and threw into relief the white masses of mountains which encircled its head, the Piz Roseg, the Glusheint, and the Monk. They spoke quietly, but always with a reserve of humour, of indifferent things—the noise of the Germans in the lounge from which one had somehow to escape—the absurd conduct of the Italian Count who had pretended to run away from his American wife and had then turned up foolishly and unexpectedly at dinner—the morrow's climb. Then, when they found themselves on the bridge they stood together leaning on the wooden parapet and watching the play of the moonlight on the foaming waters below.

Now, Honoria was a flirt. Moreover, she was that most subtle and seductive of all kinds of flirts, a serious woman, and what is worse, a good woman. It is much more difficult to tell when a serious woman is only flirting than it is when a frivolous woman is in question. When she does flirt, the former cannot help flirting with her soul as well as with her heart, which the frivolous woman is unable to do because she does not happen to possess such an article. And if any fair reader exclaims that good women with souls do not flirt at all, why I can only hesitate and doubt as to whether such reader is a good and serious woman. I can at least positively assert that she has never been to Pontresina. The plain truth then is that whilst Honoria loved her lover Duncan, and in her heart was true to him, there was in Walden's more complex nature something which appealed to her—his whimsical humour—his fundamental loneliness. And as Duncan was there and on the spot, and knew *nearly* all that she was doing, and was, besides, safely hers; and as it was only Pontresina, she was rather—as the phrase is—"letting herself go." It was the usage of the place. As an engaged woman, after all she was as much entitled to a certain freedom in this respect as Mrs. Wilmot-Hill herself. And no harm ever came to the latter or to anyone else through her innocent ongoings. Thus it came that Honoria stood on that little bridge just past the stalls where by daylight the Tyrolese stockings are sold at double their value. As they stood there, Walden put his great hand lightly on the small one which grasped the rail. Honoria did not move, nor did she withdraw. Instead she gazed up the valley which stretched in front of them to the foot of the great mountains and exclaimed lightly, "What an awful face! It is dreadful! A monk, too! I should not like to have him for my father confessor!"

"He is mine," said Walden, in a hoarse voice trembling with feeling.

There was something in the tone which suddenly transformed the whole scene. Here was the note of tragedy. None could have known it better than Honoria. She started and sought to withdraw her hand. "We must go back," she said. "Come, Mr. Walden."

He held it fast. "Let us stay," he said, "a few moments longer. I must tell you. I must indeed."

Honoria could not move; she just glanced at his drawn face. "Very well," she said.

"Ten years ago," said Walden in a low, hurried voice, "I climbed with two comrades in the Himalayas. I was a subaltern— a mere youngster. They fell on rotten rock. In desperation, when I could hold no longer"—here Walden's voice fell to a mere whisper —"*I cut the rope!* Of course, we should all have been killed," he added. "I wish to God we had." Honoria did not speak. Only he felt her hand on the rail tremble in his and turn over. "You understand now," he went on painfully, "how it comes that that hideous brute over there became my father confessor."

Honoria glanced up the valley at the malignant face livid in the moonlight, cowled like a holy priest, and shuddered. She understood it all now. Then her disengaged hand slid on to the hand which still held hers on the parapet. Her head bent over till it rested on the three thus placed one over the other, and she cried a little. Although for the time being the representative of the power of goodness in this world, you see she was, after all, only a woman. And true goodness will manifest itself in many unconventional ways.

But, man-like, Walden did not understand. He spoke passionately now. "It is useless, I know, but I love you. I need you. If there is goodness in the world, you were meant for me." Honoria shrank backwards. "Ah! but you despise me," he cried, "and there is no one else." It was a cry of despair.

"It is not that," she said quickly; "oh, what do I care for that? I honour you for the torments you have endured. But I could never help you as you thought."

"I love you," said Walden, "and I believe you love me."

"Oh, no, no!" she answered eagerly. "Think of the face of the Monk when we had betrayed your friend. Oh, how could I redeem you from one dishonour by leading you to another! Oh, you must be strong! You must redeem yourself! You are no coward, and you will conquer in the end!"

Then in a low voice she added, "I love Duncan, and so do you."

THE MONK'S FACE

"I love you," repeated Walden passionately, "and I need you. It is nothing to him. But it is useless. Let us go." And so, in silence, these two beings, both fundamentally good, both humanly frail, turned back to the hotel. And the Monk, with hollow eyes and fixed derisive smile, stared impassively from the mountains.

*　　　*　　　*　　　*　　　*　　　*

No one who has ever experienced it can forget the weird feelings of traversing a glacier by candle light. It was a new experience to Honoria. The white ice glimmered faintly, and upon it the black shadows of the legs of the members of the party advancing in single file crossed and intermingled strangely. Seeing that each one of the party had to keep his eyes more or less constantly fixed on the ground, this curious effect of quivering shadows was a perpetual accompaniment of their advance, and all around one felt the presence of the great mountains, which seemed to be looking on and waiting eternally. More than once old Reuss, who was leading, had turned back with much muttered bad language, from some impossible crossing. Old Reuss, I may say, was thin and rather gruff. André, on the other hand, was huge, with a face like a leg of mutton, and perpetually good-humoured. Finally they came to a dead stop in the ice falls, and a consultation took place between the guides. Old Reuss yielded up the lead to André, and by this change Duncan became second on the rope and Walden became third. Then André, in order to cross a wide crevasse impeding their progress, led the way on to a solid tongue of ice which ran diagonally across it almost to the other side.

Between the end of this tongue and the wall of ice beyond was a space of some two or three feet. Standing on the end of the tongue Hans managed to cut a step in the ice wall beyond, which was considerably higher than the tongue itself, and crossed safely over. Duncan followed at once; but the step, probably damaged already, or in the darkness imperfectly cut, gave way under his foot, and with a crash he disappeared in the crevasse. Both Hans and Walden, of course, had the rope tight on either side, and he did not go far, but the shock just missed dragging Walden from the tongue of ice on which he stood. Duncan himself never for a moment lost his head, and, aided by the rope and by some projections in the ice, he soon appeared again upon the surface of the glacier. But an irreparable misfortune had happened. He was without his ice axe. It had been dashed from his hand in the fall. When old Reuss realised that the "verdamte pickel" was lost he stood for a time growling and muttering strange oaths into his straggling beard. "Never, never, never should one let go one's pickel. That was of all things the most disastrous." And once more father and son conferred together in the darkness. Evidently André thought the matter serious. Finally André turned once more to lead the way, Duncan being doomed to rely upon his power of balance without any instrument of support whatever.

It was altogether a truly unfortunate beginning of this nocturnal invasion of these realms of ice and snow. A faint light of dawn was by this time beginning to show itself. Honoria glanced round at the forms of the surrounding masses of mountains. There on the right, faintly discernible, she perceived once more the great fixed face, the diabolical smile she knew so well. For a time the exacting nature of the route had dispelled the image from her mind, though the oppressive sense of its presence had remained with her all the time. For the expedition was indeed a strange one. She had invited Walden to take them upon this climb, and after what had been brought about by her own action she deemed it proper to face it. It was the right thing to do. And thus it came that these three beings whose destinies had been so strangely entangled through the mysterious influence of a fourth—the motionless and malign figure near them—were now, as it seemed, invading his domain and the stronghold of his sway. She believed implicitly in the triumph

THE PIZ ROSEG

of good and the ultimate escape of Walden from the remorseless grip of evil power so dreadfully symbolised by the Monk. And yet now she turned from the face with a shudder. The protruding lips seemed, as Walden had found, almost to speak to her and to smile with cruel derision.

The party now pushed steadily forward, and soon the morning, from a clear sky, broke upon the mountains. What is there of earthly splendour to equal that one supreme moment of the climber when the first dazzling beams of day strike the summits of the great amphitheatre of snow-clad mountains! By magic he finds himself the inhabitant of a wonder-world of strangest beauty. What climber has not dreamt of its glory and solitude, and where is he who has ever experienced it to whom the vision does not send a thrill of excited longing! Wherever he be, in crowded city or smiling country, who can resist the call that gorgeous moment makes to the jaded soul!

Then came the first breakfast on the ice—the attack of the lower rocks, the ascent of the couloir, the merry blows of the axe, and the stream of sparkling, jingling chips struck from the ice as the staircase is carefully formed by the leader. There followed the glow of success when the first and lower peak was attained and nothing separated them from the summit but the narrow arête which joined the double peak of the mountain. Here the party rested, and André began to grope in the ruck-sacks for the last bottle of red Swiss wine. Here for the first time its members, so strangely related, really threw off the cloud which separated them. The pure calm of the great mountains seemed to have entered Walden's blood. In spite of the words of passion he had spoken, a sense of peace filled his mind. He had confessed. He had drunk at the great human source of goodness, and for the first time for ten years he had realised intimately its power and reality. It was as if he had been shriven.

"Does he know?" he said to Honoria quietly, and pointing to Duncan.

Duncan himself nodded. "She told me," he said. "I'm sorry, old chap."

"Thank God I met her," Walden said. "I think I see my way through now." And that was all. They talked joyously together for the rest of the time.

When the party began the traverse of the last part of the arête leading directly up to the summit of the mountain, old Reuss took the lead. Walden followed on the rope; then came Honoria, followed by Duncan and young Reuss who brought up the rear. A short and somewhat steep descent for which steps could be kicked had first to be made. Then came in earnest the narrow arête or ridge which on the left dropped away rapidly in vast slopes of scarcely ruffled snow down to the glacier below—a scene of terrible and inspiring beauty. The snow cornice which overhung the right of the arête was a very slight one, and the face of the mountain on that side was bare rock and very steep for a considerable distance downwards. Beyond the level stretch the arête rose suddenly in a sharp curve showing a good deal of rock, making the final part of the ridge both easy and interesting. They were now at the most exciting moment of the climb, and Honoria's eyes danced with the thrill of adventurous action. She came of an open-air breed, and the blood of generations of hunters and fighters coursed gaily through her veins. She stepped coolly and carefully in the steps prepared for her.

It was just when the dangerous traverse was almost completed and the ridge had begun to make its final rise, that the accident happened. Hitherto there had been little or no cornice. But just at the curve a short one of only a few feet had formed and broadened out; and under the foot of old Reuss it suddenly gave way. As he fell, dragging Walden with him, young Reuss, who came last on the rope, with the instinct of his race instantly flung himself on his face down the slope of the opposite side and dug the spike of his ice axe into the snow. This arrested the fall, for the rope held; but the situation was a desperate one. Upon the rocky slope on the right hung old Reuss, Walden, and Honoria. On the other André Reuss clung desperately to the handle of his ice axe whilst Duncan lay without his ice axe helpless on the icy slope. The strain on André was terrific.

" Can you hold on ? " shouted Walden.

" A little time only, Herr," came the answer from André's clinched teeth.

Honoria heard Walden say something in a low tone to old Reuss who lay against the smooth rock beneath him at the extreme end of the rope.

" Ja, ja, Herr," came the answer. " It is the only way now. Just do it."

" Shout before you let go," cried Walden to André, making at the same time desperate efforts to find a hold on the icy slab.

A terrible silence ensued. " Ich kann nicht mehr ! " came at last in a despairing cry from André.

Scarcely was it heard ere the rope between Walden and Honoria was severed, and he and old Reuss disappeared into the gulf below. The lives of the others were safe. For the second time Walden had *cut the rope*. His path to honour had been short. He had redeemed his name.

STRANGE STORIES OF SPORT

XXXVIII.—A 'PLANE STORY

BY L. H. DE VISME SHAW

DESMOND SHORTHOUSE started up in bed. At the same moment he heard the sound of the tiny bell of the receiver which reposed in the breast pocket of his coat. He glanced at the clock : it was nearly half-past nine. He had overslept himself. His servant had orders never to disturb him in the morning. Desmond, like most young men with plenty of money and no profession, usually kept late hours when in London, and adopted the wise course of allowing himself plenty of sleep.

"I wonder what Mollie wants," he said to himself as he sprang out of bed.

For many months he had kept in constant communication with Mollie by means of a pocket wireless telephone. Desmond always carried his transmitter and receiver with him, but Mollie kept hers in the wardrobe of her room, so that no one could hear the bell if Desmond called her up and she happened not to be there. Their 'phone had been tuned by Marconi himself, and was said by him to be the most minutely toned apparatus that had ever passed through his hands. The chances against any other 'phone picking up its sound-waves were millions to one.

Desmond took the transmitter and receiver from the pocket of his coat. Holding the one to his mouth and the other to his ear he said :

"Good morning, Mollie—I was in bed when you rang me up."

"Oh, Desmond ! " came Mollie's voice from the receiver, " a dreadful thing has happened. About half an hour ago that *hateful* man came in his new aeroplane—such a magnificent one—seats four besides the planeur. After a few minutes my father came to me and said he would tolerate my obstinacy no longer. Then he said Mr. Woolf was going to marry me at twelve o'clock. Mr. Woolf brought a clergyman with him in the 'plane," Mollie's voice went on, "and has got a special licence. Probably the clergyman is some unscrupulous rogue he has bribed with a large sum. I suppose our chapel in The Hall is just the same as a church for marriages. My father says that even if I refuse to repeat my part of the service the clergyman will pretend he has heard me say the words, and that it will be a legal marriage just the same!"

"I don't believe it would," Desmond muttered.

"My father has locked me in the chapel," Mollie continued. "I have just been through the outer door into the Queen Anne garden, but the garden door is locked too. I cannot escape—I cannot climb a wall fifteen feet high, and there is nothing I could move out of the chapel to stand on. Oh, Desmond! what shall I do?"

Then came the sound of a sob.

"Give me a minute to think, Mollie," Desmond said.

Lady Mollie Tressler's father, the Marquis of Sincourt, was merely the nominal owner of the estates which had belonged to his family since the Conqueror's time. His father, a *roué* to the last, had left the property heavily encumbered; he himself, a *roué* of no less degree, had squandered money right and left till at last he became hopelessly insolvent. Some six months before the time of this story, Lord Sincourt met Mr. Phineas Woolf, an American multi-millionaire, who at once fell in love with Mollie. Woolf was a heavy-jowled man of about fifty. The more Mollie turned the cold shoulder upon him, the more persistent became his wooing. She and Desmond had already told their loves to one another.

Needless to say, Lord Sincourt favoured Woolf's suit. A multi-millionaire son-in-law would save him from the Bankruptcy Court and give him the means wherewith to carry on a life of unrestrained dissipation. All his persuasion and threats, however, could not turn Mollie from her determination not to marry Woolf.

At last a compact was entered into between the two men. Woolf was to marry Mollie—by stratagem, even by force if necessary—and in return was to redeem all mortgages on the Sincourt property. This would place Lord Sincourt in possession of a rent-roll of about twenty thousand a year.

"What do you think, Desmond?" came Mollie's voice from the receiver.

"I have thought it all out, dear," Desmond answered. "I am coming to you at once in my racing 'plane, the yellow and red one.

She'll be good"—he glanced at the electric wind-gauge on the chimney-piece—"for only a hundred miles an hour against the wind that's blowing now, so I cannot hope to reach you much before half-past eleven. About that time you must look out for a yellow and red 'plane. When it is quite close to the Queen Anne garden you must run to the middle of the garden, and I'll swoop and pick you up. There's plenty of room to clear the wall when I've got you—my new planeur is a splendid man. Are you quite sure you will make no mistake?"

"Quite sure."

"All right. Now I must scramble into my clothes and rush off to the Park. Good-bye, darling."

"Good-bye, Desmond dear; I am longing to see you!" came the reply.

Desmond rang the bell. His man appeared.

"Tell Perks to go on to the Park without losing a moment, and get the racing 'plane out. He is to wait there till I come. Then bring me something to eat here—anything."

Desmond dressed hurriedly, eating a few mouthfuls of breakfast meanwhile. He left the house and jumped into a taxicab.

How strange Hyde Park must look now to anyone who has not seen it since 1908! Only a few years ago there was not a building in it. To-day there are upwards of two thousand 'plane-houses—not counting the Government, Post Office, and Police blocks—and more than a mile and a half of concrete starting strip. It is difficult to imagine how life would go on if this concession to public feeling— the erection of 'plane-houses and the laying down of starting strips— were now repealed.

The charge made to the 'plane owner is strictly reasonable, and in return he has the exclusive use of a well-built 'plane-house opening on to the starting strip. I believe I am right in saying that there is not now a single town of the slightest importance where one does not find a starting strip and good accommodation for one's 'plane. Our municipal authorities have moved with the times in this respect.

Yes, Hyde Park is very different to-day from what it was so few years ago. Then there was nothing to mar the rural beauty of the landscape. Restfulness reigned. Now from dawn till dark, and after, the busy flight goes on: 'planes coming, 'planes going—ever coming, ever going. It took man long to conquer the air. What conquest could be more complete now?

"Everything ready, Perks?" Desmond said as he stepped into the 'plane.

"Everything, sir."

" All right—let her rip.   North-north-west."

Perks touched a lever, and the red and yellow 'plane, after rushing some twenty yards along the starting strip, shot upwards into the air.   She was one of the speediest machines in existence. Desmond had flown second in her in the Farman Cup race from London to Madrid only a few weeks before.

Desmond took a Colt repeating pistol from his pocket and loaded it.   A daring gang of air pirates had already begun their work, and were publicly threatening to sink the next 'plane the occupants of which refused to place all their valuables in the purse-net which they were in the habit of lowering from their own flyers.   Desmond had declared that if he were molested by them he would cripple their gear with his Colt and chance whether or not they returned fire.

" What are we making now, Perks ? " Desmond asked as London began to fade away behind them.

" A hundred and ten miles an hour, sir," the planeur answered, glancing at the dial of the speed recorder.

" Good.   Let me know if we drop below a hundred."

Desmond knew that Mollie, from the fact of her having rung him up when she was locked in the chapel, had the pocket 'phone with her, but of course he did not dare to communicate with her, as the bell might be heard by her father or Woolf.   He felt sure, as she had not again rung him up, that one of them was with her in the chapel.   With the 'plane in such skilful hands as those of Perks, he had no doubt about his ability to pick her up if she could make her way to the middle of the Queen Anne garden at the right moment.   The only thing in doubt, and this troubled him a good deal, was whether Lord Sincourt or Woolf might not be able to intercept her.

Onward they sped on their north-north-westerly course.   They saw only a few other 'planes.   The heavy red Post Office machine carrying His Majesty's mails, which could make no more than about forty miles an hour against the fresh head wind, they overtook and left far behind.   A little later a blue police patrol 'plane crossed their bows not a hundred yards ahead.   Prompt action on the part of the police had become necessary, and the idea of putting patrol 'planes in the air was being adopted.

" Only ninety-nine now, sir," said Perks.

Desmond looked at his watch.   " We shall do it comfortably," he said, " if you can keep over ninety.   Let me know if we drop below that."

Then he told Perks what he was going to do.   Lady Mollie was to be in the middle of the garden as the 'plane swooped.

"What's the length of the garden and the height of the wall, sir?" Perks asked.

"The garden is a hundred yards square, and the wall fifteen feet high."

"Then I shall come over the wall, sir, only just clearing it, at five miles an hour, stop the engine for the swoop, and clap on full speed for the rise the moment you pull her in. The fifty-yard glide after we come over the wall will take us by her at about six miles an hour. There's no fear about our clearing the wall going out, sir."

"And there's no fear about my getting her into the 'plane if I touch her," Desmond rejoined.

As he spoke the bell of the receiver sounded in his pocket. He whipped it out and put it to his ear, holding the transmitter before his mouth.

"Yes, Mollie?"

"I am still locked in the chapel. The outer door is open. Where are you?"

"In sight of Sincourt Hall. We shall be with you in three minutes. Be sure you are ready."

"To the left now, sir?" Perks asked.

"Yes—sharp to the left—full speed. Look through the glasses. That's the place—the large red-brick house beyond the further wood. The garden is at the back of the house. There, now you can see the wall."

"There'll be no mistake, sir. I shall stop the engine three hundred yards from the wall, and then regulate speed to top the wall at five miles an hour."

The 'plane shot through the now still air at high speed, about two hundred and fifty miles an hour.

Three hundred yards from the wall the engine stopped. Slower, slower, slower grew the pace. The 'plane came over the wall with not a foot to spare. Already Mollie stood in the middle of the Queen Anne garden. Then there came a shout from the direction of the chapel door. Desmond turned his head for an instant. He saw Lord Sincourt, followed by Woolf, rushing towards Mollie. Perks also glanced at them for an instant.

"They can't do it!" he exclaimed. "Be ready, sir! Now!"

Desmond seized Mollie by the arm. She sprang at the same moment. She was safe by his side. The 'plane shot upwards at full speed and cleared the further wall with six feet to spare.

"Thank you, Perks—a fine piece of work," Desmond said.

Then he whispered in Mollie's ear, "Now I have you safe, my darling."

"We are not out of the wood yet," Mollie answered, casting a frightened glance behind her. "Oh, Desmond, look at them in the front of the house! They are running to the starting strip—that other man running is Mr. Woolf's planeur. They are coming after us in the 'plane."

"A stern chase is a long chase," Desmond answered reassuringly as he looked through his glasses. "We shall have at least seven miles start, anyhow. What's she making, Perks?"

"Two hundred and fifty-one, sir."

"Good—we've nothing to fear. If they do all they can we shall be out of sight in half an hour."

"I heard Mr. Woolf tell my father that his new 'plane was built for racing," Mollie said.

Both Desmond and Mollie kept their glasses fixed on Woolf's machine. As Desmond had said would be the case, they had quite seven miles start.

Desmond expected to see Woolf's 'plane quickly drop behind. He watched it steadily for two or three minutes. At last he said:

"You were right about the thing being a racer, Mollie. She seems quite as speedy as mine."

"Do you think they will catch us, Desmond?" she asked, turning pale at the thought.

"I am quite sure they will not unless they have any fire-arm on board. If it comes to the worst I shall pepper their gear with my Colt till something or another gets smashed up enough to bring them to the ground. That cardboard box has two hundred and forty-three cartridges in it, and my Colt the remaining seven."

Just then a sharp gust from the south met the 'plane. The wind strengthened rapidly. Their speed dropped to a hundred, seventy-five, fifty miles an hour. Stronger yet grew the gale. Forty miles an hour—thirty—twenty—ten. At only this low speed they battled against the wind for nearly half an hour.

Woolf's 'plane showed itself a far better wind traveller than the other. Ever since the gale sprang up it had gained steadily. At length no more than three hundred yards separated the two.

"What do you think now, Perks?" Desmond asked.

"The one question is, sir: Must you go on to London?"

"It is not strictly necessary."

"Then the only thing, sir, is to turn and run before the gale. It's as likely as not we shall be as much better than her with the wind as she is better than us against it."

"What do you think, Mollie?"

"Please turn, Desmond. Anything—*anything* to escape from them."

" Then bring her round, Perks, please."

"She'll tilt a bit badly coming round, sir, so mind your balance—and you, too, my lady. The sharper we turn, the more we gain; I wont't go up to a really dangerous angle. Now mind, please.''

The 'plane swept round on what seemed to Mollie a terribly dangerous tilt, and shot away before the gale at a speed of not less than three hundred miles an hour. Woolf's planeur did not dare to take so sharp a turn. Desmond's 'plane had gained nearly a couple of miles before the other settled down again to a straight course.

On they sped, pursuer and pursued. As Perks had thought probable, Desmond's proved itself the speedier 'plane down wind. It gained steadily on the other. Mollie's spirits—ever since Woolf's 'plane began to gain she had kept tightly hold of Desmond's arm —revived in a wonderful manner.

Thus, at a speed approximating three hundred miles an hour, they raced northward for some two hundred and fifty miles. Woolf's 'plane was by now some seven miles behind. It was at this point that Perks said :

" I've kept from mentioning it as long as I could, sir, but I'm getting anxious about the petrol. If my calculations are right, we can't keep on the wing for more than about half an hour longer. Do you mind looking at the tank, sir ? "

Desmond looked. The tank was nearly empty.

" You must not be frightened, Mollie," he said. " They have beaten us in the race, but they've not got you yet. I think I can see the winning move."

Mollie did not answer. She only clung to his arm again, and watched the 'plane behind them.

Then Desmond said :

" I know this country well, Perks—I've shot over it half a dozen seasons. Bear a trifle to the left now. Just over those hills six miles away there's a level strip of moor without heather. We'll drop there. I will point out the spot when we're over the hills."

Quickly afterwards the 'plane was over the hills and gliding down to the spot indicated by Desmond. Directly it came to a standstill Desmond handed Mollie out. Then, giving his Colt to Perks, he said :

" Keep near the 'plane, Perks. If you have half an opportunity, take the petrol from their tank and put it into ours. If you are caught at it, fire two or three shots through their tank, close to the bottom. Under any circumstances they must not be allowed to get on the wing again."

" I quite understand, sir."

Desmond drew Mollie aside, and led her to a spot some fifty yards from where the 'plane lay at rest.

"You must do exactly as I tell you, Mollie," he said. "If I raise no objection to your getting into Woolf's 'plane, you must get in. We cannot tell yet how things will turn out."

As he spoke Woolf's machine appeared over the hills. It glided down, and came to a standstill not twenty yards from the other.

The three men sprang out and advanced together towards Desmond and Mollie.

"You can take your choice, Desmond Shorthouse," said Lord Sincourt, on coming within speaking distance, "whether you give up my daughter to me quietly or whether you make a fight of it. You've made a sporting run, but the game is up. We are three to one, remember—at least I suppose your seven-stone planeur doesn't count," he added, as he turned and glanced at Perks, who, his hands in his pockets, stood critically looking on.

What Desmond did then literally astonished him; or rather, I ought to say, it was the way in which he did it, the way in which he displayed oratorical powers, his possession of which had hitherto never been even suspected, that astonished him; for the lengthy allocution he made was a part of his scheme. In response to Lord Sincourt's words, he launched into a vehement speech of appeal to the three men standing before him. Gesticulating wildly in order further to emphasise what he said, now raising his voice almost to a shout, now lowering it as he dwelt on some pathetic point, he kept them spell-bound under his torrent of words. With hand pointed to the heavens he appealed wildly to Lord Sincourt to consider his daughter's feelings, her future, what life would be to her with a man she did not love; he appealed just as wildly to Woolf to think what he would be doing in marrying a woman who did not love him—a woman who thus married could have nothing but unhappiness before her—he appealed even yet more wildly to Woolf's planeur to take his side, to fight for him, to do what any *man* would do to prevent a woman being torn from the one she loved and wished to marry, and married to the man she hated. None of them could put in a word against Desmond's impassioned stream of verbiage. It was not till he noticed Perks strolling aimlessly about near his 'plane that at last he lapsed into silence.

"You ought to be in Parliament, Shorthouse," Lord Sincourt said, with undisguised sarcasm. "This sort of thing is rather wasted out here. If you have really quite finished, we will say good-bye."

"Will nothing, Lord Sincourt," Desmond said more calmly, "turn you from this atrocious thing you are doing?"

"Nothing in the world."

"Nor you, Mr. Woolf?"

"Certainly not."

"Nor you?" he continued, turning to the planeur. "I'll make a final appeal to you to help me."

"I'm my master's servant," the man answered, gruffly.

"Then, Mollie, we must part. I suppose I may at least have the pleasure of seeing you into Mr. Woolf's 'plane?"

"Oh, no objection at all," said Woolf, with a grin.

The party walked in silence toward Woolf's 'plane. Desmond handed Mollie in while the others took their seats.

"All right," said Woolf.

The planeur touched the lever. The 'plane ran feebly along the ground for half a dozen yards, and then stopped.

"You'll all have to get out, please," the planeur said. "I know what's wrong—she's done it once before at starting."

All left the 'plane again. The planeur turned up his sleeves, and crept underneath. Lord Sincourt and Woolf stooped down and peered at him. Desmond and Mollie strolled towards the other 'plane—at least they strolled till within ten yards of it, and then they spurted for all they were worth. The instant they were in it the 'plane rushed forward and rose in the air. Desmond turned and waved a farewell to Lord Sincourt and Woolf.

"All is plain sailing now, my darling," he whispered in Mollie's ear as he slipped his arm round her waist and drew her to him. "The marriage shall be by special licence to-morrow."

And so it was.

STRANGE STORIES OF SPORT

XXXIX.—THE REVENGE OF KASIMOTO

BY GEOFFREY WILLIAMS

"How ripping this is!" murmured Stephen Rising sleepily from the depth of his big folding chair. "Now I know what a pipe of peace really is. I feel too angelic to quarrel even with my worst enemy. Though," he went on after a pause, "I should be hard put to it to name him. I don't seem to run to enemies somehow."

"How about yourself?" growled his companion as he bent forward to kick the log fire and send a shower of sparks floating up into the clear darkness. "Most of us can do ourselves enough harm without calling in the assistance of outsiders."

"What a gloomy chap you are, Lane!" cried the other, waking up slightly. "Beyond boring myself at times when alone, I don't think I've done myself much damage. But do try to be cheerful. Ever since we started on this trip to Lake Garika you've grown more and more captious and dismal, till now nothing will please you, and yet we've had a grand six weeks and the best shooting I ever dreamed of. What is the matter with you?"

The elder man kicked the fire again by way of reply and relapsed into a thoughtful silence which, judging by his expression, did not appear to be raising his spirits.

There certainly did not seem to be any very good reason for his depression. A comparatively junior policeman in the Central African Service, he had been selected over the heads of several others to settle the disputed question of the marriage of Jarili, the daughter of one of the most important men in Garikaland. He had been allowed to choose his own assistant in the person of Stephen Rising, and the problem, as he found on arrival, was quite easy of solution. Jarili had been taken as wife, in full accordance with native custom, by her cousin Saro, and the attempt of Mashami, chief of Garikaland, to take her himself was obviously a high-handed proceeding without a shred of justification. The case was to be decided the next morning, and the way was clear; yet Rudolph Lane continued to glower into the red-hot coals as though a mighty and distasteful decision was before him.

The truth of the matter was that Lane was in desperate straits for money. When he left Headquarters a cataclysm seemed inevitable, but now a way of escape had opened out, a way that could only be taken at the expense of honour and self-respect.

Rudolph Lane was not a man with strong feelings on these subjects, but even to the most lax and casual the first step down comes hard, and though he felt already that the end was inevitable, the struggle was a bitter one.

He had risen that morning troubled indeed and anxious, but honest in thought and act, yet in one short hour everything was changed. For Mashami had come round directly after breakfast, ostensibly to put his side of the case, but really, as Lane found when they were alone, to make an outrageous proposal.

Mashami's store of ivory was well known throughout that district, and Lane now knew that if he should give his decision in favour of Mashami and against his own conviction, enough of that ivory would find its way into his possession to remove fully and entirely all the money troubles that had poisoned his life. He knew the ropes well enough to anticipate little difficulty in disposing of the stuff, and though he had refused indignantly, Mashami had gone away content, knowing that his cause was won. Lane's eyes had been a sufficient answer.

So Lane meditated and Stephen smoked till the collapse of a charred log woke the latter from dreams very different from those of his companion, and warned him that the hour was late.

"Come," he yawned, slipping his pipe into his pocket. "It's time we turned in if we want to be up for the great decision to-morrow."

"Yes," said Lane heavily. "Good-night," and he turned slowly and wearily into his tent.

" There's something up," murmured Stephen to his departing back. " I wonder what it is. However, it's no use worrying about it. I suppose I shall find out some time ! "—which he did sooner than he expected, and with considerable surprise.

When they arrived next morning at the place fixed upon for the consideration of the great case, they found fully half the tribe assembled in long impassive lines, waiting to hear the decision. For feeling ran high over the matter, and a large party sympathised strongly with Kasimoto, the father of Jarili, who was much liked by the more moderate and law-abiding of the population.

Lane took his place on the raised seat provided for him, with Stephen by his side, and gazed out over the throng with a face so expressionless and set that Stephen felt more than ever certain that there was something seriously wrong with him. Witness succeeded witness with their long-winded dissertations upon side issues after the native custom, repeating volumes of irrelevant matter from which the Judge must extract the few points bearing on the situation ; and as the long morning wore on Stephen gradually awoke to the fact that Lane asked no questions save such as were calculated to prejudice the case of Kasimoto, harried no witnesses save those supporting him. It seemed impossible ; and yet there was no mistaking the trend of criticism, and Stephen grew cold as he realised that a great injustice was going to be perpetrated. It was terrible to sit there and see it coming, to know that every native present, no matter which way his sympathies lay, would recognise that the unfaltering justice of the White Man had failed at last, and yet to be able to do nothing. More than once he whispered to Lane a suggestion for a question which would obviously discredit the testimony of some witness for Mashami ; but Lane turned a deaf ear, and went on his way as though he were being forced to speak by some influence altogether outside himself.

At length the interminable stream of asseveration and contradiction drew to a close, leaving no doubt whatever as to where the right lay, in spite of Lane's ingenious attempts to twist the testimony of Kasimoto's witnesses ; and, after both Mashami and his adversary had summed up their respective cases in eloquent and impassioned harangues, silence fell, and the great assembly waited breathlessly for the decision.

As the crucial moment drew near Lane showed signs of agitation, but when he stood up to deliver judgment he was as cold and calm as ever, and Stephen began to cherish a wild hope that his extraordinary conduct while hearing the case had been due only to a desire to give the weaker side a fair hearing. But this hope was soon shattered. In a few terse sentences

Lane summed up the various points at issue, showing the same unaccountable bias as before, and ended by declaring his verdict in favour of Mashami.

The pronouncement was received in dead silence. Kasimoto showed no sign of what he felt, and at a wave of Mashami's spear the long lines of watching warriors melted away, leaving the two alone on their raised dais. Stephen remained for a few moments staring at the other as he stood, grim and unapproachable, still in the attitude in which he had given judgment; and then, realising that they were bound to endure each other's society for the long weeks of the return trip, and that anything he might say could only make an awkward situation worse, he rose and remarked coldly: "Well, now it's all over we had better get back and have some lunch."

In silence they returned together to their camp, but as they drew near the tent Stephen saw a pile of ivory lying beside it which had not been there when they left in the morning.

"Hullo, where did those come from?" he asked quickly.

Lane scowled at him for a moment, then, "What's that to do with you?" he snapped, and passed on into the tent.

Stephen looked after him in astonishment for a moment, and then he saw. The whole disgraceful bargain became as clear to him as if he had been present at its making, and Lane's biased questions and unjust decision were a mystery no longer.

He shook his head sadly as he moved off to see to their lunch. "What a pity!" he muttered half aloud as he went. "What a grievous pity! And to have to stand by and see it all happen without being able to raise a finger to alter it is the hardest part of all." For the two had been long enough together for Stephen to realise that Lane's character was such that any interference would only anger him, and cause him to go his own way for good or ill more firmly than ever.

But however good your resolutions may be, it is difficult to behave under such circumstances as though nothing was amiss, and for the next hour or two the atmosphere was sufficiently strained for Stephen to welcome with heartfelt relief the sudden appearance of the injured Kasimoto to break their solitude *à deux*.

It seemed probable, however, that this unexpected call portended trouble. Lane's expression showed that he expected as much, and it is hard to say which was the more astonished and relieved when Kasimoto's salutation showed that he came with quite friendly intent.

He made no reference to the events of the morning beyond stating impassively that the white man's word was law and should be obeyed, and immediately passed on to what appeared to be the main object of his visit.

"You have worked hard," he said, and there was no trace of sarcasm in his voice, "to give us justice, and we would show you some return before you leave us. It is for me, as the loser in the quarrel, to prove that there is no wish to dispute your wisdom," and if, as Stephen thought, his eye fell as he spoke on the pile of ivory behind the tent, he gave no sign of surprise or understanding. "Therefore I would show you sport before you leave us. In the reeds of Lake Garika are certain great buck, the like of which you have not seen, nor has any white man yet been told of them. Few know the paths which lead to where they lie, but if you please I will be your guide to-morrow, and you shall have sport which will give you cause to remember Garika and its people."

Lane thought a moment, and then looked up.

"We will come," he said shortly, and at his words Kasimoto saluted silently and retired.

"Well, I'm hanged!" remarked Stephen, in astonishment. "Talk about coals of fire! But I don't quite like it. It isn't natural or human that he should be so much attached to us, with that wretched girl probably crying in his hut at this very moment."

Lane winced slightly, but took no other notice of this thrust.

"I don't like it either," he said slowly, "but it will never do to show it. I know these people, and I believe we may have trouble. I wish I hadn't brought you into it. If I were you I'd stay at home to-morrow."

But this seemed to Stephen a quite unnecessary and alarmist view, and he refused to hear anything more of staying behind. After the first shock of surprise the story of the strange animals seized his imagination, and the uneasiness he had felt at first soon faded away. He was reminded of it again that night when Yola, one of his boys, who had been standing by when the invitation was given, came and begged him not to go, saying that he knew the country well, and feared there was danger.

But Stephen's first inquiry was whether he had heard of the beast in the reeds, and when Yola admitted that he believed they really did exist, he would hear no more of dangers which could not be defined.

With Rudolph Lane, however, it was different. He knew native tribes and their ways from long and close association, and knew that injuries are not overlooked in the meek and Christian spirit shown by Kasimoto. For many hours that night he lay and thought over the situation, speculating on the various lines on which Kasimoto's taste in revenge might run. Whatever happened Lane was convinced that nothing would be done openly, or in such a way that it could be traced, and before he slept he determined to be well on his guard for every moment of the coming day.

In the morning they were up well before the sun, a very necessary proceeding if decent sport is to be expected in Central Africa, but in the thick blankety darkness that comes before dawn in those parts, half night and half wet mist, the huddled forms of Kasimoto's followers were to be seen, a group of shadowy indefinite figures, while near the fire stood Kasimoto himself, ghostly and impassive.

A few minutes sufficed to swallow a hurried breakfast of porridge and cocoa, and it was still dark when the shooting party tramped off on their way to the lake and its possibilities.

Lake Garika, it should be explained, is a strange and unusual place, and far from being the sheet of water that its name would imply. Legends existed among the tribes on its borders that in some remote past clear water had stretched from bank to bank, but of this there can be no certainty. Now, at any rate, water there is none. As far as the eye can reach stretches a dark formless expanse of reeds and papyrus, not even marshy underfoot except in heavy rain; and what lies beyond them, whether more reeds, water, or dry land that once formed islands in the great lake, no man knows, though many and various are the legends and rumours. For reasons of their own, even the natives living on the banks will not plunge far into that sea of reeds, and it is seldom that they will even enter it at all.

Stephen Rising had, of course, known of this for some time, and therefore, as he trudged along in the first breaking of the dawn, he felt that his day's shooting would probably be worth remembering, whether the strange buck existed or no.

The camp had been pitched at no great distance from the lake, and the sun was only just rising over the reeds as they reached the edge, and halted for a few moments before plunging into the unknown.

The scene was not exactly beautiful, but it was none the less worth looking at, and both Lane and Stephen stood awhile in silence, watching the great ball of the sun springing from behind its green coverlet. The immense area of vivid green stretching away as far as the eye could reach was vastly impressive. The monotony of dead level was for the moment broken by rolling ragged clouds of mist that shifted and changed as they shrank and wavered before the power of the sun. In the almost imperceptible morning breeze the tall feathery papyrus heads shivered, and the reeds rustled as they swayed lightly to and fro, giving the place an uncanny air of life.

Lane evidently felt this strongly, for he started sharply from the abstraction into which he had fallen, and ejaculated, "Come, let's make a start. If we look at the place much longer it will get on our nerves, and we shan't go in at all." Stephen agreed with emphasis, and they plunged down the slight slope and into the reeds at the heels of Kasimoto, without further ado. For the next two hours they wandered along paths that seemed interminable and that led to nowhere, objectless winding tracks, apparently made by large game of some kind, probably waterbuck. The eternal reeds and papyrus, rustling and nodding far above their heads, cut off all view, and it was impossible to form any idea of where they were, or how far from the shore.

"Good Heavens, what a ghastly place to be lost in!" began Stephen at last, but an imperative gesture from Kasimoto stopped him sharply. Staring in the direction of their guide's outstretched arm they waited breathlessly until at length, in a place where the reeds seemed a little thinner, they saw something move, and in another instant a large buck emerged into the path, and was gone in a flash before either could fire. "By George!" whispered Stephen excitedly, "it *is* a new buck! There is nothing recorded with horns like that." But there was no time for discussion. Obeying Kasimoto's whispered instructions, they hurried along on the spoor of the retreating beast, whose slaughter meant such triumph for them on their return to Headquarters. Stephen forgot the great injustice of the day before, and even Lane forgot his caution and his resolutions for a hot exciting half-hour, during which they passed swiftly and noiselessly along the green shady paths, breathless and eager. Suddenly Lane stopped. "Hallo!" he cried, "where are the others?" Stephen looked behind him—not a man was following—gun-bearers, water-carriers, everyone had melted away, and they and Kasimoto were alone in this vast sea of reeds.

In surprise he turned again, only to see Kasimoto flying up the path at a pace they could not hope to equal. In an instant all was clear, and he swung up his rifle and covered their flying guide. But before he could pull the trigger his arm was knocked up, Lane's voice hissed in his ear, "You fool, you'll kill the man!" and in another instant he had brought down the runaway with a neat shot in the leg. "Quite a good shot at a running object," he remarked calmly as they walked up to the prostrate Kasimoto, "but it was a near thing. If you had killed him we should have been no better off than if he'd got away. Now let's see what the beauty has to say for himself. Well, my friend," he went on, "as your little plot hasn't quite come off, perhaps you'll show us the way home without any fuss."

"Never," groaned Kasimoto. "You have dishonoured me and all my house, and you shall pay the penalty. Oh yes, I shall die here, too; but what is that to me who have nothing but scorn to return to? And death will come quickly to me, but not to you."

"Oh no, my good fellow," Lane replied calmly, "not at all. I'm going to make it so unpleasant for you that you'll have to show us the way. Stephen, you had better go a little way off, you are too young for what I am going to do."

"What," began Stephen, looking from one to the other in surprise, "what are—oh, you are going to torture him! You—you can't do such things in these days, you know."

"Can't I?" replied Lane grimly. "Would you rather sit here and watch him die and then slowly follow suit, or will you leave me to get us out of this mess? Now clear off as I've already told you, and don't come back till I call."

Stephen went off reluctantly, in obedience to a will and purpose stronger than his own, to spend the longest quarter of an hour he had ever known. No sound came to his ears, though his nerves were strained to such a pitch that all his senses were preternaturally acute, and when at length the promised summons broke the spell, he sighed with a relief greater than he had known for years.

"Come along," cried Lane, "I don't think he'll give us any more trouble; but time is short, and though his leg isn't broken we shall have to help him along. He's a bit shaky for several reasons."

"What have you done to him?" asked Stephen as he came up.

"If I were you I wouldn't ask any more questions than I could help. It will give you less to dream of afterwards. Now help me carry him along," and Lane leant down and lifted up the inert figure of the wretched Kasimoto, who seemed to have become an old man in that quarter of an hour.

"What a brute you must be!" exclaimed Stephen in spite of himself, as he looked at the wreck before him.

"If you are so particular you had better stay here," returned Lane savagely. "I did my best to spare you as much as I could. Do you think I enjoyed doing what I have done, you idiot?"

There seemed nothing to be said to this, and for over an hour they plodded on in silence, till they began to feel as if they were in a new and original purgatory, doomed to walk for ever beneath endless reeds and papyrus, along paths that began and ended in nothingness. But the dull monotony of their progress was suddenly and strangely broken.

For miles Kasimoto had struggled along between them in spite of his wound, which was not severe, and helped by his captors as much as the narrowness of the paths admitted. He seemed perfectly resigned to circumstances, to be sunk in a sullen impassive calm which effectually concealed his bitter anger and determination for revenge, and the fact that he was biding his time for action. Presently they began to pass through a belt where the reeds were taller and greener than elsewhere, and here he chose the moment for the attempt he had been meditating during all that weary return journey. With a sudden spring he seized Lane, who was in front, round the waist, and before Stephen had time to realise what was happening, had leapt with him into the long green stems beside the path. They crashed down together on the ground a few yards from the bank, and Stephen noticed with relief that Lane instantly freed himself from his enemy's embrace without difficulty, and began to struggle to his feet. But even as he heaved a sigh of relief a strange thing happened. With an odd crackly sound the apparently solid earth began to sink beneath the double weight. Right up to the edge of the path it sank slowly and steadily, and Lane, who was now standing up, turned pale as he realised what was going on. He tried to spring towards safety, but with the effort he only accelerated the subsidence, and in an instant was submerged up to the waist. Stephen frantically held out his gun, but it was too short, and Lane's outstretched hands failed to reach it. For an instant they stared at each other in speechless despair, and then Kasimoto's voice broke the silence.

"You cannot escape," he cried, with a shrill laugh of satisfied malice. "The floor of the lake on which you have been walking is nothing but a crust of dead reeds, and beneath it is bottomless liquid mud. The buck know where to walk with safety, but elsewhere it is death to tread. I am glad to go since you go with me. It is a——" and his words died away in a choking gurgle as he sank for ever beneath the still black mud, that now showed plain where so short a while before the graceful papyrus had shivered in the breeze overhead.

Stephen turned faint with horror, but he pulled himself together as he heard Lane's voice, calm with the calmness of despair.

"It is just," he said, "and native justice is not tempered with mercy. I don't believe in theatrical last words, but send back that ivory if you ever find your way back, and try to undo the harm I have done."

"Can nothing be tried?" cried Stephen wildly. "Can't you think of something?"

"There is nothing possible," returned Lane, "there are no reeds to cling to, they have gone down with the rest. And, after all, my end may be better than yours, at any rate it's quicker."

As he ceased speaking, Stephen hid his face in his hands, and when he dared to look again all was over, and the slimy black pool was winking at him in the sunlight. How long he lay there stunned and sick with horror he never knew. Vaguely he grasped the fact that to wander on alone through that tangled maze of paths leading to nowhere would only exhaust his strength; but he was far too unstrung to attempt to form any plan of action. The shadows of evening came stealing down through the reeds, and the night breeze began to whisper strangely above his head, while a thousand weird noises broke the stillness that had reigned throughout the day. One of the great buck he had been so keen to shoot when he started off in the morning—so long, long ago!—stepped out into the path, stared at him inquisitively awhile, and then vanished into the shadows; but still Stephen never moved, and when a voice suddenly spoke in his ear he jumped as if he had been shot. Looking up he saw the boy Yola who had tried to dissuade him from this ill-fated expedition.

"Where did you come from?" he inquired dully.

"I knew there would be trouble," answered the boy, "so I followed behind the rest as you did not tell me to come. When all returned but you three I guessed what had happened, for I know the lake, and I followed and tracked you here. It was easy. The others are there. Is it not so?" and he pointed to the pool of mud that gleamed sullenly in the moonlight.

"Yes," returned Stephen, shuddering. "Now take me out of this place, and never speak of it again."

The walk back to the camp was a nightmare, but it came to an end at last as such things do, and when Stephen had recovered sufficiently from the shock he sent back the ivory and reversed the famous judgment that had had such a terrible sequel, before he left the shores of Lake Garika for ever.

The girl Jarili is happy with her lawful husband, and Mashami soon found others to console him for his disappointment. Few remember the great case and its consequences save Stephen himself, who still dreams of Rudolph Lane as he last saw him, slowly sinking into the pitiless depths of the accursed lake.

STRANGE STORIES OF SPORT

XL.—THE MYSTERY OF YMER'S DEEP

BY JOHN SANDERSON

It was Time's morning
When Ymer lived :
There was no sand, no sea,
Nor cooling billows ;
Earth there was none,
No lofty heaven ;
No spot of living green ;
Only a deep profound.
THE ELDER EDDA.

IT was past two o'clock on Lake Ulva. Stretched in the stern of a boat, Vernon Gwilt, thoroughly enjoying himself, lay smoking and idly waiting for the ripple which would come with the afternoon breeze.

The last breath of wind had fallen as usual about mid-day, and, so far as he was concerned, there was really nothing to do but wait for its return. All around the exasperatingly glassy surface of the water was broken by the " plop " of the rising grayling and trout. These fish were comparatively safe in "plopping" for the present, but in the bottom of the boat near the bow lay a gleaming mass of mixed silver and gold.

Frederic, the boatman, small, ruddy—his gentle Scandinavian weather-beaten face hard set with the lust to kill—was casting assiduously over the distant fish as they rose. He was fishing, of course, with wet fly, and Gwilt watched him admiringly for a time. How the line shot out in the motionless air, as if propelled by a force within itself! He watched the upper fold of the curved line rolling itself out almost parallel to the lower, and the flies finally alighting upon the surface of the water one after the other in beautiful sequence from the bobfly to the tail.

Then would come a gentle drag of the flies through the water, not by any motion of the rod, but simply by drawing in the line slowly with one hand. Then, sometimes, there would come a gurgle, then a furious splash, and the rod would be bending to the rushes of the captured fish. But this sort of thing, as the best angler knows, cannot be kept up long, and at length even Frederic's enthusiasm had to give way to sheer fatigue, and he sat down perspiring in the bows of the boat which lay almost motionless on the waters of the great lake.

"Frederic," said Gwilt, suddenly, after a long silence, "I suppose nothing has been heard of Sigrid this year? No news from Paris yet to anyone here?"

"Ah," replied Frederick, sadly, "you are thinking of her still!"

Gwilt uttered a short laugh at Frederic's answer and said nothing. Frederic had once been to England, having been engaged by some English proprietor for a year as a gillie. He had hated the country and had come back to his beloved Stuefenheim in three months' time. But, being a sportsman to his finger-tips, he had a respect for the English sportsman in general and for Vernon Gwilt in particular, amounting almost to idolatry. When he saw a stray Christiania angler on the lake, he spoke of him contemptuously as "Norwegian trash."

After another silence, Gwilt began again.

"I suppose, Frederic," he said, "you never at any time in your life made an attempt to get outside of the days of the week—into the eighth day? Do you know that that is what Sigrid did when she went to Paris?"

"There are seven days in the week," said Frederic, "and no more; and, of course, it is all nonsense to try to get outside of them." Then, after a pause, he went on, with a strange deprecating smile, "The people here say that in Ymer's Deep, in the Molma River, time stands still altogether, and that nothing ever happens there. They say that it is outside the world; but no one has ever been down there, so we cannot tell."

"What are you talking about, Frederic?" said Gwilt, hastily raising his head to look at the speaker. There was something so unexpected and strange in the serious way in which Frederic had spoken. Gwilt's purely metaphorical question had received a startlingly concrete reply. "You don't really believe that ancient legend, do you?" he asked, curiously.

"I say I do not know," said Frederic, shortly, "no one even can tell. From the top of the fall one can see far, far away only a little of the dark water below. There are fish in Ymer's Deep; but no man has ever fished there or ever will."

Vernon Gwilt's thoughts were back again to the scene which had suggested his whimsical question to Frederic.

He saw himself once more standing, that evening three years ago, just before he left for England, on the top of the stone steps leading to the door of Stuefenheim Farm. Seated on the lowest step, a young woman, Sigrid Stuefenheim, was giving a reading lesson to a child. He himself was waiting impatiently till it should be over. He could hear once more little Etty, in childish treble, reading her lesson from the Norwegian reading book :—

"There are seven days in the week—Sunday, Monday, Tuesday, Wednesday, Thursday, Friday, Saturday—and then we are at the beginning of another week" And then he could see once more Sigrid's scornful eyes, as she glanced up at him and said "Just the life for you, eh, Mr. Gwilt? Plod, plod, plod, and then we are at the beginning of another week. No, thank you! for me! There are at least eight days in the week for those who know how to find them. Etty, you have done very well; you may go off now to bed."

"There is only one way, Sigrid," he had said, "for me to get outside the days of the week." And she had blushed furiously, and then, like a fool, when, of course, it was hopeless, he had poured out his story, and had been refused, just as his friend Halstan had been before. The next day, Frederic, with the fat yellow pony, had taken him down in two days to the little steamer on the fiord. And the following year, when he came back to Stuefenheim, Sigrid was gone, and lost sight of entirely. She was a niece only of the Stuefenheims, and, having inherited some means of her own, she had set out upon that eternal search of youth since time began—for the week's eighth day. And for this purpose she had gone to Paris.

From these thoughts Vernon Gwilt was recalled by Frederic's voice. "The breeze is coming now, Mr. Gwilt," he said, with his eyes first on the birches of the little island hard by, and then on the quivering glitter of the surface of the water gradually widening from the western shore of the lake.

Gwilt mechanically stretched out his hand for the rod to prepare for the fray.

"What time will Mr. Halstan be back to-night?" he asked.

"He will be there when we get back," replied Frederic.

"I suppose he will not bring a wife with him this time from Christiania?" said Gwilt again.

"No," replied Frederic, beginning to pull the head of the boat round, "I think Mr. Halstan is like you. He does not forget. I hope Sigrid will never come back at all, for neither of you will ever yield to the other. I know you both. Here is the breeze at last."

*   *   *   *   *

The farm at Stuefenheim belongs, of course, to the Stuefenheims. As elsewhere in Norway—probably the most democratic country in Europe—the peasant proprietors have territorial names. A Norwegian equivalent of "de" and "von" is not in use, but these farmers trace their descent back through hundreds of years, and they marry almost entirely in those districts within their own class. The Stuefenheims lived a quiet and frugal existence far from the outer world, and the only variation in the monotony of their lives—and that a recent one—was the occasional accommodation of exploring strangers from England or Christiania who might chance to hit upon this secluded valley of the Molmadal amongst the high mountains. Vernon Gwilt and Albert Halstan had been the only two regular visitors year after year.

In the ravine in front of the farm, the waters of the Molma were preparing for the first of their desperate plunges through the riven entrails of mountains downwards to the plain where dwell the salmon-fishers from England, and where the tourists from the steamers disport themselves ashore. The salmon, like the tourists, only come up as far as the first waterfall, and that is many mountainous miles away. Above that fall, the country rises in masses of stupendous rock formed into terraces, until at length is reached the marvellous landscape in front of Stuefenheim Farm, where outcropping rock studded with firs gave the appearance of a huge overcrowded and long-disused burial-place of giants.

When Vernon Gwilt entered the parlour of the farm with its huge stone fireplace in one corner, Albert Halstan was walking feverishly up and down the room. When he saw Gwilt, who came forward with an eager face to greet his old fishing companion, he accepted his hand sullenly and his hard face did not relax for a moment. Gwilt noticed at once the transformation in his looks. He looked pale and almost haggard, and there was a strange light in his eyes which he evidently sought to hide by avoiding Gwilt's gaze. The latter realised with a pang of dismay that it looked uncommonly like the light of hate; and he instantly stopped short in his greeting. The two men confronted each other for a moment in silence.

"Sigrid," said Halstan, shortly, "is coming back to-morrow."

There was a pause. This information suddenly launched at him in this way by his friend was so unexpected that it seemed to paralyse for the moment the function of Gwilt's mind.

"Sigrid," he repeated, mechanically, "is coming back to-morrow." And then, recovering himself, and with a flash in his eye which met Halstan's squarely, he demanded: "To stay? To live here?"

Halstan nodded. "A telegram has just come," he said. Again there was a silence between the two rivals. Halstan moved to the front of the great fireplace and stood gazing at Gwilt. "I have been thinking," he said at length in a low tense voice, "that we two cannot remain together in the farm when she is here. That would be a brutal thing for her. One of us must go."

Vernon Gwilt laughed savagely, "Yes," he said, "one must go. I'm glad you realise it." And he stared truculently in Halstan's face. His blood was singing in his ears. His whole being was roused with the primal passion to battle for the woman he had chosen.

"There needn't be bloodshed, you know," said Halstan, sourly, and controlling himself with all his force to the conduct he had evidently planned. "The girl, so far as we know, cares for neither of us. We have both already been sent away with the basket. And we are both going to try again. Very well. I'd toss you for the first chance; but I find I can't face the mere spin of a coin. It's too sudden. I'll fish you for it to-morrow. Whoever gets the least weight of fish in the Molma shall leave Stuefenheim for a month and come back for his chance alone after that. I've thought it all out," he went on, after a pause. "The alternative is a hell on earth for Sigrid when she comes home. So you had better agree if you have any sense of decency in the matter at all."

Vernon Gwilt all the time was realising the restraint that Halstan was putting upon himself in making this extraordinary proposal. And he felt he was right in what he said. For both to remain would be hateful; and, after all, what was to be decided was not the right to the girl, but only to the first chance. As Halstan had said, it was only decency that one of them should give way to the other for a while. Any fair way of deciding it would do. "I agree," he said at last, "on the condition that Sigrid be told that the loser is expected at Stuefenheim in a month's time."

"Very well," said Halstan, "let us start at six o'clock. And both must be back here by eight o'clock, and Frederick shall decide the weighing. I'll toss you for who goes up the river." And it fell that Vernon Gwilt should go down. And so they parted for the night.

*   *   *   *   *

Long before six o'clock on the following morning Vernon Gwilt had found himself upon the rocky banks of the Molma just below the farm. He had never closed his eyes all night, and his state of nervous tension whilst the hours passed had been almost unendurable. Like most Norwegian rivers, excellent for salmon in the lower reaches, the Molma afforded poor prospects for other sport owing to its rocky channel and consequent poor feeding grounds for trout. And Gwilt knew that with the prospect of under a dozen medium-sized trout or grayling to each rod, a single half-pound fish might decide the issue of the day.

As soon as the agreed hour had come, he had begun feverishly casting his flies down stream with a long line, searching every corner of the great rock basins which mainly constitute the bed of the river. His success had been deplorably scanty, and the thought that the day was now already half over, and the anticipation of what Halstan might have done in comparison, gave him a sick sense of failure. For the first time he stopped to looked about him. Around on all sides the rocks of the plateau were crumpled and folded, twisted and dislocated. Some, covered with dense herbage, rose in great fortress-like structures, whilst gigantic boulders lay littering the whole surface of the land. It was a scene of cosmic destruction; a place which suggested most a battlefield of Ragnorak, the primal conflict between the chaotic powers of giants and of gods.

At this point Vernon Gwilt had captured exactly five small trout averaging perhaps half a pound—a catch which at this rate of progress he could scarcely now hope to double by eight o'clock. A dull despair had settled upon his heart as he crouched behind the boulders and drove his cast across the tail of every stream. The banks, however, were becoming almost impossible of approach, and Gwilt began to realise that he was nearing the great series of cataracts by which the Molma tore its way towards the distant valley below. And already upon his ear there sounded the dull roar of the waterfall of Ymer's Deep. And, with a pang like a knife in his heart, there flashed upon his mind the thought that Frederic had some time or other said that *there were fish in Ymer's Deep;* and they would be big fish probably, for there no man had ever cast a line. And then his teeth met and his jaw bulged a little at the corners, and Vernon Gwilt swore to himself that in Ymer's Deep he would fish that day, though it should thereby become his last on earth.

He sat down and took off his cast and wound up his line. Then he took his rod to pieces and placed it in its cover. With a stout cord he fastened the rod and landing-net to the belt of his creel and made his way to a point to the left of the waterfall where, having doubled a castellated rock which in appearance might have been the abode of a race of giants, he obtained a partial view of the yawning deep below. There he stood and gazed into the void. On his right, from above, the Molma poured its raging waters over the precipice which on all sides seemed to form the walls of an irregularly-shaped chasm, perhaps a hundred yards wide. At least a thousand feet below, he caught sight on one side of the greenish gleam of waters touched faintly by the rays of the midday sun; on the other he saw nothing but the blackness of the abyss. And there came into his mind the strange legend of the district. Ymer's Deep was believed to be all that remained of the great timeless void, Ginungagap, out of which the first being, Ymer, took shape and substance, and into which his body had again been dragged by the powers of spirit and of will. This was the beginning of all things. And this chasm was strangely believed to have remained outside of time—as Frederic had put it, "outside the world." "What a weird idea!" said Gwilt aloud, impressed in spite of himself in the suggested presence of the unknown. So much belongs to the region of the unknown—or, if you will, of the unknowable—that the serious suggestion of its presence must always exert a terrifying or at least a sobering influence. After all, one never knows. So much, so very much, is beyond.

All the time, however, he was scanning with a climber's eye the face of the precipice at his feet and all around. It seemed absolutely hopeless for any man to live through such a descent. And yet his eye had caught and was following the course of a rupture or crack in the precipice to his left which led diagonally downwards and outwards to a projecting mass of rock which seemed to overhang the space below. There the crack came to an end. And beyond that point no human eye could reach. The precipice sloped out-wards to that point, and some roughnesses in the rock might pass for hand-holds. But what was beyond? Once there—should it lead merely to blank space—would it even be possible to turn again? On the other hand there was just the possibility of something better beyond. As a climb it was far from being a fair risk. None could have known it better than Gwilt. And in the Alps, like all good climbers, he was a rigid adherent of the doctrine of the limit of risk. But what had doctrine to do with it here? The fever in his veins was driving him. And who can tell how much was due to his love of the woman, and how much to the spirit of the male roused to fury at the presence of a rival? At any rate he did not hesitate long; and, getting with extreme difficulty the point of a toe into the beginning of the crack, and with his face to the cliff, he began his perilous undertaking. As he proceeded diagonally downwards the crack widened somewhat, but at times the angle was so acute that his feet had to be successively wedged in order to find foothold. He moved almost automatically. He had ceased to think of anything. And the movements of his feet and hands and the balance of his body might have been those of a machine. And it was only after what seemed an age that, by his realisation of the extreme outward bulge of the rock, he became aware that he had actually achieved the first perilous object of his enterprise and had reached the hood of rock where the crack ended. This was the most terrific moment of Gwilt's life. The question was, what came after? Unless there was a way onward it was the end. He scarcely dared to peer over the verge. Then with a thrill of fierce joy he perceived that the rocks hidden below the hood were more or less jagged and broken, and that there was some prospect of further descent. With infinite difficulty he succeeded in circling the edge of the projection and finding foothold beneath, and so continuing his downward climb. The strain upon heart and nerves was terrible, but for an hour his tense will prevailed; and, when at length his last ounce of energy seemed exhausted and he felt he could stand the strain no more, he found he had arrived. He had descended upon a broad ledge which ran along the foot of the precipice and which formed the edge of a huge "kettle" or basin, into which plunged the tumultuous waters of the Molma from the height above. He was absolutely exhausted by the dreadful strain, both physical and moral, which he had undergone. He flung himself down and groped almost blindly for his flask and for the food which was stowed in the inside pocket of his coat. Somewhere on the other side the waters seemed to find their exit; but it was not visible from where he sat, and the waters as soon as they escaped from the tumult of the fall assumed a strange quietude as if here they had suddenly come to rest. An air of extreme stillness pervaded the marvellous scene, a stillness which the thunder of the torrent only rendered more acute. The twilight which prevailed deepened into blackness where the sides of the basin seemed to fall away again into unimaginable deeper gulfs below. And to Gwilt there recurred the long-forgotten lines of the Edda—

It was Time's morning
When Ymer lived . . .
Earth there was none . . .
Only a deep profound.

And with ever greater insistency there pressed upon his mind Frederic's foolish but serious belief that in Ymer's Deep there was no time, that it was "outside the world." A strange sense of the remoteness of outward things overcame him. This incredible idea that somehow in this abyss, leading he knew not where, and in which he found himself utterly alone, time was not, and had never begun at all, became more and more a terrible and haunting reality. In the endless roar of the fall Vernon Gwilt seemed to hear time rushing past him and all other things "hastening to their day of doom." He himself seemed to be outside of it all, and he pictured it all as a sort of flowing web in which all things lived and moved except himself. Sigrid and Frederic and Halstan and all the others seemed within the nexus and he himself outside. It was all nothing now to him, he was outside the world.

But suddenly he realised that work was to be done. Time or no time, there were fish in the "Deep." In its clear waters dark and torpedo-like forms could be seen cruising about near the surface of the water and circling round and round in search of surface food. Gwilt knew well that in the pellucid waters of these Norwegian "kettles" the fish are frequently as visible as goldfish in a bowl. But only sometimes will they take the fly. He hurriedly prepared his tackle. Casting with the wall of rock immediately behind him was impossible; but by edging towards the fall he was able to get his line carried out in the breeze it created. Then, waiting his chance, he dragged his flies across the course of an approaching fish. It turned instantly to the nearest moving fly. Gwilt struck backwards and the fish was hooked. His pulse bounded to the thrill of the touch as he drew him hurriedly to the side. A grayling it was, small even for the Molma; but to Gwilt it meant victory. It meant the right to be with Sigrid—the winning of the first round of the contest. The sombre forms of much bigger fellows were to be seen. The next, indeed, when he took the fly, almost upset the fisher on the slippery surface of the ledge. It was a trout, and fought gamely. Twice had Gwilt to give him his head, and finally when he began to come in it was only in short and fiercely-fought stages. A pound and three-quarters he weighed, Gwilt thought, at least, as he placed him carefully in the basket. And so the sport, which in this case was a feverish and almost blind obsession, proceeded, and the basket gradually became almost full. One comparative monster had so far by sheer evil fortune eluded the angler's wile. Every time this fish approached Gwilt had hoped to reach him; but again and again he had turned just as he appeared to be about to enter the danger zone. Then once more he saw him some distance away swimming

an inch or two from the surface and just under the ledge on which
Gwilt stood. The flies happened to be already in the water at
that moment, and had only to be drawn gently along the surface
ripple caused by the fall. Suddenly the trout saw the moving
objects, and the next moment the line was whirring from the reel
and the rod bent and quivering to the keenest tussle of all. What a
glorious fight it was, for a two-and-a-half pounder, a fight which
Gwilt never forgot. This was the last fish in sight, and when
at last it had been laid safely in the creel the rod was taken down
again and packed. Then Gwilt started violently, realising all at
once that darkness was beginning to fall on Ymer's Deep. He
was a man, as we have seen, by no means lacking in nerve; but the
idea of spending the night in this timeless deep filled him with
tumultuous horror. He hastily slung the basket of fish over his
shoulder, fastened his rod and net as before, and then instantly
every faculty of his mind was concentrated in accomplishing his
desperate ascent to the upper world.

* * * * *

When Albert Halstan reached the farm after his day's fishing
he found himself in a fever of alternate hope and anxiety. But
in his heart hope predominated. In his basket he had eleven
silvery trout from a quarter to three-quarters of a pound in weight.
It would surely, he thought, be an extraordinary thing if Vernon
Gwilt had taken more. And, hope being uppermost in his mind,
Halstan, who was a good fellow, even experienced an occasional
pang of pity for his friend Gwilt, born of the haunting idea of
his own misery, should it be his fate to have to make way for
his rival on the morrow.

But Gwilt, he found, had not arrived, and only twenty minutes
remained for his arrival at the hour agreed for the fateful decision
of the day. He went to the kitchen and borrowed the scales from
Beret, and then he flung himself restlessly upon the bank in front
of the farm to await his rival's approach. Then he saw Frederic
chopping wood near the stable, and called him to him impatiently.
Frederic looked with smiling curiosity at the scales lying beside
Halstan on the ground.

"Mr. Gwilt and I," said Halstan, nervously, "have had a
fishing competition in the Molma to-day. Do you think he can
have beaten that?" And he hurriedly poured the silvery catch
upon the ground before him, a lovely, glittering mass. Before
Frederic could reply, Vernon Gwilt suddenly emerged from the
thicket and stood before them. Both men stood in amazement
at the sight of him. He was gasping with exertion and streaming
with sweat. His clothes were torn and covered with réd clay;

his eyes bloodshot, and in them was a wild look, which changed to one of fierce triumph as he gazed at Halstan's little heap of glittering fish.

"That is yours, is it?" he exclaimed, truculently. "Then you have lost! You may leave to-morrow! Here are mine! There is glorious fishing in Ymer's Deep!" And, unfastening his basket, he turned it upside down before the two men. And out of his basket there dropped upon the ground five small fish—*the five trout he had caught before ever he had descended into the abyss.* There was a motionless pause—a moment of absolute silence as the three men gazed first at the five trout and then at each other. Then Vernon Gwilt swayed upon his feet and fell insensible full length upon the ground.

*   *   *   *   *

When Gwilt came to himself he found he was in bed. Halstan was watching beside him. It was night, and a shaded lamp shed a dim radiance in the silent room.

"Halstan," he said, feebly, "what has happened? Where am I?"

"All right, old man; you have been ill, but you will be all right now. You must go to sleep. I'm looking after you, you know."

And Gwilt, too feeble then to ask more, did as he was told. But sooner or later the question had to come.

"Is Sigrid here?" he asked.

"Yes," replied Halstan, grimly. "She arrived a week ago with a yellow and black French anarchist, who is her husband."

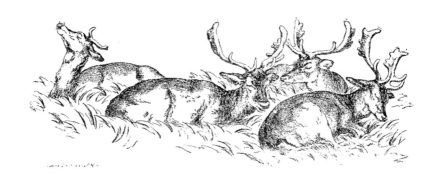

STRANGE STORIES OF SPORT

XLI.—SPOKEN IN JEST

BY N. M. PHILLIPS

DESTINY was busy weaving the threads of many a strange story during those eventful years when South Africa staged the drama of war, with its pregnant opportunities and far-reaching consequences, to individual histories as well as national interests. Such possibilities having naturally occurred to the novelist as affording a welcome fresh field for enterprise, it has been exploited accordingly, fact and fancy alike contributing to countless plots dependent for basis on the war, and its convenient chances for the revelation of heroism in the hero and the final disposal of villainy in the villain. But with this flood of literature, in graphic detail bringing home the pictures of lonely outposts, stirring battles, messages bravely borne through a hail of bullets, rescues, escapes, sieges, sudden deaths, and promotions, the impression of the life of the garrison established where the whirlwind had passed by is scarcely truthful, though picturesque. The outside world never realised how calmly men and women pursued their ordinary occupations and pleasures, under but slightly different conditions, whilst that bitter conflict of two obstinate nations dragged on. Thus there were incidental happenings, only indirectly concerning the war, yet scarcely less rich in human interest than those more intimately connected with it; for Life went on, hearts were broken and mended, careers made and ruined, fortunes won and lost, as they are every day in countries new and old, in years of peace and war. The imported garrison, with its varied and cosmopolitan elements, was a new factor—that was all. In a fashion nationally characteristic, it settled down and proceeded to amuse itself exactly as if the wave of strife had not but recently passed over and a sudden call to arms might not at any moment interfere with the programme of organised work and play.

The Englishman and his Colonial cousin are alike in one touch of nature that shows them kin—an extraordinary capacity for discovering and developing the sporting possibilities of any place they may happen to find themselves in. In South Africa, whenever there was the faintest chance of seeking something of the sort, it was sought—strange fish were caught on stranger tackle, weird birds shot with weird guns, curious cricket played on curious pitches. Collecting a "pack" of animals bearing more or less resemblance to the dog, if not the hound, a gallant officer would sally forth and have a jackal-hunt, quite undeterred by the strong possibility of a stray band of the enemy at any moment changing the respective rôles of hunter and hunted.

But it was racing, ever a most popular sport in South Africa, that was the most potent attraction, and the inevitable prominence of the soldier element alone distinguished from the ordinary numerous meetings held just as usual. Needless to say, the officers, debarred by circumstances from hunting, seized with avidity on this consoling opportunity, and stables were organised as if by a miracle. Contests varied from the improvised pony races of an isolated garrison, over a course where piled sandbags did duty for hurdles and the going was a trifle rough, to the smart and fashionable gatherings at Jo'burg, Cape Town, and Kimberley, differing scarcely at all from similar meetings "on the flat" at home. Much money was lost and won, for the magnates of the mines plunged heavily, and the soldiers liked to "have a bit on," if only to relieve the monotony of existence.

Now, a well-known soldier-sportsman, whom we will call Captain Martin Miller, was appointed on a commission concerning commissariat details and the settling of compensation claims, which kept him at Kimberley and permitted him some leisure. He got together, by the exercise of judgment and the power of determination, a useful string, and did very well indeed, not a little to the annoyance of some of the natives. In those days Kimberley was just settling down after its relief. Hardly had the tide of war swept on, leaving the town high and dry once more, with its garrison added to its wealthy diamond people, its cosmopolitan inhabitants, containing drift-wood thrown up from the whole world's ebb and flow, than the usual race-meetings were started as of yore. Captain Miller's particular interest brought him in contact at this time with all the well-known Turf people in the country; and quaint characters some of them were. Among those in racing circles whom he became very friendly with was an Irishman named Solly, who possessed the Hibernian knack of charm to an extraordinary degree. By profession a mining engineer, he had drifted to South Africa fifteen or twenty years before, and had been connected with many concerns and enterprises during that period. Sometimes he was in very low water—a typical rolling stone minus any moss; at others he flourished amazingly, and enjoyed life accordingly, with no cares for the past or the future, but a keen sense of the possibilities of the present. Nor was he unduly concerned if an unkindly turn of Fortune's wheel left him stranded—it was no use worrying, sure; something would be turning up. A sportsman to the backbone, with a strong and vivid personality, a quaint wit, and a remarkable knowledge of things entertaining if not improving, he was the best of company and a man of many friends. He was one of those rare persons always recalled with a smile and a delightful impression: Martin Miller struck up a considerable friendship with him, and would listen to his stories by the hour.

At that time Solly had a nest-egg, having of late been connected with a thriving company and had a stroke of luck. The war had brought his business affairs to a standstill, and idleness suited the little Irishman to perfection; so he was engaged in dispersing it as well as he could in such troublous times, for money always burnt a hole in his pocket. In appearance he was a small, thin man, with an ugly, nice, clean-shaven face, grizzled hair, and twinkling blue eyes a girl might well have envied. It was a great joy to him to find congenial spirits and friends of long-lost friends in the old country amongst the officers, and he talked horse to them all to their hearts' delight. Captain Miller was a very fine rider and a rare judge of pace; he generally rode his own horses, and about this time he fairly swept the board at one of the big meetings, greatly to the annoyance of the magnates who pervaded and patronised it. Needless to say Solly followed his soldier friend's luck, and the nest-egg swelled to such pleasing proportions that the little Irishman declared he could live like a lord till the war should end and business be resumed; meanwhile he had a great time.

One morning Captain Miller was sitting in his office in Kimberley, at work on some official papers, when he looked out on the street to perceive a soldier on horseback drawing rein. Martin Miller strolled out and took the message in person, casting the glance that was a natural instinct over the horse as he did so. The messenger was an Australian Yeoman, one of those sons of Greater Britain who crossed the seas to help her in the hour of need, and he was on a waler, for these Imperial Yeomanry justified their designation, and were really recruited from the ranks of Colonial farmers, many of whom had brought their own horses with them. Miller's expert eye lingered on this particular jaded steed, despite his ragged hips, his visible ribs, and wretched appearance.

" Waler—good old horse ? " he asked.

The Colonial smiled, and a flash of that understanding which makes all horsemen kin passed between the English Cavalry officer and the Irregular trooper. He spoke proudly. " Won a race or two out home, has Kangaroo, in his time—yes, I brought him over—wish I hadn't—we've got orders for home."

Captain Miller walked round the weary-looking, half-starved animal, and his age, capacity, and condition were jerkily discussed. The Yeoman looked contemplative in response to a suggestion concerning the trouble of taking him back to Australia, and the risks of the journey. He was disposed to avoid them if a suitable offer was made. Captain Miller made one, according to his conception of the case. It was met by a resolute head-shake. Finally, after a conversation that need not be inflicted in detail, Kangaroo's fate was decided, and he stayed in South Africa. Forty pounds Martin Miller paid for him, and a good change for Kangaroo it was. From a half-starved, ill-dressed troop-horse he became a pampered racehorse, and in a month his late owner would not have known him. In two his new one scarcely did. Captain Miller was, as has been hinted, a pretty good judge of the raw material, and he made singularly few mistakes, but he never closed a better bargain than when he picked up Kangaroo. He could gallop and stay, he was a hard sort and a good doer, and he came on in amazing fashion and pulled off several small races, the stakes alone trebling and quadrupling the original outlay on him. Solly watched the horse's progress with the keenest interest from the first ; there was a touch of romance in the circumstances of his acquisition that appealed to the Irishman, and he made up his mind he was a great horse and would win a big race. Often he and Miller would watch him at his work, and when he won his first race Solly's delight knew no bounds.

Then for a time business recalled him to Cape Town, and Miller heard nothing of him for awhile. Early in the New Year, which is of course the rainy season, there came the big meeting at Kimberley, a five days' affair, equivalent in importance to the First Spring Meeting at Newmarket or the Liverpool week at home. Martin Miller was very fully occupied ; he had several horses running, and had entered Kangaroo for the Kimberley Stakes, the big race on the first day, in which he proposed to ride the horse himself. It was a dull, very hot, very still day, with ominous thunder-clouds hovering about, and a most oppressive atmosphere. The crowd in the Grand Stand looked limp ; everyone longed —vainly—for a breath of air. It was a very similar sight to a big meeting at home; the smart ladies of Kimberley society sported the latest fashions, and the bright sunshades and pretty frocks gave a gay note to the festive scene. Miller was not a big plunger—he raced for the love of the sport and the pleasure of riding; still, in a steady, quiet way, he backed horses and he was in luck, nothing he touched going wrong, so that he had won a good deal, and strolled through the crowded paddock a short while before the Kimberley Stakes were timed, in a flush of confidence justified by the ascendency of his star. It only needed the supreme gratification of riding a winner in an important race on the horse he had absolutely picked up in the rough to fill his cup of satisfaction to the full, and he had at heart a strong conviction that nothing could prevent his pulling it off.

He was glancing at the sleek yet wiry waler, the centre of many admiring glances as he was being promenaded, looking in the pink of condition, when someone smote him with no little violence, and he turned with a start to perceive his friend Solly.

"Hullo! back again?" he said, smiling as they only smiled who knew that delightfully inconsequent person.

They chatted most cheerily for a few moments, and then the soldier inquired how things were going. Solly smiled, and his blue eyes were like a naughty child's; he made a little wry face and then confessed.

"Well, it could not well be much worse," he whispered. "I don't mind tellin' you, dear fellow; I've dropped a big lot to-day, and I dropped a bigger in Cape Town last week—in fact," he continued, calmly flicking a speck off his coat, and raising his hat with a most charming smile to a lady—"Ah, isn't she quite sweet now, Miller? —in fact, only a big coup can save me from bankruptcy this time."

Captain Miller whistled. "My dear chap, I'm awfully sorry; I thought you were rolling—you can't mean it?" he said.

"I do," replied the other; "it'll be an absolute smash this time; but don't you be worryin', sure the luck will be changing!" he added, complacently. "Going to thunder, too, by Jove. It's so hot it can't be hotter *anywhere*, that's one comfort."

Miller could only laugh, though he was genuinely concerned; it was a bad time to go under, as he well knew, for the country would be full to overflowing with men after jobs when the war should end, and meanwhile there was nothing doing.

"Well, now for Kangaroo. I've got a feeling about that horse," said Solly, and together they looked at him long without a word. Suddenly Solly touched Miller's arm. He dropped his voice. "I know you'll give me the straight tip, old man," he said; "it's really serious, and I've a good mind to put every farthing I've got left, which ain't much, alas! on the horse, and trust to him to pull me through. What d'you think?"

Martin Miller hesitated; ten minutes ago he would have recommended any friend to back the horse confidently enough; but this was being asked a big thing—Solly's fortunes hung in the balance, depending on his answer. He knitted his brows, and spoke slowly. "Well, there are a lot in, and it's a goodish race. There's Ginger, and Mazeppa, and several cracks; 'pon my word I shouldn't like to say!"

But the engineer persisted. "Are you on him yourself?" he asked.

Captain Miller explained that he had already done very well on the meeting, and was only putting a trifle for luck on Kangaroo. He preferred to let well alone, and though he thought the horse had a very good chance, where so much was involved he felt reluctant to express an opinion; so he hummed and hawed, whilst Solly listened and looked, but did not change his mind, as the other fervently hoped he would.

"Well, you're riding, and I'd as soon risk my all on you as anybody," said Solly. "Come now, if I don't win something over this I'm done; if you think the horse has a decent sort of chance yourself I'll back him."

Captain Miller thought rapidly for a moment; then his reluctance vanished. After all, he was himself positive Kangaroo could do it. With a sudden thrill of renewed assurance, that seemed wrung from him by the force of conviction almost in spite of himself, he spoke emphatically.

"Well, in my own mind I *am* certain that he will win," he said, "unless he drops dead—so there!" he added with a laugh; and Solly, heaving a little sigh of relief, joined in it heartily.

"That I will risk," he responded as lightly; "it seems a pretty soft thing I do think; thanks awfully!" and they parted.

Miller went and got ready to ride; Solly arranged matters; and half an hour later, just as the former was riding out of the paddock, he caught sight of a beaming face and stopped to receive a good wish and to hear "It's all right; I've got £1,500 on; four to one; go in and win!" Miller was slightly troubled with a sense of involuntary responsibility, but he put it from his mind and passed on, nodding cheerfully.

Meanwhile the bank of violet clouds had gradually moved up till the whole sky was dark with them. The atmosphere was unbearably heavy, with that extraordinary stillness which so often precedes a violent storm in Africa; people crowded the stand and deserted the rails in fear of what was coming. On, on, swiftly now, crept the indigo cloud-masses, changing as they advanced to inkiest black : then came a rumble of distant thunder—and the horses were at the starting-post. They were drawn up in line just as the storm broke in all its blinding fury. The jockeys could not see their horses' ears when the signal was given and they were off! Only those who have seen it can picture the sudden vehemence, the tropical rain, the torrential force, of such a thing : the downpour wiped out the landscape, and swept down like a veritable tornado. Captain Miller gripped Kangaroo, bent right down in his saddle, and just let him romp. Maddened by the deluge, the horses tore down the course, scarcely under control, and Solly, watching anxiously from the stand, could just make out the pink cap and white jacket shooting out from the rest as a vivid flash of lightning illuminated the whole scene in most dramatic fashion for a moment.

The racecourse at Kimberley is circular, and this race was once round. Miller rode superbly, keeping his head despite the dis-traction of the fearful storm, which was too much for three or four of the runners, who dropped out of the impossible contest, their jockeys unable to face the onslaught of the elements. It was a wild ride indeed : the thunder crashed and reverberated in a manner beside which memory of the fiercest storm ever witnessed in an English summer would fade into utter insignificance. It was practically dark, with the peculiar thick darkness of a tropical storm, save when every few seconds lightning blazed and streaked right across the sky, permitting a glimpse of the race to the hushed onlookers. On, on, dashed the leading horses, first Kangaroo, the pink cap plainly to be identified, then a chestnut, and close behind two others, Ginger and Mazeppa, both good and known horses. Half-way round Miller glanced back : the chestnut was creeping up. But he knew Kangaroo, and did not ease him to wait on the others : he had the gift of judging pace, and knew exactly what he had in hand. In this case he meant to hold his position and let his horse out the whole way. Round the turn they all went, a bunched flash of colours ; then were lost to view for a few minutes on the far side of the course through the blinding rain that never ceased. People on the crowded stand crammed forward, craning out their heads, forgetful of the terrible lightning and the risk in their eagerness to catch the first glimpse of the field rounding the last corner and coming up the straight. Not one in that vast throng of closely-pressed humanity watched with straining eyes more anxiously than Solly. His heart hammered with excitement ; not merely because he stood to win or lose all on this one chance, but because he was a born gambler and an Irishman, and the excitement of the moment gripped him with an intensity almost unbearable. His hand shook a little as he lowered blurred glasses and concentrated his unaided gaze on the white rails by the turn.

Ah! at last they were coming! The pulse of those massed hundreds throbbed as one in that moment of breathless suspense : there was dead silence : then one roar—for one was leading by lengths, then came three close together—and, a mere blur in the distance, a straggling line right back. Solly peered and drew a deep breath—it was but an instant and the cry of the course was the cry of the stand—it was " Kangaroo ! Kangaroo ! " from a thousand throats. There are few things on earth more thrilling than that moment when the crowd shouts the name of the leading horse as with one voice. Solly heard it, and went mad for an instant, shouting with the rest. Miller, sitting so still in his saddle, with the big horse going strong as ever under him, galloping gloriously, heard it too. Someone next to little Solly on the stand turned to him—" Goin' to win in a canter ? "—and Solly, with an excited little laugh of triumph, replied as Miller had replied to him, " Rather ; unless he drops dead ! " Then suddenly there came a terrific flash of blinding brilliancy—forked lightning—a drift of torrential rain that hid the course from view, and a peal that seemed to crash the earth asunder. The yells of " Kangaroo ! " changed to a sudden silence ; then they arose again, altered to " He's down ! he's down ! " and as the chestnut and Mazeppa went flying past the stand, racing neck and neck, the fickle note was changed to the rival strains of " Ginger ! Good old Ginger ! " and " Mazeppa ! " Which of them won Solly never knew. In that most dramatic moment he had only time to realise the one fact that Kangaroo was a crushed and huddled heap before the sheets came down again, blotting it all out.

There were many who only waited for the slightest abatement of the storm to rush and throng the rails by the spot where the horse lay so strangely still. Solly was one of the first of them. Captain Miller, unhurt, was up again, standing over the horse, and a veterinary surgeon quickly joined him ; but the briefest examination sufficed, and both shook their heads. A thunderbolt or a fragment of one had fallen close by. But exactly what happened would never be known. Whether the shock of that terrible crash of its coming caused the horse to cross his legs, or whether the lightning actually struck him, he was beyond all doubt stone dead. In a flash as that word spread from mouth to mouth Solly remembered that " saving clause," uttered so carelessly twice within the half-hour—" He'll win—unless he drops dead." He had laughed ; but this time he did not laugh, for there's many a true word spoken in jest, and true words are sometimes bitter things.

STRANGE STORIES OF SPORT

XLII.—BESS

BY J. M. DODINGTON

" Where the deuce is that dog ? "

From the seething maelstrom of excited travellers, crimson-faced guards, vociferating servants, and frenzied dogs, which surged amongst mounds of boxes and mountains of gun-cases on Perth platform that fair August morning, there emerged a perspiring porter, dragging a brace of pointers on the couples, and a retriever which walked, sedately, alone.

"And where the dickens is the spaniel ? " I cried.

The porter pointed to a great rent in his nether garments.

" I dinna ken where she *is*, sirr," he replied, " but fine do I ken where I wish she'd been afore ever I took a haud o' her ! "

My heart sank—for well I knew my Bess !

At King's Cross the polite guard had pointed out to me the advisability of coupling retriever and spaniel together, as I had done in the case of the pointers.

"They'll travel better singly," I replied ; " they are not altogether friendly at times." (Which was one way of putting it !)

" Really, sir ? " with an incredulous air. " This one, at any rate, seems a gentle-mannered creature," and he patted Bess's head. Bess turned her melting brown eyes upon him and lovingly licked his hand, while a tear of gratitude rolled down her cheek.

At York I was aroused from my peaceful slumbers by the same guard, pale and quivering with rage.

" I will thank you, sir," he stammered, truculently, " to muzzle that dog of yours, or out she goes on York platform ! "

" Which dog ? " I asked, in innocent surprise ; but instinctively my hand sought the strap which I carry for such emergencies. The guard disdained reply, but led me to his van.

There sat mild-eyed Bess, beaming affection on all around. One loving glance at my face—and she rolled over on her back, and prepared for the inevitable. . . .

When the strap had satisfactorily fulfilled its first mission, it was adjusted muzzle-wise on her patient countenance. Throughout Bess had emitted no murmur of complaint, but in her liquid eyes was a look of such patient reproach as melted even the heart of the justly-incensed guard.

" I don't think she meant to hurt me, sir," he mumbled, as he sucked his bleeding thumb ; " it was more playfulness than anything."

The same playful spirit, the porter now explained, had goaded Bess—the strap having been removed by the soft-hearted guard—into setting her teeth into the calf of his leg. A well-directed kick backwards had induced her to loosen her hold with much promptitude, and she had disappeared amongst the crowd.

I had to wait half an hour for the slow train which did not disdain a halt at my little junction ; but, instead of enjoying the substantial Scotch breakfast to which I had been looking forward all the way from Edinburgh, the whole of my time was spent in hunting every hole and corner of the station for Bess. But neither hint nor hair of her was to be seen. . . . My train backed, slowly, up to the platform. The injured porter deposited my rugs in a carriage, and, in the few minutes that remained, we had a last look round for the lost dog. But in vain. . . . So there was nothing for it but to leave my address with the station-master, and to give urgent instructions for a renewed search to be made.

" 'Deed, sirr," said the porter, as he locked me into my compartment, " I wadna fash mysel' nae mair aboot her. Ye're weel rid o' a deil o' a beast like yon."

But my heart was sore for my lost dog ; and as I gazed, with unseeing eyes, upon the green pastures and waving cornfields of the fair Vale of Perth, mentally I wove her elegy.

A cross-bred spaniel she, in whom the Sussex predominated ; with a nose for game which I have never seen equalled. From a running pheasant to a diving duck, nought escaped her. And she was steady as a rock. After all, what was such a minor offence as the occasional disappearance of a leg of mutton or a sirloin of beef from the larder, and the consequent bloated appearance of Bess as she mildly, but firmly, asserted her right to the foremost place on the smoking-room hearthrug? What was a playful snap at the stranger's obtrusive leg or over-patronising hand? All high-spirited dogs are given to such impulses. And I heaved a long, grief-laden sigh. . . . A cold, wet something touched my down-dropped hand; from under the seat projected two nut-brown paws.

"Bess!" I exclaimed, in incredulous joy.

She crawled out, weeping, slobbering, imbecile with delight. She licked my boot, then laid her chestnut ringlets upon it, and looked up into my face.

"How could I submit to be parted from you, my heart's delight? How could I endure the long, long night shut up in a darksome den with the fiend who had taken me away from my beloved master? How could I allow myself to be dragged out into that Pandemonium where was no sight or sniff of him who is the lode-star of my life? And, for my devotion, what is my reward? . . . Ah, cruel, cruel! But I love you still the same, and will adore you till I die!"

All this, and more, said those melting brown orbs.

"Bess, Bess, you unspeakable hypocrite!" But my hand strayed over her curls, and Bess's heart was stayed and comforted.

That year I had taken a small grouse-moor in the Black Water district, attracted there, in part, by the fair shooting at a modest rental suited to an equally modest purse; but, in even a greater measure, by the fact that in a neighbouring glen, four miles away as the crow flies, double that distance by road, dwelt the lady on whom my affections had been unalterably fixed ever since the day of our first meeting at the Inverness Gathering of the year before. I had seen a good deal of Betty Gordon in the interval. She had a brother in London, essaying to tread the thorny path of literature, to whom I had been able to render some slight assistance, and during a memorable month which she spent with him in town Betty and I had arrived at a most blissful understanding. . . . But, alas! Betty had a father—a queer, cross-grained old fellow he was, with occasional flashes of humour of a recondite and disconcerting character. The whole household trembled before the Laird, and even my bonny, bright-eyed, high-spirited Betty "heeded the shake of his thumb."

The Laird was a dour obstacle to the course of our true love, particularly as he had a leaning towards another of Betty's admirers, Andrew Musgrave, a glib-tongued Edinburgh advocate, with a long pedigree and a profitable little estate in the border country to back his suit.

He had been invited to Craigdhu for the first week of the shooting; I had not had that honour, but, when the Laird heard that I had taken Glencray, he sent me a curt invitation to drive over on the morning of "the Twelfth" and help swell the day's bag. (Without boasting, I may here indicate that I am a fair shot.)

"And bring a dog with you," he added. "I am short of retrievers; none of your flashy dogs, but one that will leave nothing behind. I hate waste."

Now Nell, my handsome black retriever, was a scion of a very distinguished race, and an excellent dog, as dogs go; my first impulse was to take her. But as I whipped the moorland burn on the day that intervened between our arrival at Glencray and the great day of the festival—with but small success, for the water was low—my mind misgave me. Great things were at stake, and, staunch as Nell was, I _had_ known her lose her head over a rabbit. Let this happen but once under the grim eye of the Laird, and my fate was sealed! No, I dared not risk it; I would take Bess, the "spannel." Beautiful as was my Bess of the chestnut curls and the melting brown eye, she was not a spaniel of any breed in particular—no, she was, emphatically, a "spannel"; that, and nothing more.

And there was not, in the whole length and breadth of that Empire on which the sun never sets, a prouder dog than she when, at eight o'clock next morning, she was hoisted into the dog-cart. She sniffed the cartridge-bag, she nosed the gun, she lifted up her voice and made hill and glen resound with her shrieks of delight. And oh! the loftiness of her mien as she passed the kennels without deigning a glance at their howling, heart-broken occupants.

The light mists were drifting up the steep sides of Craig-na-Brattan; from behind a passing cloud a shaft of sunlight played over the rounded crest of Knock-Auli; the harebells by the roadside shed sparkling dewdrops as the breeze swayed their slender stalks; the birch trees shook their perfume in my face. Above the moors on either side of the lonely Kirkmichael road, the larks poured out their hearts in song, and the challenging "Ke-bec- Ke-bec-bec- bec-bec" of the cock-grouse awoke the echoes of hill and glen. . . . It was "the Twelfth," and I was going to see my sweetheart: life seemed very, very good! I added my _basso profondo_ to the diapason of nature, while Bess laid her head against my knee and snuffled.

I found the shooting-party gathered round the door of the castle. The Laird gave me a short, dark greeting, and ostentatiously pulled out his watch. Betty, radiant as the morning, whispered, as she gave me her hand, "Never heed him; you're well up to time, but he's always fractious until he gets everybody off."

I paid but little attention to the other guns; my mind was concentrated on Musgrave, who was standing close to Betty. He was a good-looking fellow, I must say, and, I was told, a famous shot.

I noticed a sardonic grin flit over the Laird's hard-bitten countenance as he glanced at the three of us. He walked over to where we stood.

"Well, well," he said, "I'm thinkin' there'll be a fine report to send in to the papers wi' twa such grand guns as you, gentlemen. I would like fine to lay a bet on which o' ye makes the best bag afore lunch-time—I think little o' the afternoon's shootin', the mornin's the time. What do you say, Betty? Shall we offer a prize to the best shot o' the twa? I wonder what they would like best? Just you think about it when we're gane."

And, as if by accident, he lifted her hand, turned it over thoughtfully, then, with a keen glance, first at Musgrave and then at me, dropped it and stalked away.

Betty flushed crimson and turned to pick a rose from the wall.

"Come on, come on!" shouted the Laird, impatiently.

As I lingered yet an instant, Betty whispered: "Go, go; but for heaven's sake shoot your best, he's in one of his daft moods this morning."

Now I am not, at heart, a jealous shot, nor do I believe that Musgrave was—he was much too decent a fellow. But, foolish as it may seem, the veiled suggestion of the artful old Laird had fired the already heated blood of two rivals, and not even Lord G——— and Count M——— could have noted each other's hits and misses with more lynx-eyed vigilance than did Musgrave and I.

By accident or design—the latter most probably—his place in the line was next to mine; the birds rose to us fairly, and the fortunes of the day were first to one and then to the other.

The dogs worked magnificently—and, say what you will, is there any form of shooting that comes quite up to the good old-fashioned sport of shooting over a highly-intelligent, thoroughly-trained dog? —the weather was glorious; but for the anxiety gnawing at my heart it would have been the most perfect "Twelfth" of my experience.

Betty was to drive up the moorland track, with the luncheon, to the Lady's Pond, so named from the fair English girl who, in bygone days, had married a "gay Gordon." She sent for water-lily bulbs from her home in the south, and planted them in this sullen pool amongst the moss-hags. Strangely enough, they took root, grew and flourished exceedingly in that cold, northern clime. For two successive summers the gentle lady watched them bloom and fade, and then she, too, faded out of a wearisome world. For her gay Gordon had been very, very gay, and the happy southern bride was a broken-hearted woman when she lay down to die.

But the lilies still bloomed on the face of the Lady's Pond, and by its brink we were to meet for luncheon.

We came within a hundred yards of it ; I saw Betty, shading her eyes with her hand and gazing over the moor towards us.

I do not expect to be believed, but it is nevertheless an absolute fact that at that moment Musgrave's score and mine were identical. Fourteen brace of grouse had fallen to his gun, fourteen to mine ! It was in the highest degree unlikely that any more would be put up now—so near the luncheon-cart and its attendant gillie. My attention wavered for a moment, and, at that very instant, with a loud defiant chortle, up whirred a cock-grouse. Before I could raise gun to shoulder he was well away. It was a very long shot, but I could have sworn I saw him carry on, and drop just over the crest of the hill.

I walked quickly to the spot.

" Hi, seek, Bess ! " I cried.

With fluttering nostrils and quivering tail she sought. I do not believe she left an inch of ground unquartered within an area of a hundred yards, but never a feather did she find.

" Hi, lost, old girl ! Hi, lost ! "—and lost it was.

I gave it up at last and gloomily wended my way to the pond— Bess, in dire disgrace, trailing despondently at my heel. They had almost finished luncheon when I reached them ; the game had been packed in the cart, keepers and gillies were clustered at the back of the knoll, indulging in pipes and low-voiced conversation till the " chentlemen " should be ready to resume sport.

" I tell you, Donal' "—I recognised the voice of a black-visaged, hungry-looking Highlander who had taken Musgrave under his especial care—" they may search till the judgment-horn blaws, but neffer a bird will they get, for nae bird is there, whateffer. He's chust sittin' on the tap o' Clach More, lauchin' at them."

Apparently the Laird was of the same opinion. " Not picked him up after all ? " he said, with affected concern, " an' wi' such a grand dog, too ! But even she canna flee after him through the air," and he laid a patronising hand on Bess's head.

" Down, Bess ! " I cried sternly, for I had seen the spark in her eye. I was only just in time—the Laird hastily withdrew his hand, and Bess slunk back amongst the heather.

" Deil tak' the beast," growled the Laird, a trifle disconcerted.

Betty handed me the pie, and poured out my beer like the pitying angel she was, beer more delightful from her hands than Bollinger of its best year.

By the time I was lighting up I had recovered my composure. After all, it was only a case of " As you were, gentlemen."

I had but drawn my first whiff, when the pipe fell from my mouth. Through the tussocks of heather, head borne proudly aloft, stalked Bess. She looked neither to right nor left, but, with eyes fixed steadily on mine, advanced to my knee, and there stood rigid, the corpse of a cock-grouse in her mouth.

" By Jove ! " exclaimed Musgrave.

The Laird snorted.

Betty blushed crimson as I held her looks with mine.

*   *   *   *   *

Next morning I again traversed the eight long miles which divided me from Betty. I had determined to brave the Laird in his den, and ask him, man to man, to give me his daughter. After all, he could but show me the door.

But he did not. He listened in silence, then contemplated me thoughtfully.

" Musgrave's awa'," he said, unexpectedly.

" What ? Is he ? I don't understand."

" Oh yes, he's awa'. Betty's sent him off wi' a flea in his ear." There was another meditative pause. " Maybe ye'd better see what she says hersel' ; after a', it's her that will hev to suffer for her mistakes, no me."

I needed no second bidding, but, stammering my thanks, made for the door.

" And I'm thinkin'," he added, as my hand was upon the latch, "that, if ye bring over that dog o' yours to-morrow, we might pick up a cripple or twa. Man, she *hes* a nose, deevil though she be ! "

*   *   *   *   *

Let those asterisks denote the events of the first blissful half-hour with my Betty—mine henceforth in the face of the whole world. And now I take up my tale at that precise moment when she buried her face in the breast of my coat, while her whole form shook convulsively.

" My darling ! " I exclaimed in alarm, " what is it ? "

No reply.

Putting a hand on each side of her bonny face, I forced it backwards and scrutinised it anxiously. Tears, not of sorrow, but of mirth, rolled down her rose-red cheeks.

" Bess ! " she gasped.

" Bess ? " I echoed, in amazement.

" Good dog, Bess—dear dog, Bess ! " she stammered.

" What ? "

With a great effort she controlled her laughter, and I dried her eyes—*not* with my handkerchief.

"Yesterday," she said, "you remember her bringing the dead bird?" and again she laughed.

"Of course I do. Isn't she a nailer?"

"She is indeed," fervidly replied my Betty, "for when she slunk away in disgrace I watched her, and what do you think I saw? She got round the knoll, and then she stood for a moment with a sad, sad look on her face, as if pondering over the miserable injustice of this weary world; then she turned, ran up to the game-cart, seized a bird, circled round the brae, and came stalking up with it to your knee."

"Impossible!" I exclaimed.

"It's as true as true! I could not have believed it, if I had not seen it with my own eyes."

But I could—for well I knew my Bess!

STRANGE STORIES OF SPORT

XLIII.—THE FIRST ASCENT

BY JOHN SANDERSON

IT was our last night together in Switzerland. In one corner of the little old-fashioned restaurant attached to the much more modern and pretentious hotel a few of us still lingered late into the night. We were climbers to a man, and it was our custom every evening to desert the somewhat commonplace allurements of the greater Alpine establishment to gather together in this bare little " Gastzimmer," furnished with its ancient French " billiard " and wooden tables, and known amongst ourselves as the " House of Lords." Here it was our wont to discuss our various doings on rock and snow, and to argue together—sometimes with no small heat—concerning the technicalities of the most companionable and, as we considered it, by far the most satisfying sport in all the world. There are few ties for the souls of men like that which is knotted by the Alpine rope. It endures; I am persuaded that it grows more vigorous even when the ear has become deaf to the ring of the axe and the tinkle of the falling ice and the most valiant heart has ceased to thrill to the glory and peril of the precipice and peak. My friend Denys was an example of this truth. We were climbing together at this time, and were everything that friends can be; but I knew then, as I know still better now, that an old fellow student, Edward Archer, who fifteen years before had been lost in the Alps, and who had been his first youthful companion upon the mountains, was bound to him by a subtle and imperishable bond of fellowship which seemed to grow stronger as the years went by. In the Alps he thought of him continually.

We had some big climbing men amongst us, and the gradations of authority were well defined and recognised. Occasionally some stranger might join us for a night—perhaps a pair of climbing German professors with tasselled ties and green feathered hats whom some of us might happen to have encountered in some Alpine hut the previous night. But for the most part we were English, and knew all about each other and what each had done and what each intended to do, unless of course some new route was projected, when the secret was only revealed after its glorious accomplishment. To-night a middle-aged Englishman whom none of us had seen before had chanced to enter into conversation with Denys and me as we sat together somewhat in the outskirts of the circle. He was a small, heavily-built, grey-bearded man, with the appearance of one who might have spent his life in over-exerting enormous natural strength. His cheeks were sunken and ghastly in their pallor, and his eyes had that strange filmy appearance which comes only after long and serious illness. He was clad in the ordinary climbing attire, and I could not help noticing that upon the toe of one of his black and heavy climbing boots there were a couple of brown patches of chamois skin such as might have been inserted by some remote village cobbler in an emergency. For the most part he sat silently listening to the talk; but by the shrewdness of some rare remark upon the questions raised, and by the quiet assurance with which it was uttered, no one could help recognising in him an old master of the craft. The discussion happened to have fallen upon the eternal question of reconnoitring for a route, and the surest way of ascertaining the state of the rock which it was proposed to climb. Everyone of course had some special theory of his own, and it was not until the subject had become somewhat languid that our strange acquaintance suddenly began to talk.

"As a young man," he said with a faint smile, "and upon my very last climbing tour in the Alps, I had a strange experience in reconnoitring. It occurred in this very district. I have never spoken of it before, partly because I have never since met with climbing men like yourselves, and partly because one does not usually tell this sort of thing at all.

"Years ago I stayed in this little inn in which we now sit. For days I had been secretly reconnoitring the Glockenspitz from the south-east—'the impossible side,' as it is called in the village. Over and over again, ensconced amongst the seracs of the glacier, I had searched with my field-glass every visible crevice and ledge of that great frowning mass of rock and ice. On that side of the Spitz there was little snow, and no one so far had thought of attempting the ascent. The angle is, as you know, extremely acute, the dip of the rocks is the wrong way, and the base is difficult to reach at dawn from any of the huts in the neighbourhood. In fact no one ever comes near it. The first part of the route I had already settled in my mind. I had seen how from the top of the lower buttress a traverse might be made to the great rock-rib running up the centre of the face of the whole mountain. Once there, for fully half-way up the mountain the ridge of the rib was almost certain to be possible. But then almost half-way up there came a gap in the rib which rendered further progress by it impossible, and I was not at all certain of finding a traverse from the gap to the parallel chimney or gully which, in turn, must constitute the route up to the arête near the summit of the mountain. It was this gap which worried me, and which had worried me all along. It was as if a great slice or wedge had been cut out of the rib, leaving a smooth glistening rock-face which renders direct progress from that point impracticable. Finally, one afternoon, I resolved to climb the buttress itself in order to see how the problem looked from that point of view.

"It proved an arduous scramble, and to my disgust when I reached the top of the buttress the sun had sunk behind the mountain masses in the west, and already the glacier was touched with that dead whiteness which means that night is close at hand. I was rather exhausted with the hurried rush, and sat down for a time and looked around me. I felt terribly lonely all at once, I know not why, for I am accustomed much more to solitude than to company. I sat there motionless for some time. Suddenly I stood up, for, gentlemen, a marvellous thing happened—I heard voices upon the mountain. They came from above, far up the precipice above me. The tone was the furious one of climbers strained beyond the pitch of endurance, of men in straits raging at each other. Some of you gentlemen must know that tone as well as I did. It is not pleasant to hear. It has been my fate to be in such straits myself once; thank God only once in all my experience.

"'Give me more rope,' came a voice, furiously; 'I tell you I can't stay here. Blast you! Quick; give me rope.'

"And the answer came, shouted with brutal emphasis:

"'Shut your mouth, will you? I can't move myself. Go slower, or go to the devil; I don't care which.'

"In the night air, amid the deathlike silence of the darkened peaks, the tense voices rang clearly out, attenuated only by the distance above from which they came. The so-called impossible side of the Glockenspitz, gentlemen, was, it seemed, being climbed by starlight. Then there came a dead silence for a time—the silence, as I knew, of men fighting for their lives. Away up on the face of the mountain I believed I could dimly distinguish the dark forms of three climbers moving far too close together for the kind of rock on which they were. But in that I may have been mistaken. In what I heard, however, there could be no mistake. Again the fevered voice rang out:

"'Quick; good God! give me rope. I must have it—quick!'

"'Must you?' came the answer, brutally. 'Then cut the damned thing and be done with it. That's the proper thing to do!'

"'Is it?' came the answer; 'then, by God, I will!'

"Then there came a loud cry, and something else was said, but the sound was too faint for me to distinguish the words. The voices faded away, and utter silence once more dwelt upon the mountain.

"I was alone again, and I tell you, gentlemen, I was afraid. My limbs shook uncontrollably under me. I had to lie down on my face and fight for self-possession. For the thought had come to me that there was no other sound whatever except the voices; nothing stirred. No boulder came ricocheting down the gully beside me. Although I had heard the warning shout, no sound of a single stone had fallen upon my ear, and stones should have fallen on rock like that. In time, of course, I reasoned that, after all, these might easily have been diverted by some projecting rock about, and so fallen upon the other side of the great rib altogether. That idea steadied me a bit, and at least restored to me the power of locomotion. I made my way down the rocks and round the base of the mountain in the moonlight to the Alpine hut—I forget its name—perched upon the rocks far up the neighbouring glacier. I have never touched an ice-axe since that day."

When the stranger had finished his recital a silence fell upon the whole company of us. I suppose no one knew exactly what to say. This man had a dignified and even impressive manner. He was obviously an expert, and had just been relating to experts the manifestly incredible concerning a mountain which each one of us knew, at least from a distance. His description of its least-known face was also no doubt perfectly accurate, though none of us had ever seriously examined it. And it shocked us to hear a man, obviously sober, pitching at a lot of strangers a yarn of this impossible kind. There was an uneasy sense of constraint all round. It was old Whetham who first ventured to break the spell of silence which had fallen upon us all. Whetham was one of those intrepid climbers of a past generation who had ceased to climb, but who was totally unable to modify his original idea of what constituted a holiday. Year after year he continued to haunt his old favourite climbing centre, and was regarded with great outward respect as more or less of a pompous nuisance. He loved to fill the ears of a younger generation with mysterious hints of danger in any climb about to be undertaken, and with solemn and private warnings against dangerous qualities he had discovered in the chosen companion of each of his hearers in succession.

But this was too much even for Whetham. And when he bluntly remarked that high altitudes sometimes had extraordinary effects upon the senses and brain of unhealthy people, he gave frank if somewhat bald expression to what after all was in the minds of most of us there present. It cleared the air for us all, and made us feel rather less constrained and uncomfortable. That the redoubtable south-east side of the Glockenspitz had been climbed at all none of us in these days had thought of imagining, but that it had been climbed, as alleged, by starlight, with a comfortable start in the early evening and the whole night to do it, as it were, was the sort of tale which the most solemn oaths would not induce the Alpine Club Committee itself to admit to the archives of that august society. We were only too glad to change the subject and spare the man, and the conversation drifted into visions seen by guides in the mountains, strange sounds heard, beliefs in the existence of happy valleys hitherto undiscovered, legends of enchanted sheep and cattle, and, in short, into all the varied store of romance connected with the high and secluded corners of the Alpine ranges. To all this our stranger contributed not another word. And in the midst of it all he must have silently stolen away, for when I turned to look at him he had disappeared.

*   *   *   *   *

Denys and I had been making the ascent of the Gipfelhorn, which is, of course, to the south of the Glockenspitz; and upon our return the following afternoon we left our guides, and out of pure curiosity made a detour so as to pass along the base of the latter mountain. I confess it gave me quite a shock to see the great rock-rib running up the centre of the south-east face with the large gap near the top which our stranger had so accurately described. There, too, was the lower buttress on which he had stood, and away near the summit was the gully which he had hoped to reach after he had entered the gap. The whole cliff was illumined at that moment by the level rays of the setting sun, and its surface glowed as if lit by a large searchlight established upon the western heights of snow.

Then Denys spoke to me what was in his mind. "King," he said, seriously, "I am going to climb that face."

Somehow I had divined what he was going to say, and I answered quietly enough, "That man talked sheer insanity. Besides, you could never get beyond that gap in the rib. He thought so himself."

"It is the gap I mean to reach," he replied.

"Then," I said, "you could never get back, you know that as well as I do."

"Two men," he replied, strangely, "could go on where one could not; one man could get neither up nor down."

"Denys," I said, suddenly, "what on earth is in your mind?"

"I cannot tell you," he answered, feverishly. "I do not really know. I cannot get that infernal story out of my head. Come with me, King," he continued. "I know it will go all right, or I should not ask you. The route that stranger described is the right one, and with two of us it will go all the way. I shall go myself if you do not."

And with that I had to be satisfied. Of course I agreed to go. As I said before, we had climbed a lot together; and besides, I knew nothing would alter his resolve. We kept our design secret, and began to interview our guides. But when we came to broach the matter to old Gruhl we met with a grievous disappointment, for he refused point-blank to have anything to do with the project. Everyone had thought Gruhl would attempt anything in decent weather and with adequate pay. We argued in vain. The thing might be done perhaps, but he was not going to do it. What mysterious reason prevented him we could only guess, and no reason would he vouchsafe, in spite of everything that we could urge in its favour. So we resolved to fall back on Schnutze. But here again we were no more successful. It was not meant to be climbed by living men, Schnutze declared. That was the full substance of his objection. Only one other guide was worth asking, for this was not then one of the big climbing centres, and from him we had a similar reception. It seemed to be conspiracy. By this time my own unsuccessful arguments with the guides in its favour had at least had the effect of imbuing me with a profound belief in the possibility of the ascent, and I was now just as keen as Denys himself to carry the project through. Moreover, the mystery which had suddenly and unexpectedly invested this familiar mountain became first a fascination, and finally a real obsession, and Denys and I resolved to proceed alone and without informing anyone of our intention.

Two days later we set out together. The glorious day drew to a close as we reached the spot we had chosen for our resting-place during the hours of darkness. We had resolved to spend the night under the shelter of a rock at the base of the mountain, and for that purpose had transported thither the necessary coverings. With a spirit lamp we heated our "Maggi" soup, and as we settled down to smoke and talk the darkness drew down upon us and the gorgeous beauty of the ice-falls and of the mighty peaks around us faded slowly away under our eyes, and the whole world glimmered darkly to us under the starlit heavens.

What a solitude it was! Every climbing hut in the Alps that night would have its cheerful and familiar throng of climbers with their guides. Here, on the bare ground, amid the silent waiting mountains, it seemed as if we alone of the human race inhabited this fantastic world of glimmering shadows. There was no moon, and silence hung round us with that appalling insistence upon the mind which is only experienced in lifeless regions of ice and snow. Do what I would my thoughts turned persistently to the terrible scene upon the rocks above which the stranger had described—the mysterious climbers in the moonlight cursing each other brutally as they struggled for their lives.

"Denys," I exclaimed, "you don't believe in that rubbish about the midnight climbers, do you? You don't believe he really heard them?"

"I don't know," said Denys, shortly; "we shall see. Let's turn in."

Quickly sleep fell upon us both, and with the first faint line of dawn upon the mountains we rose refreshed from our shelter in the rocks. And as soon as the handholds became visible we prepared to start. Denys led, and we started with 60 ft. of rope between us. It was difficult to manage, but we had been well warned. The need of freedom of motion had been stamped into our minds in a way we were not likely to forget. It was well it had been. Soon we had 100 ft. of rope between us, and Denys was out of my sight during large portions of the climb. Except for the direction which Denys gave, and which he seemed to pursue himself unerringly, each really climbed for himself, and over and over again as one weary slab succeeded another with scarce a resting-place where one could breathe in security, one realised the terrible tension of nerve which the fear of the slightest jerk of the rope from below must have brought to those who might find themselves upon that mountain-face. A short rope upon that mountain-face meant death and nothing else. The animal rage of climbers desperate with anxiety was after all but the inhuman mood of men in hopeless battle, when the bravest soldier may lose his self-control. To tell the truth the time came when I ceased altogether to believe that we could come out of it alive. And I cursed furiously to myself the folly of the sport, and vowed that if only by some miracle I should escape it would be the last time I should find myself upon an Alpine rope. At climbers' vows Jove laughs. Who has not made such a vow? I have climbed many a tricky slab since then, but never have I made that vow with such conviction and sincerity. For it was touch and go all the time without intermission. And that is not sport at all. It becomes torture, and nothing more.

At length a joyous shout from above informed me that Denys had actually reached the gap in the great rib we had been climbing, where there must be rest for aching fingers and overstrung nerves. The thought of it filled me with a tumult of happiness. For the moment at least we were out of danger, and Denys firmly fixed upon the platform above. Recklessly I hurried over the intervening slab of rock, the worst, I think, of all, and at length my eyes came upon a level with the floor of the gap torn in the sides of the mountain. And there stood Denys, white as death, leaning with his face towards the mountain wall. There never was a steadier head than Denys's in the Alps, and the cause of his emotion was certainly not the dizzy depth of space around us. I knew that, and sought for it elsewhere. Lying upon the floor of the gap was the skeleton of a man. His garments had entirely disappeared except his boots, which were a pair of heavy English climbing boots with serrated iron edges almost eaten up with rust. Around his shrunken form was an Alpine rope, which had been severed some two feet from the knot, and beside him lay an English hunting-knife, likewise rusted almost to the core ; and upon its handle were the letters E. C. A., the initials of Denys's friend's name.

Well, that is the real end of my story. We just managed to reach the gully from a point below the gap by means of a spare rope. And a few days later the remains were reverently buried in the little village churchyard. And only then did old Gruhl confess the evil reputation of the mountain—the dreadful voices heard by night, the vision of climbing spectres.

There are chains now on the Glockenspitz, as every climber knows, and the climb is done every season. And without them or a rope no man could escape from that platform alive. As for the strange rumours of the midnight voices, I reserve my judgment upon that, and ever shall. But I will guarantee this : that the gap in the rib on the south-east face of the Glockenspitz was never reached by starlight by living mortal man.

STRANGE STORIES OF SPORT

XLIV.—THE DEVIL'S DISH

BY M. ALEXANDER

THERE was excitement among the members of the Carrow-Shinnagh Hunt. The new R.M., Captain Lafayette, had appeared on a new horse—a horse not bred or made or owned by any in the wide wild precincts of Carrow-Shinnagh—a horse about which no man, woman, or child knew a single thing. The first person at the meet to perceive the fact was Matt Brady, who had dismounted half a mile from Carrow Cross to mend his throat-strap with a piece of much-sucked string. He looked up at the sound of hoofs and observed the phenomenon.

Matt was a person of resource—not for worlds would he have divulged the curiosity that filled his breast. After one sidelong squint at the approaching R.M., he fell to a searching examination of his grey's hairy near-fore fetlock.

"A fine soft mornin', Captain," he remarked, affably, as Lafayette passed. "I was in dhread this one might be after getting' a thorn in him." Then, mounting, he followed the R.M. up the bohereen, covetously eyeing the black horse's hocks and quarters.

"I seen a baste the dead spit of that one in Cork 'ere last week," he said presently, edging alongside Lafayette. "I was near buying him too, only for the price they had on him—three times his value they were looking—'Sure,' sez I to the fella that owned him, 'ye'll need to be scraping Ireland for a fool before ye'll part him at that money.'"

The R.M. laughed. He knew his countrymen. Matt Brady, as an individual, might be new to him, but with Matt Brady as a type he was well acquainted. It was, moreover, not the first time he had ridden a strange horse in a strange country, and he could assume that nice combination of reticence and tacit brag which the situation demanded. Matt's veiled inquiries were but the precursors of many more, for Carrow-Shinnagh was frankly inquisitive about other people's concerns in general and their horses in particular.

Later in the day, when a straight-necked mountain fox was leading hounds at a rare pace across the small light fields of the barony, the general curiosity gave place to a violent breach of the tenth commandment. Jealous eyes were cast on the new-comer. Envy filled the hearts of every man and woman out, and many a rough-coated little nag of the "butty" type common to Carrow-Shinnagh received an unwonted dose of the stick. The R.M., of course, was in the seventh heaven of delight. The black horse was a trifle too fast for the country, and more than a trifle too flippant; but he gave his rider the indescribable "feel" of breeding, and he had the proverbial spare leg.

"Struck oil this time," thought Lafayette, as he pulled up on the edge of a small fir-wood, where hounds had marked their fox to ground in a rabbit-hole after a racing forty minutes.

"Not a bad horse, that new one of yours," said the Master, when he arrived five minutes later; but the non-committal, somewhat patronising tone was nullified by the glance he cast on the black.

"Yes, he seems all right," returned Lafayette, with suitable indifference. "Bit too fast for this country, perhaps."

On the road home he again encountered Matt Brady.

"I see that colt's put you down," said Lafayette, as he passed.

"Is it the colt fall? Not at all!" exclaimed Matt, who was caked with mud from the crown of his hat downwards, having been in three boggy dykes in succession. "Sure ye couldn't knock this one. If ye went to throw him into a fence itself he wouldn't fall. The thrifle of dirt that's on me I got strapping Miss O'Malley's girths."

He then waxed confidential, and imparted to the much-bored R.M. several dark secrets connected with his neighbour's stables, until Lafayette, partly to get rid of him, turned into Kilmoneen, where his *fiancée*, Lucy Barry, was staying.

To avoid a certain satisfaction in talking of his new purchase would have been more than human, and Lafayette dilated to Lucy on the black horse's perfections to such an extent that the girl begged for a ride, to which the R.M., being very much infatuated, and comparatively ignorant of her capacities as horsewoman, readily agreed.

The following Tuesday saw Royalty side-saddled and double-bridled, standing before the mounting-block in Kilmoneen stable-yard, while Lucy wrestled with a safety-skirt. Lafayette had taken her assurance that she "could ride anything" in absolute faith. His first doubt awoke when she gathered up a curb and a snaffle rein and left the other two in loops on Royalty's neck.

"I never can remember which is which," she said, airily, when he commented on this fact.

It was a warm, grey, autumn morning, with a suggestion of sunlight filtering through the pearl-coloured clouds and wisps of mist on the blue horizon. Their way lay across a curious bit of land known as the "Devil's Dish," a huge, shallow, saucer-shaped depression, all short grass like the Curragh of Kildare, with patches of gorse. dotted on its green surface. A thin screen of fir trees, about eight hundred yards long by fifty wide, which grew at one side of the Dish, formed a favourite nesting-place for the herons of the district. The century-old furze harboured now and again a wily greyhound fox, but as a rule the place lay too open and wind-swept to attract animal life.

Lucy rode along happily, sitting very crooked, and hanging on firmly by the curb reins in a manner vexatious to Royalty. Just as they reached the shelter of the screen, Lafayette pulled up for a second to light a cigarette, and she rode on ahead of him.

It was at this unpropitious moment that a heron chose to fly suddenly out of the fir-trees, uttering the Banshee scream of his tribe. No self-respecting horse can stand the unexpected approach of a large bird.

Royalty shied violently and deposited Lucy in a bunch on his withers. Those who have been in a similar position will know the undignified, slithering descent that inevitably follows. Miss Barry landed softly on a tuft of rushes, and grabbed it with hands that should have been otherwise occupied.

Royalty, after a second's stare of shocked inquiry, flung up his head, found the reins loose, and trotted gingerly away from her. Miss Barry made no attempt to stop him. She sat placidly among the rushes, re-arranging her hat, until Lafayette galloped up full of breathless inquiry.

"Oh no, I'm not a bit hurt," she reassured him, sweetly. "But—what happened? The horse suddenly went from under me. Does he often do that?" She was genially certain that the fault lay with Royalty.

"You weren't sitting tight enough, and anyhow I think he's a bit too much for you," said the R.M., suppressing the inquiry as to why she had let him go, which would rise predominant in his mind. "If you're sure you're all right, I'll go after him. This is the deuce of a place to catch a loose horse."

"He went through the wood," she answered, waving her hand at the fir trees into which Royalty had disappeared a moment earlier.

Lafayette flung himself into his saddle and went in pursuit. There was a good deal of undergrowth round the stems of the firs—dwarf holly and bramble, and great patches of russet-coloured bracken—and it took the R.M. three or four minutes to work through it in Royalty's wake, where his tracks were plainly visible. The black horse had evidently crossed the little wood and jumped out over a wide boggy dyke on the opposite side. There were his hoof-marks on the mossy bank—the long brown smear which showed where he had slithered on landing.

Lafayette urged his snorting chestnut mare over the same place, and then pulled up to look for the fugitive. Before him lay the Devil's Dish—wide, green, and bare under the high October sky which met it on every side. Nothing living moved on all its surface.

"Where the dickens can the brute have gone?" muttered the R.M., shading his eyes with one hand. He peered round the whole horizon, hardly at first able to realise the fact that Royalty was actually not visible. It seemed on the face of things too incredible, for the Devil's Dish was three miles wide by two and a half long, and a horse cannot gallop three miles in as many minutes. Yet the fact remained that Royalty had disappeared. He was not in the wood, he was not on the sky-line, he was not anywhere on the flat "sheep-land." The broad clumps of low-growing gorse which dotted the Dish at intervals were not of sufficient height to conceal more than his legs.

The R.M., utterly bewildered, scoured the whole place, but in vain. Royalty had vanished—vanished in the space of four minutes, on an open plain, in broad daylight.

After an hour's exasperated and futile search, Lafayette gave it up as a bad job. The spongy grass carried no tracks, except just under the little wood. He could only imagine that Royalty possessed a most extraordinary turn of speed, and that from the moment he landed over the dyke he had laid himself out to gallop in a manner most unusual in a loose horse. There was nothing for it but to take Lucy home and then tell the police.

The R.I.C., by dint of diligent examination of the Devil's Dish, were able to establish one fact, and that was that Royalty had apparently never left the place. There was a low bank all round it, too wide for a horse to clear, and so rotten that he must infallibly have left the mark of his passage on its crumbling sides—and there was no such mark. But where, then, was the horse?

This question agitated Carrow-Shinnagh for a fortnight, during which Lafayette was daily subjected to exasperating rumours, hints, and speculations. In the end he had to accept his loss as cheerfully as he might.

Matt Brady, who was loudest in lamentation and foremost in search in all out-of-the-way corners of the barony, opined that Royalty "was after galloping straight to the say, and sure ye wouldn't know what 'ud happen him in that backward place— maybe he'd get clifted, or fall in the wather. Wasn't there a grand young heifer, and she picking along the rocks, and what would happen her only to shlip in one o' them clefts that does be below there, and whin they went looking for her, what did they get in it only her bones and skin?"

In course of time Lafayette himself adopted this conclusion. It did not fit in with facts, but then few conclusions do in Ireland. And, after all, the manner of Royalty's demise mattered little, now that his demise appeared proven. He dismissed the whole business from his mind except on those occasions—which were not infrequent —when Royalty's unworthy successor refused an awkward place, or landed with a neck-dislocating jar over a stonegap. At these moments it was impossible to avoid a sigh of regret.

Months passed—winter, summer, autumn—until the morning of late October on which the R.M. and Lucy returned from their honeymoon to her father's place.

" Papa's got a present for you, Jim," she remarked, as they drove from the station. "You're to be given it after lunch. It's a horse."

Lafayette expressed suitable delight, being conscious at the same time of inward misgiving. The Barrys, having sold their Irish property, lived in Somerset, and he knew how the average English horse comports himself in Ireland. It was therefore with modified joy that he followed his father-in-law to the stables.

"I think you'll like him," said Mr. Barry, confidently. "He was bred the other side of the Channel, and—well, here he comes."

"By Gad," began Lafayette, in a tone of unqualified approval; and then, "Why, great Scott, it's Royalty!"

*   *   *   *   *

Mr. Barry could do nothing towards elucidating the mystery. He had bought Royalty from one of the best-known dealers in Ireland, a man above suspicion, who in his turn had got the horse at a small fair, and who could not furnish the name of the previous owner. That he had been stolen was obvious—but how, or by whom?

The R.M. recalled certain sums of money which he had received anonymously during the past year, with the one word " Restitution " inside the envelope. They had all been posted in Dublin, and gave no smallest clue to the sender.

On his return to Carrow-Shinnagh he instituted inquiries—openly, and in those secret methods that are the most productive of success in Ireland—but, for all that, two years elapsed before he learnt what had happened, and then only by the merest chance.

He was riding home one August evening across the Devil's Dish when a sudden thunderstorm swept down on him from the hills. It was accompanied by those floods of tropical rain which mark July and August in our island. An old man, driving an ass laden with turf, was the only other living thing visible, and as Lafayette overtook him he turned and pointed to the grey veil which came flying towards them out of the lowering slate-coloured west.

" Yes, we're in for a wetting, Martin," said the R.M., recognising a relation and bitter antagonist of Matt Brady.

" Begob, it's spilling rain, so it is," said old Martin. " Still an' all, we'll get grand shelter in here, your honour. Come on now till I show you."

He hauled the ass's head round towards a clump of gorse on their right hand, a low, close-growing, dark green patch of some two acres in extent.

" That, man? Why, there isn't shelter there for a goat! " said Lafayette, but he followed Martin nevertheless.

The storm swooped on them with a crash and a flash of steel-coloured light that made Lafayette's young mare snort, and before they could reach the gorse the rain was hissing off the ground.

Old Martin drove straight into the furze bushes, one arm extended, the other hauling at his long-suffering ass. The R.M. followed gingerly, half blinded by the flying drops, conscious only of the reluctant parting of the wet, wiry bushes as the mare clove through them. It was with sudden surprise that he felt his wrist pricked, and, looking down, saw that the furze, which a minute earlier had only touched his girths, was now up to his mare's withers. She went forward slowly, snorting at every step.

" Where the deuce are you taking me, Martin? " cried the R.M., angrily; but before the words were out of his mouth a sudden rattle of thunder overhead dispelled the mare's caution; she plunged at the bit, stumbled and lurched on to her knees, shooting Lafayette out of the saddle.

"Ye have a right to be careful, sir. Horses is very apt to trip with the obstacles that's in it," came Martin's voice warningly out of the green gloom.

The R.M. scrambled up and looked about him curiously. They were in a natural tunnel formed by a fall of the ground, and roofed by the meeting of the gorse bushes overhead. Before him lay a dip like a quarry hole, filled with the dry, upright, twisted stems of century-old furze. Shafts of light filtered down weirdly from above, and now and again, when the wind blew the bushes aside, a sudden gleam of daylight illumined the brown earth and the eerie forest that grew out of it. The place was like the illustration in a fairy tale of the witches' wood. A gleam of lightning zigzagging across the upper world showed Lafayette the black mouth of a cave in a wall of bog-mould which lay just ahead.

Martin was standing in the opening, "heartening" the ass with resounding whacks.

"Bastes does be frightful here," he announced, apologetically; "in dhread of the dark they are, but ye'll get grand shelter in it. 'Tis aqual what rain 'ud be falling wid'out sorra a drop 'ud come here."

In silent astonishment Lafayette entered the cave, which was large enough to admit the mare also. It ran back evidently for many yards, and out of the darkness came a trickling sound of running water.

"'Twas here they hid away horses they'd steal in the ould days," said Martin. "Poulagaddy is the name they have on it—the thieves' hole. I heard tell there'd be as many as fifty horses hid wid'in, and if St. Pather himself was travelling the place above a week, he'd not get any sign of them—an' by the same token——" He paused dramatically.

"Yes?" said the R.M.

"D'ye mind Matt Brady, that's me father's cousin by the mother's side?" said Martin, after a pause, which the thunder filled with stage effect.

"Yes."

"Be cripes!" Martin whacked the ground with his stick. "Be cripes, I could tell your honour things about that one ye'd be hard set to believe!"

Lafayette, recollecting a vehement dispute between the raconteur and Matt Brady over a legacy of twelve pounds and a mountain ram, nodded in silence.

"That one 'ud disgrace any family in Ireland, so he would," continued Martin. "'Tis he was the rogue ever and always—and as to talk, the dear knows ye'd be stunned with the talk that's out of him—sure he wouldn't regard the truth no more nor an ould cobweb. Maybe your honour remimbers the way he hunted the barony hither and over after the black horse that went away from the young lady in the wood firnint this place. Begob 'twas he had the great hunting! and the horse widin in the back of his own cowhouse all the while!"

"What! Matt Brady?" exclaimed Lafayette.

"Deed aye! It was this way, sir. The morning you lost the horse Matt was widin in the wood, walking down to Carrow Cross. He seen the horse throw the young lady, and he stopped quiet like, watching to see would she ax to chase it—an' presently the black horse came trotting through the place that's thick and throng with ferns and all sorts, right up agin the tree where Matt was. Matt caught him aisy enough—sure wasn't yourself helping the lady, and with divil a one there to pass any remark at all what 'ud hinder him? He lept up on the black horse's back then and faced out at the gripe, looking round and about to see would your honour lay eyes on him. He wasn't only just widin the gorse here when he seen you leap over the drain after him, and sez he to me, and we talking of it afterwards, 'I was in dhread to breathe,' sez he, 'for fear the Captain 'ud see me.' He kep the horse in here until it was dark night. The pollis were after hunting the place till it had them heart-scalded. Matt was waiting on them all day, and whin the last of them was gone, out wid him and away—an' as soon as he had the horse at his own place, in to the back of the cowshed, he wint up to see your honour, and tell ye it was what he thought the horse must be clifted. He took him away the second night to Clashcunnihy, and left him for his cousin to mind. I don't know rightly what he got for him, but he was a great baste. Ye'd sooner be looking at him than ating your dinner—and as to lepping! Well, I declare to goodness, he'd make but one lep of the Shannon!"

There was a silence of some moments' duration, while the R.M. slowly digested the remarkable facts of the case.

Presently Martin spoke again.

"There wasn't one in the barony knew," he said, regretfully. "'Twas only 'ere last month himself told meself, and he having drink wouldn't know rightly what he'd be saying. But in regard to the wish I have for your honour, I thought bad not to tell ye; so I did."

"Umph!" said Lafayette, dryly, wondering whether he would ever have learnt the truth had not the house of Brady been torn with internecine strife. There was nothing to be done now, he reflected. The charge was almost unprovable, since Martin confidential and Martin in the witness box would be two very different people.

To change the subject he handed the mare's reins to the old man, and began with a box of vestas to explore Poulagaddy. The cave was evidently one of a kind common in Ireland. It ran back into dark galleries and strange holes like gigantic fox-earths. In one of these Lafayette found the confirmation of Martin's tale—there, covered with cobwebs and gnawed by mice, lay Lucy's saddle and the bridle which Royalty had worn on the day of his disappearance.

"It's grand out now, your honour," came Martin's voice from the doorway; and then, as they emerged into the forest of gorse-stems, now shot with golden gleams of sunlight and hung with the fairy lace of wet cobwebs, he added, feelingly, "Sure, Matt was only a common fella always, he got no great edgication—the likes of him wouldn't know the way to behave at all."

STRANGE STORIES OF SPORT

XLV.—NO-MAN'S-LAND

BY GEOFFREY WILLIAMS

ALONE in his large airy office sat Heriot Cranworth, Assistant Colonial Secretary of the Caribbees, staring fixedly at an open dispatch that lay on the desk before him.

The little clock on the shelf by the door ticked off the minutes with monotonous regularity, but Cranworth still sat on motionless till the clear typewritten words faded into a formless blur that swam before his abstracted gaze.

When he had entered the office half an hour before, eager to open the English mail, he had been cheerful, even hopeful; but the contents of the first long envelope had changed the whole world. Yet the information it contained was simple enough. Someone had been directed by the Secretary of State for the Colonies to state "that the post of Colonial Secretary of the Caribbees, recently rendered vacant by the promotion of Mr. Andrew Brandon, had been offered to and accepted by the Hon. Amyas Carew, Sub-Commissioner of Kyria Province, Nigeria." Merely an ordinary instance of a job appointment—nothing more.

But to Cranworth it meant everything. For twenty years he had dragged out a wretched existence as Assistant in the pernicious climate of Great Caribbee, battling with ill-health, and buoyed up solely by hopes of promotion to the senior post, when he might fairly begin to indulge in rosy dreams of a governorship in some bright healthy colony where he could find in middle age that enjoyment of life which had been denied to his struggling earlier years. Three times he had hoped, and three times had the powers that be passed him by; but with the promotion of Brandon his real chance had come. In the locked drawer of his desk there even lay a letter from a friend in Downing Street, giving the vague hint of favours to come so dear to the official mind, and which is often the first intimation the anxious applicant receives of coming promotion. In this case it was merely a sentence sandwiched into a sheet of political gossip. "You say you cannot afford to take that new house you want, but I should advise you to wait a few weeks before deciding finally to refuse it." Practically an assurance that he would soon be drawing higher pay. But Carew, a man with no claims whatever, save those of a great name and important relations, had stepped in at the last moment and all was over.

The disappointment was paralysing, and when at length Cranworth moved uneasily in his chair and picked up the fatal dispatch in his trembling fingers there was an added droop about his shoulders, a new expression in his deeply sunken eyes. With a slow deliberation which was painful in its restrained intensity, he tore the stiff paper into minute fragments and dropped them one by one into the basket by his side. As the last bit fell fluttering down he rose and laughed lightly, a laugh which would have made his acquaintances look curiously at him had they been by to hear.

"Good news should be celebrated," he murmured, half aloud. "I think I'll make a holiday of it and go and see what my little friends by the sea have to say. They are sure to be interested," and, turning with an air of decision, he passed swiftly through the corridors and emerged into the hot and crowded streets in which the motley negro population plied its daily avocation with much noise and fluster.

Plunged in his own thoughts, and ignoring the friendly salutations thrown to him from time to time, he hurried on and soon left town behind him. His way lay through fields of tall green canes, the leaves of which rustled faintly in the brisk trade wind, and here and there were gangs of blacks engaged in getting in the crop and singing monotonous hymns the while, as is their wont. But Cranworth passed on, noticing nothing until, leaving the canes behind, and with them all signs of civilisation, he emerged upon a vast and desolate tract of sandy soil, on the further side of which the open sea stretched away into the shimmering haze of the horizon, its white horses dancing and gleaming in the sunlight. A more depressing spot it would have been hard to find, and the brightness of the day only seemed to accentuate its gloom.

The poverty-stricken soil was dotted with patches of sickly vegetation in unwholesome greys and yellows, while here and there grew hideous and almost leafless bushes, whose cankered stems and twisted branches bore witness to their struggle for existence. As the walker neared the sea even these feeble attempts at growth died away, till at length, in a world neither sea nor land, surrounded by tortuous watercourses, stagnant and festering in the great heat, he sank down on the sand, and with his head resting on his hands, gazed out over the dismal prospect with a look of expectation in his strained face.

Beneath his feet and all around the sand was pitted with innumerable small holes, apparently empty; but, as the intruder sat on motionless and silent, into the mouth of first one and then another there crept up a hitherto invisible tenant, a brilliant scarlet land-crab. Resting half in and half out of their burrows, eagerly watching for food, their cruel eyes glittering as they moved to and fro, the uncanny creatures gave the one touch the landscape needed to make it completely horrible—a touch of furtive, menacing life. Now and again a crab would issue from its burrow and scuttle away with its stealthy sideways gait in pursuit of some unseen prey; but for the most part they remained quiescent, giving an impression of inexhaustible patience and tenacity of purpose.

On Cranworth's overwrought and morbid imagination the advent of these strange creatures produced an immediate effect. The strained expression he had worn since approaching their haunts deepened rapidly, and soon, as though he were mesmerised by the thousand tiny wills beside him, he began to mutter to himself in a hoarse, breathless undertone.

" Good little friends," he whispered, " I knew you would come as you always do to put your wisdom at my service. As you sit there waiting, ever waiting, teaching me a lesson in patience, you learn the answer to Life's riddles. The world rolls on, playing out its trifling comedy or tragedy, but you neither laugh nor weep. Still you sit and watch and wait. And to me alone of men it is given to learn of your wisdom—wisdom born of the experience of a thousand years, you passionless lookers-on. Shall I tell you why I have come ? It is because—What is that you say ? " and he put his hand to his ear as though listening, while his scarlet-coated auditors stayed motionless as ever, save for the rhythmical waving of their projecting eyes.

Presently he went on in the same hushed voice.

" You know all about it ? Of course you do. You hear and see everything as you sit there. Distance vanishes and locked doors are not when *you* listen and watch. And you advise me to—yes, yes, the very thing ; you are always right. But we won't say anything about it—we'll keep it to ourselves." For a while he fell silent again, gazing fixedly out over the barren sand ; and then he rose, and as the myriad little scarlet bodies, alarmed at his movements, vanished down their subterranean passages, "Never fear, little friends," he cried; "wait patiently a little, oh, so little longer—a few days or a few weeks are neither here nor there, and soon I will come back. But not alone; not alone." And, laughing discordantly, he turned and retraced his steps across the stagnant waters towards the homely canefields.

As he approached them the wild look faded from his eyes, and it was merely an ordinary-looking rather haggard man who returned home to his solitary lunch.

The ill-health consequent on repeated attacks of fever had for some time past made Heriot Cranworth somewhat strange in his ways, and of late he had contracted the habit of resorting alone to the No-Man's-Land between the canefields and the sea to brood over his troubles, real and fancied. Always the scarlet crabs sat watching in their burrows, purposeful and stealthy, till he began to regard them as friends who took a kindly interest in him, and liked to hear all his affairs. A man with few acquaintances, and no real friends, it was a relief to him to unburden his mind and indulge himself in unfettered speech. But such doings are good for no man, least of all in a climate like that of the Caribbees, and Cranworth had not realised the risk he was running by giving his imagination free rein. At each visit he slipped unconsciously a little further, lost a fraction of his self-control; but never had he gone so far as now. The shock of learning that he had lost the appointment from which he hoped so much had had a far deeper effect than appeared on the surface. As the days passed which brought the coming of Amyas Carew nearer he showed no signs of the inward fever which was consuming him. The manner in which he accounted to his Chief for the destroyed dispatch was calm and convincing; and if at times there was an expression in his eyes which sound men should not wear— well, people are accustomed to that sort of thing in the tropics, and if they notice anything are content to suggest Home Leave as a panacea for all ills.

Every day when the office closed he would walk down through the canes and commune with his horrible auditors in the sand; but what they heard no one knew. If he planned and schemed and thought the unthinkable under the unholy influences of those countless black and beady eyes, he brought no sign of it to his daily work.

When the fateful mail arrived he even went to meet his new Chief, a man younger than himself and with only a dozen years' service to his credit, and the necessary words of welcome came quite easily to his lips.

Carew, a kindly but tactless man, lost no time in referring to the sorrow that he felt at taking up a post which should so much more properly have been given to a man who knew the Colony so thoroughly; but Cranworth felt no difficulty in making the deprecating answer with which one meets such perfunctory regrets. In fact he showed every desire to be on the best of terms with the man who had come between him and his hopes, and in a few days Carew was ready to declare that he could do nothing without "that invaluable fellow Cranworth."

The evening visits to No-Man's-Land had to be discontinued, for there were a thousand and one things to be done—a house to be taken, servants to be found, horses bought, and so on—and who could manage all these affairs so well as the indefatigable Assistant Colonial Secretary?

Time slipped by rapidly with so many interests, and it was three weeks after Amyas's arrival when Cranworth suggested, in a casual way, as they left the office together, that they might take an afternoon off and go down to the open sea. Carew, tired by a long, hot day of work, closed eagerly with the proposal, and they were soon trudging along past the tall, murmuring canes, deep in conversation. Cranworth was in high spirits, and his rather sardonic humour kept his companion so well amused that it was with a sensation of surprise that he suddenly realised they had left the fields behind and were on the threshold of the open waste.

"What a ghastly spot!" he cried, as he looked round over the uninviting prospect. "I never saw such a dismal country. Why do you bring me to such a place?"

Cranworth laughed. "It has its charms," said he, "at least for me. I always come here when I'm out of sorts or depressed."

"Well, I can't say I'm likely to follow your example," muttered Amyas, with a shiver of distaste. "I don't think I'm at all likely to come here again."

"I don't think you are," said Cranworth, with a harsh laugh that made the other look up at him uncomfortably for a moment.

"I hope you won't, in fact," he went on, a trifle hurriedly, "for the solitude is its chief charm for me. But I think it will interest you this time. I have friends here, and you shall see them. Though they are not human, you may find them entertaining. Let's hurry on a bit," and he quickened his pace over the sickly herbage.

The sun was setting straight ahead of them, and the fading light seemed to bring out all that was sombre and menacing about the place. The stunted bushes waving stiffly in the strong breeze looked like bunches of writhing snakes, and the villainous grey and yellow grasses as they lay over to the wind seemed to be striving to lift themselves bodily and move to kindlier soil. As they approached the watercourses the last rays of the sun fell on the grass slime within them, while the tropic evening chill came over the flat, and Carew shivered and buttoned his coat preparatory to suggesting that it was high time they turned back.

But Cranworth had stopped, and throwing himself on the sand pulled the other down beside him.

"Stay quiet for a few moments," he whispered, "and you will see these friends of mine. They have waited a long while to make your acquaintance, and you must not disappoint them."

There was a new and strange ring in Cranworth's voice, and the odd words and manner made Carew suddenly feel unaccountably nervous; but, putting this down to the surroundings working on his imagination, he shook off the unpleasant impression and waited in silence. Soon the scarlet shells became visible in every hole around, and Cranworth whispered, "These are my friends. Watch, I am going to feed them."

So saying, he pulled out a piece of raw meat from his pocket and threw it a few feet away. In an instant from all the holes for yards around the crabs rushed scuttling out, their antennae bristling with excitement and their eyes protruding to their fullest extent as they fell on the tempting morsel and tore it swiftly to shreds.

"Pretty things, aren't they?" murmured Cranworth. But the other was already on his feet.

"Horrible!" he cried. "I can't think how you can watch them. I'm going home at once, and only hope I shan't dream of them."

"I don't think you quite realise the situation," said Cranworth, getting up and standing opposite Carew; "my little friends are hungry. I have not fed them for three weeks, and they want more."

Carew felt a sudden return of his uneasiness, and looked up at the face of his companion, a good six inches above his own. In an instant he turned to run; but it was too late. Casting all restraint aside and giving a free rein to the insanity he had held in check so long, Cranworth was upon him. Naturally a weak and delicate man, Carew had no chance in a hand-to-hand struggle, and almost before he had realised anything he was on his back on the sand, with the other thrusting a handkerchief into his mouth as a gag.

"You shall be their meal!" he cried. "For weeks they have waited, and now their time has come. When I told them you were to be sent to take the post that was mine by right they said, 'Bring him to us,' and I promised that I would, and I have done so. It will be long now before they are hungry again."

Spurred by fear, Carew renewed his struggles to escape, but without avail. He was a child in the madman's grasp, and in a few minutes, his clothes torn off him and thrown in every direction, he lay helpless at his captor's mercy.

"My little friends would have found those clothes of yours in the way," cried Cranworth, as he worked. "*Now* they will find their task easy. But I must tie you up first to these two stakes which you see I've had all ready for you. I can't let you roll about and kill my little friends. And I've got a splendid idea which has the elements of poetic justice in it. Red tape, you know, has ruined my hopes and sent me mad. It is stronger than iron chains. Nothing can break through red tape, so I'm going to tie you up with that," and he pulled a hank of official tape from his pocket and proceeded to bind Carew's hands and feet and tie him to the stakes.

"One strip will be enough," he went on, "one little yard is stronger than any chain; no one can break through it, no one can break through it. It is stronger than Fate, more relentless than death."

So he chattered on, wildly cursing at the powers of red tape, and all the while with busy fingers tying a knot here, a knot there, till at length the wretched Carew was trussed tightly between the stakes, one at his head and the other at his feet. Exhausted by his struggles and paralysed by the horror of his position, he heard nothing till, after viciously tying the last knot, Cranworth bent over him and hissed into his ear:

"Now all is ready, and I leave you to my little friends. You will not be lonely. They will look after you!"

Carew, half distracted by terror, rolled his eyes despairingly in a last silent appeal; but Cranworth was now beyond the pale of aught human, and with a last low laugh of satisfied malice he sped away across the watercourses towards the sea.

Left to himself, Carew strove valiantly to regain his self-command, feeling that come what might he must die sane. But as time wore on the strain grew well-nigh unendurable. The rising mist from the marshy tracts chilled him to the bone and sapped his courage.

Lying on his back and unable to move, he could see nothing save the swiftly darkening skies; but his imagination peopled the holes around with their ghastly scarlet occupants, resting, as he had first seen them, in their burrows, trying to subdue their instinctive fear of man and advance to the attack.

Soon he began to grow light-headed, fancying he heard exultant whispers of anticipation, and as night fell and shut away the outer world he strained his ears to hear the movements of some more daring one among his enemies cautiously approaching over the loose sand. How long he lay there he did not know. Time had ceased to have any meaning for him, but as he drifted slowly away into the ocean of unconsciousness a sudden twinge broke the spell. In an instant a thousand small but powerful claws seized him wherever his body touched the sand, and, excited by the blood drawn by their first attempt, the crabs swarmed over him in vast numbers, ravenous and savage.

The attack brought Carew sharply back to a full realisation of the horror of his position, and frantic with pain he writhed and strained in his bonds till of a sudden something seemed to give. Hardly daring to hope, he redoubled his struggles, and to his unutterable relief the supreme effort was successful and his hands were free. In another moment the tapes were lying on the ground and he was on his feet once more, sick and giddy from loss of blood, but safe. The crabs had completely cast aside their natural timorousness, and were tearing fiercely at his legs and feet; but an awful fear lest he should faint and fall once more into the seething mass below gave him unnatural strength, and seizing such of his clothes as he could find in the darkness he set off towards the canefields with what speed he could muster. Behind him he fancied he could hear the steps of Cranworth, wild at being cheated of his revenge, and the fear lent him wings till exhausted nature had its way and he fell in a heap by the canes at the roadside, to be found in the morning by a party of blacks on their way to their work in the fields.

When Carew had recovered sufficiently to tell his story a search party went to look for the unfortunate Cranworth, but a day and a night elapsed before he was discovered, lying half in and half out of one of the watercourses that meandered over No-Man's-Land. The fate he had planned for another had fallen upon himself, and the men who found what was left will never speak of what they saw.

Amyas Carew escaped with nothing worse than the pain of his wounds and a sharp attack of fever brought on by exposure; but he never again visited No-Man's-Land. Nothing but Cranworth's strange delusion as to the strength of red tape had saved him from an awful death, and at the earliest possible moment he took an exchange to a colony where land-crabs are not, and where there was nothing to remind him of the past. He performs his duties efficiently and well, but if you run short of red tape you will never find any on his office table.

STRANGE STORIES OF SPORT

XLVI.—THE HEALING OF MISSY KATE

Being the Episode of the Sorcerer and the Sacred Tiger

BY E. A. MORPHY

KASENA's heart was full of terror as she left the house for the jungle path, but her resolve never faltered. The Mem wondered why the old nurse wished to leave her for even an hour when the Missy Kate was so ill, but Kasena was obdurate in her request to be allowed to go.

There was no doctor; the Tuan was away in the *ulu*—the jungle —whither his wife knew it was no use sending men to follow him. The work of administration had to be carried on, justice had to be administered even to malefactors. But the doctor of Primpanu had broken his leg, and the other doctor, a day's march beyond at the Kuala, had gone off on leave to the Settlements, so Mrs. Pownatt was alone in the bungalow with only her native servants and the child that was so cruelly ill.

As Kasena left the house the last sound she heard was the Missy's fevered whimpering. The noise of it now dogged her along the *jalan tikus*—the "mouse-path," through which she burrowed into the jungle—and spurred on her steps as she hastened in quest of the Pawang, the magician. The Pawang dwelt far off near Tarempang, and there was no assurance that he would be at home.

Neither was there any assurance that he could help her. For it was of common report that the white people were outside the pale of ordinary spells, and even their babies might be immune. Still, there was no white doctor, and the Missy Kate was ill. Moreover, Kasena had her big gold *krosang* (or brooch) in a cloth under the fold of her *sarong*. It weighed twice as much as a silver dollar, and it held five of the blood-red stones that were so costly. Assuredly that would be enough to pay him to come. So Kasena pushed on through the mouse-path.

Kasena knew what was really the matter with mother and child, though the Mem would not permit herself even to guess at it. She knew that one night of the full moon, three months before Kate was born, the Mem had heard a noise on the verandah, and had crept from beneath the mosquito curtains, and peered out through the slits in the shutters, and looked into the eyes of the great tiger. It was no ordinary, timorous, jungle tiger that walked up and down on a verandah at that time of night, and sniffed at white people through the *jindelas*. It was the *Rimau Kramat*—the Tiger of the Strange Powers—and it had bewitched the Mem and her unborn babe.

On that occasion also the Tuan had been away. The Tuan was always away when evil fell upon the house.

The Mem's terror of the tiger had passed into the soul of her child, and now the Mem had seen the tiger again—seen it twice in the daytime, and once at the bud of dawn, when it came prowling about the house of the District Officer. She had not screamed, she had pretended to no fright or uneasiness; but Kasena had noted the white face of her mistress getting whiter, the apprehensive glances over the shoulder more frequent. She noted, too, that the nervous question and command to herself and to the other servants was iterated again and again every hour after the passing of the day: "Are the doors open? Shut all the doors!" "Are the *jindelas* open? Shut all the *jindelas!*"

When many miles had been left behind the *jalan tikus* widened. Other mouse-paths converged into it, and Kasena knew that she was approaching the Tarempang main road. She also knew that when she reached the main road it was only another couple of miles to the great white trunk of a fallen forest giant that marked the path to the hut of the magician—the Pawang. Once there—why, then the matter rested in the lap of Allah. The *krosang* was of true gold, and they said that the red stones in it were of great worth. They were real *batu delima*—the rubies of the Tuans. They had belonged to the father of her husband that was dead, and that father was an *orang laut*—a man of the sea, and a *prompa* at that—a pirate—who only hoarded articles of indisputable intrinsic value. It was a big fee even for a wizard. To an old woman it was only a dead toy, whereas Missy Kate was a living one. Missy Kate dead would be —— !

"Augh! Hurry, Kasena, thou lazy one! Pick up more quickly those feet of a sick snail! Hurry, hurry, hurry!"

The tropical sun had been two hours gone when Kasena returned that night to the house of the District Officer. She had heard no baby's whimpering as she approached the bungalow— nothing but the phantom wailing that had been in her ears all day— and for a moment she feared that death had come in her absence, and that the wizard doctor would be too late after all. But, as she drew nearer and peeped through the *jindelas*, the awful dread went away. The child lay on the great double bed with her mother. The tiny legs and arms were huddled up under her as she crouched with her head on the pillow, in the attitude of a little white-clad toad. She was fast asleep, and the pale mother slept beside her.

"Of a truth," said Kasena, "the Pawang understands. He has given them sleep and drawn away the dread of the tiger."

She then went out to her own quarters in the row of little houses where the servants lived, and there she awaited the arrival of the magician who had followed her from his lair in the jungle. Presently he appeared; a shrivelled old man, with coarse white hair, and a coarse white stubble growth on his chin, and a myriad of leathery wrinkles. He was woefully thin, and his ribs showed out like the bars of a bird-cage. His brown hands were as those of an old woman, long and fine. The stamp of age sat upon him majestically, despite the stoop of his shoulders. His eyes blazed strangely behind the slits that framed them.

"I must look at the Missy," said he to the ayah, as he seated himself on the raised platform which formed the main living half of Kasena's room. "It will suffice if I see her from a little way off, though in any case she shall not be frightened of me. It would be well also that I should see the Mem. Why need she ever know that I am a *tukan ubat*? There are many old men about who are not medicine men, and she will not think it of me. It were well that I should see her if I am to take away from her also the terror of the tiger. Otherwise, of a certainty, she will again give the terror to the child, and the spells will be useless. Therefore, Kasena, show me the mother as well as the child."

"And what wouldst thou do to the mother, Pawang?" asked the nurse.

The Pawang gave a laugh like a sigh. "Look at me, Kasena," said he, "and learn to believe that the things that old men say are true!"

Kasena looked at the eyes of sunken fire.

"Look at me well, Kasena, so that you may the better remember!"

Kasena looked intrepidly at the dark eyes, for to her the fire in them seemed kindly; and as she did so, the magician smiled again.

"If you now look outside, Kasena," said he, nodding to the open doorway and the lights of the big house across the compound, "you will see The Terror as it sits on the heart of your Mem—Nay, peace, woman. Thou art even as a child!" and he laid a thin hand on Kasena's trembling arm. The old ayah's jaw dropped in fright, her narrow eyes bulged from their sockets.

"*Rimau! Rimau!*" she panted, "the tiger! the tiger!"

"Nay, shriek not, mother!" warned the old man, "tell me gently what you see."

"I see the tiger, the devil tiger!" whispered Kasena: "He is on the verandah at the back, and he is sniffing at the *jindelas*. He smells the Mem. He is a great and a terrible tiger. He is bald: his tail is like a great earth-worm, slimy and purply, and mottled with pink. His whiskers are like the quills of a porcupine, and at their ends there are horrid drops of yellow matter. The inside of his mouth is green and rotten. His eyes have no lids, but they gleam like lanterns, and there are maggots where the lids have been! Pawang, Pawang, spare the Missy Kate! Pawang, Pawang——"

"Peace, woman!" interrupted the Pawang. "The tiger is not there. You have seen but a vision of the Mem's terror. Come, let me look at her so that I may take it away."

He stretched out his hand to her as he spoke, and took her by the arm unresisted. Then, barefooted and silent as ghosts, they crossed the compound to the back verandah, where Kasena softly opened the slats of one of the *jindelas* and let the Pawang look into the room where her mistress lay asleep with her sick child.

For a long time the Pawang stood like a bent statue, his face glued to the open *jindela*. He held Kasena's hand as he watched, and she felt the grasp of his thin fingers on her work-worn hand like a vice of iron. She, too, could see into the room, through the slanting *jindelas*. The lamp was burning high on the other side of the apartment, and the great bed with its veiling of mosquito curtains lay between. Nearest to them crouched the child on all fours, like some tired animal, its curly head buried in its arms. The mother rested on her side with her arm out as if to protect the baby, who had eluded the caress in her fretfulness. As the Pawang watched them, Kasena noticed that Missy Kate relaxed her crumpled attitude, and seemed to roll over naturally on her side.

The little bare legs stretched out, the arms straightened. Something approaching a smile supplanted the tense expression of care on the face of the mother.

" Pawang," whispered Kasena, " are they now truly asleep ? "

"They sleep," replied the Pawang; "come away."

And the strange old pair crept back to the narrow abode of Kasena.

" You tell me, Kasena," said the Pawang, when they were again on the ayah's mat, " you tell me that the tiger has been about again, and that the Mem has seen it ? "

"Yes, Pawang," admitted Kasena, " the Mem has seen it, and she gave the terror to the child. Her heart is as water because the Tuan is away."

"Her heart will become strong again presently," said the Pawang, "for I have taken the terror out of it, and I shall carry it back to the jungle, and put it into the heart of *Rimau* himself, and he will never again frighten the Mem or the Missy. I shall now depart, for I have elsewhere to go, and many spells to work by the dawn in order that I may put back the fear in the heart of the tiger."

So speaking, the Pawang made his farewell *tabeks* to the ayah, and, turning out of the compound, was immediately swallowed in the shadows.

Next afternoon the District Officer returned. He came two days earlier than his official schedule had planned ; for a messenger, about whom nothing was mentioned to his wife, had gone after him into the *ulu* to tell him that the child was ill, and that the Mem was red-eyed with weeping. So he had come back.

Thank God, the Missy Kate was better, and the Mother Kate's eyes had known a whole night's rest.

" I don't know what it was, dear," explained the wife, "except that God answered my prayers. Kasena would go away yesterday morning. She would not tell me where, but the syce's wife helped me to nurse the child. Kate was crying and crying, and I cannot imagine how Kasena had the heart to go; because she was always so fond of her. About three o'clock in the afternoon baby seemed to get better, and the queer thing about it is that I did too; I have not been quite well, dear, you know. I am sure I am a very silly woman ; but I am still afraid of the tiger, and he was back here again since you left. It is so ridiculous ; but I could not help being frightened. Kate is the same way. She catches the fear from me. I am sure that was what made her sick. But now the fear is gone."

They were sitting on the front verandah, and it was the heavenly time of the later afternoon. The heat of the equatorial day was passed, and the cool air of the evening had not yet got chill. The District Officer, after the roughness of his tour, and the ghastly apprehension of loss that had ended it, was lolling back happy and at his ease, when an untoward incident disturbed them.

A stalwart Sikh orderly in hobnailed boots was crunching up the gravelly drive from the main road to the bungalow. He halted in the covered carriage-way before the verandah and saluted. It was a matter of small importance he had to communicate, but one withal which the Sahib might like to know. The Tarempang road was blocked by a tiger.

In an instant all the shikari instincts of his race blazed up in the breast of the District Officer. A tiger!

"Has it a kill?" he asked the orderly.

"I do not know, Sahib; but the people are afraid. They say that the road is held by a tiger at the first milestone beyond the *jalan tikus*, which is the short cut from here to the Tarempang road. I tarried not with the *khubbar*, but hastened with it to the Sahib. As the Sahib knows, when the natives bring *khubbar* of a tiger in this country, the news is invariably true."

The District Officer was on his feet by this time. In his eyes was the gleam of the hunter's desire. The stately havildar noted the gleam; and through the punctilious gravity of his own demeanour he reflected it, subdued but burning.

"Richard," said the wife, "must you go? We have been so ill, dear."

The District Officer wheeled about. "Oh, I nearly forgot, little woman," said he. "No, of course I won't stir out to-night. It would be too late for this evening anyhow, unless the brute is guarding a kill. Maybe we'll have more news to-morrow. I'll stop home and look after my two duchesses to-night. Where's our Kate?"

The apprehensive eyes of the wife lighted up again as she called for the ayah and the child.

The District Officer turned to his orderly in a slightly shamefaced way. "Never mind, Tota Singh," said he, "you shall have the reward for the *khubbar*, but the Mem and the Missy are sick, and I have been long away, so I do not hunt to-night. If there be fresh *khubbar* to-morrow, bring it to me."

The havildar saluted and left.

At six o'clock next morning, as the District Officer was pottering about his verandah, pyjama-clad, there was again a scrunching on the gravel, and again Tota Singh stood before him at salute.

"More *khubbar*?" queried the District Officer.

"Yes, Sahib; strange *khubbar*; the tiger still blocks the road to Tarempang."

" Where ? "

" At the same spot, Sahib.   It is difficult to believe, but it is truly so.   I have made drastic investigations.   No, Sahib; the brute is neither sick nor wounded.   But they say it is the *Rimau Kramat*, the sacred tiger.   They seem afraid to speak of it, and they believe in magic.   It is not in order or proper for a healthy tiger to block one road for a day and a night.   Behold, Sahib, here come men with fresh *khubbar*.   They are those I have sent to inquire."

Two Malays of the *ulu* were standing grinning by the entrance gateway.

Whatever the Malay's moral or intellectual deficiencies may be, it cannot be charged that he lacks sporting proclivities.   He would sooner hunt than eat; and it was obvious to the most casual observer that these two children of the wilds at the gate were keen as mustard on the prospect.

" Come hither, brothers," called the Sikh, and the two little men approached, still grinning.

" Explain to the Tuan," he ordered; and the little men proceeded to explain: There was a tiger on the Tarempang road. The whole country knew thereof.   It was doubtless a sacred tiger; otherwise how would it remain without fear in the highway?   No man dare pass.   They had come by the jungle paths.   Many had come by the jungle paths.   The postman even was afraid.   These men, the newsbearers, were honestly afraid; not that they feared *Rimau*, the tiger, in his natural state; for they would joyously attack him with spears if they found him.   But *Rimau Kramat* was totally different.   He was a *hantu*—a spirit—and a tiger as well.   His wisdom was as that of Suliman, and his vengeance was as the wrath of Allah.   He forgot no slight or injury; and being immortal, he was not to be killed by men.   It was a most complicated situation to have such a visitation on the Tarempang or on any other road; but the matter lay in the lap of Allah, or in the hands of the Tuan District Officer, which, as everybody knew, was precisely the same thing.

The District Officer wondered whether there were precedent for such an act on the part of a *Rimau Kramat*, or any other sort of *rimau* in that part of the country.

There was not.   The incident was entirely novel in every respect.   His senior informant, Hassan, knew the *ulu* like a book, knew it from Siam to Singapore, and he had never heard of such behaviour on the part of any tiger.   He would be loath to believe it, even on the word of a Tuan, had not his own eyes assured him. The tiger was there.   It had been there on the preceding morning at this identical hour.   It was still there two hours ago.   He had run hither like a deer, for he had seen a miracle, and he should desire to have his vision authoritatively corroborated. Of a truth he would accompany the Tuan to the spot, *instanter*.

"Very peculiar," commented the District Officer. "Can you explain the matter at all, Hassan? You know that this is unusual. Is there nothing to hold the brute? Is there no kill, no trap, nothing?"

Hassan fumbled his fingers, his more youthful companion looked aside. Two schoolgirls caught fibbing could not have seemed more obviously guilty. The cleverest Malay is at best a miserable liar, and the jungle folk, if questioned, cannot even begin to suppress the truth.

There was nothing—nothing whatever that could detain a tiger, nothing, that is to say, that ought to delay one over a day and a night, and hold it like a tree or a statue, spellbound. The only thing that they had noticed in any way out of the usual—save and except the presence and demeanour of Rimau himself—was perhaps the fact that there was a man there too. Yes, they had utterly forgotten the circumstance, it was such a small matter, but there was a man there too. He was an old man, but he was not hurt, much less eaten. He was seemingly interested in the tiger, and ——. But, if it was quite and entirely at the pleasure of the Tuan, the matter was one which they would rather not discuss. There were matters which they found it safer to taboo conversationally, and this was one of them. The man was there, and it might be that the man was detaining the tiger. At any rate, as they had before stated, they were wholly willing to accompany the Tuan and show him everything. They would prefer that their responsibility should rest at that.

Richard Pownatt had lived too long in the jungles of Malaya to be amazed at anything; but this was a matter of more than casual interest. What a pity there were not a few other fellows to hear the story. For his own part he believed it; though he could not make head or tail of the mystery.

"What do you take it to be?" he asked Tota Singh.

"I think, Sahib," responded the orderly, "that it may be the Pawang—the magic doctor from the Tarempang *ulu*. I am not yet sure, Sahib; but I think that the Pawang was here the night before last. It may be that the tiger tracked him hence, for there has been a tiger hereabouts. I have spoken nothing about the matter, lest alarm should come to the Mem; but I have been inquiring as to what mischief may have brought the Pawang to this side of the country. They say that he has strange powers over all manner of forest beasts."

"At any rate," said the District Officer, "we will see what it means at once."

Half an hour later, Pownatt was on his way through the same jungle path which Kasena had threaded two mornings earlier. With him, by special permission, came Tota Singh, the havildar orderly; with him came Hassan and his comrade of the jungle; with him came his own "boy" or body servant, Noor, proud in his capacity of gun-bearer. Two other Malays followed with the *barong*—the baggage—which included the tiffin basket with refreshments for the day. The pony trap, it had been arranged, should go round by the road, and wait at the entrance to the *jalan tikus* until Pownatt had bagged the tiger.

Shortly after the start was made, Hassan disappeared down a side track that seemed scarce wide enough to give passage to a weasel.

"He is gone for fresh *khubbar*," explained Noor.

A couple of hours later, towards the end of the jungle path, Hassan rejoined the expedition.

"He is there still, Tuan."

"And the man?" asked Pownatt.

"He is there too, Tuan. Bid them halt."

The party halted, and Noor came forward with the guns, a heavy tiger rifle and a double-barrelled 12-bore gun, which is as good as any rifle at close quarters.

"The Tuan can go close to the tiger," said Hassan, as he looked at the battery with the comprehensive eye of an old shikari. "Therefore that might be a good gun, especially if the Tuan has the bullets that swell." He pointed to the 12-bore.

"Then you may take the rifle," said Pownatt to the Sikh orderly; and with assurances from the jungle man that there was no fear of losing their game, they broke off the path they had been following, into a narrower track that ran at right angles to it and parallel to the main road. Presently they came to such a clearing in the forest as is left by the wandering Sakais when they scratch a patch of land for a harvest. At the lower end of it the light shone through the wall of trees, and they could discern the red track of the high road. Hassan pointed a knotted brown finger. "They are there, Tuan!"

Nobody who has ever stalked a tiger, or has awaited one on a *machan* over his kill, or who has otherwise approached him on murder bent, can boast of having done so without some thrill of emotion. It is the love of that thrill which makes your true shikari. Pownatt had been on many hunts, but he did not remember ever before having felt so queer in approaching his quarry.

Whether it was the fret and worry that had come with the news of his sick child, or the reaction when he found her better, or the nonsensical yarns about the *Rimau Kramat*, that so excited him, he could not tell; but he felt his heart throbbing like a pump as he picked his way through the long *lalang* grass and over the snags and stumps of the clearing to the trees that fringed the road.

"There, Tuan!"

With gun poised, the District Officer let his glance follow the pointed finger of the Malay. Almost dead in front of him, not thirty yards from where he stopped—crouching, glaring, tail almost straight along the ground, in the supreme attitude of a spring—was an enormous and loathsome tiger. It was almost totally bald with age and mange, and its hideously hairless face and head was fringed with a dishevelled mane. Great scabs fretted its body, and there were streaks of clotted blood where he had scratched the sore places with his claws. His fangs were bared in a snarl. The effulgent apotheosis of hate and malignity that seemed to burst from him was curbed, as it were, by an overlying veil of terror. Why did he crouch so? Why was the spring not made?

On the ground in front of the brute, some half a dozen paces nearer the District Officer, was squatted a shrivelled, white-haired Malay. His back was towards Pownatt, his left hand was pressed to his breast as though saluting somebody, while the right was extended menacingly at the tiger as if in the pronouncement of a malediction.

Like the tiger, he was absolutely motionless. Both figures seemed pregnant with instant life and pulsing action, but man and beast remained still as statues.

Then Pownatt remarked a thing that amazed him. It was a very small thing, and it doubly amazed him that he should notice it at all under the circumstances. Withal the item that impressed him most in the astounding spectacle was the tip of the tiger's tail. It was curled ever so little sideways, in just such a twitch as a tiger gives when preparing to spring, and it remained curved that way.

He noted the matter, reflected upon it, raised his gun and fired, all in a single instant; for in the chase of big game it is wise to shoot quickly when at close quarters.

With smokeless powder, a Meade shell, and a trusty 12-bore at thirty yards, it is easy to hit a big tiger that is three-quarters face on.

Pownatt paused with his finger on the second trigger. Would the brute spring in his death struggle?

The echoes of the report reverberated through the clearing and the surrounding forest, the Sikh stepped forward with the precision of a soldier on parade, the sporting rifle lifted to his shoulder, ready to shoot should his master's safety demand it.

The tiger still crouched rigid as bronze—still malignant, still glaring, still on the edge of its spring.

"*Kramat! Kramat!*" cried the Malay. "*Kramat!* Run, Tuan! He cannot be hurt by bullets."

Then Pownatt saw another thing. Not only was the tiger still undisturbed, unhurt, motionless, but the old Malay was the same. Even as the tiger crouched and glared at him, so sat the Malay, squatting, one hand on his breast, the other extended in a sinister anathema at the horrid brute that menaced him.

Pownatt let his gun fall to the rest, appalled. Mechanically he broke the breech and drew another shell from his pocket. As he did so, the discharged cartridge popped out beside him with a click. He rammed home the new shell with his thumb, and took careful aim and fired. The side of the tiger's face seemed to disappear, there was a little jerk, and the brute rolled over on its side like a thing of wood or metal. The front paws were still extended, the hind legs at the spring. The tail remained rigid with the little hook-like curl at the end.

With his right hand extended towards the spot where the tiger's face had been, the Malay still squatted in the roadway, unmoved.

Pownatt stepped out from the shade of the trees, still holding the gun, and the Sikh followed him. The tiger lay absolutely still. In his chest near the left shoulder was the hole where the first shell had entered, and on his right side, by the lower ribs, was a hole as big as a hat where the exploded shell had emerged. The left side of the head and face was gone. The shell had probably struck the bone under the eye, and blown half the head off.

Pownatt turned to the Malay, who still squatted with menacing hand extended.

" He is dead, Sahib!" said the Sikh. " Of a truth there has been witchcraft here!"

" How? dead?" gasped the District Officer. " What has killed him?"

"Thy servant doth not understand, Sahib," replied the Sikh, " but that he is dead I am assured. Behold, the ants are running in and out of his ears and under his eyelids. It is not for me to voice opinions in the presence, but I think this man bewitched the tiger, and was then himself bewitched. I have seen many dead; but never have I seen any quite like this before. Does the Sahib observe that the tiger is not bleeding? He was dead before the Sahib fired!"

Pownatt looked again. What the orderly said was true. No blood came from the torn corpse of his quarry, and already the scavenger ants were in full possession, though there was as yet no sign of putrefaction.

"It is queer!" said Pownatt to himself. "It's a pity there are no inquests in this country. Don't know enough, or I'd hold a post-mortem myself. A pity Jalland's leg is broken!

"Call the men, havildar."

The Malays, who still remained afar off, were called, and the District Officer gave instructions. A man was to go to Tarempang at once and find out who the dead man was. He was the Pawang? Eh? Well, his friends were to be found, and he was to be decently buried. He was first to be searched here and now, and his property, if any, was to be brought to the office of the District Officer for administration. The tiger was not fit to be skinned; but he, the District Officer, wanted the claws brought to him. The whiskers might go to the Malays as charms. There was doubtless a Chinese doctor at Tarempang who would pay well for the liver. It was for Noor to do with it as he pleased. The men who brought the *khubbar* could do what they liked with the rest; they would also be well paid for the news. Full inquiry was to be made as to how the Pawang came to be on the road, and how he encountered the tiger.

When the District Officer got home in his trap that afternoon he was still thinking and thinking. The mystery was utterly beyond him. Hypnotism of sorts, no doubt, he concluded; but it was more than extraordinary for all that. One thing, however, superseded his worry over the mystery and more than compensated for it: Never in months had the wife he loved seemed so well, never for weeks had he heard the same ringing laughter from the curly-headed Missy Kate as that which she chortled out when she flew to kiss her dada.

It was not until after dinner that night that the mystery of the *Rimau Kramat* was again brought forcibly to his mind; and that was when again the havildar Tota Singh sought an interview with "the presence" on the verandah.

The men had come back from Tarempang. The Pawang had no friends, and no man could tell what had killed him. People said he could bewitch animals and mortals alike, and make them see visions and obey his will. There was another Pawang, however, who feared that this Pawang was not strong enough to bewitch a *Rimau Kramat*, and he also believed that the *Rimau Kramat* had pursued the deceased along the road, and the deceased had sought to save himself by bewitching the monster and had partially succeeded. While he was so doing, however, the monster had also bewitched the Pawang, and the strength of their bewitchments was so great that both of them had died. Such was the word of the Pawang, which doubtless the Sahib knew well to be only a lie. He, Tota Singh, gave it for what it was worth. He had also brought to the Sahib the few small trifles that had been found on the body of the dead Malay, and among them was an ancient gold *krosang* set with rough rubies.

"There is but one such *krosang* in this country," said Tota Singh, "and that belongs to the Mem's ayah, Kasena."

"Bring Kasena hither," said the District Officer, "but do not frighten the Mem."

Kasena was brought around from the back of the house, diplomatically, and was commanded to explain how and when she lost or gave away the *krosang*, and whether she knew aught about an aged Malay who was known to be a Pawang—a sorcerer—and who lived in the forest near Tarempang.

Yes, Kasena knew. She would tell everything. She was very sorry, but she feared much for the Missy Kate, and she knew it was the tiger that was in her soul. She had only the *krosang*, and——.

And Kasena told the whole story of the Pawang, and how he had given her a vision of the *Rimau Kramat*, and how she had let him look at the Missy and the Mem through the open slats of the *jindela*.

"You had better come and tell it all to the Mem herself," said Pownatt, at the close of the story. "I have no doubt but that it will entertain her. Come on."

They went into the sitting-room where the Mem was reading, and Kasena told her story again. When she had finished, Pownatt saw that his wife was silently crying; and Kasena, who also noticed it, crept out very softly.

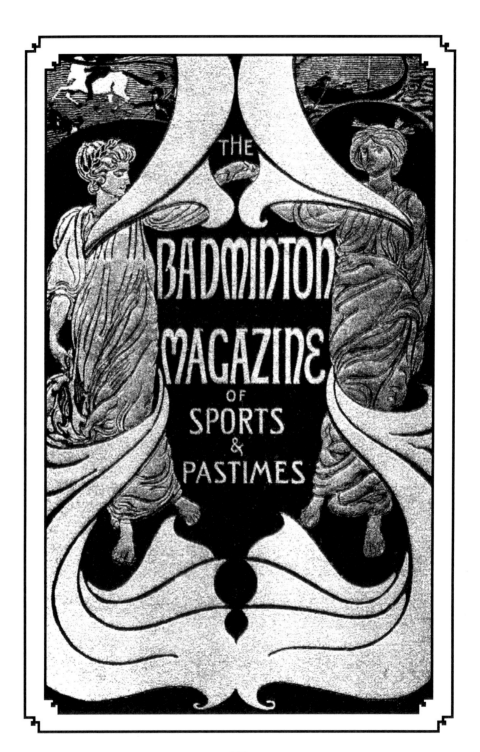

THE

BADMINTON

MAGAZINE

OF
SPORTS
&
PASTIMES